Science, Truth, and Meaning

From Wonder to Understanding

Dear Nicholas,

immense gratitude for your generous review of my first (and perhaps only) book.

I hope my references to your work herein do justice to it.

Thanks so much for your support.

Best wishes,
Ben

Science, Truth, and Meaning

From Wonder to Understanding

Benjamin L J Webb

*Genome Institute of Singapore, A*STAR, Singapore*

NEW JERSEY · LONDON · SINGAPORE · BEIJING · SHANGHAI · HONG KONG · TAIPEI · CHENNAI · TOKYO

Published by

World Scientific Publishing Co. Pte. Ltd.
5 Toh Tuck Link, Singapore 596224
USA office: 27 Warren Street, Suite 401-402, Hackensack, NJ 07601
UK office: 57 Shelton Street, Covent Garden, London WC2H 9HE

British Library Cataloguing-in-Publication Data
A catalogue record for this book is available from the British Library.

SCIENCE, TRUTH, AND MEANING
From Wonder to Understanding

Copyright © 2022 by Benjamin L J Webb

All rights reserved.

ISBN 978-981-123-189-6 (hardcover)
ISBN 978-981-123-307-4 (paperback)
ISBN 978-981-123-190-2 (ebook for institutions)
ISBN 978-981-123-191-9 (ebook for individuals)

For any available supplementary material, please visit
https://www.worldscientific.com/worldscibooks/10.1142/12152#t=suppl

Printed in Singapore

In this ambitious work, Benjamin Webb describes a large part of western philosophy, modern physics (including relativity and quantum mechanics) as well as biology, genetics, evolution and the neurophysiology of the brain. He then brings all these strands together to show how they underpin our relationship with the world and our own nature. He does not shirk from tackling issues that are still controversial, such as the quantum measurement problem and the "hard problem" of human consciousness.

> Alastair I.M. Rae, Reader in quantum physics,
> University of Birmingham; author of
> 'Quantum Physics — Illusion or Reality'
> (Cambridge University Press), &
> 'Quantum Mechanics' (Routledge).

Benjamin Webb has written a remarkable and unusual book that delves into fundamental questions about science and meaning. The book has an astoundingly broad scope and starts with a detailed review of philosophy and science, covering the early attempts by Plato and Aristotle, via the logic formulations of Gottlob Frege, Bertrand Russell and Kurt Gödel, to the more pragmatic theses of Thomas Kuhn, Paul Feyerabend and Karl Popper. Webb then focuses on the status of modern scientific theories of physics, biology and evolution. His analysis of the classical and quantum views of physics includes Albert Einstein's major contributions not only to his creation of the special and general theories of relativity but also to the birth of quantum mechanics. After a familiar account of how Niels Bohr, Werner Heisenberg and Max Born crafted the Copenhagen interpretation of quantum mechanics, Webb devotes much more space to the implications of Schrödinger's Cat for the quantum measurement problem, and of Bell's inequality for hidden variable theories. Although these may seem deep and confusing matters for most working physicists, quantum entanglement and decoherence are now of direct relevance to quantum computing. As a working biochemist it is not surprising that his account of modern biology and the implications of the discovery of DNA — with Francis Crick's postulate of gene expression and the 'central dogma of molecular biology' — is thorough and detailed. After a discussion of modern views on Darwin's theory of evolution and the puzzle of the Burgess Shale, Webb moves on to the more controversial topics of consciousness and free-will. The book concludes with a wide-ranging discussion of knowledge, Artificial Intelligence and the nature of reality. In summary, Webb's book covers an amazing range of topics and provides the reader with a fascinating overview of deep questions about the limits to our scientific understanding.

Professor Tony Hey, CBE, FREng, FAAAS,
FACM, FIET, FBCS, FInstP, C.Eng.
Chief Data Scientist,
Rutherford Appleton Laboratory STFC,
Didcot, OX11 0QX, UK
Senior Data Science Fellow, eScience Institute,
University of Washington, Seattle, WA 98195, USA

Contents

Acknowledgements xvii
List of Figures xix
Introduction xxi

1 Philosophy and Science 1

  Philosophy and the Origins of Modern Science 1
  The Philosophers and the Philosophical Movements 10
    i) Idealism 10
      Plato (c428/423–c347 BC) 11
      Immanuel Kant (1724–1804) 12
    ii) Logic and Logical Positivism 14
      Logic 14
      Logical positivism 18
      Aristotle (384–322 BC) 20
      Gottlob Frege (1848–1925) 22
      Bertrand Russell (1872–1970) 23
      Georg Cantor (1845–1918) 30
      Kurt Gödel (1906–1978) 34
      Incompleteness and why Principia Mathematica failed 37
      Ludwig Wittgenstein (1889–1951) 38
      Scientific method: Kuhn and Feyerabend 52
      Thomas Kuhn (1922–1996) 53
      Paul Feyerabend (1924–1994) 54
      Karl Popper (1902–1994) 55

iii) Rationalism	60
René Descartes (1596–1650)	60
Baruch Spinoza (1632–1677)	66
Gottfried Wilhelm Leibniz (1646–1716)	68
iv) Empiricism	70
John Locke (1632–1704)	70
David Hume (1711–1776)	73
v) Dialectical Materialism	75
Georg Willhelm Friedrich Hegel (1770–1831)	75
vi) Pragmatism	78
Charles Sanders Peirce (1839–1914)	78
William James (1842–1910)	79
vii) Phenomenology	80
Edmund Husserl (1859–1938)	80
viii) Existentialism	81
Søren Aabye Kierkegaard (1813–1855)	82
Martin Heidegger (1889–1976)	83
Jean-Paul Sartre (1905–1980)	86
ix) Other Important Philosophers	87
Arthur Schopenhauer (1788–1860)	87
Friedrich Wilhelm Nietzsche (1844–1900)	89
Michel Foucault (1926–1984)	90
Jacques Derrida (1930–2004)	90
Concluding remarks	92
2 Physics and the Classical World	**97**
i) In the Beginning	99
ii) Relativity, Quantum Theory, and Reality	105
Questioning the Universe	110
Parsec	114
Redshift and size	115
Fate of the Universe	119
iii) Special Relativity	120
Ernst Mach	123
Details and effects of special relativity	124
Twin paradox (and summary)	134

iv) General Relativity	140
What is spacetime?	141
General and special relativity in action: Homage to John Archibald Wheeler	142
Interval	144
Discovered or invented?	148
Block universe	149
Three worlds	150
Spacetime curvature	152
Spacetime and black holes	156
Ageing	157
Planetary motion	157
v) Universal Conditions	159
Martin Rees	166
Our Cosmic Habitat	170
Other life	170
Fate of the Universe and multiverse	173
Multiverse modelling	176
3 The Quantum World	**181**
i) The Worldview Before Quantum Theory	182
Modern terminology	183
The Copenhagen interpretation and beyond	185
ii) From the Old	188
Thermodynamics	190
Atoms and molecular mass	192
Ludwig Boltzmann	194
The problems	197
1. Black-body radiation	197
2. The photoelectric effect	203
3. Bright line spectra	205
Quantum numbers	208
The Balmer series	209
Wave/particle duality	215
iii) To the New	220
Schrödinger's cat	227

QED	230
Uncertainty	233
The quantum problem	235
Decoherence	236
Entanglement and the EPR paradox	237
Hidden variables	242
John Bell	245
Difference between entangled and relativistic effects	260
Delayed-choice *gedanken* experiment	261
The collapse of the wavepacket, the measurement problem, and reality	265
David Bohm	267
Realism	271
Robert Nadeau and Menas Kafatos	273
Bernard d'Espagnat's veiled reality	274
Julian Barbour	276
What is real?	277
iv) Subatomic Particles, GUTs, and Nuclear Power	279
Subatomic particles, forces, and the search for a GUT and TOE	279
Fermions and bosons	280
Hadrons and leptons	281
Fundamental particles	283
Forces	289
The Higgs boson	291
Models and theories	294
String theory	295
Lee Smolin's five fundamental problems	300
Closing the loophole	302
Nuclear power	303
4 The Biological World	**307**
i) How a Cell Works	313
Early studies on the cell	313
Cells and organisms	315
The protein world	317

Protein functions	320
Enzyme catalysis	320
Myoglobin and haemoglobin: allosteric interactions	322
Protein modifications: regulating protein activity	325
Molecules of the immune system	328
Cell membranes and compartmentalisation	329
Energy generation and storage	331
Glycolysis, the citric acid cycle, and oxidative phosphorylation	332
One metabolism	334
Molecular motors: movement and life	336
The DNA world	341
DNA makes RNA makes protein	342
The exacting nature of DNA	343
Chromatin and chromosomes	346
The molecular biology revolution	347
DNA replication	349
DNA replication in the test tube: the Polymerase Chain Reaction	351
Reverse transcription	353
ii) Gene Expression	355
Synthesis of RNA (transcription)	357
Promoters and enhancers: Creating binding sites for transcription factors	359
Synthesis of protein (translation)	362
Analysing gene expression in the 'omics era	365
Gene regulation: layers upon layers of control	367
Chromatin modifications	369
Alternative RNA splicing	370
MicroRNAs	371
Stem cells and gene editing	372
iii) Development	376
Dynamic random processes	376
Development and evolution	381
Transcription factors in the formation of body plan	382

Hox genes determine body plan in *Drosophila*	385
Hox genes in vertebrates	387
Ontogeny and phylogeny	390
Multicellular development	392

5 The Evolving World — 395

i) The World Before Darwin	395
The anthropic principle: How likely is life?	397
The origins of life	399
ii) Evolution	401
Charles Darwin	401
Darwinism and natural selection	405
Adaptive radiation	408
Neo-Darwinism	410
Methods and insights of the theory of evolution	414
Evolution and development: Comparative anatomy	414
Species and populations	416
Coevolution	416
Stephen Jay Gould and punctuated equilibrium	417
Wonderful Life: Decimation and diversification?	419
The Burgess fauna	425
Burgess: Cause and effect	429
Extinctions	431
Burgess interpretation by Gould	435
Burgess interpretation by Derek Briggs and Richard Fortey	435
Differences between Dawkins' and Gould's opinions	438
From Dawkins's viewpoint	439
From Gould's viewpoint	442
Richard Lewontin and the role of environment	446
The Doctrine of DNA	447
Adaptationism	450
Consciousness	450
The Triple Helix	453
Norms of reaction	455
Adaptation revised	456

Cause and effect?	457
Size matters	461
iii) Mathematics and the Natural World	463
The golden ratio	463
Fractals and chaos	470
Concluding Remarks	473

6 Consciousness and the World — 479

i) Introduction	479
ii) The Unconscious: Accessing the Inaccessible	485
Carl Jung's unconscious	486
iii) Consciousness: Accessing the Knowable?	489
Neurons	491
Gerald Edelman	495
Summary of Edelman's process	498
Language: Consequence for consciousness — Edelman's thoughts	499
Bernard Baars	500
Francis Crick	501
Roger Penrose	503
John Searle (and more thoughts on Crick, Edelman, and artificial intelligence)	510
Nicholas Humphrey	517
Philosophical zombies	521
The Inner Eye	522
Soul Dust	531
Knowledge of qualia and reality	532
Problems with knowledge of qualia and reality	535
Physical description of subjective experience	536
David Papineau	538
Knowledge from the scientific method	540
I	542
iv) Free will	544
Predeterminism and free will	547
John Bell: predeterminism, free will, and entanglement	550
Physicalism, predeterminism, and free will	551

Quantum measurement	554
Sam Harris	558
Free will as illusion?	560
Gerard 't Hooft's view	563
The predetermined self	565
Predeterminism, TOE, and life on Earth	568
Kurt Gödel and fatalism	570
Role of the human mind in predeterminism	571
Types of free will	572
Incompatibilism	572
Metaphysical libertarianism	572
Free will by chance and determination	573
Compatibilism	573
Free will as unpredictability	573
Influences	575
Questioning free will	577
Ilya Prigogine	581
Colin McGinn	582
CALM	586
View from nowhere	588

7 Mind-Knowledge-Meaning — **591**

i) Are We Asking the Right Questions?	591
ii) Mind	594
Memory	596
Mind, matter, and knowledge	598
iii) Limits of Knowledge	601
Numbers and the infinite	602
Gödel and Tarski: Logic, truth, and intuition	604
Implications of Gödel's theorem	612
Douglas Hofstadter and artificial intelligence	613
Alan Turing	616
Strange loops and artificial intelligence	619
Reality	623
iv) Mental Prowess	624
Early man	624

	Modern man	627
	Learning	628
	Thought	628
v)	Can We Know Reality?	630
	Niels Bohr's insight	631
vi)	The Quantum Versus Real Division	631
vii)	Concepts That Limit Our Knowledge of the World	633
	Relating to our physiology	633
	Relating to our access to reality	634
	Relating to our knowledge about reality	635
viii)	My Position	638
ix)	What Am I?	642
x)	Man and Reality	644

References — 647

Index — 667

Acknowledgements

I am indebted to Nigel Brand for all his suggestions, criticisms, editing, and enthusiasm. He was an intellectual sparring partner with whom to bounce ideas. As my drafts of the book progressed, his thoughtful suggestions helped shape it into its current form. I doubt I would have published it without him.

I am grateful to Nicholas Humphrey, John Leslie, Tony Hey, Andrew Whitaker, and Andrew Briggs for their support, and Alastair Rae for, among other things, his patience in helping me understand special relativity. I thank Sook Cheng Lim for her help in bringing this book to publication.

Authors of books encompassing broad subject matter like this invariably pass it through the filter of many professional colleagues. My book reflects the fact that it was written from the perspective of someone trained in the biological sciences, but for whom physics and mathematics hold great interest, and whose importance is integral to the book.

Finally, this book took many years to complete, and the patience, love, and understanding of my family gave me the space to do it. Thank you mum and Premelaa.

I dedicate this book to my grandparents, and my son, Suryan.

List of Figures

Figure 1.	Generating hypotheses	57
Figure 2.	Definition of a Parsec	115
Figure 3.	Relativistic effects between inertial frames	132
Figure 4.	Einstein's train	133
Figure 5.	2-dimensional length	144
Figure 6.	Interval	145
Figure 7.	Circle limit (IV) — M.C. Escher (1960)	162
Figure 8.	Black-body radiation	202
Figure 9.	The Balmer series	210
Figure 10.	The Periodic Table	212
Figure 11.	Orbitals	213
Figure 12.	Electron orbits	215
Figure 13.	Double-slit experiment	217
Figure 14.	Feynman diagram	232
Figure 15.	Polariser alignment	243
Figure 16.	Scheme to test Bell's inequality	247
Figure 17.	Graphs of $\sin\theta$ and $\cos\theta$	253
Figure 18.	Graphs of $\sin^2\theta$ and $\cos^2\theta$	253
Figure 19.	Mach-Zehnder interferometer	259
Figure 20.	Delayed-choice experiment	261
Figure 21.	Hadrons	286

Figure 22. The eightfold way	287
Figure 23. Standard Model of elementary particles	288
Figure 24. Forces	290
Figure 25. Construction of a TOE	291
Figure 26. Amino acid notation	319
Figure 27. Protein kinase signalling	327
Figure 28. Striated muscle contraction in skeletal muscle	338
Figure 29. Deoxyribonucleotide (dNTP) group (triphosphate form)	344
Figure 30. Double-stranded DNA	345
Figure 31. DNA base-pairing and replication	350
Figure 32. The flow of information	354
Figure 33. mRNA splicing	356
Figure 34. Gene expression	358
Figure 35. The genetic code	363
Figure 36. Establishment of anterior (A) to posterior (P) axis in the *Drosophila* embryo	378
Figure 37. Key transcription factor gene families	383
Figure 38. Probability for albino offspring	413
Figure 39. Example of a simple cladogram	437
Figure 40. The shell of the nautilus	467
Figure 41. The compatibility of free will and determinism	544
Figure 42. Knowability of reality	583
Figure 43. Hypothetical plot of the relationship between level of intelligence and degree of consciousness	585

Introduction

The purpose of scientific knowledge isn't only to improve the quality of our lives. It also provides a factual foundation to help answer the deeper questions that have plagued humankind since the dawn of civilisation. What am I? What is life and existence?

After writing early drafts of sections of this book, I showed them to relevant academics to obtain their comments. Some philosophers responded with "why have you included so-and-so, and not such-and-such", so I initially altered my writing plan according to their suggestions, only to be reproached later by others for removing some "important contributor to man's understanding of reality". The same occurred with the input from scientists. I soon realised that their comments were their own views on contentious issues, and in trying to satisfy everyone, I would both be facing an impossible task and, more importantly, not be true to my conclusions. We are all subjective beings who are susceptible to our own opinions and prejudices, skewed as they are by our own experiences and knowledge. This book represents my view, and any perceived flaws reflect my lifes experiences and how they influenced me.

If we ponder the nature of understanding and knowledge, we need to consider the possibility that there are limits to our capacity for understanding, imposed perhaps by the structural makeup of our brains or even the nature of the Universe. Since we have gaps in knowledge, there *is* no 'is' only opinion on what may be right, and thus opinions vary among individuals over what or who is important. We are not working our way along the route to a known, defined, goal. As such, this book represents just one viewpoint. Since there is no universal truth (where 'truth' means 'being in accord with fact or reality') for the totality of reality, all such books could be considered flawed, or perhaps as something that may shed light on a different viewpoint. Most scientifically accurate books tackling the 'Big Questions' of existence are written, either professionally or for the intelligent layperson, by philosophers. Some are written by physicists with a philosophical bent. They write with a skew towards the position of their own particular expertise — they cannot help but introduce an element of personal bias (in terms of beliefs and knowledge, and hence worldview).

The motivation to write this book was the realisation that my vocational training in biochemistry and molecular biology provided me with little insight into what it means to exist as a sentient being, which then led to extensive reading and thinking about metaphysical issues. From my reading, I detected a paucity of attempts to reflect on mankind's relationship with reality that was holistic in its approach. That is, one that considered the human biological organism against which all knowledge reflects back on.

To me, it seemed strange or even wrong to attempt to discuss our relation with reality without addressing the particular limitations and peculiarities that we humans possess. We must understand who and what *we* are as well as our limits before we have any chance of understanding what reality means to us. We are, after all, asking the questions. This book is my attempt to encompass this important consideration.

The book title reflects how science defines truth and asks whether truth is possible and can provide more meaning to our lives. The word 'meaning', in general use, is the way something is understood by an individual. Furthermore, 'meaning' is subjective and has many meanings. For example, it can be existential and touch on the value of life, or it can be linguistic where words define meaning. In the context of this book, 'meaning' is meant in an existential sense. Does knowledge, truth, and the understanding of reality that science provides enhance our lives? Do answers to questions such as "why are we here?" and "what is the purpose of existence?" provide reassurance and, indeed, meaning?

'Meaning', covered in detail in Chapter 7, is our attempt to understand our place in a 13+ billion-year-old Universe in accordance with scientific truths. It is to appreciate the issues faced by conscious entities occupying a physical world and to be mindful of our limits as sentient beings.

'From wonder to understanding' is a paraphrased quote from Albert Einstein (1879–1955), who described the search for scientific truth as "… a continual flight from wonder to understanding". In this respect, the book moves from the wonder of metaphysical philosophers about how the world works to how their questions were addressed by science to reveal usable truths. My aim is to show that there are different meanings of truth and knowing. To know oneself is to know in a way that no one else can know. The subjective experience of the self represents a type and depth of knowing that is inaccessible to science. This is an important consideration when discussing meaning and truth.

This book aims to better understand our place within the Universe using science as our guide. Science deals in exactitudes, and yet there are things that science cannot address. Just as philosophers disagree with each other, so do scientists about what we know. Difference of opinion drives the refinement of what we know to reflect more closely how things actually work. Whether we are on the path to truth or just a model that mimics it, time will tell. We cannot, however, escape the fact that science enables advancement in every aspect of human life.

This book intends to illustrate the scientific achievements and, thus, the sheer potential of man. It appreciates that there is much to know and that there are things we may never know. But modern science has changed life in diverse areas, whether they are biological (e.g., the 'human genome project' and its ramifications) or physical in nature (e.g., the Large Hadron Collider). A common misconception is that they are *completely* separate sciences. The scientific achievements, be they medical, biological, astronomical, chemical, or physical in nature, have all evolved from the same foundations of knowledge. Through a systematic process of formulating hypotheses, experimental testing, and using the data obtained to refine those hypotheses, this *scientific method* changes lives like nothing else on Earth. That advances in physics, chemistry, and biology rely on the same fundamental principles and extends from one another serves as convincing evidence that they are likely to be correct.

Yet, within this framework of effective knowledge, intrinsic factors exist that *limit* our knowledge of physical reality. This book seeks to clarify them and, in doing so, link philosophy to the biology, chemistry, and physics that constitute modern science. Accordingly, relevant scientists and philosophers are discussed, starting with some of the philosophical schools of thought that have shaped our thinking over the last two and a half thousand years.

Key advances in our understanding of the physical world from the work of English polymath Isaac Newton (1643–1727) through to Albert Einstein and Niels Bohr (1885–1962), for example, were built upon the knowledge of previous generations. In the scientific community, it is physicists with their attempt to generate a *Grand Unified Theory* (GUT) of everything that might seem most qualified to contribute to these questions. Yet philosophers often pour scorn over their *reductionist* approach, arguing that life is more than a mere set of equations. Could equations encapsulate what love is, what beauty is (it seems very unlikely within the framework of science and mathematics we have constructed). How can such subjective experiences be encoded and understood in terms of the objective scientific methods we use to explain our reality? In turn, physicists may criticise what to their ears is untestable philosophical mumbo-jumbo which, though being non-falsifiable, lies beyond the realms of science. Is such a viewpoint narrow-minded?

We recognise that we may be able to define, for example, the physical processes that constitute a conscious experience, but *that* understanding does not give insight into the quality of such experiences. Hence, does greater understanding of ourselves require more than what objective science is capable of providing? Objective scientific method leads us on a path to understanding the relations between the external physical world and a human mind that is limited both temporally and spatially — recognition of that limitation within the objective paradigm must allow for acceptance of other conceptual limitations.

Over the course of this book I aim to show that, since we are finite beings, the scientific truths we reveal about the Universe are constrained to the limitations our physical and mental makeup impose on how we can address problems. Some questions may be beyond our abilities and comprehension to solve.

Arguably, the most remarkable fact of reality is that matter and force has, over time, enabled a being to arise that is alive, intelligent, and conscious, and that possesses qualities that transcend mere material construction. Thus, even if we can never solve the riddle of existence, the mere fact that we can think, feel, reason, and understand at all is a marvel in itself.

The purpose of this book can also be described more specifically in terms of chapter content. The physical world is discussed in Chapters 2 and 3 through the development and details of the two major disciplines that gave us our modern picture of the nature of physical reality. *Classical* and the later *quantum* physics are, in essence, conflicting theories. They describe with incredible accuracy the behaviour of the largest and smallest objects in the Universe. Yet, fundamentally, they are incompatible. It is the great goal of physics to unite these areas into one grand theory of everything. Though such a theory would not describe many aspects of nature, which will be covered in Chapters 4 and 5, it would explain how force and matter interact to produce physical phenomena. It is the journey that led to these theories, and their details and problems, that are discussed here.

Classical physics refers to our understanding of the Universe in non-quantum terms. This represents a deterministic world. Deterministic science has influenced philosophical thought for hundreds of years. In the 17th century, the English philosopher Thomas Hobbes was convinced by the certainty of mathematics and constructed a mechanical model of the Universe. He believed that the Universe could be described using the science of motion. This is the pre-1900 world, the world in which Newton's discoveries on gravitation so accurately fitted observation, and which formed the foundation from which Einstein developed his theories of relativity. Though these theories remain within classical thought, they so accurately describe phenomena from the atomic level to the motions of stars and galaxies that they are still applied today. Nevertheless, they cannot explain effects observed at the subatomic level.

Most of the sciences, apart from some physics, can use classical concepts in their descriptions, but underlying them is the world of the quantum. From the early discoveries of the *quanta* by the German physicist Max Planck (1858–1947) through to more modern issues such as the *Copenhagen interpretation*, non-locality, and the *correspondence principle* and complementarity, the world of the quantum describes so accurately what we observe at a subatomic level that we conclude that it either cannot be false or must at least be on the path to describing how physical reality actually is. Thus, the quantum revolution has been described as humankind's greatest intellectual achievement. However, it is incompatible with the classical world.

Quantum theory defies common sense, yet its counterintuitive conclusions show perfect agreement between theory and experiment. A popular anecdote about the apparently absurd implications of quantum theory stresses that anyone who is not shocked by it has not understood its meaning. There are many such quotes relating to its intrinsic contradictions and difficulty. Indeed, Bohr, one of it's founders, said that "every sentence I utter must be understood not as an affirmation, but as a question". This contradiction is what I hope to project in this book — that the wonder of philosophy and science is that we are limited beings made of matter and yet are capable of asking questions to make sense of our existence.

Despite the great accuracy of both quantum theory and relativity, they describe different aspects of reality. The search for a single theory of everything (TOE) that can define reality under one model is ongoing, but it remains elusive. It would unite relativity with a unified field theory, creating a GUT. Such a theory would incorporate the effects of all the current known forces:

1. Electricity.
2. Magnetism.
3. The weak force.
4. The strong force (which comprise the GUT), with gravitation.

Roger Penrose, whom we will meet many times throughout the book, is an English physicist, mathematician, and philosopher of science. His main professional contributions have been to cosmology and relativity, but his work has also added to the debates on *consciousness* and quantum theory. Many of his ideas in these areas have been presented in books such as *The Emperor's New Mind* and *The Road to Reality*. He believes that for us to make progress in unravelling a TOE/GUT, we need a new kind of physics that is not yet known (or perhaps even beyond us).

It seems remarkable that though fewer than a hundred elements occur naturally in the Universe, these same elements can constitute such a great diversity of physical constructions, from stars to living conscious entities. Life on Earth is primarily formed from arrangements of the simple elements carbon, hydrogen, nitrogen, and oxygen. From these elemental building blocks, and under specific environmental conditions, the process of evolution acting in a chaotic and unpredictable arena over huge timespans has enabled the emergence of the countless diverse forms of life that populate the Earth, from unicellular organisms to ourselves. Yet the physical processes of all biological life are very similar and linked to chemical processes, which are ultimately linked to physics.

Chapters 4 and 5 are to life what Chapters 2 and 3 were to physical reality — the classical physics of the very large (e.g., galaxies) and the quantum physics of the very small (e.g., atoms). Here, the 'very small' is the mechanism of the living processes within a single life. The 'very large' is the billions of years of evolution of life on Earth that led to the existence of our species.

Chapter 4 focuses on the biological world and describes the physical mechanisms that enable a living entity to live by reviewing some of the basic cellular processes of life — how proteins work and the nature, replication, and expression of DNA. The chapter concludes with an overview of how development is programmed by evolutionary-conserved mechanisms of gene expression. Of course, these mechanisms evolved over many millions of years, so after we discuss the minutiae of life's processes, the theory of evolution itself is considered in Chapter 5. There I discuss aspects of the theory of evolution and how we came to exist on Earth, from the ideas of Charles Darwin to the more recent debates on the finer details of the theory by English evolutionary biologist Richard Dawkins, the palaeontologist Stephen Jay Gould (1941–2002), and Harvard evolutionary biologist Richard Lewontin (1929–2021). We end that chapter with a look at how mathematics informs and shapes the world around us.

The conditions on Earth were favourable for the emergence of sentient life. Through unpredictable and catastrophic events, the species *Homo sapiens* evolved to be different from all other terrestrial life. Human beings contemplate, and indeed question, their own existence and place in the Universe. We are able to leave a record not only of what we are but also of what we have created (and all this from a collection of matter that billions of years ago existed only as a constituent of stars). In human form, this matter integrates to produce qualities that transcend material construction. The quality that is most striking is consciousness, the subject of the final two chapters.

Without mind there would be no questions, no answers, no relevance. Without mind, things just 'are'. The previous chapters laid the foundations for an understanding of what we are, our physical nature and how we came to be, and the nature of the Universe in which we exist. From our analysis, we can celebrate humankind's achievement of using reason and science to uncover so many mysteries of our existence. Yet, as the philosophical sections of Chapter 1 discuss, there is much we do not know; indeed, there is much we may *never* know. We can know objective knowledge about a thing, but never encapsulate the *essence* of the thing. This difference is the distinction between the subjective knowledge of 'being' a self, and objective scientific knowledge of what constitutes *that* physical being. How the mind and physical reality relate homogenises the totality of existence. We are connected to, and are part of, the world.

Scientific progression is not a blind and undirected advance. Instead, it is focused on identifying problems that can be solved because we want to use this knowledge to improve the quality of all our lives as well as to satisfy our insatiable, unique need to understand our own existence. Chapters 6 and 7 discuss these issues. Integral to this discussion is an understanding of concepts such as consciousness, *free will*, and *determinism*, which are discussed in detail to illustrate that questions are not purely objective, but relate to a being embedded within reality.

As a final note, each chapter can be read individually as primers for their respective subjects. However, when read in conjunction, I hope they allow the reader to assess the knowledge we have of ourselves and the world in which we are embedded, and to analyse what this means in the context of truth.

1 Philosophy and Science

Philosophy and the Origins of Modern Science

The roots of science lie within philosophy and ancient man's curiosity about himself, the world that surrounded him, and what lay beyond. A modern misconception is that science and philosophy are very different things. The average person may feel that they could hazard a guess at what a philosopher does more readily than what a scientist does. But if we go back to the time of Plato and Aristotle, we would see that the ancient philosophers were asking some of the very sorts of questions that engage scientific minds today. So what is philosophy? It can be described as the study of the nature of reality, ethics, knowledge, and existence using the method of rational enquiry. That description also might be applied to science, with the ethical dimension being most pertinent to biomedical research, where questions arise around issues such as animal experimentation, genetic modification, and personalised genetic profiling.

    As an individual, I am a scientist with a great interest in philosophy. Scientists, when acting in a scientific manner, are trained to be objective. Hence, few scientists have time for philosophical thought, which I consider a shame since I believe that a philosophical perspective in all of the sciences is beneficial. Scientific thought and rational interrogation of our world to a large extent grew out of philosophy. So, before discussing the objective reality of man and his world, I will provide some insight into western philosophers who have attempted to question (and answer) what makes man and the world. Thus, in this Chapter, I discuss the philosophers who were interested in understanding the world in accordance with the objective vision of science. I discuss these philosophers from an *approximate* chronological order, in accordance with the philosophical movement(s) that they represented (if they can indeed be associated with one). From their questions came insights that were applied to address these questions. I hope to show the reader how man applied his mind to understand himself and the world he found himself living in.

Philosophy has long been a discipline for understanding the human form and our place in the wider world. Pythagoras (c570–c495 BC) believed that a harmonious world of numbers underpinned and explained the abstract world of appearances. Two hundred years later, Aristotle would acquire information on a subject and logically analyse it before making theories and conclusions (much the way science is done today). As such, many of the philosophers of Ancient Greece, for instance, made serious attempts to understand not only the nature of the physical world — the movement of the sun and planets, for example — but also the nature of the human body and its workings. These were attempts to rationalise and categorise matter, and both of these approaches are central to scientific thought and progress.

The Greek physician Hippocrates (c460–370 BC) postulated in his medical theories that there were four humours affecting human behaviour and personality:

1. blood
2. phlegm
3. black bile
4. yellow bile.

In a healthy individual, these four bodily fluids were thought to be in balance. They were also believed to have a direct influence on four traits or temperaments:

1. Sanguine, which describes a person who is optimistic and social in character (blood).
2. Phlegmatic, the characteristic of a calm and contented individual (phlegm).

3. Melancholic, which is quiet, inward, and analytical (black bile).
4. Choleric, which describes a person who is driven and prone to shortness of temper (yellow bile).

Ancient Greek and Roman physicians believed that excesses or deficiencies in these distinct bodily fluids directly influenced temperament and health. This approach to medicine was seen as holistic — each patient was said to have their own unique humoral make up — and showed similarity to the Indian Ayurveda system of medicine as well. The four humours and temperaments were also linked to the four elements of air, earth, fire and water, and even the four seasons!

It seems astonishing to us now that this pseudoscience dominated Western medical thinking for over two millennia until the birth of what we consider to be modern pathology and medicine during the Age of Enlightenment. As the French Nobel laureate Charles Richet commented in 1910, "What can we say of this fanciful classification of humours into four groups of which two are absolutely imaginary?"

Anyone wishing to pursue a career as a scientist undertakes a course of research-based study in a particular area leading to the award of a *Doctor of Philosophy* (PhD; also called a D Phil). Typically, this work is presented by writing a thesis that will be examined by a panel of experts on the subject. This higher degree confers on the recipient the academic title of doctor and is a prerequisite for many academic careers (in both teaching and research).

When talking of academic degrees, which are principally awarded in the fields of the sciences, it is used in the context of its original Greek meaning which is 'love of wisdom'. The PhD has its roots in medieval European universities, though the first Doctorates in philosophy were awarded in Germany in the 17th century. In Britain, Durham University introduced the Doctor of Science in 1882. In their training, PhD students learn how to pose meaningful questions in order to further knowledge and test them experimentally. The process starts by constructing a theory (hypothesis), then testing it experimentally and analysing the results obtained to see whether they prove or disprove the hypothesis. The conclusions drawn can then add to our accumulated knowledge on the subject and serve as a basis for the construction of new hypotheses that can take the process further.

If new scientific knowledge cannot be experimentally and theoretically falsified, it is considered an addition to our understanding.

Humankind's written record of hypothesis, experiment, and result — reported and scrutinised in many thousands of peer-reviewed specialised scientific papers — ensures that our knowledge of physics, biology, and chemistry (and their offshoots) adds to a continuing interconnected knowledge base with which we enhance our understanding of our world, and hence ourselves.

I was trained in the biological sciences and hold a PhD. I am not a philosopher by profession, possessing none of the skills that a philosophical training imparts, yet I consider myself a philosopher in the sense that I ask philosophical questions. Not possessing a doctorate *in* Philosophy does not mean that I cannot ask and address these questions — I feel the same need for answers as philosophers do. However, my life and my education give me a different perspective from theirs. To a scientist, many philosophical treatments aimed at understanding human 'being' are found wanting. They often ignore scientific facts about reality. Within science, physicists often ignore the biological element. Ultimately, we are, after all, biological organisms asking questions about our own existence. Thus, a biological perspective opens a different window to these issues.

This book is a personal journey stemming from my vocational training and my wider interests. To be an expert in all the topics covered in this book is impossible and, therefore, as mentioned earlier, some experts in one field or another might feel aggrieved that 'their' subject is not treated with the emphasis they believe it deserves. This disagreement could indicate the incompleteness of human understanding, since if no debate were present then no conflict of opinion exists. But if we ponder the nature of understanding and knowledge, we need to consider the possibility that there are limits to our capacity for understanding, imposed perhaps by the structural makeup of our brains or even the nature of the Universe.

Perhaps the Universe is innately unknowable. What we think of as true may merely be an interpretation of reality that makes sense to a limited, finite organism. We understand the concept and reality of infinity, but to capture it mentally as we do a finite object, for example, is outside the contemplative capacities of our likewise finite minds. Yet we apply and incorporate such ideas to our understanding of the physical world, from which we have created the technological civilisation that surrounds us. We pride ourselves in what we do know, and as we advance our knowledge ever further, we assume that we will reach all answers. But is that true — that is, is it possible? Even the foundation of our current knowledge is constructed with uncertain ideas like chaos, *indeterminism*, and unknowability.

Science is objective — it is knowledge of a different kind, where knowledge of one thing is relative to some other thing. For example, we know that the chromosomes in our cells are made of DNA and that the genetic code they contain is responsible for making all the proteins of the body (this will be reviewed in Chapter 4). We can know all objective knowledge about a thing but not its *essence*. This gap reflects the difference between the subjective knowledge of 'being' a self and the objective scientific knowledge of what constitutes *that* physical being.

Some things that are inanimate in nature do not have a self, so is it true to say that a complete physical understanding constitutes all there is to know about them? Is knowledge merely a 'reference point' and not an indication of what 'is'? When we define what a stone is, for example, our definition reveals as much about us as about it. What we find is skewed according to what we are.

It is possible that the Universe is unknowable and that our knowledge of it is merely a biased construction to help us make sense of it. If it is unknowable, this explains why we cannot know it. But if it is knowable, we do not yet know it is knowable, because to do so would require our ability to describe ever process within it. If one day we think we know it, how do we know whether this truth that answers all the questions we can ask is 'the' truth or just a limited model that fits our capabilities? The human mind may be incapable of knowing a knowable universe.

Why would we assume that just because we know things, we can know everything? That is as illogical as it is arrogant. Of course, within the framework of language, we can make statements such as "this is my hand", and as we define 'hand' in a way that encapsulates an incomplete knowledge of what a hand really 'is', then we can with confidence acknowledge that this is my hand. However, if I were to say "the Universe works this way" before defining a model, then such a statement implies meaning. It uses language to suggest that what is defined can encapsulate the Universe. I am saying that though the statement intends to demonstrate the Universe is as it says, the Universe may not be as it says.

The application of the scientific method through integrated disciplines utilising a common set of expanding proven principles and rules enabled us to start to delineate the processes of the Universe. Yet, since science is constrained by the rules governing the interaction of force and matter, philosophical enquiry did and continues to enable us to probe possibilities limited only by the creativity of the mind. Hence, philosophy is always a guide as to what might be, whereas science seeks to determine what is. The scope for knowledge is limitless, but that which I present here has allowed our species to progress on many levels. For the individual, it enables one to gain a greater insight into one's existence. Philosophy puts this knowledge in context by showing what knowledge is as well as what we really can know.

Some readers may think that there is a paradox connected with the decision to begin with a chapter devoted to philosophy. However, everything discussed in this series must have an element of truth, in a scientific sense, in order that the Earth give rise to creatures capable of reason and understanding. And yet it is only because humans possess reason and understanding that, in another philosophical sense, they were capable of engaging in scientific research — if we had not evolved as a species, we would not have done these things. In effect, this circularity signifies the essence of this particular book.

We can marvel at how our brains produce a mind that is capable of determining how we came to exist in a world that we can quantify and understand. The knowledge our minds gain of the reality in which we are embedded may not reflect absolute truth, but as we can manipulate it for our benefit, it is a version of reality that must possess an elemental truth. In short, we have developed an incomplete but consistent scientific description of our world. It is feasible, however, that another form of science, unknown to us and different in fundamental description, could provide a better explanation of reality. Perhaps one day we will produce this, or maybe such a description would be impossible for us finite beings. Furthermore, it may be fundamentally impossible as a property of nature itself.

The science I discuss in this book is specifically western science, which dates from its origins in the seventeenth century. To be sure, science of various kinds also existed in the ancient Islamic world, ancient Greece, and other locations, but what I talk of here arose from the ideas and intuitions of the 16th century Italian scientist Galileo Galilei (1564–1642) and the French philosopher René Descartes. Metaphorically, science is the full bloom of the seeds they planted.

When people talk of the greatest human minds ever, many will place philosophers (e.g., Immanuel Kant, his fellow German Friedrich Nietzsche, and the Austrian Wittgenstein) and scientists (e.g., Isaac Newton, Charles Darwin, Albert Einstein) on their list. Perhaps this is because we are appreciative of the complexity of reality and thus celebrate those who make significant advances in our understanding or our ability to interact with reality. As we advanced our understanding throughout the latter half of the 20th century, the scientist became increasingly specialised — 'niche' science, if you will. The era of the all-encompassing philosopher-scientist, such as was evident in the Age of Enlightenment (18th century), has well and truly passed.

The philosopher and scientist can address the same issues, even with similar perspectives, yet with different methods of address. Simplistically, the philosopher is the thinker and the scientist is the doer, though that is of course not always the case. What links them is an attempt to find answers to questions posed by the world, including some of the 'big' questions such as "where do we come from?" Scientists tend to reflect on a portion of reality and, as mathematician and historian Jacob Bronowski said, this inevitably involves ignoring that which is necessarily involved. They seek truth, but what is truth? Definitions vary, but pragmatists say that it is the "satisfactoriness of belief" whereas some philosophers see it as the coherence between propositions. In fact, it is debated whether truth is a quality or a relation. Perhaps we intuitively 'feel' what truth is.

Philosophy has traditionally been taught in western universities according to a long-standing programme — René Descartes and Immanuel Kant, ethics and *epistemology* (the examination of the nature and limits of knowledge, and comparison of knowledge with belief), philosophical logic and the philosophy of mind. Wittgenstein's destruction of what we think can be known, as described in the logical propositions of his *Tractatus Logico-Philosophicus*, marked a change in direction to some extent, although he as well as others ultimately came to refute the ideas of that work. Before Descartes, western philosophy incorporated theology and developed in accordance with Christian dogma. In the medieval period, God was the focus because theories of creation make the creator more important than the creation. Man had a mind to ask questions, but there was no natural science to address them, so God and his role in all that 'is' took centre stage.

Descartes changed this viewpoint and based his assumptions on *reason*. He was a rationalist, constructing his philosophy from the idea that everything can be doubted except that one is thinking (hence his famous line, "I think, therefore I am"). He believed that the human mind, as created by a perfect God, provides insight into truth. By being created by perfection, it cannot be deceived. Half a century later, the British empiricist John Locke questioned this, claiming that access to the truth came from experience, not reason. He thought that sensations from experience give us ideas, and that what we consider to be innate ideas are in fact ideas from reflection on experience.

However, the Irish empiricist Bishop George Berkeley brought God back into the picture by realising that if knowledge of the world comes from experience, then how do we know it exists when we do not perceive it? He said that as God is omnipotent, 'He' perceives it and confirms its existence at all times. However, although Berkeley believed that perception is reality, the source of these perceptions could have been something other than reality itself, such as God, which means that a material world (realism) was not a logical certainty.

In the 18th century, the Englishman David Hume began to question the validity of trusting experience or thought alone as a window to truth. He said that just because something happens the same way many times (e.g., the rising of the Sun) does not provide a logical basis to reason that it would happen again the same way. We cannot use inductive logic to reason from experience that something causes something else, merely because one event always precedes the other. Logically, it is equally valid that they are not causally related.

Later, Kant used the ideas of Hume to distinguish the world as it is in itself, the *noumenal* world, from the world that is accessible to human reason and sense, the *phenomenal* world. So, was that the end of the story? No. After the German philosopher Georg Hegel failed in the last attempt at an all-encompassing philosophy, others tried to reduce questions of metaphysics (the study of the nature of reality) to the issue of linguistic meaning (e.g., Wittgenstein and the logical positivists), thus ignoring or bypassing deeper questions by claiming their meaninglessness. Others, such as Heidegger, claimed that we had to understand human 'being' (he used many different terms for 'being' — relating to the being of human being) before such issues can be addressed, using self-imposed rules of such obscurity that it was either ignored or difficult to criticise according to the usual rules of philosophical rigour at the time.

Despite philosophical inquiry leading to a general conclusion that there was no universal concept of reality, let alone a way to define it exactly, science progressed in its search for truth through a standardised mechanism of constructing a hypothesis and then testing it experimentally. The data obtained then feeds into and shapes the knowledge base. Although we are finding that there are limits to what we can know about reality and that it may well be more complicated than we can even imagine (as the English astronomer Martin Rees puts it), science continues to make advances in both our understanding and quality of life.

In 1943, the English physicist Sir James Jeans (1877–1946) tried to link science with philosophy to ask whether the world we perceive is the ultimate reality. His book, *Physics and Philosophy*, now over 70 years old and still one of the best on the subject, shows how much we struggle, scientifically and philosophically, to find complete answers as well as to accept that, possibly, there are things we do not know and maybe cannot know. Science and philosophy were once inseparable — Newton called his physics *natural philosophy*, and some consider that the Age of Enlightenment or Age of Reason has its origins in the works of Newton, Spinoza, and others from the mid-17th century. However, there has been a drastic reversal since the start of the 20th century due to the development of natural science. Science can address the questions posed by philosophy, but from a stance of physical verification and refutation of hypotheses.

Philosophy is distinct from science in that although it integrates with science, the methods it uses to address fundamental problems are different, being less physically invasive yet instructive about how we might best access the truth. As such, I will concentrate in this chapter on the philosophers and philosophical movements that attempted to address the crucial 'big' questions — "what is everything made of?" and, fundamentally, "who are we, and why do we exist?" Of course, we have yet to find an answer to the latter question, and there may never be an answer acceptable to all.

Philosophy sought how to find answers, and science evolved to address them head on. As natural science and philosophy progressed, the role of God in all phenomena was continually — and reluctantly by those destined to lose influence — reviewed, revised, and diminished. Descartes was the pivotal figure in the reappraisal of God. Although his ontological argument harks back to medieval times, his commitment to objectivity laid the foundations for the scientific revolution that made God a redundant hypothesis.

Following Descartes, the only philosophical movements that seemed to fit with science are *empiricism*, positivism, and pragmatism, which will be discussed in detail later. However, other philosophers associated with different philosophical movements, such as existentialism and phenomenology, are discussed too because they either showed a new perspective of how to view phenomena or, by presenting them in a new light, they directly or indirectly (albeit fruitfully) forced science to address problems from an alternate position. Let us now turn our attention to the achievements and stumbling blocks that humankind has encountered in its quest to understand the world.

The Philosophers and the Philosophical Movements

i) Idealism

Idealism, which dates from the work of Plato, is a philosophical doctrine that gives metaphysical priority to the mental over the material. The only things that really exist are minds, mental states, or both. Idealism asserts that only 'ideas' exist. Thus, it follows that the empirical world does not exist independently of the human mind.

It contrasts with realism, which proposes that universal concepts exist in their own right, outside of the human mind that perceives or identifies them. Idealism is opposed to the philosophical doctrine known as *nominalism*, which denies the reality of the concept of real entities, or *universals*. Nominalists believe that what we know of things is not what the thing is in itself, but our conception of it through reason and empirical evidence.

Plato (c428/423–c347 BC)

Plato was, with Socrates (470/469–399 BC) and Aristotle, one of Ancient Greece's greatest and most famous philosophers. Although much of Plato's works evolved from those of Socrates, it was also influenced by pre-Socratic thinking. Many of the early Greeks showed an interest in trying to explain the world around them. Democritus believed that the world is comprised of atoms. Xenophanes stated that a man could not know the complete truth about anything because even if he did state it, he would not know that he had done so. These and others, such as Pythagoras, influenced Plato.

Like a true rationalist, Plato thought that knowledge and understanding must come from reason and not experience. The truth is revealed by the mind, and the senses can be wrong. He believed the world to be different when we describe it through language versus how we conceive of it through experience. Central to Plato's philosophy was his *Theory of Ideas* (or *Forms*). By this he means that the world around us is merely appearance, and true reality is the ideas from which appearance derives. The world of appearance is in constant flux whereas the realm of ideas is unaltered. He explained this in the famous story about people living in a cave and watching the images their bodies made against the cave wall, reflected there by a fire. He said that we take the reflections as reality, but only when we turn our back to the reflections and walk out of the cave can we see true reality.

Plato considered the world of senses to be surpassed by the permanent world of real forms. For example, we know and recognise a yellow banana when we see it because it shares the forms of 'yellow' and 'banana'. This was the beginning of modern logic. He was of influence to many modern physicists and mathematicians, and will permeate ideas discussed later.

He considered time to be "a moving image of eternity". Kant, however, added that time was intrinsic to our perception of and ability to infer from the world, and that time and the Universe began simultaneously. It is to him we now turn.

Immanuel Kant (1724–1804)

Kant was, arguably, the most important modern European philosopher, mainly due to the publication in 1781 of his *Critique of Pure Reason*. He was able to bring some sort of order to the philosophy of his time by performing (in his critical period) a synthesis of empiricism (the doctrine that holds that all knowledge comes from experience and that there are no innate ideas) and *rationalism* (the doctrine that holds that reason serves as the only basis for beliefs).

He asked himself, "what are the necessary preconditions for having any experience at all?" He considered our knowledge of the outside world to be dependent on the mechanism by which we perceive it (e.g., sight and sound). He wanted to know which knowledge we have of the world rests on the physical abilities we possess to unravel its truths and which is not due to God-given insight. His work was divided into three periods.

The first *pre-critical* period dealt with investigating the proper method of metaphysics and with looking at fundamental questions in science. This work was scientific and naturalistic in character and consisted of, among other published works, the *General History of Nature and the Theory of the Heavens* (1755). He was concerned, during this time, that rationalism could not demonstrate existence (despite Descartes's belief that he had done so). Kant was worried that empiricism could not show how experience becomes knowledge either, so he aimed to address these problems in his *Critiques*.

The middle period, known as the 'silent decade', was in preparation for his most important work, *The Critique of Pure Reason*. Here, he attempted to address whether metaphysics could exist as a separate science (which Hume denied could happen). Early on in his philosophy, Kant believed that space was absolute (as Newton suggested) rather than relative (as was the opinion of the German polymath Gottfried Willhelm Leibniz).

The third period produced three versions of the critique and set out to determine the capacity of thought.

In the *Critique of Pure Reason*, written at the age of 56, Kant considered the phenomenal world as "transcendentally ideal". That is, it is the world as we can only know it, as allowed by our mental abilities, physiology, and the spatio-temporal arrangement as we interact with the world.

Kant's philosophy of idealism tried to determine the meaning and boundaries of human knowledge. It consists of synthetic propositions and *a posteriori* knowledge. Rationalism holds that knowledge comes from logical and rational deduction, and that innate ideas are the only stable basis of knowledge. It consists of rational propositions and *a priori* knowledge. Kant introduced the term *a priori* such that *a priori* knowledge comes purely from reasoning and is independent of experience. In contrast, *a posteriori* knowledge derives from experience. This world differs from the world *as it is in itself*, which is independent of the things that allow us to know it. Hence, the world we know is only that which is openly visible to our mental framework and abilities. The world as it is, the world of *noumena*, is the world as a God would know it. Kant fused the ideas of these philosophical movements such that synthetic *a priori* statements are possible. Hence, cause and effect take on a deterministic mathematical treatment.

Rationalists claim that reason gives us knowledge of the world, which exists independently of the human mind. What we know of reality is derived from the material world. Empiricists believe that we can have no knowledge of what really exists, and thus cannot know if it really does exist. We can only have knowledge of our perceptions and experiences. Kant bridged this divide with his account of the noumenal and phenomenal worlds. The domain of timeless truth was called the noumena or 'things-in-themselves' (in other words, they have an existence independent of our ability to perceive them), whereas phenomena are 'things-as-they-appear'. Through phenomena, noumena are experienced, and our mental faculties make sense of this information.

For Kant, metaphysics meant the understanding of philosophical knowledge that transcends experience. He believed that such knowledge was both created and *a priori*. Kant sought the knowledge of final truths beyond the confines of everyday existence, epitomising the tradition of Plato, but he also saw knowledge as a synthesis of experience and concepts.

We have to experience an object to be aware of it, but at the same time we must understand it in order to conceive of it. He thought of space and time as *a priori* intuitions, and that we possess *categories* of thought to structure how we make sense of physical reality.

The twelve fundamental judgements (categories) that Kant defined were substance, cause/effect, reciprocity, necessity, possibility, existence, totality, unity, plurality, limitation, reality, and negation. These, together with space and time, are imposed by the human mind on the existence of phenomena encountered in order that man can make sense of the real world. By imposing categories on existence, all that human knowledge can achieve is a systematic knowledge of the phenomena that are presented to the mind. Yet he thought that even if we could bring our perceptions to the highest degree of clarity, we would not be closer to the constitution of things-in-themselves. The limits he set to knowledge whereby appearance (the phenomenal world) and reality (the noumena) are different meant that the thing-in-itself is unknowable. Thus, traditional arguments about God, the soul, and immortality transcend reason. What we think we know bears no relation to the world of noumena.

Kant was influenced by Newton, and in turn, he influenced those whose ideas followed the logical branch of philosophy. Kant also produced important works on science, morality, legal theory, geography, political theory, logic, anthropology, and pedagogy. The German school of idealism grew after Kant's death, whose exponents included Johann Fichte (1762–1814) and Friedrich von Schelling (1775–1854).

ii) Logic and Logical Positivism

Logic

The term 'logic' implies that the argument for a deduction is faultless. Logic represents a branch of philosophy associated with reasoning and argument. It is the study of inference (the process or product of reasoning) and the rules of valid inference. *Abstract patterns of inference* generate an indefinite number of inferences of the same logical form. For example, 'No A is C' infers 'No C is A', and 'A is red' infers 'A is coloured'. *Deductive* logic defines how one thing, said or written, follows from another. *Inductive* logic occurs when larger conclusions are made from singular or simple facts. *Symbolic* logic, also known as mathematical or modern formal logic, uses symbols that represent defined propositions and how they connect to other propositions.

Mathematical logic concerns concepts expressed using formal logical systems. A formal logical system comprises a fixed formal language and a deductive system consisting of inference rules and/or *axioms*. An axiom (or 'postulate') is a proposition that is not proved but considered to be self-evident and a starting point for deducing truths. *Theorems* are derived by principles of deduction from axioms — one expression is derived from previous expressions within that system. So, an axiomatic system is a set of axioms (systems of assertions) from which a few initial propositions can be used to logically derive further inferences and theorems.

First-order logic is a formal logical system that has proof-theoretic properties. In 1931, the Austrian logician Kurt Gödel, through his first and second *incompleteness* theorems, established limits on first-order axiomatisation.

Basically, the first incompleteness theorem states:

> that no formal logical system can be proven to be internally consistent. The first incompleteness theorem states that no consistent system of axioms that can be presented like a computer programme (e.g., the ideal of the *Principia Mathematica*) can prove all facts about *that* system from within the rules of its own axioms — there will always be statements that are true and unprovable within the system. Hence, it is incomplete, and essentially so.

The second incompleteness theorem shows:

> that if such a system is also capable of proving *certain* facts about the system, one truth the system cannot prove is the consistency of the system itself. The second theorem extends from the first since the unprovability of truths *is* an inconsistency.

Logic has been applied to a multitude of philosophical conundrums that have vexed man since time immemorial. An example is the question of how things change through time. When I change my hairstyle, I am still me. Even if I lose a limb, I am still me. The 'me' that exists now looks and thinks differently from the 'me' of twenty years ago and is made of different matter (as our constituent cells are continually changing), yet I am still the same person. It can be argued that when a change is made to something, the old thing ceases to exist and a new thing comes into existence (sharing some of the properties of the old thing). However, logic says that this mistaken conclusion is based on the ambiguity that is is the distinction between objects and properties. So, as I change over time, I as the object remain the same whereas my properties change. I change in terms of material constitution over time, yet the thing that proves my continuation as the same person is memory — I remember events a year ago and know it is me.

The term 'proof' is used in everyday language, but often incorrectly. To prove something is to attempt to convince people of the truth of what is being said. Yet truth is absolute whereas proof relates to the rules of a finite system. We assume a proof denotes the absolute truth of what has been claimed as proven, but what is accepted as proven in one generation may differ in another. Euclid's *Elements of Geometry* were formally deduced from basic axioms, yet it was discovered some 1,200 years later by the German mathematician David Hilbert (1862–1943) that the deductions were incomplete.

Some proofs are accepted now, yet do not seem to be as 'set in stone' as others. For example, the *four-colour conjecture* is a hypothesis that basically states that if you draw boundaries around imaginary countries (of any size and shape) on a piece of paper, it is possible to colour the countries with just four colours so that no boundary is linked on either side by the same colour. This has been proved, disproved, and reproved over the last hundred years or so. The current one thousand-page proof needed over a thousand hours of computer-time to check the 1,936 possible exceptional cases. Here, the 'proof' was not by logic or deduction, but through trial and error of possible examples. It is a humbling case of human ingenuity.

Modern logic involves induction (reasoning by generalisation), deduction (conclusions that necessarily follow from premises), validation, truth, self-reference, probability, paradoxes (statements that appear acceptable yet possess unacceptable contradictory consequences), inference, postulates, propositional and prepositional calculus (truth-function theory), *quantification theory*, and more; the list goes on. These terms define methods and aspects of how modern logical analysis addresses problems posed to man by man or nature. I include the paradoxes, which is important since they describe problems that logic cannot deal with.

We must accept that ultimate truth, for us, may be meaningless. Kant and the German philosopher Arthur Schopenhauer showed this with the descriptive difference between the noumenal and phenomenal world where, as mentioned earlier, noumena underlie our phenomenal experience of the physical and mental world, not objects of possible experience.

Logic, with its rigidity, meets problems in what appear to be the simplest of cases. For example, if I define a bacterium as 'A' and it divides to create two more identical bacteria named 'B' and 'C', then 'B' and 'C' were 'A' but are now distinct. Thus, things that are the same are not necessarily always going to remain the same. Leibniz had stated that if two objects are the same, then a property of one is a property of the other. This statement is not a law as it does not hold for all cases, but Leibniz did not see it as he was more concerned with attempting to formalise things. This formalisation continued and reached its peak in the 1930s. However, we are learning that reality is more complicated than can be easily and rigidly formalised by our order-seeking minds.

As we will go on to see, Wittgenstein realised that a formalisation of language into simple logical rules could not explain what we can say — our reality is simply too complicated for any formal system to be able to describe it as a whole. Both rationalism and empiricism, while being mindful of the trappings of language, appear necessary to describe the world we inhabit. Therefore, rationalists such as Leibniz, Berkeley, and Descartes and empiricists such as Locke and Hume failed in producing an all-encompassing metaphysic. Kant was so highly regarded because he was the first to link rationalism and empiricism in his *Critique of Pure Reason*.

There is a particular type of paradox called a *sorites paradox*. For example, at the age of four years a person is a child, and each second later, he or she is still considered a child. So when is the exact moment they change into an adult? There is vagueness between childhood and adulthood. Another example would be if I named my ageing car 'old Ben' and started replacing all of its constituent parts. Later, the car would still be called 'old Ben', despite the fact that all its parts are now different from when it was originally named. Here, we see that the object is the same (design and name) as are the properties, but the vagueness comes from the term 'is'. One explanation is through something referred to as *fuzzy logic*. When one thing (e.g., the child) fades into the other (e.g., the adult), logic has to deal with the inherent vagueness. If I say "my car is new", there is vagueness to that statement. It is new 'now', but a moment later it is less new, and 'now' even less new.

Truth values are used in logic to deal with vagueness. A sentence is true in a situation if its truth value is greater than or equal to a contextually determined level of acceptability.

Logical positivism

Logical positivism represented a philosophical movement that was popular in the 1920s and 1930s. Its goal was objectivity, where knowledge must be scientifically verifiable. Positivism uses a rigorous treatment of ideas, hence its association with logic. It sets out that in nature there are laws that can be known, but the causes of things cannot. A proposition that cannot be reduced to a simple statement is meaningless. It states that only relations between facts can be known. Positivism itself is a philosophical doctrine stating that positive knowledge, such as scientific fact, can be obtained through direct experience. However, we need to be careful how we define the foundation of logic.

The French philosopher Jacques Derrida (1930–2004) criticised the western philosophical search for a fixed point of origin of truth. His *deconstructionist* view acted as a suspicion against such thinking. That only verifiable scientific propositions have meaning was a key principle of logical positivism. Thus, meaningful statements have to be analytic (where truth or falsity can be assessed through the words and symbols used) or open to observation. All other statements, according to logical positivism, are meaningless. For example, "God is omnipotent" is a meaningless statement because it is neither true by definition nor true or false by experience. There is no test.

Many notable logical positivists (including Moritz Schlick, Rudolf Carnap, Otto Neurath, and Hans Reichenbach) formed what was known as the 'Vienna Circle' of logical positivists, so-named due to the location of their meetings where they discussed philosophical logic. As a guest of and influenced by the Vienna Circle, the young British logical positivist A. J. Ayer (1910–1989) was to bring the *verification* principle to a wider audience principally through his book, *Language, Truth and Logic* (1936). He was also strongly influenced by David Hume. *Language, Truth and Logic* represents a concise exposition of the tenets of logical empiricism. Ayer suggested that the distinction between a conscious man and an unconscious machine is the distinction between "different types of perceptible behaviour". This argument anticipates the Turing Test, conceived by the British computer scientist, cryptanalyst, and 'father of modern computing', Alan Turing (1912–1954) in 1950.

One interesting problem for Schlick and the Vienna Circle was that if a statement is only meaningful if verifiable or by definition, then this principle defining whether a statement is meaningless is itself meaningless because it is neither a definition nor empirically testable. It has been said that the Vienna Circle took Wittgenstein's *Tractatus Logico-Philosophicus* to be their 'bible' on logical positivism. What separated Wittgenstein, of whom more later, from the Vienna Circle (which he refused to join) can be crystallised in the proposition from his *Tractatus Logico-Philosophicus* which declared that "that which cannot be shown must be passed over in silence". Here, to Wittgenstein, everything that cannot be shown *is* what is important. The *Tractatus Logico-Philosophicus* was just a tool to disseminate that which can and cannot be shown.

In typical Wittgenstein style, he informed those of the Vienna Circle who were impressed by the *Tractatus Logico-Philosophicus* that they had misinterpreted its meaning, stating that the book's point is an ethical one. The work consisted of two parts — that which was presented in the book and that which was not written. And it is precisely this second part that Wittgenstein considered important. The Vienna Circle saw the *Tractatus Logico-Philosophicus*'s purpose as clearing the way for science by removing irrelevant philosophical nonsense (analyses of things that cannot be shown). The irony was that Wittgenstein had little time for science, and all interpretations of his book seemed to annoy him.

The logical positivist movement faded as it became clear that logic alone could not solve the 'problems of philosophy'— such as meaning, knowing, the eternal questions of "what am I?" and "what can I know?"

and the like. However, a number of philosophers who placed emphasis on logic *have* made a lasting impression on human understanding, and they are discussed below. We start with a return to Ancient Greece.

Aristotle (384–322 BC)

At the age of seventeen (although some reports state that this was at the age of thirty), Aristotle travelled to Athens to study under Plato. He stayed there for twenty years until Plato's successor, Speusippos, added a mathematical bias to the philosophical teaching, which Aristotle did not agree with. This is ironic, since mathematics and logic are so inextricably linked, and Aristotle was considered the founder of logic. Western philosophy based on logic began with Aristotle, who was the last of the great Greek philosophers and the first to attempt a categorisation of knowledge. Only recently through the explosion of science have we seen a fading out of this categorisation along predetermined paths. Although Aristotle was taught by Plato, his metaphysics was opposed to Plato's idealism. Plato was more religious than Aristotle, who considered that the world around him was real and can therefore be analysed scientifically.

Aristotle expected to succeed Speusippos after his death as head of the Academy and was affronted when the position was given to Xenocrates. This decision annoyed Aristotle so much that he set up his own teaching institution, the Lyceum. There, he studied and wrote on many topics including logic, ethics (in which he rejected Plato's absolutism), metaphysics, mathematics, botany, history, literary composition, meteorology, oratory, religion, zoology, the physical world, political science, and psychology. No subject seemed unworthy of his analysis. He was perhaps the first taxonomist, believing that every feature of an animal was there for a function. The Lyceum survived until it was finally closed around the year 500.

Aristotle's early works have been lost (though his lecture notes from the Lyceum have survived), but they were based on the futility of existence and the joys of the afterlife. His later philosophy was based on research, reason, and inductive logic, which was a far cry from the dialectic method of his predecessors. None of Aristotle's theories and conclusions were considered by him to be final but, rather, formed a summary of evidence at that time, always open to refinement and improvement as new information and knowledge was applied to the problem. This approach seems astonishingly modern.

Aristotle believed that all knowledge could be obtained from observing the thing to be explained, and that something could only be understood and explained through its causality. To describe causality, Aristotle considered the ideas of actuality (what happens) and potentiality (where something has the *potential* of qualities). He proposed that substance (e.g., a house) was the product of matter (bricks) and form (the design of the house). Thus, he set out four causes:

1. The Material cause — defines an object's substance.
2. The Formal cause — defines its design.
3. The Efficient cause — defines its maker.
4. The Final cause — defines its function.

The function of a thing was the most important cause to Aristotle. He was the first to develop deductive inference for which he defined syllogisms (deductively valid arguments). He concentrated on perfect syllogisms, which consisted of two premises and a conclusion from them. For example:

1. If all men are mortal, and
2. Socrates is a man, then
3. Socrates is mortal.

However, Aristotle did not realise that knowledge of the truth of the statement "all men are mortal" is achieved by induction. He was not sure what such logic was telling us. Did it relate to the objective world directly, or did it only tell us about how language or the human mind itself works? Aristotle devised different types of syllogism, but they all consisted of the same basic structure — a major premise followed by a minor premise, and then a conclusion.

Although not all arguments can be formed according to Aristotle's syllogistic logic, it was formed in accordance with his metaphysical goals, which were to develop a logical theory of language that could describe the fundamental objects required for a complete understanding of reality.

Aristotle said that for a sentence to be true, it must correspond to the facts. This later became the *correspondence theory of truth*, where something said (e.g., "snow is white") is deemed true if the statement corresponds with the facts in the world (that snow *is* white). Yet if someone agrees with the statement, it does not make the statement true, merely that his or her opinion is that the statement is true. This theory was largely replaced by the *redundancy theory of truth*. Here, if I say "water is a liquid", then that is how it is believed to be.

So who was the greater philosopher, Plato or Aristotle? It has been suggested that they were equally talented metaphysicists. Aristotle was a master of ethics and epistemology, yet Plato was the ideas man (with Aristotle suggesting answers to Plato's questions).

Despite his greatness, Aristotle made some serious errors. For example, he believed the Earth to be the centre of the Universe, despite evidence suggesting that it orbited the Sun. We now move two thousand years forward from Aristotle to the next great logician, mathematician, and philosopher, Friedrich Ludwig Gottlob Frege, who marked a transition in logical philosophy.

Gottlob Frege (1848–1925)

Frege's importance was only really recognised after his death when he was recognised as the founder of modern symbolic logic — now termed *analytical philosophy*. In fact, his work on mathematical logic led to the development of the computer. His goal, however, was to derive all mathematics from logical assumptions that have been derived from deductive reasoning. He wanted to use logic rather than epistemology as the starting reference point for philosophy. He removed unformulated reasoning from mathematics, placing it on strong foundations. Furthermore, he showed mathematics to be a branch of logic. Frege proved wrong Kant's theory of mathematical propositions as synthetic *a priori* knowledge.

Frege's most important work was his *Begriffsschrift* ('*Concept Script*'), published in 1879, which formulated a new logical calculus that set out to clarify logical relationships concealed in ordinary language. By applying mathematical logic to language, he showed how an argument could be presented rigorously. Freed from metaphysical language, Frege's arguments could be constructed with logical meaning. However, the British philosopher/logician Bertrand Russell and Gödel were to show, later, that his work was riddled with contradictions, although that does not detract from his contribution.

Frege defined the difference between *sense* and *reference*. The sense of a word is a proposition and can have different colourings (e.g., the word 'river' conjures up different images in different people), whereas the reference, the actual river, is constant. This distinction was influential to Wittgenstein and Russell. The *Begriffsschrift* contained the first systematic formulation of prepositional calculus, where laws are derived from simple primitive principles. Frege developed quantification theory, which was used to render validity to expressions such as 'all' and 'none' in symbolic logic. Quantificational logic revolutionised the field and replaced Aristotle's syllogistic logic in university syllabuses.

His interest in logic was to help him with his philosophy of mathematics, where his most important question was: "do mathematical proofs depend on logic, or do they need the support of empirical facts?" In his attempt to answer this, he wondered how far he could go in arithmetic using logic alone. The work of Russell and, later, Gödel was to reveal limits for the formalisation of mathematics that would shatter Frege's goal.

Bertrand Russell (1872–1970)

Russell, or his full title, the third Earl Bertrand Arthur William Russell, was a Welsh philosopher who was made famous for, among other things, his many contributions to the public understanding of philosophical and scientific issues as well as his support of the emerging anti-nuclear movement in the early 1960s. In his long life, he was awarded the Nobel Prize for literature, made the philosophical world aware of the importance of the work of Frege, and was a teacher and mentor of Wittgenstein — perhaps one of the few who knew him well. Between the time of Descartes and Russell, the main branch of philosophy was epistemology, which is basically the study of what we *can* know. It examines the nature and limits of knowledge and compares knowledge with belief. Russell developed new approaches to epistemology.

Russell's philosophy, rooted in logic and empiricism, always incorporated science. He invested great effort in the field of epistemology and he wanted to know the relation between our knowledge and the external world. Our senses are mental experiences of the external world, and science is the application of the mind to increase our sensory experience, yet science does not tell us about the thing in itself. The questions that have hounded western philosophy since Plato, such as "what can we know for certain?" and "can certainty be formulated on logical foundations?" were the ultimate focus for Russell rather than those relating to being and existence. Hence, we can follow the train of thought relating to the foundations on certainty from Plato through to the conclusions of Wittgenstein (that it is all a problem of language), whereas those of 'being' currently appear to be accepted as unaffected by Wittgenstein's criticisms (if one follows Heidegger's arguments), since being underlies everything.

Russell's work can be placed into three different areas — philosophical logic, the foundations of mathematics, and finally epistemology and metaphysics. In fact, his work, *A History of Western Philosophy* (1945), was his best-known philosophical publication and demonstrated his wide-ranging knowledge of philosophy. It showed that no two philosophies are mutually exclusive. However, his most influential idea was that relating to meaning and quantification.

Modern philosophy, in the form of the Derrida and Michel Foucault (also a Frenchman), attempts to say that there is no such thing as universal truth (Derrida) and that knowledge relates to its era and cultural or geographical origins (Foucault). It seems that as scientific knowledge increases, there is no philosophical foundation to relate this expansion to.

We tend not to think about the foundations of knowledge, what can we know for certain, our mortality, or our existence in essence; rather, we know that science works in the sense that we can extract more and more use from it and, from a material and capitalist sense, this is enough and thus it is acceptable to avoid deeper questions. Russell's work to find a philosophy of logical certainty was irreparably damaged by Gödel's incompleteness theorem, which revealed the internal inconsistency and incompleteness of formal axiomatised systems. In such systems, for example, Gödel demonstrated that contradictory statements could be shown to be both true and false. Of importance to Russell, it showed that not all true statements could be proved, which is a theorem that is universally accepted.

Wittgenstein's linguistic philosophy, to a lesser extent, also damaged Russell's plan. Though not universally accepted as correct in every detail, Wittgenstein did show that many of the problems of philosophy are, through the nature of language, rendered meaningless. However, this was much later, and when Russell asked his questions about certainty, the solutions seemed to be attainable through the application of clear thinking, rigour, and logic.

Essentially, when Russell realised the foundations of mathematics were not as solid as he had expected, he thought that he could use logic to strengthen these foundations. It is now believed that there is no proper knowledge or truth in mathematics — it represents convenient ways of manipulating abstract symbols that 'make possible' the genuine knowledge acquired using the physical sciences. However, there was debate as to whether mathematics is a science of mathematical objects and concepts that are real and Platonic (as Frege saw it) or a system of techniques for the manipulation of mathematical signs — a tool for making 'showable' reality clearer (as Wittgenstein saw it). Einstein, Georg Cantor (the German mathematician, and creator of *set theory*), and Gödel, but not the influential physicists Niels Bohr and Werner Heisenberg (1901–1976), believed that mathematical objects and properties exist objectively and independently of knowledge of them by the human mind. For example, a square is a square independent of our conception of it. The question is whether it only has existence when perceived and conceived, and is a square always a square, independent of the type of perceiving construction?

While at Cambridge University, Russell's first connection with philosophy was a metaphysical system based on Hegel's idealism. This, he hoped, would provide the answers he sought. However, he rejected this idealism as he saw it as illogical. He began to see things more in terms of what we experience, as was the view of another eminent Cambridge philosopher, George Edward Moore (1873–1958). Thus, he adopted an empirical materialist view. But this did not help him on his question about the foundation of mathematics. Euclid's axioms formed the basis of geometry, yet the basis of the axioms were not logically defined. So, after Russell met the

Italian mathematician Giuseppe Peano (1858–1942, famous for *Peano arithmetic*), who had been working on the logical foundations of number, he set about using what he had learned to produce a logical foundation for number. Russell was not entirely convinced by Peano's methods and set about devising the notion of *class* (or *set*, as classes are now known).

Class is a logical distinction that identifies something. Something cannot be itself and not itself. A set is something which everything under that definition belong — 'all houses' or 'all people', for example, are sets. That is, every person is included in the set 'all people'. Russell showed that the notion of class is prior to that of number. For example, the class of 'all bananas' can be conceived without collecting all the bananas in the world and counting them. Russell used the notion of class to form the concept of number. More importantly, he showed that the truth of mathematics could be reduced to the truth of logic. He published *The Principles of Mathematics* in 1903, showing that mathematics was reducible to logical forms. Firmly concentrated on logic, he still believed that science could not as easily be reduced to logical form as mathematics.

The Principles of Mathematics was written in English, so Russell decided to put his ideas on logical analysis into symbolic form, which was not open to linguistic interpretation. This work resulted in the publication of the three-volume *Principia Mathematica* (1910–1913), which took Russell and co-author Alfred North Whitehead ten years to complete. Russell used the logical formalism of his *Principia Mathematica* to reassert problems in their logical form. He stated that mathematical truths could be translated into truths of pure logic, and once in their logical form could be proved by logic alone.

Relatively early in this project, Russell encountered a problem that he thought he could quickly overcome but proved to be more difficult. This problem is now known as *Russell's paradox*, which goes like this. Let us first define a 'normal' class as one that is *not* a member of itself (e.g., the class of 'philosophers', since the class of philosophers is not a philosopher), and a 'non-normal' class as one that *is* a member of itself (e.g., the class of 'thinkable things', since the class of thinkable things is a thinkable thing). Then, let 'N' be the class of all normal classes. Here we encounter the paradox when we ask, "is N a member of itself?" If we say that it is, then it is normal by the definition of 'N'. However, by being a member of itself, it is also non-normal by the definition of 'non-normal'. Yet it cannot be both normal and non-normal at the same time as this leads to a contradiction.

When Frege's Vol. 2 of the *Grundgesetze* was about to go to press in 1903, Russell wrote to him explaining that Russell's paradox could be derived from Frege's Basic Law V. It is easy to define the relation of *membership* of a set or extension in Frege's system. Russell then drew attention to "the set of things x that are such that x is not a member of x". Because the system of the *Grundgesetze* states that the set characterised *both is and* is not a member of itself, it is inconsistent. Frege honestly, and famously, wrote of the depressing and crushing realisation of the implication of Russell's insight.

So, it seems that logic and language are not necessarily consistent all the time and, although Russell tried to fix this, it was not until the genius of Gödel that the reason why such problems were doomed was placed on solid foundations. His conclusions were somewhat disconcerting. They upset Hilbert's programmes for formalisation or axiomatisation of arithmetic and all that followed (though the Gödel Theorem is not the direct reason that Russell and Whitehead's *Principia Mathematica* is a dead letter). Hilbert wanted to show that mathematics could be consistent (i.e., following the rules of the system would never lead to a contradiction), complete (i.e., for any true statement, the rules of the system can be used to prove it), and decidable (i.e., a test must exist that can decide whether a mathematical assertion is provable). Gödel showed that no system of mathematics could be both consistent *and* complete. He did this by constructing a mathematical assertion that said, "this assertion cannot be proved". If proved, there is a contradiction and the system is inconsistent. If it cannot be proved, then even though the assertion is true, the system is incomplete as it cannot be proved. Thus, Gödel showed that consistency and completeness are mutually exclusive. A few years later, Alan Turing, who we will return to in the final two chapters, addressed the decidability issue with similar conclusions.

Russell's *theory of types* attempted to 'fix' the problem and avoid incompleteness paradoxes by stating that sets could only enter a set of higher order. However, this approach was not rooted in logic and was crushed by Gödel. Russell wrote to the French mathematician Henri Poincaré (1854–1912), who likened the problem to *Epimenides's Paradox*. The Cretan Epimenides' statement was "all Cretans are liars", which is a self-referential paradox. If all Cretans are liars, then what he is saying is untrue and all

Cretans are not liars, as he who says it *is* a Cretan. That is, he is not a liar, making the statement false. However, if all Cretans are not liars, then what he is saying is true, so all Cretans are liars, making the statement true. If it is false it is true, and if true it is false. A similar issue occurs when I write "this sentence is false". If "this sentence is false" is true, then the sentence is false, which means it is actually true. Yet this also means it is false. This reasoning is cyclic *ad infinitum*. If, however, we choose to believe that "all Cretans are liars" is false, then the statement is true which means it is false, but this would also mean it is true. This reasoning, too, is cyclic *ad infinitum* and has been called *the liar paradox*.

Russell overcame the class definition problem with the ingenious invention of the theory of types. Here, he distinguished between different types of class such that what was true for classes of individuals (e.g., humans) was not true for classes of classes (e.g., mammals). With the theory of types in place, the *Principia Mathematica* took only another seven years to produce (largely by Russell alone due to Whitehead's teaching duties). The logic of this work formed the foundation of the logical positivism movement in the 1920s.

Russell's method of philosophical logic is less popular now than it was in the last century, though its effects were profound on the development of logic. His *theory of descriptions* was of great importance for defining the meaning of sentences. For example, the phrase "the king of France is bald" makes sense, but in the French Republic there is no king, so the sentence is meaningful in its construction but also meaningless in reality. The Austrian logician Alexius Meinong stated that such a sentence could exist in the world of logic, yet this allows us to deny its existence in the world of reality. From this perspective, the "bald king of France" is real in the sense of logical reality. Russell wanted more order than these ideas implied, so he invented the theory of descriptions to resolve this. For the "king of France is bald" example, Russell's method breaks it down into three parts:

1. There is a king of France.
2. There is only one king of France.
3. Whatever is king of France is bald (which shows similarity to Aristotle's syllogisms).

By exposing this logic, Russell was able to show that the statement makes sense but is false. It enabled logical assessments of the sense and reality of all sentences.

Russell's discovery that a proposition can be logically correct but meaningless led logical positivists to show that there are three types of propositions:

1. Mathematical and logical propositions are tautological (one part of the proposition explains the other, such as "blue is blue").
2. Some propositions are verified by experience.
3. Some propositions are metaphysical and thus meaningless. "God exists" is a meaningless proposition as it cannot be verified. More worryingly, all ethical propositions, such as "murder is wrong", are logically meaningless — rather, they are opinions.

Put another way, genuine propositions are either formal propositions, which are tautologies if true and contradictions if false, or factual propositions, which are tested empirically. Statements that fit neither case are meaningless. The meaning of a proposition is its method of verification. This was the conclusion of logical positivists, but it resulted in a paradox that could not be as easily removed as the 'class' issue. Gödel eventually resolved it by showing that complete mathematical systems, such as the *Principia Mathematica,* are not only incomplete but are *essentially* incomplete. Therefore, mathematical statements exist that lie beyond proof and disproof.

According to the philosophers Ernest Nagel and James Newman, although Gödel's proof showed that a finitistic absolute proof using the logical formalism of *Principia Mathematica* was impossible, it did not eliminate the possibility of finitistic proofs *per se*. That is, those not mirrored inside *Principia Mathematica* are theoretically possible, although no one yet knows what such proofs will be like. Thus, we will assume herein that his theorem applies to all known formal logical systems.

Gödel's incompleteness proof has been bracketed in the same league of scientific merit, ingenuity, brilliance, and importance as Einstein's theories of relativity. He showed that complete axiomatic systems are intrinsically paradoxical. However, despite this putting an end to Russell's dream, science is still able to function despite limitations (e.g., *quantum indeterminism* and the uncertainty principle; see Chapter 3). Russell later considered the *Principia Mathematica* to have been a waste of effort as he noted that only six people had read it in its entirety. However, it was important for his later work on the meaning of language.

Ultimately, Russell wanted to unite philosophy and science. However, he realised that if the material world is constructed from sensory information, then we do not know what it is in itself — one is left wondering if the material world exists outside the mind. Russell considered the sensory data that our mind receives about the external world as 'atomic simples' and our knowledge was constructed from their logical construction. Hence, his philosophy is one of *logical atomism*. More specifically, deciding whether a statement is true requires breaking down the construction into logical atoms and seeing whether the construction is logically correct. Here was a link with Wittgenstein.

Whereas Wittgenstein insisted on the fundamental importance of logic in understanding reality (and how language relates to this), Russell was increasingly insistent on epistemology and the real world applications of science. Hence, we can understand the Austrian philosopher Karl Popper's admiration of Russell (and his insistence of Wittgenstein's irrelevance). There are two sides to the argument. Russell and Popper accepted the failings that linguistic analysis, Gödelian incompleteness, and quantum indeterminism, for example, said about our access to knowledge of reality. Yet, if science works, then the world is still in a 'good' state despite our knowledge limitations. Wittgenstein was convinced that we realise the fundamental importance of what we can and cannot say about reality — language structure reveals world structure, but science was not his concern. However, Russell was central to the transfer of philosophical interest from epistemology to the philosophy of language. He placed great importance on language because he considered words to be the lenses through which we access the world and our thoughts.

Georg Cantor (1845–1918)

Cantor spent much of his (what turned out to be) miserable existence trying to understand what the great mathematicians before him had tried and failed to do. He wanted to know what infinity is and, in doing so, created a whole new area of mathematics known as *set theory* and drove himself to the brink of insanity. There were two reasons for this. First, his work was in fierce contradiction to that of the leading mathematician in Germany at that time, Leopold Kronecker (of whom Cantor had been a pupil at the University of Berlin), and second, his obsessive compulsion to delve ever deeper into the infinite abyss took him ever further from reality. He was, like Gödel after him, pitching the finite mind of man against a concept that has no limitation. So what was Cantor's great contribution?

If we take a list of the first ten natural numbers (ordinary counting numbers 1, 2, 3...) and try to link them to the first ten odd numbers while excluding one, like so:

1→3
2→5
3→7
4→9
5→11
6→13
7→15
8→17
9→19
10→... *ad infinitum*

we see that there is a one-to-one correspondence between the two sets. The two sets are infinite, of the same size, and referred to as *countable* infinities.

Cantor also showed that fractions created by dividing one whole number by another are also infinite. He created a theoretically infinite table that excluded the possibility of missing any possible fractions. The inclusion of all possible fractions was due to the following ingenious table construction:

1/1
2/1, 1/2
1/3, 2/2, 3/1
4/1, 3/2, 2/3, 1/4
1/5, 2/4, 3/3, 4/2, 5/1
6/1, 5/2, 4/3, 3/4, 2/5, 1/6, ... *ad infinitum*

Along each row in this table, the sum of the denominator plus the numerator of each number add up to the same number. Take row 3 for example. For 1/3, 2/2, and 3/1, $1 + 3 = 2 + 2 = 3 + 1$. This definite order for counting all fractions ensures that *all* fractions are counted. Cantor realised that there are as many fractions as there are single numbers. There is a one-to-one correspondence. These too are countable infinities.

Before Cantor, it was thought that there is only one type of infinity, and we cannot have any comprehension of what it is other than that it is unknowable. Thus, we had best leave it alone. Cantor, however, began to realise that there is not only one type of infinity. He showed that the number of natural numbers is not a natural number, but a *transfinite* number.

This transfinite number, called *aleph null* or *aleph nought*, is the smallest of infinite transfinite numbers (infinities, or *cardinals*). Hence, he introduced the concept of 'cardinality'. The cardinality of a set is a measure of the number of elements in the set. If a set, $A = \{1, 2, 3\}$, contains three elements, then A has a cardinality of 3. 'Aleph nought' is the cardinality of the set of all natural numbers and is the first transfinite cardinal. The smallest infinities that can exist, according to Cantor, are also called $\omega 0$ infinities (like the countable infinite sets shown above). There are no infinities between type $\omega 0$ and $\omega 1$. To be clear, for $\omega 0$, numbers have a one-to-one correspondence — like the even numbers to odd numbers. There are an infinite number of both, so they are both $\omega 0$ type infinities.

Where did Cantor go from here? He looked for higher order infinities, something previously unheard of. There are infinite natural numbers (e.g., 1, 2, 3 ...) and infinite real numbers (including the rational, such as 42, and irrational, such as $\sqrt{2}$), but there are more real numbers than natural numbers. So, there are different orders of infinity. If you take a number, 1, and the next number, 2, then is the set of all decimals between them a larger type infinity? The answer is yes — it is a ω1 type infinity. Why? Cantor showed it this way. If we take the following correspondence:

1→ 1.1354356
2→ 1.14536785
3→ 1.15467567
4→ 1.165556

by underlining the first numeral after the decimal point of the correspondent to the first natural number of the sequence, then the second number after the decimal point of the correspondent to the second natural number in the sequence, and so on accordingly as shown above, we make this a number:

1.1445

and then we add 1 to each number after the decimal point to give:

1.2556

then this number cannot exist in the series because we have added 1. So a one-to-one correspondence between each infinite set cannot occur, meaning that the second set is a larger and denser infinity than the first. This is an uncountable' infinity.

In fact, there are infinite orders of infinity. If you have an infinite set, then you can generate one that is infinitely bigger by considering the set that contains all its subsets (e.g., the set A, B, C has 8 subsets = 0, A, B, C, AB, AC, BC, ABC). This is the 'power' set. The power set of ω0 is p[ω0]. There is a power set of p[ω0] *ad infinitum* up to 'absolute' infinity.

If a set is defined A, B, C, then it contains three members. Its power set is 0, A, B, C, AB, BC, AC, ABC, which contains eight members. The power set of this set contains 0, A, B, C, AB, AC, AAB, ABC, AAC, AABC, BC, BAB, BBC, BAC, BABC, CAB, CA, CB, CBC, CAC, CABC, ABA … and so on, and contains 256 members. The power set of a set contains 2^n members, where the set has n members. So the power set of each infinity contains more members. Thus, some infinities can be larger than other infinities. For power sets, ω0→ω1→ω2 and so on.

Cantor's hypothesis is:

> The number of points on a line, $2^{\aleph_0}$, is the next infinite number, $\aleph_1$, after the smallest infinite number, $\aleph_0$, which is the cardinality of the set of all natural numbers. Thus, $2^{\aleph_0} = \aleph_1$.

Gödel finally showed that Cantor's hypothesis, which Cantor could not prove, could not be disproved (arguably a marked improvement).

There are mathematical infinities. For example, the logarithm (log) of any number of a defined base is the power that the base must be raised to produce the number. The log of 10000 to base 10 is 4, since $10^4 = 10000$. A graphical representation (on a vertical y-axis and horizontal x-axis) of $\log_{10}$ (logarithm to the base 10) functions, like all log functions of any base, approach the y-axis but never reach it because of the mathematical singularity at $x = 0$. We can say that the graph reaches the y-axis at infinity.

There are physical infinities, which are infinities of the physical universe. The nature of space, in the context of infinite space and time (*spacetime*), cannot be contemplated. Is space infinite? The two-dimensional surface of Earth is finite, but one could, hypothetically, walk around it forever. Cosmologists believe that the universe may have a similarly folded (albeit dimensionally more complex) topology. Thus, travelling in a straight line may return one to the same point. It may also be beyond our finite comprehension.

Great minds have made their opinions known as to their beliefs about the different forms of infinity. Russell, Gödel, Hilbert, and Cantor all believed in mathematical infinity. Only Russell and Cantor believed in physical infinity, whereas only Cantor believed in absolute infinity.

Kurt Gödel (1906–1978)

The great Greek mathematician and 'father of geometry' Euclid was active around 300BC. His *Elements* is still available today (in modern form of print, of course). He aimed to combine numerical and geometric observations into a system whereby *a priori* elementary axioms would lead through rigorous proof to theorems. This became the methodology that mathematics after him followed.

By 1900, David Hilbert laid out the idea that because mathematics had the tools of formal logic (thanks to Frege and the like), mathematics itself could be examined rigorously. Hence, the method of axioms → rigorous proof → theorems should be applied to theories according to formal logic. As such, all true statements should be formally provable. Russell and Whitehead's *Principia Mathematica* aimed to achieve a complete formal and deductive proof theory of mathematics, but it was incomplete as it could not show the completeness of mathematical theories. Thus, within a large axiomatic system, if a problem exists that is unproven, it is not known whether the problem is unprovable or just difficult (Turing showed this).

It was Gödel who had shown why this unprovability is the case. He demonstrated that every unproved statement could be unprovable. In particular, he showed that:

1. There are proofs that cannot be shown as true using that system's axioms, thus demonstrating the incompleteness of sufficiently large axiomatic systems, and
2. One proof that cannot be shown is the consistency of the system.

The implications were far-reaching in many areas. At the time of Gödel's publication, mathematicians became concerned that some *a priori* axioms were potentially wrong (with consequences) and some problems were unprovable. Take the Riemann hypothesis, named after the German mathematician Bernhard Riemann (1826–1866), for example (all non-trivial zeros of the Riemann zeta function have real part ½), and the Goldbach conjecture, named after the Prussian mathematician Christian Goldbach (where every even number greater than 2 can be expressed as the sum of two primes). Both are intricately linked to number theory. These theorems remain unproven, but are assumed to be correct. However, until proven (i.e., right or wrong), we do not know if they are provable (but difficult) or unprovable.

We know that Gödel's theorem is far-reaching, but how does it work? He made a system where formulae and theorems could be expressed as numbers (Gödel numbers), and the method can be performed in different ways. Basically, the symbols (vocabulary) of arithmetic were assigned a unique Gödel number', and numbers were given to numerical variables, sentential variables (replaceable by formulae), and predicate variables. With this, any arithmetic sentence can be expressed as a single number. For instance:

$$1 + 1 = 2$$

is written as:

$$s0 + s0 = ss0$$

(where 's' means "the immediate successor of", and 1 is the immediate successor of 0).

So, since s, 0, +, and = each have a unique Gödel number:

s0 + s0 = ss0 can be written as 7611765 776

(where 's' is assigned the number 7, '0' the number 6, '+' the number 11, and '=' the number 5).

Then, successive prime numbers each raised to the power of each number in the above sequence when multiplied together gives:

$$2^7 \times 3^6 \times 5^{11} \times 7^7 \times 11^6 \times 13^5 \times 17^7 \times 19^7 \times 23^6 = ?$$

Now, taking a step back, it was Gauss who, in his 1801 book *Disquistitiones Arithmeticae*, proved the unique factorisation theorem. Here, every integer (whole number) greater than 1 is either a prime number or a product of primes (up to the order of the factors).

For example, 1200 is a composite number (a whole integer that is not a prime and thus can be produced by the multiplication of other whole numbers; e.g., 30 × 40). 1200 is also, according to the unique factorisation theorem, a product of primes:

$$1200 = 2^4 \times 3^1 \times 5^2 = 3 \times 2 \times 2 \times 2 \times 2 \times 5 \times 5$$

So, going back to the value of our other number (represented by $2^7 \times 3^6 \times 5^{11} \times 7^7 \times 11^6 \times 13^5 \times 17^7 \times 19^7 \times 23^6$), there is a unique way of deconstructing it into prime factors. So, if we were given the Gödel number of the value of the equation $2^7 \times 3^6 \times 5^{11} \times 7^7 \times 11^6 \times 13^5 \times 17^7 \times 19^7 \times 23^6$, we could deconstruct it uniquely to reproduce the formula 1 + 1 = 2.

This seems complicated, but by using unique prime factorisations, any formula or equation of a formal axiomatic system can be uniquely constructed. In essence, arithmetic sentences can be constructed into a Gödel number and back to arithmetic sentences. The practicality of this was irrelevant, whereas the significance was great because metamathematical statements about a formal axiomatic system could be constructed using the axioms of the system (represented by the Gödel numbers). It should be remembered that "1 + 1 = 2" is a mathematical statement (an equation), whereas "1 + 1 = 2 is an equation" is a metamathematical statement, and both can be expressed by Gödel using the rules of the axiomatic system.

It is possible to generate a Gödel number for a sufficiently complex formal axiomatic system that corresponds to a metamathematical statement that says "formula X, with the Gödel number x, shows that there is a formula within the system that is not provable using the rules of that system". This was Gödel's first incompleteness theorem. Thus, 'truths' logically constructed using a system's axioms cannot be proven true using the axioms of the system. The second incompleteness theorem then follows in that such a system cannot prove its own consistency. Gödel showed that these systems are both incomplete and inconsistent. There are many ways of saying this, but the profound truth is the essential incompleteness and inconsistency.

When Bertrand Russell tried to plug the gaps in his *Principia Mathematica* (with the aim of generating a complete and consistent system such as geometry), the added axioms would not produce this result. Rather, a deeper level 'meta-metamathematical' (*ad infinitum* in theory) Gödel number would produce a sentence of inconsistency and incompleteness.

Incompleteness and why Principia Mathematica failed

The logical path that led to Gödel's theorem is thought to have begun with the conflict between the intuitionist approach of Dutch mathematician Luitzen Egbertus Jan Brouwer (1881–1966) and the formalism of David Hilbert. The two key logical controversies in mathematics that existed at the time were the invention of transfinite arithmetic by Cantor and Frege's effort to reduce mathematics to logical formalism using set theory.

Russell was to show that Frege's method to achieve his goal would fail, just as Gödel was to do the same for Russell's effort to create a theory that would derive all mathematics from logical axioms. From Russell's work, two key questions remained:

1. Could a contradiction be derived from the *Principia*'s axioms (relating to consistency)?
2. Are there mathematical statements that are unprovable in the system (relating to completeness)?

It was Gödel's theorem that addressed and answered these questions.

The resolution of Russell's paradox affected the status of Cantor's transfinite arithmetic since Cantor's logical methods to prove his results were similar to those used in Russell's paradox. Cantor had developed naïve set theory to study infinite sets, but this method used a natural language that is typically used for human communication as opposed to a formal language designed for mathematical logic. He used transfinite numbers to show that the set of natural numbers cannot be completed — they are an infinite set. Therefore, *any* list of real numbers is incomplete. Russell's paradox showed that non-formalised axiomatic systems such as his lead to contradictions.

Since non-formalised axiomatic systems lead to contradictions, axiomatic set theory was developed to determine operation limits. Many axiomatic systems have been developed since Gödel that can avoid paradoxes such as Russell's. Ernst Zermelo and Abraham Fraenkel attempted to develop a theory of sets free of paradoxes (e.g., Russell's Paradox). They developed 'Zermelo-Fraenkel set theory with the axiom of choice', which is now the standard form of axiomatic set theory. Zermelo-Fraenkel set theory and its included Peano arithmetic are subject to the same limitations as *Principia Mathematica*, but is alive and well (thriving in fact).

Ludwig Wittgenstein (1889–1951)

Ludwig Josef Johann Wittgenstein was an analytical philosopher whose work, as stated earlier, affected the development and progress of what was to become a defunct philosophy, logical positivism. However, his influence was far more profound and wide-ranging. Despite being unconventional in many ways, such as his limited traditional philosophical training and dismissal of what he considered irrelevant, his work affected diverse philosophical areas of inquiry even to this day.

Rather than suggesting answers to specific philosophical problems, perhaps Wittgenstein's greatest influence was the ability of his deep, penetrating mind to uncover problems we were unaware of in order to clarify how to address certain philosophical issues or, indeed, whether they were addressable or even worth addressing. He was interested in language, and by penetrating its essence and meaning, he cast his scathing and critical eye over poorly defined philosophical conundrums. Hence, he aimed to show what could or could not be said meaningfully.

Wittgenstein has, therefore, been given more space than any other philosopher in this book. Although the opinions of many philosophers are presented on subjects they specialise in, Wittgenstein's work permeates many questions and represents deep insights into the struggle of man in relating the mind to the external world.

The early work of Wittgenstein was influenced by a number of philosophers, including Frege, Russell, Schopenhauer, and Baruch Spinoza. His *Tractatus Logico-Philosophicus* was written as a tool, a metaphorical ladder to climb and then discard once ascended, providing not answers but mental tools and clarity with which to address problems. Once written, he lost interest in philosophy and left the field. However, far from 'solving the problems of philosophy' as he claimed at the time of writing, he came to reject this work and as a result returned to philosophy and focused on the same problems but with a less analytical bent. This later work did not seem to stem from any philosophical view, as would be the case for most philosophical writing, but was clearly the result of years of intense rethinking about similar issues. With his unique style, clarity, depth, and insight, Wittgenstein's work was yet again met with a mix of confusion and admiration. The later work, however, continues to be of great influence and interest to those working in diverse disciplines.

Russell, to whom Wittgenstein was a protégé, considered Wittgenstein to be the most perfect example of genius as it is traditionally conceived that he had ever known. Russell stated that he was passionate, profound, intense, and domineering. Perhaps his personality made his work less prone to criticism by his contemporaries than would otherwise be the case. The style that Wittgenstein employed in his philosophy (especially the later work) made it notoriously difficult to follow at the level he intended. Even renowned philosophers such as Norman Malcolm (who both studied under and was a close friend of Wittgenstein) said it took three terms of lectures at Cambridge University by Wittgenstein before he had any idea of what was being talked about!

Wittgenstein probed the very limits and essence of logic. This difficult subject together with Wittgenstein's highly regarded intellect and difficult manner did not help with comprehension. His views are much debated even today; such is the difficulty and perhaps lack of clarity of his interpretations and deductions. It seems that Wittgenstein was either very highly regarded or not at all. Those who did not rate his work highly seem to consider those who did as suffering from excessive adulation and hero worship. Those who *did* rate him believed that those who did not were just incapable of understanding his insights.

As Wittgenstein received no formal training in philosophy whatsoever, his analyses were not constructed of the form common to philosophers, adding to its difficulty in interpretation. For example, in his earlier work, he did not give examples to demonstrate or back up his conclusions. Despite this, the fundamental importance of the issues he considered and his insights into them drew attention and admiration.

His principal concern was the nature of language and logic and how it represents reality. His linguistic analysis can be seen as a modern-day version of Socrates's dialectic, such that it demonstrates how little we do know and what illogical assumptions we make. The linguistic philosophy he developed was a successor to logical atomism and logical positivism, which was the guiding principle of his earlier work. Thus, the positivism of Wittgenstein's first book, *Tractatus Logico-Philosophicus* (1920), was later succeeded by the linguistic methods that led to his *Philosophical Investigations* (first published in 1953). The latter expanded and developed the ideas of the first book, which Wittgenstein himself came to reject.

Wittgenstein's work can be divided into two stages based on both the time when they were written and the content of the work. Russell named these stages:

'Wittgenstein I' for the earlier work, which was presented in the *Tractatus Logico-Philosophicus*.

'Wittgenstein II' for the work leading to the posthumously published *Philosophical Investigations*.

In the *Tractatus Logico-Philosophicus*, Wittgenstein considered himself to have solved all philosophical problems by stating what we can and cannot know — quite a bold claim for a twenty-six year old. Certain problems that had worried philosophers for centuries were considered meaningless according to the logical analysis and conclusions of the *Tractatus Logico-Philosophicus*.

After completing that work (and happy with the response to it within the philosophical and logical community), Wittgenstein gave up philosophy and turned to other things, such as designing houses and teaching schoolchildren. However, it became clear that Wittgenstein had not solved all the problems of philosophy (e.g., what a person can know, what is meaning, what is existence, what is knowledge, and other questions of metaphysics) and that language was more complicated than he had considered.

A logical analysis of the construction of language and a formalisation of language into simple logical rules clearly could not explain what we do say or what we can and want to say (or think). Therefore, unhappy and discontented with the renewed disorder that faced him in language analysis, Wittgenstein was drawn back to philosophy and started developing new ideas about the language-reality relationship. These ideas were posthumously published in books entitled, among others, *The Blue Book, The Brown Book*, and *Philosophical Investigations*.

The *Blue* and *Brown* books were originally circulated among his Cambridge University students following his dictation (they were never formally published in his lifetime) and the ideas in these books led to the publication of books including *On Certainty* and — generally considered most importantly — the *Philosophical Investigations*. Despite reaching his sixty-first birthday before succumbing to cancer, Wittgenstein was reluctant to publish any of what came to be called Wittgenstein II during most of his philosophical lifetime.

Before we deal with the details of the work under the general heading of Wittgenstein I (the *Tractatus Logico-Philosophicus*), it is interesting to note that if one went into a quality bookshop (or searched online) to look for titles relating to Wittgenstein, one would find many about him, a number credited to him (e.g., his translated teaching notebooks), but only one published during his lifetime.

Why did he publish only once in his lifetime — the *Tractatus Logico-Philosophicus* — and then nothing officially during the following thirty or so years? The reasons given are that he was never entirely happy with what he had written, and he was also afraid of having his ideas stolen. Thus, by allowing the work to be quasi-published from dictations by students who attended his lectures, his ideas would be made known, yet not prone to critical analysis since their publication was not official.

Wittgenstein's initial aim, presented in the *Tractatus Logico-Philosophicus*, was to resolve philosophy finally and completely. He wanted to put an end to it because he considered it to be non-deductive and merely descriptive. Applying what he had learned from Frege and Russell, he wanted to describe the logic of language by showing how language works. In doing so, the problems of philosophy would be revealed to be meaningless because they fall out of the domain of logic that language can describe. This theory of logical simplification of language was later criticised (also by Wittgenstein himself) as being wrong, but it was accepted along with the logical movement of the time it was written in.

The *Tractatus Logico-Philosophicus* was so well constructed and, within its own limits, correct that it was difficult to refute. While the work in it analysed the relationship between thought, language, and the physical world, a wide range of subjects were also touched by its conclusions (e.g., knowing, being, reality, existence, truth, and meaning).

In relating reality to language, the book argues that just as the 'world' is made up of 'facts' which are constructed from states of affairs, and states of affairs are, in turn, made up of 'objects', there is a parallel in language to describe this. Language is constructed from propositions, which are made of elementary propositions, which in turn are made up of names. Thus, language basically relates to the world, propositions relate to facts, states of affairs relate to elementary propositions, and names relate to objects.

Accordingly, one name stands for one thing, the combinations of which describe a state of affairs. Wittgenstein uses these analogies to create a picture theory of reality. A picture shows its 'sense'. That is, the sense of a proposition is the situation in reality that it portrays. The only significant propositions are those that are a picture of reality, showing how things are in the real world. Thus, propositions about the problems of philosophy are not a picture of reality and are, therefore, meaningless. This idea is central to the *Tractatus Logico-Philosophicus*.

The *Tractatus Logico-Philosophicus* was originally entitled *Logisch-philosophische Abhandlung* by Wittgenstein, but was retitled (by G. E. Moore) to be more in tune with an earlier important work by Spinoza in which he stated that the world was the totality of facts, not things. The world breaks down into independent facts that divide up the world. Wittgenstein attempted to delineate that which can be talked about in a meaningful way. He questioned the nature of language and said that language can only give a picture of the world. Thus, language is a picture of reality. He referred not to the world we experience in space and time but to logical space, where a statement such as "this chair" is not independent of the surroundings and thus is not a fact, whereas "there is a chair in this room" *is* a fact. Such thoughts led to many such discussions in his later life with philosophers such as Moore, Russell, and Frank Ramsay (an influential philosopher to both logic and Wittgenstein himself, and who died in his twenties).

The emphasis on the interpretation of language was a lifelong source for analysis by Wittgenstein. In later life he criticised his earlier work, stating that language is more affected by context than by its logical and formal relation to reality. Thus, it is mistaken to consider meaning as tied to the nature of reality. Meaning is connected to the activity and behaviour of language users, which reflect and explain the meaning of words.

Russell considered the later ideas of Wittgenstein to be trivial and that the resulting *Philosophical Investigations* presented no important wisdom, but today, the later work is generally acknowledged to be his most significant. It is clear that in the *Tractatus Logico-Philosophicus*, Wittgenstein attempted to say things that he later realised could only be shown. Thus, the idea of language as presenting a picture of reality in Wittgenstein I was replaced by the idea of language as a tool in Wittgenstein II. For example, we cannot say anything about God because language pictures only reality. Wittgenstein said that God exists, but things such as God cannot be said or thought because they cannot be put into words.

In the Wittgenstein II period, he became more obsessed that people use the correct words, as he considered language essential to meaning. For example, the word 'game' has no essence because it can mean many things that do not interrelate. If I were to say "I am hungry", it means that I desire food, not that "I am known as hungry".

The *Tractatus Logico-Philosophicus* was, in effect, an attempt to show that philosophy can only fail to find a unified resolution of all things as it relies on language, which is inefficient at describing the world. In it, Wittgenstein showed that propositions describing the nature of things and the metaphysics of the world are nonsense. Thus, it attempted to show the correct logical point of view and to demonstrate the necessity of logic and logical truth. It stated that a logical proposition is true or false, independent of its constitution. If one says "this car is blue or not blue", then it is a tautology as it is always true. If one says "this car is neither blue nor not blue", then it is a contradiction as it is always false. If a method were found to determine whether a logical proposition is a contradiction, tautological, or neither, then a rule could be formed to define the basis of all logic.

So, Wittgenstein wanted to create a perfect logical language such that everything could be stated precisely. He thought that the only necessity that exists is logical necessity, and that the entire modern conception of the world is founded on the illusion that the so-called 'laws of nature' are the explanations of natural phenomena. Thus, to Wittgenstein, causality is not a law that nature obeys but the form in which propositions of science are made. He showed that any form of representation of reality is not answerable to reality. Thus, words mean the words, not necessarily what they are intended to represent in the metaphysical reality. For example, a fact could be presented that there is no cake in the room. But one *might* be in the room, so possibilities must be grasped independently of their realisation. We can picture the fact in our mind and, through language, it can give meaning to justify the fact that there is no cake in the room.

To enable this logic, the world must consist of simple objects that fit together to form *states of affairs*. Reality is the existence or non-existence of these states of affairs. Meaning only associates with propositions that are pictures of reality. Thus, nothing can be said of ethics or religion according to the logic it describes. If language were simple and purely logical, then this work of Wittgenstein's would logically have solved the problems of philosophy. However, language is more complicated than simple propositional relationships.

The rise of the Vienna Circle of logical positivists, whose meetings and movements were coordinated by Moritz Schlick, led to views that analysed reality from a logical perspective. Schlick managed to bring Wittgenstein back to philosophy after he thought (incorrectly) that the *Tractatus Logico-Philosophicus* had solved all the problems of philosophy. The *Tractatus Logico-Philosophicus* is still read and the *truth tables* devised within it that determine the conditions under which a sentence is true or false are still used, but it is the later Wittgenstein II work that confirmed his reputation (although Russell might not agree).

An example of where the application of propositional logic to language breaks down can be shown when we apply what is called the *conditional*. Take for example the logical deduction:

> If you go to Barcelona, you will be in Spain,
> If you are in Spain, you are in Europe,
> Hence, if you go to Barcelona, you will be in Europe.

The logic makes sense and the statements have real and correct meaning. So where is the problem? Before we analyse this example, let us look at a rule of logic. It is general practice in the terminology of logic to use the symbol $\rightarrow$ to denote 'if ... then ...' (the conditional). That is, $x \rightarrow y$ means 'if x occurs, then y will happen'.

Let us convert the statements above to a general logical form using the letters a, b, and c to represent the statements such that "go to Barcelona" will be denoted as 'a', "be in Spain" as 'b', and "be in Europe" as 'c'. Now, the logical terminology tells us that $a \rightarrow c$ means that if a occurs, then c will follow (if you go to Barcelona, you will be in Europe). Thus, this inference can be formulated as follows:

$$a \rightarrow b \; b \rightarrow c / a \rightarrow c$$

However, an important point to make is that inferences of this form can produce invalid language constructions. The conditional logic can break down with regard to actual meaning in the real world. For example, suppose there is a move within the British Conservative Party to replace the Prime Minister Theresa May and she is challenged by Boris Johnson. Consider the inference (according to the above formula):

> If Mrs May dies before the election, Boris Johnson will win. If Johnson wins the election, May will retire and take her pension. Hence, if Theresa May dies before the election, she will retire and take her pension.

Clearly nonsense!

There are many examples, not necessarily of this form, where language defies logical analysis and is shown to be something that must be lived and experienced before its many rules can be understood (and this does not yet include the variations of inflection, posturing, emphasis, tone, situation, and so on, all of which can affect meaning). Language is clearly something that is used and experienced as a living thing. For example, consider that I told you that I could not understand how to work my DVD player, and you responded that you have a manual. Now, I understand you to mean that you have a manual that explains the operation of my DVD player, yet there is no logical reason that your comment — that you have a manual — does not relate to one describing how to build a rabbit hutch instead.

Logic is essential to our scientific understanding of the world. For example, Francis Crick, the co-discoverer of the double helix structure of DNA, formulated a logical central dogma that 'DNA makes RNA makes proteins'; that is, the flow of information in the *genes* encoding the proteins of the body can only pass one way — from gene to protein — via an intermediate made of RNA. Advances in logic have enabled us to see why certain assumptions we make about reality are not necessarily correct, or to demonstrate that logical analysis shows that there are some things we cannot know.

Logic consists of its own growing language, terminology, and symbolism that are characteristic of a developing system — terms such as truth values, disjunctions, conjunctions, negations, particular and universal quantifiers, tense operators, and probabilities describe certain types of language meaning in logical analysis. These may be "it must be the case that…" or "it has always been the case that…"

Ultimately, the purpose of the *Tractatus Logico-Philosophicus* was to clarify the limitations of meaningful language. It failed. Since language could not be logically formulated, the problems of philosophy are open again to analysis through thought and language. Wittgenstein's thoughts about the purpose of philosophy were clear — it explains or deduces nothing, yet shows what is possible before discovery or invention. Science differs from this in that it consists entirely of true propositions; it studies the existence or non-existence of states of affairs.

So why are we discussing the work of someone who was opposed to the claims of science? The reason is that Wittgenstein aided our understanding of what is, or is not, knowable and thus how we can place scientific deductions about reality in the context of ultimate truth. He is, therefore, closest to the goal of this book and deserves the greatest coverage.

Science may reject Wittgenstein's conclusion but accept his method. In the *Philosophical Investigations*, which Wittgenstein claimed was the result of sixteen years of philosophical investigation, he attempted to set the limitations of language. He developed the term 'private language' to not only describe a language that is intelligible only to its user (as it uses private sensations and psychological states), but also demonstrate that there is no such thing. Language is a public experience as it is governed by rules which are learned and checked through the use of language itself. However, let us not get caught up in semantics. When one has learnt a language, one can have internal private dialogue with the self and through a language process (from a biological and philosophical perspective) in which there is no way of determining whether any other person shares it.

In *Philosophical Investigations*, Wittgenstein sees the connection of words in language like a net that consists of many pieces of interconnected string. Understanding becomes knotted when we misuse a word, so language can only present an incorrect picture of the world. Before we look into the details of the *Philosophical Investigations*, let us be more general in our consideration of language as a means to communicate ideas.

Wittgenstein thought that language limits our interpretation of thought — he was concerned that language presented a barrier to its comprehension. "If a lion could talk, we couldn't understand him," he said, because we do not share the same makeup as the animal. As for human language, he wondered how well we can infer correctly what another person means. The assumed simple process of communication is in fact very complex. When thinking of an idea, and wanting another person to comprehend it, thoughts must move through different states of consciousness. From full consciousness, the mental images and words transfer to the form of speech. Language is shared, has rules, and thus cannot completely translate the intended meaning of thought. The recipient hears and translates the words into conscious thoughts and understanding. Can we be certain that the understanding is the intent?

Verbal language is obviously the primary way of passing ideas between individuals, yet the transfer of information constitutes far more than this. The tone and mannerisms of speech, together with inflections, define or even alter meaning. The complexities of language are learned as an integrated living experience. As such, language is constantly changing. When we speak of language here, we mean the form of communication of ideas.

There are many languages, some more complete than others in their ability to explain the world. Languages change over time to correspond to the world they represent. Thus, some languages that once existed are no longer in use. Some languages that suffice for certain parts of the world would not work in others — they have a place of use only in a specific time and space.

Complex modern languages such as English, French, and German can explain similar complex phenomena in a similar way. When translating from one language to another, subtleties in meaning are lost or changed, demonstrating that a language is somehow more than the sum of its parts (e.g., it has been said that Heidegger's masterwork, *Being and Time* (1927), cannot be translated correctly into English because its central issue of 'being' has many forms in German that cannot be sufficiently translated). Great works of literature are often translated, and a thorough understanding of the original text by the translator would benefit the intention more than an uninformed direct literal translation. Here, understanding means that rules can be manipulated.

A person is more likely to grasp the meaning of an expression when the rules for its use are understood. Wittgenstein understood this in both the *Tractatus Logico-Philosophicus* and the *Philosophical Investigations*. It was the realisation that the rules are more complicated than mere logical relationships that changed his view after Wittgenstein I. Furthermore, in the *Philosophical Investigations*, Wittgenstein denied that the rules form a single rigid system. He said that the rules are not independent of us, as opposed to was stated in the *Tractatus Logico-Philosophicus*. Thus, the active use of language is important in the process, which means that an individual who has never met another human being in his or her life cannot have an internal language system.

The calculus that describes the language rules in the *Tractatus Logico-Philosophicus* are replaced in the *Philosophical Investigations* by a language game (but not in the usual sense that we understand the term 'game'). Although one calculus describes the whole of language in the *Tractatus Logico-Philosophicus*, many different games describe a communication-dependent language in the *Philosophical Investigations*.

Here is an example — the sentence "I didn't order the cheese" seems to have one meaning. Yet, if we emphasise one particular word in that sentence when spoken, the meaning changes — "*I* didn't order the cheese" might mean someone else ordered it. "I *didn't* order the cheese" might mean that cheese was presented but not requested. "I didn't *order* the cheese" might mean that the way it was requested was rude. "I didn't order the *cheese*" might mean that an order was made, but not for cheese. The same words, with different emphases, give wholly different meanings. Language is a lived thing, after all.

Italian economist Piero Sraffa (1898–1983) was instrumental in Wittgenstein's change of thought that led to the *Philosophical Investigations*. Famously, when Wittgenstein insisted that a proposition and that which it describes must have the same 'logical form', Sraffa responded by making a rude Neapolitan gesture and asked, "what is the logical form of that?" to disprove Wittgenstein's argument. Language, meaning, and understanding are clearly more than a simple singular interpretation of a string of words, and Wittgenstein realised that his work was flawed.

Paralleling intelligence, human beings appear to be unique among organisms in their ability to deeply understand language (there has been some evidence very recently that dolphins are able to conduct conversations with whistles and clicks, with one animal waiting for the other to finish before replying). This makes it difficult to discern whether we possess an innate language organ.

Some insights from the American linguist Noam Chomsky into the evolution of human language were:

1. For natural languages, such as English, there are a finite number of rules to learn. These generative grammar rules, if correctly applied, enable the formation of all grammatical sentences in that language.
2. Children are able to learn any language.
3. If an adult has a mother tongue, they can learn other languages. This is because there is a general ability to cope with any generative grammar; this is called *universal grammar.*
4. Universal grammar has a strong innate element.

So, we are theoretically able to create billions of meaningful variations of word combinations (with variable length) because these are encapsulated in a finite set of rules that are 'hardwired' into us. Yet the operations of the mind are constrained by certain innate structures. Chomsky went on to speculate that logic could be hardwired too. Some might state that advanced animals like the dolphin understand language, but it is almost certainly not in the way we do. Dolphins in captivity can be taught to act appropriately toward sentences comprising up to five words, such as "put ball in basket". On this basis, some people credit them with sentence comprehension. However, three points should be noted relating to this 'understanding':

1. It is easier to understand than to explain. The dolphin can do what is intended, but explanation is beyond it.
2. The dolphin does not produce sentences in such experiments.
3. It is not known if dolphins use words or syntax in the wild.

Certain primate can understand simple language. For example, some species of African monkey have been shown to have different distress calls for different threats. Furthermore, some species of monkey understand another species' distress calls — this has to be learned. Having made these points about the distinction of human language abilities, let us return to Wittgenstein's later work.

To Wittgenstein, there are no philosophical propositions and no philosophical knowledge. For example, Moore had attempted to prove that a person can *know* he has a particular sensation (e.g., pain) or that he has two hands. Wittgenstein opposed this view, believing that the concepts of knowledge and certainty could not be applied to one's own sensations. Wittgenstein's perception and clarity of thought were exceptional. Yet he himself was amazed that anything should exist at all. Certain aspects of his thought had a 'Heisenbergian' feel. If I want to observe my desires, for instance, then I must know what they are in order to observe them. So how does one know that by observing, they are not altering what is being observed?

Philosophical problems come from the tangled mess of linguistic rules relating one term to another. That is, there is limitation in language as to how words relate to one another and whether this represents the conscious understanding of the relation that is intended and inferred by language. Thus, Wittgenstein was continually interested in the limits of meaning and language, because only from this understanding can one hope to address other problems of philosophy and science with any degree of certainty.

In language, names combine to represent reality. They correspond to the linking of objects that make up the substance of the world. However, names only occur in the context of a proposition. We only understand conceptual relations by logical analysis of sentences. Language does not have to be explained. We speak, and those who listen, learn.

Wittgenstein was also interested in the meaning of thought, which is a logical picture of the facts, and propositions are expressions of thoughts. A thought shares a homologous form with reality because it depicts the facts of reality in another representation. Logic and logical thought both enable true and false statements to be made about reality, but science and common sense tell us what is in the world.

Wittgenstein considered philosophy to be the bewitchment of our intelligence by language. That is, language hinders our thinking because attempting to convey a thought verbally converts the thought into another form. When we think of matters such as life, space, mind, and free will, we become bewitched by language. The words have their natural place in speech, but by assuming that they refer to some essence of that which they try to define, we take the word out of its place and forget the application of the word.

Toward the end of his life, Wittgenstein looked at certainty — what *are* we certain of? To him, this equates to a lot less than we think. As stated earlier, if I say "I have two hands", am I sure that I do? If I look at them and see them, I would think so. But the proposition is no less certain after I look at them than before. Basic propositions are taken for granted in normal conversation — they are the frameworks of ordinary behaviour, the background from which learning and questioning are referenced. Wittgenstein's work demonstrated *that* part of our cultural progression by the fact that, just as it happened for alchemy and astrology or maybe even God, we are learning to do without philosophy.

Karl Popper was considered perhaps the greatest philosopher of science, so before we look at him, we need to understand a bit about science and the approach through which science progresses — the scientific method — something we will come back to later.

Scientific method: Kuhn and Feyerabend

Considered the creator of scientific empiricism and regarded in his own day and even in ours as the godfather of the scientific revolution, Francis Bacon (1561–1626) was an English philosopher who is famous for his *Novum Organum* (1620), a treatise on logic and syllogism. In this treatise, the *Baconian method* (or 'scientific method') was developed. It replaced the syllogistic methods put forward in Aristotle's *Organon* and consisted of procedures to isolate the form, nature, or cause of a phenomenon by employing the method of agreement, method of difference, and method of concomitant variation.

The Oxford English Dictionary describes the scientific method as a "method or procedure that has characterised natural science since the 17th century, consisting in systematic observation, measurement, and experiment, and the formulation, testing, and modification of hypotheses".

For nearly 300 years, scientific understanding of the mechanism of all aspects of physical reality has progressed according to this process. It is an extension in the scientific domain of humankind's ability to make itself the master of the planet (through language to writing, agriculture, industrialisation, and so on).

The scientific method is the best approach that humans have formulated to distinguish truth from lies and delusion. There are many minor variants to the process, but basically it proceeds as follows:

1. Consider and observe some aspect of the Universe.
2. Generate a tentative description, called a *hypothesis*, that is consistent with what is observed.
3. Make predictions from the hypothesis.
4. Test these predictions through experiment or observation and modify the hypothesis based on the results.
5. Repeat steps 3 and 4 until there are no discrepancies between theory and experiment and/or observation.

Thomas Kuhn (1922–1996)

Of course, there has been much criticism of this process, most prominently in this century in that the whole construct of the scientific method is flawed as it is inevitably constrained by human limitations.

In 1961, the American philosopher Thomas Kuhn wrote that if a scientist has a theory about some process before designing and undertaking experiments to make empirical observations about it, what happens is that the "route from theory to measurement can almost never be travelled backward". What follows from theory to measurement seems 'logical' because of the loaded process, whereas the reverse (measurement to theory) does not follow because the loading was from the initial idea. Thus, the way in which a theory is tested is dictated by the nature of the theory itself — it has every reason to succeed. The repercussion of this is that once theories that have been validated by the scientific method are adopted by a profession, no theory is testable by any quantitative tests that it has not already passed — it has been defined by the original idea.

Kuhn published *The Structure of Scientific Revolutions* in 1962, which was primarily a book about the history of science. In it, he made clear that progress from the scientific method is not a continuous, flowing process. He distinguished between various phases:

> **Phase 1** is the *pre-paradigm phase* and it occurs only once. Here, different scientists may work on different theories that are often incomplete and incompatible with other current theories. During this phase, if one particular conceptual model is chosen and there is consensus on the methods, terminology, and experiments that will increase insights from this model, this leads to …
>
> **Phase 2**, where solutions to scientific problems are addressed according to 'normal science'. However, as more information is gathered, data deviating from a current paradigm may result such that the model is considered weakened.
>
> **Phase 3** is the phase of crisis. Either crises are resolved within the context of normal science, or science enters the next phase.
>
> **Phase 4** is the 'Scientific revolution', where the assumptions of the current paradigm are re-evaluated to the point where a new model is established.
>
> **Phase 5** is where the new model is accepted and scientists return to addressing problems within the framework of this new paradigm.

Of course, if science experiences these phases too often, it would impede progress within a paradigm.

Perhaps Kuhn was saying that science progresses in a way that is similar to the *punctuated equilibrium* theory of evolution (as discussed in Chapter 5), which states that species change over time through jumps and starts, with periodic changes in equilibrium.

Paul Feyerabend (1924–1994)

Since the human mind is finite in space and time, it is finite and limited in capability too. The way the mind attempts to understand reality is essentially constrained and skewed towards these limitations. We will see later that although the scientific method may well be the most appropriate way by which we are capable of understanding the physical world, it may not lead to truth because a) truth may not be in the form of laws and b) the Universe may be more complicated than we imagine.

Austrian-born Feyerabend argued that the scientific method of modern science is not a truly methodological process. In his book, *Against Method*, he criticises the belief that adherence to an accepted method leads to scientific progress since one can always find historical occurrences where its violation has also contributed to progress. By blinkering ourselves to one particular scientific problem and not seeing scientific progress holistically, we can be unaware of proofs of facts that occur through means that are at odds with the current paradigm. Feyerabend, in his mocking contempt of what he considered to be scientific arrogance, suggested that the rule of scientific method is 'anything goes'.

Karl Popper (1902–1994)

Logical positivists placed emphasis on verifiable assertions, but Popper pointed out that if verifiable assertions are to be meaningful, then any discussion about the concept of meaning must possess meaningless statements. The logical positivists had no strong response to arguments like these. So, Popper was not a logical positivist. Indeed, the British philosophy populariser Bryan Magee called him an anti-positivist. To demonstrate that Popper differed from the positivists, Magee used the example of the statement "God exists". Although the positivists would say that the statement is meaningless, Popper would say that the statement has meaning and could be true, but because it cannot be falsified, it is not a scientific statement. So, Popper was a scientific philosopher who applied logic to real world issues (he was the strongest critic of Marxism, for example).

Induction is the method of basing general statements on accumulated observations. Inductive reasoning is a part of logic. Hume questioned this process and stated that just because the Sun rose every morning in the past does not mean that it is any more likely to rise the next day. Russell correlated this example with the story of a man who feeds his chickens every day. One day, the man wrings all the chickens' necks. The chickens had expected to be fed just as they were every other day, but they should have had "more refined views as to the uniformity of nature".

Popper demonstrated the use of inductive reasoning by showing the asymmetry of the scientific method. Specifically, no number of experiments can prove the validity of a scientific theory as inductive reasoning shows that the next experiment *could* prove the opposite. Popper suggested the term *falsification* rather than the verification process used by the Vienna Circle. That is, a scientific theory cannot be proved (verified), but it can be shown to be untrue (falsified). Later authors would argue that falsificationism does not account for many newer theories in science, but it *is* the fundamental principle of most science (indeed, it is illogical in most cases to deny its rationale).

Deduction is fool proof, producing the right inferences if the premisses of the inference are correct. Induction can lead to errors. However, science uses induction, where if several repeated experiments give the same result, then that result is taken as correct. Science could not survive on deduction alone, because a positive result from a limited sample cannot be extrapolated to the whole. A negative result from the sample can, however, lead to the deduction that the theory is false. Hence, science uses induction.

Newton's gravitational theory made predictions for the planetary orbits, but the orbit of Uranus was found to be different from that expected. This apparent falsification of Newton's model would imply that Newton's model was wrong (and, according to Popper, should be rejected). However, John Couch Adams and Urbain Le Verrier independently chose to consider the Newtonian model as correct, and sought to find other reasons for the deviating orbit of Uranus. They found a new planet, Neptune, whose gravitational effect on Uranus explained Uranus's orbit. What is important, is that what they did was not reject the original theory based on its falsification, but use it as a foundational truth from which to find reasons to explain the data deviation, and then having done that, re-confirm the original theory.

In modern times, subatomic theories in their many guises present theories that are impossible to test experimentally, and thus in some sense fall outside the remit of traditional scientific method.

Realists believe the aim of science is to describe all reality. Anti-realists believe science can only explain the observable, macroscopic, part, and that inferences about the non-observable realm are not definitive. In cases

Low resolution	High resolution
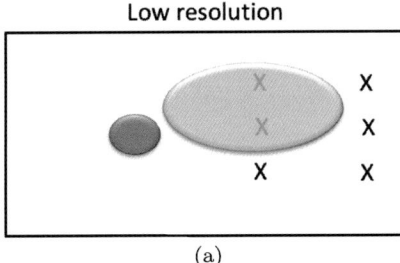	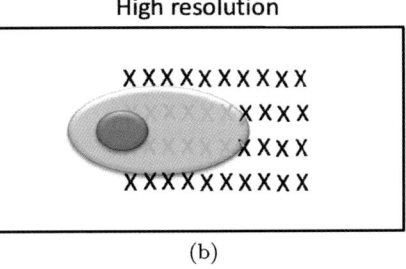
(a)	(b)

Figure 1. Generating hypotheses. Exploration of an undefined space using (a) low-resolution, or (b) high-resolution information illustrates the increased likelihood of defining a hypothesis that correctly explains a complex observation. In this figure, the hypothesis is shown as the large blob and the solution or truth is shown by the oval. The crosses depict the extent of the knowledge base against which the hypothesis is generated. Taken from Nabel (2009).

such as the results of subatomic collisions in the Large Hadron Collider, the data can be explained by many incompatible theories. This causes anti-realists to believe that theories relating to unobservable entities are 'underdetermined' by the data (unlike clear results of macroscopic tests).

Religion lies outside of science, so such theories are not applicable. Another idea that cannot be falsified or verified, and which lies closer to science, is that of free will. This subject will be examined in depth in Chapter 6, such is the importance of the relationship between theory and truth that the word 'verisimilitude' specifically relates to the extent to which a hypothesis approaches the 'truth' (whatever that is). Gary Nabel stated in an article that was published in 2009 in the journal *Science* that "there is synergy between hypothesis generation and hypothesis testing — if well designed, these efforts complement one another and can lead to fundamental breakthroughs. But how do we strike the right balance?" In what he describes as the 'coordinates' model, the exploration of hypotheses — as potential models for a mechanism — defines an unknown space with greater precision. Explored at low resolution, the solution to a problem could lie in a gap in the knowledge space (Figure 1).

However, increasing the density of information increases the likelihood of defining the coordinates of a hypothesis that encompasses the solution. Popper's philosophical impact on analysing how science is done and what we can logically expect to achieve by scientific endeavour is profound. Aspects of his philosophy of science have significantly influenced many great western scientists. In a number of sections of this book, I discuss how various areas of science have progressed through systematic observation, test, theory, and experiment. Popper analysed this process and provided insights that resolved the issues that had concerned philosophers and scientists before him.

In science, experiments are often designed to represent what happens in nature, but under laboratory conditions. They are repeated several times and if the results are identical, they are deemed representative of how the process under investigation will always behave under those conditions. However, irrespective of the difficulties of trying to represent what happens in the *real* system as well as the difficulties of interpreting that data, the scientific method does not resolve, address, or even consider important (through necessity) Hume's dilemma. Yet the fact remains that repetitions of the same result does *not* logically imply that it will happen the same way the next time.

The scientific method is 'aware' of Hume's dilemma. However, science has to be performed in the only way that it can be done and thus cannot capture the true unknowable intrinsic cause of any process. Although we may claim that when event 'x' follows event 'y', it is because of 'y' and we *believe* it to be as such, we also know that we cannot prove it and must accept that we have merely observed a progression of events. In fact, science works through statistical likelihood, not inductive logic. The results of investigations help us to infer by induction the future behaviour of a system. Although logically flawed, this is how much of science is done, and it works because it has produced all that we have achieved.

The problem for the more deep-thinking scientist is the paradox that science, though worthwhile in that it manages to advance our knowledge or the world, improve the quality of life, or reduce suffering, is but a complex marriage of hypothesis, experiment, verification, and falsification, whose whole construction is grounded in illogical assumption. This is not pessimistic but an aspect of our interpretation of reality that we accept and incorporate in our (methods of) understanding.

As Bryan Magee stresses in his book *Popper* (1973), Popper showed a logical asymmetry between verification and falsification. In terms of the logic of statements, if we take the example of observing if there are any white swans and we were to observe no white swans, no number of observations of white swans allows us to logically derive the statement "all swans are white". However, the observation of one black swan does allow us to logically derive the statement "not all swans are white" — hence, the allowance of a falsification, but not a verification. Popper said that induction is meaningless, dispensable, a myth — there is no such thing. By analogy, science progresses by making the statement "all swans are white" after seeing a handful of white swans. However, according to this analogy, if a black swan appeared, we would later reappraise our deductions.

Popper saw that the way that knowledge advances is through problems and our attempts to solve them. Repeating a result a million times adds verification to the result, but does not, in fact, increase its probability of being true. Popper did not receive the notoriety he deserved, partly because this idea was misunderstood. Popper said that we can *never* prove what we think we know to be true because it could turn out to be false.

Newton thought that he was right about gravity, but his ideas were superseded by those of Einstein. With all probability, Einstein's ideas will also be revised in due time. Indeed, there are regular publications (often reaching the public domain) of theories claiming to disprove Einstein's *special* and *general relativity*. None as yet have been proven right.

So, our knowledge comes closer to representing the reality it explains, yet we cannot know if it achieves this. To attempt to try and prove the truth of a theory or justify belief in it is impossible. What scientists can do is revise and improve on knowledge. Of profound importance to the scientific method is that Popper showed that observation cannot be prior to theory such that a theory can be presupposed by an observation (Einstein agreed with Popper about this). To Popper, the failure to recognise this and the belief by scientists that a theory can be presupposed by an observation is a flaw in the foundations of empiricism.

Wittgenstein was obsessed with the meaning of language whereas Popper considered what language enables us to do as most important. It is easy to see that the two characters were totally at odds with one another, and their single brief meeting was not a pleasant encounter by all accounts. Of course, both their contributions to philosophy and modern human thought are profound.

If I make the statement "today is Monday" and it is indeed Monday, then it is correct. If I make the statement on Tuesday, it is incorrect. If the word 'Tuesday' actually means Monday somewhere in the world, then the reverse is true there. Thus, the meaning and association of words is important. Wittgenstein delved into the essence of meaning, ignoring common sense or reliance on assumptions about whether understanding is achieved. Magee considers Popper's view of what Wittgenstein did as akin to a carpenter spending all his time sharpening his tools, only never to use them except on one another. Hence, to Popper, language is an instrument and what is important is what is done with it.

Popper's extension of ideas to applications of course required some level of assumption about the level by which we understand words and their association with other words, otherwise we could not say anything regarding some external issue as we would be spending all our time defining terms used in the attempt to say it. Put another way, a discussion would be impossible because the incessant necessity to define terms would never lead preliminaries to more.

Just as there are developmental noise and random and indeterminate mechanisms that define each organism's individuality, we evidently must accept that understanding is unique to each individual. Each human mind is unique, and unique in its capabilities. If we were to incorporate the ideas of consciousness (at all its levels) with Wittgenstein's endeavours, then I see no way that ensuring intention of meaning would produce the desired effect. Any test to prove otherwise would be subject to Popper's idea of falsification.

iii) Rationalism

Rationalism is the philosophical doctrine that claims that the nature of the world can be established by wholly non-empirical demonstrative reasoning. Hence, it is diametrically opposed to empiricism. It is also known as *apriorism* because it is derived from *a priori* knowledge.

René Descartes (1596–1650)

Descartes was a French philosopher who laid the foundations for what is seen as the modern scientific age. He is considered to be the first to have created an acceptable foundation for scientific thinking, and was perhaps the most original philosopher since Aristotle.

Descartes compared the whole of philosophy to a tree (presented in his *Principles of Philosophy*), with the roots as metaphysics, the trunk as physics, and the branches as the specific sciences. Widely thought of as the father of modern western philosophical ideas, he attempted to produce an all-encompassing philosophy of the Universe. His methods of deduction and intuition affected modern metaphysics.

His interest in philosophy was roused by the Dutch philosopher, Isaac Beeckman. The Netherlands provided a liberal working atmosphere at the time, which was important to philosophers since the church, which had greater power elsewhere, would punish those who presented work that diminished the role of God in any process. Descartes, Locke, Spinoza, and Leibniz all spent time working in Holland. Here, Descartes's vision of an all-encompassing philosophy and science of knowledge was conceived.

Common-sense analysis of phenomena is not enough according to Descartes — we must probe the interactions between the smallest particles of the physical world to know what is happening. Thus, he was a reductionist. He was also part of the philosophical *Enlightenment* together with such philosophers as Hobbes, Spinoza, Leibniz, Locke, Berkeley, Hume, and Kant. The Enlightenment was the beginning of the *Age of Reason*, which set a conflict between the church's dominance over intellectual life and the mind's search for truth through reason. The Enlightenment taught some essential ideas:

1. Man is not inherently depraved.
2. The aim of life is life, not the afterlife.
3. The essential condition for the good life is freeing the mind from ignorance and superstition.
4. By achieving the third point and freeing oneself from arbitrary state power, man is capable of progress and perfection.

Descartes published many works on a wide variety of subjects throughout his relatively short life. *Le Monde* concerned cosmology and physics and would have been published in 1633, yet was withdrawn since it contained subject matter similar to that of Galileo (it questioned the powerful role that God was conceived to have in all physical processes) and thus would have put Descartes in a difficult position with the Church.

The *Discourse on the Method* (the full title being *Discourse on the Method of Rightly Conducting One's Reason and Seeking Truth in the Sciences*) was published in 1637 and contained his famous statement "cogito ergo sum". This was followed by the *Meditations* in 1641. The *Discourse on the Method* presented the less controversial aspects of his *Treatise on the Universe*. Descartes considered all matter in the Universe to be the same, that there was no difference between terrestrial and celestial phenomena, and that the Earth was part of a homogenous Universe. His *Treatise on the Universe* attempted to explain meteors, geometry, and a whole range of scientific subjects.

The *Discourse on the Method* displayed his skills both as a mathematician and philosopher. In it, he discussed the foundation of knowledge, God's existence, and the difference between mind and body. It contained the core of the *Cartesian* system, which was expanded in *Meditations on First Philosophy*. The Cartesian coordinate system (so-named by Leibniz, but was of Descartes's doing) influenced much of the mathematics that followed after him. Descartes also invented algebra, which was used to solve geometric problems and again influenced the direction of mathematics (some universities that wanted to ban the teachings of Descartes on account of his philosophy could not because of his mathematics).

The *Principles of Philosophy*, published in 1644, presented Descartes's metaphysics and his view on the *mind-body* distinction that minds can, and do, exist apart from bodies. He was not only interested in how the mind and body interacted but also where it occurred. He decided that this was in the pineal gland in the brain (its function is currently still not known). He considered mind and matter to be different and independent entities.

Descartes is most famous for the proposition *cogito ergo sum*, which can be translated as "I think, therefore I am" or "I am thinking, therefore I exist", where man is only sure of his existence when he is thinking. This was the most fundamental truth that Descartes considered could not be wrong (our perceptions may be illusions, dreams, or 'tricks' by a superior being). From this, Descartes supposed that the essence of being was thinking, and hence the mind and body are separate (Milan Kundera's modified *I feel, therefore I am*, which he thought was better, is nonsense since making such an assertion requires thought — the 'cogito' is primary). Is *cogito ergo sum*, as the starting point for Descartes's philosophy, a valid position? The

German scientist Georg Lichtenberg believed that Descartes was only really entitled to claim that "thinking is occurring", not his assertion about the 'I'.

To show that the thinking being could know about the outside world, Descartes had to prove the existence of God so that we know that our ideas are true and that we are not being tricked by some 'demon'. He argued that the idea of a perfect God must have a cause and that this cannot come from us, so God must be the cause of our ideas of him. From this circular logic flows his philosophy.

Descartes believed that truths about reality were 'revealed' truths. He said that we discover the principles of physical reality by the light of reason, not the prejudices of the senses. He believed that the evidence for the principles could not be doubted, and that only real things that are external to ourselves could be described in the quantitative terms of mathematics whereas all other qualitative aspects of reality were subject to the confusion of the senses. Thus, he described two categorically different types of 'substance':

1. The extended substance (*res extensa*) where geometry and mathematical forms reside (physical reality), and,
2. The thinking substance (*res cogitans*) which relates to human subjectivity.

Res cogitans is right about *res extensa*, he believed, because God created the world according to mathematical principles, and our minds — designed by God — are made to understand it in the way that God wanted. Descartes considered God to be the sum of all perfection and since existence is perfection, it cannot be separated from the essence of God. He stated that reason is God-given and as long as we use it correctly, we cannot err.

Antoine Arnauld, a contemporary of Descartes, argued that if we had to prove God's existence in order to underwrite the reliability of the human mind, then how could we be certain of the reliability of the reasoning that was needed to establish his existence in the first place? Descartes attempted to counteract this argument by saying that God's existence was self-evident and thus something we can be sure of.

Once God's existence is established, in whom all the answers lay hidden, Descartes could establish a systematic approach to science through pure mathematics. It was a rigorous system built on weak foundations that were of course made necessary by the religious climate of his time. Since the mind owes its existence to God, it has innate ideas that correspond to reality, thereby putting us on the right track to understanding. This argument was developed in *Principles of Philosophy*.

Wittgenstein thought that the *cogito* could not be the starting point of what we can know. If *cogito ergo sum* is to have meaning, there has to be a prior acceptance of what thinking is and how thought is used (as that is how language is used). With this deconstruction, Wittgenstein suppressed the search by philosophers for ultimate certainty.

Incidentally, it has been suggested that in 1581, the Portuguese philosopher Francisco Sanchez published a treatise, *Why Nothing can be Known*, that presented the same method of Cartesian doubt as Descartes, but sixty years earlier. However, Descartes's interest was to show how the physical world could be mathematically described and mapped out independently of the misleading view produced by our sensory organs. That is, the senses can deceive us. Whereas Aristotle believed that science can only be based on experience, Descarte denied that evidence from the senses can provide us with definite true knowledge about reality. Descartes proposed that the Universe's physical processes, and those of biological life, could be calculated and predicted once the mechanics were understood — today, we use calculations to predict accurately the actions of subatomic particles.

From Descartes's primary assumption of the validity of *cogito ergo sum*, he went on to discuss the nature of the thing that thinks. He assumed that everything entering his head could be considered no truer than his dreams. Yet, despite this, he felt that no sceptic could deny the validity of *cogito ergo sum*. His method of philosophical writing was such that he presented the process of his thought, so the reader feels involved. This stands in stark contrast to the usual philosophical method of presenting analyses of conclusions or aphorisms (Wittgenstein and Nietzsche) or dialogues (Plato and Nietzsche).

Descarte proceeded from the primary conclusion to surmise that mind is immaterial and therefore separate from body. The 'I' is independent of the physical world and thus could survive the destruction of the body. However, he did not deny that thought may be accompanied by brain processes. He proposed that the whole of life could be a dream or that some "malicious demon" had attempted to deceive him about the true reality. However, even if the demon did exist and was doing so, Descartes must first exist for it to be able to do so, so the 'I am' aspect is true (considering that "he who thinks" is asking this very question).

Descartes's reasoning for the unquestionable validity of his *cogito ergo sum*, notwithstanding the fact that the existence of his body may not be true, is not in fact entirely logical. He stated that because he could doubt the existence of body but not the existence of mind, therefore mind can exist without body. While his arguments fitted his examples, they are not thorough or all-inclusive and are thus not logically sound.

As John Cottingham stated in his excellent book *Descartes* (1986), Descartes made the error of reading truth about *ontology* from epistemological truth. Metaphysics is a branch of philosophy that is concerned with the nature of reality. Ontology is the part of metaphysics that is concerned with the study of being and is thus more specific in focus than metaphysics.

The Cartesian system falls apart when thought is included, since Descartes considered mind to be completely distinct from matter. The mind-body problem that interested him, as well as how these separate entities were connected, was resolved when he believed that they operated by communicating to produce a singular regulated function. This dualistic approach is present in all of Descartes's work and is the result of his distinction between 'thought' and 'extension'. Thus, there are two kinds of entity — thinking and extended. Extended substance is that of the three-dimensional physical world and thinking substance consists of thought.

As thinking has its own motion, Descartes considered animals not to have minds, but were merely mechanical automata. Furthermore, he thought that the body was just a mechanical system. This poses a question that is still pondered today — how do the two interact? What is consciousness and how do we solve the mind-body problem? Descartes held that the thinking substance is inexplicable by the quantitative language of physics.

Although Descartes separated mind from body, he was insistent on their interdependence. As he aged, he realised that he could not separate them completely. The mind reads signals from the body, so the human being is the amalgam of mind and body. Some have inferred from Descartes's writings that he eventually rejected his mind-body dualism (i.e., accepting mind and body as one). He thought that the relationship of the human being to the mind and body is like that of water to oxygen and hydrogen. Things are experienced in us that refer neither to mind nor body alone. So, we are not just thinking things, but beings who are bound to bodily states. Descartes may not have solved the mind-body problem (how the inner workings of the mind relate to the physical world of reality), but he did instigate this line of thought, which is the ultimate test of an all-encompassing model of scientific thought.

Baruch Spinoza (1632–1677)

Baruch, or Benedictus de, Spinoza was a Dutch-Jewish rationalist philosopher. He spent his life philosophising, but this did not earn him a living, so he became an expert lens-grinder. Inhaling glass dust over many years might have been the cause of his eventual premature demise at the age of 44.

He published two books in his lifetime, the *Principles of Descartes Philosophy* and the *Tractatus Theologico-Politicus*, although other works were published posthumously (e.g., *Ethics*) because he feared that they might be construed as demoting the role of God in reality and the Christian church would punish such blasphemy with death. The *Tractatus Theologico-Politicus* was a preparation for people to receive his masterwork, the *Ethics*, published in 1677. He studied the scholastic view of Aristotelian philosophy as well as the commentaries on Aristotle by Moses ben Maimon and Chasdai Creskas. Here, he attained the view that matter was eternal and the Universe was infinite. The Universe has no meaning, yet is its own meaning. He studied Descartes's work and was greatly influenced by him too.

Spinoza's work influenced Nietzsche, Russell, Leibniz (who allegedly plagiarised the *Ethics*), Einstein, and Hegel — who saw his philosophy as a stage on the road to his own ideas. Spinoza's *Short Treatise on God, Man and His Well-Being* was an early version of later work presented in extended form in the *Ethics*, which was an analysis and presentation of a new deductive system. This work was written in Latin, yet was contorted to a 'geometric' style. It was a reduction of Descartes's system. Here, his mature philosophy was presented as a series of definitions, axioms, propositions, and proofs.

Like many philosophers who succeeded him, Spinoza created his own complete philosophical system to explain reality. As his view of the world was an extension of Descartes's own rational system, it was also decidedly a rational one. However, we know that the world is anything but rational. Little was he to know that his system was doomed to failure. This system was superseded by Locke's empiricism, which in turn was destroyed by Hume (cause and effect is but a succession of events we have become accustomed to). However, Hume had no answer to reality, and both Kant and Hegel tried and failed to produce complete philosophical systems. Such things are probably impossible.

As the human mind has limited access to ultimate reality considering the linguistic, physiological, and physical limitations we possess, it has only an incomplete picture of the phenomenal world. Scientifically, with our limited tools, we create an ever-increasingly complicated model of the Universe in the hope that it will 'reveal' beautiful simplicity. Philosophers and scientists know that it is futile to search for ultimate truth (Kant's noumenal world) — rather, we can only seek our own truth. The model we create is a limited view of a limited part of the Universe made using limited tools. With this in mind, perhaps we overcomplicate our model, and a more rational view would be revealed if our limitations — *the* limitations — were incorporated as intrinsic to our model.

In Spinoza's writings about the Universe, he devised a system that set out eight basic assumptions: 1) a thing which is its own cause, 2) a thing which is finite in its own kind, 3) substance, 4) its attributes, 5) its modes, 6) God (a substance of infinite being, essence, and attributes), 7) freedom, and 8) eternity.

Spinoza's concept of existence is one where every logical possibility must exist. He believed that all mind and matter are modes of the one substance, 'God' or 'nature'. He 'proves' that there is one substance — God *and* nature; thus, God *is* nature. No two substances can have the same attributes. However, a perfect substance has all attributes, leaving no attributes for any other substance. So, except God, no substance can be conceived if there is a God. For Spinoza, the physical world is God's body — the physical aspect, not the totality, of God. From this, Descartes's problem of how the mind interacts with the body is overcome.

To Spinoza, mind and body are two aspects of the same thing. Cause and effect is a logical necessity and is the same as the order and connection of ideas in reason. His entire philosophical system stands on the validity of his assumptions and definitions. Spinoza used variations of the Ontological Argument to prove the existence of God. There are various versions of this argument. Basically, it says that God is the greatest idea we can conceive of. If this idea does not include the attribute of existence, then there must be a greater idea that does. Thus, the greatest possible idea must exist. Therefore, God exists. However, as described in the section on logic, we see that this argument is not particularly rigorous.

Gottfried Wilhelm Leibniz (1646–1716)

The rationalist Leibniz, whose original surname was Leibnutz but was changed at the age of twenty, profoundly affected the ideas of the rational and logical philosophical movements. He was also a mathematician (who independently co-invented calculus with Newton) and an inventor of many ingenious devices, the match if anything of Leonardo da Vinci. In addition, he made contributions to geology, linguistics, and physics. Leibniz published only one book on philosophy, the *Theodicy* (1710), but most of his philosophical work was published in journals (or kept in a trunk, to be discovered 150 years after his death!). Russell considered Leibniz to have produced two philosophies — one was a simple form for private consumption, the other a more complex, logical system.

Descartes used mathematics, reason, and science to create a mechanistic vision of the world. This mechanism was considered to have been started by God. Leibniz believed that God creates, conserves, and concurs in the actions of the substances he creates. Leibniz thought that Descartes's vision was flawed because he saw that it presented a uniform Universe that was at odds with what comprised it. Thus, the Cartesian system for the measurement of a location could not determine if something was stationary because it faced problems in defining a reference point for the location. From this, Leibniz began to formulate his own rational metaphysical system. Leibniz believed that some concepts are innate to the human mind. He believed that space did not exist, only things did. How things appeared to us depended on our relativistic reference point. Only God could see things as how they 'are' from a viewpoint independent of time and space. Thus, the Universe was thought to consist of a hierarchy of components, and God was at the pinnacle of it (evil was considered to be motivated from the hand of God).

Leibniz saw things as consisting of infinitely small points, called *monads*, which have no temporal or spatial relevance, yet which mirror the Universe. These infinite monads make up everything in the world. They have no extension and are, thus, not material. Therefore, the world is made of metaphysical points that cannot interact. They do not conform to the laws of physics that apply to matter. The interaction between monads is due to 'harmony' that God created and which exists between them. He classified entities within three levels of existence:

1. Ideal entities.
2. Well-founded phenomena.
3. Actual existents.

These were considered as monads with their own perceptions, interacting through God's will. Leibniz also considered there to be three types of truths:

1. Those that can be defined.
2. Identical propositions as in mathematics. Truths derived from reason can be reduced to these types.
3. Empirical propositions that are not logical, but contingent.

However, some truths do not fit into these categories (e.g., if $x = y$ and $y = z$, then $x = z$). Leibniz reckoned that science must accept his three forms of truth if it was to progress. He developed his principle of sufficient reason, suggesting that nothing happens unless there is sufficient reason for it to do so. He also developed a principle of contradiction for defining what is logically possible. Despite these great contributions, he struggled (like Nietzsche, Spinoza, Marx, and others) to make a living, and his philosophy was largely ignored (again, like Nietzsche, Spinoza, Schopenhauer, and others) during his lifetime. There is debate as to whether all his ideas were his own or pillaged from others. However, a case can be made that he took ideas (e.g., from Spinoza) and refined them so much that he considered them his own.

Leibniz presented the theory of monads in the 1714 edition of *Monadology*, where every monad is deemed unique using his 'identity of indiscernibles', because if they were indiscernible, they would be the very same thing (one can think of modern physics — quarks and quantum numbers — which is addressed in Chapter 3). Leibniz went on to consider that each monad contains within it a consciousness of its entire existence. It seems possible that a rational system was created and considered fine, yet when analysed, certain flaws evolved. However, rather than modify the system to remove the flaws, the original creation was considered to be true, so the same system was fitted to allow for the original hypothesis. Here, the consciousness of the monad seems to be such an attempt to 'fit'.

One wonders, with the monad theory, how the material world consists of immaterial objects. However, we know from atomic structure that the nucleus presents the material and the electron orbit/cloud presents the immaterial, forming the structure of what we see in the world. For example, you or I, if reduced purely to our atomic nuclei constituents, would be barely visible. Leibniz wondered how much we really know about the world and how this 'knowing' is determined by the way we think (a problem still considered today). He thought that what we perceive is not the ultimate reality. What we perceive is dependent on the senses, especially sight. Scientific instruments merely give us better tools to extend the range of our senses. By stating that we cannot have access to ultimate knowledge of reality, or indeed reality itself to assess, Leibniz paved the way for future philosophical attempts to answer this question.

iv) Empiricism

This is the theory that all concepts derive from experience. Thus, all statements have meaning if derived from, and justified by, experience. It's the opposite of rationalism. The process of modern science verification is empiricism, in essence.

John Locke (1632–1704)

Locke lived in the time of and shared ideas with the great chemist Robert Boyle and Newton. His most famous work, *An Essay Concerning Human*

Understanding (1690), presented his philosophical ideas. This work, together with Newton's *Principia*, was accepted at the time as a valid alternative to Descartes's Cartesian philosophy. That is, Locke believed that knowledge about the world must be obtained through experience (epistemology), whereas Descartes considered reason (rationalism) to be enough.

Locke thought that the senses provide knowledge about the physical world that does not need to be confirmed or interpreted by the intellect. He argued that the way we conceive of the world and ourselves is determined by the way we experience the world. There is a difference between the way something is in itself and the way we conceive of it. He was convinced that conclusions cannot be made about how a thing is based on its observation, since how it is intrinsically may be (and probably is) different from conclusions from observation. That is, the object being sensed may be very different from the way we conceive of it on the basis of that experience.

Locke argued that the senses provide knowledge in the form of phenomenal knowledge about experience; beyond this lies speculation and probable conclusions. Descartes's statement that intellect alone enables us to grasp completely the principles governing physical reality — and without the need for experience — was rejected by Locke. Whereas Descartes rooted his philosophy in the infallibility of human reason (under God's guidance), Locke's appealed to the limited human sensory abilities. He disagreed with the concept of innate ideas, considering the mind to attain ideas as a result of experience alone. Thus, when one is born, one is a blank receptive instrument — a *tabula rasa* — for ideas of sensation and reflection.

As we age, the mind actively forms complex ideas from simpler ones. Locke posed the scenario that a blind man can distinguish between a cube and sphere by touch. If he gained sight, could he still distinguish between them without touching them? Would he know which was which? Locke suggested that objects and ideas differed in that objects have qualities that produce ideas in the mind. Since there exist what he called 'primary' and 'secondary' qualities, where primary qualities exist in the object and secondary qualities produce ideas in the mind, Locke attempted to distinguish between appearance and reality. A person born blind cannot know what 'blue' or 'yellow' means, but heat is a different concept. Even without being able to feel heat since it is a natural state, the meaning of heat can be understood because it is linked to physical reality. Colour is semantically different as it is linked to sensory appearance.

Primary qualities are objective and scientifically measurable, whereas secondary qualities are subjective and depend on the perceiver's sensory apparatus. An apple has mass, which is a primary quality, while its smell, taste, and colour are secondary qualities. Thus, a physical object would possess the same primary qualities to any advanced species analysing it, but most likely different secondary qualities. For humans, we share knowledge of the primary qualities, but our sensations of primary qualities are personal — I do not know for certain if your sensation is the same as mine when perceiving the same object.

The bishop George Berkeley believed that all experiences are mental ones created by God. There is no distinguishing between primary and secondary qualities, and God combines all primary and secondary qualities of a thing to create a coherent whole that makes the illusion tangible. When things are not perceived, their existence is maintained by God's omnipotence. Berkeley's idealism of God-created illusions could be seen as more complicated than the perception of a real existant world though sensory apparatus.

Although Cartesian philosophy was deeply dependent on God, Locke required a more logical explanation for phenomena. For example, the Cartesian view rejected the existence of spirits. Locke wondered how, if spirits did exist in space, they would interact with material things. If they do not occupy space, what is their spatial existence, and can they affect this reality? How can we know of something that is not a part of physical nature? If something is not connected with this reality, what constitutes its existence in another reality?

He considered the world to be intelligible if it is thought of as being composed of a uniform matter that made up 'corpuscles'. This bears resemblance to a simplified version of atomic theory. Locke thought too about the mind-body problem — we tend to think that the mind exists independently of the body and that there is a duality. The mind-body problem is immense, posing questions such as "how does the mind and body interact?", "is the mind independent of our interactions with the physical world?" and "is objective truth possible?" These questions are still being asked today. Locke argued about dualism and whether thinking has a mechanical explanation. He deliberated over whether thought is independent of mechanical process. He thought it possible that we are ignorant of something essential to thought or mechanical processes and that knowing it can resolve the mind-body interaction problem.

David Hume (1711–1776)

Considered by many to be the greatest British philosopher (barring Russell perhaps), Hume continued the empiricist tradition of Hobbes, Locke, and others. This led to variations by the English utilitarian philosophers Jeremy Bentham and John Stuart Mill before leading to the analytical philosophy of Russell himself. It could be said that Hume was both the inventor and ultimate destroyer of empiricism. Immanuel Kant, perhaps the most influential philosopher of all, was said to have been "awoken from his dogmatic slumbers" by Hume, so we at least have him to thank for that. As an empiricist, he stated that our thoughts have no content and our words have no meaning unless they are connected to the world of experience.

Hume was extremely knowledgeable about the humanities but knew very little about science and mathematics, yet he applied his reasoning with considerable effect to a huge array of subjects (e.g., morality, scepticism, aesthetics, causality, existence, economics, and anything in the philosophical domain). He wrote on a large number of subjects and his favourite work was *An Enquiry Concerning the Principles of Morals* (1751).

He held philosophy in the highest esteem and judged the study of human understanding above all others. He was hugely influential on the principles of induction and causality. If we throw one ball at another and the second ball moves, we think that this is the result of the action of the first ball. Hume suggested the throwing of the ball and the hitting of the other ball are separate events occurring at different times and are, thus, separable in thought. So, he questioned causality. We associate the two events as cause and effect, but is this really true or just a habit of our mind, conceived from past experiences of the results from such experiments?

Human belief in causality is an example of another idea — inductive reasoning. For example, if all men we meet are mortal, then we reason by induction that all men are mortal. Hume's scepticism of this method, together with causation, undermines the process of the modern scientific method. Perhaps Popper's idea of falsification is the most promising solution to the scepticism of Hume.

Hume divided the perceptions of the human mind into two distinct kinds:

1. Impressions — strong perceptions entering the mind with force and violence.
2. Ideas — less intense images of thinking and reason.

Every object of human reason could be also divided, according to Hume, into two distinct types:

1. Relations of ideas — Pythagoras's rule (the square on the hypotenuse equals the sum of the squares on the other two sides) is an example of this kind. They relate to mathematical rules and are discovered by mental process.
2. Matters of fact — these present propositions for which the opposite fact to that stated are feasible (though practically unlikely). An example is that the Sun will rise tomorrow. The opposite — that it will not rise — is unlikely albeit possible.

These ideas led him to question our belief that every event must have a cause as well as why the cause must have the effect we assign it from a few (compared to the infinite possible number of) epistemological examples. He did, however, believe in cause and effect, and that chance was really the effect of an unknown cause. If we ask whether a table is in front of us, we can use neither reason nor experience to answer it (Descartes and Locke would have disagreed). However, Hume argued that when we look at the table, look away, then look back to find it there, we are in error to believe that it is the same table. It *probably* is, but not definitely. Empiricism fools us, as does reason. We fill in the gaps of time with an expectation that, if fulfilled, confirms our assumptions. Hume challenged these assumptions.

When analysing one's own inner assumptions, one finds a confused, chaotic linkage of perceptions, assumptions, and feelings. Locke believed that memory relates a life of experience into a single mind. However, Hume argued that memory does not make an identity but discovers it. He said this because if I were to judge if an idea is from memory or imagination, I must first know whether the experience remembered was mine. So memory makes us discover our personal identity by demonstrating the relations between cause and effect among our different perceptions.

v) Dialectical Materialism

Dialectical materialism is both a scientific theory and the philosophical basis of Marxism. It states that everything is material and change results from the struggle between opposites according to definite laws. Of its various applications, the main one has been in the analysis of human history and it evolved from *Materialism*, a system of philosophical thought that explains the world based on matter. Materialism proposes that nothing exists other than matter — and that would also include God. Thus, materialism contrasts with idealism. Materialism proposes a material world that is independent of experience, and that the mind derives experience from physical reality. Nature lies behind sense experience and is causally responsible for sense perception.

The dialectic system starts with a *thesis*, which is a position proposed for argument. The opposition to this is the *antithesis*. From this evolves the *synthesis*, which resolves and embraces both the thesis and antithesis. The resultant synthesis becomes the new thesis, requiring a new antithesis and, hence, synthesis. The process repeats until, theoretically, we achieve an ultimate synthesis.

Georg Willhelm Friedrich Hegel (1770–1831)

Hegel was a prolific writer whose definitive works exist as fifty volumes of dense text. He is widely regarded as the greatest German idealist philosopher and his influence on philosophy is still present today. It was he, not Nietzsche, who declared that "God is dead". His breadth of knowledge was enormous. Like many great philosophers, he had his fair share of illnesses, suffering from smallpox, malaria, and the standard philosophical afflictions of depression and cholera at various points in his life.

He was influenced in his time by Holderlin (a German lyrical poet) and Schelling (a German romantic philosopher). However, his greatest influence was Kant and his *Critique of Pure Reason*, which Hegel considered the greatest event in German philosophy. The reason for this was because Kant produced a positive reaction to Hume's conclusions, which were that since experience is our only source of knowledge, and the only way to build on this knowledge is through causality (which Hume deemed to be an illusion), then philosophy is at an end. Kant said that causality is only one of the ways by which we can understand the world and used reason to build an entire philosophical system.

Hegel was also influenced by Spinoza. From reading his works, Hegel was convinced that all parts of the Universe are linked and interdependent, which is interesting considering the modern analysis of universal interconnectedness as demonstrated by *Bell's theorem* (or *Bell's inequality* as it is also known, which I discuss in more detail in Chapters 3 and 6). Hegel was to use this vision of an interdependent Universe (considered as a whole) to create an all-embracing philosophical system. He put these ideas together in his most complex work, *The Phenomenology of Mind* (1807). This difficult work describes the route taken by the human mind to reach 'absolute knowledge' through simple consciousness, self-consciousness, reason, spirit, and religion. The book has been interpreted in different ways and formed the grounding for phenomenology, existentialism, and Marxism.

Hegel's method of dialectical reasoning was a strong influence on Karl Marx, who cemented the ideas of Hegel into his own form of dialectical materialism. However, neither Hegel's nor Marx's systems could see how history unfolds. Their systems tried to predict the future based on the past, yet we realise that history has no predetermined pattern and the outcome is very much in our own hands. We do not trust in dialectical metaphysics; rather, we trust in the hands of science and the application of our technological ingenuity.

Hegel was a monist, believing in one totality, which is the absolute spirit. His writing is seen as the most impenetrable of the important western philosophers, but yields insights into many ideas including those of social and political orientation. He believed that the ultimate reality was mind and spirit. As we age, the mind generates an ever-expanding consciousness of itself. Thus, philosophy allows the development of self-awareness and the ability to free ourselves from lack of reason and that which results from partial knowledge.

Hegel rejected Kant's idea of the noumena, arguing that whatever *is* is knowable. Thus, everything is interconnected and nothing is unrelated. Hegel saw reality as being constructed by the mind. The mind thinks that reality is external and independent of itself, but when the mind recognises reality as its own creation, it knows reality as it knows itself and becomes at one with itself. He argued that ordinary logic governed by contradiction is static and lifeless. For him, the process of dialectic reasoning could explain all of history, the history of thought, and the notion of morality and being.

His dialectic method begins with a thesis. One example of a thesis is 'existence'. Hegel said that the thesis will undoubtedly be incomplete and an antithesis is generated (in our example, this is represented by 'non-existence'). Two opposites form a synthesis (in this case, 'becoming'). The synthesis retains the rational elements of both the thesis and antithesis, resulting in a higher level of truth. The synthesis may become the thesis of another stage of the process. As the series of thesis-antithesis to synthesis is repeated, we see an achievement of greater rationality. The more rational the knowledge achieved, the more spiritual it is. The final synthesis reaches 'ultimate knowledge' and, hopefully, perfection. This dialectic method was what Hegel called logic.

Logic, to Hegel, was to be dialectical, or involved resolution by means of conflict of categories. He defined dialectics as spiritual or logical, and its difference from traditional logic (see Aristotle's syllogisms) is that whereas traditional logic speaks only of itself, Hegel's dialectic reasoning unveils an ascendance to 'absolute spirit'. By refining this method of the dialectic from traditional syllogistic logic, Hegel created a study of how the mind works, which reveals how the world works.

Hegel was of influence to Edmund Husserl and the phenomenological movement. Hegel believed that all human intellectual development is the mind getting to know itself, not through Aristotle's syllogism but through dialectical logic. His *Encyclopaedia of the Philosophical Sciences* (1817, later revised in 1827 and again in 1830) is a summary of his philosophical system.

Hegel had argued in *The Phenomenology of Mind* that thought is objective reality. Thus, logic directed toward thought is logic directed toward objective reality. He believed that his dialectic method mirrored the mechanism of the mind. The problem with his dialectic method is that, despite some theses and antitheses leading to obvious syntheses, often the choice is arbitrary. Thus, he was right to disassociate it from traditional logic, though his reasons were different from the fact that it was indeed less rigorous. However, he should be credited for attempting to produce a complete philosophical system, as with other great German philosophers such as Kant and Heidegger. Some have claimed that Hegel possessed a deep internal division in his psyche, which was probably due to the schizoid extremes of his dialectic method.

For all his achievements, Hegel was the least scientific of philosophers in that his system rejected logical rigour. That said, he did try to make sense of reality. He was influenced by Kant, but the difference is that Kant saw the world in terms of 'is' whereas Hegel saw it merely as a historical progression.

vi) Pragmatism

The American philosophical school of pragmatism stresses that the truth about a proposition has no grounding until its practical use or value has been determined. It attempted to formulate the meaning of concepts according to their practical significance. That is, how do thoughts and actions relate?

Charles Sanders Peirce (1839–1914)

Peirce was an American philosopher, scientist, logician, and leading exponent of pragmatism, which he explained in a series of six articles. A difficult man, he described himself as a 'laboratory philosopher', where laboratory experience encouraged him to apply his pragmatic approach. He proposed to begin his method from the scientific experience of inquiry and investigate from that basis the norms that control cognitive processes. He stated that the aim of inquiry was to replace doubt with settled belief. Inquiry begins when one of our previously settled beliefs is disturbed and ends when a new answer addresses the question that has disturbed the individual.

Pragmatism clarifies and reveals the features of the concepts and hypotheses of scientific investigations. It serves to dismiss some metaphysical hypotheses and clarify our conception of truth and reality. Peirce believed that pragmatism would eliminate ontological metaphysics and that scientific progress would necessitate scientific metaphysics, in which deterministic laws do not govern the Universe. He understood statistical laws and reasoning which, when related to science, demonstrated that observation could not establish scientific laws as absolutely true. He was also interested in the scientific study of signs and symbols. Most of his work was published well after his death.

William James (1842–1910)

James was an American philosopher and psychologist. In *The Principles of Psychology* (1890), he correlated thoughts and feelings with conditions of the brain. He avoided metaphysics in this world, such that the physical world was independent of the mind. The mind is consciousness, perceived through introspection. James's opinion of free will was "the sustaining of a thought because I choose to when I could choose other thoughts". Thus, consciousness cannot control ideas presented to it, but it can control those that affect behaviour.

James won notoriety for pragmatism, but actually credited the concept to his friend Peirce. However, Peirce named his work on this philosophy 'Pragmat*ic*ism' to distinguish his views from James. In James's *Pragmatism*, he considers truth to consist of practical ideas that can be utilised to encourage useful behaviour and emotion. Thoughts are tools through which we do things, and truth determines what is pragmatically useful. Hence, pragmatism (the philosophy) defines a method for living.

James stated that emotional feelings stem from sensations of a state of the body. Thus, emotions follow from the state of the body. He rejected materialism and can be considered to have taken a phenomenological materialistic view of mental processes, such that they represent consciousness of physical states of being. He believed in radical empiricism where the constituents of knowable reality are ultimately pure experience. It is related to pragmatism because knowledge is thought of as the way the experience composing a mind leads it to successfully negotiate with experience beyond it.

vii) Phenomenology

Phenomenology was founded by Husserl and it led to the development of existentialism. It is grounded in the view that philosophy should focus on human consciousness. Its ideas contrast to that of empiricism and deductive logic as it focuses on the description of subjective experience through intuition rather than through analysis. Thus, it is the investigation into how things (e.g., objects and ideas) appear in our consciousness. Explanations are of less interest than the immediate experience. Phenomenology removes the object from its place in physical reality and suspends it as we experience it in our consciousness.

Edmund Husserl (1859–1938)

Husserl was a German philosopher who studied human consciousness and how it relates to objects. He was particularly interested in the structure of experience. For him, philosophy must proceed like science. In his *Logical Investigations* (1900–1901), he suggested that logic is not reducible to psychology. He was convinced that knowledge of one's own consciousness is the one certainty. His phenomenological method was to find what was intrinsic to thought and then discard the mis-suppositions. This reduction then leads to the essence of an experience, after which one is able to look at the logic that led to this essence. Husserl believed that the study of humanity lay beyond the abilities of science and psychology and that it is only possible with the use of his phenomenological reduction.

To focus on consciousness, Husserl removed particulars that are not essential to the structure of the conscious mind. Real objects are for scientific analysis. One must ignore objects and acts of consciousness, such as memory. The resultant pure consciousness is a part of absolute being. An example of Husserl's thinking is — if I am thinking about love, then my thinking is an act that is distinct from other acts of thinking, but the love I am thinking about may not be a particular love, but love in general.

Husserl felt that logic describes the interrelation between intended objects of consciousness.

The way that experiences are consciously perceived was a problem considered by James. Husserl thought, for example when considering musical notes in a melody, that we have no awareness of the notes before and after a moment in time. He considered that as time advances through the melody, the notes that recede in time appear in 'retentional modifications' — thus, the notes and the order are retained in the consciousness, explaining our appreciation and analysis of music.

Husserl talked of 'essences' as objects of consciousness, and phenomenology is the study of essences. He emphasised that the 'intentional' object that thought is aimed at may be real or unreal. In later life, it was thought that Husserl considered the 'I' to be unknowable and, if this is so, it posed the question as to what can be known. Other philosophers have used his methods to serve their own, but his hope of resolving philosophical disagreements were unfulfilled.

viii) Existentialism

Existentialism and phenomenology were the dominant philosophies in France in the 20th century. They were directed towards the understanding of experience, the subject, consciousness, and meaning. Existentialism consists of several philosophical systems that are concerned with the nature of being and of existence. In accordance with existentialist ideas, it has been suggested that the greatest insights into existence occur during occasions of extreme experience. There are two kinds of existentialists — the Christians and the atheistic existentialists (including, most famously, Heidegger and the French existentialist Jean-Paul Sartre) — and it is the latter type I mean when I refer to existentialism in this book (unless otherwise stated).

Existentialism has lost its public and philosophical following in modern times. Once of primary focus, its dwindling interest since the 1960s was because, perhaps as Mary Warnock stated, it moved towards social anthropology and sociology (i.e., moving from the inner focus of human existence to its outer experience). However, the insights it provided into the " 'being' of the human condition were extensive.

Søren Aabye Kierkegaard (1813–1855)

Kierkegaard was a Danish philosopher who is regarded as the founder of existentialism. He was interested in a certain form of truth which he called 'subjective truth' (or existential truth). This truth cannot be communicated but involves insights about the individual's life. Like that of Socrates, Kierkegaard presented his ideas by developing a form of indirect communication. He also often wrote under pseudonyms (e.g., Johannes Climacus and Nicolaus Notabene), partly due to his wish to conceal his ill-ease with his views of the church. He saw knowledge as abstract — only existence was real.

Here, we need to distinguish *objectivity* from *subjectivity*. Objectivity is the idea that a pure form of description exists that is not affected by human subjectivity. Science needs objectivity because the scientific method aims to provide an accurate description of worldly phenomena. As the French phenomenologist Maurice Merleau-Ponty saw it, objectivity is impossible because it requires a multitude of simultaneous perspectives.

To be objective rather than limited to the perspective allowed by our senses, physical location, and physiology, we would have to be everywhere at once (e.g., that which is only possible according to the notion of God). Subjectivity is harder to define but, put simply, it is to base something on personal feeling. The concept is essential for the understanding, application, and analysis of the doctrines of phenomenology and existentialism (e.g., the works of Husserl, Kierkegaard, and Sartre).

These traditions state that the extent to which the world is created subjectively by an individual is as real and true to the individual as the 'reality' outside the self. Our knowledge of reality is limited by our mind's capability and our physiology, size, molecular composition, and so forth, as well as our being bound to the temporal flow. So, we are constrained to deal with the subjectively constituted world of meaning since this is what we create and relate to as our interpretable version of absolute reality. Thus, Kierkegaard's writings don't lead to anything objective since he considered only inner existence as real.

All of Kierkegaard's works lead back to the self of subjective truths. Existing, being, and the nothingness that pervades being are pondered subjectively. Kierkegaard distinguished between objective and subjective truths. Objects (things) can be thought about because they can be conceptualised. However, Kierkegaard thought that existence cannot be thought about because it is concrete and never abstract. Thus, when all is said about that which can be thought about and conceptualised, the existence of that which thinks is that which remains (since it cannot be thought).

Existence must be *lived*, and in living it is related to thought. Since living is action, then the thought that is related to the doing of existing is called subjective thought. Objective thought, which encompasses things such as science, can be tested. It focuses on the object or the thing. The individual does not change if the objective truth is different. Subjective truths, not objective facts, are related to one's existence, so they affect the individual if they are different. Morality is a subjective truth because what we think is right or wrong relates to our self. Kierkegaard considered subjective truth to relate to *how* rather than *what*. By this he meant that if we *really* believe in something, it will be shown in how we behave.

Kierkegaard believed that objective truths about the world could be derived scientifically. When we are conscious of something as being something (e.g., a hen's egg as brown), there is the simultaneous possibility of it being something different (e.g., the egg is white). There is a constant duality between what is actuality and possibility; what is and what isn't. Consciousness presents many possibilities and the denial of this is what Sartre termed as living in 'bad faith'. It is escaping the responsible freedom of being-for-itself.

Existing, and even consciousness itself, presents terror to the individual when they realise the possibilities of life from their acceptance of life. Kierkegaard accepted that religious belief would save himself from terror and doubt. However, one wonders about the depth of his belief since he realised that even this belief presented its own doubt.

Martin Heidegger (1889–1976)

Heidegger was considered important in the development of existentialism. He considered himself a phenomenologist, but was widely thought of as an atheistic existentialist. He developed his existential ideas as a progression Kierkegaard's and in conjunction with the phenomenological ideas of Husserl, under whom he studied. He initially agreed with Husserl's phenomenological analysis before probing deeper into existence. He wanted to know what existence means. What is 'is'? Like Nietzsche, he rejected the Cartesian division between the subject and external world. The world is not external to a conscious observer — rather, he is embedded in it. Before any philosophical question can be asked, Heidegger asked the simplest question of all, "why is there something rather than nothing?" His philosophy took on a religious form, but devoid of God.

Heidegger's viewpoint can be seen as an extension of Aristotle's logical categorisation of being. Heidegger was interested not only in the being of entities themselves, but also of the surrounding context. Thus, he wanted to understand the very nature of being and how it leads to such diversity of type. Being has been a question for philosophers since the beginning, and Heidegger realised that he had to define what being is in order to answer this.

He agreed with Kant that how things *are* depends on how we contribute to them, and that *we* are concrete and real, not just consciousness. Heidegger claimed that no proof had been given for things existing outside of us. It is what Kant referred to as "the scandal of philosophy" that we have a problem proving the existence of minds other than our own or the reality of the external world. The problem for Heidegger was not that the proof had not been found, but rather that it was expected and had been attempted to be found many times.

Heidegger wanted to understand the meaning of being that would explain existence. To do so, he devised an entirely new philosophy that was seen as either revolutionary or meaningless depending on one's viewpoint. Like the American pragmatist John Dewey, Heidegger did not accept the subject as an isolated spectator in an external world but, rather, that we are embedded in an environment that we must manipulate to our own benefit.

At the turn of the 20th century, the problems of philosophy were approached and analysed from points of view that each led to uncertainty. Two independent and mutually exclusive traditions of philosophy developed during this period and they addressed why such uncertainty existed. Each, however, considered the other as nonsense, meaningless, or wrong.

One was linguistic analysis, which was derived from Wittgenstein and addressed what can or cannot be asked. Here, problems arise from the misapplication of words. We cannot know the meaning of existence according to this line of thought because 'meaning' and 'existence' cannot be applied together. For existence to have meaning, meaning would need to exist outside of existence, which is not possible.

The other tradition (devised by Heidegger) asked about the meaning of existence and being in a way that could not be reasoned away by the methods of linguistic analysis. Here, the idea is that existence is prior to rational thought.

To Heidegger, being is more fundamental than any existent being or object. It precedes its appearance. *Dasein* is Heidegger's word for human 'being' or 'human existence'. He defined Dasein as "the entity which in its being we know as human life". The being of Dasein is understanding its own being. From this, the being understands the being of other beings, which are other than its own being. Heidegger referred to Dasein often in his work. This term, which could mean 'being-there', is his term for human reality and is the essence of human being.

The English language derives from Latin, so derivations for Dasein have less meaning than in German. Thus, even though Heidegger's and Wittgenstein's philosophies are diametrically opposed, the concept and importance (and ambiguity) of meaning is epitomised by our inability to get to the essence of the word Dasein in English. Dasein goes beyond logic and syntax to the fundamentals of intuition. Here, existence is even deeper than Descartes's basic assumption, *cogito ergo sum*.

More fundamental than this is my 'being-in-the-world', which is ultimately what Heidegger wanted to tell us. Dasein is existence in essence and, as such, is beyond our access. We cannot stand back and see it because it is us. Heidegger thought that philosophy had ignored this, and he realised that humankind had lost the concept of being. This removal of the centality of 'being' was due to the demise of the work of the pre-Socratic ancient Greeks (e.g., Anaximander), who studied the essence of being. Socrates, Plato, and Aristotle, the forefathers of modern western philosophy, focused the tradition in the wrong direction. Furthermore, Heidegger saw that languages such as English, French, Italian, and Spanish are derived from the primordially dead Latin. Only German, derived from ancient Greek, is consequently the language that encapsulates the essence of being.

Heidegger criticised Kant's critical idealism in favour of critical realism. He was concerned with how the self-awareness of humans is associated with death and the concept of time. Since human beings inhabit life, Heidegger was interested in being rather than existence. He argued that western science and philosophy are condemned to non-rational beliefs. For example, he believed, as did Wittgenstein, that arithmetic is founded on counting and measurement instead of the logic of Russell and Frege. Heidegger saw modern philosophy as being unaware of the notion of 'being', let alone its importance for philosophical foundations. Science and technology have reduced society to nihilism, where our non-understanding of being is matched only by our non-awareness of the concept.

Heidegger had to create a new language of being to make its importance understood within the western philosophical framework. This language is the function of his *Being and Time*, though this work was never finished, and it is considered by many philosophers to be among the most influential of philosophical works, in the same league as Kant's *Critique of Pure Reason*, Plato's *Republic*, and Nietzsche's *Thus Spoke Zarathustra*. In it, Heidegger analysed, with his knowledge of all of western philosophy, the correlation between being and time. He started by saying that we have no definition or notion of what we mean by the term 'being'. Some say that such probing of existence is not necessary in today's age.

Science works despite fundamental gaps in our knowledge that are due to either technological infancy or nature being illogical. We work within the framework of what is revealed to us. With concepts such as quantum indeterminism, however unappealing it is to our desire of attaining total knowledge, we strive on within these confines.

Jean-Paul Sartre (1905–1980)

Sartre was perhaps France's most famous and best-loved philosopher. He was also a novelist, literary critic, and, in his later years, a Marxist political activist. He wrote much about being and consciousness, which have been scrutinised against *Being and Time* by Heidegger and *The Phenomenology of Perception* by the other great French existentialist Maurice Merleau-Ponty (1908–1961).

In his masterwork *Being and Nothingness* (1943), Sartre argued that consciousness belongs to a different ontological category than the physical world. He claimed, wrongly according to some, that consciousness is associated with an unspoken self-consciousness. One definition he gives for consciousness is that it is the "behaviour of behaviours". He attempted to apply Husserl's phenomenological methods to the study of the imagination, perceived as a distinctive mode of intentional consciousness. The contents of the imagination should be viewed, according to Sartre, as inner objects.

Our ability to imagine what isn't the case (i.e. that which could, but doesn't, happen) offered Sartre proof that we are not subject to the determinism that governs the development of all other Earth entities, for which their existence is governed by their essence (what they are destined to be). Sartre made the division between 'being-in-itself' and being-for-itself. The 'in-itself' relates to pure objects that possess 'fullness', as Sartre calls it. Here, objects such as a chair are complete; they are what they are and nothing else. The 'for-itself' is Sartre's version of consciousness. There is no fullness in this category as we are not only here, but are aware of being here, which is reflected back to our consciousness. We cannot achieve full equivalence.

ix) Other Important Philosophers

Arthur Schopenhauer (1788–1860)

Schopenhauer's doctrine of the will opposed the idealism of Hegel. Schopenhauer believed that will is more basic than thought in man and nature, and he was a realist — nothing exists without the mind. The intellect creates the world of material things by applying the principles of cause and effect to sensory information received. However, the intellect is secondary to the will.

Schopenhauer was influenced by Kant and Plato, and he was one of the few western philosophers who was also influenced by Hindu and Buddhist ideas. He was an atheist and his work was of great influence to Nietzsche. Schopenhauer considered the world to exist for the subject of knowledge. All knowledge of the world is a product of the kind of animal we are. The world is purposeless, in which the will blindly strives forward towards something. He thought that universal determinism held true for the phenomenal world, or the world of phenomena.

The four volumes of his greatest work, *The World as Will and Representation* (originally published in 1818), sees Schopenhauer follow Kant's reasoning of the distinction between the 'thing-in-itself' (noumena) from the phenomenon, where Kant saw the thing-in-itself as not responsible for our sensations of the phenomenon. Kant argued that our behaviour represents itself as phases of a will. Schopenhauer, however, thought that we are still able to get insight into the nature of the thing-in-itself. He considered the thing-in-itself as corresponding to the will.

Schopenhauer's subject of representations is neither part of the objective world, in space and time, nor affected by causality. Kant thought that our experiences represent a collaboration between us and a reality we know nothing of other than that it exists. He thought that by distinguishing the phenomenal world (that we experience) and the noumenal world (i.e., the world as it is in itself), he would be able to show that many traditional philosophical problems cannot be answered. By limiting our reason, Kant believed that he had made way for a reason to have faith. However, is this an example of bad reasoning where a conclusion is made (that there is a God) before an argument is created to support the conclusion?

Schopenhauer was not prepared to disregard as 'appearance' such elements as pain and death, which was the attitude of many philosophers before him (hence his pessimistic view). He thought about the body and the will as such: I am aware of myself objectively as I am aware of other things as objects extended in space and time. But I am also aware of myself subjectively, as feelings — as will. Awareness of the body differs from awareness of the external. The body and the will are one. The body is will — it is the manifestation of will to life. The brain is the will-to-know, the foot is the will-to-walk, and so on. Knowing myself as will is to feel the inner unity of life, and as a separation from external space and time.

Since Schopenhauer knew that all knowledge is relative and our intellectual knowledge of the world is incomplete and fragmented, he saw the intellect and the will as total opposites. The attributes of the will come from a basic urge to live, whereas the intellect consists of other attributes, such as consciousness. He saw the body as the outward form of the will and the will as the inward form of the body. Since all objects are the outward form of an inner will, then what we feel as our true being is the true being of all things. Thus, Schopenhauer thought that there is an outward world of events (a phenomenal world) and an inward world of everpresent will (a noumenal world). He claimed that we know the world of appearances through the will. His idea of the one will was his most important philosophical creation.

His work is an interesting attempt at an all-encompassing philosophy, but it did not stand up to scrutiny as well as Kant's efforts. Sadly, for all his insight, he is confined to history as the great pessimist.

Friedrich Wilhelm Nietzsche (1844–1900)

Nietzsche was of great importance to western philosophy — "Every philosophy conceals another philosophy" is an example of his way of thinking. He was originally a philologist (the science of the structure and development of language) with no formal philosophical training. He realised, as Wittgenstein did fifty years later, that language cannot convey objective truth about external reality. When Descartes said "I think, therefore I am", he had ignored the body.

In his book *Beyond Good and Evil* (1886), Nietzsche criticised many assertions along the line of certainty about knowing it is 'I' that thinks. He accepted the phenomenal world in the traditional sense, but considered another one. This phenomenal world is an unknowable one where 'truth' is the will to be master over sensations. He saw logic as an attempt to comprehend actuality by means of a scheme of being that we have proposed. Furthermore, he believed that we prefer untruth to truth, in that our instinct for self-preservation teaches us to be superficial.

Nietzsche speculated on metaphysical theories that assess the nature of reality using reason alone. He thought that there could be a metaphysical world, but we behold things in it through our heads. He then asked, "If we cut off this head, would the world be there?" Theories to answer this question are outside the scope of our investigation — he thought that the existence of a metaphysical dimension would be the most useless of all knowledge. He was a profoundly positive thinker who sought ways to enhance life from the collapse of traditional values.

His writing method of brief reflections makes him difficult to read and hides the complexity of his ideas. Furthermore, his writing is so forcefully put and so well presented that often one is driven to believe the content beyond what might be considered rational based on ideas alone. He believed that science is unable to yield anything like absolute knowledge, thus criticising the claim of science to explain the world. To Nietzsche, science isn't explanation but description. It distinguishes from earlier stages of knowledge by describing better, but explaining no more. For example, the progress of science has enabled us to give better descriptions of things like thought and fire, but it has explained nothing about them.

Michel Foucault (1926–1984)

We have seen how philosophy had taken two directions — Wittgenstein's reduction of the problems of philosophy to linguistic errors and Heidegger's continental philosophy. Foucault was influenced by the Heideggerian tradition, through which he saw how philosophy and forms of knowledge arrive at their own version of truth (since there is no ultimate truth or ultimate reality).

Importantly, Foucault was to show that truth, in its limited sense, is based on assumptions that are indicative of the age of their creation (but perhaps that is the very nature of progress — incorporating accepted ideas). Hegel influenced Foucault because of his interest in linking philosophy with history. Foucault could see that a correct understanding of the present is based on how we view the past. He was also interested in the work of Sartre and, in fact, his own ideas were a reaction to those of Sartre, Heidegger, and Hegel.

Jacques Derrida (1930–2004)

Derrida was a deconstructionist and he claimed that "there is nothing outside the text". His philosophical beginnings saw him follow Sartre's nihilistic existentialism (existence precedes essence). He moved on to Heidegger and Husserl before formulating his own philosophical direction.

In 1962, he published a large introduction to Husserl's *Origin of Geometry*. Husserl's work questioned the basis of knowledge on intuition. Furthermore, if knowledge is beyond science and reason, how do we know truth that is not intuited? Derrida thought that Husserl saw geometry as a type of perfect knowledge, irrespective of intuition. By analysing this work, Derrida started developing his 'questioning of philosophy'.

Unlike other philosophers, Derrida's work proves difficult to interpret and, as such, opinion is divided as to its importance. Derrida regarded Husserl's notion — that geometry presents a truth that is not grounded in experience — as inconsistent. How do we know that truths such as geometry are waiting to be discovered? Does it come from logic or intuition? Such questions get to the essence of western philosophy. Wittgenstein wrote many off as linguistic errors. The other philosophical tradition of dealing with such problems came from Heidegger, who thought that certain assumptions exist about the foundations of knowledge. This metaphysical assumption lies beyond the phenomenal world and cannot be removed by reference to Wittgenstein's linguistics. Heidegger showed that western philosophy and science is based on the belief that truth can be validated. Derrida saw error in this western philosophical assumption. No finite intellect, with its limited intuition, can know whether what its limited intuition intuits is absolute truth. Thus, Derrida said that not even philosophy can exist, so he did not see himself as a philosopher.

Hume had stated that all knowledge is based on experience while Descartes said that we can rationally extract the truth about reality. However, Derrida again found fault in Descartes and claimed that he was bound by the language of his thought. Thus, he could not fail to see a distorted view of reality. Western philosophy found faults in both systems as a route to universal truth and sought truth through logic. When this failed, we saw philosophy diverge with Wittgenstein on one path and Heidegger on the other (yet science works, and we use it to our technological benefit in so many ways despite Derrida and Heidegger destroying the notion of scientific truth).

Derrida published prolifically. *Of Grammatology*, published in 1967, attacks the indecidability of philosophy. He attacked the logic of language, believing rather that understanding comes from experience. Derrida was aware of Gödel's incompleteness theorem, the success of science, and Wittgenstein's linguistic philosophy. He knew that we express our knowledge through language, yet that this is not logical as it is full of contradictions and ambiguities. Language is a lived thing, and Derrida wanted to show that what is written can be interpreted in many drastically different ways. Yet my saying "give me some cheese" does not mean "hit me" by any stretch of the imagination. The meaning of language is communication. Rather than seeing the limitations about what we can derive from language, as commented by Wittgenstein, Derrida chose to deconstruct it to show how little it can *really* tell us.

Does what Derrida did have any use? It does not say what a text means, but says how it achieves meaning. Philosophy wanted to eliminate ambiguity in knowledge. Derrida wanted to show how philosophy works — it reveals its assumptions of truth and shows that language revolves around the ambiguity of these assumptions. Derrida's linguistic relativism and Foucault's cultural relativism are in accord and also part of the French movement of post-structuralism. Here, knowledge is considered as relevant to something and not absolute. However, Foucault's emphasis on the context of the text was later criticised by Derrida, and Foucault considered Derrida's work as intellectual nitpicking. This split the post-structural movement.

Derrida remained convinced that we cannot attach a single fixed meaning to a text. It is interesting to see that Wittgenstein and Derrida both claimed to have put an end to philosophy, yet their approaches are diametrically opposed. Derrida did so by showing the ambiguity of language and that coherent philosophy is impossible. Wittgenstein attempted unsuccessfully to 'construct' language rules, yet later attempted to show what can and cannot be meaningfully said as well as how the application of language leads to confusion and meaningless propositions.

Concluding remarks

The traditional understanding of the history of science was as a continual, fluid progression of knowledge that moved steadily closer to the truth. Thomas Kuhn argued that the historical progress of science is far from continuous.

Indeed, different periods of investigation presented scientific ideas that caused re-evaluations of current understanding. He was not suggesting that it was a stop and start progression but rather that there were paradigm shifts that caused a revision of particular scientific models. An example is Einstein's theory of relativity which replaced Newton's laws of gravitation.

Paul Feyerabend moved from the ideas of logical positivism and Popper's falsificationism to extend Kuhn's thesis of *incommensurability*. Rather than scientific progress oscillating between periods of 'normal' science and 'revolutionary' science, he saw science as always being revolutionary. This is because science proceeds with multiple concurrent and differing hypotheses existing at any one time, all vying for the position of not being falsified and being accepted as 'currently' correct. Feyerabend considered 'facts' not as statements of truth but as representations of what people believe.

The American philosopher W. V. O. Quine (1908–2000) thought science to be the "final arbiter of truth". Only science tells us about the world, and what it can tell us about it is that our knowledge of it is constrained by our sensory stimulations. He rejected Kant's attempted synthesis of rationalism and empiricism, arguing that theory and experience work together to produce our best theory of the world. That is, what exists is what our best theory says exists. Thus, to Quine, physical objects are *posits* of our best theory and their existence can be denied in light of recalcitrant experience. Quine acknowledged our fallibility and that what we believe is true is taken as true until a better version is accepted as the new truth. Thus, no truth we reveal can be stated as noumenal truth.

The French philosopher Jean-Francois Lyotard (1924–1998) proposed that science is best understood in terms of Wittgenstein's language game. It is a language game with the following rules:

1. Only descriptive statements are scientific.
2. Scientific statements are different from those which constitute the social bond.
3. Competence is only required on the part of the sender of the scientific message, not the receiver.
4. A scientific statement exists within a series of statements, which are validated by argument and proof.

5. It follows from 4 that the scientific language game requires knowledge of the existing state of scientific knowledge. Science does not require a narrative for its legitimation as its rules are immanent in its game.

Lyotard suggested that for the progress of science, each new scientific statement (e.g., axiom) must win the approval of other scientists within the same field of research. We know this process as 'peer review'. Understandably, science progresses through time to an increasing level of complexity in terms of how well we understand the phenomena under investigation. With science today, we see a crucial role for technology in producing the maximum output for minimum input. Lyotard called this process the "principle of performativity", which dominates the modern scientific language game because scientific discoveries require proof, which costs money. Thus, the relevance and predicted success of scientific endeavors are important considerations.

There is the belief that the most well-funded research is most likely to produce the 'best' results. It is true that certain types of research require much more money than others due to their nature. Some scientific disciplines require expensive machinery and reagents to function (consider the Large Hadron Collider, for example). However, the quality of the output relies on many things including money, skilled scientists, good ideas, intelligence, and perhaps a bit of luck too at times.

Lyotard stressed that since only those with wealth can fund research and the wealthy profit from it, power and knowledge are therefore more linked today than ever before (and increasingly so). As we study scientific phenomena, we aim to get closer to the 'truth' of the process. If truth is found, then results cannot be falsified. However, when Newton embarked on classical works on gravitation, little was he to know that science would progress to understand reality as being fundamentally indeterminate in nature. Thus, in our quest for the type of truth we hoped for, we have revealed within our narrow framework of understanding that such truth cannot be found. Nature, it seems, is not innately knowable. On the other hand, it may be knowable, but in a way that cannot be comprehended by our finite minds.

Some philosophers consider philosophy to have reached an impasse — the problems of philosophy cannot be answered. There is no metaphysics according to Wittgenstein and Kant, and the French philosopher/physicist Bernard d'Espagnat showed that parts of reality are unknowable to us. Science and philosophy were once seen as the same thing. Now, while philosophy struggles to find out what it is, what it wants to know, and how to address it, science continues to produce results. It is not surprising that science has taken centre stage. We can manipulate it for our own good. Although it deals with the phenomenal world, science has to ignore, by necessity, parts of it that are not within the focus of its analysis. Thus, we study one aspect and ignore another, even though the other may impart an effect on the analysis. As a result, our conclusions are merely approximations, assumptions, theories, and models.

As I mentioned earlier, science fits with our modern context of an increasingly technological age. Think of the human genome sequencing project, the search for the Higgs Boson at the Large Hadron Collider, or the detail of our Universe gleaned from the Hubble telescope. But philosophy isn't dead — it in fact remains the deepest intellectual pursuit. Indeed, young researchers graduate from universities with the degree of Doctor of Philosophy (PhD). Now that we have reached a stage where we can exploit science for our benefit, let us not forget the questions we have asked since the time of Socrates and earlier, and which got us started on our quest for knowledge, such as the nature of being and consciousness — "What am I?"

These questions have led us to the need for and construction of a methodological scientific approach to obtain usable knowledge of the world. Consciousness is a subject of both the scientific and philosophical domains, and until we can resolve the mind-body problem objectively (which is probably impossible), it will remain so.

The link between this chapter and the following two which consider the physics of the Universe can be encapsulated in a memory of mine. As a child, I asked myself, "What does 'now' mean?" When I look at a distant star, I am thinking of it as it is 'now', but in fact I see it as it was billions of years ago because that is how long its light takes to reach me. The thought and image have different points in time. But if I talk to people, see them, hear them, and think about them, these events seem to occur together, yet they actually also occur at different moments. Physics describes how light and sound travel at different speeds. We see things before we hear them. The physics of relativity explains *time dilation* effects — fast moving things shrink and time slows down. Quantum theory determines finite measurable limits in the Universe — the 'Planck time' (named after the German theoretical physicist Max Planck) is the smallest passage of time that has any meaning. This is a thousand trillion trillion times shorter than the shortest passage of time we have been able to measure. This is how the reality in which we are embedded is. However, when consciousness is involved, it too imparts constraints on our knowledge of time in relation to things when they happen.

Consciousness, though experienced by everyone, is a difficult phenomenon to address both scientifically and philosophically. We probe its meaning in many contexts, and for each there is much disagreement. This lack of consensus indicates how much we still have to learn about it. What *is* agreed is that, essentially, it is not a thing but rather a process that occurs in our brains. It relates to the physical world in which it is embedded. It cannot touch or experience reality directly, yet its existence, to the 21st century scientist, is regarded to be a result of physical neuronal processes. It is the flow of sensations that gives life meaning, rather than just existence.

What we mean by 'now' can only be a passage of time with blurred limits and knowledge of a finite point in time is an illusion. Why is this? Knowing anything requires consciousness and it requires the passage of time to function because consciousness is a *process*. Like any process, consciousness has a past, present, and (possible) future. If we bring relativity into the equation, two conscious minds existing in different parts of spacetime are subject to relativistic effects that cause minute differences to what 'now' is to each of them. The constant flow of time means that, for consciousness, 'now' is a working integration of what was (past) as well as what will/can be (future) sensed as the present. An object can be known if we dissociate it from time and let the process of consciousness act on the thing. Time itself is a part of spacetime. If the question "what time is it?" is asked and one wants to answer this scientifically and not in the social sense, the answer is clearly "it's relative".

And it *is* relative — to objective reality, the conscious mind, and the relation between these things. In essence, reality merely 'is' whereas understanding reality, for humans, requires a process. It is through this process that the nature of reality that 'is' is revealed and becomes known.

2 Physics and the Classical World

Science and philosophy have been linked for over 2,000 years in European history. Aristotle was renowned not only for his logic and metaphysics, but also his prowess as a scientist, particularly his observations on biology and zoology. But science perhaps saw its real flowering during the Renaissance and the Enlightenment, the age of Galileo and Newton, the Polish astronomer Nicolaus Copernicus (1473–1543), and Bacon. This was the period when serious attempts were made to understand the nature of reality through the application of the scientific method, which was not without its dangers.

These were, of course, times when the Church wielded enormous power and to suggest that God was not at the centre of the Universe was seen as heretical. Great scientific minds such as Galileo were forced to deny their findings for fear of death or excommunication. Philosophers too had to tread carefully, either publishing their work in countries that had a more liberal and less suspicious attitude to new thought or finding a way to incorporate God into philosophy, as Descartes did with his famous proposition *cogito ergo sum* ("I think, therefore I am"), which makes God the cause of all our ideas.

Physics is the most fundamental of the sciences; from it extend the physical laws from which all science is derived and to which all can be reduced. Wittgenstein, however, might have had something to say about the claims of 'truth' derived from the sciences despite all its practical successes. This and the following chapters discuss the physics of the large-scale (physical) and small-scale (quantum) Universe. The former is revealed by *classical mechanics*, incorporating Newtonian mechanics, which describes the motion of macroscopic objects, whether it be a bullet, an apple falling from a tree, or the movements of satellites, planets, stars, and galaxies. The incorporation of special relativity enabled the description of objects traveling at close to the velocity of light, while general relativity enabled a deeper understanding of the effects of gravity. When married with *quantum mechanics*, which describes the subatomic (small-scale) level of the Universe, a complete description of the physical laws describing the behaviour of matter that comprises physical reality is produced.

While the behaviour of all living organisms is determined to a great or total degree by their genes and their relationship to the physical environment, as we shall see in Chapter 4, their intrinsic processes also accord to these fundamental laws. Although the physics of the large- and small-scale Universe differ, together they complete the physical description of the laws of the Universe. The search is on for a *Theory Of Everything* (TOE) that can describe all of physics under *one* paradigm.

Scientists like Richard Feynman and Stephen Hawking (1942–2018) have sought to explain to lay readers what to many outsiders often seems a challenging and difficult area. In that tradition, I hope that this and the following chapter can stand on their own as a primer for those with little prior knowledge of theoretical or quantum physics. They present a conceptual and partly historical description of both relativity (special and general) and quantum theory. The beauty of each theory suggests truth, yet their incompatibility begs the questions of whether reality is determinate, indeterminate, knowable, or definable under one theory, and whether *our* minds and methods of address are capable of answering such questions. Being able to ask the right questions does not imply ability to answer them.

Describing the physics portrayed in these chapters necessitates neglect of much of the work that led to it. The nature of man and scientific process is that success is rewarded while failure is not. However, a path of research is never initiated with the belief that it will fail. Failure is an inevitable possibility we all face when accepting a challenge, and yet a failure can be viewed as a success from a different perspective. It may close off one potential route of research, yet make another avenue more appealing and perhaps more likely to succeed. Such is the nature of science.

Quantum theory is over a hundred years old, though its form has changed over time. However, it would not have emerged without the work of the classical sciences from which it evolved. Indeed, the science of the classical period has covered far more of humankind's scientific history than that devoted to quantum theory. The 'language' of quantum physics, though, is far removed from that of common speech. Thus, the non-physicist may be in awe of this work due to the apparent incomprehensibility of the notations used to express its ideas. To make quantum physics understandable to a wider audience, its mathematical symbolism must be translated into common language without altering the meaning of the mathematical relations it describes. Quantum theory cannot yet be extended to incorporate the entire sphere of classical mechanics. The special and general (or *geometric*, as the American physicist John Archibald Wheeler (1911–2008) preferred to call it) theories of relativity, formulated by Albert Einstein towards the beginning of the last century, form a link between Isaac Newton's determinate classical picture of reality and the quantum revolution. They certainly demonstrate the ingenuity of the human intellect. Indeed, as an indication of our intellectual achievements, and as a description of the scientific principles underlying our reality, relativity is applicable to both.

i) In the Beginning

The first person to look up at the sky and wonder what was out there was so far back in our history that it preceded forms of communication. Perhaps questions were formed in the mind of early man in an abstract way, not logically formulated due to the lack of language, but driven by feelings of awe and wonder. I am talking, of course, about questions such as "who am I?" and "what's out there?" I believe that feelings equating to these questions arose before the concept of gods or religion. These feelings, together with the need to survive and reproduce, must have aided the development of the brain, intelligence, language, and culture.

The early hominids, predating even those species that were on the direct evolutionary path to *Homo sapiens*, might have had the ability to ask such questions in a simple way. Thought is possible without language. Despite simplistic communication, they could have visualised concepts that were understandable to themselves in a unique and specific way, which then enabled them to reason, rationalise, and think about their existence beyond the basic necessities for survival (e.g., eating, surviving, reproducing). They were the dominant species due to their brains. One look to the sky and their intrinsic insight of perspective would show them, in their own way, that there lay a great space physically unavailable to them. One thought equating to "what's it for?", which is the kind of thinking they might have regularly used for survival when encountering an unusual object, and they would have questioned the meaning of life in a simple way. The irony is that despite all our advances, the first questions that got us started on our quest for truth are still unanswered and are the most difficult.

You might ask, "Is it important what or who was the first to think of these things?" Perhaps we do not need to know the exact individual hominid or human who first pondered such things. But when these thoughts began in us, I imagine that a momentous change occurred in our mental make-up. We made the leap from addressing local necessity to comprehending and mastering other non-essential phenomena. The non-essential for one generation becomes essential for the next. The benefit from mental evolution and understanding for future generations was not a conscious consideration at first but rather a genetic consequence of the mind's capability and intrinsic to its inquisitive nature. I think it was also a factor that drove the necessity for communication.

The theories of relativity presented a transcendental leap in our understanding of our place in the Universe, but they were not the first of such leaps. From humankind's first wonderment at our place in the Universe, we have tried to formulate a truthful paradigm of what 'here' is. In about 140 AD, Ptolemy Claudius of Alexandria presented his view of the 'world picture' in his work *Almagest*. This Ptolemaic scheme of the Universe essentially placed Earth at the centre of the world. Thus, the importance of man was emphasised in that we must inhabit the centre of all things. Although Ptolemy knew that the Earth was spherical, he thought it impossible that the Earth was moving — he believed that the heavens and stars were moving around it. Not knowing the huge interstellar distances that exist, Ptolemy's reasoning seemed logical and his conception of the Universe held for over a thousand years. Without the opportunity for advancement in scientific understanding, in all the intervening time there was neither data nor reason to doubt it. Furthermore, his ideas fitted with humankind's belief in its universal importance.

It was not until the 16th century that the next great leap forward was made. The main work of Copernicus was not published until after his death in 1546 in the form of his *Doctrine of the Rotation of Celestial Bodies*. Here, he made the bold conclusion that the Earth rotates around its own axis and that the stars do not move with the great velocity that Ptolemy predicted in his own system. He calculated with high accuracy the movement and radii of planetary orbits. Although he thought that planetary orbits were circular, he knew that the Sun, not the Earth, was at the centre of what we call the solar system (in fact, he knew that the Sun was slightly off-centre within the solar system).

It was the Danish astronomer Tycho Brahe (1546–1601), utilising ingenious astronomical instruments of his own design, who noted that planetary orbits are in fact elliptical. His student, the German Johannes Kepler (1571–1630), advanced this work into a law of planetary motion about the Sun. His meticulous measurements of planetary motion showed that while a planet's elliptical orbit around the Sun varies in velocity with respect to distance from the Sun (faster when closer to the Sun and slower when further away, an effect we know today as being due to gravitational attraction), the total area of sweep per unit time remained constant. Kepler went on to devise three laws of planetary motion:

First law — a planet moves about the sun in an elliptic orbit, with one focus of the ellipse located at the sun.

Second law — a straight line from the sun to each planet sweeps out equal areas in equal times.

Third law — the time required for a planet to make one orbit, when squared, is proportional to the cube of the major axis of the orbit (distance from the Sun).

Galileo made the next great advancement over Kepler's vision, and this was again due to advancement in the means of astronomical observation. Indeed, telescopes in the year 1920, for example, were 20,000 times more revealing than those used by Copernicus. Galileo's telescope was at least 100 times better than Copernicus's device. In terms of the development of the theories of relativity, it was Galileo who first investigated the laws of falling bodies. He was the father of mechanics and formulated the basic laws of motion. He discovered that all bodies fall equally fast, and that every body that is not affected by external forces moves in a straight line at uniform velocity, indefinitely. Based on these facts, Isaac Newton would go on to construct his laws of the mechanics of movement of heavenly bodies.

Newton's three physical laws of motion are the basis of classical mechanics. They are:

1. A body at rest stays at rest, and a body in motion stays in motion, unless an external force acts upon it.
2. Force equals mass times acceleration, $F = ma$ (or, alternately, force equals the rate of change of momentum with time). Newton's equation, $F = ma$, was originally of the form $F \propto \Delta (mv)$, but as change in velocity is acceleration, it was the Swiss mathematician Leonhard Euler who generated the equation we know so well today.
3. To every action there is an equal and opposite reaction.

Newton, therefore, succeeded in combining the results of Copernicus, Brahe, Kepler, and Galileo into one complete system. He built on the laws of inertia established by Galileo, adding that there is a force responsible for every change of motion. Importantly, the presence of forces indicates that a body is not in uniform but in *accelerated* motion.

Newton discovered that the power of attraction between heavenly bodies diminishes with the distance between them. Thus, the Sun attracts the planets with a power decreasing in proportion to the square of the distance between them. Through measurement and theory, he was able to show that the attraction between the Earth and the Moon was responsible for the motion of the Moon around the Earth. Thus, the Copernican theory of the motion of the planets and Kepler's laws concerning their orbits, aligned with Galileo's laws of falling bodies in a gravitational field, were integrated into a universal explanation of planetary motion. Indeed, Newton showed that his laws of motion combined with his law of universal gravitation explained Kepler's laws of planetary motion.

Newton's law of universal gravitation, $F_g = Gm_1m_2/r_2$, stated that gravity exists in all bodies universally, and its strength between two bodies depends on their masses and inversely as the square of the distance between their centres. It was a chance meeting with astronomer Edmund Halley that set Newton to work on formulating the law. Halley had shown a keen interest in the motion of a comet (Halley's comet), which showed an elliptical path. Newton had predicted this from equations, yet it took some time to formulate them properly (as a law of universal gravitation) since they led to a larger body of work, the *Principia* (1687).

Robert Hooke, the curator at London's Royal Society and Newton's nemesis, had suggested to Newton that the attraction between bodies varies according to the inverse square law. For this, he later claimed rights to the laws of universal gravitation. True, Newton did apply Hooke's method of analysing curved motion (through seeing it as the combination of straight-line centripetal force and inertial motion), but it was Newton who realised the relation between all bodies of mass. He linked Kepler's laws to each other and to the fundamental concept that all bodies are attracted to all other bodies (not just those under consideration).

This view of the motion of planets held for over two hundred years, yet many questions lay unanswered. For example, what was the motion of the planets relative to? Was there a background, an invisible aether, against which movement was measured? It took the genius of Albert Einstein to construct a new worldview or paradigm of reality from all the data that had amassed in the years before him. His visionary construction of reality represented perhaps the greatest leap forward in understanding the nature of reality. How was Einstein able to this?

In the words of the philosopher Hans Reichenbach, "There seems to exist something like an instinct for the hidden intentions of nature; and whoever possesses this instinct, takes the spade to the right place where gold is hidden, and thus arrives at deep scientific insights. It must be said that Einstein possesses this instinct to the highest degree. His assumptions cannot be justified in a purely logical way; yet they introduce new ideas quite in the right place." Einstein was the quintessential genius.

Classical physics is somewhat Platonic in viewpoint — it deals with a world of absolutes. At the turn of the century, physicists were so sure of their ideas about the nature of matter and radiation that any idea that was in contradiction to this classical picture was disregarded. The mathematical formalism of Newton and the Scot James Clerk Maxwell (who unified electricity and magnetism into electromagnetism, the first step in unifying the forces of nature by describing the properties of light) was impeccable — predictions made from their theories were confirmed by experiments. Experimental verification was, and is, the scientific way of testing theory and generating physical truths since Galileo demonstrated that experiments could be devised to test the predictions of mathematical laws. It is the hallmark of good physics and science in general. So, we can say that classical physics is the physics of the late 19th century, rooted in the mechanics of Newton and the electromagnetism of Maxwell. During the 18th and 19th centuries, Newton's laws of motion were tested and confirmed by many kinds of reliable experimental and theoretical methods, but mainly experimental. His laws of gravitation predicted the measured movements of the planets with great accuracy.

Maxwell's prediction for the existence of invisible light waves in his *electromagnetic wave theory* was proven correct when electromagnetic waves were shown to reflect and refract like light. The mathematics of both Newton and Maxwell were correct, and measurements based on their theories corroborated their predictions, proving to them and those of their time that they were right. They had little reason to doubt themselves (it should be noted, to avoid confusion, that light waves and sound waves are fundamentally different sorts of phenomena. Sound waves are elastic vibrations in a medium (air) and do not propagate in a vacuum. They are not fields. Light is electromagnetic radiation and thus propagates in a vacuum, such as space). However, two things revolutionised this classical picture — relativity and quantum physics.

We will discuss the development of quantum physics, its mechanisms and applications (e.g., nuclear power), and how it contrasts with the classical deterministic worldview in Chapter 3. For the world it describes, it is as accurate as classical deterministic physics when comparing its predictions for subatomic and, potentially, larger-scale phenomena with the results of experiments that tested them.

Einstein's theory of relativity describes the same world that Newton's mechanics describes. However, it is far more accurate and is thought, by some, to be a true representation of the reality it describes. They think that the relativistic equations explain the fundamental universal framework (or are, at least, an incomplete version of the correct type). If this is true, we have revealed what was set at the moment of the Big Bang when the observable universe began (the observable universe is the spherical region of the Universe that comprises all matter that can be seen from Earth. It is deemed 'observable' because electromagnetic radiation from all objects within it has had sufficient time to reach Earth since the Big Bang).

For many phenomena, relativity theory produces similar results to those from Newton's laws, such as the motion of Jupiter around the Sun. However, where the two differ is when gravitational effects (explained by the general theory of relativity) or effects seen at velocities approaching that of light (explained by the theory of special relativity) are taken into consideration. Here, Newton's laws of universal motion fail as they become inaccurate, indicating an inadequacy or omission in their formulation. Einstein's theories, like Newton's (and unlike quantum theory), are still deterministic such that if the state of the system is known at any one time, it is completely fixed at a later (or earlier) time according to the equations of the theory. Neither relativity nor quantum theory alone can fully describe the behaviour of a system.

At present, without a unified theory, both are required. The problem with the acceptance of quantum theory is the fact that intrinsic to its nature is the lack of absolutes, which indicates limits to our ability to determine absolute truths.

ii) Relativity, Quantum Theory, and Reality

The theory of relativity was poorly received when it was first presented. New ideas usually are, and relativity *was* radical. The general and special theory presented a new vision of reality, but they were based on extensions and extrapolations of the laws that existed at the time. They are as applicable now as they were when formulated. When quantum theory appeared, opinion was that it could replace relativity and generate a singular set of laws of nature. However, no quantum theory of gravity has been developed that can replace general relativity despite a hundred years of knowledge of the quantum world. How gravity fits with the quantum world is needed to enable a deeper understanding of nature.

To understand the relationship between forces and matter as well as relativity and quantum physics, we need to know what happened in the first moments after the Big Bang (a term given by the cosmologist Fred Hoyle to explain a version of the Universe's origins that he did not like) when the observable Universe came into being. Scientific progress enables us to understand events ever closer to the Big Bang. We know that immediately after the Big Bang, all forces were combined, yet they separated at 10^{-43} s, 10^{-36} s, and 10^{-12} s after the Big Bang into the different discrete forces we understand today. A major challenge of physics, fundamental to the understanding of reality itself, is to generate a TOE that unifies these forces under a single paradigm.

Nearly 13.8 billion (+/− 21 million) years have elapsed since the Big Bang. One might, therefore, assume that the radius of the observable universe is at least 13.8×10^9 light years, equivalent to the most distant and earliest light that we can see reaching us. However, this does not take into account the very earliest moments of the Universe when the laws of physics were different. Expansion violated special relativistic rules. Indeed, those stars that emitted the earliest and most distant light we can detect are now, in fact, roughly three times further away than might be expected by physical law, at about 46.5 billion light years according to the latest estimates, therefore putting the diameter of the observable Universe at 93 billion light years.

The American astronomer Edwin Hubble (1889–1953) is popularly credited with discovering that the Universe is expanding. The mutual recession of celestial objects from one another as a result of the cosmological expansion of the Universe is called the *Hubble flow*. In fact, it was the Belgian astronomer (and priest) Georges Lemaître (1894–1966) who proposed the Universe expansion theory before Hubble did, and he was the first to derive what came to be known as Hubble's law and the Hubble constant (the rate of expansion of the Universe). Lemaître's analysis of Einstein's general theory of relativity convinced him of a Universe with a beginning consistent with the idea of a Big Bang (which he called the 'cosmic egg'), rather than the static Universe favoured by Einstein at the time.

The rate of expansion is dependent on time, which is relative, but it is possible to define the rate, which is the same throughout the Universe, by expressing it in terms of *'comoving time'*. If we consider comoving observers to move with the Hubble flow, then they are the only ones who can perceive the Universe as *isotropic* (i.e., same throughout). Isotropy defines a special local frame of reference called the *comoving frame*. The comoving time coordinate is the elapsed time since the Big Bang according to the clock of a comoving observer and is a measure of cosmological time. The Universe is 13.7 billion years old as measured in cosmological time. The special theory of relativity enables us to define time in a universal context, beyond the constraints of human existence. It has practical applications (e.g., satellites and particle accelerators) and, together with the general theory which incorporates gravitational effects to describe how large-scale matter behaves, provides deep insights into the nature of reality.

Relativity explains why *black holes* exist. These are the ultra-dense singularities found in the centre of galaxies and other regions of space, which may possess the mass of billions of our suns (note — if the Earth were 1 cm wide, on this scale our Sun would have an impressive 109 cm diameter. However, the largest star, VY Canis Majoris, would dwarf them both with a staggering 2.3 km diameter. This supergiant star contains the volume of over 10^{19} (10,000,000,000,000,000,000) Earths). Black holes occur when a large sun completes its fusion processes (see later) and shrinks into a dense *neutron star* consisting of compressed nuclear material. If large enough, and having attracted matter through gravitational attraction, it may collapse under its own gravitation to form a black hole. This term, coined by Wheeler, implies that it does not even let light escape. However, it does emit *Hawking radiation* (named after the English physicist Stephen Hawking who theorised it).

Gravitons are the theoretical particles that support the gravitational field. These have not been detected yet, but the prediction is that they will be in time to come. Einstein believed that gravitational waves exist, despite a brief relapse in 1937 as to this certainty. Russell Hulse and Joseph Taylor received the 1995 Nobel Prize in Physics for indirect evidence that gravitational waves do exist. In February 2016, gravitational waves were detected for the first time. They were emitted from the inward spiralling and merger of two black holes into a single black hole. The 2017 Nobel Prize in Physics was awarded for the successful development of the Laser

Interferometer Gravitational-wave Observatory (LIGO). Half of the prize was awarded jointly to Caltech's Barry Barish and Kip Thorne, and the other half was awarded to Rainer Weiss.

A unified field theory that accounts for electricity, magnetism, the nuclear weak and strong forces would define a Grand Unified Theory (GUT) of nature. Incorporating gravitation into this GUT would result in a TOE and represent the unification of classical and quantum physics. A number of quantum models look promising, but incorporating gravity into the same theory to produce a TOE is proving difficult. The reward from such a theory, however, would be the ability to account for the interaction between all matter and forces under a single paradigm. From a reductionist viewpoint, all phenomena will be derivable from a TOE.

In practice, not *all* interactions can be explained or predicted due to reality's intrinsically indeterminate and chaotic nature. Indeed, understanding the complex nature of physical reality does not follow from identification of the fundamental laws of physical reality. The necessity for high computing power would also limit its scope, and much of biological function would be beyond its remit. Quantum computing is an area that is proposed to simulate things that classical computing cannot. It is in its infancy in terms of the practical application of theoretical possibilities. When considering whether we can control the huge number of continuously variable parameters defining the quantum state of a useful computer, physicist Mikhail Dyakonov's answer was "no, never".

However, a TOE would be humankind's greatest achievement because it relates to the innate nature of reality, extending all the way back to the Big Bang. The matter that constitutes the complexity of all structures in the Universe, including life forms, was once compressed in an infinitely small volume of infinite density. Thus, we must understand what happened in the very first moments after the Big Bang in order to understand how and why the Universe is as it is as well as what is knowable — and perhaps know the ultimate fate of the Universe.

The quest by physicists for beautiful equations and a TOE that can account for all physical phenomena is the result of the belief that nature can be explained from fundamental laws. This search is motivated by the idea that since all that exists in the Universe resulted from the Big Bang, then the rules that defined this point in spacetime modelled the evolution of all complexity that extends in space and time. The belief is that since all that *is* should be explainable from this point in time which was infinitely small and dense, then a fundamental theory should define what it produces. This, according to a reductionist's logic, is the TOE. Quantum theory is indeterminate in nature, however, and it is possible that indeterminism is fundamental to the framework of the Universe — indeterminacy determined within the first 10^{-6} seconds following the Big Bang.

Until a TOE surfaces, it is clear that we need all the classical and quantum components that underlie it, both for their practical application and for explaining our current understanding of the Universe at every level. If a TOE remains elusive, the great J. B. S. Haldane (1892–1964) may have been prophetic when he stated that the Universe is not only stranger than we suppose, but probably stranger than we *can* suppose.

The use of quantum physics enables us to calculate subatomic reactions with high accuracy and can even be extrapolated to explain simple molecules. However, chemistry is the science we use for determining molecular interaction and while it is not as accurate as the potential of quantum theory, its application not only suffices but excels for its uses. For molecular interactions, chemistry is quicker, more accurate, easier to apply, more predictable, and more cost effective. Chemistry can be practically applied to explain *all* molecular, atomic, and ionic (charged particle) reactions, which is clearly beyond the scope of quantum theory for reasons of cost, time, and computing power. The mere fact that the quantum formulae work is proof of their validity, if not universal applicability.

Quantum theory is a successful albeit possibly flawed theory. Its formalism may not represent subatomic 'reality' but rather an accurate 'representation' of it, in a similar way that relativity may represent large-scale reality. If so, it is interesting then that both theories developed from the same physical and mathematical knowledge that was present at the end of the 19th century — both are extremely accurate, yet are incompatible in terms of unification under a single paradigm.

Both quantum theory and relativity are difficult subjects to comprehend because the 'worlds' they describe are inherently different from everyday experience. To *experience* the results of special relativistic effects requires velocities that we are unlikely to encounter (in our lifetime at least). Quantum theory is even more difficult as it describes an innately unknowable world.

The Danish physicist Niels Bohr (one of the founders of quantum physics) once said, "Anyone who isn't shocked by quantum physics hasn't understood it." To emphasise its bizarre nature, Physics Nobel Laureate Richard Feynman similarly said, "If you think you understand quantum mechanics, you don't understand quantum mechanics." That these deterministic and indeterministic theories describing different aspects of reality are so different in formalism yet each so accurate implies that either one or both is wrong, or that a single TOE is impossible.

The reality I speak of is the Universe we occupy. There are a number of theories proposing that this is one of billions of possible (or actual) universes. Scientists such as Neil Turok, Burt Ovrut, and Paul Steinhardt have 'concluded' that the observable Universe is one of an infinite number of bubbles in hyperspace, created by the collision of parallel universes. If so, one wonders whether each has its own laws of physics.

Reality constitutes matter embedded in nothingness. The concept of 'nothingness' is difficult for humans to contemplate because it plays no part in our lives on Earth. We think of the invisible air around us as nothing, when in fact it is a dense collection of different gases. Within the Earth's atmosphere, we are protected from the cold vacuum of space in a shroud of warm, life-giving gases. This is in an incredibly small region of absolute space, compared to all space. The precious region of life we call Earth is tiny in the context of space. It is special, rare, and unlikely; yet everything that exists on it is deemed less wondrous than it really is because we are complacent.

How unlikely *is* life? We will discuss this later as well as in Chapter 5 which deals with evolution and the nature of the biological world. The retired British cosmologist and astrophysicist Martin Rees stresses that life on Earth is the result of an extraordinary chain of events. Ten million, billion, billion stars are within range of our telescopes. One wonders whether conditions that allow intelligent life to develop exists on any planet orbiting one of these.

Questioning the Universe

In the 1800s, Willhelm Olbers demonstrated an example of our historical interest in how the Universe can be interpreted. His simple but brilliant experiment proving that the Universe is not infinite became known as *Olbers's paradox*. It goes like this:

> If you drew spheres around the Earth at ever increasing distances, but with the same factorial increase in radius from Earth, say, one light year followed by two light years and so on (one light year is the distance travelled by light at a constant velocity of 186,000 miles per second in a year — thus, one light year equates to light travelling a distance of 5,900,000,000,000 miles), then the volume of space encapsulated by the spheres increases as we move away from the Earth. With spheres spaced at defined distances as we move out, the number of stars in each sphere increases. At these distances, they increase by a factor of four in successive spheres, but the luminosity of these stars were observed as having an intensity of only one quarter to that of the next inner sphere. Thus, as we move away from Earth through each successive sphere, theoretically, out to sphere infinity, each sphere presents the same relative luminosity as viewed from Earth.

Thus, if we compare sphere number three to sphere two, sphere three has four times as many stars as sphere two, but they are farther away and so they appear a quarter as bright as the stars of sphere two. As $4 \times 1/4 = 1$, the luminosity of the stars is the same from both spheres from Earth's viewpoint, and this ratio is the same for comparing all spheres. Each sphere of stars gives the same relative luminosity as each other, from sphere number one to sphere infinity, when seen from Earth. So, where is the paradox? Well, if the Universe is infinite, then there can be infinite spheres, and as each sphere gives the same luminosity of light from its stars, and stars are randomly dispersed throughout space, then the sky should be completely lit up with starlight, with no dark areas. There would be no room in the visual field for darkness because an infinite distance has infinite stars and, thus, infinite starlight.

The theory is correct — stars give off light (as radiation) and the star luminosity calculations were correct, therefore the conclusion was that the Universe is not infinite but finite. It informs us not only about the size of the observable Universe but also whether it is contracting or expanding. If the Universe is contracting, then night should be brighter than day since more energy would be received from the background than from the Sun's emission. If the Universe were stationary, then night and day would be equivalent in light intensity. If, as it is, the Universe is expanding, night is darker than day. Thus, from Olbers's Paradox alone, we can conclude that the Universe is expanding and it is of finite size. In 1909, Jacques Fournier used the science of fractals to resolve this issue. Millions of dollars have also been spent to confirm this using *redshift* analyses (described below).

In the beginning of the observable Universe, all matter was compressed into an infinitely small point in space, but it was of a different form from that which we observe in its current state. The Big Bang 'exploded' into potential space, spreading out into and creating the observable Universe. As the expansion continued and the temperature and pressures lowered, the atomic matter we see today (protons, neutrons, electrons, etc.) formed from *exotic* particles that existed only in the extremes of temperature and pressure close to the Big Bang event.

Physics has progressed so far that it is now known what processes occurred from just a fraction of a second after the Big Bang. However, although we know most of the processes of the expansion, the events of that first fraction of a second — which remains hidden from us — may hold the key to the observable Universe's outcome. Will it collapse, expand, or reach a point where it is at a steady state? Here, the force of the Big Bang is balanced against the gravitational attraction that exists between all matter.

Particle accelerators are used to attempt to produce exotic particles that mimic those of the initial universal conditions in the hope that we might understand the Universe's beginnings. Why are initial conditions so difficult to analyse? After the Big Bang event, space was expanding at (at least) the velocity of light, unconstrained by special relativity. During these very early times, matter was of a form consistent with such extremes and comprising particles not present in an expanded and cooled Universe. Later, as the Universe expanded from this infinitely small volume of infinite density, particles evolved into forms that we understand as atoms in a fraction of a second.

Understanding the complex initial conditions and components and interpreting them in terms of a model that encompasses both what existed after the Big Bang and today presents the greatest challenge to physicists. Although we do not know its fate, we know that the Universe will be here for at least several billion years. As matter expanded in all directions after the Big Bang, the temperature and pressure of the Universe decreased. As it expanded, the Universe created spacetime from nothingness. The *observable* Universe has been expanding for some 13.7 billion years in a manner defined by the initial conditions. That which happens in the Universe is controlled by gravitation on the large scale and other forces on the subatomic scale.

Gravity makes the observable Universe less uniform as time advances from the Big Bang event because of the contrast it generates in temperature and density. The force of gravitational attraction is weak, but unlike the other forces, it acts over large distances. This ultimately brings the dispersed matter of the early Universe together into clumps to form moons, planets, asteroids, stars, galaxies, black holes, and other objects. From the Big Bang, all objects are moving outward and away from each other, but that is not strictly correct. Gravitation causes pockets of attraction and association within an overall expansion. Our solar system is part of a huge galaxy called the Milky Way which comprises billions of solar systems, each of which orbits around a central core. The core almost certainly consists of a huge black hole that acts as a gravitational attractant and, hence, an axis of rotation for the entire galaxy.

The Earth spins on its own axis as it orbits the Sun, and the solar system itself rotates as it moves with the swirl of other systems within the galaxy's rotation. The Milky Way is about 100,000 light years across, containing over 100 billion stars. This galaxy is part of the local group of 54 galaxies, some 10 million light years across. This group of galaxies is part of the Virgo Supercluster of galaxies, containing over 100 similar clusters. The Virgo Supercluster is 110 million light years across. However, it only forms a small lobe of the Laniakea Supercluster, containing 100,000 galaxies and 520 million light years across. Zooming out further, even this structure is just one of millions more that are present in the observable Universe.

So, we see that galaxies clump to form clusters of galaxies which, in turn, clump to form superclusters consisting of millions, if not billions, of galaxies. Thus, the geometry of the Universe can be likened to foam. There are expanses of vacuum (space) and the gravitationally clumped matter that constitutes the stars exists on the bubbles of the foam. Hence, the Universe appears fractal in nature.

For our particular solar system, the Sun is approximately 93 million miles from Earth. We orbit the Sun every 365.25 days. The Moon and Earth orbit a shared gravitational centre every 28 days approximately. Other planets (Mercury, Venus, Mars, Jupiter, Saturn, Uranus, and Neptune) also orbit the Sun, and their motions too are controlled by gravity. The Earth remains approximately the same distance from the Sun during its orbit, which is not as elliptical as those of some of the other planets (especially Mercury).

Pluto was demoted from planetary status in 2006 because other objects of similar mass have been identified recently that orbit the Sun, and which also could be regarded as planets if we consider Pluto as one. They are Eris, also known as 2003 UB_{313} (discovered by, among others, David Rabinowitz of Yale University in 2003), Quaoar (found in 2002), and Sedna (detected in 2004).

By 2012, Pluto, Ceres (which lies between Mars and Jupiter), and the trans-Neptunian objects Haumea, Eris and Makemake, are considered dwarf planets. Advances in detection mean that nearly 600,000 new asteroids have been detected in the solar system since 1980, although the total mass of orbiting objects makes up only 0.14% of the solar system's mass.

Parsec

To measure distances on Earth, we use units such as centimetre (cm) and kilometre (km). In space, distances are so great that other units need to be used. Even our closest star other than the Sun, Proxima Centauri, when measured in km, produces enormous numbers when measured in these units. It is 39,700,000,000,000 km away (to put this in perspective, it would take a space shuttle at reentry speed 160,000 years to reach it).

Proxima Centauri is 4.2 light years away (the distance that light travels at 300,000 km/sec in 4.2 years). Astronomical units (AU) are used to define such distances, and 1 AU is approximately the distance of the elliptical orbit of the Earth around the Sun. However, even this is inadequate. Another way of defining its distance is in *parsecs*. Parsec is an abbreviation of 'a distance corresponding to a *parallax* of one *second*' (parallax is the apparent shift in an object's position when viewed from one point then another). Thus, a parsec is the distance from the Sun to an astronomical object that has a parallax angle of 1 arcsecond (Figure 2).

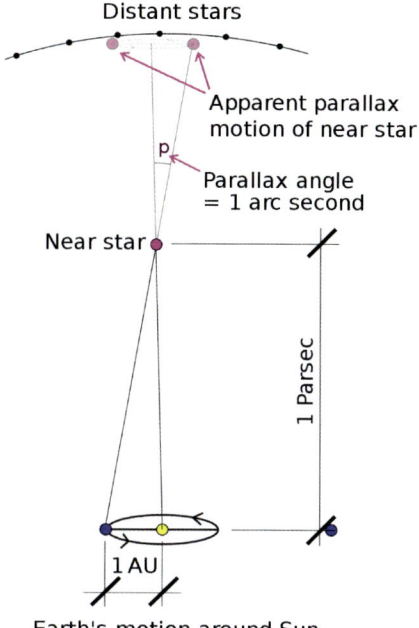

Figure 2. Definition of a Parsec. A parsec is a unit of length that is used in astronomy. It is 3.26 light-years or 19 trillion miles. 1 degree = 1/360 of a circle. 1 arcminute = 1/60 of a degree. 1 arcsecond = 1/60 of an arcminute (1/296000 of a circle). In this visual illustration of a parsec, Earth is shown, not to scale, as a blue sphere orbiting our Sun (yellow).

Of course, kilo-, mega-, and gigaparsecs are also used to describe very large distances between objects in space (the Milky Way is about 30 kiloparsecs in diameter). Proxima Centauri is 1.29 parsecs away.

Redshift and size

Redshift is a term used often in quantum theory and relativity. If one looks at the Sun, the light emitted from it can be split into its constituent wavelengths using a prism. If we look through a telescope at a star from a distant galaxy and split its spectrum, we will see a broader red light line than that achieved from looking at our own Sun. Its spectrum of light is shifted to the red end, hence the term 'redshift' — the amount the wavelengths are stretched.

All galaxies (apart from most in the same cluster as us) are moving away from us and from each other. The more distant the object, the faster it is receding from us. The redshift is the measure of this recession velocity and it is larger for more distant objects. So, the greater the redshift, the further the star is from us and the greater the distance it has separated from us since the Big Bang.

At distances greater than a billion light years, another recently discovered force called *cosmic antigravity* causes objects to move apart faster than theoretically predicted. As a star recedes at a fraction of the velocity of light, the light from it returns at the velocity of light. Therefore, we can calculate from the degree of redshift how fast it is travelling away from us, the distance it is from us, and the distance in time from whence the light was emitted.

If a red-shifted spectrum predicts that an object is ten billion light years away, then the light has taken ten billion years to reach us. What we see is ten billion year-old light and, hence, how the object *appeared* ten billion years ago. The light we see from the most red-shifted objects in the Universe emanates from the most distant objects. This light is from a point in time relatively close to the Big Bang. A highly red-shifted spectrum might indicate a star travelling away from us at 99% of the velocity of light, for example. The star is receding at close to the velocity of light, but as light is emitted from the star at the velocity of light, the spectrum is pushed further away from the spectrum than we would achieve when we observe our Sun. Conversely, if it was travelling *toward* us at huge velocities, we would observe a blue-shifted spectrum. Thus, when we observe stars in the night sky, the light we see could have been emitted billions of years ago.

What we observe is where the source of light was when the light was emitted, ignoring gravitational effects on light. However, this source has already moved to a new position following universal expansion and the intervening time during the light's journey to us. Such is the size of space and the huge difference in distances of each source from us that the pattern of the night sky bears no resemblance to where the object is *now* (if 'now' has any meaning).

The special theory of relativity limits the speed for any form of communication or causal process to the velocity of light. Thus, within *that* paradigm of causal links, where we see a star 'now' is where it *is* (relative to us) because we cannot see it at any earlier time. But what does that mean? It means that that is how the laws of physics apply when we try to perceive or *know* about reality. The reality of the situation is that when we see light from a star, its position reflects where the star was when it emitted the light, and it has actually changed position to one determined by the amount of relative motion between it and us during the time of transit of the light we see. Thus, more distant objects are actually further removed from where they appear to be than are closer ones. Indeed, the greater the distance from us, the less accurate the light position is as a description of where it is now (relative to us).

But there is another sense of understanding 'now'. When light travels to us from a star, it takes a certain amount of time to reach us according to the distance travelled. When looking at this star, if we were to suspend reality and subtract from our perception the time taken by the light for the journey, then the emission of light from the star and our seeing that light are *simultaneous events*. If reality is like this, then where the emission source is 'now' is exactly where we see it to be 'now'. Of course, this is physically impossible because reality *is not* like that since we know that light travels at 186,000 miles per second (in a vacuum — it is slower elsewhere). But if we were to remove the constraints according to special relativity, then we can imagine the version of reality that we intuitively *feel* exists, even though we know through physics that this is not how reality really works.

The physics of reality, as well as human communication and *knowledge* of an event, conform to special relativity. Perception and sensation only provide a sense or experience of the immediate. Human intelligence, applied through science, has clarified that the sensation of 'now' is but an illusion. We are tied to the laws of physics of the reality in which we are embedded. Perceptions of reality are experienced as occurring 'now' in a way that violates special relativity, yet they are also reasoned as conforming to the laws of physics. To complicate matters, quantum physics tells us that, innate to reality, there *are* some special cases where events can occur together in time in this way and in violation of the rules imposed by the special theory of relativity. Such 'entangled' events for special particles imply a deep connection of the Universe that we do not really understand. These points will become increasingly clear as we go on.

When we speak of the Universe, we mean the observable Universe, which comprises all that constitutes the physically existent Universe that has been expanding since the Big Bang. Possible previous universes that might have existed prior to the Big Bang, due to the very nature of the Big Bang/'Big Crunch' theories, are unknowable. Any matter existing prior to or after the Universe we inhabit would not be constructed from the same matter as it is now. It would be annihilated at the Big Crunch, which is when the Universe collapses back in on itself.

One view is that the Universe was not a singularity at the moment of the Big Bang, whereas the observable Universe was. This distinction between the 'whole' Universe and the 'observable' part of it that we see and exist in is important as it leads us to ask, "What is the observable Universe expanding into?" Putting *multiverses* (i.e., more than one Universe) aside until later, it is a misconception to consider the observable Universe as a sphere embedded within higher dimensional space and that the observable Universe is expanding into this space. We have no access to that which does or might exist in this space outside the observable Universe. All measurements apply to the boundaryless observable Universe. Indeed, as we have no way of defining or knowing if the observable Universe is expanding into *anything* (since we cannot see it), we cannot think about what the observable Universe is expanding into in a meaningful way.

Everything that we can measure is within the Universe and says nothing about a hypothetical higher-dimensional space. There is neither boundary nor centre of expansion of the Universe. The Universe is not expanding into anything we can access, so the Universe is all there is. Perhaps, after the Big Crunch, if a new Universe evolves, it will have different laws of physics. Each Universe presents the possibility for different laws of nature. In this respect, we do not know if the observable Universe possesses *its* laws for 'this' Universe, or *the* laws for 'any' Universe.

Different theories have been put forward that suggest a multiverse concept or an endlessly cycling Universe theory. The British physicist and philosopher Roger Penrose recently proposed a Universe that expands indefinitely until all matter decays, so space and time have no meaning. It differs from the traditional cycling model in that there is no Big Crunch, but the process of expansion evolves into the next Big Bang *ad infinitum*. For both the multiple parallel multiverse model and the endlessly cycling model of one Universe leading to another, the possibility of the existence of at least one Universe evolving that can support life as we know it presents itself as not particularly unlikely — in an infinitude of time, anything is possible.

Fate of the Universe

Under the influence of gravity, will all the matter finally compress into an infinitely small space (the Big Crunch)? An infinite Universe cannot be comprehended. However, a finite Universe presents the possibility for comprehension, albeit also for many different forms. Is it contracting, expanding, or static, and what lies beyond its boundaries?

As mentioned previously, Edwin Hubble (in whose honour the Hubble Space Telescope was named) showed that all galaxies are moving away from one another, proving — for now at least — that the Universe is expanding. In 1929, he showed that nebulae are receding with a velocity proportional to their distance. More specifically, he demonstrated an approximate linear relationship between their velocity and their distance. Hubble's law relates redshift to distance and tells us how much the Universe has expanded while the light is travelling towards us.

The observable Universe is huge. We are aware of the properties of the smallest objects (approximately 10^{-15} metres wide) that constitute all else that exists within the observable Universe (10^{27} metres wide). We are also aware of the lifetime of the shortest-lived particles (10^{-23} seconds) to the age of the Universe (about 10^{17} seconds).

If we compared both our size and lifespan to the size and age of the observable Universe (the largest and oldest thing), as well as to some subatomic particles (the smallest and shortest-lived things), we would find that we live long but that our size is not so great. Compared to the age and size of both the Universe and some subatomic particles, we can say that we are small but stable — we live much longer than would be predicted by our small size.

It is intriguing that we are exactly of the size that does not directly feel the effects of quantum and large-scale relativistic processes. That is, we are too large for quantum effects and too small for large-scale relativistic effects. This is viewed in the light that we are a reasoning species evolved from inanimate matter attempting to uncover the truth of the universal forces and about existence. We attempt to understand our fate and that of the observable Universe through the application of physics. Yet due to our physical makeup, we also live our lives too slowly to feel the influence of special relativity's extension of Newtonian mechanics — that is, the effect of velocity on time dilation. There is a degree of irony in the fact that the nature of reality is being revealed by an organism whose physiology is the least well equipped to experience its subtleties!

Questioning the fate of the Universe taps on our desire to understand our place in it, our purpose, and meaning. To know the answer requires understanding reality further, and from our attempt to do so extend solutions that will improve the quality of life. That reward is the purest of reasons to financially support research into the framework of reality. Psychological effects from knowing the answer are merely a bonus (despite being the career motivation for most of those who achieve the answers). Humankind would not have advanced without the inquisitive, deep thinker (e.g., Einstein). When applied in an integrated, technologically advanced collective setting, the advantages are obvious. Science feeds off and adds to itself, producing the capacity for future ethical, scientific, and economic decisions to be based more on fact and knowledge than unknowns (and humans fear the unknown).

iii) Special Relativity

To think that Einstein's major contributions to science were his theories of relativity — special *and* general — would be correct. However, even without these, he would have been a scientist of international fame. Without detailing all his contributions to science (see *Subtle is the Lord* by Abraham Pais), such was his genius that he could possibly have received the Nobel Prize for four different areas of theoretical research — the *photoelectric effect* (for which he *did* receive the Nobel Prize), Brownian motion of molecules and atoms, special relativity, and general relativity (which, surprisingly, were not rewarded by the prize).

His most famous equation, $E = mc^2$ (or $E = \sqrt{m_0^2 c^4 + p^2 c^2}$), resulted from his general theory of relativity. It is often publicly misconstrued that this equation led to the atom bomb (Einstein was a pacifist and, like Bertrand Russell, a champion of nuclear disarmament). By stating the equivalence of mass and energy, this equation explains the enormous energy locked inside the rest mass of matter (hence the link to nuclear weapons). Just one kilogramme of matter can potentially release the same energy as that obtained from burning a million tons of coal.

Another consequence of this formula is that when matter, such as that which comprises a future space rocket, is pushed close to the velocity of light, the energy required to achieve this velocity increases greatly. We know that the velocity of light is the ultimate speed limit in the Universe (300,000 km/s), but for example, 220,000 electron volts (eV) would be required to accelerate an electron to 90% of this speed, and over 4 billion eV to 99.999999%.

As the rocket's velocity increases, so does its mass. However, mass here is not defined as 'amount of matter' because the same amount of matter has a different mass at different velocities (although mass *is* amount of matter, such that the mass of a human is the same on Earth as on the moon, weight is relative to gravitational fields. Hence, a man on the moon weighs less than on Earth). The relativistic mass of a faster moving object is greater than that of a slower one due to the extra kinetic energy, even though the same matter has the same mass relative to its own frame of reference. All changes in energy involve a mass change (in chemical processes this is very small). The large energy released in a nuclear reaction is due to the huge energy stored in the strong interactions, and the measurable mass change is a consequence of this, not a cause.

To reach the velocity of light would require infinite energy and cause the matter to have infinite mass, so the velocity of light, c, is the maximum velocity attainable in the Universe. If it were not, according to Einstein's theories, a number of bizarre phenomena would occur, such as travelling back in time. Hence, an accident could be undone — something that is clearly impossible.

The structure of the Universe is such that the velocity of light is the maximum limit defined by the Universe. More than this, the velocity of light is only finite from the perspective of the observer from a different frame of reference. From the perspective of a photon, though it is travelling at the speed defined by the Universe, it is as if time has frozen and everything outside this frame is ageing very quickly. The photon 'experiences' ageing as it would if it were (theoretically) ageless, but this ageing is dilated relative to an external frame, to be observed as if halted.

At velocities between stationary and that of light, the degree of relative dilation effects increases. We will go on to see why this is so. It is said that Einstein became interested in the physics that led to his theories of relativity after he wondered what would happen to light if he were moving alongside it at the velocity of light. It was thought prior to Einstein's theories that light was 'fast' but not of a constant velocity that was independent of the velocity or location (i.e., frame of reference) of the observer.

The velocity of electromagnetic waves in a vacuum is the velocity of light, and this was calculated using Maxwell's equations (it was the British scientist Oliver Heaviside who rearranged Maxwell's equations into the form known now as 'Maxwell's equations'). Through the work of Maxwell and Hermann von Helmholtz, it was thought that electric and magnetic fields were transmitted through a medium that supported the (electromagnetic) field. This medium was termed the *luminiferous aether* (or *ether*). The idea of the luminiferous aether was accepted for about forty years, where it was considered to fill space and permeate bodies. The idea of the aether was somewhat contradictory in that it was supposed to be completely permeable to all material bodies and yet infinitely rigid in order to support light.

In 1887, the American Physicists Albert Michelson and Edward Morley tried to detect the presence of the aether (the famous 'Michelson-Morley' experiment resulted in the 1907 Physics Nobel Prize for Michelson) using a huge stone block immersed in mercury and connected to a measuring instrument called an interferometer which was placed on the block. Without going into the specifics of the experimental design, they compared the amount of time taken for light to travel the same distance on perpendicular paths and return to the same position. One path was perpendicular to the direction of motion of the proposed aether (but this is true only at particular times during the year when the earth's orbit is parallel or perpendicular to the direction of motion of the aether); the other path was with it. If light had constant velocity relative to the aether, it should take less time to travel a set distance across it than to travel the same distance against and then with it. The consensus of opinion was that they detected no motion of the Earth through the aether.

So, Einstein had to deal with the idea that the aether existed but could not be detected. The principal argument that led Einstein to the theory of special relativity was not the need to resolve the conflict between the Michelson-Morley experiment and the aether theory but rather, independent of this, it was the need for truth as a result of his rejection of 19th century views on classical physics as being both artificial and unconvincing.

To introduce special relativity and its central concern, let us take the example where Einstein wondered that if he were travelling with a wave or beam of light and held a mirror in front of him, what would he see? The dilemma is that if he were travelling at the velocity of light, the light could not catch up to the mirror in front of him and so his image would disappear. This is the scenario if the aether is accepted as existent and correct and that light travels relative to the aether (as does Einstein on his hypothetical wave). With such a view, the light is not moving relative to the observer. Einstein rejected this view of absolute space and motion and became interested in the work of Ernst Mach.

Ernst Mach

Ernst Mach (1838–1916) was an Austrian physicist and philosopher whose influence was wide ranging, both in the philosophy of logical positivism and in physics with his criticism of Newton. His philosophy affected his views on physics and vice versa. By recognising only sensations as real, the new physics at the beginning of the 20th century that defined atoms as discrete entities was, to Mach, wrong. Indeed, Mach seemed to reject the physical theories of a scientist based on his opinion of their philosophical outlook. Einstein realised this about Mach's objection to some of Newton's theories on space and time. But leaving it at that would do a disservice to his influence on the way many great minds viewed science at a time of major transition, specifically the introduction of quantum theory.

Mach believed that any physical theory should be free of metaphysical constructions. Mach was an ultra-positivist and anti-metaphysicist and disregarded all that was not attainable by the full senses. He challenged the accepted ideas on mechanics by believing that physical theory should be based on primary sense perceptions. Thus, he never accepted atoms as real since they lay beyond direct sensory perception (he was never supportive of the great German physicist and father of statistical mechanics, Ludwig Boltzmann).

Mach's work was instrumental to Einstein's development of special relativity in the context of frames of reference. However, rather than pointing to what was right, in some ways Mach's work helped Einstein by allowing him to ignore what was wrong. With this as well as the fact that no one could detect the aether, Einstein rejected the idea of the aether altogether. He believed that whatever the method light used to travel from place to place, his image in the mirror should not disappear. But common sense then suggests that to a stationary observer on the ground watching Einstein travelling on the light wave, the light between him and the mirror would be travelling at twice the velocity of light.

Despite not knowing about light having a defined velocity or the actual velocity of light, it was not acceptable to Einstein and others that the same light would have different velocities for different observers. These thought experiments, or *gedanken* experiments as they are traditionally named, enable physical impossibilities to be theorised without experiment.

Details and effects of special relativity

According to wave theory, sound (as sound waves) travelling from an approaching train toward a stationary or moving observer moves at the same velocity irrespective of the velocity of the train. If the train was moving at a velocity greater than that of sound, we would see it pass us before we hear it (as seen when the Thrust SSC car broke the sound barrier in 1997).

Maxwell's equations on electromagnetism predicted the same for light. Thus, the light leaving Einstein's face to the mirror would, to the ground observer, leave at the same velocity irrespective of his velocity. If Einstein was moving at the velocity of light, he would be moving at the same velocity as that of the light leaving his face. Thus, he would not see his face in the mirror as the light would, according to the theory, never reach the mirror. But if he does see his face, then light reaches the mirror in the same way as when we look at our face in the bathroom mirror (there is no gradation for light, unlike the train), so the observer on the ground would see the light moving at twice its velocity. Whichever way you look at it, it is inconsistent. Einstein was determined to see if there was a way for the velocity of light to be the same for both him and the ground observer, and this specific problem was key to enabling him to develop his theory of special relativity.

Galileo had been one of the first scientists to take an interest in motion and apply scientific principles to try and understand it. Of relevance to

Einstein's ideas, he stated that all steady motion is relative and cannot be detected without reference to an outside point. However, Galileo's motivation for understanding these phenomena was different from Einstein's. Under political pressure, he was interested in its application for war, particularly in calculating cannonball trajectories (or rather he had been told to!). He realised that the motion of objects such as cannonballs could be analysed by treating their horizontal and vertical motions separately. By combining these motions, he found that an object will fall to the Earth's surface at the same rate as an object fired horizontally at high velocity. An interesting ramification of this idea is that if an object is fired horizontally at a velocity of five miles per second, then it will continue to circle the Earth. Satellites do this. The rate of fall is exactly compensated for by the curvature of the Earth, so the object remains the same distance vertically from the Earth's surface as it progresses in a horizontal direction.

The Earth's surface is a frame of reference, as could be any vehicle in which we are travelling and attempting to calculate relativistic effects. The Earth's surface is considered to be an *inertial* frame of reference since Newton's first law of inertia holds in this frame. This law states that objects at rest stay at rest and objects in motion stay in motion (with the same velocity and vector) unless acted on by another force. In fact, due to the Earth's rotation, it is actually an accelerated (noninertial) frame of reference, but due to the slow rotation, it is, in effect, inertial.

Galileo's principle of relativity stated that it is not possible, when moving within an enclosed vessel, to know whether you are moving smoothly or standing still unless you look to an external frame of reference. This principle relates to the equivalence of inertial frames of reference for the laws of mechanics. Galilean transformations allow us to calculate the position of an object in one frame if we know its position in another frame, the time, and the relative velocity of the two frames in question. Einstein used this argument for the aforementioned mirror problem. He believed that he should still be able to see his image normally even if moving at the velocity of light, because if the image was not there in the mirror, he would know that he was travelling at the velocity of light purely by its absence and without having to look at an external frame of reference. This violates the Galilean principle of relativity, which states that the laws of mechanics are the same for all inertial frames of reference (we will see later that the time interval between events in different frames is not the same in Einstein's relativity whereas it is in that of Galileo).

Using the principle of relativity as a reference point, Einstein wanted to show how the light leaving his eyes towards the mirror could be the same beam and velocity for him travelling on the beam of light as for the ground observer. To do this, he needed to re-evaluate the concepts of space and time. In 1905, in the physics journal *Annalen der Physik*, Einstein presented two key papers.

One paper was on Brownian motion which used the new theory of atoms to describe macroscopic behaviour. This treatment of atoms as 'real' objects would have showed Boltzmann that he was right about them and that his nemesis Ernst Mach was wrong. Boltzmann had been driven to suicide before this partly, it is thought, because of the scientific community's rejection and at times ridicule of his ideas about atoms as real things, rather than as conceptual tools to help describe behaviour. Einstein used Boltzmann's mathematical realism to good effect in his description of macroscopic behaviour.

Einstein also presented his ideas 'on the electrodynamics of moving bodies' in the same journal edition. Here, he suggested that the principle of relativity should work for light as well as for ordinary motion. As such, everyone should observe the same velocity of light irrespective of their frame of reference. This proposition meant that the luminiferous aether was to be rejected and that conventional ideas on time, length, mass, and velocity needed to be drastically reappraised. Einstein made two postulates on this:

1. Irrespective of how light propagates when you are standing still, it propagates the same way when you are moving, *or* the laws of physics take the same form for all inertial frames.
2. Light is propagated in empty space with a definite velocity (denoted 'c') that is independent of the state of the emitting or receiving body. An observer on the ground sees light moving at the same velocity as does the moving observer, *or* in any given inertial frame, the velocity of light is the same whether light is emitted by a body at rest or by a body in uniform motion.

The physicists Heinrich Rudolf Hertz and Maxwell had shown that electromagnetic effects take a defined amount of time to act. Einstein proposed that there are no instantaneous interactions *at all* in nature. This is the physical application of his second postulate. That is, every interaction takes time to go from one place to another. Einstein stuck with this view throughout his life despite facing evidence to the contrary. One implication of quantum theory is that instantaneous action is possible. Thus, this fuelled Einstein's mistrust of this view of the world (we will discuss this later).

Einstein devised *gedanken* experiments based on relativistic views to disprove aspects of quantum theory, such as the *EPR* paradox (named after its creators, Albert Einstein, Boris Podolsky, and Nathan Rosen — discussed later). As he was convinced that there is no instantaneous interaction in nature, this logically meant that there must be a maximal speed of interaction. This maximal speed equates to the velocity of light, or the velocity of electromagnetic interaction. If this maximal speed of interaction is the same for all observers irrespective of their own velocity, then his second postulate implies that the maximal velocity of interaction is the velocity of light and it is a universal constant, c. It was a difficult concept to accept — nothing can go faster than light, and light travels at the same velocity for everyone. As we will see, an EPR experiment cannot be used to transmit information — this has been described as a 'peaceful coexistence' between special relativity and quantum mechanics.

When dealing with a single frame of reference, it is easy to make calculations using Galilean relativity for problems relating to velocity. Only when we compare different frames of reference do we encounter strange effects. Einstein realised that if the velocity of light is constant, then it is perhaps *time* that is the variable component for different observers.

In our daily lives, we understand how velocities (e.g., 70 mph) are calculated and know how they feel through experience. The velocity is the distance covered divided by the time taken to cover it (though we do not consciously think of this calculation when experiencing it). With this idea, a moving person could observe (hypothetically) light travelling a distance, d, over a span of time, t, to give a constant velocity of light, c, whereas a stationary person could observe the light travelling a different distance over a different span of time but still obtain the same velocity of light, c.

If time is the variable, we have to understand the idea of *simultaneous events*. For a train arriving at a station at midday, simultaneous events are the pointing of the hands of my watch to the number twelve and the arrival of that train with this event occurring on my watch. Simultaneous events in one frame of reference are not necessarily simultaneous when viewed from another frame of reference — this is called the *relativity of simultaneity*.

Imagine a train carriage moving at constant velocity along a track. By constant velocity, we mean constant velocity vector (a vector is a direction of movement or position). The carriage is one frame of reference and the platform of the station is another. Imagine that at the exact centre of the moving carriage, a torch shines towards the doors at either end of the carriage, which open when light hits a sensor. To a passenger on the train, the doors open simultaneously, but to a person on the platform, the back door opens first as it is travelling *to* the light while the front door is moving *away* from it. This *gedanken* experiment depicts the theory's principle.

The theory shows that which door opens first is dependent on the observer's frame of reference. The velocity of light is constant, so an event that is simultaneous for one frame of reference (in the train) is not for another (on the platform). Since velocity is distance divided by time, velocity is constant (with regards to light), and time is variable, then distance is also variable in different frames.

To gain further insight into special relativity, let us consider the following — if I walk to the front door in the moving carriage, I have walked half a carriage's distance from the train's frame of reference, but of course a much greater distance has been travelled in that time with respect to the platform's frame of reference. Although I have walked the half-carriage distance to the door, I have also travelled the distance that the train covered during the time in which I walked to the door. Once we understand this and accept that velocity is constant, then the time effects are obvious (from the relationship 'velocity is distance divided by time'), if only a little harder to visualise.

If a clock were placed at the front of a moving object, say a train moving at constant velocity, and another at the rear, then in the direction of motion, the clock at the front will be behind (time-wise) the clock at the rear according to the equation:

$t = (dv/c^2)/(1-v^2/c^2)^{1/2}$ (where t = time, d = distance between the clocks, v = velocity of the train, and c = velocity of light).

If on the train I fire a bullet from the rear clock to the front clock, then the velocity of the bullet relative to the train would be the same as it would be relative to the ground if fired from the ground. However, the velocity of the bullet relative to the ground if fired on the train is:

$v_1 = (u + v)/(1 + uv/c^2)$ (where v_1 = bullet velocity relative to the ground, u = velocity of the train relative to the ground, c = velocity of light, v = velocity of the bullet relative to the train).

This shows that the bullet can never reach the speed of light relative to the train or the ground, thus adhering to Einstein's second postulate.

As the train moves along the track, it will shrink in length when viewed from the frame of the platform and the clocks on the train will slow down. If travelling at uniform velocity with a constant course (vector), the contraction and time dilation effects can be calculated according to the same type of equation called the *Lorentz transformation* (named after the Dutch theoretical physicist Hendrik Antoon Lorentz (1853–1928), who devised it. For an excellent account and its derivation, see *Einstein's Special Relativity* by Ernie McFarland). The Lorentz transformation converts spacetime measurements for different frames of reference so that they are consistent. It is intrinsic to the formulation of special relativity and enables us to calculate temporal and spatial effects between different frames of reference.

Lorentz was perhaps the greatest positive influence on the life of Einstein — he was someone Einstein respected both as a person and as a scientist. The Irish physicist George Francis FitzGerald (1851–1901) sometimes has his name associated with Lorentz's work (as the *Lorentz-FitzGerald contraction*) even though his insights were independent of those of Lorentz. FitzGerald proposed in his 1901 paper titled *The Ether and the Earth's Atmosphere* and published in the journal *Science* that if all moving objects were shortened in their direction of motion, it would account for the results of the Michelson-Morley experiment. However, it was Lorentz who formulated the conjecture rigorously. Before Einstein's death, he was asked whom he admired most. He considered Newton, Ernst Mach, Hendrik Lorentz, and Max Planck as his true precursors, with Maxwell included as a fifth.

Returning to the example of the train on the track, if we consider length first, the Lorentz transformation tells us the fractional shrinkage of the moving train relative to the ground (the rest frame):

$l_1 = l\sqrt{1-(\frac{v}{c})^2}$ (where l_1 = length of the train relative to the ground, l = length of the train relative to the train, v = velocity of the train relative to the ground, c = velocity of light).

Thus, if the train is 100 metres long when measured at rest and travelling at 25% of the velocity of light, then its length relative to the train is 100 metres, whereas its length relative to the ground is:

$$100\sqrt{1-\left(\frac{0.25}{1}\right)^2}$$
$$= 100 \times 0.97$$
$$= 97 \text{ metres.}$$

So, the train travelling at 25% of the velocity of light has shrunk 3 metres in the direction of travel.

The slowing down of the clocks on the train travelling at 25% of the velocity of light are given by a similar equation:

$t_1 = t\sqrt{1-(\frac{v}{c})^2}$ (where t_1 = relative passage of time on the train relative to the ground, t = passage of time on the train relative to the train, v = velocity of the train relative to the ground, and c = velocity of light).

Thus, again, if the train is travelling at 25% of the velocity of light, then, say, 10 seconds of time as measured by the clocks at rest will measure as t_1 relative to the clocks on the ground, which is:

$$10\sqrt{1-\left(\frac{0.25}{1}\right)^2}$$
$$= 10 \times 0.97 = 9.7 \text{ seconds.}$$

So, for a train travelling at 25% of the velocity of light, 10 seconds of ageing on the ground produces only 9.7 seconds of ageing on the train.

This means that for every second that passes according to the moving train's clock, we can calculate how many seconds pass on the ground clock according to:

$$t = 1/\sqrt{1-\left(\frac{v}{c}\right)^2}$$

So, for the above example, every second on the train's clock results in 1.03 seconds passing on the ground clock.

Moving clocks indeed run slow and are contracted in length (as is the train and everything in it) in the direction of travel. For a train passing through a station at 25% the speed of light, from the station's frame, time on the train is dilated and the train is contracted. From the frame of the train, the station is contracted and time is dilated.

It is believed that humans have approximately 2 billion heartbeats in a 70-year lifetime. Imagine that somehow you were cloned and there are now three different versions of you that are identical in every way. From birth, one of you is sent on a rocket into space at 80% of the velocity of light, another at 40%, and the third stayed on Earth. Without knowledge of relativity, it is agreed all of you will meet on Earth in 50 years' time after the rockets departed as measured by an Earth clock. However, what would happen is that the you who stayed on Earth would age faster than the clone who had been travelling at 40% of the speed of light, who in turn would age faster than the clone who had travelled at 80% of the velocity of light. Each would return to the launch site at different times, having experienced 50 years in their own frame of reference. We will return to this later in our discussion of the *twin paradox*.

Do moving clocks really run slow? It is real in that special relativistic effects on time are fundamental to the fabric of reality. In *It's about Time*, N. David Mermin states that moving clocks really do run slower and moving objects really do shrink if the concept of the rate of a clock and the length of an object are to have any meaning at all. Thus, the rules of quantum mechanics (which we will come to later) are 'Lorentz covariant', meaning that since clocks and length really do slow down and contract, respectively, at high velocities, then the laws of physics do change with the velocity of particles.

OBSERVER FRAME	OBSERVED FRAME	LENGTH	TIME	EFFECTS
Space rocket	Earth launch pad	The rocket sees Earth contracted in length in the direction of travel as are all objects on Earth (no longer spherical)	The rocket sees clocks on Earth run slower than when measured on the rocket	Launch pad and contents appear contracted and ageing more slowly
Earth launch pad	Space rocket	Earth sees the rocket and its contents contracted in length in the direction of travel relative to their length as measured on Earth	Earth sees clocks in the rocket run slower than when measured on Earth	The rocket and contents appear contracted and ageing more slowly

Figure 3. **Relativistic effects between inertial frames.** A rocket moving without turning or changing velocity is, like Earth, an inertial frame and experiences the same relativistic effects relative to the launch pad as the opposite. Both are equally valid as rest and moving frames.

Let us use an example to illustrate relativistic effects. Why does the moving frame appear contracted to the rest frame *and* the rest frame appear contracted to the moving frame? In his book, *What is Relativity?*, the Russian physics Nobel laureate Lev Landau uses the example of the 'Einstein train' moving through a station to explain why. In this *gedanken* experiment, a 2,400,000 km long train (measured at rest) passes through a station platform of the same length (also measured at rest) at a velocity of 240,000 km/s (i.e., 80% of the velocity of light).

When the train enters the station platform, a person in the carriage shines a torch from the floor of the train vertically up to a mirror and the light is reflected back to a detector on the floor (defined as position A in Figure 4). The path of the light relative to the passenger is denoted by the dashed line.

An observer on the platform has measured that 10 seconds have elapsed between the departure of the light at A and its return to the torch at C. Since light travels at 300,000 km/s (186,000 miles per second), then in 10 seconds the light has travelled 3,000,000 km. As the train is travelling to the right at 240,000 km/s, then relative to the platform observer, the light has travelled the path A to B to C. We know that A to B is the same distance as B to C, so the distances AB and BC are 1,500,000 km

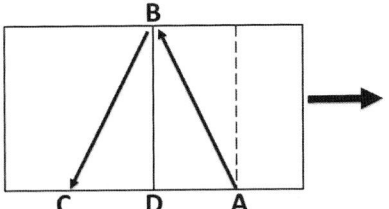

Figure 4. Einstein's train. A train travels in the direction of the arrow at 2,400,000 km/s through a station platform of the same length as the train (at rest). Which is longer when the train is moving? The text below will explain.

each. We know that in 10 seconds the train has travelled 2,400,000 km since distance = velocity (240,000 km/s) × time (10 seconds). Thus, the distance AC is 2,400,000 km. As AD = CD, then the distances AD and CD are 1,200,000 km each.

Notice that we have two right-angled triangles in Figure 4, namely ABD and BDC. Pythagoras taught us that the square of the hypotenuse is equal to the sum of the squares of the other two sides. Thus:

$$AB^2 = AD^2 + BD^2$$

We already know the lengths of AB and BD from the speed of light and that of the train. Now we want to know the length of BD. We can rearrange the Pythagorean equation to give:

$$BD = \sqrt{AB^2 - AD^2}$$

We can then substitute the numbers that we have already deduced into this equation:

$$BD = \sqrt{1,500,000^2 - 1,200,000^2}$$
$$BD = 900,000$$

Thus, the distance that light travels in the carriage relative to the passenger's frame of reference is 2 × 900,000 = 1,800,000 km (from D to B to D). As light travels at 300,000 km/s, we can state that for light to travel 1,800,000 km, it would take (1,800,000 / 300,000) = 6 seconds. This tells us that when the train is travelling at 80% of the velocity of light, 6 seconds of elapsed time from the passenger's frame of reference (where time dilates) is experienced as 10 seconds of elapsed time from the stationary observer's frame of reference. But what is longer, the train or the platform?

From the train's frame of reference, 6 seconds elapsed as it passed through the station platform and travelled at 240,000 km/s. Therefore from the *train's* frame of reference, the platform is 6 × 240,000 = 1,440,000 km long. This is shorter than the 2,400,000 km-long train measured from the moving frame (which experiences the same effects of motion as the measurer), so from the passenger's frame, the platform is shorter than the train by 60%.

However, from the *platform's* frame, the situation is different. We know that the platform is 2,400,000 km long. We also know that the formula $l_1 = l\sqrt{1-(\frac{v}{c})^2}$ enables us to calculate lengths of moving objects relative to stationary ones, so the length of the train from the platform's perspective is:

$$= 2,400,000\sqrt{1-\left(\frac{0.8}{1}\right)^2}$$
$$= 2,400,000 \times 0.60$$
$$= 1,440,000 \text{ km.}$$

So for the stationary observer, the train is also shorter than the platform by 60%. From the frames of reference of both the train and the platform, they observe the other frame as contracted in length and dilated in time. Through the example of the twin paradox, we will investigate this further.

Twin paradox (and summary)

An interesting paradox of time dilation is described by the thought experiment known as the *twin paradox*. Here, twins live on Earth and one twin decides to take a high-velocity trip on a spaceship into space at a significant fraction of the velocity of light. When this twin returns from the trip, which twin is younger? Is there a paradox at all?

Einstein's critics used the twin paradox to try and prove that the special theory of relativity was wrong. They concluded that both the travelling and stationary twin would have aged more relative to the other, which is not possible. We will see that this conclusion is clearly wrong and how special relativity resolves the problem.

Let us first imagine identical clocks, a and b, in two inertial frames that pass each other in a straight line at constant velocity (like the aforementioned train and the station). Clock a 'sees' the time of clock b as running slow (i.e., time dilated) and the dimensions of clock b as shrunk (i.e., contracted) in the direction of movement. Clock b 'sees' the time and dimensions of clock a in exactly the same way — running slow and contracted. They are both experiencing special relativistic effects in the same way relative to each other. In *that* scenario, which *is* slow? It is the same scenario as the train and the station earlier. In fact, it is a meaningless question — as far as each clock is concerned, the other is slow and that is all we can say about it.

Let us say a pair or twins, A and B, have identical clocks a and b, respectively, and twin B travels with clock b while twin A stays at home with clock a. As before, twin B takes a high-velocity trip into space at a significant fraction of the velocity of light. From the description above, wouldn't each twin expect the other to be older? And couldn't both twins consider themselves, in a relativistic sense, to be the traveller? This was the reasoning of Einstein's critics.

The answer to this 'twin paradox' is if twin B was travelling relative to twin A at constant velocity and yet experience an acceleration to achieve this velocity (the spaceship launch), then we know that twin B is the moving frame (as it experienced a non-inertial acceleration) and twin A is the stationary (rest) frame. As well as the initial acceleration, the travelling twin also experiences the acceleration he must undergo in order to turn around and return to be compared with the stationary twin, whom he will eventually find to be older than himself. It is only after experiencing this acceleration that a stationary clock can be observed to be faster than a moving clock. If there was no acceleration with both remaining in inertial frames and no return flight, then each sees the other's clock as moving slowly.

Here, twin A sees clock b as running slowly (time dilation effect) and twin B sees clock a as running fast (relative to how fast clock b is running). Additionally, twin A sees the dimensions of clock b as contracted in length in the direction of travel (as explained by the Lorentz contraction equation), and this is an actual contraction.

The moving twin might have experienced acceleration for anything from a small moment to the entire trip (depending on how advanced the ship is). However, what is certain is that for some moment, the ship was in a non-inertial frame and thus the person on the ship will have aged less than the person in the stationary inertial frame, as would be clear when they meet again. If the moving ship accelerated for a large proportion of the trip, then the ageing would take place during this time, whereas if it accelerated for only a tiny fraction of the trip's duration and the remainder of the trip was inertial, then all the ageing effects relative to the stationary, inertial frame from where the ship departed would occur in this accelerating part of the non-inertial frame of the trip. Thus, the 'paradox' that seemed present when the trip was considered as the relation between two inertial frames evaporates when one frame is correctly seen as non-inertial.

There are a number of different solutions to the twin paradox. Some attribute a crucial role in explanation to the acceleration of the travelling twin at the time of the turnaround. What the acceleration for one twin *does* show is who is moving and who is stationary. The acceleration and change of frame are enough for us to calculate the time dilation effects.

Some explanations of the twin paradox include the fact that when one twin experiences acceleration and the frame becomes non-inertial, special relativity alone ceases to apply and we need general relativity to explain the time dilation effect and mass increase during the acceleration. Some consider the relativistic Doppler effect on the return journey of the twin in addition to the time dilation effect, but for all intents and purposes, it is the change of frame due to acceleration that removes the 'paradox' of both twins ageing and explains why the travelling twin ages less.

Is time dilation real? At CERN in 1977, experiments on muons proved it to be real. On average, muons exist for only $2.2e^{-6}$ seconds, and in an experiment where they travelled at 99.94% of the velocity of light, the travelling muons existed for nearly 30 times as long as the stationary muons. So, yes, it is real.

The way an object appears depends on not only the length contraction but also how long the light takes to reach the eye from different parts of the object in view. If we observed a cube passing nearby at high velocity, light from different parts of the front face of the cube would take different amounts of time to reach us. The complicated effect would result in the sides appearing curved. The front face would be contracted in the direction of motion and the top and bottom edges would be straight lines.

Prior to the Lorentz-FitzGerald contraction, the laws of electromagnetism were predicted to not be the same for all frames of reference. The Lorentz-FitzGerald contractions allow the laws of electromagnetism and mechanics to hold for all frames of reference — they removed contradictions between classical mechanics and electromagnetism. It took Einstein's insight to apply this. Special relativity explains spatiotemporal effects between inertial frames. General relativity is an extension of special relativity, but being geometric in nature, it incorporates gravitational effects and applies to non-inertial frames.

The credit for devising special relativity has been rightfully attributed to Einstein, though Lorentz (who inspired him) also has his name associated with it through the Lorentz-FitzGerald contraction. However, when Einstein published the theory, he was unaware of Lorentz's work on spatiotemporal contraction. It has been reported that the Irish physicist Joseph Larmor (1857–1942) had known of the ideas or principles of the Lorentz-FitzGerald contraction before Lorentz himself independently elucidated them.

Assignment of due credit in its minutiae is practically impossible, yet fortunately this is rarely an issue. However, sometimes when the discovery is important, disputes arise over where credit is due. The historical record of science is littered with disputes over who was first or who did what with regards to a particular discovery. Examples are the disputed inventor of calculus, Newton or Leibniz, and the discoverer of the HIV virus, Robert Gallo or Luc Montagnier. Often, the *real* discovery is the result of one person's particular insight into the application of another's work, as was the case for Einstein and special relativity.

The French polymath Henri Poincaré must also be considered alongside Lorentz as playing an important role in the theory's construction. Although he did not fully appreciate the subtler aspects of what special relativity meant, he was instrumental in constructing the necessary mathematical geometry of spacetime along with Bernhard Riemann. Riemann himself had constructed a geometry that provided insight into the possible shape of the Universe as well as the formalism necessary to construct special and general relativity.

Interestingly, although both Riemann and Poincaré worked in many areas of mathematics, they were responsible for creating specific mathematical problems that have confounded mathematics for over a hundred years. In 1900, David Hilbert named 23 mathematical problems that he considered would pose great difficulty to the greatest mathematicians in the century ahead. By 2000, seven remained. In 2000, the Clay Mathematics Institute in the USA offered one million dollars to anyone who could solve or resolve any of them. These so-called 'millennium problems' and their current status are:

1. **The Riemann Hypothesis** asks if there is a pattern to the distribution of the prime numbers, related to something called the zeta function — UNRESOLVED.
2. **Yang-Mills Theory and the Mass Gap Hypothesis**, whose solution would help us understand why the electron has mass (named after the Chinese American Chen-Ning Franklin Yang and the American Robert Mills) — UNRESOLVED.
3. **The P v NP Problem** aims to understand the types of problems computers can analyse by trying to determine whether problems can be broken up into two groups: easy to find answers (P) and easy to check answers (NP) — UNRESOLVED.
4. **The Navier-Stokes Equations**, which are differential equations governing fluid dynamics and yet do not have known general solutions — UNRESOLVED.
5. **The Poincaré Conjecture**, a topological problem for 3-D objects — SOLVED (2003).
6. **The Birch and Swinnerton-Dyer Conjecture**, which relates to whether a particular class of equations have solutions — UNRESOLVED.
7. **The Hodge Conjecture**, a complicated work in analytic geometry — UNRESOLVED.

Poincaré is famous for many mathematical concepts, but he is perhaps most well known for the Poincaré Conjecture. It asks whether the surface of a 3-D sphere is simply connected. It concerns a space that locally looks like ordinary 3-D space but which is finite in size and lacks any boundary. The conjecture claims that if such a space has the additional property that each loop in the space can be continuously tightened to a point, then it is just a 3-D sphere. The implications of the result have ramifications on the large-scale structure of the Universe, special and general relativity, and the TOE. This 100 year-old problem had been solved for higher dimensions, but proved difficult for three. It was proven in 2006 by the Russian mathematician Grigory Perelman. He rejected both the Fields Medal (the mathematical equivalent of the Nobel Prize) and the Millenium Prize for this. None of the other five problems have been solved.

Riemann and Poincaré did work relating to relativity, but it took the physical insight of Einstein to link and apply abstract concepts to the real world. Both Poincaré and Lorentz missed the discovery of special relativity by being too concerned with the considerations of dynamics. Only Einstein saw the crucial point of the need to reject the aether. Poincaré stated that when light leaves a star, it is not at its destination and not in the star. Thus, it is 'somewhere' and supported by some material. Poincaré clearly believed in the aether. He was aware, however, that clocks in uniform relative motion would not mark the *true* time; rather, they would represent *local* time. Aware that simultaneity had been questioned, Poincaré was close to elucidating the full theory.

Before the publication of the special theory of relativity, Lorentz had managed to create the hypothesis that implied the complete impossibility of determining absolute motion. It was not as if Einstein was alone in his quest to find the truth. Anyone who accepted the aether could also see its failings. However, even Einstein believed in it until 1901. Some consider Lorentz to have deserved equal credit with Einstein for relativity since he was the first to have found the mathematical content of the relativity principle. However, the consensus is that although the key figures were Einstein, Poincaré, and Lorentz, Einstein's contribution was by far the greatest.

Einstein was always reticent to acknowledge the Michelson-Morley experiment in his thinking, Lorentz never could let go of the idea of the aether in his, and Poincaré never really understood relativity in its final form. Lorentz was a true classical physicist and, thus, though he was capable of imagining the velocity of light as being c, he could also imagine it being, for example, one mph faster. Although he understood relativity mathematically and conceptually, he could not let go of his classical ideas.

Poincaré lacked some fundamental understanding of the theory, however, as demonstrated in his comment that the theory was based on three hypotheses — that no body can attain velocities greater than that of light, that the laws of physics are the same for all inertial frames, and that a body in translational motion suffers a deformation in the direction in which it is displaced. The third hypothesis, however, is a consequence of the first two and is therefore not another unique hypothesis. Poincaré either never understood or never fully accepted relativity. Einstein did not rate Poincaré highly as a scientist as some did, the possible reasons for which are discussed in Abraham Pais's *Subtle is the Lord*.

Acceptance of Einstein's theory of special relativity was bolstered by Arnold Sommerfeld's relativistic calculations concerning the spectral lines of hydrogen. Although a different model is now used for explaining these phenomena, Sommerfeld's work linked special relativity with the beginnings of quantum theory.

iv) General Relativity

Einstein's general theory of relativity was an extension of special relativity and dealt with accelerated frames of reference and gravitation. The German mathematician Hermann Minkowski (1864–1909) reformulated Einstein's special relativity in terms of four-dimensional (4-D) spacetime — essential for the latter development of general relativity. The story of the development of special relativity (completed in 1905) was a rather simple historical tale whereas the production of the completed general theory (1915) was a far more convoluted one. Einstein considered the latter to be his greatest achievement.

The test of the theory that pleased him the most was its ability to account for the strange orbit of the planet Mercury around the Sun, which could not be explained by Newton's laws of gravitation. Mercury's perihelion, or the point in its orbit when closest to the Sun, had been measured to advance by 38 seconds per century. Newtonian mechanics predicted no such advance, but Einstein's theory predicted it to advance by 45 seconds (+/− 5) per century. It is now known by measurement to be 43.11 seconds (+/− 0.45) per century. Thus, Einstein's general theory resolved this within statistically acceptable margins of error. He was allegedly so happy that he could not work for three days after the discovery of this result.

This section focuses on both the special and general theories together. Even on a purely classical level, nobody can claim to have a full grasp of the dynamic content of the non-linear dynamics of general relativity.

What is spacetime?

When we think of something occupying space, we consider the three dimensions of length, breadth, and height, and that time is a different category of dimension. We inhabit three dimensions and move within these through time. However, in space, there isn't space *and* time but rather spacetime, and this is fundamental to the general theory of relativity.

Spacetime is any mathematical model that combines space and time into a single construct called the spacetime continuum. Space and time are conceptually different in the context of what they mean to our everyday lives. We cannot go forward or backwards in time, but we are tied to its flow. Space is more flexible — we can go here and there, but we can only be in one place at a time. The construction of spacetime enables a deeper understanding of reality and how the common-sense understanding of time and space are, indeed, relative.

The general theory of relativity modified Newton's gravitational laws by allowing for the treatment of rapidly moving objects. The theory also enabled the determination that energy (as well as rest mass) is affected by gravitational fields. It predicted that light should be gravitationally attracted by masses. Thus, our observation of stars is not representative of their true position, but the result of the light from them being bent while on its path to us through attraction by objects (e.g., other stars). This is not strictly true because we also have to bear in mind that the actual position of the star relative to an observer will have been different from where it was when the light was first emitted.

Experimental confirmation of special and general relativistic effects has been plentiful. In 1923 for example, the 'Compton effect' (the scattering of *photons* by electrons, named after the American physicist Arthur Compton) confirmed the relativistic laws of conservation of energy and momentum, and it was important in demonstrating the quantised nature of light (as we shall see later). Time dilation was first demonstrated in 1941 in an experiment on subatomic particles.

General and special relativity in action: Homage to John Archibald Wheeler

Einstein's theory of special relativity included the completion of the work of Maxwell and Lorentz. It was the result of 10 years of thought about the properties of light. His general theory involved the completion of Newton's theory of gravitation and incorporated Mach's vision of the relativity of all motion. This itself was the result of eight years of thought about gravitation. But that is not to say that this was *all* he thought of scientifically — he was also deeply imbedded in the growing areas of quantum theory (as a sceptic) and statistical mechanics. Maxwell as well as others before him and after could never resolve the cause of gravitation. He saw it as attractive and that to align it with electromagnetic theory, gravitational energy needed an additional minus sign. This led to a paradox that he could not solve since gravitational force is attractive and dense bodies should influence the medium by reducing gravitational energy.

John Archibald Wheeler was instrumental throughout the 20th century in the continual development and application of both quantum theory and relativity (and, thus, gravitation). To make relativity understandable to the layperson, he wrote *A Journey into Gravity and Spacetime* (1990), which described the special and general theories of relativity using explanatory tools that I will at times apply here. Special relativity relates to temporal and spatial contractions as a result of high-velocity movements at uniform velocity between frames of reference. With this theory, Einstein rejected the concept of the aether, though he still considered space to be flat. For his general theory of relativity, he was going to have to review this idea.

If we look at the Earth's surface, it seems flat. Of course, we know that it is actually spherical. If we draw a circle around the widest part of the Earth (i.e., the equator) and then take points on that line and draw perpendicular lines towards the north, all the lines will converge at the North Pole. To an individual who cannot directly sense the curvature, he will think that he is walking in a straight, flat line. Only from the knowledge obtained by multiple walks from different points on the equator meeting at the North Pole will he realise that the surface is curved and spherical. In a similar way, space that appears flat is in fact curved.

Why does space curve? The reason, as Wheeler put it, is that "spacetime grips matter (mass), telling it how to move and matter (mass) grips spacetime, telling it how to curve". In essence, that one sentence sums up general relativistic effects. The more matter there is in a particular region of space, the greater the curvature of space around that region. Conversely, the extent of curvature decreases with increasing distance from the body of matter. It is similar to visualising a polythene sheet used to represent spacetime and a ball placed on it to represent a star. The deformation that the ball makes in the polythene represents the spacetime curvature caused by the star.

This is, of course, a 3-D model of a four (or more) dimensional reality, but it helps us to visualise the effect. If we rolled a smaller ball across the polythene towards the 'star', its course would be altered by the polythene deformation caused by the larger ball (of equal density). The smaller ball would be attracted to the larger one due to the curved indentation in the polythene caused by the latter. Similarly, a meteor passing near to Earth will be attracted to Earth due to spacetime curvature caused by Earth's mass.

Once we have considered spacetime, we can understand the concept of *free-float*. When you jump from an aeroplane, you are thought to fall. However, this is really free-float under the motion-directing force of gravity. Spacetime around the Earth is curved due to the mass of the Earth, so when you leap from the plane, you are being directed to the centre of mass causing the curvature — the Earth.

Consider the *gedankan* experiment where we throw a ball inside a house. The moment we let go of the ball, it is in a free-float frame of reference. If we threw the ball in exactly the same way again from the same position, but at the moment we let go of the ball, we let the house free-float, the ball would track a straight line and not fall as both the ball and the house would be in free-float. Furthermore, the track path of the ball will be identical in both cases, but it just 'appears' to arc in the first example because the house is resisting free-float whereas the ball is not.

In the first scenario where the ball is thrown inside a house that is standing on Earth, if balls were thrown at different velocities, they would appear to arc differently. The arc is variable in space but identical in spacetime. If we were to compare the arc of the balls in 2-D, up-down, and past-future spacetime, all ball arcs would be identical. This is irrespective of the mass or density of the ball. Remember, we are considering this to be occurring in the (near) vacuum of space and not with the wind-resisting effects of the atmosphere, which are not incorporated in relativistic effects. A feather would drop slower than a ball bearing only because of wind resistance. However, it has been established to a precision of one part in 10^{11} that aluminium and gold (which differ in density) fall at identical rates in a vacuum. Thus, Einstein was right in thinking that the medium and not the mass determines motion.

The next concept we come to regarding the general theory of relativity and spacetime is *interval*. There are different versions and meanings of 'interval', but the one we refer to is a 4-D spacetime interval.

Interval

Events in the real world are separated in time and in space. For this, the term 'distance' will not suffice. Separation in spacetime is called *interval* and can be space-like and time-like.

As we saw earlier, time-like events can cause each other to happen, like throwing a ball and hitting a bottle. The order cannot be changed — the ball is thrown and then the bottle breaks; it is never the other way round. A time-like interval contrasts with space-like intervals in that enough time passes between events for a cause-effect relationship to be possible. Space-like events are slightly harder to visualise.

Using Figure 5, in 2-dimensional space, the distance, *l*, between two points, A and B, can be presented in terms of length projections *x* and *y* according to the Pythagorean equation:

$$l^2 = x^2 + y^2$$

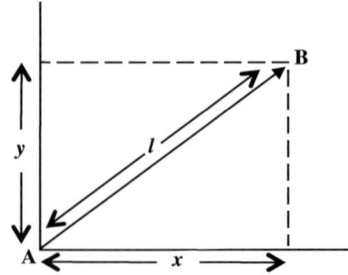

Figure 5. 2-dimensional length.

This reveals the equation for length *l* as:

$$l = \sqrt{x^2 + y^2}$$

This can be extended for a distance, *l*, in 3-dimensional space by using a third spatial axis, *z*, which is at right angles to *x* and *y*. In 3-dimensional space, the equation for length *l* is:

$$l = \sqrt{x^2 + y^2 + z^2}$$

Things get a bit more complicated when we look at 4-dimensional spacetime (i.e., 3-D space and time), and we need to define the distance between points in a way that is observer-independent. To do this, we exploit the fact that the speed of light, *c*, is constant so that we can define time, *t*, in units of distance (metres). Then distance, or interval *S*, is defined by:

$$S = \sqrt{c^2 t^2 - x^2 - y^2 - z^2}$$

This equation tells us how events are causally related in spacetime. If $c_2 t_2$ is dominant, then interval is termed *time-like*, whereas if the spatial component $x^2 - y^2 - z^2$ is dominant, then the interval is described as *space-like*. A time-like interval between events means that there can be a causal relationship between them, whereas a space-like interval precludes this (Figure 6).

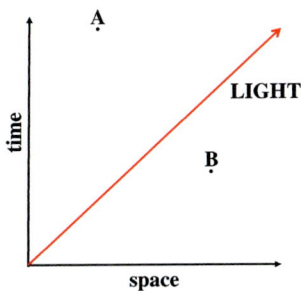

Figure 6. Interval. In a spacetime diagram, the red line represents the movement of light through spacetime from a point designated by the graphical origin. Point A represents an event that can be causally connected to an event at the origin, such that the emission of light from the origin and event A are separated by a time-like interval. Point B represents an event that cannot be causally connected to an event at the origin, such that the emission of light from the origin and event A are separated by a space-like interval.

Let us consider things in a slightly different way, using words to replace the symbols shown in some of the preceding equations. On Earth, the spacing between points, or nearby events, can be given by:

$$(\text{distance})^2 = (\text{east-west separation})^2 + (\text{north-south separation})^2 + (\text{up-down separation})^2$$

Space-like events preclude connection by a light signal — a photon generated at event A will still be moving towards event B when B occurs. Thus, a space-like interval is one that separates events that do not occur in each other's future and past (quantum *entanglement*, as we will see in the next chapter, is linked to this concept). There is no causal relationship between events because there is not enough time for light to cross the spatial distance between the events to make them possibly causally related. To calculate a spacetime interval, we have to consider the separation in spatial dimensions (as for distance) and also the temporal separation. By subtracting the temporal separation, if the product is positive, then it tells us that the separation is space-like. If it is negative, the separation is time-like.

Revising the earlier equations but in word form, these intervals can be calculated thus:

1. $(\text{space-like interval})^2 = (\text{east-west separation})^2 + (\text{north-south separation})^2 + (\text{up-down separation})^2 - (\text{separation in time})^2$
2. $(\text{time-like interval})^2 = (\text{separation in time})^2 - (\text{east-west separation})^2 - (\text{north-south separation})^2 - (\text{up-down separation})^2$

Using this concept of interval, we can calculate special relativistic effects (as in the previous section), but this time using the terminology of spacetime and general relativity, enabling an easier transition to general relativity and its effects.

Consider that I am standing on a table and I roll a ball from one edge of the table to the other side three metres away. The ball has rolled three metres relative to the table. If, while I am rolling the ball, the table is moved four metres sideways to the direction in which I roll the ball, then the ball has moved three metres relative to the table and five metres relative to the Earth, because it has rolled the equivalent of the hypotenuse of a 3:4:5 triangle.

Let us replace the ball with a beam of light that is emitted from one end of the table and bounced off the other using a mirror. Let us also imagine that the table moves sideways at 80% of the velocity of light. Now, when the light moves to the mirror and back, it has moved six metres from the table's frame of reference and 10 metres from the ground's frame of reference using the 3:4:5 triangle of the previous example. We can now calculate the time-like interval for the two frames of reference.

From the table's perspective, the (separation in time)² for the time between emission, reflection and return, is 36m². From the ground's frame, it is 100m². The (separation in space)² is 0m² from the table's frame and 64m² from the ground's frame. Thus, from the equation above, the time-like interval for both frames is 6m². As such, *interval is independent of the frame of reference*. Separation in space and time is observer-dependent, whereas interval — the separation in spacetime — is observer-independent. Furthermore, events that are separated by space-like intervals cannot influence one another (due to the limit of the velocity of light) whereas those separated by time-like intervals can.

Let us apply this idea to another *gedanken* experiment that is similar to the one discussed earlier. Suppose that in the future, a man was to travel from Earth to a planet that is 95 light years away and his velocity is such that, based on Earth's time frame, it will take 100 years to reach the planet. That is, he travels at 95/100 (95%) the velocity of light. Would he live to survive the duration of the trip, there and back, and would those who bid him farewell eventually still be there to meet him? We can calculate the answer to these questions as follows:

> The separation in space for the return trip is 95 + 95 light years = 190 light years. This means that relative to Earth, light would take 190 years to reach the destination and be reflected back to Earth. The separation in time is 100 + 100 light years = 200 light years, which means that relative to Earth, the spaceship would take 200 years for the whole voyage.

These relate to Earth's frame of reference. However, it is different from the traveller's frame of reference. Using our equation:

$$\text{Interval for outward journey} = \sqrt{(\text{separation in time})^2 - (\text{separation in space})^2}$$

The (time separation)^2 is $(100)^2$ and the (space separation)^2 is $(95)^2$, or $10000 - 9025 = 975$. So, the interval is $\sqrt{975}$, which is equivalent to 31.22 years. Therefore, the round trip would take 62.44 years. What does this mean? As interval is independent of frame of reference, travelling to and returning from a star that is 100 light years away at 95% the velocity of light would cause the traveller to age 62.44 years. That is, according to his spaceship's clock, he would experience 62.44 years of ageing on his trip and arrive back on Earth 62.44 years later. He would experience time on the spaceship as he did on Earth, but when he gets off his spaceship when he returns to Earth, he would notice that the Earth clocks are 137.56 years forward $(200 - 62.44)$. Moreover, those he left on Earth would have died as 200 years would have passed.

Discovered or invented?

Events unfold in time. Nothing changes in spacetime, yet time is a part of spacetime. The equations of 4-D reality imply that the past, present, and future exist equally, rather than the past having happened and the future not having happened yet. This disconcerting picture means that everything I have done, am doing, and will do exist, but my consciousness, now, is scanning the immediate present to define the now. One might think that this picture of reality means that fate is essentially encoded and predefined or predetermined.

One also wonders, then, what is real? One hundred years ago I did not exist, nor did my parents. Was I any *less* real then than a mathematical equation that defines a physical property of the Universe (e.g., some stellar effect) that is yet to be discovered? If the equation is never discovered by consciousness, is it any less real? Does knowing something that is not physical but a true relational concept make it more real? Is a concept real? Platonists believe that the equations defining physical events are not created but discovered.

Stephen Wolfram considers the mathematics that we use now as an historical artefact, and that in the future we will discover other types of mathematics that may represent reality in a different way. It seems true that we are constrained in our analyses both by our mental framework and consequential abstract tools. All knowledge is relative to this, and data as well as assumptions and conclusions will be skewed towards it. Hence, 'truth' is more relative than absolute. When new mathematics is discovered, is it really discovered or invented? In a predetermined Universe, it would be considered as discovered. Since it is abstract, then the concepts that are realised, once realised, represent a hidden truth (or model) about some aspect of reality that is revealed. This revelation cannot be invented since it exists as a consequence of the actions (in the mental domain) of a component of physical reality (the ordered structure of the human mind).

Block universe

The 'block universe' theory sees spacetime as an unchanging block rather than a conventional three-dimensional space modulated by the passage of time. It is controversial because it goes against the intuitive feeling that time flows from a past that has happened to a future that has not happened yet. However, much of physics, as we have and will see, is counterintuitive. In the block universe, past, present, and future exist. So, for instance, a reality where I am dead exists. How can this model be true as a representation of physical reality and not just as a useful mathematical representation of what is? Perhaps it is not. Although it can mathematically define 4-D spacetime, the reason it contrasts with intuition may be that our conception of past and future *is* correct.

If our Universe is part of a multiverse and if an external Universe affects events in our Universe, then the unfolding of events in our Universe is not solely determined by the Big Bang. Yet as mentioned earlier, it is generally believed that an external universe, in a multiverse context, does not affect our Universe. So, there is no external influence on the causal determination of future events by our Big Bang. Even if there were influences on our Universe from other universes, the 4-D spacetime mathematics and block model would still relate to a future defined by knowable and unknowable influences acting on the particles and forces that exist in our Universe. With such input, free will could still be an illusion and predeterminism would still exist as the determinism would emanate from the Big Bangs of both our and other influencing universe/s.

The British astrophysicist and science writer John Gribbin (and the British physicist David Deutsch) has a view that the block universe model restores free will. The future, past, and present are equally real; it is just that we are consciously experiencing the present. Gribbin believes that the nature of quantum physics restores free will in the block universe because all quantum states that correspond to all moments in time exist. If there is one block, we have no free will, but if a branching multiverse universe is added whenever decisions are made, then all futures can exist. Here, it is the choices we make that determine which future exists and becomes real.

Many models where human consciousness (decisions) has deep ramifications on reality have been devised (and are discussed later in the final two chapters). The issue with inciting branching whenever a decision is made is that a conscious being in this Universe is used as the tool to generate the infinite universes that allow for the free will of the very same being that is required to cause the branching, which is a somewhat circular argument.

Three worlds

Let us digress slightly and mention Plato again. Plato was above all a rationalist who believed that knowledge and understanding could only stem from reason and not experience. Truth is revealed by the mind — the senses can mislead us. Thus, the appearance of our physical surroundings can mislead us. Roger Penrose stresses that there are three 'worlds':

1. **The Platonic world** — the physical world is appearance. True reality is the ideas from which appearance derives. Though not physical, the Platonic realm of ideas is unaltered — it is the ideal against which reality is measured. If we take the idea of a sphere, for example, this idea is a perfect sphere.
2. **The physical world** — in the case of the sphere, it is a real and physical approximation of a sphere and thus never perfect.
3. **The mental world** — the mind is part of the physical world and can think of the Platonic Realm. Indeed, we can think of a sphere (i.e., both the idea and the real thing — a mix of 1 and 2).

(These differ somewhat from the three worlds as described by the philosopher Karl Popper, namely World 1, the physical world; World 2, that of mental states; and World 3, the products of the mind.)

Penrose's view is that the world of ideas (Platonic), the physical world, and the mental world interrelate in a complex and mysterious way. The physical world maps onto the mental world, the mental world onto the world of ideas, and the world of ideas onto the physical world. Each world seems to emerge from a tiny part of the one that precedes it — the physical world is a part of the totality of Platonic ideals, the mental world (the mind of man, for example) is a part of the physical world, and the Platonic world is a part of the mental world (we can think of other things). The mystery is how they interrelate.

In a scientific context, Platonic existence would be that of an objective external standard independent of human opinion — in other words, an absolute. Penrose believes that as the Universe exists, it must exist according to some laws, and human attempts to understand those laws (e.g., whether such laws actually exist or are within the capacity of human intellect) is debatable. The understanding we do have explains a lot of what happens, but as it is an incomplete understanding (there are things we cannot explain), we do not know whether our models are on the right path to 'truth' or not. Perhaps the Platonic ideal is described by a form of mathematics beyond human comprehension.

From human intellectual endeavour, we may find an equation that describes some physical process, but is it invented or discovered? If it is an *approximation* of the truth (e.g., Newton's laws of gravitation), is it an invention? Conversely, if it were a Platonic 'truth', innate to the laws of the Universe, is it not therefore discovered? If it is wrong, it follows that it can only be an invention, yet how can we know if it is right or just something whose flaw we have not yet seen?

Since physical things possess physical being, we may not fully understand them, but we are certain of their existence. Relationships (equations) between matter and force also exist, but in a different sense. Intelligence is needed to probe reality to uncover them. Yet, although we assume that there is a Platonic ideal for certain relationships, there is no physical presence of matter in their makeup to show us that they exist — they may be wrong and just an invention of the mind, or right and an invention of the mind that is also a discovery about reality.

If, hypothetically, there are one million equations that exist in a Platonic sense to define all universal physical events or relationships, yet only half a million will ever be known by conscious entities, then the unknown equations also exist and will still be part of the Platonic mathematical world. That matter — organised in the form of the brain of an intelligent, conscious entity such as mankind — has discovered half of them and not the other half may just mean that, innate to the laws of the Universe, the forces and matter that constitute it cannot form a consciousness that can comprehend all of it. In other words, there are some ideals of the Platonic World that will remain undiscovered or undiscoverable. That is, all Platonically 'true' relationships exist, whether they have been discovered or not.

Spacetime curvature

To understand Einstein's concept of gravity as the manifestation of spacetime curvature, Wheeler discusses a phenomenon known as *boomeranging*. This effect demonstrates the difference between Newton's and Einstein's visions on gravitation. To explain, let us cut an imaginary hole though the Earth from one side to the other and passing through the Earth's centre. We then release some sort of craft under free-float through the hole. It would increase in velocity as it travels to the centre, reaching 17,700 mph (a similar speed to that of a space shuttle as it enters the Earth's upper thermosphere) before decelerating until it reaches the other side (42 minutes later).

Einstein stated that we must observe the motion of two nearby boomerangers relative to each other to observe gravitational effects, not just the motion of one relative to the Earth, whereby we are focusing on *local* physics, not action at a distance. This idea of *locality* is of fundamental importance and will be discussed in more detail below (and also in Chapter 6).

For Einstein, the motion is free-float through curved spacetime. For Newton, all matter in the Universe attracts every other particle of matter with a force proportional to the product of the two masses and inversely proportional to the square of the distance between them. For the boomerangers, as they descend to the centre of the Earth, only the mass in front of them would exert an attractive effect. To Einstein, the two close-by boomerangers would free-float according to the straightest *world lines* that they can through curved spacetime. If space were flat, they would move further apart from one another. However, spacetime is curved due to the mass of the Earth gripping it. The effect is that the world lines meet 42 minutes later at the end of the journey at the surface (i.e., on the opposite side of the planet from the starting point).

On a surface, parallel lines that remain equally spaced display no (or zero) curvature. If the lines diverge, the surface displays negative curvature. If they converge, the curvature is positive. In 4-D spacetime, the warping inside the Earth is positive spacetime curvature. As Wheeler puts it, gravity is a local 'something', which is spacetime curvature. Let us ask what appears to be a simple question but is one that, in fact, has an unexpected answer that provides further insight into general relativity: What is the shortest route between two points in space?

If we took two points and separated them using a tightened piece of string, the straight line caused by the string would not represent the shortest route between the points. A *geodesic* represents a free-float world line and it is the shortest route. It may appear to curve, but actually follows the curvature of 4-D spacetime through free-float. Non-geodesic lines may be straight or curved, but they are considered non-geodesic since they do not follow the free-float world line. Nearby geodesics that bend towards one another represent positive curvature; bending away represents negative curvature. In the trip to the distant planet that was discussed earlier, the geodesic world line causes the greatest ageing. The world line trip that travels at the velocity of light causes maximum kink and does not age at all — there is zero interval between departure and return.

It is possible to measure the curvature of spacetime caused by mass. This requires assigning to each region of spacetime its responsibility for geodesic bending. The greater the mass, the greater the geodesic bending and the larger the effect on the velocity of a free-float object close to the mass. Spacetime curvature is different inside the Earth than outside of it. Inside the Earth, it is 'contractile' whereas outside it is described as 'tide-driving'.

The German mathematician Karl Schwarzschild explored the consequences of Einstein's general theory of gravity. He found a solution to Einstein's equations for the region of space around a spherical region of mass (e.g., a planet) as well as for the interior of a sphere of uniform mass. The tidal force of gravity can be detected by considering the forces on six test masses arranged in an octahedron. If inside the Earth, all six masses are pulled together. So, spacetime curvature inside the Earth is contractile such that the six points lie closer together than in empty space. Outside, they are pushed apart as the geodesic deviation of spacetime (or tidal effect) is seen. In other words, spacetime tells matter how to move whereas matter tells spacetime how to curve.

Wheeler encouraged us to sense spacetime in its full four-dimensionality: east-west, north-south, in-out, and past-future. *That* is the real spacetime surrounding us. Mass inside the Earth causes it to bend the spacetime inside the Earth, thus causing it to be contractile spacetime. This is similar to the deformation of a trampoline caused by someone landing on it. The contractile spacetime inside the Earth forces bending on the spacetime geometry surrounding it, which is the reason why spacetime can be curved in regions that are free from mass or matter. Although the spacetime curvature outside the Earth is non-contractile, it is tide-driving non-contractile spacetime. The contractile bending within the Earth causes tide-driving spacetime curvature outside the Earth — if it did not respond, spacetime would tear.

Thus, where there is a mass, curvature is contractile; where there is no mass, it is non-contractile. But the influence of mass on one region of spacetime is felt in another region of spacetime. Even though the Moon is 400,000 km from the Earth, the tide-driving effect of the Earth's mass on the Moon is enough to cause a one-kilometre deformation in its sphericity. The tide-driving effects of the Sun and the Moon on Earth can also be seen in extreme high and low tides.

As mentioned, mass grips spacetime, telling it how to curve. Spacetime curvature is proportional to the mass that produces this curvature. By gripping mass, spacetime keeps an object moving when free. Furthermore, it enforces the conservation of energy and momentum in a matter collision. Wheeler likes to consider momentum and energy as *momenergy*, just as space and time is considered as spacetime. It is a fact of nature and of spacetime that spacetime grips mass in a way that conserves momenergy. Therefore, momenergy is proportional to the mass of the object. Momenergy is conserved whereas mass is not — for example, a hot object weighs more than the same object when cold.

If we take any four-dimensional region, the grip of spacetime never permits any change in momenergy. The sum content of momenergy in any bound region of spacetime is zero. The content of momenergy within a region of spacetime is detected by spacetime itself as a consequence of the grip on spacetime by mass. To understand this as well as the generation of Einstein's *geometrodynamic field equation* (which explains all the effects of gravity), Wheeler uses the example of a cube:

> At the boundaries of a cube, the mass inside grips spacetime outside. Conversely, the spacetime grips the boundaries and drags the cube down to the centre of mass. We can think of the interior of the cube as being orientated. On a particular face, consider a direction of an arrow around the edges of the face close to the boundary as representing the boundary of the face of the cube. For each of the six faces, there is a similar boundary. The boundary orientations are determined from within the cube, and whose properties are determined by spacetime.
>
> For each point on the boundary, there is a direction of orientation from one face in one direction and from another face in another direction. For each line, each boundary, the face, and adjacent-face boundaries cancel each other out. Thus, the 1-D boundary of the 2-D of a 3-D region is zero. A 4-D block of spacetime is surrounded by eight such cubes, each consisting of six 2-D faces possessing boundaries as described. The boundary of each cube's 2-D face reveals the momenergy within. The total of 48 (6 × 8) 2-D cube faces reveal the conservation of momenergy within the 4-D region of spacetime as a result of the self-annihilation of the 2-D boundaries.

From this, the Einstein-Cartan geometrodynamic field equation (named after the French mathematician Elie Cartan, who helped Einstein with the mathematics) is revealed:

> (the sum of moments of rotation for the face of a 3D-cube) = 8π (amount of momenergy within that cube)

This equation, which is the crux of Einstein's 1915 paper on the general theory of relativity, can be used to explain how momenergy grips, bends, warps, and deforms spacetime. Although the momenergy is zero in regions of emptiness, the free-float worldlines are not free from rotation. If they were, there would be no gravity, no planetary orbits, and therefore no life.

Spacetime and black holes

The near-sphericity of Earth, other planets, and stars is due to the effect enforced on mass by gravity. It is a feature of gravity to pull matter into a spherical form, which is the smallest volume of spacetime that can be occupied by matter. The geometry of spacetime surrounding a sphere of matter is called *Schwarzschild geometry*. In 1916, the German physicist Karl Schwarzschild showed that if a large-enough star collapses on its own gravity, its spacetime is so severely curved that nothing can escape its *event horizon*. This is called a *Schwarzschild singularity*. The 'Schwarzschild radius' is the term given for the distance from a black hole that matter or light can reach, but if it passes this point, then it is a one-way ticket. The gravitational attraction from the black hole is so intense that it will not let the matter or light that has passed the Schwarzschild radius back out of the black hole.

We know that the curving of spacetime around an object can be imagined as the curving of a trampoline outside the zone of a jumper's impact. Wheeler likens the space part of Schwarzschild's geometry to the visualisation of a jar on a potter's wheel with its external surface of negative curvature. At the centre of the wheel is the axis of rotational symmetry, though it is not part of the jar. Schwarzschild's geometry is 4-D space with a curved 3-D space geometry embedded in it, yet this embedding has nothing to do with time. It is impossible to visualise — it is empty of momenergy and has zero moment of rotation, so by compensating, the curvature on the faces of the cube must be zero. The compensation of curvature is only possible when the cube exists in a space whose shape follows a parabolic curve. This parabola generates Schwarzschild's geometry.

The main difference between the geometry of the sides of the jar and of Schwarzschild geometry is that the jar is the balanced curvature of two one-dimensional lines, whereas Schwarzschild geometry is the balanced curvature of six 2-D surfaces (i.e., the faces of a 3-D cube). A spaceship travelling through Schwarzschild space geometry travels through curved 3-D space embedded in an imagined 4-D space. The 'Schwarzschild radial coordinate' provides information about the location in curved space geometry. However, this is the non-existent world of 4-D embedding space and needs to be converted to the real world of curved 3-D space. The surface and space curvature are what matters to gravity. The force of gravity acts where spacetime geometry is curved. When there is no momenergy to act on, the grip of spacetime acts on spacetime itself.

Another equation known as the 'Schwarzschild metric' tells us the distance in curved 3-D space between points. The distance between a point and another nearby point do not indicate the geometry; they *are* the geometry. The Schwarzschild metric allows us to move from curved space to curved spacetime by elucidating the geometry of spacetime. Thus, spacetime exerts its grip on mass through interval, and this is revealed through the metric. In spacetime surrounding an attracting mass, the grip balances out (with no momenergy for spacetime to grip on to) and cancels to the sum of zero.

Ageing

The ageing measured by Earth-bound clocks is less than the ageing of far-away clocks. That is, higher clocks (e.g., within an orbiting satellite) run faster than clocks sitting on the surface of the Earth, and this has been tested using atomic clocks.

In the previous sections, we discussed interval and temporal dilations between frames of reference. With geometric considerations, temporal effects are encapsulated within the Schwarzschild metric. If I throw a stone into the air so that it returns to my hand two seconds later, the moment I let go of the stone puts it in free-float, a phenomenon that we encountered earlier. For minimal ageing, the path must have maximum kink or a *null* interval. However, the free-float of the toss results in maximum ageing. There is the age-lengthening effect of moving to its highest point and the age shortening effect of its return to my hand. The principle of maximum ageing also governs the motion of the Moon and the planets.

Planetary motion

When a ball is tossed into the air, it goes into free-float. The motion of a planet around a sun must deal with twice as many options in its motion from event A in spacetime to event B. The planet must know the best instant to arrive at each Schwarzschild radial coordinate circle on its trip from A to B as well as how far around the sun it will have passed along that circle. In its orbit around a sun, the planet sweeps out the same area per unit time irrespective of its position in its orbiting path. As the area remains constant, the velocity of the orbit may change. This is the law of conservation of angular momentum.

Calculating angular momentum is akin to pushing a hinged door. Angular momentum is the linear momentum (the push on the door) multiplied by the distance from the axis of angular momentum (the distance from the hinge). We know that it is harder to push on a door or gate at close to the hinge than at the edge where the handle is located. The door acquires the effort I transfer to it with the push, thereby conserving angular momentum.

A planet retains a fixed angular momentum throughout its orbit. It speeds up as it approaches and slows down as it recedes from the sun. The rate of these processes has a net effect of an equal area of sweep per unit of time. The motion of a planet has two components — directly toward and away from the sun (in-and-out motion) and motion perpendicular to the sun (transverse motion). The two straight-line motions in balance generate the curved orbit. The energy for this motion is a consequence of the principle of maximum ageing — the conservation of energy.

Newton thought that he could explain this through two forms of energy: kinetic energy (which depends on velocity, not position) and potential energy (which depends on position, not velocity). When Earth has reached its furthest distance from the Sun, it has stored lots of potential energy that, as energy is conserved, depletes the kinetic energy. This kinetic energy is of in-and-out motion as well as kinetic energy transverse to this. The planet cannot draw on this, so it recedes to its most innermost point- so executing the orbital path.

Newtonian gravitation accounts well for orbits, especially those similar to Earth's, which is relatively circular. However, as we have discussed earlier, Mercury's orbit is more eccentric than that of Earth and requires Einstein's gravitation to bring out the truth. This theory explains all the speeding up and slowing down as well as the in-and-out motion as a consequence of the straightest line through curved spacetime.

At odds with Newtonian gravitation, Einstein's general theory of relativity shows that any satellite that possesses angular momentum (e.g., Earth) will never crash into the centre of gravitational attraction (in the case of Earth, our Sun). This can be explained by the *'energy hill'*. In Newtonian language, there are two energy demands made by planetary motion — the energy to climb out of the Schwarzschild radial coordinate against the pull of gravity, and the transverse motion kinetic energy required for maintaining the angular momentum.

Put simply, the energy hill shows that planetary motion makes planets unable to fall into the centre of gravitational attraction (e.g., the Sun) and unable to break free from orbit. As a planet orbits a sun, always in the same direction, it is fastest when close in and slowest when far out. The in-and-out motion is forever reversing. This change in Schwarzschild radial coordinate goes fastest in midcourse and slows when nearing the outer and inner extremes of the values of the Schwarzschild radial coordinates of the orbit, as if the planet were climbing a hill — an energy hill. These features follow from the simple principle that a free-float object makes its way through curved spacetime along the straightest worldline possible.

When Kepler derived his three laws of planetary motion in the 1600s, little was he to know that he was describing the very effects that are explained by Einstein's general theory of relativity.

v) Universal Conditions

Time flows in one direction from the past to the future. Yet there is nothing in Newtonian physics that prevents the reverse from happening — backwards is as good as forwards. It was not until the 1990s that the physicists Kip Thorne and Stephen Hawking showed that any form of time machine that could be made would be forbidden by the laws of physics. A circulating beam of what are called *vacuum fluctuations* would destroy any time machine at the moment of construction. Thus, time travel is impossible.

The *second law of thermodynamics* states that the entropy of a system increases with time. It also states that heat does not flow spontaneously from cold to hot objects, and that it is impossible for an engine that converts heat to work with 100% efficiency. Entropy is basically a measure of disorder of the system. Every action and event is associated with an increase in entropy. Travelling back in time moves to a point of less entropy, but as any action increases entropy, any form of time travel would therefore violate the second law of thermodynamics.

The moment of least entropy was immediately after the Big Bang. Does this mean that if the fate of the Universe is a Big Crunch, then there will be a conversion from maximum entropy (resulting from all universal processes preceding the Big Bang) to a singularity of minimal entropy, where a newly formed Universe with increasing entropy unfolds? Penrose believes not and believes that the Big Crunch model is wrong.

Clearly, there is debate as to whether the Big Crunch will occur at all. Some consider that the Universe will expand forever, others imagine that it will contract into a Big Crunch, while some believe that it will reach a point of equilibrium. General relativity states that the shape of the Universe (curvature of space) is determined by the amount of matter in it. The fate also depends to some extent on the amount of matter in the Universe. Currently, there appears to be too little to close the geometry and result in the Big Crunch. If there is enough matter in the Universe, then the gravitational attraction between particles will draw them together, counteracting the force from the Big Bang. If there isn't, then it will go on expanding.

Current research is trying to calculate the amount of matter in the observable Universe to resolve this point of contention. This calculation is difficult because much of the matter is *dark* and could constitute a large percentage of all universal matter. *Dark matter* describes random particles in particular regions of space which, when added together (considering the vastness of the Universe), is of fundamental importance for calculating the total amount and for trying to attain a correct conclusion for the Universe's fate. Dark matter is hypothetical — it neither emits nor reflects light — but is considered real due to its gravitational effects on visible matter.

There is an interesting story concerning our knowledge of the Universe's expansion. In 1917, the Dutch astronomer Willem de Sitter proposed a cosmological model of Einstein's general theory of relativity suggesting that the Universe is expanding. Later, in 1922, the Russian mathematician Aleksandr Friedmann (also called Friedman) proposed that it is either expanding or contracting, but it is not static. Einstein rejected both ideas, but since they were consistent with general relativity, he introduced what was known as the *cosmological constant* to counteract the expansion and collapse effects predicted by general relativity. Later, after Hubble's experimental proof in 1929 of the expansion of the Universe, he recanted this constant (the vacuum energy), claiming it to be the 'greatest blunder' of his career.

So, the Universe may expand to a point of stasis, continue expanding, or end up at the Big Crunch. The three key Friedman models of the Universe's expansion are that it will expand and then contract (at a Big Crunch) or expand indefinitely (with two versions of this outcome). Each version begins with the Big Bang, which is valid both because as the Universe is expanding now, it must have been doing so since its point of origin (the Big Bang) and because the measured microwave background of the Universe is evidence of an infinitely hot, dense, and distant past.

In each Friedman model, the Universe looks the same in all directions for any observer in any place. However, the nature of its structure and what the Universe's fate is differs between them. We know that the Universe is not totally uniform. Solar systems are grouped as galaxies and galaxies as superclusters, for example. Thus, as the Universe evolves, the irregularities of matter congregate into stars, galaxies, and black holes over time, and this is due to gravitational effects. How do the three Friedman models accommodate these structures?

For a closed Universe that terminates in the Big Crunch, the structures that develop during the Universe's life, such as stars and black holes, finally come together as a singularity from a point of maximum entropy. This model displays, at its end, none of the initial uniformity that was resultant from the Big Bang. The low entropy beginning terminates in maximal entropy, which does not happen in the other Friedman models.

For the indefinite expansion Friedman model, there are two versions. Some believe that the expansion is Euclidian in nature. In Euclidean (flat) geometry, the angles of a triangle add up to 180°. In Euclidean space, Euclid's fifth postulate — no straight line can cross another straight line more than once — is true. If space is flat (Euclidian), then the apparent uniformity of the Universe is described by a rapid inflationary phase of expansion from the minimal entropy immediately after the Big Bang followed by a slower expansion. However, Penrose believes that this model of expansion will not lead to the level of uniformity we see in the Universe.

He thinks that it constitutes the wrong type of geometry and considers the nature of the expansion to be *hyperbolic* (or Lobachevskian, after the Russian mathematician Nikolai Lobachevsky who first worked on this type of geometry). Penrose believes that the Universe is an open, hyperbolic one. This view is the second model of indefinite expansion.

In Lobachevskian space, Euclid's fifth postulate can be violated; therefore, it is non-Euclidean. This space, whose geometry corresponds to what the Lorentz contraction achieves for special relativity, can be represented by drawing a triangle on a piece of paper and then fitting it inside a bowl. Here, the angles of the triangle do not add up to 180°. Some of the Dutch graphic artist M. C. Escher's etchings (e.g., *Circle Limit (IV)* shown in Figure 7) provide a 2-D (Euclidean) visual representation of what Lobachevskian space looks like.

However, although Penrose believes that the Universe is hyperbolic in nature, he admits that we do not have a complete description. To have

Figure 7. Circle limit (IV) — M.C. Escher (1960).

produced a Universe resembling the one in which we live, a 'creator' would have had to aim for a volume of 'phase' (multidimensional) space 1 in 10 to the power 10 to the power 123 of the entire volume for the location of the Big Bang event. Such is its unlikelihood.

Penrose thinks that we need a form of physics that unites the quantum and classical worlds in order to generate a theory of the Big Bang, probably based on the hyperbolic symmetry, that describes the Universe as we see it. This includes the black holes, their near homogeneity, and their fate. The explanation of the form of the Universe should flow from the theory naturally such that we do not have to rely on the unlikelihood of the precise location for the Big Bang event. As I discuss further in Chapter 6, this physics will also, according to Penrose, describe the functioning of the human brain.

If the Big Bang had been different, the Universe would be different now and perhaps nothing conscious could have evolved in it to ask questions of its origin. If this is the *only* Universe and it possesses the only initial conditions that could result in life, then that *might* support a role for a creator in the Big Bang. However, different initial conditions could have resulted in different life. Furthermore, if this is just one of infinite universes, each with different conditions, then this one just happens to be one where sentient life of a form that can ask such questions evolved. The role for a creator here is less apparent.

As the Universe had to naturally evolve *a* form, why is it *this* particular form? Our minds, finite in form and imagination, understand the Universe in ways that make conceptual sense to us. However, the *actual* solution may require knowledge that lies beyond our comprehension. We are back in the territory of Plato's truths. The British physicist Brandon Carter introduced the *anthropic* principle, which proposes that the Universe must be compatible in terms of age, particles, forces, and constants with the conscious life that observes it.

The weak anthropic principle states that the observed values of all physical and cosmological quantities are not equally probable but have values restricted by the requirements that there are sites where carbon-based life can have evolved and that the Universe is old enough for this to have happened. The strong anthropic principle, proposed by Carter, states that the Universe must have properties that allow life to evolve in it at some stage. This implies the possibility of an ensemble of different possible universes, and that we exist in one that contains the permutation of properties that enable life as we know it to evolve.

The *many worlds* hypothesis, named by American physicist Bryce DeWitt (1923–2004) and also of Hugh Everett (1930–1982) and Wheeler, states that the observable Universe is just one of billions of universes. The parallel universes envisaged by this theory resolve many of the problems of quantum theory while opening up new ones. This hypothesis uses the existence of other universes to explain ours. Arguments against this hypothesis are many, though the most basic one can be reduced to this — it adds more variables (more universes) than is absolutely necessary to explain what *is*. The Universe may be explainable in terms of what is present (Occam's, or Ockham's, razor — attributed to the 14th century Franciscan Friar, William of Ockham — is a principle stating that explanations of any phenomena should make as few assumptions as possible).

If we reject the many worlds hypothesis to explain our own Universe, then how can we explain life, the velocity of light, and all the phenomena and physical laws that apply here? This Universe had to contain something, so why not life? The velocity of light had to be some velocity, so why not 186,000 miles per second? Each physical constant had to be such and such, so why not accept that it is what it is? If any of these had been different, either we would not be here or we would have questioned why they are as they are. Each has to be something, so none are remarkable as they are what they are according to the reality that *is*. The question of life is somewhat harder to accept on these grounds. Yet under these conditions, which permitted the *possibility* for life as we know it, time and random events here on Earth turned possibility into reality.

If we were somehow able to rerun the Universe from the Big Bang to the present day, would things have turned out differently? This type of question is deeply connected with determinism and, by extrapolation, concepts such as free will. We will discuss these further and in Chapters 6 and 7. Suffice to say, if the unfolding of the Universe is not intrinsically predetermined as a function of the interaction of force and matter over time, then how likely is sentient life? Is our existence not only unlikely in space and time but also within the context of the conditions in which it has come to exist?

There could be different levels of sentience or life somewhere else in the Universe, from omnipotence to organisms that we consider as borderline life, like some viruses which are merely amalgams of genetic material and protein. Life may exist in a form that we cannot even comprehend, it being so different from the framework in which we judge things to be living or not.

Sentient life is important to us because, through awareness of the size of the Universe and our own fragility, confirmation of its existence elsewhere would appease both our sense of curiosity and loneliness. Perhaps we overestimate the importance of sentient life over other aspects of reality because we believe that only material life with sentience has the capacity to ask questions, care, feel, and so on (as we do). To belong to a category that possesses qualities that transcend their material construction and to be able to recognise the importance of such qualities gives 'meaning' to things. Other categories of reality merely 'are'.

Although the discovery of simple life elsewhere would be of great significance, to find beings that possess qualities that we regard as consistent with higher-order consciousness (e.g., 'value') would be the greatest reward. From this perspective, we consider ourselves different from simple life in the same way that simple life is regarded as different from inanimate matter. However, despite the fabric of reality and our lifespan, which limits our possibility to communicate over great distances, there is no reason why one would understand another intelligence even if it was there. We consider life and sentience based on own personal experience of it. Life may also exist (or have existed) in ways that we do not understand and can never comprehend. Intelligent life forms we are, but maybe just *a* form, not an example of *the* form. There are other possibilities (e.g., antimatter, exotic particles, pure energy).

I believe the question of life and its reasons cannot be answered satisfactorily based upon the knowledge that we presently have or may never have. Intuition steers me to believe that we are a chance event. Simple life is likely to be a consequence of chemical processes under the right conditions operating over enormous periods of time. But *intelligent* life represents such a degree of complexity that it may well be a chance event and, if evolution (like the Universe itself) were rerun, we may not have evolved at all.

What preceded the first Big Bang? Was there a 'first'? Perhaps the answers to these and similar questions are unanswerable or lie beyond human intellectual capabilities. Certainly, if understandable, they would require principles alien to everyday existence. Indeed, much of physics uses mathematical language to describe the physical reality it *can* make sense of, yet this is either incomprehensible to those not initiated in its minutiae or distorted when reduced to the formal language we use in conversation (just like the conversion of thought to language).

Mathematical descriptions of reality impose seven or more dimensions than we can mentally conceptualise in order to make reality make sense. But when 'understanding' extends beyond what makes sense to the mind to that which makes sense only within the confines of a complex, abstract model, then regardless whether this model is consistent with the facts, if it cannot be conceived, we have fallen short of our goal of making it comprehensible. Some things can be comprehended, some cannot. In between is the murky world of theorising and modelling. History and scientific method will reveal the unknown boundaries, the fine line between nonsense and deep insight.

Martin Rees

Martin Rees (born 1942) is a British astrophysicist and former President of the Royal Society who has held the title of Astronomer Royal since 1995. He is a proponent of the Search for Extra-Terrestrial Intelligence (SETI), although he believes that the chance of finding evidence of other sentient life in the Universe is small. Rees describes six key numbers that relate to the fundamental conditions of the Universe we live in and how these have enabled the possibility for life to even have had a chance to evolve.

These numbers demonstrate how finely balanced the existence of the observable Universe really is. Locked within these numbers are the laws and conditions that govern the observable Universe. They determine such matters as "why structures exist as they do", "the permanence of physical matter", and "how our existence is possible". The numbers integrate physical constants applicable to the observable Universe with consequences of the reality in the observable Universe that they shape. Basically, the numbers are:

1. λ (Cosmic repulsion) — this represents cosmic antigravity or *dark energy*. It does not fit current models of reality (which means that current models are wrong). It permeates all of space and accounts for 68.3% of the total mass-energy of the Universe. Indeed, ordinary matter comprises only 4.9% of the energy of the Universe (with dark matter responsible for the other 26.8%). One form of dark energy is the cosmological constant, which is equivalent to the *vacuum energy*. This is a repulsive effect that occurs over distances greater than a billion light years.

    The value is very small and is as yet unknown. Cosmic antigravity is a recent finding following the observation that although gravitational effects are, in effect, non-detectable at small distances (gravitation is the weakest force and only exerts its attractive effect over large distances such as between planets and their moons), over even greater distances the effects reverse and an antigravity effect is seen. This is why distant objects have recently been calculated to be receding faster than we had originally anticipated. Edwin Hubble observed and measured recession rates for relatively close objects. Those that are over several billion light years away from us or any other object recede faster than anticipated by application of gravitational effects alone. Thus, as there is a short distance between matter (atomic scale), then strong and weak nuclear forces as well as electromagnetism are the forces that apply here. At great distances, gravitational attraction is the dominant force.

    At huge distances, gravity is reversed and matter repels. In the early Universe (before 10^{-43} s after the Big Bang), the fundamental forces were all the same strength and were different aspects of a single unified force. They then divided after expansion and assumed their current strengths. At one Planck time, 10^{-43} s, gravity separated from the other forces. At about 10^{-36} s, the strong force separated from the electroweak and, later, around 10^{-12} s, the electroweak separated into the weak and electromagnetic forces.

2. Ω (Ratio of actual to critical density of matter in the Universe) — this represents the amount of material in the Universe. It has been calculated that if we were to average out all the matter in the Universe, there would be only 0.2 atoms in a cubic metre of space (equivalent to a grain of sand held in the volume occupied by the Earth). This value compensates

for regions of zero density (space) and regions of variably high density (e.g., stars and planets). The actual density of 0.2 atoms per cubic metre of space divided by the critical density of five atoms per cubic metre of space (which is the value calculated to bring cosmic expansion to a halt) gives a value of $\Omega = 0.04$. This number determines the fate of the Universe — whether it will expand, shrink, or reach equilibrium. It relates to the search for dark matter (or latent energy in space), which will help us to calculate the observable Universe's destiny.

It is thought that 95.2% of the Universe's mass is dark matter and dark or vacuum energy (26.8% and 68.3%, respectively), even though we do not know what they are. There are detectors in deep mines to determine what dark matter is. We know that it exists since it responds to gravity, and without it spiralling, galaxies would fly apart if this additional mass did not exist.

Additionally, it does not respond to electromagnetism. Dark energy, like dark matter, is hypothetical, but it is a component of the *Standard Model* of physics (see later) and is used to explain the rate of the Universe's expansion.

3. **N** (Gravitational ratio) — this is the relationship between electrical repulsion and gravitational attraction within an atom. The value is approximately 1×10^{36} (in favour of electrical repulsion, of course). If it was different, atoms would not retain their stability and we would not be here. If the ratio were ten powers of ten less, the Sun would last for only a year rather than ten billion years. It should be stated that nuclear stability is really measured as the ratio of the strong force (rather than gravity) to the electromagnetic force as well as the neutron/proton ratio and the total number of nucleons in the nucleus.

4. **Q** (Ratio of gravitational binding force to rest-mass energy) — this number relates to the amount of energy required to break up matter divided by its rest-mass energy (mc^2). Its value is approximately 10^{-5}. The value of Q determines the stability of the Universe. If Q were smaller, the Universe would be inert; higher and it would be violent and dominated by black holes.

5. ε (Nuclear fusion efficiency) — this number determines the firmness of atomic binding and it is valued at 0.007. With stellar fusion, where hydrogen is converted into helium by the fusion of hydrogen molecules under conditions of high temperature and pressure, 0.007 of the rest mass is converted to energy. This is very efficient compared to what we can achieve artificially in nuclear reactors on Earth, and it enables the Sun to burn for the length of time that it has (and will). If the number was different, then the Sun would not have provided the thermal conditions on Earth and stability that were necessary for the processes of evolution to have occurred, processes that we know have taken billions of years for the development of species such as man.
6. **D** (Spatial dimensions) — this is the number of dimensions we exist in and it is valued at three. Time gives four, but has direction — future, not past. There would be no life with two or four dimensions. The GUTs (and TOE) impart multiple dimensions on reality, but they are embedded.

With these numbers, constants, and ratios in mind, it is easy to see that our existence is the result of a finely tuned system and that the presence and possibility for life seems unlikely. This does not imply an anthropological or creator-dependent view for the actuality of existence. What we can say is that if the conditions were not right for us to have evolved, we would not be here to discuss it. The physical conditions of the Universe have enabled life to form, and yet, as we will see in Chapter 5, even with the development of life on Earth, there was much chance involved in our actual evolution. Replay the tape of the Universe and perhaps the conditions would turn out the same for our universal physical environment, but the conditions for human life might not have been the same.

Physics may fail to develop a TOE because it may fail to model a reality that is governed from the Big Bang and external influences (like other universes) — the rules are always changing. In the next section, we will analyse the likelihood for a Universe that enables life and how the multiverse concept relates to this issue as well as the observable Universe's fate.

Our Cosmic Habitat

Our Cosmic Habitat by Rees (2001) describes how unlikely the conditions are that enable the possibility for life such as that which exists on Earth, unless one accepts the possibility that we exist in one of an incalculable number of universes (multiverse). Here, the observable Universe is part of an ensemble of universes, or a *multiverse*, where most others do not present the conditions that enable the generation of life. Thus, the laws of physics are only bylaws applicable to the observable Universe, imposed after our Big Bang.

As Rees implies, if the multiverse concept is right, then in an infinite ensemble of universes, the existence of universes 'seemingly' fine-tuned for life would occasion no surprise — our particular cosmic habitat would just belong to this subset that does present the possibility for the generation of life. This idea explains why *all* the laws that appear to be biophilic (i.e., attractive for the generation of life) are as such — we have evolved in one of the few universes where they happen to be so, and because of this. It does not follow that intelligent life will inevitably evolve in a Universe that can support life. Chance, of course, plays *its* role.

Other life

As we are proof that the observable Universe supports life, and intelligent life at that, why haven't we obtained any proof of its existence elsewhere? The search for simple biological life is limited to our primitive means of transport, which is localised to within our solar system. Probes landing on Mars or on a passing comet can conduct simple chemical tests and transmit the information back to us on Earth — assuming they land successfully, that is, as we have seen with the failure of the Beagle 2 and the Schiaparelli Mars landers.

We have sent messages into space to contact intelligent life. Conversely, aliens may have done so too. The vastness of space and the limitations for contact with intelligent life due to the velocity of light would render communication a very slow process. The nuclear-powered Voyager 2 probe launched by NASA in 1977, for example, has only recently left the solar system. Maybe we have missed any alien signals, having evolved to a level where we can listen for and understand them only too late. Perhaps the messages are there, but we are unable to detect them and distinguish intelligent, extraterrestrial information from background noise. It is possible that we simply are not technologically advanced enough to be capable of understanding an extraterrestrial signal.

Some stars formed five billion years before our Sun did. Bearing in mind our own rapid technological development in the past hundred years, any alien civilisation developing on planets around those stars would certainly have had a head start on us. However, planets could not have formed until galactic oxygen and silicon built up to a certain minimum threshold level. Yet, this still gives other potential civilisations two billion years of a head start on us.

Despite this, we cannot compare that time scale to that of our recent development in the past hundred years. The time taken on Earth for simple *eukaryotic* cells (from which we evolved) to develop from *prokaryotic* cells (even simpler cells, including bacteria) was probably at least one billion years, if not two. So, it is possible that on some planet in a solar system with a two billion year head start on us, the evolutionary course to intelligence is halted at a similar hurdle. If Earth is an example of what is necessary for intelligent life to evolve, not only do the Universe and local galactic conditions have to be ideal but also, within that context, the ideal ingredients for such life must let time and chance reveal whether the result is indeed intelligent.

The *Drake equation* enables us to calculate the probability for life existing or having evolved elsewhere. Since it is constructed entirely from variables that correlate to all conceivable aspects that affect the generation of life, it is not possible to calculate with certainty whether life evolved elsewhere. Depending on how optimistic or pessimistic one is, the answer can be anything you want (from definitely 'no' to definitely 'yes'). The definition and explanation of the terms for the Drake equation are:

$$N = R^* \times fp \times ne \times fl \times fi \times fc \times L$$

Key:

N = number of communicative civilisations (i.e., civilisations in the Milky Way whose radio emissions are detectable).

$R*$ = rate of formation of suitable stars (i.e., stars with a large enough 'habitable zone' and long enough lifetime to be suitable for the development of intelligent life).

f_p = the fraction of those stars with planets (the fraction of Sun-like stars with planets is currently unknown, but evidence indicates that planetary systems may be common for stars like the Sun).

n_e = the number of 'Earths' per planetary system (all stars have a habitable zone where a planet would be able to maintain a temperature that allows for liquid water to form. A planet in the habitable zone could have the basic conditions for life as we know it).

f_l = the fraction of those planets where life develops (although a planet may orbit in the habitable zone of a suitable star, other factors are necessary for life to arise. Thus, only a fraction of suitable planets will actually develop life).

f_i = the fraction of life sites where intelligence develops (life on Earth began over 3.5 billion years ago, so intelligence took a long time to develop. On other life-bearing planets it may happen faster, it may take longer, or it may not develop at all).

f_c = the fraction of planets where technology develops (i.e., the fraction of planets with intelligent life that develop technological civilisations, i.e., technology that releases detectable signs of their existence into space).

L = The 'lifetime' of communicating civilisations (i.e., the length of time such civilisations release detectable signals into space).

Although we have not detected alien life, absence of evidence is not evidence of absence. However, the only type of intelligence we can detect would be one that led to a technology that we can recognise. We are limited in our search because we are constrained by what we can understand. This limitation brings to mind the American logician Douglas Hofstadter's comments about intelligence and AI — our comprehension is limited by the speed of the processes we use to apply intelligence. Despite the extension to perception enabled by technology, we are limited to a tiny fraction of what reality is and, thus, what other intelligences might have access to.

Fate of the Universe and multiverse

What is the observable Universe's fate and how does the multiverse concept fit in? As mentioned, the fate of the observable Universe is either contraction, expansion, or stasis. It depends on the amount of matter in the Universe and its effect on the battle between gravitation and expansion (and cosmic antigravity).

Let us look at the progression of events from the Big Bang to where we are now, as well as to where this might take us. To start with, we must get an idea of the temperatures and densities after the Big Bang event. Even after hundreds of thousands of years of expansion following the Big Bang, the Universe's average temperature was hotter than the surface of the Sun. We know that much of what was expelled from the Big Bang formed the particles that later formed the structures that exist in the Universe.

However, dark matter also exists which does not form structures, yet is present in such quantities (estimated to be roughly a quarter of the mass and energy of the observable Universe) that it enables galaxies to maintain their form. These chargeless particles constitute a greater quantity of matter and hence gravitational influence than all of the ordinary matter constituting stars, planets, and cosmic matter combined. Attempts have been made to find out what dark matter is, but it has not been definitively detected yet. As the Universe expanded, some regions consisted of a greater density of matter than others, resulting in a stronger influence of gravitational attraction. From this, gravitationally bound systems (i.e., galaxies) formed. This is proof that the Big Bang-determined beginning of the Universe was not uniform, since this gravitational effect could not have occurred if it was.

The inference from what the ratio Ω represents is that the density of the Universe is less than that required to bring the expansion to a halt. If all of the matter in the Universe that we are aware of (e.g., stars, planets, comets and interstellar dust) was dispersed evenly throughout space, including an equal quantity of diffuse intergalactic gas that is considered present, then the density would still be 25 times less than that required to bring expansion to a halt — the actual/critical density ratio would have to be greater than 1. However, this does not mean that eternal expansion is the definite fate of the Universe. The undetectable dark matter plays an important role in the fate.

Galaxies would not maintain their structure unless there was up to ten times more matter than is observable and this matter is thought to be dark matter. But if ordinary atoms constitute only 4% of the critical density and dark matter a further 22%, we are still 74% short of the quantity of matter required to halt the expansion.

The dark (vacuum) energy is the reason why the Universe is so big — it drove the *inflationary phase* of our Universe's early expansion. This exponential expansion continued until the rate we observe now (with 10^{120} less magnitude). Here, some of the dark energy was converted to ordinary energy, enabling the formation of gravitationally driven structures.

So, the Universe started expanding in an inflationary way and then slowed to how we see it now, with additional rapid expansion over large distances due to cosmic antigravity. The dark energy present in space reinforces the deduction that cosmic repulsion should be much greater than it is. Early in the Universe's life, the repulsion was as fierce as predicted by λ, but it is not known why this energy that drove the rapid expansion is now so weak. Dark energy plays no part in galaxy and star formation, but if it can account for the mass-energy that brings the ratio of actual density to critical density to 1, then accounting for this 74% of mass-energy contributing to gravitational effects will render the geometry of the Universe flat (where the relation between distance and angles is Euclidean).

Recent results, including data from the European Space Agency's Planck observatory platform which measured, among other things, the cosmic microwave background, indeed appear to confirm that the Universe is flat.

Ultimately, for the fate of the Universe, we need to know what happened in its formative moments. This is from when it was 10^{-44} seconds old. We know that before this time, the energy was in the form of a black hole. The specificity of this time scale is determined by the rules of quantum physics and the uncertainty principle (see next chapter). The smallest length possible that will not implode into an inaccessible reality according to quantum physics is known as the Planck length (10^{-33} cm). When this length is divided by the velocity of light, it gives us the Planck time (10^{-44}

seconds). Thus, the moment from the Big Bang to when the Universe was 10^{-44} seconds old is unknowable, but from this moment to when it was 10^{-36} seconds old, some of the important formative processes of the Universe occurred. A lot happened during this one hundred million-fold ageing of the Universe. Here, the Universe underwent accelerative expansion, particle formation, and cooling.

Later in this book, I will discuss the conditions on Earth that have enabled life to evolve and how this relates to the conditions presented to Earth in this Universe. How does this relate to the multiverse concept? Our existence ultimately depends on conditions encoded in the Big Bang which enabled the Universe to:

be large enough with respect to its constituent particles;

be long-lived enough compared to atomic processes;

have gravity effective at the ideal level of force, with cosmic repulsion at a sufficiently low level;

have the relative strength of the fundamental forces to each other to be at the 'ideal' level.

Together, these conditions enabled the generation of life as we know it. So, assuming that the multiverse concept is true, let us consider whether the possibility for life here is genuinely unlikely or not. There are different 'credibility horizons', as Rees puts it, for different aspects of reality and whether we can address them satisfactorily. First, there is the limit reachable by our telescopes. A more real limit is that reachable by light emitted since the moment of our Big Bang (the Hubble radius). Zero mass photons (and possibly neutrinos, if they are shown to have zero mass) move at the velocity of light, but matter in the form of galaxies is receding from us and other galaxies at below the velocity of light. However, beyond this 'real' limit, there are regions that are never observable from our own dimension. If the cosmic expansion is accelerating, these regions are becoming more distant. Such regions are beyond our horizons of accessibility according to the laws of relativity.

There is another level — universes beyond our dimension known as *disjoint* universes. Galaxies in these universes would not have evolved from the same Big Bang as us. Such explanations bring the idea of multiverses into play. It has been predicted that such universes sprout out of Big Bangs into disjoint regions of spacetime.

Rees believes that if the underlying laws governing the multiverse allow for variability among universes, then we are living in one of a particular type. Why should we really consider ours to be the only one? If we agree that the multiverse concept is possible and that we live in one of an infinite number of possible universes (some habitable, some not), it is no longer surprising that we just happen to live in one of the habitable ones. The number λ is important here because a small λ is required for the possibility of life. An accurate measurement of λ would have some bearing on the credibility of the multiverse concept. It is possible that there are only a few universes where λ is below the threshold that allows galaxies to form. But if the observable Universe is one from a multiverse ensemble where λ can take any value, we would expect ours to not be too far below the threshold value of λ that allows them to form.

If the Universe is accelerating as it is predicted to be, then λ is only up to ten times below this value. Thus, as we are only in the tenth to 20th percentile of universes where galaxies can form, the observable Universe is no more special, with respect to λ, than our emergence demanded. It would be extraordinary if our minds were matched to all aspects of the external world. Thus, some of nature may never be explainable or understood. Indeed, what we *do* understand about reality is knowledge founded on indeterminism at the lowest level. Nature presents limits to how much we can know of it at the fundamental level.

Multiverse modelling

The multiverse is a hypothetical set of multiple possible universes. There are many different types of multiverse described, each including the Universe we experience, which comprises all space, time, matter, energy, and physical laws that exist within our cosmological horizon (a potentially causal connection with us). Recent findings of inconsistencies in dark matter radiation across the Universe have been proposed as evidence of other universes. That is, they are exerting their effect on ours from outside.

Swedish-born cosmologist Max Tegmark has constructed a multiverse classification system depending on the nature and structure of each Universe within the multiverse model and how the Universe in that multiverse relates:

> **Level I** — beyond our cosmological horizon. These universes exist beyond where light from those objects has had time to reach us since the beginning of the cosmological expansion. Although these will contain variations of physical laws and distribution of matter, they will ultimately contain some universes with the same configuration as ours.
> **Level II** — 'Bubble' universes with different physical constants from our own. Our Universe is just one of the bubbles. If one considers the multiverse as a whole, as it expands *ad infinitum*, some spatial regions stop and form bubbles. These various regions experience different spontaneous symmetry-breaking, resulting in different universal properties.
> **Level III** — many worlds interpretation of quantum mechanics (as proposed by the American physicist Hugh Everett III). Here, possible observations correspond to a different Universe.
> **Level IV** — Tegmark's own 'Ultimate Ensemble' hypothesis where most universes describable by different mathematical structures are considered equally real.

There are other interpretations as well:

> **Cyclic theories** — these describe a series of infinite, self-sustaining cycles (like the cycling of Big Bang-Big Crunches).
> **M-theory** — this is a multiverse describable in terms of *string theory*. String theory is ambitious in scope since it attempts to link the Standard Model with gravity under the framework of fundamental strings. It is essentially an attempt at a 'Theory of Everything'. In this theory, the so-called 'fundamental' particles of the Standard Model are really just manifestations of one basic object — a string. Strings are extended one-dimensional objects rather than point particles with no dimensions, such as electrons or *elementary particles*. Whereas an electron is considered a point with no internal structure, if it were actually a loop of string, then this opens up possibilities as to how it moves or oscillates. The type of oscillation of such a fundamental 'thing' determines whether what

we observe is the string manifestation of an electron, photon, quark, or other particle.

Mathematically, string theory can provide convincing support for itself, yet there is no direct experimental evidence that it is a valid description of Nature despite continuous modifications and variants (described in more detail in Chapter 3). In M-theory, universes are formed by collisions between so-called 'p-branes' in multidimensional space. The universes in the M-theory multiverse take the form of a 'D-brane' where D stands for dimension — that is, they consist of strings and membranes (D-branes). These multidimensional surfaces move through the eleven dimensions of M-theory. D-branes exist up to nine spatial dimensions. A point is a D0-brane, a string is a D1-brane, a sheet is a D2-brane, and so on. A D2-brane wrapped around another dimension looks like a cylinder, and this D-brane can appear to be a one-dimensional string moving in ten dimensions. So, 11-dimensional M-theory is like 10-dimensional string theory. Matter within each Universe is confined to its D-brane, but can interact with other universes via gravity since this force is not restricted to D-branes.

Anthropic principle — as mentioned earlier, the anthropic principle is an idea that the Universe must be compatible in terms of its age, particles, forces, and constants with the conscious life that observes it. As such, the Universe as it is becomes no surprise. These are different 'strengths' of the anthropic principle depending on the level of force of argument for anthropocentric reasoning.

To define the weak anthropic principle, physicists John Barrow and Frank Tipler propose that "the observed values of all physical and cosmological quantities are not equally probable, but they take on values restricted by the requirement that there exist sites where carbon-based life can evolve, and by the requirements that the Universe be old enough for it to have already done so". For the strong anthropic principle, they state that "the Universe must have those properties which allow life to develop within it at some stage in its history".

One can imagine a single, finite, or even infinite (conceptually at least) Universe, but what about a multiverse where other universes coexist with ours, but which are so distant in space from ours that they cannot communicate with ours and have different laws of physics? Further models of the Universe have been proposed. When there are no means to physically test the theory and the limit is mathematical and physical hypothesizing, many complex and bizarre models are thrown into the arena. A 'simulated universe', such as the one depicted in the *Matrix* movies, is unlikely. John Barrow and the physicist David Deutsch believe that if we lived in such a Universe, the simulation would reveal itself as glitches in the laws of physics. John Gribbin is a proponent of the 'Designer' Universe theory, which is a Universe that could have been made deliberately by members of an advanced civilisation in another part of the multiverse, but which has been left to run uninterrupted after the Big Bang. New universes could be manufactured from black holes within universes.

Earlier in this part, I referred to classical physics as the physics of the late 19th century with its origins in the work of Newton and Maxwell. It is a physics dominated by forces acting over large distances. We must now turn our attention to physics that is very much 20th century in origin and whose focus is at the very smallest level — the world of quantum physics.

3 The Quantum World

There is no doubt that quantum theory is one of humankind's greatest intellectual achievements. But before we move from the world of classical physics to the development of quantum theory, we should bear in mind the fundamental assumptions of the classical physics that preceded it and why it seemed to reflect reality. In most applications of classical mechanics at the macroscopic level, the speed of light is so large that relativistic effects are negligible. Similarly, the quantum of action at the microscopic level can also be disregarded because it is so small. However, all that occurs at the macroscopic level obeys relativity and quantum theory. As such, classical mechanics 'approximates' reality and seems to work only because the velocity of light is so great and the quantum of action is so small.

When people talk of making a *quantum* leap, they are implying an extraordinarily large leap, but this is actually a total misunderstanding of the term. 'Quanta' refers to packets of energy and a 'quantum' of energy is the smallest possible packet of energy. Max Planck, the father of quantum theory, realised early in the 20th century that energy was related to the frequency of radiation, and from this the concept the term 'quanta' arose. There is a minimal finite amount of energy (a quantum) which relates to its frequency by a factor that Planck introduced, h, which is now known as *Planck's constant* and relates the energy of all radiation to its frequency. Its value is very small: 6.63×10^{-34} Joule seconds (Js^{-1}) — no smaller number exists when relating energy to the frequency of its radiating source.

Physicists talk of Planck length (10^{-43} metres) and Planck time (10^{-43} seconds) to represent the smallest possible extremes of length and time in the Universe that have any real meaning. Mathematically, smaller numbers of course do occur, but due to the 'packet' nature of quanta, a meaningful lower limit is set. Thus, the term 'quantum' actually refers to the smallest possible difference.

It is not possible to describe quantum theory without the use of terms uncommon to everyday language. Indeed, in our survey of the key breakthroughs in the foundation of our current understanding, we will encounter the *matrix mechanics* of the German physicist Werner Heisenberg, the *wave mechanics* of the Austrian physicist Erwin Schrödinger (1887–1961), the *quantum algebra* of the English mathematician and physicist Paul Dirac (1902–1984), the resultant Copenhagen interpretation, and other subtly diverse constructions that aim to help describe how reality 'is' at a fundamental level.

i) The Worldview Before Quantum Theory

We discussed determinism in the previous chapter, so let us see what scientists thought they were sure about with regards to the material world prior to the development of quantum physics:

1. The Universe was considered to be huge and set in a framework of absolute space and time. Movement within it can be understood as simple movement of the workings of the Universe's constituents, even if they cannot be seen.
2. Newton's laws of mechanics implied that all motion has a cause. The view of cause and effect (i.e., causality) had not been doubted since its formulation.
3. If the motion of an object was known at one point in time, it could be determined at any other point in the past and future. This is determinism — there was no uncertainty.
4. Maxwell's electromagnetic wave theory completely describes the properties of light.
5. There are two models of energy in motion — a particle, represented by an impenetrable sphere, and a wave, such as a wave on the ocean but of a more consistent pattern, such as the shape of a sine wave or

as represented by the oscillatory motion of a skipping rope. Waves and particles are mutually exclusive — energy is either a wave or a particle.
6. It was possible to measure to any level of accuracy any property of a system. Atomic theory was thought to be no exception to this rule.

Strict Newtonian causality states that if the position and velocity of a particle were known at one point in time, it could be calculated at a later point. However, quantum theory implies that whatever instrumentation is available to us, the *exact* position and velocity can never be known simultaneously. In fact, all the statements listed above were thought to be true, but by the time an acceptable formulation of quantum theory (called the Copenhagen interpretation) was presented, all the propositions would be in doubt.

Before we look at the Copenhagen interpretation in more detail, we first need to get to grips with the terminology in the quantum world.

Modern terminology

Quantum theory is another name for quantum physics. It is the study of the relationship between matter and energy at the simplest and most fundamental level of subatomic and elementary particles. Elementary particles are subatomic particles that cannot be subdivided into anything else. They are the constituents from which everything that exists is constructed. They consist of *bosons, mesons,* and *leptons* as well as their constituent antimatter particles. *Antimatter* represents the hypothetical counterpart to matter and consists of anti-particles. These have the same mass but opposite electric or magnetic properties to their corresponding particles. Thus, the hydrogen atom consists of a proton and electron plus its anti-particle constituents, an anti-proton and positron, respectively.

Quantum mechanics is the use of quantum theory to explain the behaviour of subatomic elementary particles. It describes the behaviour of electrons in matter. *Quantum electrodynamics* (QED) was developed to incorporate the theories of quantum mechanics in order to explain the interaction of subatomic particles with electromagnetic radiation. It was developed so that electromagnetism would be consistent with quantum mechanics. Since it treats light as particles and not waves, it compromises a theory of how things happen for the benefit of calculating highly accurate probabilities of what will happen. QED is a relativistic *quantum field theory* (QFT) of electromagnetism. QFT extends quantum mechanics from particles to forces which permeate space and time. The electromagnetic field, like the gravitational field, is a classical (non-quantum) field. Applying quantum mechanics to the electromagnetic field gives rise to the simplest QFT, QED. QFT can reproduce the results of classical physics, but the calculations can contain infinite answers.

QED is so successful in accounting for the electromagnetic interaction that it is considered the best of the QFTs and an archetype for all other new quantum theories that are being developed to explain particle interactions.

Quantum chromodynamics (QCD) is the study of the fundamental nuclear constituents, *quarks*. It is the theory of the strong nuclear interaction, which is a fundamental force describing the interactions of the quarks and particles known as *gluons* within *hadrons*. Quarks are assigned 'colours' and 'flavours' according to laws that govern the formation of subatomic particles. These concepts will be discussed later as we progress through the history of how quantum theory was conceived and developed.

To achieve testable predictions of results from theory, the finite probabilities must be extracted through a process called *renormalisation*. Kenneth Wilson received the Nobel Prize in 1982 for his "theory for critical phenomena in connection with phase transitions", which showed that infinities arising from the application of QFT at infinitely short distances can be discarded. This is not some trickery but a function of correct theory. However, QFT is very complex and produces approximate answers.

Perturbation theory is the process by which calculations are made. QFT, in the form of QED for electromagnetism (the interaction of light and matter) and QCD (describing quarks and the strong force), constitute the Standard Model of physics and are quantum theories that predict nature with high accuracy. However, the fact that the Standard Model is not simple or elegant and fails for gravity means that arriving at a TOE still requires a paradigm shift in thinking. Interestingly, gravity is non-renormalisable. We will come to these later.

The Copenhagen interpretation and beyond

Having seen how we saw the world around 1900 and taken a glimpse at the terminology of modern quantum mechanics, we can look at the work that led to this shift in thinking. Quantum mechanics consists of theories that have proven to be more accurate, when compared to the experimental evidence testing them, than classical theories on Euclidean geometry, Newtonian mechanics, and Maxwell's electrodynamics.

QFT, which incorporates Maxwell's electrodynamics, quantum mechanics, and Einstein's theory of special relativity, is accurate to one part in 10^{11}. When measured in *Dirac units* (named after Paul Dirac), the magnetic moment of the electron is predicted by this theory to be 1.001159652(46), whereas the measurement showed it to be 1.0011596521(93) (the numbers in brackets represent uncertainty). This, however, is still short of the accuracy of Einstein's theory of relativity with Newtonian mechanics incorporated, which has been shown to be accurate to one part in 10^{14}. Despite its accuracy in predicting events, Einstein considered throughout his lifetime that quantum theory was only a preliminary to a true story and that relativity itself was on the correct road to an all-encompassing theory.

It is clear that great advances were made in theoretical physics during the second decade of the 20th century — the New Zealander Ernest Rutherford's discovery of the atomic nucleus, Bohr's discovery of the quantum theory of the atom (he had been the first to realise that β-decay is the process in which electrons are ejected from the nucleus), and Einstein's relativity. However, despite not being unified and united, these works led to highly accurate explanations for different aspects of reality.

What does quantum theory allow us to know about the physical world? It informs us as to why atoms do not collapse and why electrons do not spiral into the nucleus (which they should do according to the classical view). It shows us why atoms produce spectral emission lines, which we observe as defined wavelengths. The chemical forces holding molecules together are quantum mechanical in nature — genetic inheritability depends on quantum mechanics at the level of DNA, as we will see in Chapter 4. *Black-body radiation* is only understandable if the radiation is quantised. Lasers (<u>L</u>ight <u>A</u>mplification by <u>S</u>timulated <u>E</u>missions of <u>R</u>adiation) operate according to the rules of quantum transitions between quantum mechanical states of molecules. Superconductors allow electrical currents to flow indefinitely due to the absence of electrical resistance. These phenomena occur in metals and alloys at very low temperatures and are associated with long-range quantum correlations between electrons.

These are just some of the processes that quantum effects determine. What is extraordinary about quantum mechanics is that it enables us to test whether something might have happened but actually did not. This is called 'testing counterfactuals'. Quantum mechanics allows real effects to occur from counterfactuals. Quantum 'counterfactual definiteness' means that one can speak meaningfully about results of measurements (e.g., properties of objects) that were not actually performed. It is of particular relevance to quantum entanglement because measuring one entangled particle allows properties of the other to be known without anything being done to determine it directly.

The problem with the perception of quantum theory is that it represents one world, and observation of this world by magnifying it to the classical level changes the rules by which it operates. The process of converting a small-scale, indeterminate quantum event to something that can be seen as 'real' is called the 'collapse of the wavefunction' or 'reduction of the state vector'. Mathematically, an event becomes a calculated probability.

Like all elementary particles, electrons possess an intrinsic property called *spin*. Electrons are fermions, which are particles that make up ordinary matter, and have a spin of $+1/2$ or $-1/2$. That is, they must rotate 720° before returning to the original orientation. When an electron is measured in a detector and is detected and described as spin *up*, its wavefunction is spin *up* and the spin *down* component is gone. This is an example of collapse of the wavefunction. Upon measurement, the *superposition* of all possible states no longer exists. The probability of all states in a quantum sense becomes real and actual in a physical, classical sense. When measured, the wavefunction collapses onto a particular reality called the *Eigenstate*.

Quantum mechanics itself is not indeterministic if one remains at the quantum level. Only when we, the observer of the quantum system, make a measurement of it by collapsing the wavefunction describing it, do we render it indeterminate. This magnification to the 'real', classical level is at the cost of imposed limitations on what we can know of it. Thus, the world viewed classically is determinate.

The world at the quantum level is also determinate. The indeterminacy arises when knowledge of this quantum world is revealed to us. As such, Roger Penrose believes that there is something missing in our view of classical and quantum physics. By this he means that a correct view of the world should be incorporated in a single theory that allows for all phenomena — those on the subatomic as well as the large, universal scale.

Quantum theory, as it stands, does not work for large-scale processes because in that context gravity is the dominant force, as I outlined in Chapter 2, and there is no quantum theory of gravity. Penrose considers there to be an urgent need to understand the workings of the brain as he thinks that these processes utilise the same mechanisms that unite quantum mechanical and relativistic processes. To understand the mind-body problem is to understand the workings of reality under a unified paradigm.

Let us turn our attention now to the origins of the work that led to quantum theory, follow it through to current models, and examine the problems associated with them. Those with a passing knowledge of classical physics and quantum theory might think that quantum theory continued where relativity left off, and that somehow the relativistic work ceased to continue in favour of the newer and truer physics. This is neither the case nor is quantum physics 'truer'. Each represents our best picture of the reality they pertain to. Both quantum theory and relativity research continue to this day — indeed, they are intertwined. The cause of confusion is, I think, twofold.

First, the two areas are separated in mathematical construction since they describe different worlds — that of the very large and that of the very small. As a result, the mind automatically separates them through context. By association, relativity is seen as part of the old world and quantum theory as part of the future. We associate relativity with Einstein, through whom we begin to think of gravity and then Newton. Soon we are thinking of an ancient science.

The word quantum brings with it an implication of something new, digital, and modern, and thus right (even if Hollywood and other media keep insisting that it means something huge!). Indeed, quantum physics is newer than relativity in some sense, but Planck's initial data implying quantisation of energy was formulated fifteen years before the general theory of relativity was formulated. We must not forget the accuracy of relativity nor deny its possible role in a unified theory just because it is associated with 'old school' physics.

Second, recent interest in string theory, new subatomic particles, and the fundamental particles of matter prompts the belief that quantum theory is closer to the truth. Whether a single theory describing all reality can be constructed is, at present, unknown. It may be an amalgamation of relativity and quantum theory or, as Penrose suggests, a new physics altogether.

An extraordinary aspect of quantum theory is that indeterminism disappears when we make an observation of a quantum system. The observer appears to cause a quantum system to adopt a particular state when a measurement is made, which implies that consciousness is intrinsic to linking quantum indeterminism and classical determinism. This will be discussed later, but before we do, we need to unravel how we understand the quantum worlds to be. Through the development of quantum theory, the areas where the problems and gaps in our understanding are will be revealed.

ii) From the Old

In 1927, the annual meeting of the Solvay conference (sponsored by the Belgian industrialist Ernest Solvay who, like Alfred Nobel, made his fortune from dynamite) was held in Belgium and was devoted entirely to quantum theory. Many physicists whose names are famous to this day attended the conference — this was a defining time in the formulation of modern physics.

The conference fielded illustrious names, many of whom were awarded the physics Nobel Prize. They included Irving Langmuir (the American industrial chemist/physicist), Planck (Nobel Prize 1918), Marie Curie (the Polish/French chemist), Lorentz, Einstein, Peter Debye (the Dutch physicist), William L. Bragg (the Australian physicist who shared the Nobel Prize with his father, William. H. Bragg, for work on X-rays), Dirac (Nobel Prize 1933), Arthur H. Compton (also won a Nobel Prize in 1927 for work on X-rays), Prince Louis de Broglie (1892–1987, the French physicist who won the Nobel Prize in 1929 for work on light and matter), Max Born (the Polish-born physicist who was rewarded "for his fundamental research in quantum mechanics, especially for his statistical interpretation of the wavefunction" with the Nobel Prize in 1954), Bohr, Paul Ehrenfest (the

Austrian-born physicist, noted for his application of statistical mechanics to quantum theory), <u>Schrödinger</u> (Nobel Prize 1933, shared with Dirac), <u>Wolfgang Pauli</u> (1900–1958, the Austrian physicist who was integral to quantum theory's development, and awarded the 1946 Nobel Prize) and <u>Heisenberg</u> (Nobel Prize 1932 for the "creation of quantum physics").

We will concentrate on the ten names underlined, who were key figures in the development of quantum theory, each of whom would go on to receive the Nobel Prize for physics.

Quantum theory can be considered to have begun with Planck's postulation in 1900 that matter can absorb and emit electromagnetic radiation only in finite-sized energy bundles (quanta), whose size and frequency is proportional to the frequency of radiation. In 1905, Einstein generalised Planck's notion. Between 1905 and the Solvay conference, Einstein had been concentrating on general relativity (until 1915) but had not forgotten about quantum theory. Indeed, he continued to make contributions to both relativity and quantum theory throughout his life.

In the early developmental stages of quantum theory, Einstein showed that light always exists as quanta, which is why matter absorbs and emits it as such. Planck did not believe him despite being the one who identified quanta. At the 1927 Solvay conference, Bohr most avidly defended the strange conclusions of quantum theory. He managed to convince all those present at the conference of the probabilistic interpretation of quantum theory — well, all except Einstein! Bohr (together with Heisenberg and Pauli) was the driving force behind the Copenhagen Interpretation of quantum theory, so named because of Bohr's location during those times and, thus, the base where these ideas were formulated. The argument between Bohr and Einstein relating to quantum theory and what it represents, whether it was a truth or merely an interpretation, continued until Einstein's death in 1955. Whereas Bohr had the 'strange but true' attitude, Einstein was more of the opinion that it was 'too strange to be credible'.

Also at that Solvay conference was Schrödinger, immortalised for his 'Schrödinger's cat' scenario (which will be discussed later), but whose true contribution to quantum theory was the application of his wave equation. This equation, describing a quantum system, could be used to calculate the probability of events occurring in the real world we interact with through the reduction ('collapse') of the wave function. Pauli was also present for, among other contributions to the theory, having elucidated the *Pauli exclusion principle*, which denoted the application of a unique complement of quantum numbers to each electron in an atom.

Werner Heisenberg attended because he was instrumental in the formalism of quantum theory by introducing the *uncertainty principle* (together with his matrix mechanics), which set calculable limitations on our knowledge of the position and velocity of an electron in an atom at any one time. When applied, it states that to measure the position of an electron more accurately requires energy of a shorter wavelength and thus higher frequency. This higher energy, from our knowledge of the photoelectric effect, affects the electron such that the more we know about its position, the less we can know about its velocity, and vice versa. Indeed, Heisenberg determined a precise statistical probability equation determining the limits for this knowledge.

Dirac, the youngest scientist present at only 25 years old, would complete the Copenhagen interpretation of the theory in 1928. de Broglie (pronounced 'de Broy') attended on account of his PhD research on *pilot waves*. Finally, the last major contributor who was present and who would also later receive the Nobel Prize was Born. He was able to bring together the work of Heisenberg and Schrödinger. Despite Einstein's scepticism about the theory that was presented at the conference, it would be only a year later that the rudiments of its form were formulated. Today, 80 years on, debate continues over its validity.

How did such a strange theory come to be, one that seemed to violate common sense and was so different from the previously considered true laws of nature? What was so wrong about them to require what turned out to be not only a revision, but also a new way of thinking? It isn't necessary to go into the details of all the classical laws of physics that were accepted, rejected, or revised as a consequence of quantum theory's development, but some of them need to be explained.

Thermodynamics

Thermodynamics is the study of heat. It describes the movement of heat, which moves from a hot body to a cold one until thermal equilibrium is reached. The 19th century German physicist Hermann Helmholtz stated that when energy disappears from one place, an equivalent amount must appear somewhere else in the system. This idea led to the law of the conservation of energy, also known as the *first law of thermodynamics*, which states that the change in energy of a system is the change in work plus the change in heat (Helmholtz's work on energy conservation was actually mediated through studying the speed and action of nerve impulses).

The German physicist Rudolf Clausius (1822–1888), who formulated the law, introduced the concept of *entropy* and expressed it in terms of heat flow from a body of higher temperature to one of lower temperature. The entropy of a system always increases and reaches its peak at thermal equilibrium. It might be prudent to mention here the four laws of thermodynamics and their relationship:

The *0th law of thermodynamics* states that if two thermodynamic systems are each in thermal equilibrium with a third, then they are all in thermal equilibrium with each other.

The *first law of thermodynamics* relates to the conservation of energy. It states that energy cannot be created or destroyed; it can only change forms. In a closed system, energy is conserved.

The *second law of thermodynamics* states that the entropy of an isolated system never decreases — spontaneous natural processes increase entropy overall.

The *third law of thermodynamics* states that as temperature approaches absolute zero, the entropy of a system approaches a constant minimum.

The second law of thermodynamics can be defined in different ways. The *Kelvin statement* is that no cyclic process is possible in which heat is taken from a hot source and converted completely into work. The *Clausius statement* of the same law is a bit more intuitive and states that heat does not pass from a body at low temperature to one at high temperature without some accompanying change occurring elsewhere. These two statements are logically equivalent, although this is not immediately apparent. The concept of entropy encapsulates both the Kelvin and Clausius statements in that "the entropy of the Universe increases during any spontaneous change".

As an example, let us consider a steam engine as a form of heat engine. It has a high temperature source of energy, a device that converts energy into work, and a cold sink for discarding unused work as heat. No engine is 100% efficient. The efficiency = $1 - (T_{sink}/T_{source})$, where T_{sink} is the temperature of the cold sink surroundings of the engine, and T_{source} is the temperature of the functioning engine. Thus, efficiency can be increased by reducing the surrounding temperature of the cold sink, but 100% efficiency is, for all intents and purposes, impossible.

Without the cold sink, the engine cannot function. During function, heat is transferred to the cold sink, thus increasing its entropy (which cancels the decrease in entropy of the hot source). For work to occur, the overall entropy must increase, which is why there must be the cold sink. The engine produces work from heat only if the reaction is spontaneous, and removal of the cold sink prevents this. Therefore, entropy is temperature-dependent and results in the formulation of the idea of absolute zero. A consequence is that it is impossible to cool a system to absolute zero.

Atoms and molecular mass

The concept of atoms has been around for over two thousand years, but it was not until the theoretical calculations of Einstein and experiments by Jean Perrin that they were accepted as fact. Maxwell was a firm believer in atoms and he used this assumption to formulate his *kinetic theory of gases*. He considered a contained volume of gas to consist of billions of molecules moving around by random processes, colliding with each other and with the container walls. If we heat the gas, the kinetic energy of the molecules increases and they move faster, causing more random collisions.

In his theory, Maxwell wanted to see whether the qualitative effects of random gas motion could be predicted from a microscopic model consisting of a collection of gas molecules. His theory made the assumptions that molecules are hard spheres and the space between them is much greater than the size of the molecules themselves. He assumed that molecular collisions are random and that molecules move between collisions at a constant speed. He also stated that the position and velocity of the molecules are initially random. This theory was based on statistical averages because the number of molecules is too great to use Newton's laws.

The number of atoms in the gramme (gram) molecular mass (called a *mole*) of any element is 6.02257×10^{23} (interestingly, by coincidence, this is roughly the number of stars in the observable Universe). This number is called 'Avogadro's number', a number which Einstein was one of the first to give an accurate estimation of.

The 19th century Italian physicist Amedeo Avogadro had hypothesised that equal volumes of gases at the same temperature and pressure contain equal numbers of molecules (Avogadro's Law). The known elements range from hydrogen (*atomic number* 1) to ununoctium (atomic number 118), and the atomic number represents the number of protons in an atom. An atom of hydrogen, as we saw earlier, has one proton and one electron. The recent discovery (confirmed in December 2015) of elements 113, 115, 117, and 118 complete the *Periodic Table* (to which we will return in more detail later). Elements larger than americium (atomic number 95) do not occur naturally and have to be synthesised.

Take carbon for example. Naturally existing carbon atoms (denoted ^{12}C) consist of six protons and six neutrons, so carbon's atomic number is six (protons) and its mass is 12 a.m.u. (atomic mass units). A mole of carbon therefore contains 6.02257×10^{23} atoms of carbon and weighs 12g. In comparison, a mole of hydrogen, possessing one proton, contains 6.02257×10^{23} atoms of hydrogen (protons) and weighs approximately 1g. I say 'approximately', so let us look at this in more detail.

In actuality, ^{12}C is $^{12.011}C$ because the '12.011' refers to the 'relative' atomic mass. This is the average number of neutrons plus protons found in a carbon nucleus in nature. Although most carbon atoms contain six protons and six neutrons, some *isotopes* (atoms of the same element with the same atomic number but different numbers of neutrons) exist that contain more than six neutrons, giving a slightly higher relative atomic mass for carbon than exactly 12. An isotope is therefore an elemental variant that differs in its number of neutrons. Consequently, no element has a relative atomic mass that is an exact whole number due to the existence of isotopes. Carbon has two other isotopes, ^{13}C and ^{14}C, which have one and two extra neutrons respectively, even though all contain six protons. Some isotopes are radioactive, such as ^{14}C and tritium (^{3}H), a form of hydrogen with one proton and two neutrons.

The atomic weight of any element is standardised and defined relative to ^{12}C (as 12.000). Thus, the relative atomic mass is the ratio of the average mass of an element to 1/12 of the mass of ^{12}C. Therefore, 12 grammes of ^{12}C has 6.02257×10^{23} atoms of carbon. ^{1}H hydrogen consists of one proton (its atomic number is therefore 1), so in one gramme of ^{1}H hydrogen gas, there are 6.02257×10^{23} atoms of hydrogen. This rule can be applied to all atoms and all elements, as well as compound molecules such as water (H_2O), which is formed from one atom of oxygen (16 a.m.u.) and two atoms of hydrogen. A mole of water therefore weighs 18 grammes. With this explained, we can return to Maxwell.

With such a large number of atoms or molecules, Maxwell's statistical analysis showed that the temperature is a measure of the microscopic average velocity of the gas, squared. Thus, the motion of the molecules and the collisions cause heat — the faster they go, the hotter they get. The thermodynamic heat (enthalpy) relations were described by Helmholtz and the other 19th century German physicist, Clausius. Maxwell's theory enabled the prediction of the probable velocity distribution of molecules, hence the velocity of a randomly chosen molecule can be predicted with a certain high probability. The resultant *Maxwell distribution* predicted that at higher temperatures, there is a larger percentage of molecules with higher velocity than at lower temperatures. This prediction enabled the use of probabilities to calculate gaseous motion in the absence of information about individual atoms.

Ludwig Boltzmann

Like Cantor before him and Kurt Gödel after, the Austrian physicist Ludwig Boltzmann (1844–1906) was a man before his time. He was the leading proponent of the reality of atoms as well as how a study of their behaviour required a statistical approach. His beliefs contradicted the deterministic view of reality that existed in his day. Scientists then thought that atoms were not real; rather they were just convenient mathematical constructs used to describe phenomena.

Boltzmann's paradigm-shifting work accepted atoms as real, but argued that relating their behaviour to macroscopic reality would require a statistical analysis that was indeterministic due not so much to fundamental limitations but more so because it allowed large numbers of particles to be dealt with in a predictable manner. His idea that reality was unknowable from a practical sense, and all we can use are probabilities, encountered much disdain.

Boltzmann's kinetic theory of gases related the motion of atoms and molecules to macroscopic properties such as temperature and pressure. He devised a constant, K (immortalised as 'Boltzmann's constant'), which bridged the gap between the microscopic and macroscopic world. This equation is:

$\frac{1}{2}mv^2 = KT$ (where m and v are the mass and average velocity, respectively, of gas molecules, T is the gas temperature, and K is Boltzmann's constant)

It links atomic properties of the gas (left-hand side of the equation) to measurable macroscopic properties we interact with (on the right-hand side). With this equation, it was possible to probe the atomic world before the advent of quantum theory. Being in the wrong place at the wrong time, Boltzmann continually struggled to convince his contemporaries to accept his ideas.

Perhaps more famous is this equation of his:

$$S = K \log W$$

(where S = entropy, K is Boltzmann's constant, and W is the probability of a particular arrangement of atoms relating to another constant and a property known as 'statistical weight').

Importantly, this equation relates to the second law of thermodynamics — as entropy increases, the arrow of time is set in the forward direction. Newton's deterministic laws allow reversibility of events. Boltzmann showed that the arrow of time is always pointing forward because entropy always increases with any event; that heat passing from hotter to colder matter can be considered as that which distinguishes past from present. Boltzmann showed that this is not due to some fundamental law, but rather that it is simply the most likely thing that would happen. Atoms in a hot substance move faster than those in a colder substance, so it is statistically more probable that the hot atoms collide with cooler ones and transfer some of their energy to them. Hence, a cup of tea cools down rather than heats up over time.

Without this thermodynamic direction, many phenomena of reality appear — with our current understanding — to be reversible. The rejection of his ideas ultimately drove him to suicide. Sadly, had he persevered for a few years more, he would have experienced the due credit that his work warranted.

It is interesting to note here that there is still debate over the meaning of entropy. It can mean chaos, disorder, or missing information, for example. Arieh Ben-Naim stresses that entropy is seen both as a physically measurable objective quantity with units of energy divided by temperature and as *missing* information, or a nebulous subjective quantity. However, by seeing entropy as information and both concepts of entropy as objective quantities, then redefining temperature as energy enables the removal of Boltzmann's constant and renders entropy dimensionless and identical with information, which is quite a neat idea.

We see the relation between Boltzmann's and Maxwell's work. Boltzmann continued Maxwell's work and presented the general probability distribution law (the canonical distribution) applicable to all entities that have freedom of movement, are independent of each other, and interact randomly. He went on to formulate the theorem of *equipartition of energy*, which states that energy is shared equally among all degrees of freedom at thermal equilibrium. He showed that the increase in disorder of a heated system (whose entropy increases) can be measured.

The equation $S = K \log W$ defined the number of ways a system can be assembled from its constituent atoms. This was the beginning of statistical mechanics and enabled the properties of macroscopic systems to be calculated from the statistical behaviour of its constituent parts. Classical determinism was incorporating indeterminate probabilities to make real world predictions. Boltzmann assumed that on heating, a system evolves from a less probable to a more probable state. At thermal equilibrium, the system is in its most probable state. The probability calculation determines the most likely state that the constituent atoms or molecules will be in.

From this statistical method, there is the small possibility that all the molecules in a box containing a gas are at one corner of the box at one moment in time and a vacuum in the other. It is theoretically possible but practically unlikely. In the history of the Universe, it has probably never happened.

These and other classical works provided a great deal of information but revealed shortcomings. However, the use of probabilities and the statistical mechanics of microscopic systems to calculate macroscopic properties would underlie quantum theory.

The problems

Prior to quantum theory, there were three crucial experiments that could not be explained by a direct application of classical physics such as those we have been discussing. These are:

1. **Black-body radiation** and the *ultraviolet catastrophe* (explained by Planck's quantum).
2. **The photoelectric effect** (explained by Einstein's light particles).
3. **Bright line optical spectra** (explained by Bohr's atom).

These three problems will be discussed below. With their solutions, Planck, Einstein, and Bohr led us to a new understanding of nature. Their conclusions led to the formation of the *Bohr model* of the atom (in 1913) and what is known as the old quantum theory.

1. *Black-body radiation*

A heated object emits electromagnetic radiation (light) over a broad frequency range. If you heat a metal, it changes colour as it gets hotter due to the increase in frequency of emitted radiation. The higher the temperature, the higher the frequency of peak radiation intensity over a broad band. A light bulb emits over a broad frequency range, yet we only see and use the visible light (but pay for all frequencies). The intensity of emitted radiation of a heated metal also varies with its frequency.

A black-body is something like a box that absorbs all electromagnetic radiation entering it. With a hole in it that is too small to affect internal thermal equilibrium, such a heated black box will emit only the electromagnetic radiation that is characteristic of the properties of the box. By heating the box, experiments show that the frequency of emitted radiation gets higher, reaches a peak, and then falls to zero. Apparatus constructed to measure the radiation curves of black-body emissions show that they are similar to those of Maxwell energy distributions for a gas in a closed container. Thus, it was thought that a classical approach could solve the meaning behind the distributions achieved.

In 1860, the German physicist Gustav Kirchhoff had demonstrated that the ratio of emitted to absorbed energy depends only on temperature in the cavity and the frequency. As it had nothing to do with the physical properties of the box, such as its size, shape, and composition, the ratio implied an underlying physics about the radiation itself. However, at the end of the 19th century, it was only possible to accurately measure black-body distributions at relatively low frequencies (i.e., below the ultraviolet region of the spectrum).

Despite this constraint, late 19th and early 20th century physicists attempted to unravel the meaning behind the distributions achieved. Assumptions were made that it was possible to understand black-body radiation by treating it as Maxwell had done with the kinetic theory of gases. On these theoretical grounds, the black-body container was considered to contain waves instead of particles in the hopes that wave-like analysis would reveal the reasoning behind the frequency response to temperature changes. Between 1900 and 1905, the English physicists Lord Rayleigh (John William Strutt, 1842–1919) and James Jeans theorised that the intensity of electromagnetic radiation would increase indefinitely with increased frequency. Through a number of theoretical modifications, their *Rayleigh-Jeans Law* predicted that the spectral density (emitted to absorbed energy in the black box) increases to infinity with the square of the frequency.

When only low frequency measurements were possible, the data fitted the Rayleigh-Jeans model well. However, as experiments advanced and they could measure high frequency emissions beyond the ultraviolet spectrum, the intensity was shown to have a finite limit as the frequency increases. Rayleigh and Jeans were wrong.

By applying the statistical physics method to their theory, they had considered it possible to add more and more electromagnetic radiation (waves) to the box, which is reasonable from a classical sense. Thus, more waves imply higher frequency or lower wavelength and unlimited radiating energy emission as temperature increases. Although their predictions fitted the data for low frequency emissions, they failed for higher frequencies. In fact, Ehrenfest (who committed suicide partly, it is thought, because of the incomprehensibility of quantum theory) pointed out in 1911 that the Rayleigh-Jeans model would lead to 'ultraviolet catastrophe' — high intensity, high frequency emissions at high temperature that would kill everything. So, why was it wrong? Why did it only fit at low frequencies, and what was right?

In 1896, Wilhelm Wien also tried to explain the black-body spectral density versus frequency curves for different temperatures. He created a formula not from sound classical mechanics but from properties of the box and some additional dubious reasoning. His formula, like that of Rayleigh and Jeans, predicted patterns that correlated with experimental data that was produced by Friedrich Paschen in 1897. However, by 1900, Otto Lummer and Ernst Pringsheim showed that it only worked for high frequencies and not for low ones (the opposite of Rayleigh-Jeans).

Planck, a colleague of Wien's, had long been aware of the problem of black-body radiation. Being an expert in classical thermodynamics, he was keen to formulate an understanding on these terms. He even derived Wien's law in 1899 without the 'fiddling' that Wien had employed to make his formula work. However, that law was soon shown to be false.

Planck reasoned that the correct formula to explain the effects should contain the temperature, the frequency of electromagnetic radiation, and a constant (invariant with box or colour). He knew the black-body radiation experiment results were accurate and could be used to compare his theoretical results. He also knew that the total energy in the black box was proportional to T^4 (the fourth power of the temperature) as specified in the Stefan-Boltzmann Law. Most significantly, Planck knew that the correct radiation law he sought would be of universal fundamental significance.

By oscillating the cavity of the black box, Planck expected according to electromagnetic theory that the average frequency of the molecules, which consisted of all frequencies, would increase at higher temperatures until equilibrium was reached. Despite this, the energy distribution at equilibrium was a problem. He managed to derive a formula relating the radiation energy to the frequency (over the whole range) and temperature, which fitted well with experimental data. Legend has it that this result came to him on October 7th 1900 in response to hearing about some data by the experimental physicist Heinrich Reubens. He published the result two weeks later.

However, the use of constants that allowed the data to fit did not provide insight into the underlying physics of the phenomena. The constants (set values to fit all the data that it pertains to) were found by a process of trial and error — placing them in equations and then comparing the predictions with experimental data.

Planck tried to leverage his expertise in thermodynamics and apply classical physics to the problem, without success. One could say that, in desperation, he turned to Boltzmann's statistical version of the second law of thermodynamics (formulated in 1877), $S = K \log W$, although he was not happy with this methodology. Planck used the equation to calculate the entropy, and this was maximal at equilibrium. He used Boltzmann's method of dividing the energy of the oscillator (atoms were not known at the time and electrons would not be identified until 1897, so the box was thought of as a vibrating set of oscillators) into small finite chunks. He had to choose energy units proportional to the oscillator frequency, thus:

$E = h\nu$ (where E = energy, h = some constant which falls towards zero as the number of packets of energy increases, and ν = frequency).

Planck found that if the energy packets reached zero, the derivation got invalidated. But from his formula, he realised that he did not *need* the energy or some constant, h, to fall to zero. If the energy is discontinuous (i.e., released in discrete quanta), he found a law to explain the black-body phenomena. He proposed that the quantity $E = h\nu$ is finite and h is not zero. If h is specifically 6.63×10^{-34} J.s (the exact value of Planck's constant), he found that the formula predicted results that fit the experimental data exactly. He realised that energy is absorbed and emitted discontinuously in the small indivisible units called energy quanta. It was the prediction of continuous energy that doomed the Rayleigh-Jeans explanation and any other similar ones to history.

Planck's conclusion was derived without the knowledge of atoms, which is why he spoke of oscillators. In atomic terms, we would say that as the cavity of the black box is heated, the atoms (oscillators) of the cavity wall become *excited* — they absorb energy and so the electrons move to higher energy states. They then fall to lower energy levels, emitting electromagnetic radiation (photons) of a particular frequency. The higher the temperature, the more that energy is absorbed and then emitted. Under such conditions, electrons move to higher energy levels and then fall back to release quanta ($h\nu$) that are of a higher frequency. However, at very high temperatures, even though the Rayleigh-Jeans law had predicted high frequency emissions, it costs too much energy to release a high frequency quantum (since h is a constant), so the emissions fall to zero in this part of the spectrum.

We should note here that because electrons can occupy distinct energy levels in an atom, the excitation of a high frequency photon (emitted by an electron falling from a high to low energy level) requires energy far higher than the mean box energy at thermal equilibrium (equipartition), so it is very unlikely — it can only be either emitted or not at all. The higher the frequency, the further from the peak frequency at thermal equilibrium and the less likely it is to produce such a quantum (hence, the characteristic fall at the high frequency end of the black-body curve). There is no theoretical upper limit to the frequency of radiation, but there are practical ones.

Importantly, photons are emitted as quanta or discrete bundles or energy. Therefore, even at very high temperatures, there will always be frequencies higher than the peak frequency of emission at thermal equilibrium that can *potentially* be emitted, but which require too much energy to produce, resulting in the characteristic decline to zero that is seen on the right-hand side of a black-body distribution curve as depicted in Figure 8.

A quantum of energy of a photon of light of a particular wavelength (or frequency) is always the same. For example, a photon of blue light of wavelength 450nM always has an energy of 2.76eV. Above certain temperatures, electrons can absorb enough energy to become separated from their nuclei (a phenomenon known as *photoionisation*). Above 1 billion degrees

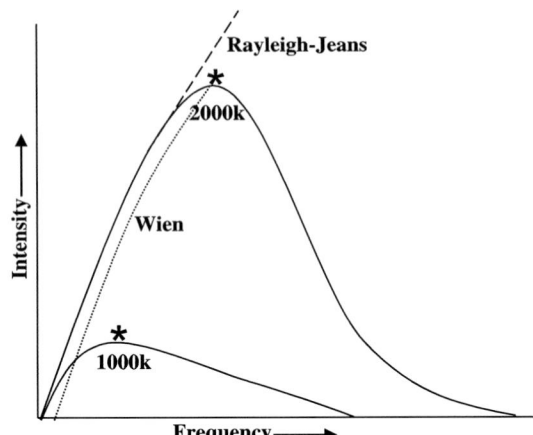

Figure 8. Black-body radiation. For each increase in temperature of the black box, the mean peak intensity moves to a higher frequency. For a given temperature of the black box (e.g., 2000 Kelvin at equilibrium, shown here), the Rayleigh-Jeans model (shown as large dashes) fails at high frequencies whereas Wien's formula (small dashes) fails at low frequencies. For each of the two temperatures (2000K and 1000K) shown, the mean peak frequency of emission is denoted by *.

(pressure-dependent), the nuclei of atoms separate into their constituent protons and neutrons, releasing huge amounts of high frequency nuclear energy in the form of X- and gamma-rays. This will become clearer later. The classical approach of Rayleigh and Jeans was sufficient to calculate energy with respect to *low* frequencies. Here, their predictions fitted well with data, as I had mentioned earlier, because since their method treated all modes of oscillation (electron energy levels) as equally likely such that, at low temperatures, any photon emissions in the box were lower than the equipartition of energy (kT). That is, no more energy is required to emit these photons than is present at thermal equilibrium (according to a statistical interpretation). However, at high temperatures, it costs too much energy to make a quantum, even though there are many 'vibration modes' that can theoretically be excited (higher frequency = more waves). With Planck's method, the high frequency photons are unlikely as they cost more energy than is likely available, whereas Rayleigh-Jeans saw these high energy photons as being as equally likely as low energy ones.

Planck's law has only fairly recently been shown to fit experiments exactly. This was determined in 1990 by comparing the energy-to-frequency ratio for the cosmic background radiation, or the radiation that is left over after the Big Bang. The curve of such a comparison matches a black-body spectrum to one part in ten thousand, proving that the matter of the Universe was once a compressed gas that was hotter than the centre of the Sun. The cosmic microwave background radiation is approximately 3 Kelvin (−270°C). This means that it is 3° above absolute zero temperature. This heat represents the residual energy that pervades all intergalactic space that resulted from the energy release of the Big Bang 13.7 billion years ago, despite the huge expanse this heat exists in. This discovery, made in 1965 by Arno Penzias and Robert Wilson, put to rest the steady-state theory of the Universe.

Temperature relates to amount of energy. There is no maximum possible temperature, although above certain temperatures matter as we know it will not exist. There is an absolute minimum limit for temperature. At absolute zero, there is no energy. It is not possible to attain lower temperatures than that because one cannot achieve less than no energy. On Earth, we can achieve temperatures close to absolute zero in the laboratory, but we can never reach it.

2. *The photoelectric effect*

The second phenomenon not explained by classical physics is the photoelectric effect. When monochromatic or single frequency light is directed at a thin metal foil, electrons are ejected from the metal. The Hungarian-German physicist Philipp Lenard (who incidentally was fanatically anti-semitic and decried Einstein's 'Jewish physics') experimented on this phenomenon. Using an apparatus that consisted of a collector of the emitted electrons from an irradiated metal plate, he could measure the photoelectric current and observe the effect of voltage on it. He showed that at a certain retarding voltage, the photoelectric current disappeared. He considered the results to be indicative of the necessity to treat the phenomena in particle terms.

When electrons are emitted from an irradiated foil, they have a defined kinetic energy. This energy is lost on their transfer through the retarding voltage. It could be concluded classically that the electrons acquired their kinetic energy from the light shining on the foil. However, Lenard found the electron energies to be independent of light intensity. There was also a lower limit of frequency from which no photoelectrons were emitted. Einstein was the one to explain why.

Already familiar with the work of Planck and Boltzmann, and together with his own knowledge of statistical methods, Einstein was able to show that radiation behaves thermodynamically at high frequencies. Recalling Boltzmann's Law ($S = K \log W$), Einstein showed the radiation to consist of quanta with magnitude $K\beta f$. Thus, the radiation of energy (E) with magnitude $nK\beta f$ behaved like light particles. Einstein's equation, $E = nK\beta v$, used several constants, namely β (derived prior to Planck's work to describe blackbody radiation) and K (Boltzmann's constant). As the equation $E = nK\beta v$ is similar in form to Planck's equation, $E = hv$, $K\beta$ can be substituted for Planck's constant h. Einstein's new equation, $E = nhv$, enables us to see that radiation energy equals the number of particles multiplied by hv (the quantum of radiation). Thus, the result extends Planck's result by stating that *all* light and electromagnetic radiation travels in packets of energy equal to hv.

Einstein showed in a paper in 1905 (the same year as his theory of special relativity) that the photoelectric effect can be explained if the illuminating radiation is considered as a collection of particles or photons. When light photons (of magnitude hv) penetrate a metal foil, the energy quanta affect the electrons of the metal. Some energy is transferred to the kinetic energy of the electrons, which are emitted. Before emission, the electron must 'work' to break free of the metal as a result of excitation from the incoming radiation. The kinetic energy of the electron is given by hv-p, where p = work required to break free of the metal surface. As each interaction of photon and electron leads to the same energy transfer, Einstein's equation showed that the electron energy is not dependent on variation in light intensity, but on the frequency or wavelength.

For light of a given wavelength, the number of electrons emitted per unit time increases as the intensity increases, but the amount of energy acquired by each electron does not change. The intensity affects the number of photons, so to prove whether Einstein was right or not, experiments were performed to determine whether the linear relationship predicted between the increase in energy of photoelectrics (measured as voltage) and frequency was observed. The American physicist Robert Millikan (1868–1953) showed this relationship to be linear, which was much to his dismay since he was a classical physicist and wanted to prove Einstein wrong. Einstein was correct in thinking that the energy of emitted electrons is independent of intensity and dependent on the frequency of the light.

3. *Bright line spectra*

The third phenomenon that could not be explained by classical physics was bright line spectra. When a gas is heated and then viewed from behind a narrow slit, distinct bright lines are visible. These lines are characteristic of the gas. We normally see the colour of the gas as an integration of its components, but the constituent properties of this colour can be broken down. The light given off is known as the *emission spectrum*.

A spectrometer allows us to visualise the unique combination of dark and bright lines that is characteristic of a pure gas. When white light (containing all frequencies) is emitted from a heated solid (e.g., a light bulb) and passed through a narrow slit and a prism which splits the light into its constituent visual frequencies, a continuous light spectrum of all the emitted light can be seen.

Newton had observed this effect for sunlight and saw that further splitting was not possible. If we now use a heated pure gas instead of a bulb, a bright line spectrum of the emitted gas can then be observed. What is interesting though, is that if we pass the heated bulb light through the same cooled gas (and the slit and prism), dark lines appear at the same positions as the bright lines when the gas was heated. The cool gas is absorbing exactly where the hot gas was emitting. These absorption and emission lines are characteristic of the elemental source.

In the early 19th century, the German optician Joseph von Fraunhofer used a spectroscope to visualise the dark characteristic emission lines of the solar spectrum, what have come to be known as 'Fraunhofer lines'. By superimposing known element spectral lines on the Fraunhofer solar spectrum, Gustav Kirchhoff and the chemist Robert Bunsen showed in 1859 that known elements surround the Sun. This method enabled the discovery of a new element, helium. Since the spectra were characteristic of each element, they informed us of the internal atomic structure of that element.

Since hydrogen is structurally the simplest element that exists, and the Swede Anders Ångström had already measured the four prominent visible spectral lines of this element in 1868, hydrogen spectra were investigated to obtain greater information about atomic structure. In 1885, Johann Balmer was able to formulate an equation that predicted the four visible lines of hydrogen:

$$F = R (1/n_f^2 - 1/n_i^2).$$

This formula would be correct if the Rydberg constant, R, is 3.29×10^{15} cycles/sec, n_f (final) = 2, and n_i (initial) = 3, 4, 5, and 6 (the n numbers here relate to whole number defined absorption or emission energy levels). Although Balmer's method was purely mathematical in nature, it hinted at an underlying physical law.

Balmer predicted more lines other than the visible, but which could not be detected. These lines were verified in 1906 (*Lyman* series for $n_f = 1$, named after the discoverer Theodore Lyman), in 1908 (*Paschen* series for $n_f = 3$, infra-red, named after the discoverer Friedrich Paschen), and in 1922 (*Brackett* series for $n_f = 4$, infrared, named after the discoverer Frederick Brackett). Another series for $n_f = 5$, or the *Pfund* series, named after August Pfund, was also later identified. The whole number change in n_f predicted calculable changes in absorption and emission energy, indicating an intra-atomic rearrangement of some kind. Despite this, as we know, at the time of Balmer's prediction (1885) there was little known about the structure of the atom.

It was the English physicist Joseph John Thomson who demonstrated that one of the atom's components, the electron, is a particle and that it possesses a charge/mass ratio. However, this did not show how electrons are involved in the atomic structure. His attempts to formulate a picture of the atom (with Lord Kelvin) as a sphere of positive and negative charges (the 'plum-pudding' model) were clearly wrong.

In 1907, Rutherford along with the German Hans Geiger (famous for his association with the radiation-detecting Geiger counter) conducted research involving particle scattering. They noted that while most particles passed through a metal sheet, some were deflected and some returned in the direction of the source. Their results indicated that the atom consists of a small but highly dense and positively charged centre (the nucleus) surrounded by negatively charged particles (electrons). Since only the particles that struck the nucleus would be deflected, they concluded that the nucleus resides in a billionth of the space occupied by the full atom (inclusive of the electron shell, orbit, or cloud). However, the atomic model was far from solved.

They did not understand how electrons are arranged around the nucleus, what the nucleus is comprised of, and why it does not explode due to the repulsive forces of its positive charge. They also wondered why the electrons do not fall into the nucleus as a result of opposite electrostatic attraction. Although it was a great discovery, it was disastrous for classical physics. Rutherford's suggestion of an atomic model similar to the orbit of planets around the Sun was not physically feasible since the orbiting electrons would lose energy and spiral into the influence of positive attraction. A 'solar system' atom held together by electromagnetic forces is nothing like a solar system held together by gravitational forces.

Now Niels Bohr enters our story, through whom the modern quantum rules were formulated. He dedicated his working life to quantum theory with the hope of producing a coherent presentation of his ideas on the subject. Despite not breaking new ground on the subject himself in later life, he was a pivotal figure through whom others could bounce ideas, knowing that Bohr's grounding in the theory was second to none.

Bohr came from Denmark to work with Rutherford in Manchester (via J. J. Thomson's Cambridge laboratory) in 1912. He started work on the atomic model and continued to do so till his death in 1962. He was convinced that Planck's and Einstein's work was valid and that classical mechanics do not apply to the atom. He reasoned that there are stable orbits for the electrons, which have something to do with the Plank/Einstein quantum relation, $E = h\nu$. When he became aware of Balmer's formula for hydrogen spectra (the atom he was considering), he proposed a new model for the hydrogen atom. This was the beginning of the quantum theory of atomic structure.

Bohr's colleague, J. W. Nicholson, had managed to quantise angular momentum and calculate it for hydrogen ($L = nvR = n\{h/2\pi\}$, where L = angular momentum, and v = velocity). Bohr acknowledged the importance of this as he believed that L can only rise or fall by discrete amounts when an electron leaves or enters an atom (or is excited). This is in accordance with the atomic significance of Planck's constant, h.

We know that linear momentum (p) must equal the mass multiplied by the velocity (p = mv). Angular momentum given by L is equal to mvr, where r = the radius from the central axis of rotation. If a rotating system continues without friction, a constant angular momentum exists. By incorporating Planck's ideas, Bohr considered that the electron can only 'jump' to another orbit or energy level where the angular momentum is either higher or lower than the one it occupies, and by a multiple of $h/2\pi$. Thus, the electron 'shells' are quantised in terms of Planck units. Bohr considered the atom to exist in a number of possible orbits without energy exchange.

Quantum numbers

These so-called *stationary states* or *standing waves*, which represent the shells, possess an angular momentum, $L = mvr = n(h/2\pi)$, where v is the speed around the orbit as Nicholson had calculated. This is the *quantum orbital condition*. The angular momentum is thus not arbitrary as defined by classical physics, but has a defined value according to multiples of $(h/2\pi)$. The first orbit has $L = 1(h/2\pi)$ when $n = 1$, the second orbit has $L = 2(h/2\pi)$ when $n = 2$, and so the multiples continue for successive orbits. The integer, n, was termed the *principal* quantum number and it defines the energy levels.

So, we see that $E = h\nu$ (from Planck) and angular momentum is also quantised in Planck units of $h/2\pi$. Bohr was able to use these equations and the knowledge gained regarding n and $h/2\pi$ to calculate the radius and energy of the orbit using Newtonian mechanics. The radius of hydrogen is the smallest when the principal quantum number, n, is equal to 1, and this state of the atom is called the 'ground state'. Furthermore, Bohr could calculate the energy of the orbital once the radii were known for that energy level. The resultant energy difference between energy levels could determine the frequencies of absorption and emission of light. The frequency of this electron transition is given by:

$h\nu = E_i - E_f$ (where E_i is the atomic energy in the initial stationary state and E_f is that in the final state).

This is known as the *quantum transition condition*. Bohr then derived the Balmer formula according to his new atom model rather than Balmer's purely mathematical methods (fitting data by trial and error to formulate an equation). He was able to use the physical orbit energies to demonstrate how the spectra for atoms originate. However, at that point, it had been demonstrated only for hydrogen. Could it work for more complicated elements?

With careful examination of the hydrogen spectra, it became clear that extra spectral lines were seen that could not be accounted for using Bohr's principal quantum number alone. The German physicist Arnold Sommerfeld extended Bohr's ideas by including elliptical orbits in his calculations, as Kepler had done for planetary motion. The resultant differences in energy transitions, accounted for by Sommerfeld's work, explained the additional spectral lines. In agreement with Bohr, only certain values for the shape of orbital energy levels were allowed. The new quantum number, *l*, termed the *azimuthal* or *orbital* angular momentum quantum number which determines the shape of the orbit (or the electron's angular momentum), was quantised in units of $h/2\pi$.

That was not the end of it though. In the 1890s, Pieter Zeeman had shown that extra spectral lines also appeared when excited atoms were placed in a magnetic field. A proper theory of the atom should account for this. It was Sommerfeld who accounted for what became known as the *Zeeman effect* by stating that orbit orientation ensured that electrons can select from more orbits angled at varying slants with respect to the applied field.

The direction of the orbits in the field were quantised as well, so the new *magnetic* quantum number (*m*), which determines energy levels available in sub-shells (or the electron's energy in a magnetic field), was added to the quantum numbers *n* and *l*. *n* determines the size of the orbit, *l* the shape, and *m* the direction that the orbit is orientated. Bohr used these numbers to determine energy level selection rules. However, it became clear that yet another quantum number was necessary to explain all the magnetic effects since *n*, *m*, and *l* could not define the energy level.

The Balmer series

From an equation perspective, since $E = hc/\lambda$, we would expect high energy photon emissions to have short wavelengths and high frequencies (and vice versa for low energy). Indeed, when we observe the *Balmer series* describing the spectral line emissions of the hydrogen atom, the absorption of sufficient low energy results in the emission of red light (656 nm). Absorbing *more* energy results in an emission of higher energy, shorter wavelength (434 nm), and higher frequency blue light.

Spectral lines in addition to those normally found were observed as a further result of magnetic effects. This was called the *anomalous Zeeman effect*. Pauli accounted for the additional magnetism-induced lines by proposing that a hidden rotation accounts for the additional angular momentum. He proposed a fourth quantum number, the *spin* quantum number with two values, which could account for the anomalous Zeeman effect and define electron spin.

Pauli thought that the hidden rotation was akin to a spinning planet rotating around a sun, but he did not pursue this idea. George Uhlenbeck and Sam Goudsmit, however, did in 1925 and their professor, Ehrenfest, submitted their work for publication and international approval. The rotation or electron spin could be either 'spin-up' or 'spin-down'. That is, unlike a spinning top whose spin can be angled, the electron is 'up' or 'down' (one or the other). However, the angular momentum of the electron was found to be half of that expected by quantum theory — it was $h/4\pi$ or spin ½, which meant that the electron had to spin around twice to get back to its original position.

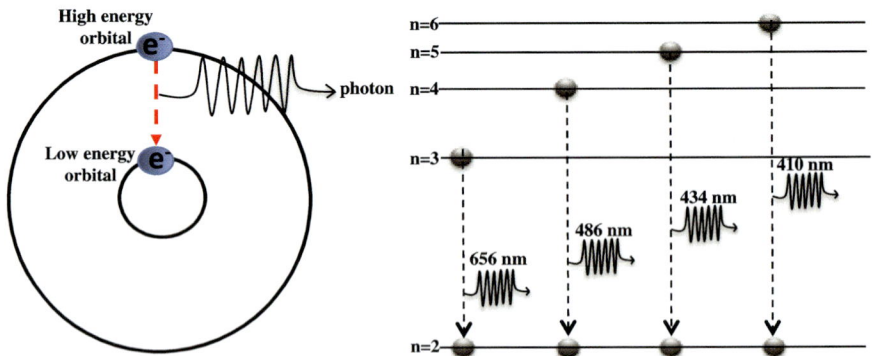

Figure 9. The Balmer series. Electron transitions to different orbitals result in light being emitted at different wavelengths.

Being an example of a 2-D state vector space in quantum mechanics, we cannot think of this *up* and *down* in usual 3-D terms. Indeed, in some quantum mechanical problems, there are possibilities for infinite-dimensional spaces that, of course, cannot be visualised, but which can be mathematically expressed as a *Hilbert space* (named after German mathematician David Hilbert).

To explain why electrons do not fall to the ground state, Pauli proposed that each atomic state (defined by the three quantum numbers n, l, and m) contains two electrons (spin *up* and *down* = $+½$ and $−½$, respectively) and requires its own orbit. This was called *space quantisation*. He went on to propose the Pauli exclusion principle in 1925, which states that each energy level quantum state can possess only one electron, not two. When an energy level is filled, the electron must occupy the next available energy level, filling up the empty energy levels from the lowest first to the highest last.

Thus, each electron possesses a unique combination of quantum numbers n, m, l, and s (or ms). The arrangement prevents the atom from collapsing to its ground state and defines each atom's characteristic structure. Furthermore, it defines why physical structures have substance. Pauli proposed that the same principle can be applied to all electrons and atoms. Of significance, the Periodic Table of elements (Figure 10) can now be understood from first principles rather than the arrangement of elements being based on chemical properties, which had been the method utilised by the Russian chemist Dimitri Mendeleev, the first to formulate a periodic table of elements.

The Periodic Table lists all the known elements and are grouped together according to electronic structure and, thus, chemistry. These elements can interact with one another to form all the substances that exist and which constitute the four states of matter — solid, liquid, gas, and plasma (plasma constitutes over 99% of the matter in the Universe and consists of free electrons and positively charged nuclei at extremely high temperatures, such as in a sun).

In the modern Periodic Table of elements, the atomic orbitals can be defined not only by their quantum numbers n, l, m, and s, but also by the letters s, p, d, f, g, and h. These are derived from the quality of the spectral lines they produce — sharp, principal, diffuse, and fundamental

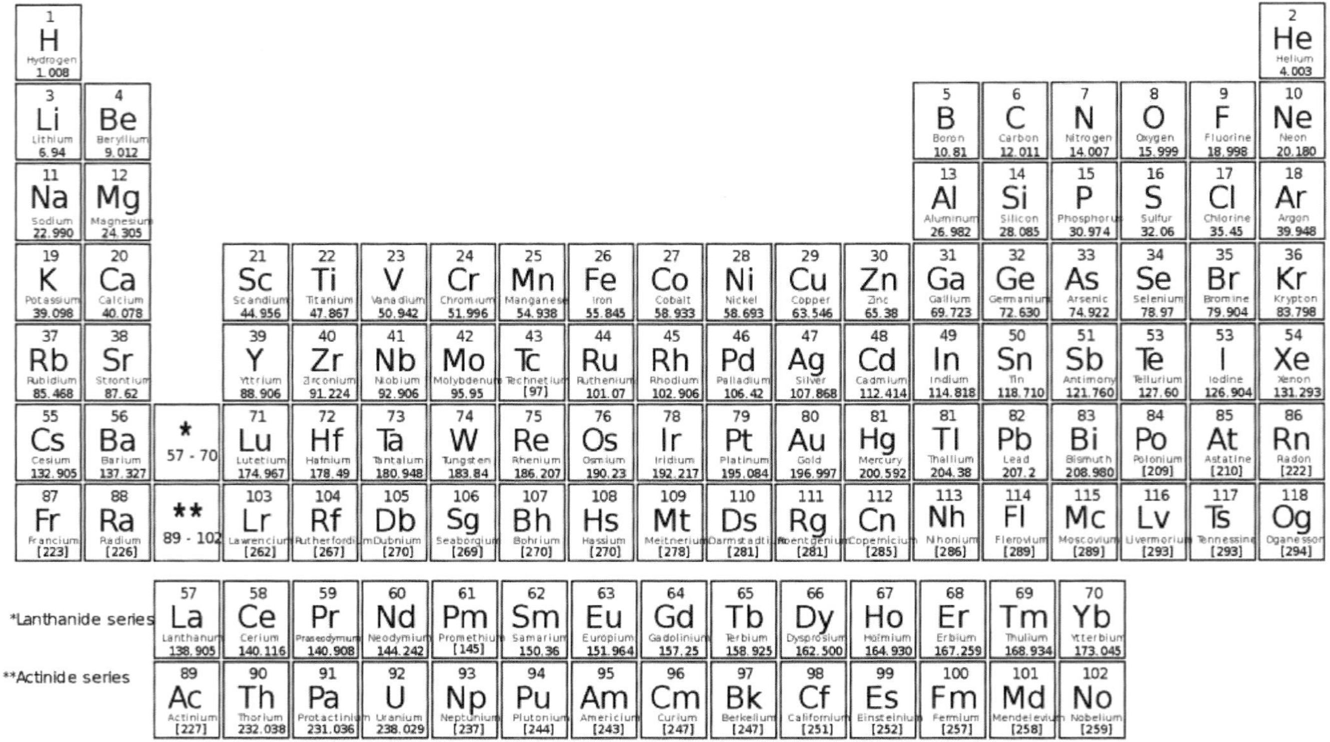

Figure 10. The Periodic Table. Each box identifies an element, shown with its one or two letter symbol. Atomic numbers (written above the symbol) denote the number of protons. The relative atomic mass (below the element name) is basically protons + neutrons. Elements in the same vertical 'group' possess similar chemical characteristics, which is the reasoning behind the presentation of the elements in this form. Chemical and biological processes extend from the electron arrangements of the elements.

	s	p	d	f	g
1	*1*				
2	*2*	*3*			
3	*4*	*5*	*7*		
4	*6*	*8*	*10*	*13*	
5	*9*	*11*	*14*	*17*	*21*
6	*12*	*15*	*18*	*22*	
7	*16*	*19*	*23*		
8	*20*	*24*			

Figure 11. Orbitals. The numbers and letters in bold indicate the orbitals. The italicised numbers indicate the order for filling. Notably, the filling order is north-easterly, as shown by the arrow, for completion before filling a lower energy orbital (e.g., 3s is filled before 3p).

(and the rest for convention purposes). These names are used in electronic configurations (Figure 11).

The shapes of the s, p, d, and f electron orbitals differ. The s orbitals are spherically symmetrical and can contain two opposed-spinning electrons. The p orbital has a figure-of-eight shape and there are three equivalent p orbitals for each n quantum number (>1). The d and f orbitals are more complex, for which there are five equivalent d orbitals and seven equivalent f orbitals. Again, each orbital can contain only two opposed-spinning electrons.

The correct electronic configuration of an atom is achieved by placing the appropriate number of electrons in orbitals in order of energy. The orbitals of lowest energy are filled first — this is called the *Aufbau principle* ('Aufbau' is German for construction). This is subject to the rule that for equivalent orbitals (e.g., the three p orbitals), the electrons are placed in each orbital until all the orbitals are half filled. This is called *Hund's rule* (after the German chemist Friedrich Hund). The upshot of this rule is that for most atoms, there is an order of energy for the orbitals:

1s < 2s < 2p < 3s < 3p < 4s < 3d < 4p < 5s < 4d < 5p < 6s < 4f < 5d < 6p < 7s…

Bohr explained the periodicity of the Periodic Table before Pauli using his orbital model of the atom. He suggested that the physical and chemical properties of an element depend on the electronic arrangement, which he thought of as layers or shells. He considered these to contain a defined number of electrons, and the chemical properties of an element are defined by how full the shell is. Inert (inactive or noble) gases — neon, argon, krypton, xenon, and radon — possess a full outer shell of electrons and hence do not become readily involved in chemical reactions due to electron shell stability in their native form.

This stable state is the electron shell 'goal', so to speak, for any reaction. Any shell can achieve this state through *covalent* or *ionic* interactions. That is, such reactions may be covalent (electron sharing) or ionic (charged particle arrangements) in nature. Carbon dioxide (CO_2), for example, possesses covalent chemical stability — the carbon atom receives electrons from two oxygen atoms for a stable shell of eight electrons. In return, the result of the oxygen atoms sharing their electrons with the carbon is that they too achieve a stable state of eight electrons. Although covalent bonds involve electron sharing, if the two atoms involved are different, then it is usual that the electron is held by one atom more strongly than the other due to different electron affinities.

Some ions possess electronic stability, but this is achieved in a different way. Put simply, electrically stable ions are atoms that have gained or lost electrons to achieve outer shell electron stability. Of course, ions also exist where their electronic outer shells are not in a stable state, yet their reactivity is due to their 'wanting' to achieve a stable electron shell through loss or acquisition of electrons.

Equally oppositely charged ions (e.g., one is +1 and the other −1) are electrically attracted, which can be seen in the crystal structure of common table salt. Sodium chloride (NaCl) is ionic because sodium (Na) loses an electron to achieve stability in its outer shell, becoming positive by one charge unit relative to its native state (denoted as Na^+), and similarly, chlorine (Cl) becomes Cl^- because it gains an electron (e^-) and becomes negative by one charge relative to the chlorine atom's natural configuration.

An atom in its usual state consists of the same number of protons in its nucleus as electrons surrounding it. Here, the charges cancel out. Ionic sodium in Na^+Cl^- has lost an electron, so there is a single extra positive charge from a proton not cancelled out by an electron due to its loss. Electrons in a covalent bond can be considered as *delocalised* over a

	N	possible *l*	possible *m*	possible *s*	states	total states
1st shell	1	1	0	+/– ½	2	2
2nd shell	2	1	0	+/– ½	2	8
	2	2	–1,0,1	+/– ½	6	
3rd shell	3	1	0	+/– ½	2	18
	3	2	–1,0,1	+/– ½	6	
	3	3	–2,–1,0,1,2	+/– ½	10	
4th shell	4	1	0	+/– ½	2	32
	4	2	–1,0,1	+/– ½	6	
	4	3	–2,–1,0,1,2	+/– ½	10	
	4	4	–3,–2,–1,0,1,2,3	+/– ½	14	

Figure 12. Electron orbits. (the progression continues in a likewise fashion for the higher orbits).

different atom's nuclei. This delocalisation stabilises the molecule and is energetically favourable over separate bond localisation.

Bohr knew that hydrogen, lithium, and sodium are chemically similar and must possess similar electronic arrangements. As hydrogen has one electron and lithium is similar chemically but possesses three electrons, it must have one electron in its outer shell with the other two closer to the nucleus. Sodium, with 11 electrons, is also chemically similar to lithium, so it has an inner level of two electrons, an outer shell of one electron, and eight electrons in between. Potassium is similar to sodium but possesses 19 electrons — one in the outer shell and 18 inner electrons. Since the inert gas electron configurations represent stability, they define a full shell.

Bohr used his theory to define the Periodic Table according to the electron requirements of each shell. However, it was Pauli's principle that automatically generated these electron requirements. Figure 12 shows how Pauli's exclusion principle determines how many electrons can fill each shell for stability (n, l, m, and s refer to the quantum numbers referred to earlier).

We now turn our attention to the concept of *wave/particle duality*. 'Frequency' is a property of radiation (the wave model), while 'energy' is a property of photons (the particle model).

Wave/particle duality

Do waves or particles best describe the nature of matter and radiation, or do we need both views? This was a question that had troubled scientists for hundreds of years. Newton considered light to consist of 'corpuscles' (i.e., particles), whereas the 17th century Dutch physicist Christian Huygens considered it to exist as waves. Each showed, without knowing it, that the answer lay with the method that is chosen to observe it. Let us first look at waves and their properties.

Waves can be considered as a pulse transmitted along a flexible string. Periodic waves occur when a pulse is repeated from one end of the string with successive similar pulses. If the pulse is transmitted from either end of the string towards the centre — that is, from different directions — a *superposition* occurs (this does not occur for particles). A superposition of opposite polarity waves cancels out. The result is that the total displacement is the sum of the individual displacements. The velocity of a wave is equal to the wavelength (length of the wave cycle) multiplied by the frequency (how rapidly the wavelength repeats in time). Thus:

$$v = fλ \text{ (or } v = vλ)$$

In the famous double-slit experiment (Figure 13), first performed in a simple form by the English polymath Thomas Young (1773–1829) in 1801, periodic waves pass through two nearby slits onto a screen. In-phase waves, which are waves from both slits whose wavelengths overlap, form what is termed *constructive interference* and create a light spot on the screen. Out-of-phase waves form *destructive interference* and cancel out the wavelengths, forming a dark spot on the screen.

When light passes through a slit of similar size to the wavelength, the waves bend around the edge, spreading the light out and causing interference. This is called *diffraction*. The interference pattern that appears on a screen after a large number of photons pass through the double-slit appear like stacked dark horizontal rectangles against a white background. The interference and diffraction patterns, together with Maxwell's electromagnetic theory, point strongly to the wave nature of light. In an interference experiment, light behaves as a wave, but with the photoelectric effect, it behaves as a particle.

However, Einstein thought that quantum theory should develop into a form that would incorporate a combination of the wave *and* particle nature of light, or the *wave/particle duality*. This was because he had been able to show wave and particle characteristics in his explanation and reappraisal of

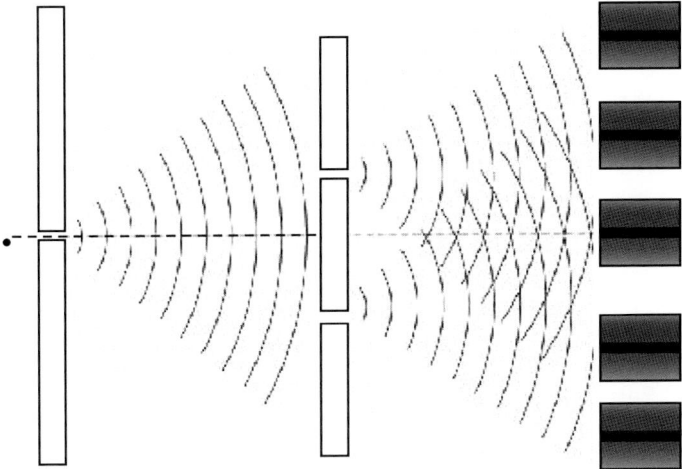

Figure 13. Double-slit experiment. After passing through the double-slit, in-phase and out-of-phase waves produce the characteristic diffraction pattern on a screen, characteristic of constructive and destructive interference respectively. The wavelike nature cannot be described in terms of probability waves, but as complex waves of alternatives. Here, rather than passing through one slit *or* the other, the photon is described by a combination of both alternatives, weighted by complex numbers (e.g., $\sqrt{(-1)}$). Thus, the state of the photon as it passes through the slits is defined by 'complex number W × (alternative A) + complex number Z × (alternative B)'. Using Dirac (*ket*, | >) brackets (a *bra*, < |, vector is the complex conjugate of the ket vector), the quantum mechanical state of the system, ψ, is given by $\psi = W|A> + Z|B>$ (where A means the photon reaches the screen through the top slit, B through the bottom slit, and |B> means the system is in quantum state B). Note: this equation is a quantum superposition (deterministic), *not* an indeterministic probability-weighted combination.

both black-body radiation and the photoelectric effect. Luckily for Einstein, who was alone in thinking about particular properties of photons, de Broglie suggested that particles possess wave properties.

The double-slit experiment exemplifies wave/particle duality because the interference is an example of the particle's requirement to have both wave and particle properties. In this experiment, the photon has passed through one slit or the other — there is no evidence for the photon splitting. Yet light passes through both slits in the form of a wave if we perform the interference experiment. So, if we treat it as a wave, it behaves as a wave, and if we treat it as a particle, it behaves as particles do.

A photon with measurable frequency interacts with one electron. de Broglie was convinced that wave/particle duality is general and extends to photons, electrons, protons, and the entire physical world. de Broglie's insistence that wave/particle duality applies to all quantum objects means that it applies, not exclusively, to matter with mass (a photon has zero rest mass, but like all elementary particles and when considered in quantum terms, it shows wave/particle duality — exhibiting wave interference with other photons but also a definite result when measurements of position are made). Indeed, wave/particle duality has been demonstrated in terms of interference for molecules.

Thus, one then wonders, since we are constituted by quantum objects possessing properties dependent on the type of measurement made, how do we as humans fit into the wave/particle measurement issue? Is what we observe just a property of a whole, which hides what is fundamentally indeterminate and measurement-dependent? How do we, as quantum objects, collapse the wave function if indeed the rules of quantum theory apply to us (the measurer) as well as the measured? We will consider this later, but in the meantime, we will continue with the physics and leave the philosophical ramifications for now.

Richard Feynman made use of the double-slit experiment in his *Feynman Lectures in Physics*. Here, he showed that placing a light between the slit and screen does 'illuminate' the position but also changes the rules and result of the experiment (the meaning of this will become clear later). de Broglie considered that an in-phase pilot wave accompanied the electron particle through space.

More recently, the American-born physicist David Bohm (1917–1992) expanded on this idea to produce a version of quantum theory that challenged the Copenhagen interpretation, in that a quantum object can be considered real at all times and is not dependent on measurement. However, to detect such waves and relate this to the particular motion, de Broglie had stated that there are velocities associated with the group wave packet (i.e., when many waves are superimposed) and the individual wave constituents (phase velocity of wave). The group velocity relates to the particle velocity and displays the energy and momentum associated with a particle. de Broglie made some major conclusions by rearranging already known formulae related to the wave and particle nature of light and electrons. Einstein's famous equation relating mass to energy is, of course:

$$E = mc^2$$

This can be written as E = (mc)c: mc is mass multiplied by speed, which is also termed momentum, or p. So, rewriting this, we get:

$$E = pc$$

We know for waves that c (velocity of light) = $\nu\lambda$ (frequency × wavelength). Thus:

$$E = (p)(c) = (p)(\nu\lambda)$$

Also, from Planck and Einstein:

$$E = h\nu$$

So, $(h)(\nu) = (p)(\nu\lambda)$. By rearrangement, $h/p = \lambda$, which applies to photons.

The implication of this work is that by decreasing the wavelength of light, the individual light photon momentum increases. This was of great importance for Heisenberg in formulating his famous 'uncertainty principle' (more of which soon). de Broglie's relation was applicable for all particles.

If $\lambda = h/p$, and for electrons $p = (m)(\nu)$, then the momentum (p) can be calculated for electrons and the wavelength predicted from de Broglie's equation. However, despite this evidence, many physicists considered electrons to definitely be particles. Einstein was highly impressed with de Broglie's work and his predictions were soon verified by experiment. de Broglie went on to state that as the electron went around the nucleus, the associated wave is stationary. Furthermore, only discrete frequencies are produced. This explained the unexplained *2π factor* that Bohr had found. If a whole number of electron waves fit around the atom, then Bohr could have justified his orbital quantisation by incorporating de Broglie's relation.

For standing waves:

$$n\lambda = 2\pi r$$

Using the de Broglie equation $n(h/m\nu) = 2\pi r$, the *quantum orbital postulate* is:

$$n(h/2\pi) = mvr$$

Thus, Bohr could redefine his term as the *quantum orbital reality*. The old quantum theory described above resulted in many successes — Bohr's orbital model of the atom, Pauli's exclusion principle, the explanation of the Periodic Table, Sommerfeld's modification of the Bohr model and its derivation of the hydrogen spectrum, and finally, the energy states of the atom as described by selection rules and quantum numbers. However, it still did not tell us whether to think of the electron as a particle or a wave. Answering this led to the new version of quantum theory.

Before moving on to further details of the development of quantum theory, we should end this section by clarifying something about other highly important but somewhat neglected interpretations of quantum theory. I say neglected because interpretation is complex and highly debated, whereas the applicable use and accuracy of the theory is unquestionable. Many avoid interpretation not only because it is difficult but also because to some it can lead to no useful answers. Yet, if there is an understanding, it would fundamentally affect how we interpret the deepest questions about our existence.

In addition to the standard Copenhagen interpretation of quantum theory and those attempts to address the 'not real until measured' measurement problem, such as the well-known Bohm pilot wave analysis and the many-worlds interpretation, many other theories have been suggested. This is indicative of how, despite the practical usefulness of the theory, the metaphysical consequences do not sit well. Proposed in 1985, the Ghirardi-Rimini-Weber theory (GRW), named after Giancarlo Ghirardi, Alberto Rimini, and Tullio Weber, is another wavefunction collapse theory that has received more attention than most and proposes a spontaneous collapse of the wavefunction, thus avoiding the measurement problem.

iii) To the New

After 25 years of confusion between the initial work of Planck in 1900 and 1925 where we take up the theory, the 12 months between June 1925 and June 1926 produced three developments in the theory that proved, on examination, to be identical in nature. These are:

Matrix mechanics (formulated by Heisenberg),
Wave mechanics (formulated by Schrödinger), and
Quantum algebra (formulated by Dirac).

Heisenberg had studied with Sommerfeld, was great friends with Pauli, and had worked with both Bohr and Born. Many great physicists spent some time working with Bohr at his 'school', including Dirac, Pauli, Max Delbrück, Carl von Weisäcker, George Gamow, Lev Landau, J. Robert Oppenheimer (of 'atom bomb' fame), and Ehrenfest. Each of these individuals made significant advances in their fields.

Heisenberg found during his time with Bohr that he did not agree with Bohr's imaginary electron orbits and, while working with Born in Gottingen, developed a code to connect quantum numbers and atomic energy states with the frequencies of light spectra. This was his quantum mechanics. For this theory, he started by considering the atom to be not a solar system but a virtual oscillator (as Planck had done when dealing with the black-body radiation problem) that had the capability of producing all the frequencies of the spectrum. He incorporated into his thinking what was known as the correspondence principle. This thought process involved both quantum and classical ideas, such that it is a requirement that classical mechanics is recoverable for large systems. This means that the behaviour of systems described by the old quantum theory reproduces classical results for large quantum numbers.

Heisenberg considered the Bohr atom at large orbits (i.e., high n number shells). Here, the orbital frequency is the same as the radiation frequency, and the atom behaves as a linear oscillator. From this point of view, he could analyse the problem from a classical physics standpoint. Linear momentum (p) and displacement from equilibrium (q) could be used. Classically, he could solve the equation of motion and calculate the particle energy in state n and the quantised values E_n. His remarkable insight allowed him to extrapolate from the largest orbit to the inner ones, enabling a formula that would account for all states.

In classical physics, p × q = q × p. We can understand this easily because three multiplied by two is the same as two multiplied by three. Heisenberg found this to not be the case in his formulation. To obtain correct frequencies and intensities for the spectral lines according to his theory, he included the quantum postulate as Bohr had done earlier. He surmised that pq − qp is not zero but = $h/2\pi i$ (where i is an imaginary or complex number = $\sqrt{-1}$). He had shown that the energy states are quantised and time-independent. They are stationary, as in the Bohr atom.

Next, Heisenberg sought Pauli's opinion on the idea. Pauli thought that the formalism was promising, so Heisenberg sent the work to Born. On detailed analysis, Born realised that it represented a type of mathematics called *matrix calculus*. A mathematical matrix is basically a rectangular array of numbers or symbols arranged in columns and rows. Together with Ernst Pascual Jordan, Born transformed Heisenberg's formalism into a systematic matrix language. Without going into the details of the mathematics of the matrices, the frequencies of the optical spectra can be represented by an infinite matrix (see below). The frequencies are associated with an infinite matrix of oscillators with momentum, p(t), and displacement q(t). The quantum postulate was added to obtain correct frequencies and intensities represented by a set of two numbers in matrix form. Thus:

pq − qp = $(h/2\pi i)$I (where I is a unit matrix) and the *quantum condition* was formulated.

By incorporating classical mechanics with this condition and when written in matrix form, a system of equations was formed that can, theoretically, calculate frequencies and intensities of spectral lines for any atom. Pauli mastered the mechanics and was able to deduct the hydrogen spectrum from them as well as lines produced by electric and magnetic fields. Thus was derived the first complete version of quantum mechanics. However, although the mechanics worked in practice, it was purely mathematical and provided no visualisation of atomic orbits, unlike the Bohr model.

Furthermore, Heisenberg considered that it was impossible to draw correlations between atomic structure and the classical world — he thought that it was not feasible to consider electrons as particles or waves. Thus, energy levels were discussed in terms of numbers. Of fundamental importance, as we will see, is the 'non-commutability' (p × q does not equal q times p) of the matrix mechanical formalism. It indicates that the *order* of measurement is important and that the *act* of measurement is critical. That is, the method of observation determines the result — treat electrons as waves and they appear as waves; treat them as particles and they behave as particles.

Schrödinger published his paper on wave mechanics in 1926 in the journal *Annalen der Physik* at the same time that Heisenberg published his paper on matrix mechanics (describing the same phenomena) in the journal *Physikalische Zeitschrift* (both German journals, quite common at that time, although most modern scientific breakthroughs are now published in American or British journals). Schrödinger's equations described the motion of electrons as three-dimensional de Broglie waves surrounding the nucleus, whereas Heisenberg's model was far more abstract. He considered the atom as comprising infinite linear virtual vibrators (or oscillators) whose frequencies coincide with all possible emission frequencies of an atom. A description of the linear vibrator is made using its mechanical momentum (a particle's mass multiplied by its velocity), p, and position of equilibrium (or displacement), q.

To construct a matrix table, let us look at basic multiplication. Multiplying 3 × 1 is the same as multiplying 1 × 3 — both give the answer 3. Thus, standard multiplication is commutative. Matrix multiplication is (generally) non-commutative. The standard form of matrix multiplication is given in the following example:

$$\begin{matrix} 1 & 4 & 6 \\ 3 & 7 & 1 \\ 6 & 2 & 4 \end{matrix} \times \begin{matrix} 6 & 4 & 3 \\ 5 & 7 & 3 \\ 2 & 5 & 9 \end{matrix} = \begin{matrix} 38 & 62 & 69 \\ 55 & 66 & \mathbf{39} \\ 54 & 58 & 60 \end{matrix}$$

To achieve these values, numbers in the horizontal rows in the 1st matrix are multiplied by those in the vertical columns in the 2nd matrix and then added. Thus, to obtain the value of 39 shown in bold, we perform the following matrix calculation:

$$(3 \times 3) + (7 \times 3) + (1 \times 9)$$

That is, the 1st number of the 2nd row in the 1st matrix is multiplied by the 1st number in the 3rd column of the 2nd matrix. This value is added to the multiple of the 2nd number in the 2nd row of the 1st matrix and the

2nd number in the 3rd column of the 2nd matrix. The final (1 × 9) calculation follows accordingly as the last numbers in the 2nd row and 3rd column, respectively. Therefore, the calculation for 54 (bottom number of 1st column) is (6 × 6) + (2 × 5) + (2 × 4).

If we switch the order of the 1st and 2nd matrices to be calculated, we achieve:

$$\begin{matrix} 6\ 4\ 3 \\ 5\ 7\ 3 \\ 2\ 5\ 8 \end{matrix} \times \begin{matrix} 1\ 4\ \mathbf{6} \\ 3\ 7\ \mathbf{1} \\ 6\ 2\ \mathbf{4} \end{matrix} = \begin{matrix} 36\ 58\ 52 \\ 44\ 75\ \mathbf{49} \\ 65\ 59\ 49 \end{matrix}$$

So, we see that matrix multiplication is not commutative.

Heisenberg used the idea that atomic spectral line emission frequencies represent an infinite matrix so that other mechanical quantities of an atom can be represented using these matrix multiplication tables. The mechanical momentum and displacement, p and q, can thus be given as an infinite matrix of the above form. He was able to calculate, as did Schrödinger with his wave equation, the intensities and arrangement of atomic spectra lines.

Schrödinger did not like matrix mechanics. He preferred the idea that we can visualise all aspects of the physical universe. He attempted to develop a version of de Broglie's wave concept by formulating an equation, known now as the *Schrödinger wave equation*, which is applicable to any physical system where the mathematical form of energy is known. The solution to the equation is a wave. The equation has solutions for particular quantised values of the electron energy. The electron cannot possess an energy lower than the lowest allowed value of the equation solution, thus avoiding the problem of the electron spiralling into the nucleus. This describes the quantum aspects of a system whereas the physical interpretation of the wave was to be a major philosophical problem. The equation is:

$$\delta^2\psi/\delta X^2 + 8\pi^2 m/h^2\ (E - V)\ \psi = 0$$

(where ψ = Schrödinger wave function, E = total energy, V = potential energy, h is the Planck constant, and the first part of the equation relates to derivatives for the position).

It describes how a probability wave associated with a particle moves through space. The Schrödinger wave equation has a solution that is a function of space and time. Squaring this value gives the probability of finding a quantum particle (e.g., an electron) at some particular location at a particular moment in time. Wave peaks represent highest probability and thus where the particle is most likely to be found. The equation used the method of *Fourier analysis*.

This method expresses a mathematical function as the sum of an infinite series of periodic functions. The Fourier technique used is the *method of eigenvalues*, where the amplitudes of each correct function are added by superposition to provide the solution. When a measurement is made, the wave superposition collapses onto a particular eigenstate (position). Thus, the wave function for the system is replaced by an infinite series of the harmonic periodic wave functions for the individual states. The replacement waves describe the individual states of the quantum system. The amplitudes determine their importance to the whole system. So, within the eigenvalue system is the fundamental underlying quantisation of the atomic system.

Schrödinger's method was accepted immediately as a great achievement and of universal significance. His method was termed wave mechanics. Experimental verification that electrons do exhibit (de Broglie) wave characteristics came in 1927 when the American scientists Clinton J. Davisson and Lester H. Germer (and, independently, the English physicist George Thompson) directed an electron beam onto a metal crystal to produce a diffraction pattern similar to that achieved by passing light through a pinhole. The diffraction phenomena of de Broglie waves in the case of atomic beams were later demonstrated by the German physicist Otto Stern.

Schrödinger's system is a conversion of the energy states in an atom to a 3-dimensional vibrating system. The quantum numbers of Bohr and Sommerfeld were now linked to the number of nodes in a vibrating system. Schrödinger's theory described fully the Balmer formula, the Zeeman effect, spectra of hydrogen, and the spectral lines induced by electric and magnetic fields. He showed that the nodes from his 3-D wave solution corresponded to the quantum numbers n, l, and m from the old theory.

Schrödinger disliked the idea of quantum jumps between energy levels, and his equations presented a continuous mathematical explanation for the phenomena that was more in line with his traditional view of physics. With the success of his equation, he proposed a classical theory of matter waves that had the same relationship to mechanics as did Maxwell's electromagnetism to optics. He wanted physics to return to the view that atomic events occur by continuous processes rather than quantum transitions. Schrödinger doubted the existence of particles at one point in space. Rather, he considered a wave packet to spread out in a sort of 3-D representation of what happens when a stone is thrown into a pond. The initial point is not a particle but the superposition of waves. The 'particle' moves with the group velocity of the wave packet. However, Lorentz pointed out to Schrödinger that although this might work in the atom, it could not describe the electron.

Despite wanting to describe all particles as the superposition of waves, Lorentz put Schrödinger right on a few points. Namely, as waves spread with time, describing particles as wave superpositions is invalid. Spectral lines will not be produced by the frequencies, and the wave equation does not fit with the classical framework of physics. It was demonstrated that the wave function does not spread with time, so Schrödinger was wrong in his hopes to be rid of the particle picture. So, how *do* particles and waves relate?

Despite disliking Heisenberg's matrix mechanics due to its lack of visualisation and the abstract mathematical formalism, Schrödinger went on to show that his and Heisenberg's theories are mathematically equivalent. John Polkinghorne, who trained under Dirac, put it metaphorically by saying that Schrödinger moved the scenery with the actors standing still, whereas Heisenberg let the actors move among untouched scenery. However, one was a clear conceptual wave model of atomic structure whereas the other said that such a model was meaningless, and yet they reduced to the same mathematics. How could this be resolved?

In the same year that Schrödinger's and Heisenberg's theories were shown to be the same (1926), Heisenberg questioned Schrödinger in a scientific meeting about how his theory could explain the quantised processes of black-body radiation and the photoelectric effect. Schrödinger realised that his theory could not. Schrödinger suggested that the wave function represented the position of the electron, or the density of electric charge. However, it was Born who presented a clearer picture with his introduction of *quantum mechanical probability*. He stated that the square of the wave function represented the physical probability of the associated particle's presence. What Born implied was that there are no defined answers, only probabilities, and that the wave function determines the *probability* that a certain quantum state exists.

Of great importance for a theoretical understanding of quantum theory, the new probabilities suggested by Born were different from those of the classical Maxwell-Boltzmann kinetic theory of gases. In that old version, averages were taken based on probabilities through ignorance of individual atomic motion and position. The new theory, clarified by Born, stated that probabilities were also involved, but not through ignorance of knowledge of the system — the probability is all we *can* know about the system. The wave function determines the likelihood an electron will be at a particular position.

Schrödinger's cat

Schrödinger did not accept the probability superposition of quantum states and considered his equations misused to prove a point that he himself did not believe. To emphasize this, in the mid-1930s he proposed a thought experiment known famously as *Schrödinger's cat*.

This *gedanken* experiment supposes that a live cat is placed in a box (the inside of which we cannot observe) with a radioactive source, a Geiger counter (to measure radioactivity), and a sealed phial of poisonous gas. When the radioactivity reaches exactly half its original value, the counter triggers the breakage of the phial, the gas is released, and the cat dies. The radioactive source is such that quantum theory predicts a 50% probability for the decay of the radioactive source to reach half its original value after an hour (there are variants on this part of the experiment, but changes here do not alter what the experiment conceptually demonstrates). Thus, after the hour, there is an equal probability for either state. The cat has equal probability to be in the alive state or the dead state. Quantum theory predicts that on the hour, the box contains a cat that is neither wholly dead nor wholly alive.

The 'Schrödinger's cat' thought experiment is still used to prove the point of the theory, despite Schrödinger's intention for it to ridicule the interpretation of his wave function. The true interpretation is that when we open the lid to see if the quantum prediction is correct, the cat is a mixture of the two states, a superposition of the two wave functions, and our act of observation collapses the superposition of the two functions to a single one, making the cat either dead or alive. Do we kill it or save its life, merely by observing it?

This scenario poses a lot of questions. It seems strange that the physical reality of the Universe is dependent on the act of observation. If we were not to have evolved, or no organism had evolved, there would be no observers. Would this mean that everything would remain in a state of superposition? Does the theory give support to the anthropic principle mentioned in Chapter 2? Does it indicate the need for a truer physics that does away with the need for the reduction of the wavepacket?

Eugene Wigner (1902–1995), a Hungarian quantum physicist and another Nobel laureate, was concerned with what causes the collapse of the wave function. He believed that it was consciousness where the collapse occurred. He later changed this so that the wavefunction of a superposition is objectively changed in the eye, guaranteeing that only final measured information is presented to consciousness. The Copenhagen interpretation, advocated by Bohr, states that every system is governed by the Schrödinger wave function. If one makes a measurement about a system, this collapses the wave function and the complementary information about that system is lost (e.g., the speed of an electron when measuring its position). But there are philosophical implications.

If consciousness of the event brings about the collapse and in certain circumstances defines the actuality of a life/death superposition, what level of consciousness can keep the event real and cause the collapse — that of a cat, a mouse, or even an amoeba? If humans cause the collapse, then when? Is it when we observe the result on the detector, or perhaps when we consciously register the observation? And if the latter is the case, then as consciousness is a process, the cause of the collapse is not a distinct point in time but some ambiguous 'span of time' that corresponds to conscious registration of the collapse.

Wigner thought that the whole idea set physics back hundreds of years. The physical and philosophical problems associated with this are hotly debated even today. However, quantum physics works, and for those who use it to make calculations, their concern is not the philosophical reason behind what causes the wave to collapse, just that it works.

Returning to our historical progression of the theory's development, by the mid-1930s there was a sense that multiple variants of the theory existed. After a presentation by Heisenberg in 1925 at the Kapitza club in Cambridge, Dirac set about trying to resolve the differences and difficulties between Bohr, Einstein, Planck, Born, Heisenberg, and Schrödinger. He realised that the non-commutability of $(p \times q) \neq (q \times p)$ is the essence of the new approach. It linked the old and new quantum physics, and with this he formulated his own ideas on quantum mechanics. Heisenberg and Born, on reading Dirac's results, realised that his was the correct result, and so Dirac's name was added to the list of those instrumental in quantum theory's formalism. By the end of 1925, Dirac published several other papers on the theory and presented these for his PhD (which, of course, was awarded).

In 1926, Dirac moved to Copenhagen to work with Bohr. Here he completed a paper on transformation theory. He showed that Heisenberg's and Schrödinger's theories are versions of his own — furthermore, they are all equivalent.

The Hungarian mathematician John von Neumann, Born, and Dirac have all been credited, historically, with proving the equivalence of Heisenberg's matrix and Schrödinger's wave mechanics. Dirac continued to work with Bohr, and then later continued his research in Göttingen where he considered emission and absorption of electromagnetic radiation. Most of the evidence at that time had favoured the wave nature of light, despite Planck and Einstein presenting theoretical evidence for the existence of light particles (photons). Einstein had suggested that, for light, there existed a wave/particle duality. However, many felt that light should be one or the other. Dirac resolved this apparent paradox.

Dirac applied quantum mechanics to Maxwell's electromagnetism to produce the beginnings of QFT. This continuous field theory allows light to be considered as waves or particles *and* be correct. The continuous field does not break up into discrete parts to interact with matter (electrons, protons, or other subatomic particles) — it acts as a continuum. Thus, if you approach a problem using the field theory and treat the subject in a particle-like way, it will demonstrate particle-like behaviour. If treated as a wave, wave-like behaviour is seen.

QED

The study of the wave and particle nature of light (QED) and its interaction with matter continued, free of paradox, under the pioneering work of Richard Feynman, the English-born mathematician Freeman Dyson (1923–2020), and the American Julian Schwinger (as well as, indirectly, the American physicists Murray Gell-Mann (1929–2019), Steven Weinberg, Sheldon Glashow, and the Pakistani physicist Abdus Salam). Each, except Dyson who was sadly neglected, received the Nobel Prize for their contribution to this work. Feynman (1918–1988) was one of the most famous modern physicists not only for his work in QED and his involvement in solving the cause of the Space Shuttle Challenger disaster, but also for his character, enthusiasm, and popularisation of physics. He is quoted almost as often as is Einstein in order to add credibility to one's own arguments.

QED succeeded in solving the interaction of light with matter. Earlier, I stated that QFT predicts accurately the value of the magnetic moment of an electron. Dirac predicted this to be exactly 1 and was incorrect because he did not take into account all the effects of the interaction between electrons and light. Around 1938, Feynman, Schwinger, and the Japanese physicist Sin-Itiro Tomonaga independently developed the theory of QED (a.k.a. quantum field theory), which gave such an accurate value of the magnetic moment by incorporating the interaction of the electron with light.

It was Dyson who proved the mathematical consistency of their work. The accuracy between theory and practical measurement that I stated earlier is equivalent to less than the width of a human hair in three thousand miles. At present, no known process in the interaction of light and matter produces results that deviate from those expected by the theory of QED, therefore theoretically, all the processes of chemistry and biology can be predicted (with a large enough computer and knowledge of the start conditions) by QED. However, macroscopic classical approaches are used because of the complexity. Furthermore, in addition to the complexity preventing its use in systems it does apply to, there are some processes it does not cover (e.g., some forms of radioactive decay and gravitation).

In the theory, Feynman was keen to stress that light is made of particles and behaves like particles. He also stressed that QED explains how nature *is*, not *why*. 'Why' is an impossible question, he thought, and pointless to ask because the quantum world is fundamentally nonsensical under logical, meaningful analysis.

To stress this distinction between quantum events and real-world interpretations, let us look at an example. If light is shone at a thin sheet of glass at some specific angle, about 4% of the photons will be reflected back whereas 96% pass through. As the thickness of glass increases, the percentage of photons that passes through increases to 16%. However, as the thickness increases further, the percentage that passes through falls back to 0%. This increase to 16% and fall to 0% continues indefinitely as the thickness of glass increases, an effect that can be explained by QED.

Feynman's book, *QED* (1985), makes much use of diagrams to give the reader an insight into the principles involved in QED. The theory explains how light seems to bend under water, the processes involved in a mirage, and of most importance, why we think light travels in straight lines whereas in reality it does not. It only 'seems' to go in straight lines because that which goes between object and observer has the greatest influence on the 'result'. Thus, the classical interpretation and result of QED analysis on a light travel event produces similar results despite completely different methods of analysis. The idea that light goes in a straight line is a convenient approximation to describe what happens in the world that is familiar to us.

Feynman said that in a crude picture of the world, light only goes where the time is least, and the least time is generally the shortest line. Calculations from QED incorporate these phenomena using the *path integral* process of Feynman and colleagues. This *sum-over histories* interpretation translates all possible events to real world interpretations and predictions. For example, light moves at different rates in water and air, which affects what is the least time and shortest route for the light and accounts for the apparent bending. This and all other light phenomena can be explained by QED.

Since light is observed to take the quickest path between two points (e.g., from source to detector), one might ask how it knows where it is going. If we know the start and end point of the light photon's journey, we can calculate the time taken for this journey. But when light is emitted from a source, it does not 'know' where it is going — so why *does* light take the quickest route to some chosen endpoint? The shortest route for light is usually the quickest (although sometimes not, such as when it passes through air and water), but QED takes into consideration all the possible journeys and from this calculates the probability of what will happen. One way of visualising this is by making a 'Feynman diagram' (Figure 14).

A Feynman diagram can be used to show every possible path for a photon between source and detector. Each individual possible path is assigned a complex number-valued probability. Feynman replaced complex numbers with spinning arrows, which start spinning at a defined speed at emission and end at detection. The arrows are aligned head to tail for all possibilities. A straight line connecting the start to the finish of all the arrows (emission to detection), squared, represents the total probability of the event, which is equivalent to classical analysis since the major contributor of the possible histories is the shortest and fastest straight line path of the photon. Our natural assumption of a straight-line path of the photon is more a consequence of incorrect common sense due to a misunderstanding of the strange nature of electromagnetic radiation. Indeed, Feynman did not explain why the amplitude arrows are fundamental to the QED description, probably because he stressed that the theory tells us what is happening rather than why.

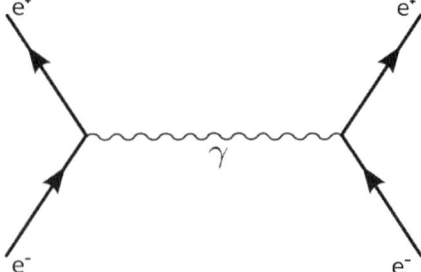

Figure 14. Feynman diagram. An electron (e⁻) and positron (e⁺) annihilate, creating a decaying photon (γ) and new electron-positron pair.

But we digress. Back in 1925, Schrödinger did not know about electron spin when he formulated his wave mechanics. He would not have been able to formulate a QFT, nor did he incorporate Einstein's special relativity into his equation. It fell to Dirac to apply quantum mechanics to Einstein's theory and generate a functionally successful wave equation for the electron. The *Dirac equation* explains electron behaviour at high speed, and predicts the experimentally verified electron spin of ½.

Spin-½ particles such as electrons (but also neutrons and protons) can have two spin states with opposite rotations, and the superposition of these states can be defined by:

$\psi = W \:|up> + Z \:|down>$ (where W and Z are complex numbers).

The Dirac equation also predicts the existence of an anti-electron, a *positron*, which has the same mass as an electron but is positively charged. This prediction, in 1930, was the first prediction of antimatter. Verification of Dirac's ideas came in 1932 with the detection of positrons by Carl Anderson, who received the Nobel Prize for this work.

Uncertainty

In 1927, in addition to his earlier formulation of matrix mechanics, Heisenberg made another great and perhaps more famous discovery based on his realisation that quantum theory limited the amount of information that can be obtained simultaneously from a measurement. He stated that the exact position of a subatomic particle cannot be found unless one accepts limitations on the knowledge that can be obtained about the particle's momentum. Conversely, one cannot ascertain the particle's exact momentum unless one is willing to accept limitations on knowledge of its position. Thus, with this statistical insight, electron behaviour can be defined more accurately when there are many electrons being measured. To locate a particular electron, one can only state the probable position within the complex superimposed wave motions of the electron group. Furthermore, the fewer the number of electrons, the more indeterminate the measurement of probability.

A quantitative relationship for the extent of this uncertainty can be asserted by simultaneously measuring the position and momentum. The equation form of this uncertainty relation is shown below. To measure position accurately, we need a short wavelength and, thus, high frequency. A greater number of wavelengths per unit of length provides more information about the content of that length within the space being considered. However, energy of short wavelength is high-energy radiation, which imparts energy that is transferred to and thus affects the momentum of the observed particle. Greater accuracy in the measurement of position makes possible a consequent reduction in quantification of momentum. The imprecision of the positional measurement of an object under magnification is limited by diffraction when interference patterns overlap. The converse is true for the effect of the momentum's measurement on position.

Using long wavelength radiation of low frequency does not significantly alter the particle's momentum, thereby enabling a more accurate measurement. But this detracts from the accuracy by which we can measure its position by an extent denoted by a defined quantum relationship. These limitations are not the result of practical experimental limitations; rather, they are *fundamental to the nature of quantum reality*. Heisenberg was able to use the two relations for position and momentum to formulate his *uncertainty principle*. That is, the imprecision in the position (x) measurement is approximately equal to the wavelength (λ):

$$\Delta x \sim \lambda$$

The minimum imprecision in the momentum measurement is approximately equal to the momentum imparted on the electron by a single photon. Thus, from the de Broglie-Einstein relation, $\Delta p \sim h/\lambda$.

The change in position (x) and momentum (p) will always be greater than or equal to ($\geq$) a certain value:

$$(\Delta x)(\Delta p) \geq (\lambda)(h/\lambda) \geq h \text{ or.... } \Delta x \, \Delta p \geq h \text{ (where } h \text{ is Planck's constant)}$$

This is the Heisenberg uncertainty principle. Put into words, the simultaneous measurement of momentum and position of a particle is greater than a fixed amount, which is approximately equal to Planck's constant. It states the limitations on how much knowledge we can have about the world at the fundamental level. In mathematical terms, if we knew both where a particle and what its momentum are, it would be in a state that is simultaneously an eigenstate of position operator x and an eigenstate of momentum operator p. The uncertainty principle tells us that the operators of x and p do not commute, so we cannot take definite values. Feynman said that every new discovery in theoretical physics since Heisenberg's uncertainty principle has been merely a restating of it.

It was Bohr who pointed out to Heisenberg in his first paper draft of the principle that a reduced change in momentum brings about a compensating added uncertainty in position. Although these phenomena do not affect our day-to-day lives in the macroscopic world, it does limit the information that can be attained from a subatomic system. The philosophical ramifications and consequences for classical physics are huge. Regarding the double-slit experiment, Heisenberg showed that the detection of which slit the photon passed through is a measurement of position and the observation of interference is like a momentum measurement. The narrower the slit is, the broader the diffraction pattern. This limits the accuracy of simultaneous measurements. The uncertainty principle, together with wave/particle duality, puts a fundamental limitation on the precision of a simultaneous measurement of physical quantities such as the position and momentum of a photon or any particle for that matter.

The quantum problem

Classical determinism was considered a true representation of reality since Pierre Simon de Laplace (1749–1827) formulated his principle of *determinism* in the 18th century. Determinism states that if we know the position and motion of the particles within a system at one point in time, we can exactly calculate their motion at a later stage. The Heisenberg uncertainty principle states that we cannot know the exact position and motion of a particle at any one moment, so determinism and the uncertainty principle cannot be accepted congruently. Quantum physics rejects the simple type of determinism envisaged by Laplace.

In 1927, Bohr made the deduction that wave and particle behaviour are both necessary to fully know the properties of an object despite their mutual exclusivity. This was called *complementarity*. It describes how measurement destroys some property of a quantum system. Thus, we see again a difference between the classical and quantum view on reality. In classical terms, if two conditions are mutually exclusive, then one must be wrong. In quantum theory, the particle or wave-like behaviour of objects depends on how you choose to view it. Bohr treated complementarity and indeterminism as fundamental facts of reality.

Bohr began to bring all the parts of quantum theory together into a single system — the Copenhagen interpretation, which included his complementarity, Heisenberg's work on matrix mechanics and the uncertainty principle, Schrödinger's wave equation, Born's probability, and Dirac's quantum mechanics. The radical aspect of the Copenhagen interpretation is that the state of an atomic system is considered undefined until measurement — it only has the potentiality for certain values with associated probabilities.

There are three levels to a quantum measurement — the way the apparatus is set up, the statistical result involving many measurements, and the result attained in a particular measurement, which is random and unpredictable. Thus, quantum physicists take the *measurement problem* seriously. This problem arises from the idea that quantum systems have properties only when they are measured. Until measured, there is a superposition of all possible states. Yet there is nothing outside of the quantum system to make the measurement; that which measures is itself a quantum system, which is why Eugene Wigner decided on our consciousness as that which closes the cycle and causes the collapse — even if, as Penrose surmises, consciousness itself may be a quantum process.

Decoherence

One wonders, in the context of what is required to collapse the wave function, whether humans can do this. Something that is conscious of the collapse, caused by the measurement, is capable of making the measurement (and does not exist as a superposition!). Indeed, could a conscious entity existing as a superposition cause a collapse? As humans are constructed of atoms that can exist as superpositions separately, why in the form of a whole human does the superposition fail?

From the above, it is obvious that we should ask why small things can exist as superpositions whereas large things cannot. The Copenhagen interpretation implies that superpositions are common, but in fact they are rare. The word 'superposition' is used freely to describe the strange properties of quantum reality so that, although the properties they describe exist, they play a small part in the reality we interact with. To maintain a superposition requires careful experimental setup, and the superposition is easily destroyed, causing collapse. Decoherence presents a reason why superpositions are rare and only really seen in atomic or small molecule systems.

The interaction of the superposition of one quantum system with that of another results in decoherence between the two and the collapse of their respective superpositions. Thus, it is clear that in a large multi-molecular entity such as a human, avoidance of decoherence is nigh on impossible. Hence, we do not see humans as superpositions. Although decoherence explains why large object superpositions are rare, it cannot resolve quantum dilemmas such as non-locality, entanglement (which we look at next), or why when we make a measurement, say of a spin-correlated photon, the value is *this* and not *that*.

Entanglement and the EPR paradox

Bohr was convinced that once two particles are connected, they are never separated no matter how far apart because they are, in quantum terms, *entangled*. This caused Einstein some problems. Central to the Copenhagen interpretation is the distinction between the microscopic quantum world and the macroscopic apparatus we use to measure it. Here we see why Einstein did not like the ideas of quantum theory and why he spent much of his later life searching, unsuccessfully, for a Grand Unified Theory applicable both to the microscopic and macroscopic world. The information we obtain about the quantum world is achieved through using an apparatus, and this very act alters the system being measured. It is unavoidable. Physical properties are possessed by the combined system of the quantum reality of the microscopic object plus the measuring apparatus.

Bohr presented his ideas 'on the principle of complementarity' at a conference in September 1927 in Como, Italy. He stated that if a set of experiments can only be interpreted on the basis of wave properties and another on the basis of particle properties, then the two sets of evidence are not contradictory. As the evidence is obtained under different conditions, it cannot be combined into a single picture — rather, it is considered to be 'complementary'. Einstein was not at that meeting, but he did attend the Solvay conference in October 1927 (mentioned earlier).

When Bohr presented the ideas of the Copenhagen interpretation there, he thought that Einstein would agree with them. Indeed, it was Einstein he most wanted to convince (if he agreed, Bohr thought it must be right!). However, Einstein did not like the probability theory. He wanted a description of the thing itself, not the probability of its occurrence. He considered the interpretation to be of only temporary use.

Einstein spent much time formulating *gedanken* experiments in an attempt to uncover faults in the quantum formulation. Bohr was always able to explain these thought experiments in terms of his interpretation of quantum theory. One of Einstein's *gedanken* experiments (out of many others) that was used to try to prove that the uncertainty principle was violated was one where a box full of light could enable an examiner to simultaneously determine the energy of a single photon and the time it was emitted (time and energy are governed by the uncertainty principle, though not the same uncertainty principle as Position X and Momentum P. In quantum mechanics, P is an operator, E is not). The experiment is as follows:

> If we weigh the box, release a photon through a shutter operated by a clockwork mechanism inside the box, and then weigh the box again, the change in mass enables the energy of the photon to be calculated from the equation $E = mc^2$. Thus, the energy change would be known as would the exact time of the photon release, which is in contravention of the uncertainty principle.

That was Einstein's thinking on the matter. However, Bohr showed that when the photon is released, the recoil will affect the clock's position in Earth's gravitational field, resulting in an uncertainty in the time measurement due to, as Einstein failed to appreciate, Einstein's own general theory of relativity. The Copenhagen interpretation stood up to that particular test.

Einstein and others continued their thought experiments. Einstein was 'certain' that the Copenhagen interpretation was wrong. He wanted to prove it through the use of hypothetical and often untestable scenarios that the rules of the interpretation could not explain so that physicists would try harder to find a theory that could explain phenomena as they were, rather than through the probabilities of events occurring. His most famous *gedanken* experiment attack on the Copenhagen interpretation was not directed at the uncertainty principle, but at another aspect of the theory. It was called the EPR paradox and it goes like this:

> Electron pairs are usually of opposite spin. It is possible to obtain a pair in a so-called 'singlet state' where the spins cancel each other out to give a combined spin of zero. If we allow two such particles, denoted A and B, to move far apart, and then we find the spin of A to be in the 'up' state, then because the two spins must cancel to zero, particle B spin must therefore be in the 'down' state.

According to classical physics, there is no problem here as we would say that B had 'down' spin from the time of separation — its spin was determined at source. However, the Copenhagen interpretation states that the spin of A has no value until it is measured — it is in a spin superposition. When it is measured, that action must have an *instantaneous* effect at B, causing the collapse of its spin wave function into the 'down' state. Thus, however far apart particles A and B are, when A is measured, B assumes the opposite spin position even if special relativity appears violated. According to the Copenhagen interpretation, apparent faster-than-light 'communication' and 'spooky' (as Einstein called it) *action-at-a-distance* appear possible, neither of which is acceptable within the classical rules of physics.

If two systems are separated and in isolation from one another for some significant but undefined amount of time, then a measurement of one can have no effect on the other. They are *non-local*, a term that implies that different parts of a quantum system appear to influence each other even when they are great distances apart and when there is no interaction between them. Non-locality is like locality, but without special relativistic restrictions. This is Einstein's 'action-at-a-distance' rule of the locality principle. Also, his theory of special relativity states that nothing can travel faster than light. Einstein, Podolsky, and Rosen were convinced they had shown the existence of and need for *hidden variables*, which quantum theory had not accounted for. They thought that a revision of the theory was needed because its statistical nature rendered it incomplete. Thus, hidden variables are just that — additional elements of reality, hidden from us, but which render reality fundamentally determinate. Spin is a hidden variable since which way an elementary particle spins is both a 'variable' (could be anything) and 'hidden' (we cannot see it).

Was the Copenhagen interpretation incomplete? Bohr had the answer that convinced himself, but not Einstein. Bohr said that even if the radius of the Universe separated particles A and B, they are still part of the same quantum system. Once the particles are connected, they are never separated — they are entangled (the modern term used to describe particles that are connected through property correlation from the German 'verschränkung', coined by Schrödinger).

Bohr stated that it was naïve to consider that *local* conditions apply to an atom. Locality applies to anywhere the quantum system being 'measured' occurs. To him, the 'apparent' violation of the theory of special relativity does not matter in the case of the quantum system of particles A and B since they are not really separated — they are the same quantum system described by a single wavefunction. Particle B can assume the 'down' spin at half the width of the Universe away immediately when particle A is measured to have 'up' spin. The entanglement (or correlation) can violate special relativity, but *knowledge* of it does not.

Let us clarify entanglement. To Einstein, for a measurement of A's spin to cause B's spin to be correlated (e.g., A is + and B is −) immediately, either the spins must be determined at source and not by measurement, or there are hidden variables in addition to the current version of quantum theory that enable the correlation without violating special relativity. If spins are determined at source, then Einstein saw no violation of special relativity for correlation as the spins are predetermined. If correlations are determined by measurement, however, then special relativity would be violated because measurement of A's spin causes B to adopt the correlated spin faster than the speed of light. That is, for A to 'communicate' with B about its spin state, it would have to do so in violation of special relativity.

Einstein thought that regardless whether the spin state is determined at source or by measurement, the Copenhagen interpretation is incomplete (i.e., if by measurement, then special relativity is violated; if at source, then measurement has no determinate feature).

Correlation does not occur at the point when A and B are made, according to Bohr. Additionally, it is the act of measurement of A that causes B to assume its correlated state. So, the argument is about hidden variables and locality. Bohr saw the particles, A and B, as entangled. They are forever linked as a correlated system, whatever the degree of separation. Einstein saw *any* form of violation of special relativity as a need for improvement of the Copenhagen interpretation. Bohr, however, was satisfied with it and thought that entanglement can be instantaneous without violating special relativity since the entanglement only applies to that which is entangled. *Knowledge* of the entanglement must conform to special relativity. Thus, to Bohr, relativity *and* the Copenhagen interpretation are consistent with entanglement being immediate. More importantly for Bohr, the Copenhagen interpretation survives the EPR paradox unscathed.

In an article *Cool horizons for Entangled black holes*, physicists Juan Maldacena and Leonard Susskind have postulated that entangled particles are actually linked by wormholes, which are natural deformations of space-time. If true, entanglement is not non-local, and no violation of special relativity occurs.

Jacob Bronowski believed that every event in the world is connected to every other event (particle entanglement is a special example of this). This may appear as purely a metaphysical statement, but it has practical consequences. If such is true, then the practice of science is incomplete. When an experiment is performed, we are decoding a part of nature that is isolated from the whole. It is separated from all that is connected purely as a result of experimental design and must be interpreted as such. As Bronowski put it, we cannot get out of our finiteness.

Dionysus the Areopagite (in the 5th century) said that God's love draws every piece of matter to him, but every piece of matter must be drawn to every other piece. Within such a theory, there can be no ultimate truth that we can find. We always have to cut off a piece of the Universe to perform an experiment. As we will see later, Bohm attempted to construct a quantum theory that treated all existence as a single connected thing. If our access to reality is finite and limited as is our physical and mental capacity, then all knowledge cannot ever reach 'truth', merely truth relevant to us and our limitations.

Hidden variables

Hidden variable theories are most easily demonstrated in situations where there are only a few possible outcomes to an experiment. One example exploits the polarisation of light. Maxwell's equations determine that the direction of vibration of an electric field is always at right angles to the direction of light travel. The electric field can change direction, but it is possible to create light where its pointing remains constant, known as plane polarised light.

Normal non-polarised light can shine onto 'Polaroid' sunglasses and emerge the other side polarised with a subsequent 50% diminishment in light intensity. By passing light through a polariser such as a calcite crystal, the light divides into two component-polarised forms — parallel (or vertical, V) or perpendicular (or horizontal, H) to a direction in the crystal. This is a random process as the H- or V-polarisation is not predictable. Thus, passing light through an HV polariser causes photons to emerge from the H channel (horizontally polarised photons) and from the V channel (vertically polarised photons).

It might seem that polarisation is a wave concept and not applicable to particulate photons. If the V-polarised photons are passed through a second HV polariser and the H-polarised photons through another HV polariser, the photons will pass through the same channel as they did through the first polariser (i.e., V through V and H through H). However, if instead of a second HV polariser, the HV separated photons are passed through individual +/−45° measurement polarisers (determining whether the light is +45° or −45°), the H- and the V-polarised photons will pass through either channel. The act of measurement has made them 'forget' their polarisation. We can see that this polarisation is an example of the superposition principle mentioned earlier.

If +45° light is passed through a HV polariser and the H- and V-polarised light are both passed from this through an exact reverse angle HV polariser before passing through a +/−45° measurement polariser, the light emitted here has the same polarisation as the initial light entering the first HV polariser. As the light entering the HV polariser has no knowledge of what polariser it will encounter, how does the light measured know that it was initially +45° when entering? Without knowledge of quantum rules, the conclusion would be that either the light passes both the H- and V- polariser channels at once (even though it is only detected in one) or that by passing one path, it knows what it would have done had it passed the other path.

The conclusion of such a hidden variable theory is that the photon does not *need* to know what is happening at the other channel. Rather than treating wave and particle models as alternatives, both are present simultaneously. Locality is preserved because the behaviour of the photon results from the wave properties at the point where the photon actually *is*.

Let us look at things a different way. Passing a light through a polarisation filter causes about half the light to be absorbed and half to be transmitted. The light that is transmitted adopts directionality, which is made apparent by passing it through another polarised filter. How this filter affects the light depends on its orientation with respect to that of the first filter that the light beam encountered. At a certain orientation, the filter has no effect on the beam, but as it is turned, it absorbs light until at 90° it absorbs all the light. As we increase the angle, light starts to pass through again until at 180° all the light passes through (Figure 15).

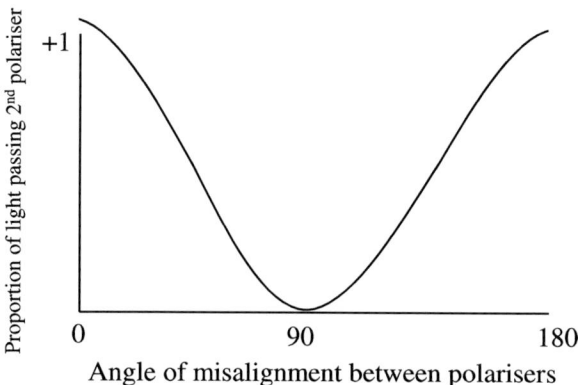

Figure 15. Polariser alignment. The angle of misalignment between polarisers determines the proportion of light transmitted.

So, for example, if the second polariser is 30° misaligned to the first, then about 75% of light will pass through the second polariser. Of course, this represents a proportion, and individual photons are either transmitted or rejected. Now, the graph for $Cos^2\theta$ (see Figure 18) looks a lot like this graph, and we will see why this is later. However, rather than determining the proportion of photons passing the filter, it represents the *probability* that each photon will pass.

In 1932, von Neumann proved to his own satisfaction that any attempt to find a hidden variable theory that agrees with quantum mechanics is doomed to failure. He predicted that such a theory would be bound to disagree with quantum theory in some of its predictions, and that all of physics is reducible to quantum physics. He suggested that when a superposition of a quantum system confronts a conscious mind, there is a collapse onto a particular property.

The problem with this idea is that at every stage from the quantum system or object being measured up to the conscious mind measuring the collapse, there exists a superposition. Thus, the measuring apparatus and the human body must exist as a superposition of states up to the point of consciousness-induced collapse of the measured system. It seems like a case of focusing on mathematical rigour while ignoring intuitive feasibility, which Einstein considered to be of utmost importance.

Von Neumann explained the measurement problem thus — if we want to measure temperature, we use a thermometer. The mercury in the thermometer enables the temperature to be measured by the thermometer. We can go further and explain it in kinetic and molecular terms — the heating and expansion of mercury. When bringing light into the equation, we can say "the image of the mercury in the thermometer is registered on the retina of the observer". Going further, we can trace the chemical reactions in the brain producing the image and say that changes in brain cells when measuring temperature this way are perceived by the observer. However, when we define the measurement of temperature, we must divide the world into two parts — the observed system and the observer. While in the former we can follow the physical processes, in the latter this is meaningless.

The boundary between the observer and the observed can be moved (be it the mercury or even the physical processes of the brain cells), but it is always there. It can neither be avoided nor removed. Thus, in an experiment, we can only say that "an observer has made a certain subjective observation" and never "a physical quantity has a certain value", since the former relates the perceiver to the perceived whereas the latter ignores the necessary and evident boundary between the two worlds. Since the boundary must be put somewhere between the observer and observed, von Neumann suggested that consciousness collapses the wavepacket. It is our perception of an event that collapses the probability wavefunction of the event onto a physically real, observed, and definitive event.

In 1952, Bohm (whom we shall encounter in more detail later on) constructed a hidden variable theory that agreed with quantum mechanics in all its empirical predictions. He adopted de Broglie's pilot wave concept in an attempt to explain the double-slit experiment.

The de Broglie-Bohm version of quantum theory (initiated by de Broglie on Einstein's encouragement and modified by Bohm) considers physical reality not to consist of particles or waves, but both. The associated pilot wave for the quantum particle guides the particle on its trajectory such that the particle possesses a real position at all times. The pilot wave enables the electron or particle to 'ride' the wave as it passes through both slits in the famous double-slit experiment. Thus, this theory avoids the superposition principle and preserves some form of realism. However, it is innately non-local (because of the pilot wave), and despite avoiding the consequences of the violation of the *Bell inequality*, it violates special relativistic realism. It is not universally accepted because the introduction of the pilot wave concept reminds some of a return to 19th century physics and the luminiferous aether. We now move our attention to Bell.

John Bell

John Bell (1928–1990) was born in Northern Ireland and was a much-lauded physicist and philosopher. He was stirred to reappraise von Neumann's proof of the incompatibility of hidden variable theories. Bell developed an inequality principle (later termed 'Bell's inequality theorem') to test the questions raised by the EPR paradox.

In 1969, Bell showed that it is theoretically possible to determine *experimentally* if a hidden variable theory that preserves locality and determinism is capable of reproducing the quantum theoretical predictions of the double-slit experiment. He demonstrated that under certain conditions, quantum theory (in its traditional form) and local hidden variable theories predicted different results for the same test on correlated or anti-correlated particles. Furthermore, this applies to *all* possible local hidden variable theories (N.B. correlated particles display the same value when measured (e.g., A is +, B is +), whereas anti-correlated particles display the opposite (e.g., A is +, B is –), but both correlations demonstrate entanglement).

Locality means that cause and effect occur at the same location, whereas non-locality means that cause and effect occur at different locations. It is possible to use angular momentum-correlated electrons or spin-correlated photons in an interferometer — an instrument that can emit, reflect, deviate the path of, and detect a particle — to determine locality. One can also exploit the polarisation effect of light. The polarisation of a transverse wave describes the direction of oscillation in the plane perpendicular to the direction of travel. Due to known predicted quantum mechanical effects, the behaviour of particles and waves can be measured and compared with Bell's predictions to determine if locality is held. Photons are spin-1 particles, so it is easier to measure photon polarisation than spin orientation, as would be the case for spin-½ electrons.

So, what *is* Bell's theorem? What does it really test, how does it do it, and why is it so important? Fundamentally, Bell's theorem actually refers to local realistic hidden variable theories rather than quantum mechanics. The theory tests the consequences of quantum theory as does the EPR paradox, for example, in that it questions how particle A affects distant particle B (particle A and B may be, for instance, separated spin-correlated photons). It is a theory that produces a set of testable inequalities whose violation following measurement would mean that no deterministic theory can explain particle entanglement. It does not mean, as some suggest, that if one gives up determinism or hidden variables, then no violation occurs. It means that if violated, *no* deterministic theory can produce the predictions that do not violate the inequality.

Experimental measurements to test the inequality on entangled particles have shown, for certain conditions, violation of the inequality. Since the inequality is generated according to local and deterministic assumptions, its violation implies a non-local universe. Quantum theory, which assumes non-locality, conforms to measurement and violates the inequality under the specific condition that measurement violates it too.

To derive the inequality, Bell used facts and ideas that he considered everyone would agree on. He assumed Einstein's condition of non-locality to be true and stated that if the inequality is violated by experimental verification, then one of the facts or ideas he considered to be true would be false. It does not really matter which one since the assumption from the violation of the inequality is that nature is non-local. He designed this experimental idea as there had been no test made of the correlation implicated by the Bell inequality. An extended Bell inequality was formulated that tested not only determinism but also many hidden variable theories that include a random element. In such an extension, any hidden variable that preserves locality is rejected.

In 1982, the research group of the French physicist Alain Aspect produced experimental results that indicated verification of the violation of Bell's inequality. The setup shown in Figure 16 is similar to that used by Aspect and evaluates a certain type of hidden variable theory. Let us say that the reader of the detectors on the left-hand side of the apparatus is 'A' while those on the right-hand side is 'B'. Let us also say that they are

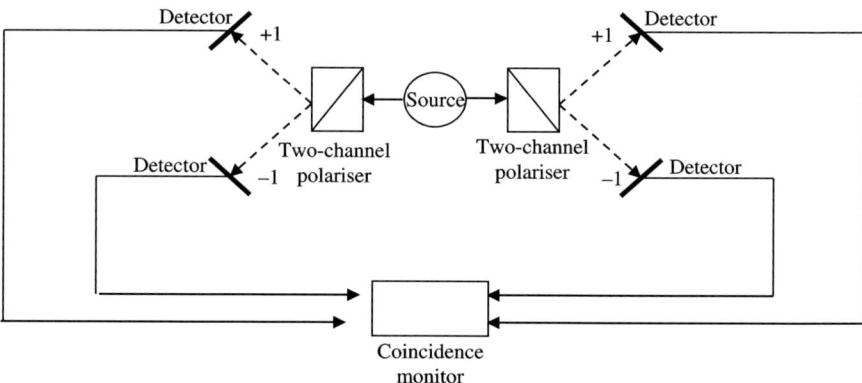

Figure 16. Scheme to test Bell's inequality. The source sends pairs of entangled photons in opposite directions. Each photon reaches a two-channel polariser whose orientation (up or down) is set by the experimenter. Signals from each channel are detected and counted by the coincidence monitor (up-up, up-down, down-up, down-down). More elaborate tests have been designed, such as the CHSH Bell test (named after John Clauser, Michael Horne, Abner Shimony, and Richard Holt), which distinguish between entanglement and hidden variable hypotheses.

measuring the spin of spin-correlated photons. Due to the conservation of angular momentum, the decay of a photon can lead to the production of two daughter photons whose spins are perfectly correlated with a probability of unity that if the spin of one photon is +1, then the other is −1. This occurs when the spins are measured along the same axis. As we will see, this is important.

According to quantum mechanics, the wave function of the pair is in a singlet state and is described by the equation:

$$\psi = 1/\sqrt{2}[(+1)_A|(-1)_B - (-1)_A|(+1)_B]$$

(N.B. the minus sign between the two sides ensures that the net spin is zero).

This function is a superposition of two states — one where the photon traveling to 'A' is spin +1 (up) and the correlated photon traveling to 'B' is spin −1 (down) along the same axis of measurement (e.g., z-axis), and the other where the photon traveling to 'A' is −1 and 'B' is +1. According to quantum theory, the wave function describing the superposition of states indicates that we cannot attribute exact values for the position or velocity of the particles — Heisenberg determined the limits for this. The wave function is a description of the entangled particle pair, and measurement of a property collapses the particles onto a particular Eigenstate or position vector.

Before measurement, particles have no well-defined spin properties but a superposition of all possible states as described in the equation above. As the entangled, correlated particles separate in space and time, the wave function continues to describe the whole system irrespective of the distance of separation. Quantum mechanics in the Copenhagen interpretation states that when observer 'A' measures a particular property (spin in this case) of their photon along one axis, observer 'B' can predict with certainty the spin of the other entangled particle with certainty and without measurement, and that this property is correlated. When a measurement is made, the equation collapses onto one of the two possibilities for correlation. This correlation applies for measurements on the same axes and it is immediate.

In this example, the Copenhagen interpretation says that the state of a particular property is not determined at the moment of decay, and that the act of measurement of that property of the particle traveling to 'A' *causes* that property to adopt a state (e.g., spin = +1 or −1, up or down) *and* for the same property of the entangled particle traveling to 'B' to immediately adopt the correlated state. Thus, the Copenhagen interpretation of quantum mechanics states that entangled particles violate special relativity (in the context of entanglement only, not *information* about entanglement) and that the Universe is non-local (not 'local'). Physical reality is non-local (entanglement), but social reality is local (knowledge of entanglement). By this I mean that useable information about entangled particles must conform to special relativity.

The English chemist Jim Baggott explains this with a hypothetical scenario. If a man and woman marry and the husband later travels to another planet billions of miles away and dies subsequently, in non-local terms they are no longer married at the point in time he dies from his perspective. In non-local terms, this is the same time for the wife too. However, in local, social-realistic terms, they cease to be married after the period of time that light takes to travel from the husband to the wife after he dies. In the world in which we interact, the marriage conforms to special relativity. It was Bell, with his testable inequalities, who provided the means to test whether any local hidden variable theories can exist.

The idea that particles exist as a superposition of states until measured is an unnerving prospect, not only for you and I but also for Einstein himself. He was not a 'fan' of hidden variable theories and wanted some form of realism. Unfortunately, he died before Bell produced his idea of testable inequalities for local realism (or 'locality', which is clearer), which enabled the likes of Aspect and later Greenberger, Horne, and Zeilinger (GHZ) to design experiments to physically test them. However, his famous EPR paper voiced his concerns that questioned the Copenhagen interpretation.

Bohr agreed that it is an unsettling fact of nature that reality is, at the fundamental level, indeterminate (if you're not shocked by it, you haven't appreciated its implications, he said). For him, the Universe is non-local. When Einstein said, "God doesn't play dice" (to paraphrase his infamous quote), Bohr retorted that Einstein should stop telling God what to do. He meant, of course, that we model the world according to how we find it, and if it is as we see it — however unsettling — that is just how it is and we should not try to fit the data according to how we 'intuitively' feel it should be. Wheeler, paraphrasing Bohr, also said that we have no right to ask what photons are doing — no elementary particle is a phenomenon until it is registered.

How does Bell's theorem help us to understand the nature of reality? Is it local or non-local, and how do hidden variable theories fit in? To reiterate, Bell's theorem uses the scenario of correlated particles to reveal facts about the nature of reality. By using correlated particles, the theorem is able to probe and evaluate the importance of measurement of a quantum state, special relativity, locality, realism, and hidden variable theories.

Quantum theory states that entangled particles are correlated for the same property measured along the same axis, and this is immediate following measurement of one particle — the other correlated and unmeasured particle 'disregards' locality and 'remembers' what it must be when it is measured, and this effect occurs from the moment the other particle is measured (and from that moment in time in its frame of reference). Yet, there is no reason why measurement must be made along the same axis. Going back to the experimental setup depicted in Figure 15, 'A' may want to measure particle spin along an arbitrary direction (d), say d_A, while observer 'B' wants to measure spin along some other direction, say d_B. From the wave function described earlier (a form of the Schrödinger wave equation), the probability that both 'A' and 'B' record +1 (up) correlated spin along the chosen direction is:

$$P(+1, d_A; +1, d_B) = \tfrac{1}{2} \sin^2(\theta/2)$$

where θ is the angle between directions d_A and d_B (we will see why later).

Since the entangled particles are correlated, $P(+1, d_A; +1, d_B) = 0$ because there is zero probability of both recording +1 spin. For 'A' to record spin +1, 'B' must measure −1 for the correlation. These are the predictions of the Copenhagen interpretation of quantum theory. However, this interpretation sees the system as a superposition until measured, at which point the particles adopt a well-defined state. Can hidden variables add to this interpretation of reality? Hidden variables are hidden properties in addition to those that can be observed. A particle may know what it will do, but if this information is unavailable to us, then such a theory is a hidden variable theory. The Copenhagen interpretation in essence states that particles do not know what they will do — it is indeterministic.

Hidden variable theories state that they do know what they will do, but that this information is hidden from us as observers. There is an essence of determinism in such theories. In a 'local' hidden variable interpretation, we assume that the particles possess well-defined properties that enable the entanglement, but that they are hidden from us and our interpretation. That is, neither stating that the entanglement is determined at source nor by the act of measurement is true. There are hidden properties that we know of, but not what they are, that cause the correlation in accordance with the rules of special relativity. If true, then the Universe is local, realism resides, and Einstein's first criticism upholds — special relativity is not violated.

Bell's theorem tests this local, realist hidden variable interpretation of quantum theory. If Bell's theorem is violated, then the Universe is non-local at the fundamental level, as can be proven by assessment of the special case of correlated quantum systems through experimental analysis of the theorem. However, a non-local theory of the Universe may also possess hidden variables, but it must explain special and general relativity as well as quantum theory. Unlike Bell's test of local hidden variable theories, there are no means to verify whether non-local hidden variable theories are correct.

For the test of local hidden variable theories, if Bell's inequality is not violated, the Copenhagen interpretation fails. If it is violated, that interpretation *can* survive intact (despite the possibility for non-local hidden variable theories, such as that proposed by Bohm, to also be feasible). To test a local hidden variable theory using Bell's theorem, we will use the simple case of 'A' and 'B' and measuring the spin of spin-correlated photons along the z-axis. Rather than describing the correlated pair using the wave function shown above, we assume for the entangled particles that:

50% of the particles can be described by $(+1)_A$ and $(-1)_B$
50% of the particles can be described by $(-1)_A$ and $(+1)_B$

So, for half the pairs, 'A' sees +1 spin with 'B' seeing −1 spin, and for the other half, 'A' sees −1 spin with 'B' seeing +1 spin — this gives a 100% correlation. This does not mean that we are stating locality, non-locality, or the reason for entanglement, just that there is total correlation for the detection of the spin-correlated photons. In other words, that there is entanglement. Quantum mechanical predictions (i.e., 'A' and 'B' see a random sequence of perfectly correlated particles) are reproduced.

Since 'A' and 'B' can measure along any axis, let us allow measurement along two axes, independently and randomly, and call the directions of measurement d_1 and d_2. So, 'A' can measure along one of d_1 and d_2, as can 'B'. Therefore, d_A is now either d_1 or d_2 and d_B is either d_1 or d_2. If we assume that each particle is created at source with predetermined spin properties in accordance with local realism (as Einstein suggested), and as we have not specified the orientation between d_1 and d_2, then correlated photon pairs detected by 'A' and 'B' can be described as fractional populations (F):

F_1 of the photon pairs can be described by $(+1,+1)_A$ and $(-1,-1)_B$
F_2 of the photon pairs can be described by $(+1,-1)_A$ and $(-1,+1)_B$
F_3 of the photon pairs can be described by $(-1,+1)_A$ and $(+1,-1)_B$
F_4 of the photon pairs can be described by $(-1,-1)_A$ and $(+1,+1)_B$

If 'A' measures spin as +1 and +1, for example, along directions d_1 and d_2, then 'B' will measure −1 and −1 along the same directions, and the proportion F_1 of the photon pairs will read as such. Measurement along d_1 and d_2 cannot, of course, occur at the same time. By writing these four pairs, we guarantee that if 'A' and 'B' measure along the same axis, quantum mechanical predictions are reproduced and the particles are correlated. For measurements taken along different axes, the quantum mechanical predictions are reproduced if:

$F_1 = ½ \cos^2(θ/2)$
$F_2 = ½ \sin^2(θ/2)$
$F_3 = ½ \sin^2(θ/2)$
$F_4 = ½ \cos^2(θ/2)$

where θ is the angle between directions d_1 and d_2. The sine and cosine equations come from a description of the amount of light transmitted when

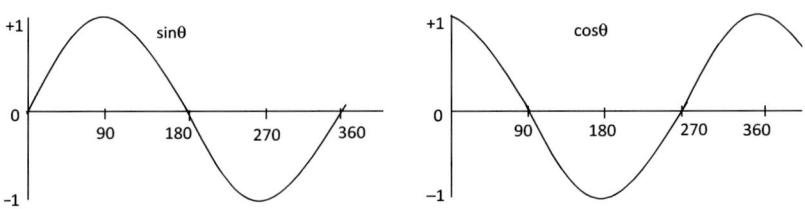

Figure 17. Graphs of sinθ and cosθ.

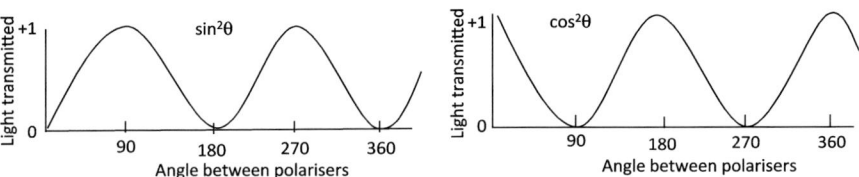

Figure 18. Graphs of sin²θ and cos²θ.

plotting a graph transmission intensity against the angle or direction of the polariser (see below).

The graphs of sinθ and cosθ are shown in Figure 17, and the graphs of sin²θ and cos²θ are shown in Figure 18:
Quantum theory predicts that:

P(+,+) = ½ cos² (angle between polarisers)
P(−,−) = ½ cos² (angle between polarisers)
P(+,−) = ½ sin² (angle between polarisers)
P(−,+) = ½ sin² (angle between polarisers)

for the values relating to the probabilities of finding photons at the different detectors.

That is, and we should refer to the 4-detector interferometer setup shown in Figure 16, P(+,+) means that the left-hand side (LHS) detects a photon in the (+1) 'up' vertical detector while the right-hand side (RHS) also detects a photon in the (+1) 'up' vertically polarised detector. P(+,−) means that the LHS detects a photon in the (+1) 'up' vertical detector and the RHS detects a photon in the (−1) 'down' horizontally polarised detector, and so on.

If the source produces spin-correlated photons and we are measuring correlation, then we are looking for P(+,–) and P(–,+) because they represent correlated photons. For example, if we see a (+) in the LHS, we want to see a (–) in the RHS to preserve spin correlation. The importance of this is that if the values from these calculable predictions violate Bell's testable inequalities, then the implication is that there is no possible local hidden variable quantum theory that can describe the photon correlation.

Now, *Malus's law*, named after the 18th century French physicist Etienne-Louis Malus, states that when a polariser is placed in a polarised beam of light, the intensity, *I*, of the light that passes through is given by:

$$I = I_0 \cos^2 \theta$$

(where I_0 is the initial intensity, *I* is the intensity to be measured, and θ is the angle between the light's initial plane of polarisation and the axis of the polariser, as shown in Figure 15).

So, if one polariser is placed at an angle of 90° or 270° to the beam of polarised light, then no light is transmitted through the second polariser. But, if put it at an angle of 180° or 360°, all the light is transmitted. Malus's law is therefore relevant to the correlation issue.

For perfectly spin-correlated photons as defined by P(+,–) and P(–,+), we expect that if the RHS detector is 90° or 270° (same effect as 90°) to the LHS detector, then we will find all the photons (both P(+,–) and P(–,+) = ½ sin² 90°). From the graph for sin² 90° shown in Figure 17, we see 100% light transmission for 90° and 270°. Conversely, for non-correlated photons defined by P(+,+) and P(–,–), we expect that if the RHS detector is 90° or 270° to the LHS detector, then we will find none of the photons (both P(+,+) and P(–,–) = ½ cos² 90°). For the angles between 0 and 90°, there will be a gradation of expectation. So, for the fractional populations, $F_1 + F_2 + F_3 + F_4 = 1$. That is, the total probability of all four cases is unity. All possibilities are covered. So, in F_3, for 'A' to measure spin –1 in direction d_1 and 'B' to measure spin –1 in direction d_2, this would occur with frequency ½ sin² (θ/2) according to quantum mechanical predictions. Here, no mechanism is given for how these populations are generated, which is the point — they may depend on hidden parameters involving the production of the particles at source, or perhaps the detectors affect the reading.

The question is whether a local theory, with or without hidden variables, can explain correlation. For measurement in two directions, it is possible to create a mechanism that explains the populations and reproduces quantum mechanical predictions in a local, deterministic way as Einstein would have liked. However, when 'A' and 'B' choose from *three* possible directions, problems arise for local, deterministic hidden variable theories.

If we define the fractional populations of particle possibilities, as measured in three directions, we have:

F_1 of the photon pairs can be described by $(+1,+1,+1)_A$ and $(-1,-1,-1)_B$
F_2 of the photon pairs can be described by $(+1,+1,-1)_A$ and $(-1,-1,+1)_B$
F_3 of the photon pairs can be described by $(+1,-1,+1)_A$ and $(-1,+1,-1)_B$
F_4 of the photon pairs can be described by $(-1,+1,+1)_A$ and $(+1,-1,-1)_B$
F_5 of the photon pairs can be described by $(+1,-1,-1)_A$ and $(-1,+1,+1)_B$
F_6 of the photon pairs can be described by $(-1,+1,-1)_A$ and $(+1,-1,+1)_B$
F_7 of the photon pairs can be described by $(-1,-1,+1)_A$ and $(+1,+1,-1)_B$
F_8 of the photon pairs can be described by $(-1,-1,-1)_A$ and $(+1,+1,+1)_B$

where, for example, $(-1,-1,-1)$ represents the spin measured along directions d_1, d_2, and d_3. If the same rules apply as before (e.g., measurement along same axis, correlated spins), then the probabilities of particular results can be presented. For example:

$$P(+1, d_1; +1, d_2) = F_3 + F_5 = [(\underline{\pm 1}, -1, +1)_A \text{ and } (-1, \underline{\pm 1}, -1)_B] + [(\underline{+1}, -1, -1)_A \text{ and } (-1, \underline{\pm 1}, +1)_B]$$

where the relevant direction measurement is underlined for (d_1, d_2, d_3). Only in cases F_3 and F_5 does particle (photon) A have spin +1 along d_1 and particle B have spin +1 along d_2.

In this situation of measuring along three axes, it is possible to write down a condition that holds *true* in our local, deterministic, and realist hidden variable theory, but which is in *conflict* with quantum mechanical predictions. We know that F_1 to F_8 each represent probabilities of particular spin measurements along particular directions, so from this we can formulate inequalities. For example:

$$F_3 + F_5 \leq F_3 + F_5 + F_2 + F_7$$

is the same as:

$$F_3 + F_5 \leq (F_2 + F_5) + (F_3 + F_7)$$

which, as before for two axis measurements, is a statement about probabilities, namely:

$$P(+1, d_1; +1, d_2) \leq P(+1, d_1; +1, d_3) + P(+1, d_2; +1, d_3)$$

This is a Bell inequality.

It follows from the assumption that each particle (spin-correlated photons, in this case) has predetermined measurable qualities from source along any measured direction, and that measurement of one particle (at 'A') does not affect the other (at 'B'). A theory of this type — a local hidden variable theory — will produce results that satisfy this inequality and never results that violate it. However, and this is the key point, for some specific angle of measurement choices, quantum mechanical predictions *do* violate the inequality. For example, take the equation:

½ sin² (90/2) ≤ ½ sin² (45/2) + ½ sin² (45/2)
(where 90 and 45 represent θ, the angles of measurement)
produces values that state 0.25 ≤ 0.146.

This is clearly false, so the quantum mechanical predictions from a local theory violate the Bell inequality (this derivation was extrapolated from the American physicist Travis Norsen's description in *Objective Science*). Thus, any local, realist, and deterministic hidden variable theory that satisfies Bell's inequality contradicts quantum mechanical predictions.

Experimentally, the quantum mechanical result has been proven right by Aspect and others, so it is not possible to reproduce the correct statistics with a theory where the particles have well-defined properties. Therefore, at least one original assumption — that the particles have predetermined properties at source, or that measurement of one particle does not affect some property/properties of the distant, other, correlated, and non-local particle — is wrong.

Quantum mechanics in the Copenhagen interpretation states that measurement determines the state, and it is not determined at source. The violation of the Bell inequality means that there appears to be faster-than-light, non-local communication between correlated particles. However, even though the result shows that any local, deterministic hidden variable theory cannot describe entanglement, this does not exclude the possibility that non-local hidden variables may still apply, as Bohm proposed. The Copenhagen interpretation cannot be *logically* rejected by these results.

Thus, Einstein's vision of a local, deterministic hidden variable theory that proves the Copenhagen interpretation wrong was shattered by tests of the violation of Bell's inequality (but not a non-local one, such as Bohm's). Either we accept entanglement as a fact of nature and that measurement does define the quantum state (i.e., measured as a particle, we see a particle; measured as a wave, we see a wave) as is the case for the Copenhagen interpretation, or we believe that non-local hidden variables exist where measurement may not cause the state.

In the case of Bohm's version of a hidden variable theory, realism is preserved and the Universe is non-local, which would have pleased Einstein since it eliminates the measurement problem. Non-locality in a non-Bohmian, Copenhagen interpretation sense means that the connection between entangled particles does not diminish with distance — it is instantaneous. Locations are linked without crossing space. If action on one photon can affect the state of another a long distance away immediately, and Bell's theorem rejects the possibility that the effect occurs from a property that is possessed by the photons when created, then where do we stand?

Although particle entanglement is a rare case, it serves as proof that non-locality is real and suggests a connection to life that is of immense significance in addition to the role of consciousness in the measurement problem (we will explore this in later chapters). However, *loopholes* have been found in Aspect's statistical analysis. Indeed, although some physicists state that experimental setups are now sophisticated enough to close the loophole (rendering local reality untenable for good), others state that loophole-free tests are impossible as a function of quantum theory itself.

So Bell's theorem is open to question and the EPR paradox (or 'theorem', as physicists prefer to call it) is still being debated. Despite this, most people working actively with the direct consequences of quantum theory are convinced that all local hidden variable theories can be discounted. If the Universe is fundamentally non-local at the quantum level, implying a preservation of instantaneous connection within a quantum system (e.g., distantly separated spin-correlated photons), then the EPR paradox does not violate special relativity because measurement correlations do not depend on any assumed travel. If non-locality is the conclusion we make about how the Universe 'is', then that is what underlies the world we interact with — one of cause and effect, and where special relativity is a limiting factor. That is, the fundamental non-locality and the quantum world itself is alien to us in an interactive sense. As living beings, the classical picture that extends from causal quantum processes is what we feel and where we reside. Only intellect enables conception of what lies beneath.

The Copenhagen interpretation states that it is not meaningful to talk of an electron as possessing a *real* position or momentum until it is measured. Bohr's interpretation was that the quantum system of two correlated photons should not be considered as separate entities until measurement of one part separates them. The superposition describing both particles collapses on the measurement of one, causing the other to immediately adopt the correlated state given that they are entangled and described by a single wavefunction, rather than two (i.e., one for each particle). If a quantity is real only when measured, then the experimenter causes and can change the real properties of a quantum system.

Bohr stressed the importance of measurement and the danger of ascribing properties to unmeasured properties of quantum systems. Before a measurement can be made in experiments such as those described here, a photon (or electron) must be detected in either channel or position. Without measurement, the physical reality of where and why is meaningless. Interferometry is a process that reveals other interesting aspects of quantum indeterminism (indeed, it can be used to test real effects from counterfactuals).

Consider a particle like a photon passing through an interferometer (like the one shown in Figure 19). If there is one possible path for each particle from the emission source to the detector(s), then the percentage of particles that are detected at each detector is as expected by tracing the only possible path. However, if the particle can take two possible paths to the mirror (denoted as C in Figure 19) and is deflected to the detectors, it is detected as 100% at one detector and 0% at the other (rather than 50:50 at each detector).

For this to occur, the path length taken by each particle from the emitter to the detector is the same. By increasing the path length of one of the possible paths by a factor of two (this is achieved by increasing by an integer number of wavelengths), the particle is detected 100% at the detector that was 0%, and 0% at the detector that was 100%. This reverses again when the path length doubles once more (with gradations of detection in between) and so on, *ad infinitum*. So, for one particle emission, we can say that it has been emitted and detected, but not how the particle got to the detector (did it go this way or that way?). When one path length is changed, it is as if the particle 'knows' and changes its behaviour (Bohm would attribute this to the pilot wave).

Looking at the situation in Figure 19 more closely, the diagonal rectangles (A and C) represent beam splitters where the thick lines represent half-silvered splitters such that half the light passes through and half is

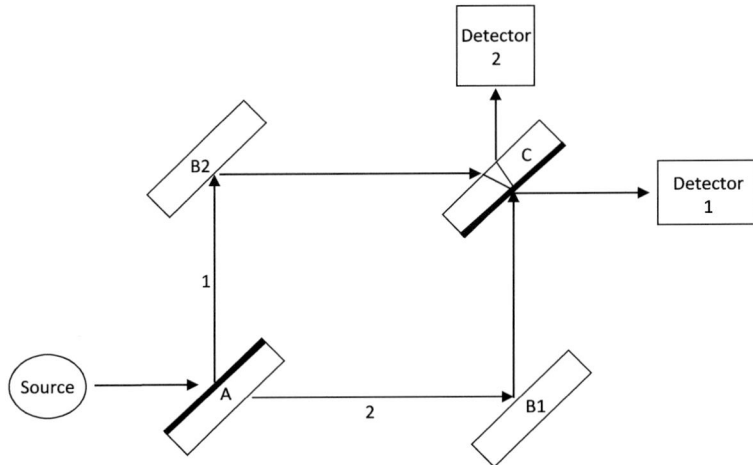

Figure 19. Mach-Zehnder interferometer. Light from the source has two paths (labelled 1 and 2) available to it. The figure shows that for each detector (labelled detectors 1 or 2), light can reach them by two different paths. With paths of exactly the same length, all the photons are detected at detector 1.

deflected. B1 and B2, in contrast, deflect all light. As stated above, if the light transit length between A and C are the same for the two paths, then all photons pass to detector 1 and none to detector 2. This is actually because of the phase changes of light when reflected and how, when recombining, the interference effect determines the direction of transit. As one path length is increased, the interference on recombination is affected such that the light moves towards the other detector. As the length of one path increases in whole number multiples of the length of the other path, the interference is cancelled out and all light moves to the other detector. This process is consistent and calculable based on path lengths due to the fact that the phase of a wave of light changes by multiples of π.

Returning to our two-channel polariser interferometer (Figure 16), if the source emits two particles that are linked as a quantum system (e.g., up/down spin-correlated photons), then the spin of one at one detector is opposite to that detected at the same time (relative to the first particle's frame) at the other detector (as we have discussed earlier). As we know, Aspect showed by testing Bell's theorem in 1982 that the correlation is non-local in nature.

Quantum theory states that a particle/wave exhibits properties once measured. Thus, although we have been addressing the correlation of spin of spin-correlated photons, we could also be looking at the correlation of wave/particle duality and the complementarity of these positions. In terms of local hidden variable theories, advocates have suggested that a photon is affected by the way the measuring apparatus is set up. The apparatus somehow adopts either wave or particle characteristics due to hidden variables that affect the outcome of what is detected. Thus, as mentioned, closing the door finally on local realism is not easy.

Difference between entangled and relativistic effects

The violation of Bell's inequality, as shown by experiments by Aspect and many others, reveals that entangled particles deviate from the classical, relativistic picture of the world in three ways:

1. The force of gravity diminishes with the square of the distance between objects. The connection between entangled particles is not attenuated, irrespective of distance between the particles.
2. The force of gravity does not discriminate. It is a force that acts between all matter. Entanglement is a specific interaction between two particles, and none other.
3. Relativistic effects are limited to the velocity of light. Quantum entanglement is instantaneous.

As George Greenstein concluded in *Quantum Strangeness*, what Bell's Theorem proves is that quantum mechanics is not a local hidden variable theory, which is another way of saying that that unlike all other sciences, quantum theory is not a theory of normal reality.

Delayed-choice *gedanken* experiment

In 1978, Wheeler devised a *gedanken* experiment known as a *delayed-choice* experiment to show the peculiarity of quantum theory (both wave/particle duality and the superposition principle). A photon passes through a double-slit apparatus, but the choice of type of measurement is made after passage through the double-slit (Figure 20). We know from our

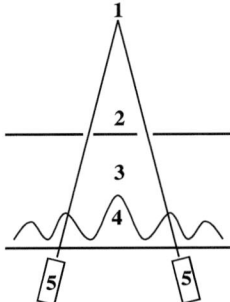

Figure 20. Delayed-choice experiment. A photon is emitted from position 1 and passes through one or both of the slits in the double-slit set up (labelled 2). After passing the double-slit, a choice is *then* made at 3 as to whether a screen at 4 measures an interference pattern, or a telescope measure a photon at either, or both, telescopes (at 5).

understanding of quantum theory that wave or particle characteristics are displayed after passing through a double-slit, and that the type of measuring apparatus used to detect this behaviour determines what it is. After passing through the double-slit, if we measure particle behaviour, that will be what we observe. The converse applies when we choose to measure wave-like characteristics.

However, if the choice of measurement is delayed until after the photon passes through the double-slit, then we can assume the photon is 'committed' to showing one type of behaviour or the other. This wave or particle behaviour will encounter the type of measurement chosen by the observer after the double-slit has been encountered (hence, 'delayed-choice'). There is no way for the photon to 'know' whether it should show wave/interference effects or particle-like properties because the characteristics being measured have been chosen *after* the photon must 'choose' whether it is a wave or particle.

If the interference screen remains after the photons pass the double-slit, an interference pattern is detected on the screen. If the screen is removed after passing the double-slit, the photons are detected at one of the telescopes (but not both) as a particulate photon in accordance with them passing through one or other of the slits. Indeed, whatever property is measured, that is the type of behaviour demonstrated even when the photon has to decide what it is before the observer decides what property it will measure.

When visualised as a temporal flow, we give the photon the opportunity to pass though one, the other, or both slit(s). We assume that it makes a choice before it heads to an unknown detector. Later, when we choose the detector type, this apparently overrides any choice the photon has made as to what it is. One conclusion is that the photon passes the detector in one form but maintains a connection with its past superposition, which then collapses onto the appropriate state once the type of measurement is decided. However, this interpretation makes no sense as it calls on a reversal of time. Bohm's pilot wave also has some appeal here.

From a quantum mechanical stance, although we rationalise the photon as passing the double-slit as a wave *or* particle and that a choice must be made by it about what it is, what actually happens is that the photon emerges at the other side of the double-slit as a superposition of both states (perhaps some sort of pilot wave enables this). In doing so, the choice of measurement collapses the superposition onto the type of state determined by the observer every time. Such a *gedanken* experiment is very difficult to test experimentally, and it wasn't until 2007 that Aspect's group verified the indications of earlier groups (e.g., those of Alley and Helmuth) that the Copenhagen interpretation is still valid.

The conclusion is that until a measurement is made, even with a delayed-choice, the wave function describes the *whole* system. Therefore, when a measurement is made, the wave function collapses and the photon adopts the properties that the chosen type of measurement measures. So, the photon passes through the double-slit and then a choice of what type of measurement is made. When measured as a particle, the photon moves from a superposition of wave/particle duality to adopt the state of a particle. When measured as a wave, it collapses to reveal the wave state in the 'real' world.

Delayed-choice experiments prove that, until measured, quantum systems exist as a superposition of all possible quantum states. We have access in the 'real' world to only one of the properties of this at one time. Experiments testing entanglement demonstrate that reality is describable in non-local terms because the entangled 'particles' are describable by the same single wavefunction. Measurement of one entangled particle collapses the wavefunction describing the whole entangled system of *both* particles, causing the other unmeasured particle to adopt the correlated spin state immediately when measured. This violates Bell's inequality and apparently special relativity too. However, as mentioned before, observer information of the entanglement conforms to special relativity whereas entanglement does not. The Copenhagen interpretation seems unsettling, but it stands up to experiment.

The EPR paper of 1935 highlighted key problems in the sense of preserving some form of reality that the Copenhagen interpretation implies. Bohr immediately countered this article in the same journal that same year. Essentially, Bohr believed that prior to measurement, entangled particles are, if they are in any sense real, a superposition of all states. Measuring one 'particle' determines *its* state *and* that of the other (revealed when measured) immediately, however far apart they are. So is EPR still right in stating that quantum theory is incomplete? Schrödinger pointed out in 1936 that quantum systems possess a *unique* property — correlation — that is not a property of single 'things' but only of correlated quantum systems. Bohr's Copenhagen interpretation states that the observer (who collapses the wavefunction describing a quantum system) and quantum systems are linked. Without the observer, there is no measurement, and without measurement, the quantum superposition defines the whole system of the correlated particles.

Take entangled particles A and B with a net spin of 0. If the spin state of entangled particle A is observed and recorded by a person at position A and particle B by a person at position B which is a light year away, the spin states will appear random to each person. Only by their communication will they see that the particles are entangled. This human communication reveals the unique correlated property of entangled systems and must do so in accordance with special relativity. However, the entanglement itself, as a quantum superposition, is described by a single wavefunction. Thus, measurement of particle A means that particle B is affected by this measurement *because* it is part of the same superposition and described by the same wavefunction.

To preserve the laws of physics, when one entangled particle is measured, the other cannot suspend these laws but must act in accordance with them. Thus, it adopts the correlated state immediately, irrespective of separation. Consciousness may be responsible for causing the collapse of the wavefunction, and to make the entangled particles 'real' while proving the correlation and preservation of the laws of physics, special relativity cannot be violated.

Do we accept entanglement as innate to the fabric of reality or are there other explanations? Are hidden variables present or do we accept Bohr's Copenhagen interpretation that has existed since 1926? There are other explanations, such as Bohm's (and de Broglie's) pilot wave model where, simply, the correlation is maintained by a quantum potential or pilot wave. Here, the electron for example exists as a particle (corpuscle) and wave. It is the wave that guides the photon along (hence 'pilot'). This removes local hidden variables and acts as a non-local hidden variable theory that does not violate relativity. The pilot wave supports the photon in the delayed-choice experiment too.

Other possible explanations are variations of the American physicist Everett's many worlds or *branching-universe* interpretation, devised in

1957. Here, every measurement of a quantum system splits the Universe into different universes (e.g., a universe where that particle has 'up' spin and one where that particle has 'down' spin). This seems too fantastic to be possible, but it has mathematical merit. EPR may be correct that quantum theory is incomplete, but gravity may be the issue, not special relativity. A quantum theory of gravity currently evades us whereas special relativity, though a fundamental constraint for 'classical' events such as travel and communication, encounters different rules at the quantum level.

Perhaps the reason for so many interpretations of quantum theory to exist is that none are right and that we are currently physically and mentally incapable of uncovering the truth. In other words, at the moment the truth is beyond the comprehension of the human brain. Indeed, we assume that there *is* a truth of how reality is because there is a world out there, and if something exists, there *must* — so we assume — be an explanation. But reality may be fundamentally chaotic and unknowable to us. If that is the case, it would explain why we cannot make sense of it. Just as we cannot unify gravity with a GUT (electromagnetism, QED, QCD) or understand infinity, we are continuing our journey to find out which things are intrinsically unknowable, which are knowable but beyond our ability to know (harder to define since knowledge of it dictates the ability to know it), and which we will delineate fully in time.

The collapse of the wavepacket, the measurement problem, and reality

The collapse of the wavepacket is the pivotal point for the transition from the quantum world to that of physical reality. It represents the instance where debate exists as to how and when this occurs. At least four different ways have been suggested:

1. To state that the wave function is not a description of a physical system but of one's knowledge of it.
2. The Copenhagen interpretation, which questions whether it is meaningful to consider whether photons actually exist until they are observed.

3. The role of the observer. Is the act of observation that which causes the quantum state to collapse? If we consider an enormous Schrödinger wave equation embracing the totality of all that is involved in the measurement process, where does it end? Does it not imply a need for its continuity through evolution? Do we assume that in the billions of years before conscious life evolved, whether on our planet or elsewhere, no wavepacket collapsed?
4. The many worlds interpretation. Basically, if we consider the Schrödinger cat paradox, rather than worry if the cat is dead or alive, there is both a live cat and a dead cat. Each cat occupies its own box in its own universe. The many worlds interpretation arises from its mathematical formalism whereas the Copenhagen interpretation requires assumptions to be made to distinguish quantum systems from the measurement apparatus. The problem with the many worlds hypothesis is that if we make an estimation of the number of quantum events that would lead to many worlds splitting since the Big Bang, then there would now be $(10^{10})^{12}$ universes. Where are they? It has been said that they coexist with our own but are unable to interact with ours as a result of the quantum measurement that caused the split in the first place. The numbers seem too staggeringly huge to be credible.

Many aspects of the Copenhagen interpretation do work, such as Schrödinger waves, Heisenberg's uncertainty principle, and the fact that it cannot be definitively refuted. However, quantum theory is continually being refined. For example, Feynman invented a way of formulating quantum theory that bypasses the Schrödinger equation and proceeds to the calculation of probability amplitudes. This is the path integral or sum-over-histories method mentioned earlier.

Despite the advancements of quantum theory, the debate is still out on its interpretation. Einstein had a deep belief in the need for the Universe to be fundamentally measurable and hence real. He did not like the idea that future events are not completely determined by how things are at present. He always sought an objective, deterministic reality as he was driven by the belief that a fundamental theory should be applicable to all physical reality. This is not possible with quantum theory in its current conception and thus, if this belief is correct, then it is not the fundamental theory.

If our analysis of photons at the quantum level shows us that contradictions arise if we attribute properties to them before measurement and, furthermore, if quantum theory is fundamental and universal, it must apply to the macroscopic measuring apparatus as well as the microscopic quantum world being measured, which it does not.

David Bohm

In *Wholeness and the Implicate Order*, David Bohm made a brave attempt at unifying all aspects of the world, both physical and abstract. Traditionally, the *explicate order* defines the reality we see all around us as constituted of independent yet interacting objects and forces. Modern science still tends to address reality through the explicate order and looks for relationships between the particles that make up physical reality.

For Bohm, to analyse reality in terms of separate components seemed intuitively flawed since he saw it as a harmonious whole. This is because underlying the explicate order is the true *implicate order*. Whether addressing the physical, mental, abstract, or indeed anything, each is a 'sub-totality' of the whole harmonious process of reality. Thus, he considered reality as 'process' rather than being made up of separated but interacting constituent particles.

Like the inherent stability seen in the vortices of a flowing stream, the implicate order describes the movement of the whole, or the holomovement, as one of harmonious flux. Any material or immaterial part of the whole — being connected — exerts its effect on the whole. In the implicate order, the movement of the whole as process can explain conceptual issues such as the mind-body problem and the philosophical implications of quantum theory.

Both relativity and quantum physics imply that the state of affairs is an unbroken wholeness of the Universe, but both theories differ in their notion of order. For relativity, movement is continuous, causally determinate, and well defined. In contrast, quantum mechanics is discontinuous and neither causally determinate nor well defined. Each theory focuses on its own fragmented mode of existence — relativity applies to separate events connected by signals; quantum mechanics applies to a well-defined quantum state. Quantum particle entanglement, when viewed from the perspective of the implicate order, represents the connectedness of everything. Special relativity defines limits for the relative movement of matter or information within the implicate order and is consistent with it. In the context of the explicate order, entanglement clearly presents difficulties. Indeed, many phenomena that pose problems when addressed with our current models, which invoke separate entities within a system, seem less impenetrable when viewed in terms of the implicate order.

The relationship between Bohm's explicate and implicate order differs from that of Kant's phenomenal and noumenal reality (or d'Espagnat's 'veiled' reality where a property of a veiled quantum system is revealed to us when measurement collapses the superposition) in that, unlike noumenal reality, the implicate order is not some unknowable concept of reality beyond our mental or perceptual comprehension. Whereas the explicate order is the world of well-defined objects, the deeper implicate or enfolded order gives rise to it.

The implicate order is the world that 'is' and which lies prior to measurement. Pure unconditioned thought is focused through adaptation according to rules, language, and society. Resultantly, thought that naturally addresses the implicate order is taught to separate reality into units that connect and, thus, becomes focused on the explicate order. Bohm applied this idea of wholeness and the implicate order not only to quantum theory and physical reality but also to social reality.

Many of the problems of today are caused by failing to realise the intrinsic connectedness of everything and everyone. Bohm asked, "What's the relationship between thinking and reality?" This is a subject that the final chapter addresses, but is applicable here because it is intrinsic to Bohm's conception of reality. Since thought is a process of movement like the flow of movement in matter, he asked if thought is a part of reality as a whole. If this is true, Bohm questions how one part of reality could 'know' another. Does thought give a representation of reality, or can it grasp the essence of living movement? He asked of how we to think of the flow of existence as a whole, encompassing thought and the external reality as we experience it. Hence, these questions are both scientific and philosophical in nature, but Bohm hoped to use the conceptual understanding of the world that we already possess to answer them.

Physicists and philosophers rarely gel. Being both, Bohm's work on quantum theory as a hidden variable theory invoking the implicate order has been largely neglected because it is perceived as linking mysticism with rigorous quantum physics. As such, it sits alone, slightly at the edge of what is considered to be scientific method. Bohm was forever frustrated by the lack of acceptance of his ideas, even as a model from which to investigate further. He knew that it was not complete, but felt that it deserved further investigation. The scientific community prefers the idea of a reality that only exists when measured to one that is a single, connected harmonious whole, and his theories in the quantum context sit alongside other 'models', such as the many worlds interpretation.

Whether we find a GUT/TOE or not, or whether it is even possible, was not the issue in Bohm's work. That search has its own merit, even though the timescale cannot be known. Bohm stated that if we do not work with and apply what we think we *do* know and merely focus on trying to find this elusive and possibly unknowable thing, it is at the expense of questions that can already be addressed with the knowledge we do have, and the repercussions of not exploring these avenues are already evident in the world around us. Bohm argued that our notions of cosmology and reality are continually developing, and that we should start with ideas that improve on what is available and then go on to better ideas.

Ultimately, Bohm's vision was one of unification of the totality of existence, which will help to unify the human race. Bohm recognised that a worldview that includes the nature of reality, cosmology, and consciousness will probably never be resolved completely. However, this did not stop his attempt to investigate proposals aimed at meeting this challenge, a train of thought that led to the charge of mysticism. He saw that the global distinction between people (e.g., race, nation, profession) that prevents mankind from working together for the common good is partly due to the type of thought that treats things as divided and disconnected. Thus, when humankind thinks of its needs, humanity is regarded as separate from nature.

By thinking of totality as independent fragments, the mind will operate accordingly. Conversely, by considering everything as a connected harmonious whole, the mind will move in a similar way. Bohm considered this to be crucial for overall order of the mind. He believed that a proper worldview that is consistent with its time is essential for harmony in the individual and for society as a whole. The proper order of the operation of the mind requires an understanding of what is known, both logically and intuitively.

This way of thinking not only provides a source of new ideas but is also needed for the mind to function harmoniously — possibly benefiting society by helping it to become (more) ordered and stable. It is often thought that fragmentation (of cities, religions, political systems, and such like) is seen as part of the reality we live in and that wholeness is an ideal towards which we can strive. However, Bohm saw wholeness as real and that fragmentation is the response of the whole to man, who uses fragmentary thought applied through fragmentary systems. Thus, as reality *is* whole, man's attempt to understand it with a fragmentary approach will be answered with a fragmentary response.

We suppose that thought processes and the content of thought are independent, thus allowing us to think rationally about thought content. However, Bohm saw content and process as two aspects of one process, like the oneness of the observer and the observed. By treating the entirety of thought as a whole and not by a mode of thought that analyses itself through a separation between its process and content, we will be more successful in resolving issues such as uniting relativity and quantum theory. As thought is fragmented, these divisions in thought are given disproportionate importance as if they represented, falsely, actual breaks in the reality that *is* and that thought conceives. Thought as a whole process with the non-existence of fragmentation removes the divisions that are not present in reality.

As an experiment, Bohm attempted to develop a new language construction which he termed the 'Rheomode' — derived from Greek which means 'to flow' — that would help to end fragmentation by creating a structure based on modern language that would not be prone to fragmentation and that encouraged flow. For example, modern language fails at addressing questions of falsity and truth as each truth is treated as a separate fragment that is fixed. Even Wittgenstein, the modern philosophical analyst of language construction, was sceptical about what language can tell us (see Chapter 1) and what we can tell about language. He said, "What's spoken can only be explained in language and so in this sense language cannot be explained."

Ultimately, Bohm attempted to develop a new notion of order — the implicate order — that applies to an unbroken universe. Space and time are not the dominant factors determining the relationships of dependence and independence of different elements in the implicate order. Here, a different basis of connection is found where space, time, and the notion of separate particles are derived from the deeper order. Clearly, Bohm's aim was immense. In terms of possible solution, he was striving for answers before their natural time. Yet Bohm was an accomplished quantum physicist with the courage to investigate possible solutions to physical and philosophical problems intrinsic to the foundations of modern quantum theory. Rather than merely accept these as fact as most did, he probed deeper with the goal of making sense of it. Hopefully, history will treat this effort better in years to come than has thus far been the case.

Realism

An often-held misunderstanding even among physicists is the meaning behind EPR and Bell's Theorem. What is at stake in Bell's Theorem is locality, not local realism. EPR and Bell's Theorem together show that locality is false. Bell's theorem shows that local, deterministic, hidden variables conflict with the predictions of quantum mechanics and (more importantly, we now know) experiment. Most physicists just focus their attention on Bell's theorem and totally miss its relation to the EPR argument.

Clearly, when viewed together, EPR and Bell's theorem show that locality is false, which is a very interesting conclusion. If you ignore EPR and only look at Bell's theorem, you start saying things like "local realism is false" because you miss the fact that locality actually 'entails' whatever 'realism' (i.e., hidden variables or whatever) is needed. We know that local, deterministic, hidden variable theories conflict with both the predictions of quantum mechanics and experiment (which are in agreement). The violation of the inequality means that nature or reality is innately non-local, but the definition of realism presents confusion.

There are several different types of realism that have been attributed to that which is refuted by Bell's theorem:

Naïve realism is the view that all features of a perceptual experience originate from a corresponding feature of the perceived object. Thus, the greenness of a green apple is an intrinsic property of the apple, reminding us of Plato's logic. That which perceives contributes nothing to the experience, which is merely a revealing of the property. Thus, quantum theory contradicts naïve realism since it states that nothing exists until measurement — there is no revealing. It has been proven that it is impossible to assign premeasurement values to all possible observables of a quantum system where measurements reveal premeasurement values, and these values are consistent with quantum theory.

Scientific realism is the doctrine that scientific theories provide truths about the world. But quantum mechanics is our best scientific theory, and Bell's theorem is not premised on the assumed truth of scientific realism. Indeed, Bell's theorem is not premised on *any* scientific theory, and it is its generality that makes it so profound.

Perceptual realism states that sense perception reveals facts about the world and judgements on perceptual experience provide truths about the world. Of course, our senses can be deluded, and yet even complex scientific theories are grounded in data that come from experience and experiment. Moreover, experiments can provide skewed answers to pointed questions. So, any scientific theory must incorporate perceptual realism.

Metaphysical realism is the acceptance of the existence of the physical world, and Bell's Theorem depends on the acceptance of metaphysical realism. The derivation of a Bell inequality depends on locality, which depends on a metaphysical reality as a background on which to act. Without metaphysical reality, there is no conception of local or nonlocal. Locality presupposes metaphysical realism. To reject metaphysical realism is to reject a physical world. Rejecting metaphysical reality in the sense that reality is only a conscious construct is wrong, since there is no spacetime and nowhere for consciousness to occur without metaphysical reality. If the realism at stake in Bell's theorem is metaphysical realism, then we cannot reject it in favour of locality, whereas the reverse is the only option in the case of the violation of the inequalities.

When describing local realism, Travis Norsen of Marlborough College believes that this term comprises of the three principles endorsed by Einstein — metaphysical realism, locality, and naïve realism. Despite the lack of clarity, it is clear from the violation of Bell's inequality that non-locality is a real fact of nature and pays no respect to relativity's prohibition on superluminal causation.

Robert Nadeau and Menas Kafatos

Science historian Robert Nadeau and physicist Menos Kafatos believe that non-locality is a fundamental property of the Universe. Since entangled particles emanate from a single source, they reason, so too must all quanta have interacted at some point in their history. The reality, the existence of which is inferred between the particles that are measured in experiments such as those conducted by Aspect, is one that underlies all physical events. Yet all we can say of it is that it manifests as an undivided whole and its existence is inferred when an interaction with an observer occurs.

They go on to speculate upon the implications of this undivided whole, whose existence is assumed 'real' when observed, by stating that it cannot be the subject of scientific investigation because no knowledge can be gained about its actual character. Science deals with manifestations of this reality (undivided whole), which are actualised when measured. When factoring in the implications of non-locality, the relationship between parts (quanta) and the undivided whole (universe) in terms of physics, biology, and consciousness can be seen as the emergent phenomena of an interconnected whole. They believe that one can conclude that physical 'Being' is 'revealed' by the wave function of the Universe. The sense of profound unity we have with the cosmos can be presumed to correlate with the action of the deterministic wave function.

Bernard d'Espagnat's veiled reality

The Frenchman d'Espagnat (1921–2015) wrote that "the doctrine that the world is made up of objects whose existence is independent of human consciousness turns out to be in conflict with quantum mechanics and with facts established by experiment". Did he mean that if no conscious entity exists then nothing exists, since there is nothing to be aware of its existence? No.

Consciousness is the measure of existence *if* we define existence as the real, deterministic reality in which we interact and that we understand in a classical, objective sense. If, however, existence constitutes how reality *is* at the fundamental level and if that proves to be indeterminate, then consciousness has no access to that. Indeed, it is the measure of what reality isn't, and how it presents itself to consciousness.

So, d'Espagnat stressed that conscious measurement gives objects existence as we understand 'existence' in a common-sense way. Thus, the world of quantum objects is inaccessible to us as it innately *is*, and revealing to our world of accessibility one type of property of their existence requires measurement. This measurement cannot ask "what are you?"; rather, it asks "are you this?" (if the answer is yes — particle), or "are you that?" (if yes — wave), as the experiment can only be set up to measure one or the other of the complementary properties. Yet an electron, for example, is neither particle nor wave. They are both complementary descriptions of the electron, yet they reflect the limitations of language that is used in and designed for a classical world to apply to the quantum world.

According to the Copenhagen interpretation, the position adopted is determined by the type of measurement made. So, material reality without consciousness of it exists as a superposition. Conscious knowledge (as we know of) necessitates that it must adopt a particular state. Thus, having knowledge of material reality at the fundamental level requires the state under measurement to change from a superposition of all possible states to that one state that is determined by the type of measurement we consciously decide to make.

As mentioned, d'Espagnat talked of a veiled reality that bears similarities to Kant's noumenal world. It is the world of existence that measurement reveals aspects of. It is inaccessible to us as a complete description since we, *as conscious entities*, do not exist as indeterminate quantum superpositions. However, this does not mean that scientific study within the constraints of what we are is useless, as we must understand the true context of the knowledge we acquire. Knowledge is relative and *our* knowledge is relative to the type of being we are.

Our interaction with reality does not necessitate knowledge of the fundamental, quantum level to provide meaningful and useable information in many areas of science. We can interpret much of the world around us through science that does not need to know of the quantum world. Biological science, as we shall see in Chapter 4 for example, concerns itself with molecular interactions in a classical, deterministic way and analyses behaviour by statistical interpretations of the study. It can disregard (while being mindful of) the underlying indeterminism, and the answers sought can be addressed using practices that avoid access to the quantum world entirely.

The absence of absolute knowledge in biological study does not obviate rigor; it merely necessitates a different approach which is mindful of the importance of interpretation. This process is the testing of hypotheses, the outcome of which adds to accumulated knowledge and leads to the formulation of further hypotheses that can then be tested. Thus, knowledge of the indeterminism intrinsic to the quantum processes underlying biological molecules is not considered essential since it does not affect the large-scale behaviour under analysis. It is this behaviour that is analysed, to which a statistical approach may be applied. This statistical indeterminism is not based on the absolute indeterminism of quantum theory; rather, it is an indeterminism based on having to take approximations from small-scale analyses and extrapolating this information to the larger context.

Of course, a TOE should be as accurate in describing 'everything' (covered by current quantum and relativity theories) as quantum theory and relativity are capable of describing the worlds that they represent. A TOE should theoretically be able to describe many biological and chemical processes too, although even if a TOE were formulated, the limitation to its use would probably be computing power. Interpretation of biological systems, for example, would be astonishingly complex and involve many variables, including chaotic systems. Furthermore, since conscious beings are an obvious reality of existence, then they should also be accounted for by such a theory, including the conscious process itself (and we have no idea how the matter of the brain produces conscious experience — the mind-body problem).

If our conscious processes are intrinsic to when the collapse of a wavepacket occurs, then a TOE that does not incorporate conscious processes is essentially incomplete. If there was no human consciousness or any consciousness at all, there would be no consciousness to formulate the TOE. Without consciousness, there is probably no collapse of the wavepacket, and if there was never the collapse of the wavepacket and quantum states only exist as a superposition, then a hypothetical TOE in that sense would not have to account for human consciousness. But human consciousness exists and there is collapse of the wavepacket, so the TOE must take account of and incorporate this concept.

Julian Barbour

Julian Barbour is a British physicist and translator whose most influential work has been a controversial look at the concept of 'time'. Time differs from the other dimensions we exist in. It defines events that occur in space, and without time, matter is just located in space. Without time, the intricacies of phenomena such as consciousness become reduced to mere constituent matter. Time enables the multitude of processes and capabilities allowed by the many variations and connections of the relatively few elements that exist in reality. Motion and the passage of time are very well-founded illusions — this is the thesis of Barbour's *The End of Time* (1999).

Barbour argues that the wave function of the Universe is static and the 'appearance' of the flow of time emerges because the wave function of the Universe is concentrated on configurations of the Universe that we recognise as a succession of *nows*. In *The End of Time*, the passage of time is presented as an illusion so that an external view into the Universe would reveal one to be static. General relativity and quantum mechanics are the most fundamental theories of physics despite possessing remarkably different structures. Time is treated in different ways in each. A quantum theory of the Universe would presumably have a single treatment of time. However, Barbour suggests that time be abolished completely.

According to Barbour, time seems to have an arrow — it moves from the past to the future through the present. Yet the equations of physics are symmetric with respect to the direction of time. They theoretically allow the events they represent to occur in both directions, though only events that correlate with an increase in entropy actually *do* occur. Barbour believes that a theory of the Universe should *explain* why entropy increases. He also thinks the theory should be devoid of the traditional conception of time. For him, rather than visualised as a continual flow, his equivalent of time is a succession of instants or 'nows', and our existence is the passage through them, each 'now' being an arrangement of the constituents of the Universe relative to each other at any moment.

Barbour suggests a simple model to help demonstrate his theory. If we suppose that there are just three particles in the Universe, at some moment they would be in certain positions relative to each other and would form a triangle. The triangle does not occur somewhere in absolute space at some instant of time; the triangles *is* the 'now'. Each arrangement of the triangle is a new 'now'.

In a universe with billions of particles, there are relative configurations of those particles and each relative configuration is a possible 'now'. In the real universe, the 'nows' are more complex than relative configurations, involving fields, but what is important is that in Barbour's universe, time does not exist. We feel as if our existence is within a framework of time. If there is no time, what does the notion of past or future mean? What also of our perception of motion? Barbour suggests that what we see as motion is really a series of 'nows' that are connected by the brain to produce an illusion of movement. Our traditional conception of past and future, including memories and feelings, are encapsulated in these 'nows' too. Whether free will can exist in such a construct of reality depends on what we accept as the type of thing that free will could be in such a reality.

What is real?

What have we learned about reality from the conclusions of hidden variable experiments? As Jim Baggott describes in the closing remarks to his book *Beyond Measure*, the anti-realists, like those who accept the indeterminism of the Copenhagen interpretation, say that the theory is all there is and it describes reality. Tests proving the violation of Bell's inequalities make a realist's case more difficult. Yet, the realists think that we do not have the whole story. Thoughts of an independent reality are either an appeal to 'faith', where faith refers to a rational character of reality, or they come from the belief that a determinate reality will reveal itself when the complete picture is realised. Here, quantum theory is seen only as a stepping stone on the path to its realisation.

Baggott believes that an unquestioning acceptance of the Copenhagen interpretation has held back alternate approaches that serve to address the divide originally characterised by the debates between Einstein and Bohr that began in the 1920s. It seems that Einstein was badly treated and perhaps we should have had more faith in his insights. Einstein believed in a local, deterministic universe whereas Bohr accepted the conclusion of a non-local, indeterminate one. At least for the time being, it seems that Bohr was right. Perhaps if Einstein had seen Aspect's proof of the violation of Bell's inequality, he would have accepted the non-local conclusion with hidden variables. So how does this relate to d'Espagnat's veiled reality?

When one property of the superposition is measured, other properties of that quantum system are no longer available to us for measurement. So, we have access to only one state of quantum reality — the true superposition is veiled. What we cannot know of reality is defined by many criteria — our mental process and physiology put constraints on how we access and interpret data about reality. Our logical axiomatic systems of analysis reveal the possibility of intrinsic unknowability and incompleteness. However, most importantly, reality itself is inherently unknowable to human consciousness because to know what a quantum superposition is would require being as a superposition.

Aside from that conception of 'knowing', our understanding of reality as fundamentally indeterminate and unknowable is because either that is how reality is or our minds are not constructed to understand how reality is — and we do not know which of these is correct. If the world is connected at a deep level, then when we measure an aspect of the quantum world, it necessitates ignoring the whole and focusing on merely a part. But if the whole is ignored and yet affects the parts under analysis (like the holomovement' in Bohm's implicate order), then what we observe is one aspect of the complementary properties of a superposition of one quantum component of an integrated whole. In essence, we exist knowing of quantum reality and its non-local implications and we realise that this world is veiled from us in terms of true accessibility.

iv) Subatomic Particles, GUTs, and Nuclear Power

Subatomic particles, forces, and the search for a GUT and TOE

When considering atoms, one usually imagines electrons surrounding a nucleus of protons and neutrons. This is one of a number of possible pictures of the atoms of elements that constitute matter. The electronic arrangement surrounding the nucleus determines the chemistry — the ability of an atom to interact with other elements, as I described earlier. This is what underlies all chemical and thus biological processes.

The Periodic Table groups all elements according to size and electronic arrangement. The number of protons in the nucleus determines the atomic number, as we saw earlier, and increases with increasing size of element. The nucleus also consists of neutrons. Elements with the same number of protons and different numbers of neutrons are called isotopes. As we increase in atomic number, the ratio of neutrons to protons increases. However, with the development of quantum theory and understanding of nuclear processes, the idea of each element comprising just protons, neutrons, and electrons and matter being comprised of these 'fundamental' particles became seen to be far from correct.

To illustrate the evolution of particle discovery, in 1932 there were three known fundamental particles, in 1947 there were six (and their antiparticles), and in 1951 there were more than 15 discovered. Now, we know of more fundamental particles than there are elements in the Periodic Table. The subsequent discovery of other particles as well as antimatter produced a far more complex picture of the constituents of matter. The theoretical discovery of antimatter was made by Dirac. He found that when combining the theory of special relativity with quantum theory, each fundamental particle must be accompanied with a corresponding particle of antimatter. When matter and antimatter particles come together, they annihilate each other with the release of high-energy photons (or γ-radiation). What follows is a description of the different types of particles that constitute matter, how they are grouped and interrelate, and ultimately how they fit into a GUT and TOE.

Fermions and bosons

There are classification systems for particles based on their behaviour. Identical particles are termed either *bosons*, with zero or integer spin, or fermions with half-integral spin. There are two kinds of fields in nature — fermionic and bosonic, which leads to what we see as a distinction between what we think of as particles and what we think of as fields. The fermionic field constitutes the physical world (matter) whereas the bosonic field produces the interactions of the material world (forces).

Fermions are named after the Italian experimental and theoretical physicist Enrico Fermi (1901–1954; in fact, Fermi was perhaps the only modern physicist who excelled both theoretically and experimentally — Rutherford was a poor mathematician yet an excellent experimentalist, whereas Einstein allegedly never did practical experiments, and Pauli was banned from laboratories as he ruined experiments). The concept of fermions is deeply entrenched in quantum theory. They are particles whose statistics require them to be in states corresponding to asymmetric wave functions. Fermions are not destroyed except in matter-antimatter collisions. All electrons are fermions. They obey 'Fermi-Dirac' statistics (after Enrico Fermi and Paul Dirac) and, from this, it can be shown that they obey the Pauli exclusion principle. No two electrons are ever in the same state of motion. Thus, if an electron is in one state, it precludes any other electron from being in that state.

From Fermi-Dirac statistics, if two electrons are in the same state, then interchanging them would mean that no change has occurred. Fermi-Dirac statistics requires a change of sign, but zero can actually be itself and also minus itself. It also means that the wavefunction vanishes and there are no states. Thus, there can never be two electrons 'here'.

Particles that do not obey the exclusion principle, such as photons, are bosons. These can be created and destroyed. Bosons are named after the Bengali physicist Satyandra Bose (1894–1974). They are essentially classical in nature, which is why Einstein was deeply involved in understanding their properties since special relativity is, essentially, classical in nature too. Bosons obey 'Bose-Einstein' statistics — they are particles whose statistics require them to be in states corresponding to symmetric wave functions. There is no bar on bosons being in the same state. In fact, they like to be in the same state together and this is the property behind lasers (light amplification by stimulated emission of radiation) and masers (microwave amplification by stimulated emission of radiation).

Hadrons and leptons

Electrons are about 1/1840 the mass of a proton. In 1937, a 'heavy electron' was discovered that had a mass of 200 times an electron and yet the same negative charge. It came to be known as a *muon* (μ^-, or mu-*meson*). Between 1946 and 1947, *pions* (or pi mesons), the first 'true' mesons, were discovered (π^+ and π^-). Earlier, I stated that fermions and bosons are ways of describing what constitutes the world and how these constituents interact. Physicists came to realise that particles could be defined by their response to nuclear forces and were grouped accordingly:

1. **Hadrons** — these are affected by the strong force. They can be bosons or fermions. Bosonic hadrons are mesons whereas fermionic hadrons are *baryons* (meaning 'heavy ones'). Protons and neutrons are the only stable hadrons. Figure 21 shows some of the many different known hadrons.
2. **Leptons** (meaning 'light ones') — these are not affected by the strong force. All leptons are fermions (including electrons and muons).

During the 1940s, new particles were found to exist under exceptional circumstances. These are not seen or encountered in everyday life as the energies required to create them were only extant in the early stages of the Universe or in stellar reactions where heat and energy is sufficient to enable such processes. The only way to 'see' such particles is by accelerating charged particles within particle accelerators and bombarding them into other particles. The hadrons κ (kappa), λ (lambda), and Σ (sigma) were detected this way.

While neutrons are stable inside a nucleus, they decay with a half-life ($t_{1/2}$) of 15 minutes if freed. Protons exist for many millions of years. Other hadrons tend to exist for only tiny fractions of a second before changing into, for example, a neutron and a negative pion according to rules that have been determined by repeated analysis of trends in the patterns of subatomic particle decay. By the early 1960s into the 1970s, physicists found hundreds of different fundamental particles and their antimatter equivalents. Furthermore, they were able to explain the patterns of their appearance and decay in terms of only a few truly fundamental particles. These were used to construct a Standard Model of elementary particles.

As mentioned above, the fundamental particles can be generated experimentally in high-energy particle collisions. Here, energy can be converted into mass — it is a conversion of form, so the subatomic rules are not broken. The overall energy of a particle is its rest energy (i.e., the energy due to its rest mass) plus its kinetic energy. The rest mass is the only unique mass that can be assigned to an object. We know about the equivalence of mass and energy, and that mass is converted into energy during nuclear reactions in accordance with Einstein's famous equation, $E = mc^2$. Thus, little mass has great energy, which explains why high-energy particle accelerators are required to bombard and generate new particles so that we may better understand the Universe, as well as the great release of energy measured when an atomic bomb is detonated.

We have exploited the high-energy release from atomic nuclei in fusion and fission bombs. Here, rest energy (or potential energy) is converted into kinetic energy, which was first shown in 1932. For a fission reaction, the total rest energy and rest mass of the products is less than the original rest energy and rest mass of the nucleus undergoing the process. By the law of energy conservation, the energy difference is released as the kinetic energy of the products. The percentage decrease in rest energy during fission is about 0.08% whereas in fusion, it is about 0.1 to 0.4%, making fusion the more efficient process.

In a particle collision, when rest energy is accounted for, energy is conserved. The particle traces of collisions between particles can be seen in so-called 'bubble chambers' as bubbles of hydrogen gas forming around ions. These reactions occur within a chamber of liquid hydrogen. Millions of traces, and hence collisions, can be mapped per second using electronic detectors. The direction of the trace and particle rules help determine the type of particle seen in a particular reaction.

Linear particle accelerators act by accelerating the charged particle across multiple voltage differences, each giving the particle an accelerative boost. Modern cyclical particle accelerators, known as *cyclotrons*, accelerate the particle through a magnetic field. The particle spirals outwards in the machine in an ever-increasing circumference. The time taken for a particle to complete its successively larger circuit of the cyclotron across a transverse magnetic field must be the same each loop despite the greater distance travelled per revolution. The energy imparted on a particle determines the type of particle collision that can be achieved, which ultimately limits the amount of information we can obtain about the fundamentals of matter. Hence, bigger and more powerful colliders, such as CERN's Large Hadron Collider, provide more information about the origins of the Universe.

Fundamental particles

What are the fundamental particles and how do they interact? The increasing size and power of particle accelerators being built enables us to gain more information relating to this question. Cyclotrons are particle accelerators that are limited to a certain energy rating because if particles (protons) are accelerated beyond certain energies, Newtonian laws no longer describe the motion and Einstein's theory of special relativity needs to be applied. Since they need to function below special relativistic energies, fewer novel particles are generated.

The *Synchrotron* is a modern version of a cyclotron and incorporates relativistic effects at high particle velocities to enable even higher energy collisions, bringing greater insights on particles. If protons are accelerated at more than the certain specified energy, their circuit synchronises with the applied voltage across the magnetic field (hence 'Synchrotron') and acceleration occurs, because compensations are made for the temporal and spatial effects of velocities at a significant percentage of that of light as predicted by the theory of special relativity. Unless compensations for special relativity are made, it would not be possible to apply the voltage at the correct moment of the particle's circuit in the Synchrotron to produce an accelerative effect.

The Large Hadron Collider (LHC) is both a linear accelerator and Synchrotron. It is the highest energy particle accelerator ever built as well as mankind's most complex machine. It started accelerating particles on 10th September 2008 and should provide the deepest insights yet. Not surprisingly, much data have been achieved as a result of hadron collisions and many patterns of reactions have been observed:

1. Electrical charge is conserved.
2. Extra pions can be created.
3. Nucleon number is conserved (though neutron and proton numbers may change).
4. The total number of some types of hadrons (baryons) is normally conserved.
5. The total number of other hadrons (mesons, which are bosons that carry forces, e.g., pions) changes after the collision.

There are some hadron reactions where a different number of baryons exist after the reaction than did before. The additional baryon created is accompanied with its antiparticle partner, an antibaryon. If all baryons are given a baryon number = 1, antibaryons a baryon number = −1, and mesons a baryon number = 0, then the following rules apply in hadron collisions:

1. Baryon number is conserved.
2. Electrical charge is conserved.

Murray Gell-Mann and George Zweig also found that hadrons are not fundamental particles but consist of even smaller particles, which Gell-Mann named 'quarks' (Zweig's naming choice, 'aces', did not stick). Basically, hadrons are made of three types or *flavours* of quarks — *up*, *down*, and *strange*. Up (u) has a charge of +2/3, down (d) has a charge of −1/3, and strange (s) has a charge of −1/3. All have baryon number +1/3 and strangeness 0 except for the strange quark, which has −1. Of course, there are the corresponding antiquarks. The stable proton is comprised of two up and one down quark.

The information gained from particle collisions, combined with theoretical analysis, produced ever-increasing lists of exotic particles. Hundreds of different types of baryons (fermionic hadrons) and mesons (bosonic hadrons) were identified and were thus grouped according to behaviour (Figure 21). Some were stable, others unstable, but some, such as δ, ε, and κ, were found to be unstable but slow-decaying. Of note, they were always created in pairs. This strange behaviour made physicists consider that hadrons possessed a quality in addition to electrical charge, mass, spin, and baryon number, which accounts for their behaviour. They named this quantifiable property *strangeness*.

Gell-Mann and Yuval Ne'eman conceived a classification system for the properties of hadrons independently using strangeness as a property. Hadrons have strangeness values of 0, 1, and −1. Strangeness can be 0, −1, +1, +2, and even larger. Gell-Mann and Ne'eman were able to group particles according to spin, charge, strangeness, and other properties, and they named this the *eightfold way* after the eight virtues of the Buddhist faith (Figure 22 below).

As the classification system developed, the existence of certain particles was predicted and thus searched for experimentally. Hence, theorists and experimenters were working together to find all the fundamental particles. Gell-Mann's and Ne'eman's system started the way to know what to look for in particle accelerator collision experiments. Gell-Mann speculated that there might be a fourth quark to pair with the strange quark, but he eventually gave up on this idea. Quarks also have a property called *colour*, so that an up red quark differs from an up blue quark. Likewise, an up red quark differs from a down red quark. The whole of the eightfold way pattern formed naturally out of the possible combinations of triplets of quarks and quark-antiquark pairs.

Baryons consist of any combination of three quarks while mesons consist of a quark and antiquark of the same or different flavour. Quarks are held together in a nucleus an exchange of *gluons*, which is thought to perhaps be the strong force (the strongest acting force at short subatomic distances). If you try to separate quarks, the collision energy increases the energy between quarks and the recoil, in effect, creates a meson in addition to the original baryon. The quarks can never be isolated singly.

In addition to the three-quark model, it was found that there is a need for symmetry in the model so that there are as many quarks as leptons. Not surprisingly, there are also six different types of leptons. The first subatomic particle that was discovered in 1897, the electron (e^-), is a lepton and its antimatter partner is a positron. Other leptons include the muon

Baryons (fermionic hadrons)	Symbol	Mass	Quarks	Charge	Spin
Proton	N^+	938	uud	1	½
Neutron	$N^°$	940	ddu	0	½
Sigma$^+$	Σ^+	1198	uus	1	½
Sigma$^°$	$\Sigma^°$	1192	dus	0	½
Sigma–	S–	1197	dds	–1	½
Lambda$^°$	$\Lambda^°$	1116	dus	0	½
Xi$^°$	$\Xi^°$	1315	uss	0	½
Xi$^-$	Ξ^-	1321	dss	–1	½
Sigma$^+$	Σ^+	938	uus	1	½
Delta^{++}	Δ^{++}	1231	uuu	2	1½
Delta$^+$	Δ^+	1232	duu	1	1½
Delta$^°$	$\Delta^°$	1234	ddu	0	1½
Delta$^-$	Δ^-	1235	ddd	–1	1½
Sigma$^+$	$\Sigma^{\rho+}$	1189	uus	1	1½
Sigma$^°$	$\Sigma^{\rho°}$	1193	dus	0	1½
Sigma$^-$	$\Sigma^{\rho-}$	1197	dds	–1	1½
X1$^°$	$\Xi^{\rho°}$	1315	uss	0	1½
X1$^-$	$\Xi^{\rho-}$	1321	dss	–1	1½
Omega$^-$	Ω^-	1672	sss	–1	1½

Mesons (bosonic hadrons)	Symbol	Mass	Quarks	Charge	Spin
Pi$^+$	π^+	140	$u\bar{d}$	1	0
Pi$^°$	$\pi^°$	135	$u\bar{u}, d\bar{d}$	0	0
Pi$^-$	π^+	140	$d\bar{u}$	–1	0
Eta	η^+	547	$u\bar{u}, d\bar{d}, s\bar{s}$	0	0
Eta prime	η'	958	$u\bar{u}, d\bar{d}, s\bar{s}$	0	0
Kaon$^+$	K^+	494	$u\bar{s}$	1	0
Kaon$^°$	$K^°$	498	$d\bar{s}$	0	0
Rho$^+$	ρ^+	770	$u\bar{d}$	1	1
Rho$^°$	$\rho^°$	770	$u\bar{u}, d\bar{d}$	0	1
Omega	ω	782	$u\bar{u}, d\bar{d}$	0	1
Phi	ϕ	1020	$s\bar{s}$	0	1
K$^+$	$K^{\rho+}$	892	$u\bar{s}$	1	1
K$^°$	$K^{\rho°}$	892	$d\bar{s}$	0	1
J/ψ	ψ	3097	$c\bar{c}$	0	1
Upsilon	Y	9460	$b\bar{b}$	0	1

Figure 21. Hadrons. Some of the (over 200) known baryons and 36 mesons, exemplifying the complexity of the particle family (adapted from *Essential Elements* by Matt Tweed (2003)).

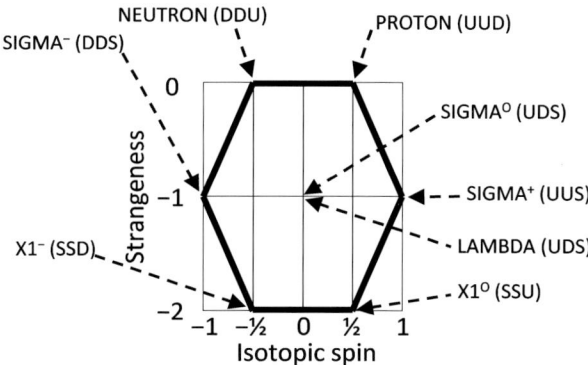

Figure 22. The eightfold way. Eight baryons are arranged to show the symmetry when strangeness is plotted against isotopic spin (**Key**: U, up; D, down; S, strange).

(mu-minus or μ⁻) and tau-minus (τ⁻). The three leptons e⁻, μ⁻, and τ⁻ have negative electrical charge and their anti-lepton partners have positive electrical charge. In addition to these, there are three neutral leptons (and their anti-lepton partners) called *neutrinos*, which stands for 'tiny neutral ones'. Pauli predicted the existence of these in 1932, but they were not discovered until 1955 by the Los Alamos physicists Reimes and Cowan.

The purpose of seeking the symmetry is that a symmetrical model is a 'beautiful' model and thus more likely to be correct. The symmetrical model should fit all bubble chamber analyses and thus represent the fundamentals of particle behaviour. New quarks were found and called *charm* (c), *top* (t), and *bottom* (b), giving a total of six quarks — up, down, top, bottom, strange, and charm. The fourth charm quark, discovered by Glashow, was the fourth quark that Gell-Mann had predicted. It is possible that quarks are fundamental particles. That is, they consist of nothing, but everything consists of quarks.

While protons are the most stable baryons, they are not totally stable. Some larger baryons decay into baryons with a lower rest mass (e.g., protons), which gives greater stability and results in proton formation. Rapid baryon decays are due to strong force interactions, less rapid ones are due to the electromagnetic force, but interactions that result in a change in flavour of a baryon's quark are due to the weak force.

We will look at the interactions (forces) and their mediators (particles) in the next section. Indeed, in the quest to understand the integration of forces and matter to produce a TOE and whose development has

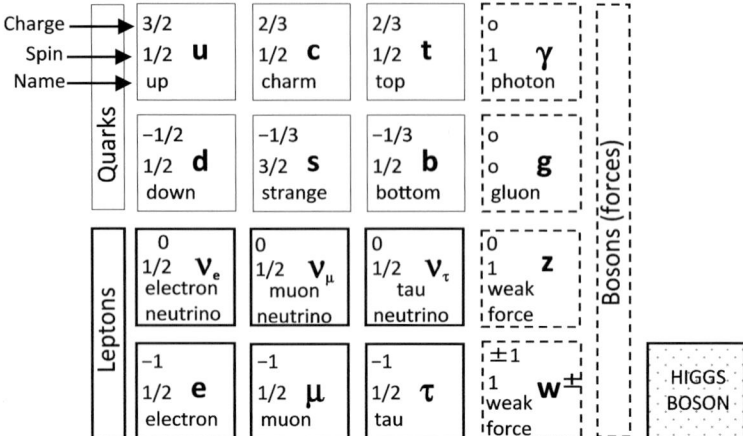

Figure 23. Standard Model of elementary particles.

gone hand-in-hand, a Standard Model of elementary particles has been constructed (Figure 23) that enables predictions for additional particles and how they might mediate their effects. For example, the weak force, also called the weak interaction or weak nuclear force, is viewed as one of the four fundamental interactions of nature. In the Standard Model of particle physics, it is due to the exchange of the heavy W and Z bosons.

The Standard Model predicted the existence of W and Z bosons (and gluons, plus the top and charm quarks), which were later proven to exist with qualities identical to predictions. The Higgs boson, which had been theorised by the English-born physicist Peter Higgs in the 1960s, was detected in the LHC, as I will go on to describe. Further, in July 2015, the LHC was used to discover a new kind of particle called a *pentaquark*. The pentaquark represents a way to combine quarks in a pattern never before observed and consists of four quarks plus one antiquark. Since the 1960s, physicists had theorised this particle, but it took experiments at the LHC to prove its existence.

I stated earlier than neutrons and protons are considered stable in the nucleus and that neutrons become unstable out of the nuclear environment (decaying every 879.6+/−0.8 seconds into a stable proton, electron and antineutrino by radioactive beta decay). Nothing lasts forever though — it has been calculated that in ordinary matter, the half-life of the proton is 10^{31} to 10^{33} years and when removed from the nucleus, it is 10^{32} years. As a result, physicists would expect to see only one proton decay in an 8000 m³ tank of water per day.

Increasing our understanding of forces and particles enables a deeper knowledge of physical processes. For example, β-decay is due to the weak force. There are two types of β-decay, one where electrons (e⁻) are emitted and another where positrons (e⁺) are emitted. β-decay of the positron variety appears to increase the rest mass energy and thus should not happen according to logical interpretations of the laws of physics. To explain how this happens, we need to look at the nuclei of certain elements. I mentioned earlier that as the number of protons increases with atomic number, the ratio of neutrons to protons also increases from a ratio of 1:1 (as for carbon) to approximately 1.1:1 in favour of neutrons as we move towards elements of a higher atomic number in the Periodic Table.

There are a number of elements that have a total nucleon mass of 101 despite having different proton/neutron combinations. One of these combinations gives a nucleus with slightly less mass than other combinations. This particular combination has the greatest mean binding energy per nucleon and is therefore the most stable. As a result, the other nuclei of this mass will tend towards this configuration through decay. Nuclei that are proton-rich relative to the stable configuration will decay through the conversion of protons into neutrons. Nuclei that are neutron-rich will decay into the most stable state; that is, neutrons converting into protons through the process of radioactive decay. Thus, proton-rich nuclei become stable by β⁺-decay, producing neutrons (and neutrons have a slightly higher mass than protons), whereas neutron-rich nuclei become more stable by β⁻-decay, producing more protons.

Forces

In addition to the fundamental particles that exist, we also want to know what forces of nature are fundamental. These have been found to be gravitation, electromagnetism, and the strong and weak nuclear forces, and they work through *exchange* particles. The particles for gravitational forces are gravitons; for electromagnetic forces, photons; for the strong force, gluons; and for the weak force, intermediate vector bosons (W and Z). Each has been detected with the exception of the graviton. It is possible that these forces are components of the underlying force, which they all reduce to.

The gravitational force is a very weak force, but it is one that can act over great distances and thus has significant effects on bulk matter but insignificant effects at the level of subatomic particles (since the force of attraction is determined by the amount of matter). The electromagnetic force (i.e., the combination of electricity and magnetism) can also act at 'relatively' long ranges and is responsible for holding electrons in atoms, for chemical bonds, and for γ-ray photon emissions. The strong force acts at short ranges and is responsible for most hadron decays. The force between hadrons is the consequence of force between quarks inside hadrons. Finally, the more recently discovered weak force can explain certain particle decays. A combination of the electromagnetic and weak forces called the *electroweak theory* was formulated to explain certain unexplainable quark behaviour.

What is the strength of the different forces and how do they relate? The strong force is 1,000 times stronger than the electric force, which is 100 times stronger than the weak force. The strong force is 10^{38} times stronger than gravity. These are shown in Figure 24 below.

Each difference indicates why it is difficult to develop a single theory that can explain all forces. We can construct a hierarchical link between the forces and how they relate to a TOE. Just as electricity and magnetism were brought together as electromagnetism, it is thought that at very high energies, electromagnetism and the strong and weak forces are of similar strength and thus essentially the same force — as in the first moments of our universe.

Interaction	Current theory	Mediator	Relative strength
Strong[3]	QCD	Gluon	10^{38}
Electromagnetic[2,3]	QED	Photon	10^{36}
Weak[3]	Electroweak	W and Z boson	10^{25}
Gravity[4]	General relativity[1]	Graviton	1

Figure 24. Forces.

(*Notes*: 1, general relativity is not a quantum theory; 2, electricity and magnetism link to form electromagnetism; 3, the strong, weak, and electromagnetic theories form the Standard Model, and a quantum theory of gravity would produce a unified quantum GUT (TOE); 4, the huge difference in strength of gravity renders it difficult to unify with the other forces under a single model).

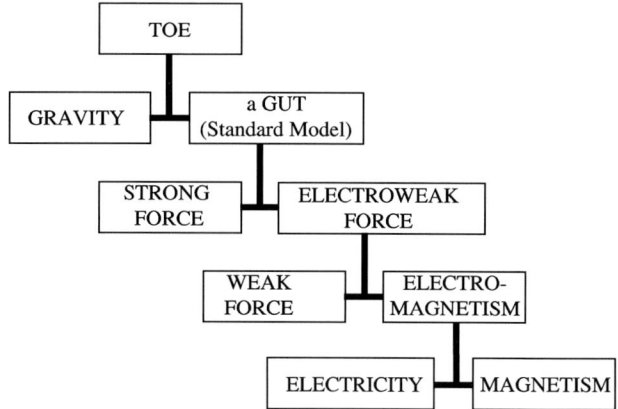

Figure 25. Construction of a TOE. Electricity and magnetism can be described by electromagnetism, which defines the physics of the electromagnetic field. The unification of electromagnetism with the weak (nuclear) force forms the electroweak interaction. To combine the electroweak interaction with the strong force would produce a GUT ('Standard Model'). Linking the GUT with gravitation would produce a TOE.

There is the hope that the TOE will incorporate the effects of all forces, explain all physical phenomena, and thus unite the physics of the small and large. Penrose thinks that this requires a revision of physics. Thus, the current theories of relativity and quantum physics are only representations of a deeper truth about reality.

So, the way the forces relate in terms of leading to a TOE is:

Electricity + Magnetism = Electromagnetism
Electromagnetism (described by QED) + Weak Force = Electroweak Theory
Electroweak Theory + Strong Force (described by QCD) = Standard Model
Standard Model + Gravity = TOE

This is shown in Figure 25.

The Higgs boson

Immediately after the Big Bang, the Universe might have been harmonious. However, something might have happened to break the symmetry, resulting in a Universe with particles and forces of different size and strength. In 1964, Peter Higgs proposed a means by which this spontaneous symmetry-breaking occurred. It required a 'Higgs Field' that permeates space. This field possessed a property of symmetry during the high-temperature beginnings of the Universe, but upon cooling, the property adopted a defined state and the Higgs Field symmetry broke.

Every particle in the Universe moves through the Higgs Field, providing particles with mass. Different particles interact with the field with differing strengths, which is why some particles have more mass than others. Some particles, such as the photon, move through the field but do not interact with it. Since photons do not interact with the field, they move at the fastest possible speed defined by the Universe itself. Accelerating particles with mass and that do interact with the field requires more energy than is available in the Universe.

The Higgs Field defines the energy state of the Universe. When the symmetry broke, the energy of the Universe changed from 'true' absolute zero to a non-zero state. Since the acquired non-zero energy caused by the breaking of symmetry is interchangeable with mass, the added mass becomes the particles with mass in the Universe. So, symmetry-breaking moved mass into particles with mass and not into those that do not have mass. However, although this theory is highly appealing, more evidence than mere theoretical speculation is needed if it is to be taken very seriously.

If the Higgs Field is real, then a remnant of this field should exist now in the form of a fundamental particle — the Higgs boson. This 'God' particle, so-called since it gives mass and physical existence to other particles, was the subject of a concerted search in the LHC. The LHC was, in fact, built specifically to search for the God particle and replaced the Large Electro-Positron (LEP) collider. The Standard Model is consistent with quantum mechanics and special relativity. The Higgs boson is important as it would help explain how matter has mass (which we sense as weight) and how massless particles convert into mass particles that constitute all physical entities with mass, including stars.

The Higgs boson was theorised to exist only at very high temperature and energy (which the LHC can reproduce), such as immediately after the Big Bang. It is thought that all particles during the period immediately after the Big Bang had no mass, and theoretical bosons *with* mass came into existence. By sticking to the massless particles, they provided them with mass. The Higgs boson gives structure and possible completion to the Standard Model, so identification of the Higgs particle in the LHC lent serious support to this theory.

How does the LHC work? The LHC accelerates two beams of protons to 99.9999991% of the velocity of light (that is, 11,000 revolutions of the 27 km circuit per second). The beams collide at four experimental areas called Atlas, LHCb, Alice, and CMS. The collisions possess so much energy that at the point of collision, the Standard Model breaks down and conditions exist as that which occurred prior to the proposed breaking of symmetry. When particles collide, detectors in the experimental areas trace and analyse the emissions of the particle collisions. Even if a Higgs boson was emitted, it decays so quickly that it is difficult to detect. Therefore, scientists have to look at the thousands upon thousands of decays (and decays of decayed particles, and so on) produced by a *single* collision and see if particle traces result that correlate with those predicted for a Higgs boson.

Hence, there is a theoretical model, and fit of the data collected with the model is deemed proof of its validity and correctness. Since particles decay into particles that can themselves decay into other particles that can also decay and so forth, the traces are difficult to interpret, especially since it is also not certain what one is looking for.

In December 2011, tantalising results from two teams at the LHC suggested that they may have found evidence for the existence of the Higgs boson. Using sophisticated statistical analyses, LHC scientists define 'sigma' as a measure of how likely a trace is due to chance. A 5 sigma rating would be a trace that signals the existence of the Higgs boson with a very high degree of certitude that this is not a chance event. Values of 2.9 and 3.1 sigma had been reported, suggesting traces indicative of a Higgs boson. Finally, a 5 sigma result was reported on 4th July 2012, meaning a new particle was discovered whose probability due to chance was around 1 in 3 million. Later, this significance was increased to 5.9 sigma, meaning a 1 in 588 million chance.

Does this finding mean that the Standard Model is right? Some think that it reveals a universal truth whereas others suggest that it is just an advancement on our current understanding and no more than a model of reality we create that is part of a path to an unknowable. Even if it is true, it is a part of reality and does not explain the elusive dark matter. Higgs and Baron François Englert were awarded the Nobel Prize for Physics in 2013. Robert Brout died in 2011, but would have been awarded too for his part.

Models and theories

Some consider the Standard Model to be ugly and that a GUT should possess symmetry and 'beauty' to be right. In fact, there are a number of GUT models in addition to the Standard Model. Each is a unified field theory that predicts that electromagnetism, the weak nuclear force, and the strong nuclear force are, at high energies, fused into a single unified field. They have rather fantastic-sounding names, such as minimal left-right model, Georgi-Glashow model, SU(5), SO(10), flipped SU(5), Pati-Salam model, flipped SO(10), trinification, SU(6), E_6, 331 model, chiral colour, and Heim theory. Other models that are not quite GUTs include 'little Higgs', preons, loop quantum gravity, and two notable ones — string theory and M-theory.

In April 2021, the UK's Science and Technology Facilities Council (STFC) said results from a 'Muon g-2 experiment' "provides strong evidence for the existence of an undiscovered sub-atomic particle or new force". There is a one in a 40,000 chance the result is a statistical fluke, and a one in 3.5 million chance is needed to claim a discovery. The specific results show that the interaction of muons are not in agreement with the Standard Model — muons were shown to wobble faster than expected.

There have also been a number of results from experiments in the US, Japan, and the LHC that point toward the need to revisit the Standard Model. Changes to the model that can explain the recent results, might also solve some of the big puzzles about the Universe (such as the rate of expansion of the Universe being due to a new force and not dark energy).

Already, before proof is found, physicists are postulating what this hypothetical particle or force might be. Names for the particle (leptoquark, Z' boson), or force ('flavour force', 'third family hyperforce' or 'B minus L2') have been 'put out there'.

Only time will tell whether any of these are correct or on the right track, but the TOE would be represented as follows:

Standard Model (or other GUT) + General Relativity/gravitation (possibly as quantum gravitation) = TOE.

The fundamental issue in quantum theory is the distinction between bosons and fermions. Bosons do not obey the Pauli exclusion principle, but fermions do. Perhaps a GUT needs to find symmetry between these fundamental particle types.

String theory

String theory has attracted much interest in the last few decades because of its claim (though ambition might be a better word) of being able to describe all elementary particles in nature and the interactions between them *in multiple dimensions*. It therefore has the potential to link all forces and particles in a unified model. Yet, despite claiming that it will be able to explain all phenomena, there are so many versions of string theory that it can neither be proven right nor wrong, and alignment of some of these can only be made through extremely complex mathematical modelling. Experimental verification is also practically impossible, at least so far.

String theory is an attempt to mathematically model the Universe through the construction of a unified theory. It has its roots in the work of the German mathematician and physicist Theodor Kaluza (1885–1954), who in 1921 published a classical extension of Einstein's theory of general relativity in which he added a fifth dimension (a fifth dimension is a common and legitimate abstraction in mathematics).

Kaluza formulated a unified field theory that incorporated gravitation and electromagnetism. A few years later, Oskar Klein, a Swedish theoretical physicist, reinterpreted Kaluza's theory with quantum mechanics, hypothesising that the fifth dimension could be considered coiled up and reduced to such a microscopic level that it becomes compatible with the physics of four dimensions. This Kaluza-Klein (KK) theory is now regarded as a precursor to string theory and its derivations, unfairly overlooked in its day due to the obsession with quantum mechanics.

String theories do not consider quarks as fundamental particles or that there is wave/particle duality. Rather, matter exists at the fundamental level as 'strings' vibrating in ten or more dimensions. So how do we define a string? Strings are one-dimensional extended objects which are imagined as lines. In contrast, classical physics refers to point or point-like particles (e.g., electrons) as zero-dimensional' objects, which do not occupy any space. These include elementary particles such as quarks, which are units that are impossible to break down further into smaller parts, and composite particles such as protons that have an internal mass, being composed of quarks held together by gluons.

String theory replaces this concept of zero-dimensional points with one-dimensional, vibrating strings instead, which in a one-dimensional representation may be thought of as a line with two definable ends. It is often likened to plucking a string under tension on a guitar, with the elementary particles being the musical notes when the string is made to vibrate at a particular pitch. (In fact, it was Heisenberg who originally proposed that strongly interacting larger particles should be viewed as extended objects rather than point-like particles like electrons.) Strings are considered 'open' (i.e., visualised as a line with two distinct ends) or 'closed', which may be thought of as a circle.

String theories have been categorised according to whether they incorporate strings in a closed loop configuration and whether fermions are included. In order to incorporate quantum gravity, a string must be close to the Planck length (10^{-33} cm). As string theories include the existence of a particle that has zero mass but two units of spin in a closed loop, this is compatible with it being the proposed unit of gravity, the graviton. The mathematics of general relativity cannot incorporate such a particle, working from the viewpoint of point mass in spacetime, but the possibility of interaction between extended objects such as strings does allow mathematical modelling to place gravitons within the framework of a theory of quantum gravity.

The beginnings of string theory lie in the 1960s with the development of bosonic string theory, whose complex mathematics requires a mind-boggling 26 dimensions to exist. It is based solely on bosons, however, and cannot incorporate fermions. This became redundant in the 1980s with the discovery of fermions, which as we saw earlier, can be elementary particles (e.g., electrons) or composite particles such as protons. This led to the development of the theory of *supersymmetry* (SUSY) in order to reconcile fermions in string theory.

SUSY relates the particles that make up matter (fermions) to those that transmit force (bosons) so that for every boson, there must be a 'superpartner' fermion. The mathematics that allow this considers strings vibrating in ten dimensions. It is controversial, in its many forms, in that unlike the Standard Model which links electromagnetism and the strong and weak nuclear forces (described so precisely as QED and QCD), they are ever changing and thus far unprovable. They were never popular with Feynman and Glashow for the very fact that in order to incorporate gravity with the other forces in a single theory, 'unnecessarily' many and unprovable dimensions are necessary to accommodate all the observed quantum behaviours and exotic particles known. In fact, the theories exceed the physical capabilities of particle accelerators to produce results that can test them. Supersymmetry partners to known particles have not been detected so far (e.g., the first run of the LHC failed to detect any evidence of supersymmetry). Such failures have been hypothesised by proponents to be because the unseen partners are too massive to detect using current particle accelerators.

In the search for SUSY, an 11-dimensional *supergravity theory* (SUGRA) was developed in the late 1970s and considered to be the most 'beautiful', but some of its proofs were subsequently found to be flawed. In this model, strings exist as a seven-sphere (seven-dimensional) loop just 10^{-32} cm in diameter. Here, seven dimensions are looped up like a coiled piece of string, yet the coil is made of coils and even those are made of coils, and so on.

Supersymmetry's 11 dimensions can be compacted onto a seven-dimensional sphere, therefore leaving the four dimensions we understand (length, width, height, and time) to operate over larger distances. Adding or subtracting dimensions is a mathematical way of making things work on a theoretical level. This is partly achieved through a mathematical process termed *compactification*. Compactification builds on KK theory and is a way of 'doing away' (from a practical sense) with the unwanted dimensions in a superstring theory so that they are reduced essentially to zero from a mathematical viewpoint and can be ignored, allowing us to reduce to the four we can more easily comprehend. (As an aside and a foretaste of the next chapter, this brings to mind, in the macromolecular biological world, how our DNA molecules are tightly compressed within the chromosomes of our cells — the DNA double helix is coiled around balls of proteins, and this beaded protein-DNA conglomerate is then itself being 'supercoiled' to form coiled threads described as having a 'beads on a string' appearance when visualised under an electron microscope).

A related theory is *$N = 8$ supergravity*. The number of dimensions is reduced from the 11 of SUGRA, and there are eight SUSY transformations necessary to relate particles with different spins (i.e., a total of 8 half-steps from -2 to $+2$, i.e., $-2, -1.5, -1, -.5, 0, +.5, +1, +1.5, +2$ — the maximum that any gravitational theory can have). Incorporating supersymmetry into string theory gives us supersymmetric string theory, or *superstring* theory for short. This led in the 1980s to a number of string theories being proposed, all of which are based on ten dimensions in spacetime. There are five main theories — Type I (open and closed loop), the closed loop Type IIA and IIB (open and closed) theories, and two heterotic forms (10-dimensional, but based on bosonic string theory travelling at one direction on a string while supersymmetry operates in the opposite direction). However, many critics of string theory maintain that although it is mathematically elegant, it is practically untestable as the machines and computing resources necessary are not likely to be developed any time soon. How *could* we detect a graviton, for example?

The renowned philosopher of science Karl Popper, whom I discussed in Chapter 1, believed that a theory is right until falsified. But if there is no initial verification for string theory, the theories exist in their own theoretical space as merely mathematical ideas, beyond the realms of reality and testability in the form of verification and falsification (unlike relativity, quantum theory in its Copenhagen interpretation, and the Standard Model, all of which have stood up to criticism through the derivation of experimental proof that supports their predictions). Thus, the harshest critics deem string theory meaningless and not worthy of the praise (or funding) that it continues to receive. The reader is directed to *Not Even Wrong* by Peter Woit, *Superstrings* by Paul Davies, and *The Trouble with Physics* by Lee Smolin for the pros and cons of string theory. A detailed review of string theory, including the mathematics of string, can also be found at the URL www.superstringtheory.com.

One inherent problem with the competing superstring theories is the general thinking that only one would be proven right to be a TOE. This led to the advent of *M-theory*, a rationalisation of string theories based on the realisation that there are, in fact, sufficient commonalities between what appear on the surface to be disparate theories — they can be reduced to one 'blended' super theoretical reduction of nature. M-theory attempts to unify the five main string theories.

Often referred to as an abbreviation of 'mother of all theories', M-theory was first put forward in the mid-1990s by Edward Witten, a theoretical physicist (then at Princeton University). He recognised that several competing superstring theories contained sufficient similarities that they could be unified through the applications of mathematical transformations called *dualities*, such that two theories can be said to be dual to one another. Specifically, these are known as S-duality and T-duality.

T-duality deals with the inherent problems of comparing distances, reconciling the very short with the long, as it were. S-duality deals with strong and weak interactions. To increase the number of dimensions necessary to formulate a single theory, it became necessary that strings are made of other components called *branes* (a contraction of membranes). These are 2-dimensional objects that propagate through spacetime in accordance with the rules of quantum mechanics. A point particle can be viewed as a brane with a dimension of zero whereas a string is a brane with a value of 1. Branes can extend in two dimensions (called *p dimensions*, hence dubbed *p branes*) from a one-dimensional string. P branes are thought to be integral components of M-theory, where we exist on a 4-dimensional membrane in a higher dimension of spacetime. This is difficult for us to comprehend as visualisation is impossible, but mathematics tells us that the possibility is there.

M-theory would unite all the universal forces into one equation. If it is true, it would realise Einstein's dream. Proof of facets of M-theory are being investigated at the LHC in Geneva. It is important work since M-theory could determine the fate and origin of the Universe. Stephen Hawking suggested that with M-theory, we may have discovered the theory of everything and it needs only to be verified by experiment. However, this is easier said than done. As mentioned earlier, suitable experimental apparatus to prove aspects of string theory are currently beyond our making and may continue to be for all we know.

It seems, then, that there is no shortage of GUT models as they are always being reworked in an attempt to fit reality. The quest for a TOE/GUT was thought to have ended with supersymmetric string theory because gravity could fit into the formalism. However, as we noted, there are some subatomic particles such as quarks which cannot be accounted for by string theories. And, of course, of the different string theories formulated, it is not possible to formulate experiments to determine which one is correct.

Are we even right in assuming that a TOE is possible? Is string theory (and other similar solutions) a representation of reality as it is, or a solution that our brains have formulated in accordance with the limits of our mental capacity? Our solutions may represent aspects of truth, but only those aspects allowed by and relating to our mental and physical constructions and limitations.

We assume that nature is presented in a way that can be calculated and known, but there is no reason why this has to be the case. Perhaps our physics and mathematics are just a tribute to our creativity within the context of what is possible by a finite mind, and their close mirroring to aspects of reality lull, trick, and convince us that they present fundamental significance. String theory conflicts with intuition, is very mathematical, and would not have been something Einstein would have embraced. For example, if many conflicting theories are mathematically feasible, they cannot all be true, if any. Yet, the fact that many can be made to work shows the disparity between what really *is* happening and what we can *make* happen within the confines of our limited capabilities and paradigms.

As a metaphor, what can happen in dreams seems real in that world, but in the light of waking logic, we can see what of the dream is nonsense. Maybe we will never know if our search for ultimate truth is a doomed pursuit due to insufficient mental tools.

Lee Smolin's five fundamental problems

The American theoretical physicist Lee Smolin, in his book *The Trouble with Physics* (2006), states that theories attempting a GUT that went beyond the Standard Model are either falsifiable (and were falsified) or untested (either because they made no testable predictions or that technology negates the possibility to test them). Many attempts have been made to test them in the realm of particle physics (e.g., supersymmetry) or spacetime (e.g. twistor theory). No experimental result produces data that would not fit with at least one theory, yet no theory fits all data. If we were to be somewhat damning of string theory, we could say it isn't a theory at all, but rather a collection of conjectures without fundamental principles or mathematical language. It has survived with such popularity not through success, but because of the beauty of its promise. Yet, science is finally admitting that little has come from it.

Smolin has clarified five clearly unsolved problems in theoretical physics:

1. To combine general relativity and quantum theory into a single theory that can explain all physical phenomena and claim to be the complete

theory of nature. This would be a theory of quantum gravity. Currently, quantum theory and general relativity theory are riddled with infinities, yet nature does not present phenomena that *result* in infinities. General relativity describes a *real* world whereas current quantum theory is of an indeterminate world, incompatible with realism. To unite the two, preferably in a realist sense, and yet remove infinities under the same model has eluded us so far.

2. To reformulate the foundations of quantum mechanics where measurement and observer have no role in describing reality by either modifying current theory or inventing a new one. It is felt that a correct theory should avoid the micro/macroscopic interface of the observer. Many attempts, most famously those of Bohm and Einstein, have tried and failed to convince a reformulation of the anti-realist Copenhagen formulation of quantum theory into realist terms. But a realist interpretation is still sought.

3. To determine whether all particles and forces can be unified in a single theory that explains them all as manifestations of a single model. We do not know if nature is actually this way (i.e., that we are seeking something that does not exist). Progress has been made to construct the Standard Model, which explains the interaction of all forces (except gravity) with all particles. It has not been improved on in the 30+ years since its formulation, but it is fundamentally flawed in that is not fundamental. It needs experimentally verified values for particles and forces. A fundamental theory should function from principles.

4. To explain how the values of the free constants in the Standard Model are 'chosen' by nature. That is, a fundamental theory should explain why they are as they are. It is believed that additional dark matter is present in the Universe, providing the added mass that affects galaxy rotation speeds, which exceed those predicted by the Standard Model. Additionally, at great distances, objects recede faster than predicted by gravitation. Here, a new form of energy — dark energy — is hypothesised.

5. Dark matter and dark energy need to be explained, or else if they do not exist, we must seek an explanation for why gravity is modified on large scales.

Closing the loophole

Loopholes represent possible explanations for why Bell's inequality can be violated and yet quantum theory in its Copenhagen guise be false. That is, 'closing a loophole' represents removing a possible (component of a) hidden variable theory as a possibility of explaining why the inequality may be violated.

The debates between Bohr and Einstein about the philosophical meaning of quantum theory (what is real, is it complete) continued from the late 1920s until Einstein's death. While the use and practical applications of quantum theory expanded, Einstein never accepted the theory and sought errors within.

The theory's tremendous useable success is encapsulated in N. David Mermin's famous "shut up and calculate" quote (credited to Richard Feynman), exemplifying the general attitude within the quantum theoretical community towards anyone asking what the theory really means. Even John Bell was fearful in the 1960s of bringing the topic of 'meaning' back to the forefront of quantum theory. Indeed, he published his ground-breaking work on the interpretation of quantum theory in a low profile journal, partly so as not to incur publishing fees for the article on his employer (they would not have wanted to pay on this unimportant topic), but also so that perhaps it would both be 'out there' and yet not be seen and stir up trouble until attitudes changed (it is remarkable that this was the attitude to what now is considered one of the most profound scientific works) The field just did not care or even considered the subject closed.

Indeed, the American theoretical and experimental physicist John Clauser (1942-) did some pioneering experimental work on Bell's Theorem, but this undoubtedly prevented him from achieving the academic path one would expect for such a scientist. His choice of interest was an example of 'wrong subject, wrong time, wrong place'. Staggeringly, it is only recently that the implications of Bell's work and the relation of quantum theory to the nature of reality has obtained any academic attention. Indeed, it was through interest by metaphysical philosophers that brought it to the wider public attention, before physics reluctantly accepted that it could not be swept under the carpet any longer.

Although Alain Aspect's experiment showed that no local hidden viable theory could reproduce the experimental results, there are other possibilities. Indeed, the number of possible loopholes seem, at present, unending. As one is closed, another opens. For example, the randomness of the choice of 'questions' the particles are asked in a Bell test may only seem random, such as the analyser orientation. Even asking a machine to make choices merely defers randomness to something that may not be random but controlled at a deeper level. Anton Zeillinger (1945–), for example, conducted an innovative experiment that showed that if there is a mechanism that controlled the randomness of the questions asked on particles, then that mechanism lies in the deep past at great distances in time and space.

More recently in 2016, Carlos Abellán and Morgan Mitchell performed the 'BIG Bell test' game, relying on human group free will to make decisions on aspects of such tests. They decided that human choice is the most random thing and thus the ideal thing to make random choices.

This, of course, falls apart if free will is actually an illusion. Here, when the human 'decides' to make a measurement of an isolated quantum system and the wavepacket collapses, both are therefore determined. Thus, the collapse may not destroy the deterministic aspect of what the collapse reveals, but due to the subject-object nature of reality, the reveal is merely incomplete information of a determined system.

Nuclear power

In this chapter, we have discussed in detail the foundations and philosophy of quantum theory. Much of the driving force that has maintained our interest in this field is not only purely for the insight it provides into the structure of reality but also because understanding atoms provides the means of being able to control them and harness (or unleash) the tremendous power locked within. From our understanding of quantum processes or at least our ability to predict their effects, humankind has utilised this knowledge and that of relativistic processes to harness the power of the atom and use it both as a source of energy and as a terrifying weapon.

Nuclear *fusion* is the method of energy production utilised by stellar objects in the Universe such as our Sun. Our understanding of nuclear processes has provided insight into the existence of elementary particles that do not exist naturally, but which did exist shortly after the Big Bang. This knowledge is due to our ability to create them artificially in controlled nuclear experiments. To understand these particles and the processes underlying their production helps us understand our beginnings and perhaps our fate too. However, this is just one aspect of nuclear and particle physics.

Nuclear power as a *fission* (not fusion, which we have not mastered for power generation) process provides benefits and hazards for society. The understanding and mastery of this power source produce financial benefits (it could be cheap once the systems are set up to achieve maximum efficiency) and the availability is potentially limitless, but there are notable pros and cons on environmental issues. The direct environmental damage caused by a nuclear power station is less than that from conventional gas or coal sources. However, there are great environmental hazards when a nuclear power station suffers, and indeed has suffered, a malfunction.

On 23rd April 1986, the Chernobyl nuclear power plant in the Ukraine underwent a reactor explosion, releasing eight tonnes of radioactive material into the atmosphere. Calculating the number of deaths due to radioactive fallout is almost impossible due to the long-term effects combined with the difficulty of correlating cause with effect. However, 25,000 local inhabitants in the region of Chernobyl have died prematurely since the event, and there has been a high incidence of birth abnormalities from which one would have little difficulty drawing conclusions.

More recently in March 2011, a magnitude 9 earthquake and tsunami off the eastern coast of Japan devastated the Fukushima 1 nuclear power plant, leading to meltdown in three out of the facility's six nuclear reactors. It is estimated that over 250 tonnes of radioactive water continue to leak from the now decommissioned plant into the Pacific Ocean daily. Environmental concerns across Europe, particularly in the wake of the Fukushima disaster and in an age of heightened global concern over terrorism, have led to nuclear energy programmes in Germany and France being scaled back dramatically.

So, what are the nuclear processes behind nuclear fission and fusion reactions? Uranium is a heavy, reactive, and radioactive metallic element discovered in 1789. However, it was not until 1938 that Otto Hahn and Fritz Strassman discovered nuclear fission by bombarding uranium-235 atoms with neutrons. It was found that uranium-235 (contributing to 0.7% of natural uranium) and not uranium-238 (contributing to 99.3% of natural uranium) underwent fission. Uranium-238 decays over billions of years, emitting protons, neutrons, and γ-rays to produce stable lead-206 (via thorium-230 and -234, protactinium-234, uranium-234, radium-226, radon-222, polonium-218, bismuth-210 and -214, polonium-210 and -214, lead-210 and -214). The bombardment of the uranium-235 nucleus with a neutron produces isotopes of the elements barium and krypton together with three neutrons. The barium and krypton fragments of the bombarded uranium nucleus undergo decay by β-emission (loss of electrons) to produce more stable and less radioactive isotopes. Thus, the fission of a uranium-235 nucleus is accompanied by a large release of radioactive energy. Hahn's long-term professional partner, Lise Meitner, was the one who calculated that the splitting of each uranium nucleus was capable of producing an enormous 200 meV of energy.

Although some isotopes decay naturally, for the energy of uranium fission to be gained, it has to be induced. Once this has happened, the neutrons released can cause other uranium isotopes to decay, starting a *chain reaction*. Fission reactions occur because the fission fragments have less potential energy and less mass than the isotope that formed them. Thus, the fragments are energetically more stable than the original isotope. Furthermore, the binding energy (a measure of stability) increases per nucleon (proton and neutron) and is greater in the combined fission fragments than the original isotope.

Fission reactions in nuclear reactors are induced by adding energy to break up the initial isotope of uranium-235. In a thermal nuclear (thermonuclear) fission reactor, it is essential that one of the neutrons released in each reaction starts another fission. The reproduction factor must be exactly one. If this is achieved, it is considered critical. Below or above this point is called subcritical and supercritical, respectively. It can be dangerous if the reactor goes supercritical, so reproduction rates are maintained carefully using control rods and moderators.

Nuclear fusion, the process that fuels the Sun, is different from fission. It is the combining of nuclei to emit energy, rather than splitting the atom. The energy release by fusion greatly exceeds that of nuclear fission and, although we have mastered fission for weapons use, we have not been possible to control it in reactors for the production of abundant and cheap energy. Atomic nuclei carry a positive electrical charge, so there is a strong repulsion between them. Only when nuclei are close enough together can the nuclear strong force cause the nuclei to join and release energy. Particles feeling the strong force are neutrons and protons (the force is carried by pions).

Some particles, such as electrons and muon, do not feel the strong force. Hydrogen, the smallest element, of course consists of a single proton in its nucleus. Hydrogen fusion brings two protons together in one nucleus where one proton then becomes a neutron. Extremely high temperatures are necessary for this to happen. In our Sun, hydrogen nuclei fuse to form the deuterium isotope (H^2). This is the slowest, rate-limiting step in stellar fusions and the build-up of deuterium is known as the 'deuterium bottleneck'. Deuterium forms helium^3, with each stage emitting radiation of high energy. These processes require very high temperatures and are contained by strong gravitational forces — if an object is less than one-tenth the size of our Sun, there is insufficient internal gravitational force to create the temperature needed to ignite the initial fusion reaction.

Further fusion reactions occur in suns as heavier elements are formed until they produce the nuclei of Fe^{56} (iron-56). Fe^{56} atoms are the most stable of all elements with respect to mean binding energy per nucleon in the nucleus. This mean binding energy per nucleon increases with increasing atomic number up to iron and then falls again. Producing nuclei heavier than this requires a net input of energy. This is something that only happens in the case of supernovae explosions — the final exit of a star's life as it releases its energy and becomes a white dwarf, black hole, or neutron star, depending on its size.

Supernovae are essential for the production of the heavier elements, and as charged forms of these elements they contribute to and are components of physiological processes within the cells of living organisms. We are all made of stars, and their death (in one sense) is that which enables life as we know it. The problem with achieving nuclear fusion on Earth is that we need to achieve temperatures of 100 million K to enable the particles to come close enough and overcome the electrostatic repulsion for the strong force to take effect. The major technical problem is finding a way to confine the hot radioactive plasma. We cannot employ the gravitational forces that exist within stars for confinement purposes, of course, but work is being carried out to try to use inertial effects and magnetic fields.

4 The Biological World

The development of quantum theory and relativity involved the efforts of many individuals, as we have seen, but history has paid special attention to a handful of physicists such as Albert Einstein and Niels Bohr who made the key conceptual breakthroughs that rapidly advanced the development of theories in relatively few years. Although their refinement has involved the work of thousands of scientists and decades of theory and experiment, the initial breakthroughs represented what the American physicist and philosopher of science Thomas Kuhn would call a "paradigm shift in understanding". Thus, for the purpose of a historical discussion of those subjects, one can relate key individuals to the important breakthroughs and present them in the context of the whole theory.

Additionally, since both quantum theory and relativity are explanations of the behaviour of matter within fields of force, understanding these theories generates knowledge of how physical matter behaves at both small and large scales. The theories are, within their context, all-encompassing explanations of why things happen. Understanding the biology of the cell differs in both these aspects.

Although it is true that quantum theory describes atomic behaviour and thus that of molecular interactions which constitute cellular activity, we cannot *use* these theories to help us predict and describe what will and does happen in a living cell. The computing power required would far exceed that which we (conceivably will) possess. Furthermore, it would only provide insight into a part of what is a dynamic and highly regulated system. The interaction of chemistry and biology has proven very effective at producing information that we can manipulate and apply. Chemistry is an extension and application of physics.

In the context of biological systems, chemistry and biology combined to form disciplines such as biochemistry, genetics, and molecular biology. Each discipline is consistent with and extends from the other such that the scientific method can expand its boundaries of application. The underlying causative physics of the behaviour of biological systems is integrated into techniques that enable scientists to unravel biological processes without applying the 'tools' of quantum theory and instead be consistent with them.

Life has been defined as a characteristic that distinguishes objects that have signalling and self-sustaining processes from those that do not. Living organisms undergo homeostasis, which is metabolism under tightly controlled conditions in order to maintain the cell, and can grow and respond to stimuli and their environment. Critically, they can reproduce, passing on their biological material in the form of genes to the next generation. In turn, this permits, over many, many generations, evolution into new forms. However, a singular, reductive 'definition' of *life* tends to either include organisms that are not normally considered as living or exclude those that are.

The philosopher Mark Bedau has suggested the possibility that that which constitutes a living being might not have a unified explanation and life may not be a basic category of natural phenomena. Therefore, although a universal criterion for the definition of life may still be possible, the answer to "what *is* a living thing" might not be simple or even singular. An example might be viruses, composed as they are chiefly of a coat of protein enclosing a DNA or RNA genetic core, which must engage in a form of parasitism and hijack the biological machinery of a living cell in order to reproduce themselves. The molecules within a cell form functional systems of great complexity, and the most complex system of cells is undoubtedly that found in the human brain — the seat of consciousness and reason.

Thus, molecules in enough number and intricacy of arrangement and through a temporal process can generate understanding in the organism which they comprise. Leaving aside whether human consciousness was a fortunate by-product of evolution, what *is* true is that this process finds solutions to problems posed in an ever-changing environment. The practical reward for these solutions is the increased chance of survival for the genes that encode them. We cannot predict biological processes; rather, we uncover the truth of their reality through experiment. Perhaps some cellular processes seem illogical and energetically expensive, but the goals of life differ from those of physics. An organism needs to ensure the integrity of all its processes in order to pass on its genes successfully, whether it is a bacterium or a human being. There is no room for error in life; a mistake (e.g., a *mutation* in a critical gene) means extinction.

The goal of biological science is to understand how our cells and bodies work and to use this information to rectify problems, maintain health, and prevent suffering. To be able to manipulate a system successfully requires first an intimate knowledge of how it works. Notwithstanding key breakthroughs such as the discovery of DNA as the chemical of heredity, our goal to understand how a cell works has been (and continues to be) an interactive, global, and increasingly multidisciplinary application of the scientific method.

A typical human cell represents a complex result of billions of years of evolution by the process of *natural selection*. Each cellular constituent and process is a refined, essential, and integrated component of a highly organised system. No theory can predict what natural selection has chosen as a solution to biological problems encountered on Earth during the struggle for existence, as we shall see in the next chapter when we consider evolution.

To understand why and how a cell works has required years of the application of hypothesis testing, verification, falsification, and analysis by hundreds of thousands of scientists. The combined knowledge of the integrated scientific community continually refines, adds, and removes from our understanding, producing an ever-clearer picture of what is happening in our cells. This knowledge is seen not so much as some quest for 'truth' but rather an accumulation of useable, consistent information that enables us to predict and manipulate, thereby allowing us to plan and act for our benefit. For example, the elucidation of the sequence of the human genome has consequences for new therapeutic prospects offered by personalised medicine, *cell-based therapies*, and *tissue engineering*.

The advent of the era of molecular biology in the 1970s brought about a journey into the realm of the very heart of the cell, the nucleus. As some scientists sought to identify all the genes carried in the chromosomes within the nucleus (*genomics*), others sought to characterise the proteins that they code for (*proteomics*) or to identify the molecules that regulate where and when genes are activated (*gene expression*). This gives the impression that perhaps the sum of the man can indeed be read in his genes, and has led to a reductionist, gene-focused viewpoint.

However, as we shall show in this chapter, it is one of the beauties of what might be termed 'inner space' that everything we learn points to the cell being infinitely more complex than we could ever have imagined, with layers upon layers of control of different sorts, tightly regulated gene expression occurring during embryonic or adult life, tissue-specific gene expression, complex feedback mechanisms within intricate signalling pathways, and a host of protein modifications acting as potent 'on-off' switches controlling protein activity. In this respect, the molecular biology of the 21st century makes one think of the subatomic world and how the description of the atom has gone far beyond the old classical viewpoint of protons, neutrons, and electrons to the fundamental particle world of bosons and quarks.

To illustrate this complexity, consider that the latest estimate for the number of genes in the human cell is only 19,000, whereas the current proteomic view is that there are probably in excess of one million different functional proteins produced from this relatively small handful of genes. I often feel that there is some of Einstein's "flight from wonder" in these findings. Although there are many specialised cells in the body (e.g., the neurons of the brain are structurally very different from those of most other body cells as a direct reflection of their distinct functions), they also contain so-called 'housekeeping' processes that are common to all cells, such as energy production and metabolism. These complex mechanisms have evolved over billions of years. Now, an organism has evolved, *Homo sapiens*, with the ability to marvel at and unravel the very mechanisms of our own biological, and perhaps mental, function.

Human cells are barely different from those of other vertebrate animals, as I will go on to describe. At the DNA and protein levels, one sees a remarkable degree of conservation when comparing animals separated by millions of years in evolutionary terms. Yet, as a whole organism, we are so different due to our conscious abilities. These abilities have enabled us to understand the world around us and our own mechanistic processes.

Could we be unique in this insightful ability due to some specific feature of our structural components, or is it through how they interact as a complete operating system? It seems the latter is true. Indeed, to understand what materially comprises our self is to link the physical with the mental.

For every biological process that we understand or investigate today, advances in computing and technology have enabled rapid progression from the initial insights revealed by the pioneering work of scientists who were unaided by such sophistication. Before such technology was available, experiments were designed according to these limitations and so the inferences and insights gained were restricted accordingly. Now, the results that advanced technology brings, including mathematical modelling of biological processes, allow for deeper insights and experimental designs with fewer practical limitations. Indeed, ideas have often now become the limiting factor for progress.

However, scientific research is driven by the search for funding both in academic and industrial settings, and it is money, ideas, and proven success that are the deciding factors for what avenues are explored and by whom. Industrial biological science is a huge global concern involving shareholders and massive corporations, such as the so-called 'Big Pharma' that drives the interaction of the pharmaceutical and medical worlds. Much of academic research is grant-funded, whether by state, charities, or industry, and there must be a proven track record of success before one is awarded money.

The quest for knowledge for the sake of advancing knowledge has become a thing of the past. With the useable foundations of biological knowledge cast as well as money as a driving force for future biological science, we will tread a careful ethical path as to what diseases or causes of suffering are pursued. Will it be the most deserving (in a 'Popperian' sense- after Karl Popper) or those most likely to generate revenue? Will it be to prevent future economic collapse as debilitating diseases such as Type 2 Diabetes, well-established in the heavily industrialised west, become more prevalent elsewhere in the world? Is it obscene to put so much emphasis on stem cell therapies and the development of expensive, personalised medicine tailored to an individual's genetic plan instead of, say, concentrating on effective vaccination programmes to combat the high rates of infant mortality in Africa?

With all our available technology and wealth of biological information in terms of understanding cellular function and dysfunction (e.g., diseases such as heart failure, diabetes, and cancer), perhaps the key issue is whether we have the moral intelligence to address the right questions in the right way. This book isn't the place to discuss the moral applications of scientific knowledge; suffice to state that we are a single species living on one planet. How one chooses to feel about how we progress and address divides in wealth and health is a personal choice.

I mentioned earlier the process of the biological evolution of solutions to problems by natural selection, but to understand our evolution and link it to what we are, we must first understand some of the key molecular players within the cell. I will show first how a cell works, looking at how proteins control many cellular functions, and review examples used in the architecture of a typical cell. We will look at how proteins act as biological catalysts for cellular chemical reactions, show how metabolism occurs through energy that is generated and stored in cells to power life's processes, and outline how a cell defends itself against infection.

I will go on to show how genetic information is conserved and passed on, not only to the next generation (the immediate goal of any organism) but in the far longer temporal context of change and evolution. The events occurring within all our cells take place throughout our lives. These processes keep us alive, all the time acting in an environment where mechanisms occur at phenomenal speeds and degrees of accuracy. Their functionality is tightly controlled; their speed, complexity, and resistance to error are proof in themselves of the power of evolutionary selection and the ideal processes that have arisen for the continuation and proliferation of life.

We have a good understanding of the mechanism of life's processes in the human and, since all living organisms possess a high degree of similarity of structural components, in other organisms too. As we have evolved from other forms of life that lived in different environments, molecular mechanisms or functional motifs within proteins have been conserved across vast expanses of time that seem to defy the logic we would apply if we were to design them ourselves. If we were to design the human eye today, would we really borrow some components from a fly's eye as a starting point? Evolution progresses not according to a logical plan, but by adapting the materials at hand and improving continually on what was already there.

On a final note, I was chatting with a couple of non-scientist friends recently and the conversation came around to genes. One asked, "How many genes do we have?" and the other queried, "A couple of thousand?" They were shocked when I told them that the number is closer to ten times that figure. "Is that more than what other animals have, like a mouse?" they asked. I replied that we pretty much have not only the same number of genes but also the same ones as a mouse. One then asked a very pertinent question: "Do we have different genes for our hair or brains compared to blood cells?" I tried to explain that every cell in the body has the same complement of genes, and it is just a question of which ones are used *where* that creates the different organs and structures of our anatomy.

Once again, as a biological scientist, I was brought face to face with a fundamental problem. Despite terms such as DNA and genes, 'designer babies', and 'Frankenstein foods' being banded around regularly in the media and often for sensational effect, the majority of people do not understand the fundamentals of what cells are and what they do, let alone why we are what we are! So, in this chapter, I may be guilty at times of belabouring a point so as to get it across, but I hope that in the process, I can provide a sound foundation as to the wonder of the inner space that is the cell.

i) How a Cell Works

Early studies on the cell

The cell is the basic biological unit from which all plant and animal tissue is composed. It is the smallest unit of life that can exist independently, and it possesses a self-regulating and self-replicating chemical system that powers its metabolic processes.

In Philip Ball's book, *Stories of the Invisible*, he likens the cell to a city and its functions to various aspects of the processes that go on in a city — movement, cooperation, communication, energy production, and so forth. This analogy is quite apt and worth dwelling on for a moment. For instance, if one imagines a medieval fortress city with strong outer defences built of stone walls, those walls can be likened to the membranes that form the exterior of any animal or plant cell. The wall contains entry and exit points for movement in and out of the city in the form of doors and drawbridges.

Our cells contain protein channels embedded in the cell wall or *plasma membrane* for the same purpose, allowing the transport of ions or small molecules across the membrane. Buildings inside would also be made of stone walls and house industries necessary for the smooth running of the city — food stores and kitchens, for example — not so different from the membrane-clad, energy-producing structures found in animal and plant cells called mitochondria and chloroplasts, respectively.

There are extended membrane structures called *endoplasmic reticulum* running throughout many cells that facilitate the orderly movement of proteins from one place to another, much like an orderly system of roads. And at the heart of such a city would have been a citadel where all the major decisions that contribute to the welfare, growth, and defence of the city are made — an apt analogy for the nucleus of the cell, which contains the genetic material or chromosome(s) wherein the genes are embedded.

The discovery of the cell is recognised as the first step towards modern biology. In *Micrographia*, published in 1665, the English scientist Robert Hooke coined the term 'cell' from the Latin word *cella*, meaning 'small chamber', to describe the small chambers in a dried section of cork that were visible to him under a light microscope. From this starting point, many discoveries and scientists have passed in the development of *cell theory*. Proposed in 1838–1839 separately by the botanist Matthias J. Schleiden and the physiologist Theodore Schwann, and then formalised twenty years later by the German researcher Rudolf Virchow, cell theory established three concepts that are obvious to us today:

1. All known living things are made up of cells.
2. The cell is the structural and functional unit of all living things.
3. All cells come from pre-existing cells by division.

The third point means that spontaneous generation does not occur, something that was experimentally proven by the Frenchman Louis Pasteur in 1862. Moreover, cell theory established that "cells contain hereditary information which is passed from cell to cell during *cell division*".

Hooke's discovery of the cell was made possible by the development of the microscope by the Dutchman Anton Van Leeuwenhoek, who used it to observe the movements of unicellular protozoa in water. Indeed, progress in biological research has depended much on technological advances. This technological dependency is true too for other sciences, but whereas many ideas about the physics of the Universe can progress with a degree of freedom through mathematical theorising (although they also require experimental proof, and the inability of string theory to do that harms its credibility as we discussed earlier), such modelling has until recently been of lesser use in biological process delineation.

While theoretical modelling now applies to several aspects of modern biological research, including delving into our evolutionary past, it is the direct access to and manipulation of that which exists that has provided the greatest advances. For example, Frederick Sanger (1918–2013, who won two Nobel Prizes in Chemistry for his work on proteins and, later, DNA) invented a method to determine the sequence of any DNA molecule. This method later became incorporated into the functioning of machines that can sequence huge amounts of DNA at one time. This development has occurred in tandem with computing advances that have allowed the vast amounts of raw DNA sequence data generated to be ordered into a complete map of our human genome. Today, we can derive the DNA sequence of entire human genomes from numerous individuals in a matter of days, even if we cannot yet completely understand the intricacies of the complex code contained within.

Cells and organisms

In describing the processes of normal cellular function, it is useful to begin with an explanation of the type of cell we are describing. In biology, no two things are alike. Every cell is different from the next, even if they are functionally the same type of cell. Liver cells, for example, differ from skin cells more so than one skin cell from the next — this is due to cell-specific specialisation of function due to cell-specific patterns of gene expression. I will describe this in more detail in later sections.

The major different categories of cells, from an evolutionary standpoint, are the prokaryotic and the eukaryotic cells. Prokaryotic organisms are comprised mainly of bacteria (*Eubacteria* and *Archaea*), so-called blue-green algae (*Cyanobacteria*), prochlorophytes, and mycoplasma. Eukaryotic organisms are plants and animals, from simple unicellular lifeforms such as protozoa up to complex multicellular organisms such as giant Sequoia trees or humans.

Animal cells, of course, differ from plant cells as the latter are able to harness the energy in sunlight to produce energy (*photosynthesis*) and can incorporate cellulose into their cell walls in order to provide rigidity and structural strength. Neither of these feature in animal cells. However, despite these differences, there are many fundamental processes within animal and plant cells that are identical. All eukaryotic organisms have their genetic material (DNA) enclosed by membranes to form the nucleus. (We should note at this point that the genetic material of any organism is organised in the form of chromosomes and can be referred to as the genome).

The prokaryotic genome tends to be a single piece of genetic material, but most *eukaryotes* possess several chromosomes in their genome. Eukaryotic cells possess many different *organelles*, such as endoplasmic reticulum (ER), the Golgi apparatus (named after the Italian Camillo Golgi, who first described it), and mitochondria, which is the site of energy production in the animal cell. Plant cells possess organelles too, such as the chloroplasts where photosynthesis occurs.

Prokaryotic cells lack any internal membrane system and thus are much simpler than eukaryotic cells. Their genomes are smaller too, roughly 500–1,000 times smaller than the human genome, yet some carry a quarter of the number of our genes (but very different genes, in the main). Eukaryotic cells either constitute the entire organism (e.g., protozoa such as *Amoeba*) or are a component of a much larger eukaryotic whole (plants, fungi, animals) and generally possess an internal volume that is approximately 10,000-fold that of prokaryotic cells. The division of eukaryotes from prokaryotes is often thought of as being the largest single breakthrough in the evolutionary history of life on Earth, such is the difference in the cellular structures of the two cell types.

The evolution of eukaryotes took place hundreds of millions or perhaps billions of years after the evolution of prokaryotes. The existence of prokaryotes dates back approximately 3.5 billion years and it is thought that cells took up prokaryotic organisms to become eukaryotes. This intriguing idea is supported by the fact that the mitochondria — those organelles within the eukaryotic cell that function as the energy production centre for the cell — looks remarkably like a prokaryotic bacterium in size and shape.

They even contain their own DNA. Similarly, chloroplasts in plant cells have been proposed to have ancestry with free-swimming, photosynthesising single-cell organisms.

The following sections describe some of the key components and functions common to many eukaryotic cells, particularly the various roles of proteins as biological catalysts (*enzymes*) in energy production, as well as more specialised contexts such as the body's self-defence mechanism, the immune response. I also consider, of course, the molecules of heredity and evolution, the nucleic acids DNA and RNA, which are found in all cells. For a more detailed insight into the biochemical functions of a cell, the interested reader should refer to the excellent undergraduate text by Lubert Stryer, *Biochemistry*.

The protein world

Of the 'molecules of life', I will consider first proteins, not only because of my own professional interest in them as a biochemist, but also because of the inference from the name. 'Protein' is derived from the Greek term *prota*, meaning 'of primary importance', and throughout this part of this chapter, it will become clear that almost all biological processes involve proteins. Some have structural functions (e.g., keratin and collagen in the hair and skin) and some have transport functions (e.g., haemoglobin, which transports oxygen in the blood). Antibodies are a specialised class of protein molecules that are central to the immune response. Some proteins can regulate cellular motion within an environment, such as the flagella on single-cell animals that are used for propulsion, or the cilia found on specialised cells lining our gut or airways. And, of course, tens of thousands of proteins regulate metabolism and control cell growth.

Proteins are made of repeating units of small molecules called *amino acids*. All proteins are manufactured from a basic alphabet of 20 different amino acids. Each amino acid consists of a central carbon atom with an acidic and a basic end (carboxyl (COOH) and amine (NH_2) groups, respectively). What defines one amino acid from another is a group coming off the central carbon atom, which is termed a side chain. Each of the 20 amino acids possesses a different side chain that varies in size, shape, charge, and chemical reactivity.

The smallest side chain, a single hydrogen atom, is possessed by glycine. The different side chains allow amino acids to be grouped according to chemical character, which is important for interaction with other amino acids, both within and between proteins, as we shall see. Some side chains are hydrophobic (i.e., water-repelling) in nature, such as leucine or valine, whereas others are able to ionise and are weakly acidic in character, such as aspartic acid and glutamic acid, or basic (alkaline), such as arginine and lysine. The aromatic amino acids possess a cyclic carbon ring-structure side chain. The 20 amino acids can be grouped thus:

1. Aliphatic side chains — glycine, alanine, valine, leucine, isoleucine, and proline.
2. Hydroxyl aliphatic side chains — serine and threonine.
3. Aromatic side chains — phenylalanine, tyrosine, and tryptophan.
4. Basic side chains — lysine, arginine, and histidine.
5. Acidic side chains — aspartic acid (aspartate) and glutamic acid (glutamate).
6. Amide side chains — asparagine and glutamine.
7. Sulphur-containing side chains — cysteine and methionine.

There is a standard symbolic notation used for amino acid naming, which is shown in Figure 26.

In any linear protein chain (also called a *polypeptide*), amino acids are joined together via a peptide bond, formed from the α-carboxyl (COO^-) group of one amino acid being joined to the α-amino (NH_3^+) group of the next one in the chain by *covalent bond interaction* (sharing of electrons). The polypeptide's linear or *primary* sequence is read from the free amino end of the first amino acid in the chain and this sequence is determined directly by the gene, as we shall go on to see later.

The true determinant of any protein's function is its three-dimensional conformation. Proteins range from simple polypeptides such as insulin or cytokines (small signalling proteins that include the interferons) to much larger functional conglomerates made of several similar or dissimilar proteins. Regularly repeating structures within a polypeptide chain called the α-helix and β-sheet are termed *secondary* structure and these contribute to the overall *tertiary* structure of the polypeptide. When similar or dissimilar polypeptides associate to form a functional protein, this is

Single letter code	Abbreviation	Name
A	Ala	Alanine
C	Cys	Cysteine
D	Asp	Aspartic acid
E	Glu	Glutamic acid
F	Phe	Phenylalanine
G	Gly	Glycine
H	His	Histidine
I	Ile	Isoleucine
K	Lys	Lysine
L	Leu	Leucine
M	Met	Methionine
N	Asn	Asparagine
P	Pro	Proline
Q	Gln	Glutamine
R	Arg	Arginine
S	Ser	Serine
T	Thr	Threonine
V	Val	Valine
W	Trp	Tryptophan
Y	Tyr	Tyrosine

Figure 26. Amino acid notation.

termed a *quaternary* structure. For example, antibodies are composed of four polypeptides, two large or 'heavy chain' polypeptides, and two smaller 'light' chains, the products of distinct genes.

The complex 3-D structure of a protein is held together by a number of processes. In addition to the strong covalent peptide bonds, secondary and tertiary structures are stabilised by the weaker *hydrogen bond* (e.g., the same forces that cause ice to stick to your hand). The hydrogen bond, which is also used in DNA, is probably the most important chemical bond in terms of life, as we shall go on to see. Van der Waal's forces (weak interactions) and hydrophobic (water-repelling) interactions also contribute to tertiary structure. Another strong interaction, the *disulphide bridge* occurs by oxidation of sulphur atoms carried on the side chains of pairs of serine residues.

Despite being composed of just 20 different types of amino acids, the variability in size, shape, and arrangement of proteins enables them to recognise and interact with many molecules and with an extremely high degree of specificity. This is particularly evident in enzymes or in receptors for hormones, drugs, or other such small molecules. Enzymes are potent biological catalysts, which are agents that speed up the rate of chemical reactions without being directly affected themselves. They are able to direct chemical reactions at high speed and specificity, binding *substrates* (molecules that are to be changed) and stabilising *transition molecules* (temporary forms that occur along the reaction path) before releasing the final products of the reaction. Enzymes are able to break and create bonds at high speeds and with high accuracy for single, specific, structurally determined reactions. We shall look at these in more detail in the next section.

Protein synthesis or *translation* occurs in the cytoplasm — the gelatinous fluid inside the cell membrane. Subsequent post-synthetic processing or modifications may be made, such as glycosylation (the chemical addition of sugar groups to the protein within the Golgi apparatus) or phosphorylation (addition of phosphate groups); both of these modifications may be critical for protein function within the cell. Ultimately, when a protein has performed its function, it is targeted for destruction by specialised proteins within the cell so that its amino acid constituents can be recycled and used in the synthesis of new proteins.

Protein functions

In the following section, I will present some examples of the wide range of different protein functions in a living organism. It is important to stress that these examples encapsulate only a small percentage of the wonderfully complex machine that nature has developed.

Enzyme catalysis

The first function we will look at is enzyme catalysis. I was drawn to this choice both by my personal scientific interest and also because delineating the enzymatic process is a typical example of how different branches of the life sciences have had to collaborate to completely explain a particular phenomenon. To start with, we need the physical principles of thermodynamics to introduce the concept of *free energy*. For a biological reaction to occur spontaneously, the free energy change ΔG (Δ = change, and G is named after the American mathematician Willard Gibbs, who discovered the concept of free energy) must be negative. The free energy change in any system is related to the *enthalpy* (ΔH, which relates to internal energy, pressure, and volume) and *entropy* change (ΔS, often described as a change to a more disordered state at a molecular level) according to the equation:

$$\Delta G = \Delta H - T\Delta S \text{ (where T is temperature)}$$

The free energy change is a measure of the amount of useful work obtained from the change being considered. Enzymes lower the free energy of activation of a reaction, thus serving to increase the reaction rate by at least a million-fold. Despite their speed, they are extremely specific in the reaction they perform and are as accurate as they are rapid. In an enzyme-catalysed reaction, a temporary *transition state* is formed between the initial enzyme and substrate starting components and the enzyme and product (altered substrate/s) of the finished reaction. The transition state is the highest energy component of the reaction but possesses the lowest free energy, making it more accessible than when uncatalysed. Furthermore, the enzyme can adopt a physical conformation that is complementary to the transition state of the reaction it catalyses.

The first step of an enzyme-catalysed reaction is the formation of an enzyme-substrate complex. The 3-D structure of the protein is tailored to provide a specific binding site for its substrate. This is termed the *active site* — a well-used biochemical analogy likens this to the precise fit of a key for the lock to which it belongs. Substrate binding is associated with conformational changes in the enzyme as a consequence. There is a model that accounts for the kinetic properties of some enzymes known as the *Michaelis-Menten* model (1913), named after its creators Leonor Michaelis and Maud Menten. The basic form of the reaction is

$$E + S \Leftrightarrow ES \rightarrow E + P$$

Thus, an enzyme (E) combines with a substrate (S) to form an enzyme-substrate (ES) complex. This then either forms a product (P) with the concomitant release of the enzyme or, as the double-headed arrow indicates, it dissociates into E and S again without catalysis.

An enzyme's *turnover number* reflects the number of molecules of substrate (S) converted into product (P) per unit time; in other words, this defines the catalytic speed of the enzyme. This speed might be over 10,000 molecules per second. The Michaelis-Menten model holds for the kinetics of simple enzyme systems, but there are many others (some more complex) that cannot be described by this model, such as *allosteric enzymes* (see next section).

Enzyme activity can be controlled within cells by chemical activators and inhibitors (molecules or ions). There are different classes of inhibitors, which can be categorised according to the method of inhibition. *Irreversible inhibitors* bind covalently to the enzyme (recall that covalent binding is the strongest interaction between atoms of a molecule, characterised by the sharing of pairs of electrons) and do not dissociate as they modify the active site. Examples include the poison cyanide, which covalently binds to mitochondrial Cytochrome C oxidase, and carbon monoxide, which irreversibly displaces oxygen from haemoglobin, hence accounting for the extreme toxicity of these substances.

Most *reversible inhibitors* bind through weaker, non-covalent interactions and dissociate much more rapidly. These include *competitive inhibitors*, which mimic the shape of the substrate so that they compete for access to the active site of the enzyme but cannot themselves be converted into product, and *non-competitive inhibitors*, which do not compete but instead decrease the turnover number by acting elsewhere upon the enzyme.

Myoglobin and haemoglobin: allosteric interactions

Myoglobin and haemoglobin are large gas transport proteins, carrying the oxygen essential for life. Oxygen, together with food (in the form of sugars, proteins, fats, and other essential nutrients), enables us to power the cellular processes that enable the continuation of life and generate energy for movement. In terms of the physiology of these individual proteins, myoglobin facilitates oxygen transport in muscles and stores excess oxygen whereas haemoglobin carries oxygen in the blood.

Structurally, myoglobin and haemoglobin consist of a protein-haem group, a porphyrin ring structure (a natural pigment in the form of protoporphyrin) containing an iron atom in its Fe^{2+} ionised form, which binds oxygen. Their structures were determined in the late 1950s by the Austrian-born British molecular biologist Max Perutz and colleagues using X-ray crystallography. This is a technique where X-rays are used to bombard a crystallised protein, and the diffraction pattern caused by X-rays bouncing off the orderly pattern of molecules in a crystal lattice is then used to infer the 3-D structure of the protein (the same process was used to determine the structure of DNA). The quaternary structure of the haemoglobin molecule is a multimer composed of different subunits. For example, haemoglobin A is called an $\alpha_2\beta_2$ multimer, as it is built up from two molecules of the α subunit polypeptide, and two β subunits, which are the products of separate genes. The quaternary structure is pivotal to the function of haemoglobin as a whole as interaction between the subunits enables *allosteric* effects to occur.

In terms of function, haemoglobin and myoglobin both transport oxygen (O_2) whereas haemoglobin also transports hydrogen ions (protons, H^+) and carbon dioxide (CO_2). The ways in which these proteins exchange oxygen can be explained only through chemistry. The state of oxidation of the iron atom determines the oxygen-binding affinity of the protein complex. Haem with a Fe^{2+} ion at its core binds one oxygen molecule, which has two electrons to share, whereas the Fe^{3+} state of iron cannot (the $^{2+}/^{3+}$ symbolism refers to the oxidation and reduction states of the iron atom, respectively). Reduced Fe^{3+} or *ferric* haem has a +3 oxidation state and is deficient in three electrons. Fe^{2+} is deficient in two electrons and is the only form of *ferrous* haem that is able to bind oxygen.

An allosteric interaction is one where a conformational change in one part of the molecule causes a subtle change in another part of it, making it more efficient at a particular function related to the bound molecules. In the case of the haemoglobin multimer, binding of the first molecule of oxygen to one subunit triggers a conformational change in the whole protein, converting it from a low affinity oxygen-binding ('tense') form, which binds oxygen very weakly, to a high affinity oxygen-binding ('relaxed') form, which binds oxygen avidly. The binding of oxygen to haemoglobin is termed a *cooperative* function, with the binding of one oxygen facilitating the binding of more oxygen molecules to other haem groups within the multimer. H^+ and CO_2 promote O_2 release from haemoglobin (of use to muscles) while O_2 promotes release of H^+ and CO_2 (in the capillaries of the alveoli, the site of gaseous exchange in the lung), which is exhaled in our breath.

In medicine, knowing both how a protein works and its structure is crucial if we are to treat human disease and understand its molecular basis. People who suffer from sickle-cell anaemia possess a variant of the haemoglobin multimer known as haemoglobin S. Here, the α chains are normal, but each of the β chains possesses a single mutation in amino acid number 6 (glutamate is changed to valine at the sixth position in the polypeptide chain — we can write this as Glu 6 → Val 6). This single change, which replaces an amino acid (Glu) with acidic character for one (Val) with a hydrophobic, water-repelling nature, has drastic consequences for protein structure — it causes a perturbation of the protein's 3-D structure, which leads to the mutant protein 'dropping out' of solution and the deposition of fibrous haemoglobin S in the red blood cells (erythrocytes). This is an extremely painful condition which leads to the destruction of the erythrocytes within the body of a sickle-cell sufferer, a pathology known as chronic haemolytic anaemia. It is interesting to note that the sickle-cell gene that encodes these mutant β chains also confers protection for these individuals against certain severe forms of malaria. Since the gene is common in native Africans and the malarial mosquito is prevalent in Africa, this suggests that there is an inherent evolutionary connection such that the mutation confers a degree of benefit.

The type of allosteric interaction found in haemoglobin is more complicated than the more basic models that are common to a number of other enzymes — these are known as the *concerted* and the *simple sequential* models.

In the concerted model (also called the MWC or Monod-Wyman-Changeaux model, after Jacques Monod, Jeffries Wyman, and Jean-Pierre Changeaux who devised it in 1965), the symmetry of the multimer (or subunit) is conserved. Here, subunits are either in one form or the other. *Ligands* (i.e., small molecules or an atom/ion) bind with low affinity to the tense form of the subunits/multimer and with high affinity to the relaxed form. Inhibitors may bind to the tense form. The simple sequential model proposes that the binding of a ligand to one relaxed protein subunit in a multimer causes a conformational change only to the subunit that it binds to, yet by doing so increases the affinity of all the other (tense) subunits for the same molecule (as we saw earlier for the binding of oxygen to haemoglobin). Thus, as each ligand binds, the probability increases that all molecules will be in the relaxed form.

Protein modifications: regulating protein activity

An inactive protein may become activated in different ways. *Proteolysis*, or the cleaving of the protein into two or more parts, can regulate an enzyme's activity; a simple example is the removal of the amino-terminal amino acids in preproinsulin, the biologically inactive precursor of insulin, to produce the active form of the enzyme. Proteolysis is also involved in protein degradation pathways either for end-of-function recycling or as a mechanism for destroying unwanted 'foreign' proteins. These mechanisms are complex, but most involve ubiquitin, an evolutionarily conserved 'marker' for degradation that is attached to proteins targeted for destruction residues by specific enzymes called ubiquitin ligases (the process is called *ubiquitination*). As a result, ubiquitin-tagged proteins are recognised for cleavage by the cell's protein recycling centre, the proteasome.

A particularly potent form of enzyme modification involves *phosphorylation* — the addition of a phosphate group, PO_4^{3-}, to a particular amino acid of a protein by enzymes called *protein kinases*. Specific kinases add phosphates to serine, threonine, or tyrosine residues and a phosphorylated enzyme can be activated, or sometimes inhibited, by virtue of the phosphorylation status of a single amino acid. Conversely, specific enzymes called *protein phosphatases* remove phosphate groups, allowing the enzyme to return to its original state and making it available for a fresh round of phosphorylation. Thus, phosphorylation can act as a potent molecular 'on-off' switch in terms of activation or inhibition of function. This process is one of the most widely used forms of reversible modification in the cell for modifying an enzyme's activity.

A major function of such phosphorylation/dephosphorylation events is in the transmission of signals picked up at the cell surface into changes in gene expression within the nucleus. Phosphorylation of protein receptors embedded in the cell membrane results in amplification of cell surface-mediated signals, such as hormones, growth signals, inflammatory signals, or stresses (e.g., exposure to excessive temperature or ultraviolet light). For example, binding of insulin to the monomeric insulin receptor, which is a member of the receptor tyrosine kinase (RTK) family, promotes receptor dimerization — in other words, two insulin receptors which have both bound insulin can now associate within the cell membrane to produce an activated form of the receptor. This then leads to the exposure of an intracellular RTK domain (i.e., a catalytic domain that is able to phosphorylate tyrosine residues on target proteins as well as self-phosphorylate) on the receptors, leading to interaction with cytoplasmic signalling proteins inside the cell. But how does this internalised signal then get to the nucleus?

It is common to find that kinases form complex *signalling cascades*, which results in the original extracellular signal being amplified several times in the cell. Such cascades include the tiered MAP Kinase pathways (Figure 27, below) which are involved in a host of cellular processes, including cell division, cell differentiation, and mediating cellular stress responses. So-called MAP3 kinases usually are the primary intracellular recipient of the signal in question and they interact with the receptor at the inner surface of the cell membrane. These MAP3 kinases then phosphorylate MAP2 kinases which, in turn, phosphorylate MAP kinases such as p38 or ERK1/2. Activated MAP kinases then target gene regulatory proteins that are active within the nucleus of the cell (Figure 27). Some of these target proteins, *transcription factors*, are able to interact directly with DNA to change patterns of gene expression, which I will discuss in subsequent sections.

So, we can see that signalling pathways are massively integrated within the cell, with single enzymes responding to multiple divergent signals in many different pathways. It is a remarkably complex but effective mechanism for controlling the integration of many extracellular inputs with intracellular functions. The process that leads to blood clot formation occurs through a sequence of events that resemble MAP kinase cascades, where the activation of one clotting factor catalyses the activation of the next (and many of these factors are proteolytic enzymes).

In summary, we can see that the control of an enzyme's activity can be mediated through a multitude of mechanisms — allosteric interactions, proteolytic cleavage, reversible covalent modification, and protein binding (inhibitory and stimulatory). Finally, it should be noted that proteins are

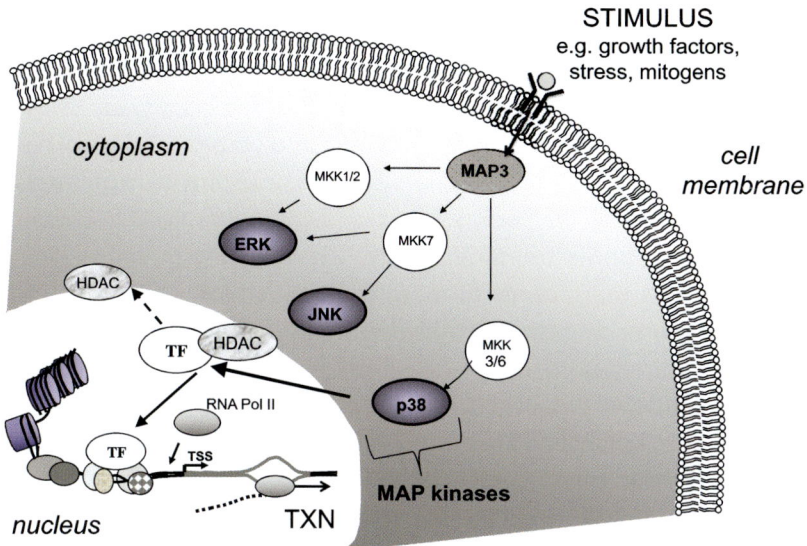

Figure 27. Protein kinase signalling. This example depicts a stimulus (small grey circle beyond the cell surface) being recognised by its cognate receptor embedded within the cell membrane. A MAP kinase cascade of signalling, which is mediated via cycles of protein phosphorylation, transmits and amplifies the original stimulus until it reaches the nucleus. Here, it brings about gene expression by modifying the function of transcription factors (*TF*), which are DNA-binding proteins that interact with RNA polymerase II (*RNA Pol II*) to drive the *transcription* (*TXN*) of target genes. **Key**: Signal is first received by a MAP3 kinase. White circles represent different forms of MAP2 kinases which then amplify the signal before passing it on to MAP kinases such as p38, ERK, or JNK. HDAC, histone deacetylase, is another nuclear regulatory protein; TSS, transcription start-site, represents the point where the messenger RNA (mRNA) will begin (here depicted as a dotted line). See text for further explanation.

not the only biological catalysts in the cell. RNA enzymes were discovered more recently than protein enzymes, although evolutionarily they are actually much more ancient. It is interesting that in the history of the development of life on Earth, complex proteins could not have existed without long DNA sequences to code for them, yet without proteins to assist the process of *DNA replication*, as I will go on to explain, only short DNA sequences could have been copied. Thus, by acting as genetic templates and as enzymes, RNA was able to resolve this problem by performing both functions.

Molecules of the immune system

Immunology can be viewed as a branch of science somewhere between biochemistry and medicine. The immune system is the body's way of fighting foreign substances, including many bacteria and viruses, and is comprised of two parts — the *innate* immune system, consisting of highly specific proteins (antibodies) that are 'primed and ready' to fight the invading body, and the *adaptive* immune system, which, as the name suggests, is a slower process that adapts to meet the needs of fighting off an infection. *Autoimmune diseases* such as rheumatoid arthritis see the immune system instead mounting an attack on our own body or 'self', mistakenly recognising our own cellular proteins as foreign.

Two key mechanisms are employed by the immune system to distinguish between the self and an invading foreign body — soluble antibodies and T-cell receptors. Antibodies — or *immunoglobulins* (Ig) as they are also called — are proteins presented on the surface of white blood cells, or lymphocytes, to the plasma around them. These surface-presented molecules act as 'lookouts' for foreign molecules borne on bacteria or viruses as well as diseased (e.g., cancer) cells in the blood.

As mentioned earlier, the quaternary structure of most immunoglobulins is composed of four protein molecules, two heavy chains, and two shorter light chains. In response to exposure to a foreign molecule, termed an *antigen* or *immunogen*, those cells that express on their surface the antibody specific for that antigen begin to proliferate and release soluble antibodies directed against it. When antigens and antibodies combine to form antigen-antibody complexes, this triggers a series of enzymatic reaction cascades called the *complement system*, which stimulates a variety of further immune processes including the release of granules containing digestive enzymes from cells known as mast cells (immune white cells) and phagocytosis (ingestion of foreign bodies) by macrophages, another type of white cell. Together, these combine to provide a complex and far-reaching system that protects the host organism from infection and disease.

For any particular antigen, different types of antibody-producing cells produce antibodies of a number of different or heterogeneous quaternary structures, grouped into five different classes of antibodies — the immunoglobulins IgG, IgA, IgD, IgE, and IgM. These may be released at different stages in an immune response or be present in different bodily fluids (e.g., the fluid and mucous of the respiratory tract rather than the blood), or released in response to particular stimuli. This differential production and release reates a portfolio of antibodies that is capable of mounting a sustained response over a prolonged period in order to neutralise a foreign invader. For example, the immune response to a typical infection will see a fast and transient response by IgM initially. This response subsequently overlaps with the appearance of a slower and more sustained IgG response to the same immunogen.

The nature of the genetics of the formation of antibody molecules is such that the genes that encode immunoglobulins can rearrange to produce 100 billion different possible immunoglobulins, easily enough to enable an organism to mount a specific attack on any potential invading foreign body.

Cell membranes and compartmentalisation

Membranes are complex protein and lipid (fat) structures that surround cells as well as many organelles within the cell, such as the nucleus and endoplasmic reticulum (ER). Our medieval city analogy would see such lipids and proteins as the equivalent of the stone, bricks, and mortar used for building city walls and buildings within alike. Membranes allow for the compartmentalisation of function in eukaryotes and enable transport between compartments. For example, many proteins are folded within the ER and then pass on to the Golgi bodies where they are glycosylated. Specific protein pumps, transporters, and channels embedded in the cell membrane (also called the plasmalemma or plasma membrane) act as semi-permeable, dynamic barriers that allow selective movement of molecules across the membrane. Similar membrane-embedded channels can allow electrical signals to pass between cells, such as in heart muscle cells called *cardiac myocytes*.

On a physical level, the plasma membrane is mainly constituted of phospholipids. These molecules have a hydrophobic (water-repelling) tail and a hydrophilic (water-attracting) phosphate-containing head. In an aqueous environment (humans are 70% water by mass), the lowest energy state for the phospholipid is a *micelle*, a structure formed by lipids forming a circle with all hydrophobic tails pointing inside, or a *bilayer* (two layers of phospholipids with the heads facing outside and inward and the hydrophobic tails linked in the middle — see the depiction of the plasma membrane in Figure 27).

A lipid bilayer forms the basic structure of the (outer) cell membrane as well as the membranes of organelles and the so-called nuclear envelope surrounding the nucleus. Glycolipids and cholesterol are also present in the cell membrane and they play very important roles, such as allowing communication between cells and maintaining membrane fluidity. The lipid bilayer of the cell membrane does not allow charged molecules or ions to pass through, yet it does permit certain proteins to associate and integrate within the structure, such as receptors, pumps, ion-channels, and transporter proteins.

Such proteins may allow signal or substance transport in an *active* (energy-dependent) or *passive* (energy-independent) way. Specific membrane proteins such as cytokine receptors facilitate the communication and energy transduction functions of the membrane, thereby allowing a cell to react to changes in its environment. Proteins and lipids can move easily within the membrane (lateral movement), whereas transverse movement of lipids across the membrane — a process referred to as 'flip-flop' — is much slower.

The proteins that span the membrane (*transmembrane proteins*) control the flow of ions and molecules across it. These proteins exist as ion channels and pumps. Channels allow charged ions such as Cl^- or K^+ to flow through the electrically charged cell membrane — the rate of this flow can be up to ten million ions per second. Channels may be composed of multiple protein subunits that can adopt both active (open) or inactive (closed) conformations. The regulation of the transition between the closed and open conformation is allosteric. This voltage-dependent allosteric regulation is in addition to the usual forms of allosteric regulation discussed previously.

The best-understood membrane-spanning channel is probably the nicotinic acetylcholine (ACh) receptor. It contains an extracellular entrance domain, a transmembrane domain much rather like a tunnel running through the cell membrane that allows substances to pass through, and a cytosolic entrance domain. This ion channel mediates synaptic transmission, which is the transfer of a nervous impulse from one nerve to the next.

Many receptors found in the plasma membrane belong to the seven-transmembrane domain (7TM) receptor family, so-named because they possess seven protein helices that span the cell membrane from one side to the other. It is predicted that the human genome contains around 800 different 7TM receptor genes; in other words, about 4% of our total complement of genes. Their sheer number suggests that they play roles in a wide variety of biological processes, including activating cellular responses to external stimuli through activation of MAP kinase or other protein kinase signalling pathways, as we saw earlier. As such, they have become major targets for pharmaceutical research. 7TM receptors include the muscarinic ACh receptors, which activate ion channels that are involved in the contractility of cardiac muscle or smooth muscle contraction; rhodopsin, the primary light-sensitive pigment in the retina of the eye; and receptors for neurotransmitters such as dopamine and serotonin, which are linked to mood and behavioural responses.

Pumps differ from channels in that they do not form a continuous pore from one side of the membrane to the other. Pumps are active transporters — that is, they require an input of energy to power the pumping process. This energy is usually supplied by the small molecule adenosine triphosphate (ATP), which will be discussed in the next section. The transport rate for pumps is slower than that of channels at about ten thousand ions per second. The sodium-potassium (Na^+-K^+) pump is the commonest pump in animal cells and is an organism's greatest drain on ATP. One molecule of ATP is needed to pump three Na^+ ions out of the cell and to pump in two K^+ ions. This pump is essential as it controls cell volume (preventing the cell from bursting, for example) and enables nerve and muscle cells to be electrically excitable (essential for their correct functioning).

Sometimes, ATP breakdown or *hydrolysis* is not essential to drive a membrane transporter system, and an ionic concentration gradient alone is sufficient to enable the pumping of ions (as is the case with the sodium-calcium exchanger).

Energy generation and storage

I return to physics and chemistry in order to provide a clearer understanding of the origin of the energy employed in all cellular processes.

According to the second law of thermodynamics, energy cannot be created or destroyed, only exchanged, as we saw in Chapter 3. Sunlight provided by nuclear fusion in our Sun is the origin of our energy. When photons reach plant cells, they excite the chloroplasts and stimulate the movement of electrons in the protein machinery within them. This process allows for the accumulation of energy in the form of a proton gradient (we will analyse later how a proton gradient is converted into energy inside every kind of cell, from bacteria to humans). This is a simplified description of the process called *photosynthesis.*

Plants use photosynthesis to 'feed' themselves, of which a fortunate side effect is that the oxygen released by the process allows animal life to survive. The source of the moving electron, 'pushed' by solar energy, is water (indispensable for all life). The photosynthetic reaction in plants is the reaction of water with carbon dioxide, which is powered by light, to produce carbohydrate (glucose) and oxygen. These products are essential for animal life as our cells consume oxygen and carbohydrate to produce energy.

Glycolysis, the citric acid cycle, and oxidative phosphorylation

Glycolysis or the *glycolytic pathway* describes the set of reactions that convert the carbohydrate fuel glucose into pyruvate, or pyruvic acid. Glucose is a ring-shaped six-carbon sugar that enters our bodies through the diet and, once in the blood circulation, is available to our cells and thus the glycolytic pathway.

The purpose of glycolysis is to generate ATP, which is used by all cells as a source of energy. Just as the hydrogen bond is probably the single most important chemical bond in nature, ATP is the most important and universally used small molecule, powering all of life as we know it. Energy is released when ATP is converted into adenosine diphosphate (ADP) through the loss of one phosphate and finally into adenosine monophosphate (AMP) by the loss of another. AMP and ADP are later recycled to regenerate ATP. Since a large number of enzymes participate in the reactions of glycolysis, there is potential for a high degree of regulation through the types of mechanisms, principally allosteric and phosphorylation regulation, discussed in the previous section.

A total of ten individual reactions make up the glycolytic pathway between glucose and pyruvate. In addition to making ATP (only two molecules of which are made per molecule of glucose entering the pathway), glycolysis provides various molecular building blocks for the synthesis of many other cellular components. Some stages of the pathway are energy deficient — that is, they require a net input of energy — but necessary for the production of pyruvate (two molecules of pyruvate are made per molecule of glucose). The small amount of energy produced by glycolysis alone is enough to support the life of small unicellular organisms like yeast and some kinds of bacteria. In yeast, for example, pyruvate is further broken down into ethanol and CO_2 through a process known as fermentation. Humans have learnt, in the process of civilisation, how to exploit fermentation to produce wine, beer, and bread.

Pyruvate is an important starting point for several processes. In the presence of oxygen, it feeds into the *citric acid cycle*; in the absence of oxygen (i.e., *anaerobic* conditions), it is converted into lactate (the cause of muscle cramps in athletes and sportsmen) and powers fermentation. It can also be directed into glucose synthesis (*gluconeogenesis*) and fatty acid synthesis.

Pyruvate is the starting material for the citric acid cycle, which is also known as the TCA or Krebs cycle after its discoverer, the German-born British biochemist Hans Krebs. The citric acid cycle, so-called because acetyl CoA reacts with oxaloacetate to produce citrate (citric acid), occurs in the mitochondria where pyruvate is converted into acetyl CoA (co-enzyme A). Although the production of pyruvate from glucose does not generate a great deal of ATP as mentioned above, the energy reward in terms of molecules of ATP generated becomes substantial when it enters the citric acid cycle in the presence of oxygen and through subsequent *oxidative phosphorylation*. Once citrate is produced, a series of enzyme-catalysed reactions reconvert the 6-carbon citrate molecule into a 4-carbon oxaloacetate, which can be used to power another round of the citric acid cycle.

Each cycle generates only one ATP molecule per molecule of acetyl CoA, but pairs of electrons are generated as by-products in the cycle and these are transferred to two so-called electron carriers, nicotinamide adenine dinucleotide (NAD^+ reduced to NADH) and flavin adenine dinucleotide (FAD reduced to $FADH_2$). These electron carriers are very important for the last step of energy production, the *electron transport chain*, whereby a far larger amount of ATP — a staggering 32 molecules of ATP, in fact, from an initial input of one glucose molecule — is produced. This important process is also known as oxidative phosphorylation, because as ADP is *phosphorylated* (to produce ATP by the enzyme ATP synthase), the NADH and $FADH_2$ are become *oxidised* — hence the name of the process.

In oxidative phosphorylation, which occurs across the membrane of the mitochondria, ATP is made as a result of the flow of electrons from NADH or $FADH_2$ to oxygen. Electrons do not pass directly from NADH or $FADH_2$ to oxygen, but instead pass through a series of electron carriers such as flavins, iron-sulphur complexes, and copper ions. As electrons (negative charge) flow through the mitochondrial membrane, protons (positive charge) are pumped out. When NADH and $FADH_2$ transfer electrons to oxygen to be reduced to CO_2 and water (which is why we release CO_2 in respiration), they lose their proton (H^+). The rate of the cycle depends on the energy requirement of the cell and, hence, the organism. As with glycolysis, there is also a high a degree of enzyme regulation at key control points in the cycle. The process is a complicated mechanism for which Peter Mitchell, the British scientist who delineated the key mechanisms, was awarded the Nobel Prize in Chemistry in 1978.

The accumulation of protons on the mitochondrial membrane generates an electrical potential and ATP is made as protons flow back across the membrane through an enzyme called ATP synthase. Thus, free energy is transmitted by a proton gradient. The net result is that the complete oxidation of one molecule of glucose to CO_2 and water (through glycolysis, the citric acid cycle and oxidative phosphorylation) generates about 32 molecules of ATP — a highly rewarding endpoint from the cell's point of view for the extraction of energy from this simple sugar.

One metabolism

Metabolism is a chemical and physical process that consists of regulated *catabolism* and *anabolism*. Catabolism is the breakdown of organic matter to release energy and organic components, whereas anabolism is the storage of energy and the building up of tissue. The main metabolic functions are the generation of ATP for energy and the generation of the building blocks for biosynthesis. Tens of thousands of enzymes are involved in metabolism. A few examples that highlight the intricate control of cellular processes help explain why we have so many enzymes dedicated to metabolic processes.

The enzymatic reactions of metabolism are controlled by multiple mechanisms such as allosteric regulation and compartmentalisation of the processes, which allow for different functions to occur in different parts of the cell as we have already described. Pathways that control opposing processes (e.g., glycolysis and gluconeogenesis, which represent the reactions for the conversion of glucose to pyruvate and pyruvate to glucose, respectively) are very tightly regulated such that when one is active, the other is quiescent. This creates an energy-efficient mechanism that underlies all reciprocally regulated (i.e., under the control of *negative feedback mechanisms*) metabolic pathways.

Feedback mechanisms are common within our cells. Certain hormones, whose release is triggered by the availability of fuel reserves in the body, profoundly affect metabolic processes that govern the fate of these reserves. When starved, they trigger catabolism of reserves. Conversely, in times of plentiful food, they trigger anabolic pathways. Hormones cause changes in reciprocally regulated pathways such as glycogen degradation and synthesis by indirectly activating key enzymes that control both pathways.

Glucose levels in the blood change throughout the day and in response to food intake. Insulin, a peptide hormone made in the pancreas, and another hormone, glucagon, are released into the bloodstream to make best use of the sugar intake. The release of insulin lowers blood sugar levels following a meal by promoting the uptake of glucose into cells chiefly through the insulin-dependent glucose transporter 4 (GLUT4) trafficking protein, which ferries glucose across the cell membrane and into the cell. Insulin also drives the synthesis of *glycogen*, which is the form in which the body stores excess sugar as an easily metabolised source of energy (in contrast, plants store excess glucose in the form of starch).

Glycogen is stored mainly in the liver and muscle in the form of cytoplasmic granules. When energy is rapidly required, glycogen is converted enzymatically into a form of glucose that can enter glycolysis so as to release energy. The pancreas releases glucagon when blood sugar is low; it targets the liver to break down glycogen and inhibit glucose synthesis. Thus, insulin and glucagon function to enable a constant blood sugar level despite large fluctuations in the daily intake.

Type 1 Diabetes (diabetes mellitus) is the most common metabolic disease, characterised by *hyperglycaemia* (high blood sugar). It is caused by a lack of insulin and an excess of glucagon. Since insulin promotes glucose uptake into cells and glucagon enhances formation of glucose in the liver, the diabetic patient releases large amounts of glucose in their urine. When blood sugar levels drop, glucose is also formed by gluconeogenesis in the liver using glycogen, proteins, or fatty acids as a substrate. Fatty acids are also released by the breakdown of triacylglycerols along with ketone bodies, which can induce coma in insulin-dependent diabetic patients.

Muscle and liver can use fatty acids instead of glucose for their energy requirements in times of starvation so that the glucose is reserved for the brain, which is the primary bodily concern for receiving sufficient fuel and oxygen. Indeed, although the brain constitutes only 2% of adult human body weight, it uses 20% of the energy production (80% of which is used to power nerve impulses). However, in times of extreme starvation, the body uses ketone bodies (e.g., acetoacetate) for fuel. These are produced as by-products when fatty acids are broken down for energy. They can be converted into acetyl CoA, which can thereupon enter into the citric acid cycle in order to produce ATP.

Hence, metabolism has backup mechanisms according to availability because its primary function is to promote survival. The liver supports the metabolic functions of the other bodily organs so that when food is plentiful, it manufactures fats and sends them for storage in adipose tissue as a fat/protein mix called very low density lipoprotein (VLDL).

Molecular motors: movement and life

Proteins are responsible for movement, both of single cells and within the whole organism. Muscles allow us to run, power our breathing, and in the case of the heart, pump blood around the body. Our body contains three forms of muscle. *Striated* muscle comprises the *skeletal* muscles, such as those found in our limbs, and *cardiac* muscle (myocardium), which is responsible for the pumping action of the heart. *Smooth* muscle lines our gut and blood vessels and is also found in many other places. We will focus primarily on striated muscles here.

Skeletal muscle cells (called *skeletal myocytes*) differ from other cells in that they fuse together to form large, multi-nucleated *myofibrils*. These contain repeating structures termed *sarcomeres* that form the basic structural unit for muscle contraction. The synchronisation of many end-to-end linked sarcomeres within a myofibril, plus the fact that myofibrils are packed together and are therefore contracting in parallel with each other, results in the contraction of the muscle as a whole.

The sarcomere contains two overlapping and interacting protein structures termed 'thick' and 'thin' filaments (so-called due to their gross appearance when viewed under the electron microscope). The thick filament consists of bundled Myosin Heavy Chain (MHC) molecules, a long filamentous protein with a densely packed globular head at one end. The MHC heads stick out along the thick filament and are complexed with much smaller Myosin Light Chain (MLC) molecules, which impart a regulatory function. The thin filament is built around long chains of polymerised actin along which, at periodic intervals, sit other thin filament proteins; tropomyosin and the calcium-sensing troponin complex (made of Troponins I, C, and T, all products of distinct genes).

The thin filaments are bound to a structure called the Z-line which marks the boundary between sarcomeres with the thick filaments lying in between (Figure 28). The two types of filaments are able to slide over each other in an energy-dependent reaction as a result of an influx of calcium (Ca^{2+}) ions. During each cycle of contraction, Ca^{2+} is released into the cell from a cell membrane-associated storage structure called the sarcoplasmic reticulum (SR). Ca^{2+} binds to the troponin complex, causing a conformational change that leads to the active site of actin becoming exposed. Once this happens, the MHC globular heads are now able to make what is referred to as a 'cross-bridge' connection with the actin, and the breakdown of ATP releases energy, which allows myosin to pull the thin filaments inwards. This causes the sarcomere to shorten, giving contraction.

This model of muscle contraction is called the *sliding filament model*, proposed in the 1950s by Andrew Huxley and Ralph Niedergerke and, independently, by Hugh Huxley and Jean Hanson. Removal of Ca^{2+} back

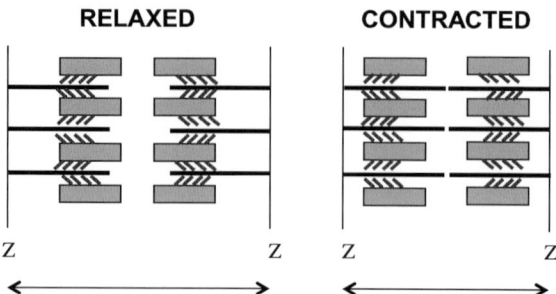

Figure 28. Striated muscle contraction in skeletal muscle. This schematic shows one sarcomere, the basic unit of contraction in striated muscle. Thick filaments composed of myosins are shown as grey rectangles; thin filaments, which are attached to the Z-line which marks the end of the sarcomere, are shown as horizontal black lines. Cross-bridge connections form between myosin heads (shown as black bars protruding from the thick filament) and the thin filament, pulling the z-line boundaries toward each other and leading to contraction. Double-headed arrows indicate the length of the sarcomere in relaxed (left) and contracted (right) states.

into the SR returns the muscle to its relaxed state. (In smooth muscle, different mechanisms are thought to control contraction).

Skeletal muscles contain a mixture of so-called fast and slow muscle fibres. Fast and slow fibres express specific protein isoforms, encoded by separate genes, of many of the regulatory components of the sarcomere such as troponins and MLCs. Fast fibres are involved in rapid movement, such as sprinting, and are packed with mitochondria in order to provide the energy needed for fast cycles of contraction and relaxation. They permit anaerobic metabolism in the absence of oxygen, though the by-product of this is lactate. However, such energy expenditure comes at a price- fast muscle fatigues easily, and we suffer cramps due to the release of lactate. Slow fibres, which contain fewer mitochondria, are able to deliver less powerful contractions, but can work over a longer period of time. However, these too will fatigue with time in response to continued work. The skeletal musculature is able to adapt to the demands of exercise, so a sprinter will have lots of fast fibres rich in energy-producing mitochondria, for example, whereas a marathon runner or distance cyclist has an increased proportion of slow muscle relative to fast.

Perhaps the most surprising striated muscle cell is the cardiac myocyte found in the heart. A similar molecular structure and mechanism drives contraction, although most of the key sarcomeric proteins are encoded by a specific 'cardiac' repertoire of genes, distinct from those expressed in adult skeletal muscle. This reflects the very different needs of cardiac muscle, which must work continuously during the lifetime of the organism to circulate blood to and from the lungs and around the body and yet be resistant to fatigue.

The cardiac myocyte is a unique cell in that it is in electrical contact and beats in synchrony with its millions of neighbours in the heart. This is a massive feat of coordination, each beat of the heart primed by a subset of specialised 'pacemaker' cardiac myocytes, which carries on throughout the life of the host or until something catastrophic such as a *myocardial infarction* or 'heart attack' occurs. This can occur as a result of *atherosclerosis*, a pathology caused by the deposition of fatty deposits within the blood vessels and subsequent immune responses that lead to narrowing or occlusion in one or more of the coronary arteries feeding the cardiac muscle. It is estimated that each cardiac myocyte is in contact with three blood capillaries, such is its demand for oxygen and nutrients. Thus, a blocked coronary artery can cut off the flow of blood to a large section of myocardium, causing myocyte death on a massive scale and rapid failure of the 'pump'.

It is believed that all mammals have a predetermined number of heartbeats in their lifetime — about one to three billion. Hence, a mouse whose heart rate is 500 beats per minute uses up its billion beats in just four years. We take on average around eighty years to use up our quota, whereas a giant tortoise may take about one hundred and fifty years. Another intriguing thing about the heart is that there have been no recorded instances of cancer affecting the cardiac myocyte. Very rarely does one come across tumours of the heart, but these tend to be tumours affecting other cell types found in the heart, such as the endothelial cells that line the blood vessels or secondary tumours that have metastasised from elsewhere.

Cancer is widely regarded as a primarily older age disease and accounts for around 40% of human deaths, and yet the heart keeps on beating right until the end. Cardiovascular disease probably accounts for an equal proportion of deaths, including life-draining pathologies such as dilated cardiomyopathies or heart failure, but even a failing heart keeps on beating under duress until, for mechanical and chemical reasons, the stimulus to beat is finally extinguished. As long as the organism has lived to pass on its genes to the next generation, then its purpose has been fulfilled, as we shall see in the next chapter. It is almost as if cardiac myocytes are blessed with some degree of immortality and only stop when their 'owner' dies. In this respect, laboratory-maintained cultures of immature cardiac myocytes can be prepared by enzymatic digestion of pieces of juvenile rat heart and maintained in a functional, synchronous beating state under suitable conditions for several days.

The final word in this section belongs to cell movement in the microscopic world. Single-cell organisms such as bacteria or simple plants can move within their environment under their own propulsion using flagellae or cilia, which are tiny cytoplasmic extensions of the cell. In higher animals, spermatazoa possess flagellae, endowing them with self-propulsion, and the cells lining our lungs propel particular matter across the airway surface using cilia (which tend to be shorter than flagellae). *Microtubules*, which are polymers of tubulin proteins, are the major components of these external organelles, indicating that these are ancient proteins. Indeed, the renowned American evolutionary biologist John Tyler Bonner (1920–2019) noted that *Homo sapiens* did not invent the wheel as bacteria managed this feat billions of years earlier in the form of a completely rotatable structure at the base of the flagella.

Microtubules also contribute to structural-supporting filaments within the eukaryotic cell that form the *cytoskeleton*, and movement within the cell is controlled by such filaments. One of the most obvious examples, readily visible through a light microscope, is the segregation of the chromosomes into two daughter cells during the process of mitosis or cell division, which is organised on a microtubule spindle.

When we consider the immensely complicated biological system that a cell is, built as it is upon a diverse array of proteins with both structural and metabolic functions, and how whole organisms are formed from millions of integrated intercommunicating cells to create a creature of singular purpose, then irrespective of the added wonders of mind and thought, it stands as testament to the efficiency of evolutionary processes. What we have become is the result of billions of years of evolution. But before we look at the process of evolution itself in Chapter 5, let us look at the building blocks of life in more detail, with a particular focus on the process of gene expression.

The DNA world

In all eukaryotic and prokaryotic organisms, deoxyribonucleic acid (DNA) is the molecule of heredity. From early observations that organisms are able to transfer part of their features to their offspring, such as the work of the Moravian monk Gregor Mendel (1822–1884) in the mid-19th century on the segregation and inheritance of physical characteristics in the common pea, the question arose, "what is used inside a cell as the hereditary material?"

For a long time, it was assumed that proteins determined everything within a cell; the chromosomes, after all long suspected of being the seat of inheritable characteristics, were known to contain proteins as well as DNA. In 1928, the British bacteriologist Frederick Griffith (1879–1941) conducted the first experiment that hinted that DNA, not protein, is the actual material of heredity. I will briefly describe his experiment because it is a classic example of the application of the scientific method.

Griffith used two strains of the bacterium *Streptococcus pneumonia* — a smooth-shaped, pathogenic strain (S) and a rough-coated, non-pathogenic strain (R). Under a microscope, it is possible to distinguish between the two strains according to the presence or absence of a polysaccharide coat that renders the R strain rough in appearance. Mice infected with the pathogenic S form died whereas R form-infected mice did not. If the S bacteria were heated for a short time, a process that leads to the unfolding and inactivation of most proteins, mice that were infected subsequently did not die.

This result agreed with the hypothesis of some protein(s) acting as the genetic material, but the strange result was that if mice were infected with the R strain in the presence of heat-treated S strain, they too would die. Griffith concluded that something else in the bacterial cells was being transferred from the S strain and it could not be protein because this had been inactivated by heating. It could only have been the DNA.

The scientific community was sceptical of this innovative result; some accused Griffith (who would die during a London air raid in the second world war) of shoddy technique and contamination of his experimental materials.

The role of DNA as the agent of heredity was not formally recognised until as late as 1952 with the experiments of Alfred Hershey and Martha Chase. By differentially radio-labelling *bacteriophages* — a type of virus that infects bacteria — through the incorporation of radioactive sulphur into the coat proteins of some viruses and radioactive phosphorus into the DNA of others, they were able to demonstrate that DNA was the true causative agent of heredity. These studies inspired the work that resulted in the resolution of the structure of DNA. We now turn to the description of the DNA molecule itself.

DNA makes RNA makes protein

James Watson and Francis Crick, together with Maurice Wilkins, discovered the structure of DNA in 1953. By interpreting X-ray crystallographic data, including that from Rosalind Franklin which were acquired without her permission, they demonstrated that DNA is composed of two anti-parallel strands (i.e., they run in opposite directions) organised along a central axis in the form of a double helix. Watson, Crick, and Wilkins were awarded the Nobel Prize for this work. Franklin might have shared the award too, but she died of cancer before the award was made. This mistreatment of Franklin tarnishes the work that heralded the start of the genetic and molecular biological revolution.

A bystander to this discovery was the renowned American chemist Linus Pauling (1901–1994; a double Nobel laureate himself, though one was the Peace Prize). It has been speculated that if he had access to all the preliminary DNA structural data that the English team had (the American Watson was working with the Englishman Crick at Cambridge University at the time), he might have solved the structure himself. Without access to decent X-ray data, Pauling thought that a triple helical structure was the correct configuration for the DNA strands. If he could have seen the data that Watson and Crick had access to, Pauling's experience as a chemist and physicist would probably have enlightened him as to the true nature of the helix.

Francis Crick (1916–2004) had his hands in many scientific pies (we will meet him again in Chapter 6 in relation to his theories on consciousness), but of particular relevance here, he went on to postulate that genetic information flows from the genes to the proteins that they encode through a riboncleotide (RNA) intermediate. This intermediate is called *messenger RNA* (mRNA) as it is an RNA copy of the genetic message imprinted in the genes and transports itself to the cytoplasm where the 'message' is decoded to make the corresponding protein.

Crick's postulate of gene expression became known subsequently as the *"central dogma of molecular biology"* and states that "DNA makes RNA makes protein". This remains true for nearly all organisms on the planet with the exception of some viruses that contain RNA genomes. For example, retroviruses such as HIV-1 must first make a DNA copy of their RNA genome by the process of *reverse transcription* as this DNA copy can then integrate into the chromosomal DNA of a host cell and pass itself off as a host gene. In this way, the invader can hijack the cell's own gene expression machinery in order to reproduce itself. Crick's central dogma states that information cannot be passed back from protein to nucleic acids. As we shall go on to see, the cell has evolved not only an encrypted triplet code using the four chemical groups of DNA to code for the twenty amino acids that make up all proteins, but also elaborate enzymatic mechanisms that enable the copying of DNA into the single-stranded mRNA intermediate.

The exacting nature of DNA

If you read any DNA sequence, you will note that it is written in a very limited alphabet — A, G, C, and T. DNA is composed of four chemical groups with a common structure; a phosphorylated sugar molecule with either a purine (adenosine (A) and guanine (G)) or a pyrimidine (cytosine (C) and thymine (T)) nitrogenous ring structure group attached to it. This sugar is not the same as glucose (which is a six-carbon or *hexose* sugar) as it is a five-carbon *pentose* sugar.

The pyrimidine or purine groups, which are basic in chemical character due to the presence of amino groups, are attached to one side of the pentose sugar and the phosphate group to the other (Figure 29). This unit, which forms the basic unit of heredity, is commonly referred to as a *nucleotide* or *base*; in its unpolymerised form, it is more properly termed a deoxyribonucleotide triphosphate (dNTP).

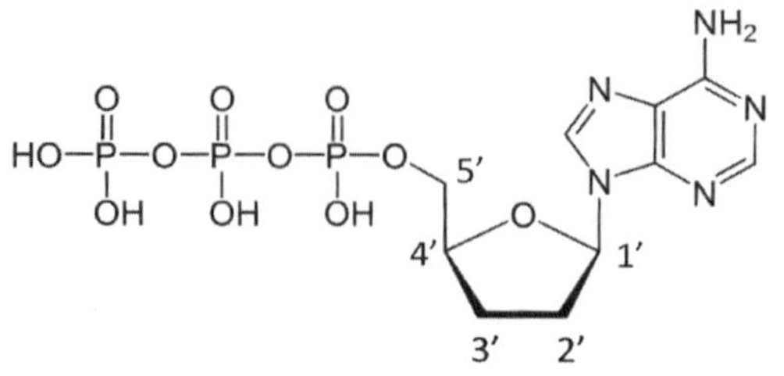

Figure 29. Deoxyribonucleotide (dNTP) group (triphosphate form). This figure shows the three main parts of a deoxyribonucleotide group or nucleotide *base* — a pentose (5 carbon) sugar ring (central) with five carbon atoms numbered 1' – 5', a nitrogenous ring structure base (to the right) located at the 1' position of the pentose ring, and phosphate groups (to the left) at the 5' position. DNA is polymerised through the creation of a phosphodiester bond between the 3' position of the sugar and the 5' phosphate group of an incoming dNTP. Thus, the convention is that DNA sequences are written in a 5' to 3' direction.

The dNTPs are linked together under the direction of an enzyme, *DNA polymerase*, through phosphodiester bonds between the 3' (read as '3 prime') position of the pentose sugar of one base and the 5' phosphate of the next base in the sequence. Diphosphate is released during polymerisation, leaving one phosphate as part of the link, which creates what is termed the 'sugar-phosphate' backbone of DNA. Consider the following example. The sequence is written and read from left to right in the 5' to 3' direction, thus:

5' - AAGCTAGATGCC - 3'

Addition of new bases, such as occurs during the process of DNA replication when a cell needs to divide and double its chromosomal content, always occurs by adding a new base to the 3' 'tail' of the existing DNA molecule. Therefore, DNA molecules always grow in a 5' to 3' direction.

As I mentioned earlier, X-ray crystallography revealed that the DNA helix is a double-stranded, anti-parallel structure. That is, it is made of two strands of DNA running in opposite directions to each other. Each strand creates a sugar-phosphate backbone for the DNA helix on the outside edge, with the purine or pyrimidine nitrogenous bases protruding into the centre of the helix where the bases associate according to strict hydrogen bond-pairing rules (often called the Watson-Crick rules) such that A always pairs with T while G always pairs with C. Thus, a larger purine is always paired with a smaller pyrimidine.

A:T pairing involves two hydrogen bonds between the bases while G:C pairing involves the formation of three hydrogen bonds. This pairing creates the classic 'spiral staircase' depiction of the double helix, with roughly 10½ base pair 'steps' for every 360° rotation of the helix (Figure 30). Thus, returning to the example sequence we just used, if we were to show both strands (though the convention is that for ease of writing, a DNA sequence is written as the 'top' or so-called *sense* strand only), we would write:

5' - AAGCTAGATGCC - 3'
3' - TTCGATCTACGG - 5'

Such is the specificity of Watson-Crick base-pairing that either strand can serve as a template for the synthesis of a fresh complementary strand during DNA replication, the process necessary for chromosome duplication

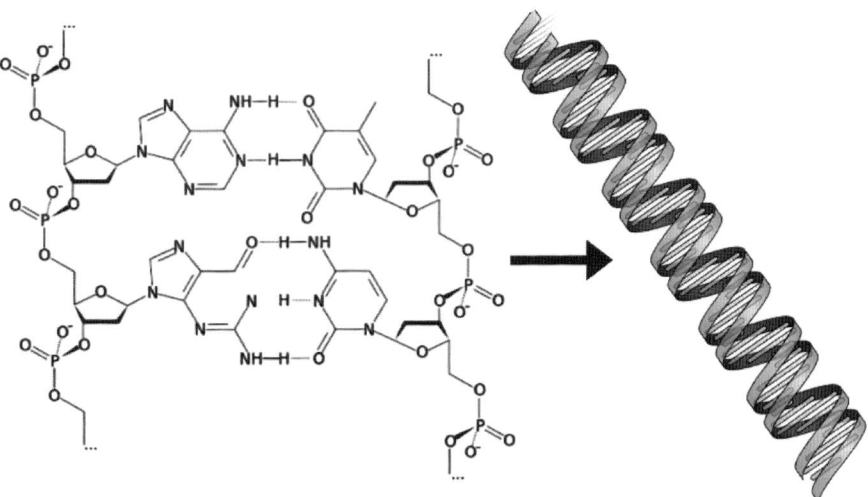

Figure 30. Double-stranded DNA. The left side shows two strands of DNA in a double helix held together by hydrogen bonds according to Watson-Crick base-pairing rules (A always pairs with T; G always pairs with C). The sequence of bases in one strand of double-stranded DNA is complementary to the sequence of paired bases on the other strand. The thousands of pairings wind around a central axis to form a helix (shown on the right).

prior to cell division. The millions of bases that make one strand of DNA in a chromosome are, thus, the direct complement of the bases in the other strand and it is this linear sequence of bases, organised into genes, that forms the basic genetic alphabet for all organisms.

The 'bottom' strand also serves as a template for the generation of mRNA (*transcription*) during gene expression. Later, we will see how this linear sequence of bases determines the precise linear sequence of the polypeptide that the gene codes for. RNA is very similar to DNA in that it has a sugar-phosphate backbone. Three out of four of the bases found in DNA are also used in RNA (A, G, and C), but thymine (T) is substituted with a related molecule, uracil (U). In terms of structure, the critical difference is that cellular RNA exists as a single-stranded molecule. Following transcription and processing, the mRNA is exported to the cytoplasm where the sequence of the mRNA directs the orderly assembly of the encoded protein, a process known as translation. Thus, we can rewrite Crick's postulate as "DNA makes RNA (via transcription) makes protein (via translation)".

Chromatin and chromosomes

A typical molecule of DNA within a human cell is very, very long compared to the dimensions of the cell. If it were possible to stretch it out, the overall length would be about 2 metres. Considering that an average eukaryotic cell diameter is roughly 10 µM (10^{-5} M), it is clear that the DNA has to be very highly compacted within the nucleus in order to fit in (DNA is about 2 million times longer than the nucleus is wide). All this material is compressed into the nucleus because of a highly sophisticated packaging mechanism termed *supercoiling* of the DNA around *histone* proteins. In this form, DNA is referred to as *chromatin*.

The primary unit of chromatin is the *nucleosome*, in which about 147 base pairs of DNA are tightly wound around an octamer of histone proteins. Nucleosomes are separated by approximately 80 base pairs of unwound 'linker' DNA, taking on an appearance rather like 'beads on a string' when visualised using an electron microscope. Further levels of compaction of this basic structure (one can imagine the small space occupied by the tangled coiled cable of an old-style telephone handset, for example) produce packaged fibres in the form of a chromosome.

Bacteria contain all their DNA on just a single chromosome, but higher animals and plants have evolved multiple pairs of chromosomes as an evolutionary result of the need to increase genetic complexity as evolution produced more elaborate organisms. Human beings, for example, possess 22 pairs of chromosomes plus a pair of 'sex' chromosomes (X, Y), giving a total of 46. All 'somatic' cells of the body (e.g., all cells excluding the gametes produced in the ovary and testis) contain two copies of the 22 chromosomes plus two sex chromosomes.

The gametes (egg and sperm), on the other hand, possess just one copy for each of the 22 chromosomes plus one sex chromosome. The reason that gametes have one set of chromosomes (referred to as *haploid*) as opposed to the two homologous copies (*diploid*) of each chromosome present in the somatic cells is so that genetic instructions in the chromosomes from each parent can combine and rearrange in an exchange of short corresponding regions between parental chromosomes, a process known as *homologous recombination*. This produces recombined chromosomes in the offspring that did not exist in the original gametes so that the offspring has genes from one or other parent but in a unique combination (except for twins) that contributes to his or her genetic uniqueness.

This, of course, was what Mendel observed in his famous studies on the inheritance of characteristics such as flower colour and plant height in the pea. Because genes are essentially spaced out from one another along the chromosomes (although Mendel did not know of genes, of course; he called the inheritable traits he saw 'factors'), they are free to segregate through recombination. Each set of chromosomes contains a complete set of all the different kinds of genes required for normal development and function. However, although each set is complete, we need exactly two sets for normal function, though the precise reason for this remains unclear.

The molecular biology revolution

Once the nature of DNA was understood and identified as the genetic material of most organisms on Earth, scientists sought ways to manipulate it in order to better understand and characterise it. The key tools for the nascent science of molecular biology were born out of studies of bacteriology and virology in the middle of the 20th century. The concept of the cell protecting itself is probably very ancient in evolutionary terms. Bacteria are prone to attack by specific viruses called bacteriophages, as mentioned earlier. Many bacteria have evolved specific enzymes called *restriction endonucleases*, which are DNA-cutting enzymes that recognise a simple, usually palindromic, DNA sequence in viral (unmethylated) DNA and cleave it. At the same time, bacteria possess enzymes called *methylases* which add methyl groups to certain DNA sequences. Restriction enzymes cannot cleave methylated DNA, so the bacterium methylates its own cellular DNA in order to prevent self-cleavage by its own enzymes. This is known as the *restriction modification system* and was discovered in the early 1950s by the Italian microbiologist Salvador Luria.

Different species of bacteria possess their own specific restriction endonucleases. For example, the gut bacterium *Escherichia coli* (*E. coli*) produces a restriction enzyme, EcoRI, which recognises and cuts the palindromic sequence GAATTC, whereas the enzyme KpnI from *Klebsiella pneumoniae* cleaves at the sequence GGTACC. Once isolated and purified, these enzymes proved to be useful tools for the molecular biologist as most DNA, when purified, is unmethylated and therefore amenable to cleavage by such enzymes *in vitro*. Thus, bacteria have given us a range of specific 'molecular scissors' to precisely chop up DNA at a range of different sequences. This allows us to cut and paste molecules together in the laboratory, enabling us to join two different molecules that had been cleaved with the same restriction enzyme, a process known as *cloning*. Let us now look at cloning in more detail.

Bacteria are able to exchange genetic material via cytoplasmic transfer when two cells make contact and engage in a process called *conjugation*. Chromosomal DNA is too large to pass through, but many bacteria contain much smaller, self-replicating DNA circles called *plasmids* which can be passed via conjugation from one bacterium to another. Many plasmids carry genes conferring resistance to antibiotics, so conjugation and exchange of plasmids is a way of passing useful traits such as resistance to penicillin to other members of a bacterial population. Restriction enzymes and plasmids, once ways had been found to purify them, became standard molecular biology tools in the late 1960s and early 1970s, ushering in the era of *recombinant DNA technology*.

As plasmids are self-replicating when introduced into a bacterial host, plasmid *vectors* are developed by engineering into them a run of useful restriction enzyme sites. Pieces of restriction enzyme-cut chromosomal DNA from eukaryotic cells can then be 'cloned' into these sites (the molecules are joined together by a bacteriophage enzyme called T4 DNA ligase). The resulting recombinant molecule can then be propagated indefinitely by introducing it into a host laboratory strain of *E. coli*, which can be grown in liquid broth culture. Once amplified in this way, the bacteria can be cracked open and the recombinant plasmid extracted and purified away from the bacterial genomic DNA for further study. The adaptation of filamentous M13 bacteriophages into cloning and DNA sequencing vectors by Fred Sanger and co-workers in Cambridge (work that gave Sanger his second Nobel Prize) later allowed the DNA sequence of any piece of cloned foreign DNA to be determined. This was the next big step forward in the molecular biology revolution at the end of the 20th century, paving the way to reading the DNA sequences of all genes in any organism.

DNA replication

All eukaryotic life starts from a single fertilised egg called an *oocyte*. When cells divide, DNA must be duplicated to ensure that each 'daughter' cell receives a correct complement of the chromosome(s). This is one of the many miracles of inner space and rests on two remarkable chemical properties that have been conserved since single-cell life first appeared on Earth. First, there is the unique nature of the hydrogen bond — it is strong enough to hold nucleic acid strands together, yet weak enough to be broken apart by heat or the displacement action of proteins that facilitate, in an energy-dependent manner, the unwinding of DNA from the supercoiled 'beads on a string' structure found in the chromatin. Second, the absolute pairing of A with T and C with G ensures that each strand, once displaced from the other, can serve as a template for the orderly construction of a new, complementary strand.

DNA is not in itself a self-replicating molecule as we have noted; the process requires enzymes and an input of energy in the form of ATP. Replication is carried out by a large enzymatic complex called DNA polymerase and the process requires several ancillary proteins. Together, their integrated activities allow for DNA replication to be performed both rapidly and with a very high degree of accuracy. Ancillary enzymes called *helicases* are required in an ATP-dependent process to unwind the supercoiled DNA, which otherwise would be inaccessible to DNA polymerase. The new strand of DNA is synthesised in the 5' to 3' direction (see Figure 31).

The replication of DNA is said to be *semi-conservative* because when the hydrogen bonds are broken and the strands separate, each strand can now serve as a template from which to synthesise a new complementary strand from the intracellular pool of dNTPs. So, if we consider a double helix to consist of two DNA strands named A and B, the process of replication first splits A-B into A and B. Strand A then becomes the template for the construction of a new strand B and, likewise, parental strand B receives nucleotide bases under the direction of DNA polymerase to form a new strand A (Figure 31). These two copies of the original DNA (chromosome) are then segregated into what become the two daughter cells.

For replication to occur, the enzyme DNA polymerase catalyses a phosphodiester bond at the 3'-5' position only if the incoming nucleotide is complementary to that on the parent strand by virtue of the A:T and G:C rule (the two terminal phosphates of the dNTP are removed during creation of the phosphodiester bond). Thus, template-directed DNA polymerase enzymes drive replication, an ancient process that is common to both prokaryotes and eukaryotes.

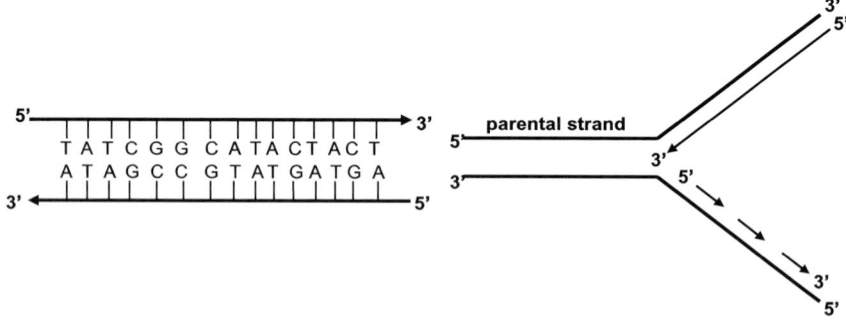

Figure 31. DNA base-pairing and replication. One strand of the double helix anneals to its *antiparallel* partner strand. For replication, both the upper strand (referred to as the sense) and the lower strand (*antisense*) become templates for the synthesis of new DNA. This new DNA is synthesised in the 5' to 3' direction either as a complete strand from the parental template strand or as fragments from the lower strand.

As the genome is so huge (three billion base pairs in humans) and replication is such a rapid process, one might predict errors to be a likely occurrence. Errors in template reading can lead to DNA mutations that might alter the genetic code and result in protein mutations, such as those where the wrong amino acid is inserted within a critical active site of a protein, as we discussed earlier for the Glu 6 → Val 6 mutation in the haemoglobin β subunit. Throughout the lifetime of an organism, millions of replication processes occur within the cells, so the process must be perfect or as close to it as possible.

Recent studies on some bacterial DNA polymerases show that the error rate is extremely low, usually in the order of 1 error in 10^5–10^6 base pairs replicated. Fortunately, evolution has built proofreading enzymatic activities into eukaryotic polymerases to prevent mispairing of bases. These detect when an incorrect nucleotide has been added to the daughter strand as the active site of the enzyme is built to accept the shape of the correct base pair, similar to the lock and key concept of an enzyme's active site matching the shape of its substrate. When an error in base-pairing is detected, replication stalls and the incorrect base is excised. DNA polymerisation then recommences when the correct nucleotide has been inserted.

Errors in DNA replication have led some scientists to theorise that the number of genes in an organism must be kept at a reasonable quantity because having a vast number of genes would increase the risk that mutations might occur. Such mutations can lead to the death of the organism or the passing on of lethal embryonic mutations to the next generation. If some (an unknown percentage) of the genome is in fact non-coding (i.e., essentially scaffolding or 'junk' DNA) as appears to be the case now that the human genome has been sequenced in its entirety, then junk DNA would act to some extent as a buffer to mutation because fewer genes and more junk DNA increases the probability that a replication error would occur within junk DNA rather than within the coding DNA of genes.

DNA replication in the test tube: the Polymerase Chain Reaction

DNA replication can be recapitulated in the laboratory using commercially available, cloned versions of replication enzymes. The *Polymerase Chain*

Reaction (*PCR*) was invented in the 1980s by Kary Mullis, who shared a Nobel Prize for this work, and it enables short stretches of DNA from a specific gene (typically from a few dozen to several thousand nucleotides) to be synthesised in the laboratory. It is the method by which genetic identity is determined in criminal investigations or paternity suits.

In the PCR reaction, a source of DNA is mixed with all four dNTPs, two short and chemically synthesised DNA molecules (*oligonucleotide primers*) whose sequences are specific to and flank the particular gene sequence to be amplified, and a DNA polymerase isolated from an extreme thermophilic bacterium such as *Thermus aquaticus*. The heat-stable properties of *T. aquaticus*, a bacterium that lives in hot freshwater pools and geysers such as those found in Yellowstone National Park in the USA, were essential to the development and automation of this now commonplace laboratory technique. The mix is heated to three different temperatures repeatedly: first, a near-boiling step that ruptures the hydrogen bonds holding the DNA together, creating two separated template strands for replication; next, a much lower temperature that allows the primers to seek out and base-pair to their target sequences; and finally, another hot step that activates the *T. aquaticus* DNA polymerase and allows it to extend the template-bound primers.

The significance of using a thermophilic DNA polymerase (other sources are now used, including bacterial polymerases extracted and cloned from deep sea, hydrothermal vent bacteria) is that the thermostable polymerase can withstand the brief exposure to near-boiling temperatures without a significant loss in activity. This allows a cyclical reiteration of the process in a closed tube system, such that following replication at about 72°C (the optimal temperature for all enzymatic processes in *T. aquaticus* in the bacterium's natural habitat), the DNA strands can then be separated again by raising the temperature to 95°C for a few seconds. Automation in a microprocessor-controlled heat block allows this whole process to be easily reiterated, and it becomes possible to amplify, within a few hours, millions of copies of a discrete DNA molecule specific to the chosen gene of interest over the course of 20–30 cycles of PCR.

PCR machines have found their way into every molecular biology laboratory and found applications in many different fields ranging from basic science through to so-called 'whole genome' DNA sequencing methodologies and routine medical laboratory procedures. So powerful is this technique that we can amplify gene sequences from often vanishingly small amounts of starting material, such as the DNA present in a spot of blood or a single human hair cell, hence its applications for forensic science. In hospital labs, PCR has replaced time-consuming and labour-intensive cell culture tests for the presence of many viruses and bacteria by instead screening for the presence of their genetic material, allowing for diagnoses to be delivered within hours, not days.

Reverse transcription

PCR has revolutionised the cloning of genes and their mRNA products. As I described earlier, 'cloning' in a molecular biology sense means the copying of genetic material *in vitro*, or in the test tube. We now turn our attention to another key development in molecular biology — the use of viral polymerases which utilize mRNA as a template from which to make a DNA copy.

Certain retroviruses such as HIV-1, the causative agent in AIDS, possess an RNA genome, yet need to pass through a double-stranded DNA intermediate form when they invade a host cell so that they may express their genes and produce viral proteins. To do this, each retroviral particle carries within it a unique virus-encoded polymerase called *reverse transcriptase*. This enzyme uses RNA as a template from which it makes a single-stranded complementary DNA copy. The DNA copy then exploits the cellular replication machinery to become double-stranded, whereupon it can insert or integrate itself into the host chromosome. In this way, it also hijacks the normal cellular gene expression machinery and its genes are expressed as if they were cellular protein-coding ones.

Thus, reverse transcriptase uses an RNA template to synthesise a strand of DNA, going in the opposite direction from RNA to DNA (this is why the enzyme is also called an 'inverse' transcriptase or retrotranscriptase). It is important to stress that this is a special case within Crick's postulates (Figure 32). DNA produces itself (replication), RNA (transcription), and through mRNA, proteins (translation). However, once protein is made, there is no reversal of the process. So, the genetic instructions (DNA and RNA) are malleable, but protein production is a final decision.

DNA→DNA	RNA→DNA
DNA→RNA	RNA→RNA
RNA→protein	DNA→protein

Figure 32. The flow of information. The *central dogma of molecular biology* (left column) was described by Francis Crick and colleagues in 1958 and again in 1970 and deals with the detailed residue-by-residue transfer of sequential information. Special cases are found in retroviruses where a DNA-dependent RNA polymerase called reverse transcriptase copies DNA *from* RNA (right column). The dogma states that information cannot be transferred back from protein to either protein or nucleic acid.

Reverse transcriptase enzymes from various sources have been isolated and made available commercially since the 1970s. They remain an essential tool for modern molecular biology with regards to the cloning and sequencing of DNA. If reverse transcriptase is presented with a pool of mRNAs that have been extracted from, say, a liver biopsy, it will produce DNA copies of all those mRNAs, allowing us to get a picture of all the mRNAs expressed in the liver. This mRNA profile would be very different from, say, that obtained from a skeletal muscle biopsy or brain tissue.

RNA itself is a rather fragile molecule that is prone to degradation when removed from the cell, whereas DNA is altogether more robust. Thus, the single-stranded DNA molecules generated in the test tube by reverse transcription can serve (in the presence of DNA polymerase) as templates to generate double-stranded DNA copies, which can then be cloned into plasmid or bacteriophage vectors and propagated indefinitely. Such cloned copies of mRNA molecules are referred to as *complementary DNA*, or cDNA for short, to distinguish from DNA originating from the genome. cDNAs generated in such a way form the basis of most cloning strategies to identify genes and their products and, as in the example just given, can be used to generate tissue-specific cDNA *libraries* representing all the mRNAs expressed in a particular tissue. Once cloned into suitable vectors, these cDNAs can then be sequenced.

PCR amplification of DNA sequences now underpins the early steps of most high-throughput DNA sequencing protocols, such as those used for genome sequencing or for identifying tissue-specific patterns of gene expression using cDNA libraries made from mRNA originating from a particular tissue or even one cell type. The nature of mRNA and the particular usefulness of cDNA from an experimental point of view will become apparent as we move on to look at the process of gene expression in more detail.

ii) Gene Expression

I mentioned at the start of this chapter that we have about 19,000 protein-coding genes, yet if one were to identify all the protein forms found in a typical cell of the body, they would probably number around a million. How can this be? Is it all because of post-translational protein modifications such as phosphorylation and glycosylation? In general, the principle is that one gene encodes for one type of protein, but the number of protein *isoforms* arising from that gene can be increased by the expression of different forms of mRNA from the gene, chiefly through a process known as *alternative mRNA splicing*.

We will examine alternative splicing in more detail later in this section, but its basis lies in the fact that the mRNA-coding sequences of most eukaryotic genes are split up into small pieces along the length of the gene. Unlike prokaryotic genes, nearly all eukaryotic protein-coding genes are described as 'split' or 'interrupted', with regions termed *exons*, which bear the sequences that end up being copied into mRNA, separated from each other by regions of non-coding DNA called *introns*, which do not contribute to the mature mRNA molecule. Apart from exon sequence at the extreme 5' and 3' ends, most of the mRNA contains protein-coding sequences. The sizes of mRNAs can range from a few hundred nucleotides to over 100,000 nucleotides, such as in the case of the muscle protein titin (which is the largest protein known, containing 38,138 amino acids encoded by 363 exons).

The general process of mRNA transcription sees the cell first make a full-length RNA copy of the entire gene — introns and all — using the antisense strand as a template. This is the *primary RNA*. Editing via RNA splicing then shortens this into the more compact mRNA form by cutting out the intron-derived RNA segments and linking the required exons together in the correct register to form the mature mRNA (yet more specialised enzymes carry this out). For the expression of some genes, alternative splicing allows choice to be made as to whether some exons are

GENE (DNA)	123456789	
PRIMARY RNA	123456789	
SPLICED mRNA	12345678	→ protein A
	125678	→ protein B
	12345679	→ protein C

Figure 33. mRNA splicing. This hypothetical gene is made of nine exons, 1–9, separated by introns (depicted as the gaps between the numbers). Transcription produces a primary RNA copy of the entire gene, both exons and introns. Splicing removes introns and joins together exons to produce the mature mRNA from this gene, which has the sequence 123456789 — note that in this hypothetical example, exon 9 is not normally incorporated into the 'usual' (i.e., predominant) mRNA form, which codes for protein A. *Alternative mRNA splicing* patterns may exclude one or more exons, as shown in the second example (B) which omits exons 3 and 4, or include an exon not normally incorporated into the predominant form of the mRNA, such as the bottom example (C) which includes exon 9 instead of exon 8. The result is that three subtly different protein variants are coded from one gene.

included or excluded from the final mRNA, thus allowing the production of several unique mRNAs and, hence, distinct protein isoforms from one gene (Figure 33).

With only 19,000 or so genes to choose from, how *do* we manage to produce over 200 different and unique cell types in the body, each with unique properties? What makes a cardiac myocyte so different from a liver hepatocyte when every one of us starts off as a single fertilised cell? The first thing to note is that all the somatic cells in the body contain *exactly* the same chromosomes and therefore the same number of genes. What is important is which genes are actually *expressed* as well as *where* and *when* they get expressed in the body.

Although many genes are expressed ubiquitously — that is, in every cell — because they perform important 'housekeeping' functions for the cell (e.g., enzymes in metabolic pathways, nucleotide scavenging proteins, DNA and RNA polymerases), there are some whose expression is activated only at specific times during development or in adult life (*temporal control of gene expression*) or in specific cells or tissues (*tissue-specific control of gene expression*). In the case of tissue-specific gene expression, this is because many genes code for specialised structural or functional components; we have no need for the expression of the muscle protein titin in the brain or our kidneys, for example, any more than we need insulin-secreting cells in our lungs. Thus, we require highly specific controlling mechanisms to eliminate the chance of inappropriate gene expression. Many of these mechanisms operate principally at the level of gene transcription.

Synthesis of RNA (transcription)

As we have seen, genetic information in normal animal or plant cells flows from DNA to RNA and then to protein according to Crick's central dogma. The DNA must first be unwound from its highly compacted state within chromatin and stripped of its associated histones and other proteins to create regions of 'naked' DNA in order to give access to RNA polymerase and other transcriptional proteins and to allow the process of transcription to proceed.

There are several types of RNA in the eukaryotic cell including:

1. Messenger RNA (mRNA) which, as mentioned earlier, carries the genetic information from the gene to cytoplasm where it is decoded into protein (*translated*) on the *ribosome*, the protein factory of the cell.
2. Short single-stranded RNAs called *ribosomal RNA* (rRNA) are associated with ribosomes, where part of their function is to scan through an incoming mRNA molecule and locate the exact start-point for protein synthesis.
3. *Transfer RNAs* which transport the appropriate amino acids to the ribosome for orderly synthesis of the protein as the message is decoded.

In addition to these main forms of RNA, there are also small inhibitory RNAs, micro RNAs (miRNA), nuclear RNAs (snRNA), and small cytoplasmic RNAs (scRNA).

Eukaryotic organisms possess three different kinds of RNA polymerase for the manufacture of the three main forms of RNA (there are also genes coding for small RNAs, of course, in the genome). The mRNA of protein-coding genes is produced by RNA polymerase II. As I described earlier, a full-length, single-stranded RNA copy of the entire gene is made initially (*primary transcript*), but it is subsequently processed to remove the non-coding introns by RNA splicing. When RNA polymerase II binds to the DNA molecule, it initiates a localised unwinding of the DNA over the

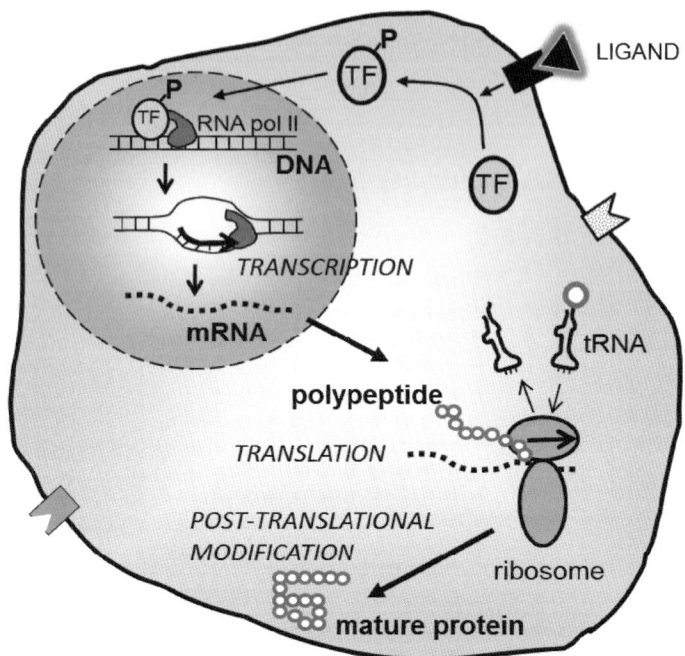

Figure 34. Gene expression. Gene expression in this hypothetical cell is triggered in response to the binding of a particular extracellular ligand (shown by the black triangle) to one of three types of cell surface receptors. Internal signaling via protein kinases (see Figure 27) leads to phosphorylation and activation of a transcription factor (TF), which is now permitted to enter the nucleus and activate a specific target gene. It does this by stimulating *transcription* by RNA polymerase II, which uses the lower strand of the gene's DNA as a template to make messenger RNA (*mRNA*). Following RNA editing (including *mRNA splicing*), the mature mRNA is exported to the *ribosome* in the cytoplasm where the genetic code for the gene is deciphered (*translation*) and the appropriate protein (*polypeptide*) is made. Transfer RNAs (*tRNA*) bring appropriate amino acids (grey circles) to the ribosome as dictated by the triplet code sequence of the mRNA. Any necessary *post-translational modification* such as phosphorylation or glycosylation then allows the mature protein to become fully functional.

5′ end of the gene, exposing the antisense strand which will serve as the template for synthesis of a complementary RNA strand. Thus, a temporary DNA:RNA duplex is made as RNA polymerase traverses the parent DNA molecule in a 5′ to 3′ direction through what may be envisaged as a moving bubble of displaced duplex DNA (Figure 34).

Short DNA sequences built into the 5′ and 3′ ends of the gene determine the exact points of initiation and termination of transcription, respectively, such that the correct length of primary RNA sequence is always transcribed from the gene. RNA polymerase II then detaches and the primary RNA transcript dissociates from its DNA template and is edited into mRNA. This process is directed by a set of splicing enzymes, forming a complex termed a *spliceasome*. Following some further modifications at the 5' and 3' ends, including the addition of a tract of adenosine bases called a *polyA tail* at the 3' end whose function is to determine the lifetime of the mRNA molecule, the mature mRNA then migrates to the cytoplasm where it is decoded into the corresponding protein sequence on the ribosome — the process of translation.

Let us now consider those short DNA sequences around the start of the gene in greater detail, as they form binding sites for many important regulatory proteins.

Promoters and enhancers: Creating binding sites for transcription factors

How does RNA polymerase II locate the 'beginning' of the gene, and what does that actually mean? Years of experimental work have gone into defining the start and end points of genes, so much so that computer software can now predict where genes lie within large chunks of newly sequenced DNA with great accuracy. Transcription always begins at a defined point on the gene known as the *transcription start-site* (TSS). This marks the position of the first nucleotide of the mRNA (designated +1), so the DNA sequence 'downstream' of any gene is numbered from this position. DNA sequence that is 5' (termed 'upstream') to the TSS is given a negative notation and numbered backwards; thus, the numbering of contiguous bases surrounding any TSS can be drawn as follows:

UPSTREAM   DOWNSTREAM
..... −4, −3, −2, −1, **+1**, +2, +3, +4 ....
                              TSS
                              → DIRECTION OF TRANSCRIPTION

The region of DNA sequence immediately upstream of the TSS is called the *promoter*. The promoter region fulfils two functions. First, it helps guide RNA polymerase II to the TSS, whereupon it will form a transcription-competent complex with other proteins that are required for full polymerase activity. Once this complex is formed, mRNA synthesis can proceed. In most genes, formation of such a complex is achieved by the polymerase first being guided onto the promoter by binding to highly conserved TATA- or GC-rich sequences located within the −35/+10 region of the gene (a similar mechanism is used in prokaryotic genes, indicating that this mechanism is extremely ancient and evolutionarily conserved). Promoters vary enormously in length and sequence (recent computer modelling suggests that most can be grouped into ten classes), but often the 5′ promoter boundary is located around 200 nucleotides upstream of the TSS. The second function of the promoter is that it contains binding sites for highly specialised DNA-binding proteins called *transcription factors*.

Transcription factors are regulatory proteins that bind selectively to DNA through the recognition of specific, conserved DNA sequences. Once bound to their cognate sequence, these factors essentially act as molecular 'on-off' switches for transcription. The viewpoint in the 1980s was that when a transcription factor bound to its target gene, it would then be able to activate transcription simply by boosting the activity of RNA polymerase II. This picture, as is so often the case in the evolving history of molecular biology, now appears to be an oversimplification!

Some transcription factors are expressed ubiquitously in every cell type of the body: the expression of many housekeeping genes, for example, is under their direction. Other transcription factors show a pronounced tissue-restricted pattern of expression, crucial for directing the expression of particular genes in specific cells or tissues. For example, many skeletal muscle-specific sarcomeric genes, such as skeletal muscle isoforms of myosin heavy chain or the muscle enzyme creatine kinase, are under the control of four related skeletal muscle-restricted transcription factors — MyoD, myogenin, myf-5, and MRF4. These four regulatory proteins have been shown by *transgenic* experimentation in mouse models to be essential for the correct formation of skeletal muscle. For example, a mouse model in which the myogenin gene was deactivated in the embryo by a gene-targeting procedure based on homologous recombination revealed that although skeletal myocyte progenitor cells develop as normal in the absence of myogenin — and indeed migrate to their correct destinations in the developing embryo — once there, they fail to proliferate and fuse together in order to form sufficient muscle, and the animal dies before birth as a result. We will return to the roles of transcription factors in more depth when we examine embryonic development.

Once they have attached to their cognate DNA binding sites, transcription factors create a 'platform' for interacting with or attracting other regulatory proteins, which allows the formation and stabilisation of a highly specific, transcription-competent environment around the promoter. This is crucial if transcription is going to begin in the right place and, moreover, is absolutely critical for activating gene expression in a particular cell type or at an appropriate stage during development. Once bound to DNA, the transcription factor makes weak (i.e., non-covalent) protein-protein interactions with other transcription factors bound to the gene. In some instances, they recruit protein *co-factors* which themselves are not DNA-binding proteins and which, therefore, need to form an association with a protein that *does* bind to DNA in order to exert their effect.

Co-factors may show a tissue-specific pattern of expression and some are known to associate with 'housekeeping' transcription factors, thereby imparting tissue-specificity to the expression of their ubiquitous partner's target genes. Another function attributed to some co-factors is the ability to form a bridge between transcription factors and chromatin remodelling enzymes (which we will review later), thus facilitating the compaction or unwinding of DNA from the nucleosomes, and hence directly influencing the local transcriptional environment of the gene.

Many promoters are compact and contain all the DNA information necessary to ensure their correct pattern of expression. The 1990s saw the cloning and identification of many promoters and their functional characterisation in the laboratory, first through analysis in cell culture conditions but now more commonly in whole animal transgenic models. Testing promoter function revolves around using them to drive expression of a *reporter gene* from a lower organism whose activity can be measured easily. Cloned promoters, for example, may be linked to a Green Fluorescent Protein (GFP) gene that occurs naturally in certain fluorescent jellyfish or the *luciferase* gene from the glowing tail of the firefly, neither of which are found in vertebrates. GFP glows green when illuminated with UV light and often is used to visualise where the native gene is normally expressed during development.

When such a hybrid DNA promoter-reporter is introduced into the nucleus of a fertilised mouse egg (which is then re-implanted in a mouse and allowed to develop) or a zebrafish egg (another common laboratory animal for transgenic analysis of development due to the transparency of the living embryo and ease of manipulation), it integrates into the chromosome and is passed on into all the cells of the resulting transgenic embryos. However, only those tissues where the promoter would normally be expressed would glow green when the embryo is exposed to UV light. Thus, a promoter cloned from brain cells might drive expression of GFP only in cells of the brain and developing nervous system, despite all the cells in the embryo carrying the GFP transgene.

The inference from such experiments is that the cloned promoter contains all the necessary information in the form of its DNA sequence to direct and recapitulate the natural tissue's gene expression. Once we have such a cloned promoter-reporter gene at our disposal, we can then introduce mutations into specific binding sites for transcription factors in the promoter and reintroduce the mutated constructs into fertilised eggs or cell cultures so as to evaluate the contribution of individual transcription factors to promoter function. In this way, scientists can tease out the nature of how a promoter works at the molecular level, using a proxy reporter gene to visualise and quantify promoter expression.

Other promoters only show full specificity of expression when linked with so-called *enhancer* elements. Enhancers are also regulatory regions of DNA which contain binding sites for tissue-specific transcription factors, but they may be located far upstream of the promoter, within introns, or very occasionally at the 3' end of the gene or further downstream. It is important to note that enhancers are never found on a different piece of DNA (e.g., a different chromosome), but only on the same DNA strand as the promoter whose expression they influence. They (or rather, the regulatory factors that bind to them) are able to exert their effect over considerable distances due to the flexible nature of DNA such that two proteins bound even several thousand base pairs away may be brought into close proximity, thereby allowing protein-protein interactions.

Synthesis of protein (translation)

Of all eukaryotic cellular processes, protein synthesis is, to me, one of the most interesting. It illustrates the complexity and functional excellence of an evolved process. Translation occurs on the ribosome, a large cytoplasmic RNA-protein structure composed of a large and a small ribosome subunit, through the coordinated interactions of many different molecules including the mRNA, transfer RNAs, and a number of supporting enzymes.

When considering that the genetic alphabet is comprised from just four bases (A, G, C, and T in DNA; A, G, C, and U in RNA) and that proteins are constructed from 20 amino acids, a triplet code is the most parsimonious to enable the coding of all 20 amino acids. A single letter code (4^1) would produce only four amino acids and a doublet code would produce only 16 different possibilities (4^2), but a code based on three bases (4^3) with the potential to provide 64 possible triplets is more than adequate to encode all amino acids. Thus, as some amino acids are encoded by more than one triplet, the code is said to be *degenerate* (Figure 35, below). Codons encoding the same amino acid are called synonyms.

Most proteins start with a methionine group at the N-terminus, which is encoded by a single codon, ATG. In addition to the codons encoding the amino acids, there are also three 'stop' codons — TAA, TGA, and

1st position (5' end)	2nd position U	2nd position C	2nd position A	2nd position G	3rd position (3' end)
U	Phe	Ser	Tyr	Cys	U
U	Phe	Ser	Tyr	Cys	C
U	Leu	Ser	stop	stop	A
U	Leu	Ser	stop	Trp	G
C	Leu	Pro	His	Arg	U
C	Leu	Pro	His	Arg	C
C	Leu	Pro	Gln	Arg	A
C	Leu	Pro	Gln	Arg	G
A	Ile	Thr	Asn	Ser	U
A	Ile	Thr	Asn	Ser	C
A	Ile	Thr	Lys	Arg	A
A	Met (start)	Thr	Lys	Arg	G
G	Val	Ala	Asp	Gly	U
G	Val	Ala	Asp	Gly	C
G	Val	Ala	Glu	Gly	A
G	Val	Ala	Glu	Gly	G

Figure 35. The genetic code. The triplet code (shown here as written in the mRNA sequence, with U replacing T) is degenerate and starts at the 5' end (first position). For example, 5' UAU and UAC both code for tyrosine (Tyr; see Figure 26 for amino acid codes). AUG is labelled **start** as it codes for methionine, the first amino acid in nearly all polypeptides.

TAG — which signal to the ribosome where translation should finish. This simple genetic code applies to all life on Earth.

Transfer RNAs (tRNA) are short, single-stranded molecules consisting of about eighty nucleotides, which assume a distinctive 'cloverleaf' shape. Each codon is associated with its own complementary tRNA which, with the exception of the stop codons, ferries the appropriate amino acid, which is attached to the 3' end of the tRNA by a specific enzyme called an aminoacyl-tRNA synthetase. The central region of the RNA is exposed to present the three-base *anticodon* to the ribosome. The anticodon is complementary to (i.e., can base-pair with) the mRNA codon which codes for the amino acid presented by that tRNA. For example, the mRNA codon 5'-ACC- 3', which encodes threonine, is recognised by the anticodon sequence 5'-GGU-3' on its matching tRNA (remembering that DNA and DNA:RNA duplexes are antiparallel like the DNA helix, so the anticodon is written backwards), thus:

$$\text{mRNA}\ldots 5'\text{- ACC -}3'\ldots \text{ CODON}$$
$$\text{tRNA}\ldots 3'\text{- UGG -}5'\ldots \text{ ANTI-CODON}$$

The mRNA is decoded in the 5' – 3' direction and proteins are synthesised in the amino (N) to carboxyl (C) direction, since each amino acid has an amino group on one side and a carboxyl group on the other. The immature end of the growing polypeptide chain therefore always presents a carboxyl group to the next incoming amino acid-tRNA. Translation occurs in three stages — initiation, elongation, and termination.

Initiation sees a special initiator methionine-tRNA called formyl-methionyl-tRNAf form a complex with the smaller ribosomal subunit. The subunit then scans an incoming mRNA in the 5' – 3' direction for the *start codon*, AUG. Here it briefly stalls as rRNA sequences embedded within it, which are complementary to conserved sequences surrounding the first AUG sequence, base-pair transiently according to the Watson-Crick rules. This creates a pause and allows the initiator tRNA methionine to be placed correctly for the next phase, **elongation**, which commences once the larger ribosomal subunit joins the initiation complex. Mechanistically, the mRNA runs through the ribosome rather like tickertape, exposing each successive codon and allowing decryption of the codon by an anticodon sequence carried on the corresponding tRNA-amino acid. Again, the specificity of Watson-Crick base-pairing ensures the specificity of the decryption of the mRNA code, thereby placing the correct amino acid in the vicinity of the C-terminus of the growing polypeptide chain. Once the correct amino acid has been added to the polypeptide chain and cleaved from its tRNA (the tRNA is then recycled and has a new amino acid attached to it by its cognate aminoacyl tRNA synthetase), the ribosome shuffles three nucleotides further along the mRNA. **Termination** occurs when the complex meets a stop codon, whereupon the completed polypeptide is released from the ribosome and the two ribosomal subunits detach from the mRNA.

The protein may then be subjected to post-translational modification (e.g., phosphorylation or glycosylation) or form a functional complex with other or similar proteins, as we saw for immunoglobulins and haemoglobin. Sometimes many ribosomes move along a single mRNA at one time. This action is termed a *polyribosome* assembly and enables large amounts of a protein to be synthesised economically. The interested reader is guided to a classic biochemistry text such as Stryer's *Biochemistry* for a full description of the translation process.

Analysing gene expression in the 'omics era

Every somatic cell in the body contains the same amount of DNA and the same number of genes. Some of these, which are essential for basic cell functions such as metabolism, are ubiquitously expressed as I have mentioned earlier. Others are expressed in a tissue-specific manner (e.g., myosin heavy chain genes are only required in muscle cells) or in a developmentally regulated manner.

Through the power of automated, high-throughput DNA sequencing and its attendant computer analysis programmes, we can now examine the genes of many different forms of life on earth and begin to build a picture of how evolution has shaped our own development. As I mentioned before, the term genome refers to the total DNA complement within the cell of an organism, be it a single chain of DNA in a bacterium or the 23 pairs of chromosomes in the nucleus of a human cell. The study of evolutionary relatedness between genes from different species is called *comparative genomics*.

The sheer volume of gene and protein expression data now being generated by many collaborative scientific teams across the globe has led to a rapid expansion in what has been nicknamed the 'omic' sciences; not only genomics but *proteomics* (determining the entire protein complement of the cell), *transcriptomics* (determining all the mRNAs transcribed in, say, a particular tissue or disease state through the DNA sequencing of representative cDNA libraries), and *metabolomics* (building a profile of all the genes involved in energy production in normal versus disease states, for example).

This endeavour is already providing new insights into molecular mechanisms, which will lead to improvements in detection, diagnosis, and treatment of disease. It will also usher in the era of personalised medicine if cost-effective and rapid mechanisms of sequencing an individual's DNA can be developed, allowing a person's individual genetic or proteomic blueprint to be read (e.g., identifying mutations in genes that may indicate a familial predisposition to heart failure or a type of cancer).

Hand-in-glove with this has gone many methodologic advances, particularly in terms of computer processing power and the development of computational biology or *bioinformatics* as it is also known. High-throughput DNA sequencing systems allow multiple DNA sequencing reactions to be run at once (made possible, of course, by amplification of starting material using PCR), and sophisticated software is needed to handle the huge amounts of 'raw' DNA sequences generated. Potential genes within such sequence data can now be predicted with a high degree of accuracy based on the knowledge we have accumulated on the structures of many individual genes from data determined by more laborious means (another good example of the utility of the scientific method).

The analysis of mRNA and protein expression has progressed from those staple laboratory techniques of the 1980s, Northern and Western blotting, which allowed scientists to look at the expression patterns of one particular mRNA or protein, respectively, at a time. Modern-day approaches allow us to analyse the expression of hundreds of different molecules at a time.

In the case of mRNA expression, this is achieved with so-called *microarray*-based systems that allow the analysis of a cell's total cohort of mRNA. The basic method uses small glass slides onto which thousands of cloned cDNAs or oligonucleotides representing known genes are immobilised in an orderly, gridded array. Labelling all the mRNA in a cell with fluorescent tags and hybridising them to such arrays allows us to identify which genes are being expressed by virtue of their hybridisation to the known genes gridded onto the array. Similar approaches using filters on which are immobilised antibodies to chosen proteins, such as protein kinases or phosphatases, are used to investigate protein signalling pathways. These methods can also distinguish products of post-translational modification such as a phosphorylated protein kinase where appropriate antibodies to phosphorylated forms of such enzymes are available, allowing comparison with the unphosphorylated form of the protein.

Gene regulation: layers upon layers of control

There has long been a reductionist viewpoint, perhaps most famously expounded by Richard Dawkins, that all we will need to know about the human cell is described in our genes. However, there is more to it than this as we will see in the next chapter. Reductionism, from the viewpoint of philosophy, is nothing new — Descartes argued in *De Homine* (1662) that animals other than man could be reduced to the level of automata, with every organ serving a particular role in the whole, rather like the cogs and wheels in a clock. (Dawkins has much more recently expressed a somewhat similar viewpoint, likening us to "lumbering robots" at the mercy of our genes).

The sequencing of the human genome was seen as a precursor to establishing the genetic plan for *Homo sapiens*. However, for the vast majority of the genome, we simply do not as yet understand whether it has a purpose or not. As some of the human genome appears to be non-coding (or junk), some scientists have speculated that it may represent inherited DNA from past ancestors that we no longer need or function as scaffolding to space genes out from one another, thus reducing the chance of DNA replication errors 'hitting' genes.

The Korean evolutionary biologist Susumo Ohno declared in the early 1970s that it was highly unlikely that the mammalian genome contained more than 30,000 protein-coding genes based on predictions according to observed mutational rates. If we had, say, 300,000 genes (a figure that a genome the size of ours could quite easily accommodate), then the chance of a deleterious mutation occurring within a critical gene would increase and, in terms of evolution (which serves to promote the 'survival of the fittest'), correspond to a higher chance that this would lead to extinction of an organism before it can pass its genes on to a new generation. Thus, it is to our advantage to have a low number of genes secreted within a vast amount of buffering DNA to which no function is attached.

Ohno's predictions have been borne out by the fact that the complete sequencing of the human genome suggests that the likely figure for man is a mere 19,000 or so genes. This does not seem like a lot considering all the basic functions of the cell of the sort that I had described earlier, let alone the tissue-specific genes needed to impart the characteristics that make a neuron distinct from, say, a white blood cell or kidney cell. What *has* become apparent in recent years though is the sheer complexity with which these genes are controlled and expressed in terms of body plan, tissue-distribution, stage of life, and the aforementioned diversity in terms of numbers of mRNAs and proteins produced from a single gene. Mechanisms of gene regulation include:

1. Modification of **chromatin**, the protein-DNA material of the chromosomes by **post-translational modifications** such as phosphorylation, acetylation, or glycosylation.
2. Direct **methylation** of DNA.
3. **Alternative mRNA splicing** where multiple, subtly different forms of a protein may be expressed from a single gene by the inclusion and exclusion of particular protein-coding exons.
4. **MicroRNAs**, or short RNAs that regulate the expression of large sets of protein-coding genes at a time by binding to mRNAs and marking them for destruction.

The net result is that these mechanisms, alone or acting in combination, bring about tightly regulated, tissue-specific gene regulation and developmental regulation, allowing genes to be activated or repressed when and where they are actually needed (this form of control may be partly or wholly recapitulated in some disease states, leading to inappropriate gene expression at the wrong time).

Chromatin modifications

Chromatin structure is highly dynamic and represents an evolutionary-conserved mechanism for the regulation of gene expression. Chromatin conformation is controlled at the nucleosome level, which is the basic unit of chromatin — the bead on the string, to use an earlier analogy, by post-translational modification of histone proteins within the nucleosome. Various enzymes modify the surfaces of histones by either adding acetyl, methyl, or phosphate groups to accessible amino acids or removing them. The most important of these are those that possess histone acetyltransferase (HAT) activity and which add acetyl groups to lysine residues. HAT activity is associated with the activation of transcription and the unravelling of chromatin. This is because histone acetylation promotes nucleosome slippage along the DNA strand and leads to the establishment of localised areas of 'naked' DNA, thus exposing the promoter as well as binding sites for transcription factors. The net result is that RNA polymerase II can now gain access to the gene. Some HATs, when bound to DNA, also appear to recruit certain transcription factors, making them central players in the activation of many genes.

Of course, there is also a class of antagonist proteins, the histone deacetylases (HDACs), which remove the acetyl groups, leading to the reformation of a compacted nucleosomal structure and resulting in transcriptional repression. Chromatin structure may be altered during development and in disease, indicating that it can impose a powerful control upon gene expression in a temporal-spatial pattern.

DNA can also be modified directly by methylation, with methyl transferases adding methyl groups to a cytosine that is followed by a guanosine. These so-called 'CpG' pairs are often clustered in runs or 'islands' within certain genes, particularly within promoter regions — computer modelling indicates that over half of all housekeeping genes contain an above-average proportion of CpG islands within their promoters. Heavily methylated genes are known to be transcriptionally repressed (i.e., switched off). Although the mechanisms remain obscure, there is evidence that methylation is important in embryonic development and plays a role in cancer. For example, recent data indicate that tumour-causing genes (*oncogenes*) are undermethylated in cancer, which therefore implies that they are actively expressed, while *tumour suppressor* genes are hyper-methylated (i.e., switched off). These sorts of external modifications to DNA that do not alter the DNA sequence are referred to as *epigenetic* modification. Epigenetics is a growing area of interest as it concerns how genes may be activated or repressed in a local cellular environment in response to external cues.

Alternative RNA splicing

We have looked at RNA splicing earlier when describing how mRNA is made. Many genes show alternative RNA splicing, often in a cell-specific manner. Splicing may seem like a waste of energy and resources, but it serves an important evolutionary function in that it can allow for greater protein diversity to occur from a single gene. Let us return to muscle and look at Myocardin, a protein co-factor that is involved in the expression of genes in cardiac and smooth muscle. Expression of the Myocardin gene sees its mRNA alternatively spliced to produce unique cardiac- or smooth muscle-restricted proteins in those muscle types: a 935-amino acid (aa) form in cardiac muscle and an 856-amino acid form in smooth muscle. Both isoforms associate with a ubiquitously expressed transcription factor called Serum Response Factor (SRF) to drive cardiac- or smooth muscle-specific expression, respectively, from genes that contain binding sites for SRF in their promoters. Thus, the responsibility for tissue-specific gene expression resides with the non-DNA binding Myocardin isoforms, which dictate in which tissues the ubiquitous SRF can bind to its gene targets.

The human proteome or sum total of proteins in a typical human cell is estimated to stand at over a million, many of which can be ascribed to alternative RNA splicing, although the majority no doubt represent post-translational protein modifications such as phosphorylation, methylation, or glycosylation. Walter Gilbert, one of the creators of the chemical method of DNA sequencing, for which he shared the 1980 Nobel Prize in Chemistry with Fred Sanger, was among the first to suggest that alternative RNA splicing could allow 'exon shuffling', particularly if different functional attributes are assigned to different exons. This method allows evolution to 'jump forward', making new genes and proteins from existing material and constructing new proteins from pre-existing building blocks, as it were. Some evolutionary theories suggest that in the evolution of a new protein, it is easier to reassign existing protein domains than to create, *ex novo*, a new amino acid sequence that encodes a new functional 3-D structure.

MicroRNAs

As I have said, the vast majority of DNA within a chromosome does not code for proteins. Recent evidence indicates that so-called 'junk' DNA does in fact contain some key regulators of gene expression in the form of *microRNA* genes. MicroRNAs (miRNA) are very short (21–23 bases), naturally occurring single-stranded RNAs that act as potent silencers of gene expression. Many miRNA genes have been identified within introns or from the intergenic regions (i.e., between genes).

MiRNAs function as inhibitors of protein expression by virtue of being complementary to particular base sequences that are present in certain mRNAs, thereby enabling short regions of double-stranded RNA:RNA complementarity to form when an miRNA finds its target mRNA. This formation of duplex RNA can have two effects. It may inhibit translation of the mRNA as translation requires a single-stranded molecule to pass through the ribosome. The second mechanism involves invoking cellular defence mechanisms that are triggered in response to invading viruses that possess a double-stranded RNA genome. Whichever pathway is followed, the net result is a blocking of the production of protein from the targeted mRNA. MicroRNAs form part of an extensive system of *RNA interference (RNAi)* mechanisms operating in the eukaryotic cell.

What makes the miRNA system such a fascinating and hitherto (until a few years ago) unrecognised way of controlling gene expression is that a single miRNA may be complementary to a highly conserved sequence that is present in many different mRNAs. Therefore, the expression of whole sets of genes may be inhibited simultaneously by a single miRNA; recent research suggests that the average miRNA may regulate 400 mRNAs at once. This provides a very specific and cost-effective mechanism for regulating the expression of whole networks of proteins associated with a particular cell type or at a particular point in development, or in the molecular pathology of a particular disease or syndrome. In this respect, miRNAs are now being investigated as markers of disease and potential targets for therapeutic intervention. Mutations within some miRNA genes have been shown to be associated with disease, indicating that the deregulation of miRNAs is related to pathology. For example, a mutation in the miR-96 miRNA gene causes a form of hereditary hearing loss. Recent estimates of the number of miRNA genes in the human genome suggest that well over 5,000 exist.

Some miRNAs are expressed in a tissue-specific manner. With regards to the heart, mice that were genetically engineered (so-called 'knock-out' mice) to be deficient in a muscle-specific miRNA gene called miR-1-2 developed a variety of morphological abnormalities before birth, including an elevated number of cardiac myocytes (*hyperplasia*), 'hole in the heart' abnormalities, and changes in properties of the electrical conduction system. These findings indicate that miR-1-2 expression in the mouse heart is essential for its normal and correct development. The hypothesis that an individual miRNA can regulate the expression of multiple protein-coding genes is well supported in this case as shown from a micro-array analysis of hearts taken from miR-1-2 -/- mice (the -/- motif shows that both copies of the gene have been 'knocked out') compared to hearts from normal or so-called *wild-type* mice, revealing upregulation of various genes associated with cardiac development. Among these were some genes encoding key transcription factors.

Stem cells and gene editing

There has been a significant repositioning of the reductionist viewpoint since the new millennium. We now acknowledge that yes, we *can* read the sum of the human being in our genes, but at the same time recognise that the workings of the cell are infinitely more complex than the molecular biologist of old had imagined, with multiple layers of control, complex networks of regulatory and signalling molecules, and a proteome that dwarfs the genome in terms of size. It is clear that learning everything about how a single gene is controlled at the molecular level is no longer enough.

This realisation led to the development of a more holistic approach to biological research termed *systems biology*. This approach relies heavily on computational and bioinformatic input to model and map out the signalling or protein-protein interaction networks operating in the cell as well as the regulatory networks provided by transcription factors and chromatin-remodelling proteins or protein signalling pathways. It has found applications in modelling tumour progression in cells that turn cancerous, particularly in mapping the pathways of cell differentiation from the starting point of a *stem cell*. These advances have all been made possible by an increasingly multidisciplinary approach to biomedical research.

British biologist Denis Noble's (b. 1936) most notable scientific achievement is, perhaps, using mathematical modelling to unravel a key mechanism in the working of the heart. However, he is also a pioneer of systems biology. He has challenged the reductionist viewpoint, and his views on evolutionary matters and the role of the gene align more with those of Lewontin and Gould, than with Dawkins.

In the excellent *The Music of Life*, Noble skilfully unravels how DNA is not life itself, but a code from which life, in all its complexity, extends. In true 'systems biology' form, life is shown to be the interplay between genes, cells, organs, systems, bodies, and the environment. The gene may set the starting criteria for limitations of what can be, but the vastly more complex interactions of higher systems that the code are what truly determine life.

It is now common for mathematicians to inform bioinformatics projects and aeronautical engineers to provide insights on fluid mechanics that may help link the turbulence of blood flow with the predisposition of certain blood vessels in the body to atherosclerosis. As advances are made in manipulating the DNA within cells — in particular, knock-out transgenic animal technologies where part of a gene on its chromosome can be replaced with a mutated version of itself in order to test its function — it becomes possible to construct testable hypotheses in an *in vivo* setting (i.e., using a whole animal) rather than *in vitro* (i.e., in a cell culture or test tube).

The very latest technologies with potential for human application are based on CRISPR (Clustered Regularly Interspaced Short Palindromic Repeats), a gene editing technology that has been adapted from what is essentially a bacterial defence system to thwart infection by other bacteria or bacteriophages. Tests in cultured human cell lines *in vitro* and in animal models have shown it to be an extraordinarily precise targeting mechanism for knocking out gene function. For example, early studies suggest that it may be of use in preventing virus infections caused by members of the Herpes virus family, and gene editing has been used to genetically engineer a particular strain of mosquito to be unable to pass on malaria. A recent report from China in 2017 described how gene editing was used to correct a single-base mutation responsible for a form of beta thalassemia, an inherited blood disorder that affects the beta haemoglobin chain in early-stage human embryos.

One of the holy grails of therapeutic intervention is to be able to grow outside of the body (*ex vivo*) replacement tissues or even whole organs that are derived from a patient's own cells. This is a field termed variously as tissue engineering or cell-based therapy. Embryonic stem (ES) cells are found in the inner cell mass of the early human embryo when they number no more than 150 or so cells in total. These cells are termed *pluripotent* as they are completely undifferentiated at this stage of development, uncommitted to any final cell lineage and, furthermore, able to become any particular type of cell if they receive the correct molecular cues. Thus, ES cells can give rise to all of the terminally differentiated (>220) cell types of the mature body. The cues can be genetic, programmed by expression of our genes, or environmental, such as contact with other types of cells or tissue matrix proteins in which the cells are embedded.

Cell division during early embryogenesis provides the initial numbers of stem cells necessary for differentiation into the progenitors of all the different cell types that will be needed to construct the body plan of the organism. Thereafter, further rounds of cell division provide more progenitors, or cells progress to terminal differentiation and specialisation in response to developmentally regulated patterns of transcription, cell movement, and inductive events, such as cells secreting differentiation molecules (*morphogens*) that are picked up by other cells in close proximity or at a distance. These stimuli allow the embryo to develop properly and grow in size. An adult no longer contains ES cells, of course, but some adult tissues retain a small population of multipotent progenitor cells, often termed *adult stem cells*, which are capable of differentiating into certain cell types in the event of tissue damage. However, these are not like ES cells which are capable of forming *any* cell type — their potency for differentiation is linked to the lineage they are already committed to.

Such adult stem cells can proliferate and differentiate as and when needed for tissue repair or for fighting infection. Classic examples include the haematopoietic progenitor cell populations found in bone marrow, which give rise to all the white blood cell lineages, and the satellite cells found in skeletal muscle which enable localised muscle repair in response to injury.

All stem cells can be characterised by exhibiting multipotency upon receiving appropriate differentiation cues and by their ability to self-renew; that is, to replenish the undifferentiated stem cell population through further cycles of cell division. Understanding how to manipulate a patient's own adult stem cells in order to make the desired type of replacement tissue is now an earnest goal of many systems biology projects. So, what are the molecular cues that one needs to invoke to get enough progenitor cells for cell therapy? And which cues are then necessary and sufficient to promote terminal differentiation into the correct end-product?

A starting point perhaps comes from the work of Shinya Yamanaka of Japan, who shared a Nobel Prize in 2012 with England's John Gurdon for their work on pluripotency. Yamanaka's team had shown that *induced pluripotent stem cells* (*iPSCs*) can be 'reverse-engineered' from terminally differentiated adult mouse or human skin cells known as fibroblasts by using viral vectors to express in them just four transcription factors. These factors, called Klf4, c-Myc, SOX2, and Oct3/4, belong to different transcription factor gene families and appeared to be necessary and sufficient to turn ordinary adult skin fibroblasts into cell types with characteristics of a progenitor cell.

This finding suggests that it may be possible in the future to take skin fibroblasts or other easily obtainable cells from a patient, back-generate stem cells from them, and re-differentiate these cells in the laboratory into whatever desired type that is needed for therapy. The precedent is clear and is being studied intensively as a result — a limited cocktail of transcription factors or other inducers could be used to turn an individual's own skin cells into a multipotent cell, which could then be manipulated further for tissue replacement.

We are as yet some way from this, although a 2013 study reported in the journal *Nature* described seeding matrix material with different types of human iPSC-derived liver progenitors, which then proliferated and self-organised into functional liver material as judged by implanting it into a mouse host and measuring several markers of liver function in the implanted liver bud. Of course, by using the patient's own cells to create replacement tissue, there is no risk of graft rejection as is seen in current transplant situations where the patient is required to take anti-rejection drugs, nor is there the therapeutic bottleneck caused by shortage of suitable donor organs.

To summarise this section, gene expression is tightly regulated in the cell, for an inappropriate signal at the wrong time in development may lead to death or at least birth abnormalities. There are multiple layers of control — from the simple limit that is put upon the lifetime of a mRNA molecule to extraordinarily complicated mechanisms for opening up discrete regions of chromatin to allow the transcriptional machinery to locate and interact with a gene promoter in a tissue-specific or stage-specific manner. Much of this information has been gained by *in vitro* studies using cell lines or by using animal models. Common animal models include the mouse, zebrafish, and the nematode worm *Caenorhabditis elegans*, for which the developmental fate of all 1,031 somatic cells in an adult male have now been mapped. Despite this disparity in species, evolution has preserved the things that are useful to it, whether they are protein motifs such as the DNA-binding domains present in transcription factors or intracellular signalling cascades, as well as conserving molecular aspects of how a body plan 'blueprint' can be executed, as we will see in the next section.

As an illustration, about a third of the genes in *C. elegans* have their counterparts in the human genome — indeed, the human equivalent can be substituted experimentally for the worm version in a number of cases. So, armed with this fundamental knowledge of how gene expression manifests itself, let us go on to look at how embryonic development is controlled with a few choice examples of some of the key families of regulatory genes involved. In particular, we will see how knowledge from studying a variety of animal models (comparative genomics) reveals a remarkable degree of conservation in the types of molecular pathways that have been used throughout evolution to create body plan and sensory organs.

iii) Development

Dynamic random processes

Morphogenesis is the process by which the adult organism arises from a fertilised egg. How is the development of the complex body plan of a vertebrate organised and implemented from such simple beginnings? The structure of the whole organism is composed largely of cells, which are arranged in an orderly pattern according to a precisely executed plan. This arrangement is due to the orderly switching on and off of genes at particular times and in the correct places.

I mentioned earlier that comparative genomics approaches have allowed us to make progress in identifying some of the key molecules in development. Thanks to technological advances in DNA sequencing and computer analysis software, the genomes of more and more species are being determined and their evolutionary relatedness revealed. However, as well as the genetic processes, such as the widespread use of transcription factors in order to activate complex, *hierarchical* patterns of gene expression (i.e., one activates another, which activates another downstream of it, rather like the tiered MAP kinase activation process described earlier), *dynamic random processes* also occur during development and, in the case of *prions*, can cause pathology in the adult.

Both early and late stages of embryogenesis reveal how dynamic processes can programme development and lay down a blueprint for structural arrangement. A very early example occurs in the fruit fly *Drosophila melanogaster*. *Drosophila* has been a laboratory test species since the pioneering work of the American geneticist Thomas Morgan (1866–1945) who used it to probe the segregation of heritable traits (i.e., genes), even though the elucidation of DNA as the material of the gene was still some decades away. It is an attractive laboratory animal for genetic studies: it has just four chromosomes, lays many eggs, and has a short reproductive cycle, and many mutations are readily visible, such as red versus white eyes, crumpled wings, or an extra pair of legs growing in place of antennae in a well-studied mutant known as *antennapedia*. Notably, *Drosophila* has been used to investigate the construction of a segmented body plan as it possesses clearly defined head, thorax, and tail regions derived from 14 segments in the embryo. In particular, *homeotic* mutations have been mapped in which a mutation leads to the transformation of one body part into a different one. *Antennapedia* is an example of this class of mutation. Comparative genomics indicates that this tiny fly shares 60% identity with man at the gene level.

The anterior (head) to posterior (tail) polarity of the *Drosophila* embryo is established in the egg even before fertilisation occurs by the laying

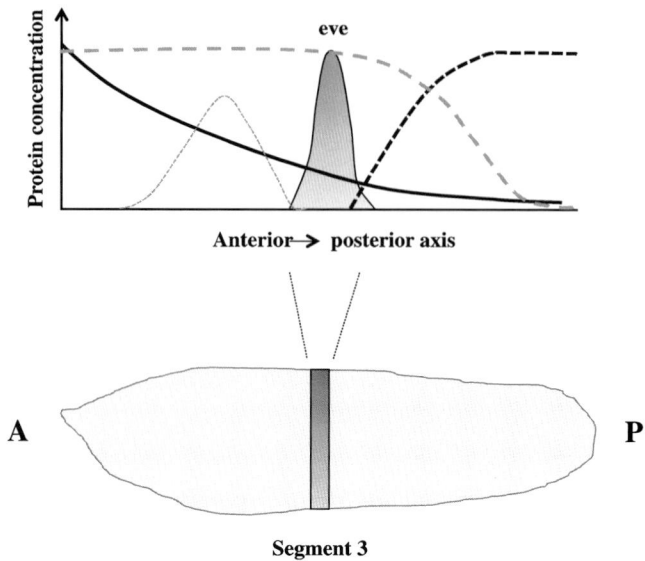

Figure 36. Establishment of anterior (A) to posterior (P) axis in the *Drosophila* embryo. An anterior to posterior gradient of the diffusible morphogen *bicoid* develops soon after fertilisation (*solid black line*). Expression of the repressor protein *nanos* (dashed black line) at the posterior pole represses translation of a widely distributed mRNA for *hunchback* (dashed grey line). These maternal effect genes establish tight boundaries of expression of downstream key proteins, including other transcription factors (e.g., gap genes such as *giant* (dotted grey line) and segment-polarity genes) in a hierarchical fashion. This process directs the development of a 14-segment body plan. The 'output' in this particular example shown at the bottom of the Figure is restriction of a pair-rule protein called *eve*, a marker for alternative segments (dark grey shaded areas), to segment 3 of the developing embryo.

down of a gradient of a diffusible morphogen protein called *bicoid*, whose mRNA accumulates in the anterior end of the unfertilised oocyte. *Bicoid* is a transcription factor that belongs to the *homeobox* class of DNA-binding proteins (we shall meet these again later). Following fertilisation, the bicoid mRNA is translated, establishing a protein concentration gradient across the A-P axis. The protein then regulates expression of other transcription factors to form tight boundaries of expression of various transcription factors, which ultimately direct the establishment of individual segment boundaries (Figure 36). *Bicoid* is termed a 'maternal effect' gene, along with a translational repressor called *nanos* which emanates from the posterior pole of the egg, and a third protein, *hunchback*, whose mRNA is distributed throughout the egg but is targeted for repression by *nanos*. Different molecules lay down the blueprint for dorsal (back) versus ventral (abdominal) development.

Other diffusible molecules are used at late developmental stages. Retinoic acid (RA) is a vitamin A derivative which is a ligand for zinc-binding transcription factors called retinoic acid receptors (RARs). Vitamin A is a powerful teratogen (i.e., overconsumption in pregnancy causes birth defects), but first it is metabolised into its biologically active form, which is RA. RARs bind to target DNA sequences known as retinoic acid responsive elements (RARE) as heterodimers with the closely related retinoid X receptors (RXRs).

Studies in chick embryos in the 1980s indicated a role for RA in determining embryonic limb development. For example, when microbeads soaked in RA were inserted into the developing wing or leg 'buds' of an embryo in mid-gestation — a stage at which none of the limb bones have formed yet — the result was a mirror-image duplication of the entire limb. However, later work has shown that RA is not a true morphogen in the sense of programming limb formation; that honour belongs to a molecule expressed before the limb bud stage, *sonic hedgehog*, an evolutionary-conserved secreted molecule with a primary role in the patterning of limb, brain structures, and teeth. RA is only involved in limb development at a stage subsequent to sonic hedgehog having initiated the limb morphogenic programme.

RA remains an interesting molecule though for several reasons. First, it is obviously involved in development as excess consumption causes fetal abnormalities. Second, cellular and tissue levels of RA are maintained by complex mechanisms, including the control of synthesis from retinol (vitamin A) via retinaldehyde to RA by two oxidative steps, (1) degradation of excess retinol to prevent tissue toxicity and (2) the presence of small retinoid-binding proteins known as cellular retinol or RA-binding proteins (CRBP and CRABP, respectively). The precise function of these small binding proteins remains obscure, but they are often co-expressed with RARs and different forms show distinct, sometimes overlapping patterns of distribution in the embryo, perhaps sequestering retinoids in an inactive form until needed. It may be that a 'supporting cast' of ancillary enzymes and binding proteins act to establish a concentration gradient of active

RA across a developmental axis, akin to a morphogenic field. At the very least, it suggests a dynamic form of control of RA within the cell. Finally, RAREs have been found within the promoters of a number of mammalian homeobox genes which, as we shall go on to see, are important evolutionary-conserved transcription factors involved in mammalian body plan patterning with their antecedents found in *Drosophila*.

Methylation of DNA is also an important dynamic factor in early development. Immediately after fertilisation, the genome of the embryo is demethylated and then remethylated. Methylation can be viewed as an epigenetic phenomenon. That is, environment influences DNA rather than information being hardwired into the DNA code. The importance of methylation in development has been shown using transgenic mice in which homologous recombination techniques were used to knock out DNA methyltransferase, an enzyme responsible for DNA methylation. All embryos resulting from such animals die at a very early stage of development. In postnatal development, there is evidence in rats that normal maternal care (e.g., grooming and feeding of young by a mother) triggers increased expression of the glucocorticoid receptor (GR) gene in the brains of offspring, something that is associated with reduced methylation across the GR promoter (we saw in the last section that activation of oncogene expression has been shown to be associated with undermethylation of these genes in some cancers).

Finally, although it has nothing to do with development, we should consider the dynamic processes by which a polypeptide can adopt its correct, functional three-dimensional form as this can have severe consequences for the organism if things go wrong. Many small proteins are able to fold themselves and adopt their correct 3-D structure spontaneously whereas others require the help of accessory proteins called *chaperones* (or chaperonins). Many chaperones act to prevent the undesired aggregation of newly synthesised proteins before they have folded correctly, and the cell has evolved intricate mechanisms for detecting, removing, and recycling misfolded proteins by involving protein-degrading enzymes called *proteases*. Prion diseases are an example of a unique pathology that arises from protein misfolding. The majority involve a small protein, Prion Protein (PrP), that can dynamically alter its 3D-form and that of its neighbours, causing some devastating and sometimes fatal slow-developing neurological conditions such as 'mad cow disease', scrapie (which affects sheep), and Creutzfeldt-Jakob disease in humans (all forms of Transmissible Spongiform Encephalopathies).

These pathologies occur when the highly conserved 208-amino acid PrP adopts an alternative, protease-resistant protein structure, possibly as a result of binding certain metal ions. This structure can then act as a template or 'seed' for altering the conformation of neighbouring PrP molecules so that the abnormal structure then spreads much rather like an infection (the term prion, coined by the Nobel Laureate Stanley B. Prusiner in 1982, is a contraction of *protein infection*). PrP is also implicated in Alzheimer's disease as it can act as a receptor in the brain for soluble amyloid beta proteins. It is thought that misfolded amyloid beta proteins can seed further misfolding around them, leading to a prion-like spread of misfolded material in the form of the distinctive Alzheimer's amyloid plaques, destroying neurological function in the process.

Development and evolution

Development is an extremely complex process, one whose fundamental concepts are being unravelled slowly. I say fundamental concepts since the development of each organism is different, yet certain commonalities have evolved. To discuss the current understanding of even the basic processes of development is a book in itself, yet what is relevant here is the conceptual parallel between the developmental changes that convert an egg into an adult and the evolutionary changes that have occurred over huge amounts of time, and which have enabled simple unicellular organisms that existed on Earth hundreds of millions of years ago to give rise to today's complex multicellular organisms through the process of natural selection, as we will go on to discuss. So, what is the conceptual similarity?

For both evolutionary and individual developmental changes, a single cell is converted into an organism with many cells. These cells are of different kinds and arranged into a complex multifunctional whole; the different functional requirements of parts of the organism are catered for by the development of specialised cells. Cell-specific gene expression dictates cell shape and function known as *phenotype*, such that a skeletal myocyte has very different physical and biochemical properties compared to a skin fibroblast or a cone cell in the retina of the eye. For *evolutionary* changes occurring over vast periods of time, natural selection ensures that organisms that are more adapted to a particular environment will go on to survive and reproduce. Their increased specialisation, at least as witnessed by the fossil record, is paralleled by increasing complexity.

Of course, the mechanisms of evolutionary and developmental change are different. The process of natural selection drives evolutionary change but not developmental change, yet they are intertwined. The accumulation of genetic information (resultant from evolution) that is encapsulated within an organism determines its development; the evolution of organisms depends on developmental changes over generations. As a species evolves, the genetic information and developmental processes change through a process of DNA mutation.

Gene mutations *per se* are changes in DNA nucleotide sequence which often have a deleterious effect on gene function. For example, a TTA codon for the amino acid leucine within the middle of the gene might be mutated in one generation to the translational stop codon TAA, which would cause premature termination of the encoded protein. This mutation, which might impair function but not prove to be immediately lethal, would then be passed on to the next generation. It should be noted though that many changes in nucleotide sequence, termed *polymorphisms*, are silent and have no phenotypic effect and may even be beneficial in promoting evolutionary change if enough accumulate within a gene over a very long timespan, as we will discuss in Chapter 5.

Evolution determines the development of an individual, and evolution as a process depends on development. As John Maynard Smith points out in *Shaping Life*, natural selection explains how information is incorporated in the genome, whereas development shows what *use* is made of it during an individual's development.

Transcription factors in the formation of body plan

How tissue-specific gene expression is controlled at the molecular level and how this is orchestrated correctly during development remains a subject of intense laboratory study. Much is under the control of transcription factors whose form and function have been highly conserved during evolution.

Before I give examples of this, we must learn a little more about what defines a transcription factor.

Transcription factors are, of course, themselves the products of genes and have been found to be organised into several large gene families (Figure 37).

GENE FAMILY	DNA BINDING SITE	EXAMPLE	FUNCTION
Homeobox	TA-rich:	Antennapedia (*Drosophila*)	Leg development
	e.g. TNNAGTG (high affinity)	Eyeless (*Drosophila*)	Eye development
	C(^{A}/$_T$)TTAATTN (low affinity)	PAX-6	
		Tinman (*Drosophila*) Nkx-2.5	Dorsal vessel development (*Drosophila*); Heart development (mammals)
bHLH	CANNTG	HIF-1	Sensor of hypoxia (low oxygen levels)
		MyoD, myogenin	Skeletal muscle development
MADS box family	CTA(^{A}/$_T$)$_4$TAG (MEF2)	MEF2 genes	Skeletal muscle development
	CC(^{A}/$_T$)$_6$GG (SRF)	Serum Response Factor (SRF)	Cell cycle regulation, cell differentiation and proliferation
C$_2$H$_2$ zinc finger	CACC(C)	Sp1	Housekeeping gene
		KLF4	Tumorgenesis; stem cell decisions
		KLF13	Cardiac development (*Xenopus*)
GATA family	GATA	GATA-1, 2 & 3	Haematopoiesis
		GATA-4, 5 & 6	Heart development

Figure 37. **Key transcription factor gene families.** Some of the major eukaryotic transcription factor families are shown along with their cognate DNA-binding sequences. Examples to which particular functions have been attributed are also shown. **Key**: bHLH, basic/helix-loop-helix; KLF, krüppel-like factor. Examples shown are mammalian unless otherwise indicated.

In each case, they are classified according to the protein sequence of that part of the protein forming the DNA-binding domain (DBD), the region that allows the factor to recognise and bind to its cognate DNA sequence within a target gene. The protein sequence of the DBD usually shows remarkable evolutionary conservation across different *phyla* (groups) ranging from yeast to fruit flies to *Homo sapiens*. The conservation of DNA and hence protein sequence is, of course, necessary in order to preserve the precise structure of the DBD. Any error introduced by mutation would alter its function and the mutated individual would most likely die before it can pass on its genes.

What has become apparent is that certain genes are not only very widespread but also extremely ancient. Their oldness is readily apparent by comparing the protein sequences of key structural elements such as a DBD across species, which may well be the only conserved part of the *same protein* from two organisms that are separated by hundreds of millions of years of evolutionary time.

One of the oldest DBD structures in evolutionary terms is the so-called homeobox or *homeodomain*, a helix-turn-helix motif that is so-called because a short turn containing a glycine residue separates two α-helices, forming a simple DNA-binding structure that can interact with the double helix in a DNA sequence-specific manner. Evolution conserves both the structure of the homeobox and the sequence that it binds to in target genes. Members of this gene family are termed Hox genes (from Homeobox). Other transcription factors contain more elaborate DBDs and examples are shown above in Figure 37.

Another ancient family that can be found in yeast are the so-called C_2H_2 zinc finger gene family, which is potentially the largest transcription factor family in the mammalian genome, comprising around 3% of the total number of genes in the human genome. The DBD of these factors is formed from conserved pairs of cysteine and histidines, which tetrahedrally coordinate or bind a zinc ion and hold the polypeptide together in a formation dubbed the 'zinc finger'. Zinc fingers are able to interact with the DNA helix and make contact with three base pairs of DNA. Zinc finger proteins are very diverse in size: some can contain as few as two or as many as 30 fingers, and the DNA targets for the vast majority remain unclear (hence the 'potentially' caveat earlier).

However, there is a well-defined subgroup of mammalian zinc finger proteins that contain just a few zinc fingers. These have been shown to bind to a simple sequence CACC or CACCC and are called krüppel-like factors or KLFs, so-called after their relatedness to a *Drosophila* zinc finger protein called *Krüppel*. KLFs are implicated in several developmental and pathological processes including skeletal muscle formation, adipose fat tissue differentiation and metabolism, and the regulation of cell proliferation and cancer. For example, KLF15 levels are raised in muscle in response to exercise in both man and mouse models; on the other hand, KLF15 expression in adipose fat is depressed in a mouse model of obesity. KLF4 functions as a transcriptional repressor in the vascular system — one of its targets in smooth muscle appears to be the SRF-myocardin complex that we mentioned earlier. KLF13 has been implicated in heart formation in *Xenopus*, and experiments on mice conducted recently in 2017 indicate a genetic role in Holt-Oram syndrome in humans, of which three quarters of sufferers exhibit a congenital heart defect.

Some other zinc-binding transcription factors that have been shown to play roles in development adopt a similar finger-like DBD conformation. These include members of the steroid/retinoid hormone receptor superfamily such as oestrogen receptors and RARs, all of which utilise four cysteines to coordinate the zinc ion, and members of the GATA family (Figure 37, above).

Other notable transcription factor families include so-called MADS box proteins such as SRF and the basic/helix-loop-helix (bHLH) factor family, whose members include the vertebrate skeletal muscle regulatory proteins myogenin and MyoD1 as well as an oxygen-sensing transcription factor called HIF-1 (Figure 37). In bHLH proteins, a functional protein dimer is made via a helix-loop-helix structure that acts as an interface for protein dimerisation. Two clusters of basic amino acids adjacent to the HLH domain are then brought into close proximity and are able to make a DBD, which makes contact with the cognate DNA-binding site in target genes, a simple palindromic sequence CANNTG (where N can be any nucleotide).

Hox genes determine body plan in Drosophila

Developmental genetics investigates how mutant genes cause their effects and thus sheds light on what the normal genes do. As noted earlier, the origins of modern developmental biology lie with the fruit fly, which has been used for about a century. Although such studies predated the discovery of DNA as the hereditary material, they allowed the clear phenotyping of fly populations based on the inheritance of recognisable traits, much as Mendel had done with his studies on the inherited characteristics of pea plants in the 19th century.

A major breakthrough in fly genetics in the 1980s concerned the discovery of the molecular basis of the *antennapedia* mutation. This mutation causes the fruit fly to develop an extra pair of legs on its head instead of antennae, a trait first noted in the 1940s. A reciprocal, 'inverse' mutation sees antennae develop on the second thoracic segment in place of the second pair of legs. Both are homeotic mutations. Subsequent use of molecular cloning techniques to identify and clone the gene responsible for the *antennapedia* mutation by Walter Gehring and colleagues at the University of Basal (published in 1983) revealed it to be the prototype of the homeobox family. *Drosophila* has a cluster of distinct Hox genes which are active early in development and play roles in the specification of the fly's body plan along the anterior to posterior axis, as I have described for the maternal effect morphogen *bicoid*.

What is notable in the fly is that the linear order of the Hox genes on the chromosome correlates precisely with where these genes are expressed along the anterior-posterior axis, a phenomenon called 'collinearity'. Furthermore, mutations in Hox genes can impose a more anterior or more posterior phenotype upon a body segment. Thus, the offending, so-called 'loss-of-function' mutation in the *antennapedia* gene, which sits in the middle of the Hox cluster, causes a pair of antennae to form mid-thorax instead of the expected second pair of legs. Conversely, a 'gain-of-function' mutation is responsible for the dramatic posteriorising phenotype of legs developing instead of antennae on the head. In other words, the normal anterior body plan instructions to 'build antennae' have been replaced by signals from a more posterior part of the fly, which instead tell it to 'build legs'. *Antennapedia* is therefore a classic example of a master regulator gene as it sits at the top of a hierarchical network of gene expression that leads to the formation of the fruit fly leg.

Hox genes in vertebrates

Vertebrate Hox gene equivalents were discovered later in the 1980s using cDNA cloning techniques. As mentioned earlier, the homeobox represents the DNA-binding domain found in all Hox proteins and is highly conserved in terms of protein and DNA sequence between family members. The high degree of DNA sequence identity between related genes enabled scientists to use one gene sequence as a probe to 'fish out' closely related sequences from a gene library by virtue of DNA hybridisation (in early days, the probe was labelled with the radioactive phosphorus group ^{32}P and was replaced later by the use of non-radioactive fluorophores). This process allows similar genes to be isolated within a species or, under conditions of low stringency hybridisation designed to identify partial matches, the identification of evolutionarily related *homologues* from other species. Such techniques enable us to clone genes from species as diverse as man, fly, yeast, and fish. That said, nowadays it is more common to determine the entire genomic sequence for an organism and map its genes using gene mapping software, after which PCR is used to derive physical copies of the gene or its mRNA.

The fruit fly contains one cluster of Hox genes. Vertebrates on the other hand contain four Hox clusters termed A-D, each containing multiple Hox genes. These are termed *paralogues* in that they are copies that have arisen by a process of gene duplication and which share some clear DNA (and hence protein) sequence identity with one another and with the *Drosophila* genes. These clusters also play roles in anterior-posterior patterning, though the situation is less clear-cut than in the fly. Paralogues of the HoxA and D clusters, for example, have been shown in mice to be involved in anterior-posterior development of the vertebrae and ribs.

Similarly, the HoxC gene cluster shows evidence of positional effects, with 5' genes in the cluster being expressed in posterior structures (e.g., the legs of the developing chicken embryo) while the 3' genes are expressed more anteriorly (e.g., in the wings of the chick embryo). There is also an interesting correlation with expression of retinoic acid. The 3' Hox genes tend to be induced by RA, their expression domains extending in a more anterior pattern, whereas the 5' genes are not inducible by RA.

Mutation of one Hox gene alone in vertebrates is insufficient to cause something akin to the homeotic mutations seen in flies, but mutating *all* Hox genes operating in a specific area does have an essentially homeotic effect. Together, these data show that vertebrate Hox genes also control aspects of anterior-posterior body plan and suggests that higher organisms have evolved through gene duplication a degree of functional redundancy, which can act as a failsafe against a mutation in a single gene causing a major developmental problem.

The Hox gene clusters exist in all animal groups that exhibit bilateral symmetry. However, there are other Hox genes in the genome that are not arranged in clusters. One such gene, *Nkx-2.5*, acts as one of the very earliest markers of vertebrate heart development. Nkx-2.5 was originally identified through its DNA sequence homology to the *Drosophila* gene *tinman*, so-called because flies bearing mutations in the *tinman* gene lack the dorsal vessel, a pulsatile tube that distributes plasmolymph throughout the embryo. This tube may be thought of, therefore, as the fly's equivalent to our heart, and 'tinman' is of course a reference to Dorothy's friend in 'The Wizard of Oz' who lacked a heart. It is interesting to note here that from an evolutionary viewpoint, the mammalian heart also starts out as a linear, pulsatile tube that is formed during very early stages of embryogenesis. Later on in development, it loops on itself to one side and undergoes significant structural remodelling to become the four-chambered heart.

Transgenic mice engineered to be defective in Nkx-2.5 expression die *in utero* due to an arrest in this looping process. In humans, mutations within the Nkx-2.5 gene, which maps to human chromosome 5, have been identified in families with congenital heart defects including atrial and ventricular septal defects (both are hole in the heart malformations) and electrical conduction abnormalities. Thus, the developmental signalling system is evolutionarily conserved, whereas the structures that develop from it and the path(s) taken are different. John Maynard Smith (in *Shaping Life*) points out that this system is the common, primitive feature shared by all animals.

To make this point even more obvious, let us take another example from *Drosophila*, a gene called *sog* that determines ventral or abdominal development. In the toad *Xenopus*, a related gene called *chordin* determines the development of dorsal or back structures. Sog and chordin are not transcription factors, but they are diffusible signalling molecules that are capable of binding to other signalling proteins and modulating their activities. Astonishingly, despite being expressed in different regions of these very different embryos — one a vertebrate, the other an invertebrate — these genes are *functional* homologues. Genetic 'swap' experiments in which the *Xenopus* gene is cloned into a suitable vector and used to replace the fly gene or *vice versa* show that sog, like chordin, can drive dorsal development in the toad and that chordin can programme ventral development on the fruit fly.

Thus, signals causing insect ventral development are identical to those causing dorsal development in vertebrates, serving as evidence that evolution has chosen the best signal for the job. One hypothesis is that at some point during evolutionary history, a partition arose in terms of the positioning of the spinal cord in vertebrates or its invertebrate equivalent, the nerve cord, with respect to body plan. In vertebrates such as amphibians, it runs dorsally; in invertebrates such as the fruit fly, it is located ventrally. The progenitor(s) of both sog and chordin therefore followed this key partitioning event, even though they then evolved independently to regulate the development of very distinct anatomical structures.

If a master regulator signal acts in a hierarchical manner by activating, say, a particular transcription factor gene whose product then switches on another and so on in a cascade, then it is imperative for the successful development of the organism that the initial signal is effective. Developmental genetics is exemplified in a famous experiment involving the mouse Hox gene known as 'small-eye' or PAX6. This is one of perhaps several master regulator genes that control mammalian eye development and is highly conserved at both sequence and functional levels across species (the protein sequences of the mouse and human PAX6 genes are identical, for example). It is notable that when a mutation is introduced into the mouse gene, it causes severe eye abnormalities.

The fly homologue of PAX6 is called *eyeless*, as gene mutations abort the normal fly eye development programme altogether. When the normal mouse PAX6 gene is transferred using a genetic vector into the genome of the fruit fly, it causes the development of extra eyes wherever the gene is directed to be expressed. However, the eye that forms is always a *Drosophila* compound eye, not a mouse eye! Therefore, in essence, the molecular signal of the PAX6/*eyeless* gene is simply telling the body plan to 'build an eye' using the fly structural blueprint and the raw materials available.

It is astounding that although hundreds of millions of years in evolutionary time separate mice and *Drosophila*, the *same* gene can be used in both species to determine that an eye is made using whatever appropriate materials are present and by acting on the appropriate downstream hierarchical regulatory networks for eye development, irrespective of species differences. Once again, the developmental signalling programme is revealed as being evolutionarily conserved, whereas the structures developing from it are profoundly different. This phenomenon also indicates that evolution over many millions of years employs an 'if it ain't broke, don't fix it' approach to useful molecules — there is no need to tinker with the DNA sequence coding for a 'useful' functional protein, as witnessed by the high degree of homology between some yeast, fly, and mammalian proteins or motifs such as a DBD. Thanks to the redundancy of the genetic code (see Figure 35), conservation of a key protein sequence can withstand a little playing around at the DNA level, with the odd nucleotide polymorphism causing no problem as long as the amino acid sequence is not changed.

Ontogeny and phylogeny

For each given animal group or phylum, there are developmental stages through which an organism passes on its way from embryo to adult. During this process, there is a conserved *phylotypic* stage that resembles that of its ancient ancestors. All fish, mammals, and birds pass through a stage where the embryo has a rigid rod along its back called the *notochord*, which is made of cartilage and supports the body in the embryonic stages of many animals. At this stage, these different species are visually almost indistinguishable. This led some 19th scientists to believe that as embryos of animals of different phyla pass through what appear to be similar developmental stages, then the obvious interpretation was that developmental history recapitulates evolutionary history.

This idea of growth or *ontogeny* recapitulating *phylogeny*, or the species' evolutionary history, dates back to 1866 following the ideas of the German zoologist Ernst Haeckel. The idea is quite compelling since it 'appears' to explain the reason for the similarity in development between different species. Haeckel's drawings of early embryos famously showed apparent similarities among species as different as human, tortoise, and dog. However, science has now rejected this theory because there is no genetic reason for it to be the case. Indeed, before the phylotypic stage, the animals may be even more different from one another than they are later. There *is* a common phylotypic stage because from this stage onwards, the organism can develop from blocks of undifferentiated cells arranged in the correct relative positions as I had indicated for *Drosophila*. The modular nature of development of an organism is thought to be the most efficient method for its generation and, furthermore, makes continued evolution possible.

Similar patterns can arise from different sets of rules. It is safe to say that as development can be divided into a series of successive processes of differentiation, the amount of shape complexity that can be added to an organism in a single developmental step is small. As differentiation of cells changes their function, a mistake in a single differentiation step can be rectified, thereby avoiding the possibility of huge mistakes occurring in the development of the organism. In *Drosophila,* as development takes place in steps and latter steps only affect localised parts of the fly, an error in a latter step that is not rectified will only affect a localised area. So, as an embryo develops, it is divided into successively smaller regions. These regions grow autonomously despite signals between regions allowing for some integration. This modularity of development enables accuracy, repair, and repeatability. Furthermore, and of consequence over generations to enabling gradual evolution, it makes possible the change of one part of an organism without affecting another part.

Advances in molecular biology and evolutionary biology mean that we tend to overemphasise and overestimate their importance in the development of an organism. However, as Lewontin and Blumberg stress in their respective books *The Triple Helix* and *Freaks*, the organism is a function of the gene and the environment, a topic we consider in the next chapter. The environment comprises the physical or molecular components present during development as well as the conditions such as pressure, temperature, chemicals, and so on. These processes are somewhat random in nature. However, it would be unwise to dismiss both the importance of the environment and the highly ordered relationship between it and the developing organism. Study of this order and relationship is in its infancy and science is, at present at least, relatively poorly equipped to resolve its minutiae. But I believe that achieving this will reveal an order of complexity and beauty that rivals the revelations that we see in the field of molecular biology. These and other mechanisms have been proposed, but we are yet to know which, if any, is correct.

Multicellular development

In this part of the book, we have reviewed some of the functional processes of a 'typical' cell of a complex multicellular organism such as a human. These processes have been refined over billions of years of evolutionary pressure, resulting in a highly efficient and integrated collection of systems. We have looked briefly at the development of an organism and discussed its parallels with the very process of evolution that gave rise to it. So, before we investigate the theory of evolution by natural selection, I will discuss briefly this critical step in the evolution of life on Earth — the jump from single-cellular organisms to integrated multicellular species.

How multicellular development emerged billions of years ago is lost in time and unknown to us — we can only speculate on it. One insight made by the American evolutionary biologist John Tyler Bonner was that all species that exist today have ancestry going back billions of years, and that the size of organisms is under constant selective pressure to be larger. Early in the history of life on Earth when every organism was unicellular, multicellularity was the key step by which they could get bigger. Perhaps, for aquatic organisms, a mutation occurred that caused a failure to separate after cell division, but this proved to be beneficial to the collective.

For terrestrial organisms such as bacteria or early slime moulds, it is possible that cells aggregated (perhaps under certain environmental conditions as is seen with modern-day slime moulds) and became mutually dependent, eventually leading to multicellularity and functional diversification of constituent cells. However that was achieved, once done, paved the way for integrated systems to evolve. Complex extra-, inter-, and intracellular signalling systems were needed for a multicellular organism to prosper. Thus, our size and complexity are the inevitable result of natural selective pressures acting on solutions to these problems over time.

What do we know of this giant leap to multicellularity? It is impossible to know what the first signals in multicellular development were since even in simple modern organisms, the initial simplicity has been lost under a mass of additional and often redundant pathways following many millions of years of refinement. Bonner had proposed that the most useful tool to reconstruct what were the first signalling pathways is mathematical modelling and by asking "what is the minimum signal needed to produce a pattern?" Here, 'pattern' might mean the stalk cell-to-spore ratio of a simple slime mould, for example.

The English codebreaker Alan Turing was instrumental in using such models to look at developmental patterns. He did pioneering work on the chemical basis of morphogenesis and published an influential paper in 1952, two years before his untimely death. This work meant that it was possible to mathematically model patterns during an organism's development and influenced developmental biology in a paradigm-changing way. These models, in their modern adaptation, enable scientists to try and reconstruct the simplest rules that cause patterns (e.g., mathematical modelling of stem cell differentiation in order to learn how to produce differentiated tissue for therapeutic cell transplantation) and enable life in the simplest of organisms. Such rules may represent those followed, in a genetic context, by Earth's simplest and oldest organisms, and from these early genetic failures and successes at multicellularity, the winners' have led to the diversity of life that exists today.

From our glimpse into a cell's processes, how an organism's constituent cells develop into the whole organism as a result of programmed self-integration, and briefly, the evolutionary leap to multicellularity — how *all* these processes came to be — forms the topic of the next chapter: evolution by natural selection. Evolution explains how all the complex organisms we see today originated many millions of generations ago from far simpler organisms existing in different environments and in response to different environmental pressures. As Bonner states, the beginnings of life were simple, and simplicity underlies all the complications we see on Earth today due to the refinements of the processes of natural selection.

5 The Evolving World

i) The World Before Darwin

The physics of the large- and small-scale Universe; the biological mechanisms of life; the thoughts from philosophers concerning what we do and can know about the reality in which we are embedded — these topics encompass our physical selves, our surroundings, and how we interact with and interpret them. Yet it remains remarkable that this knowledge and these questions result from a species that has evolved over billions of years from the simplest origins. Indeed, Earth's distant past consisted only of inanimate matter, and natural processes acting on that matter over immense time created something that has sensations and is intelligent and self-conscious. That process is *evolution by natural selection*.

The subject of evolution, whether we are talking specifically of humankind or the theory proposed by Charles Darwin (1809–1882), is one of the greatest interests in science, and this interest runs deeper than simply the desire for familiarity with the details of the process. We ponder how the diversity and complexity of life, including conscious and intelligent life, could have evolved from simple organisms and we look for similarities or differences with other species, both living and extinct. To follow the details of the theory, including the new insights provided by molecular biology and genomics as we saw in the previous chapter, is to believe and understand the power of evolution by natural selection. Whether or not the depth and insight of human consciousness is a fortunate by-product of evolutionary processes (to be discussed later), every other aspect of life certainly exists as a result of its process.

Evolution is the theory that species undergo gradual physical change in order to survive and reproduce in a competitive and changing environment. New species develop from ancestral forms as a result of gradual change according to external pressures. The definition of species varies, but the German evolutionary biologist Ernst Mayr's version considers a species as "a group of actually or potentially interbreeding populations that is reproductively isolated from other such groups".

Opinion concerning the theory of evolution has changed a lot since Charles Darwin presented his ideas in his book, *The Origin of Species*, in 1859. His theories were at odds with the then current understanding of what caused species change. Prior to Darwin, the ideas of Jean Baptiste Lamarck (1744–1829) were considered correct. Lamarck, a French naturalist, believed that adaptations were caused by acquired characteristics inherited by offspring. That is, he thought that these adaptations were caused by behaviour and passed on to offspring which, if occurring over long periods of time, produced a new species. The famous example is his belief that a giraffe acquired its long neck through each generation of giraffe stretching to reach the high leaves on a tree where no other creature could reach; therefore, the characteristic of the longer neck was passed on to future generations. This idea was called *transmutation of species* and did not hold with there being a common ancestor for all species on Earth.

The modern unified theory of evolution uses Darwin's theory of natural selection as its framework, bolstered by the disciplines of Mendelian genetics and *population genetics*, which is the study of changes in allele frequencies due to natural selection, mutation, and chance gene flow between populations. This 'modern evolutionary synthesis' was constructed during the 1940s and is generally considered by evolutionary biologists to be the correct view of how evolution takes place.

By understanding the gene, we already have a deeper insight than Charles Darwin did as to *how* evolution by natural selection works. We will see in the following sections not only how this process occurs but also how unlikely it is that we ever came to exist at all. We may well be a chance occurrence — a sentient life form existing on a rock spinning in space around one of a hundred billion suns and in one out of a billion galaxies in one of a possible infinite ensemble of universes. Thus, our existence has depended on the Universe's conditions being right for the creation of life and for there to be a planet of the necessary stability, temperature, and raw materials for evolution to act upon. Additionally, our appearance on such a planet is the result of a number of chance events that have directed the evolutionary process such that the causal chain leading to our existence, in terms of changing environments and pressures, is perhaps the most remarkable aspect of the theory of all.

So, if we step back from the evolution of life on Earth for a moment and look at life itself, how unlikely *is* it? If there is one Universe, then is it remarkable that life can exist in it, or is it in fact common? And if there are infinite universes, is it more likely that life can evolve in at least one than if there is only one Universe? And why has life evolved in ours and not another? Are such questions important, and answerable?

The anthropic principle: How likely is life?

Science and philosophy grapple with such problems, but perhaps the answer lies beyond our tools of scientific rigour and even human comprehension. According to the anthropic principle, from many possible universes which mostly comprise conditions hostile to the development of intelligent life as we understand it, we exist in one of the few that does actually support intelligent life. We can infer facts about this Universe because we have reached a stage of awareness where we can reason and investigate our environment — if the Universe was different, this would not be the case. Yet, if an infinite ensemble of universes comprise universes of infinite conditions, then those with conditions that support life that can evolve to a state where it can ponder its own existence are no more remarkable than those with conditions that support properties alien to our knowledge of our Universe. Thus, if there *are* an infinite ensemble of universes and conditions, and one such condition enables life such as humanity, then we are proof of that condition.

The computer scientist Jürgen Schmidhuber argues that all the anthropic principle really says is that the probability of finding oneself in a universe compatible with one's existence is 1. If there is just one Universe, and we know that it produces sentient life, then the Universe necessarily supports life and our existence is unremarkable. If there are infinite universes with different conditions, some of which support life, then to find life in one is, again, pretty unremarkable.

We cannot know if there are conditions within an infinite ensemble that *do not* support life. Our knowledge is only of the Universe we inhabit, so what is remarkable is not the presence of life in this Universe (as we have no case to the contrary) but whether life in our Universe is common or rare. The Universe is huge — about 136 billion light years across — and we have knowledge of only a minute portion of it. Familiarity decreases with distance. The special theory of relativity informs us of the limitations imposed on reality as to how we might obtain knowledge of this Universe. We only have intimate knowledge of our solar system and, so far, we have found no other life there. Yet, that is like examining two adjacent grains of sand in the Sahara desert in order to form an impression of the whole.

Even if we are wise and fortunate enough to exist long enough to develop technology to explore other solar systems in our region of the galaxy, it seems unlikely that we will ever be able to ascertain whether or not other life exists elsewhere in our Universe. Indeed, the vastness of space means that even if we do find life in another solar system, this might represent an unlikely coincidence of an extremely unlikely event.

In Chapter 3, we discussed the physics that enables life in our Universe and on this planet to exist, and various versions of the anthropic principle debate the philosophical meaning behind this. Whether or not a Universe supporting life is unlikely (and invoking additional universes may add credibility to the special nature of where we exist, but in fact, it is a claim beyond the realms of testability) or life on Earth is a unique, unlikely occurrence in a Universe that can support life, the fact remains that our Universe is what it is, and on one planet in that Universe, life *has* evolved. Such debates on whether we are alone in the Universe or not are thus more philosophical than scientific.

We know that conditions here are likely to be similar elsewhere as witnessed by NASA's Kepler project to identify Earth-like planets orbiting distant stars (albeit beyond our technological limit of contact), so life is likely to have existed, exist, or will exist somewhere else. Knowing this possibility without the capacity to prove it will be yet another uncertainty that the human mind must deal with. To put the sense of loneliness and frustration in context, life has also existed on Earth that we will never encounter.

However, as scientists, we use the fossil record to make strides towards understanding how we came to exist within the context of Earth's history.

What is clear is that on Earth, human beings are unique on account of our mental ability. Our capacity to reason enables us to *understand* the evolutionary process — a process that has resulted in a sentient life form with the ability to resolve and comprehend the very process of its own creation. From this, we gain deep insight into what we are, where we came from, and just how unlikely it is that we came to exist at all. Evolution provides a link between us, the planet, our cosmic habitat, and the flora and fauna that have existed and shaped our existence. The most remarkable aspect of evolution though, as I have stressed above, is that it has the capacity to enable ordered matter to produce understanding. That of all things should make one feel a sense of duty to preserve this special place where conditions are capable of producing life and its *pièce de résistance*, consciousness.

The origins of life

This chapter focuses on the origin of species, not of life. That is, the origin and cause of the variability between defined and different sets of organisms. The origin of life is a completely different problem. However, four main hypotheses have been suggested for the origin of life:

1. There is no origin to life-it coexists with energy and matter in an infinite, eternal Universe. Seeds of life are thought to travel through space to other planets.
2. Life was started in the past by a supernatural event.
3. Life happened here as a result of its arrival from another part of the Universe.
4. Life arose on this planet according to the chemical and physical laws that we understand take place on Earth.

    (Number 4 is the most widely accepted point of view).

Two key questions arise from this- does intelligent life exist elsewhere in the Universe, and did life evolve more than once on Earth? The third hypothesis obviously relates to the arrival of simple life and its evolution into intelligent life on Earth. Whether or not intelligent life exists elsewhere in the Universe is an interesting question. The step from simple non-sentient life to intelligent life is as great as that from no life at all to simple organisms and takes, on Earth at least, billions of years.

It's certainly clear that Earth's physical environment is very 'special' to permit life as we know it, as we saw in Chapter 2 with Martin Rees and his six numbers relating to the fundamental nature of the Universe. For example, our distance from the Sun permits the ideal temperature range for life as we know it; the long-term stability of our sun has enabled evolutionary processes to occur over a very long period of time; we have a stable planetary orbit of the Sun (aided by the presence of a large moon); there is the presence of other large outer planets (Jupiter and Saturn) to attract comets and prevent collisions with Earth, and our location in the galaxy is such that our distance from others suns and cosmic rays eliminates the hazards associated with them. Thus, our type of life requires very particular conditions and is, thus, unlikely. However, the sheer number of opportunities in space and time, in a single or multiverse context, means that since it has happened here, it has probably happened elsewhere. But what does that say about intelligent life of a fundamentally different constitution from our own?

Our consideration of intelligence is limited to what we understand as intelligence. What lies beyond our comprehension is alien to both definition and understanding, as our conception is limited largely by what we are as terrestrial animals and how we perceive primate intelligence to have developed. For example, we consider dolphins to be highly intelligent yet have no conception of how communication over distance underwater is achieved by these remarkable animals or other cetaceans. We do not understand how birds can migrate halfway around the world and what navigational cues they follow. To know of intelligent life elsewhere that is of a type allied to our own conception of it will require technology on their part, or significant progress on ours, to enable transfer of information relating to that intelligence. Furthermore, if the intelligent life 'out there' is less advanced than us, it falls to us to seek it out.

There is debate on the second question as to whether life on Earth evolved more than once. The method of replication of genetic material in organisms we see on Earth today involves nucleic acids, mostly in the form of DNA, as the template for inherited physical characteristics. During Earth's primordial biological beginnings, were there other methods of replication in the simple organisms that existed in our early seas that weren't based on DNA, and which didn't survive because that particular evolutionary experiment wasn't successful? We cannot know. Did all organisms we see today evolve from one simple organism, or group of organisms, into an ever-expanding tree of diversity? Or did evolution occur from independent populations of different/similar organisms that used the same mechanism of replication, but whose environmental coexistence occurred long after the initial evolutionary success of the isolated species? Such questions, with the methods we use today, are also difficult to answer with certainty.

ii) Evolution

Charles Darwin

Charles Darwin originally studied medicine at Edinburgh University before turning to theology at Cambridge. His interest in natural history was sparked during these times, but it was not until his five-year voyage on the HMS Beagle as a 22-year-old, fulfilling the roles of the ship's unpaid naturalist and geologist, that his conception of the theory of natural selection began to take shape.

The long voyage took him around the world and he tried to account for the diversity of life that he witnessed. A major reason for the voyage was to survey the coastlines of South America and make more detailed maps for navigation. In that time, Darwin spent much time on land, where he was struck by the apparent similarity between certain living animals and the fossilised remains of long-dead animals from the same regions. He also, of course, visited the Galapagos Islands on the Equator where he observed finches, giant tortoises, and mockingbirds among other creatures. When he was not suffering from seasickness, he slowly modelled a complete theory that could accommodate and account for the diversity of species and would apply for any system. Despite clarifying in his mind the elements of the theory as early as 1838, it took another twenty years of procrastination and refinement before he was to publish his work in 1859 as *Origin of Species by Means of Natural Selection, or the Preservation of Favoured Races in the Struggle of Life* (now known as *The Origin of Species*).

The theory of evolution is usually attributed to Darwin, sometimes in accordance with the Englishman Alfred Russell Wallace whose ideas were initially in agreement with those of Darwin, and whose own publication indeed propelled Darwin into hurriedly completing and publishing his own ideas. However, despite Darwin's encouragement, Wallace did not continue along a focused path as did Darwin and in later life turned more to spiritual explanations for biological phenomena.

Darwin believed that those creatures that were best adapted to their environment were more likely to survive. That is, the ones with the physical characteristics that could most ably utilise the environment in which they lived would have the greatest chance of surviving and thus reproducing. Although they do not change themselves during their lifetime (which was Lamarck's viewpoint), the characteristics they possessed gave them advantages over other individuals of the same species with respect to their environment. These characteristics also served their progeny well.

Darwin did not know of the gene or genetics as this was nearly ten years before Gregor Mendel's first publication on the inheritance of traits in the pea plant, but he knew that characteristics were retained in the offspring (again contrasting with Lamarck's view, which was that offspring acquired new characteristics as they grew, like the giraffe stretching its neck). In other words, in a changing environment, the physiology of the individuals that survived was more adapted to the environment in which they lived compared to the average level of adaptation of the previous generation. This gave those individuals a greater chance of survival, a selective physiological advantage, which was retained in the offspring. The net result is that with each generation, the species in question gradually changes to another form with different morphological characteristics from the form from which it developed in order to prosper in a changing environment. This is called *speciation*.

Ultimately, new species would result that would be unable to interbreed with the progenitor and, over long periods of time, some progenitor species may become extinct. Despite the acceptance of these ideas, Darwin did not have a clear explanation of how variation is achieved — he believed parental characteristics blended with the offspring — nor could he explain his theory experimentally. However, Mendel's work on peas overcame this weakness with the discovery of particulate inheritance.

Darwin's ideas were greeted with mixed emotions. Religious animosity to the theory began almost as soon as Darwin presented his ideas due to natural selection's indirect challenge to religious belief in the importance of man over other organisms through man's special link with God. Many were unwilling to believe its implication that we are merely advanced apes, which is something that Darwin would more strongly suggest in his later work, 'The Descent of Man'.

Proof that we evolved from the same simple ancient organisms as other living organisms using the sciences of genetics and evolutionary biology and the knowledge of DNA and protein sequence homology between organisms (i.e., similarities indicative of common ancestry) means that the fundamental concepts of natural selection are irrefutable, as I will go on to describe. Yet in Darwin's time, DNA was unknown and the idea was a theory in its infancy. He did not possess the factual arsenal that we now have to support his theory. Chiefly because of ill health, Darwin left much of the defence against the many misunderstandings of his theory to his 'bulldog', Thomas Huxley.

The religious-scientific debate has been raging in its various guises for 150 years, but in the context of man, evolution is not an attack on religion or a belittling of humankind. It is, from one perspective, a celebration of our mind and, from another, a fact of life. After all, it is our minds that define our uniqueness among the animals. If something cannot be falsified but can be verified, then — however extraordinary it may seem — science has to accept it as credible because further hypotheses as to its nature must inherently be testable. Religion, however, views scientific insights in the context of how they challenge doctrine and is often sceptical for this reason. Through necessity, it refines doctrine to accommodate scientific fact, but care is taken not to harm the role of a deity or push the limits of religious credibility.

After a long period of ignoring the theory, the Catholic Church moved to a neutral position in the 1950s and eventually acceptance later on. However, this acceptance is somewhat ambiguous in that the Church states that faith and the theory of evolution do not conflict, although humans are a 'special creation' and God is necessary for their creation. God has long had a place in man's psyche ever since such a deity was first invoked to give reason to all that seemed unexplainable. However, despite human progress in scientific explanation, rather than marvel at our ingenuity, we have often suppressed ideas that appear in conflict with religion (Galileo was a case in point). Yet without the logical possibility of ever providing a testable proof for the non-existence, or existence, of an omnipotent supernatural entity, God will continue to be ingrained in human culture, providing a sense of morality, togetherness, purpose, and meaning.

Although the theory of evolution has repelled all attempts to refute it, it still receives disapproval outside of science, such as from current Creationist lobbyists. Other 'sciences' suffer less despite standing on much less solid foundations. Why is this? Take the *Gaia hypothesis* that was devised by James Lovelock as an example. Named after the Greek goddess of life, this theory postulated that the physical and chemical conditions of the atmosphere and oceans of Earth have been actively made fit by the presence of life on it. It regards all living things on the planet as part of a single living being, and each component affects the environment's ability to sustain life. It focuses mainly on biological feedback mechanisms, which regulate and sustain conditions that support life over long, geological periods of time; in turn, these are essential for evolution to occur. However, these can be explained without necessity for Gaia.

The modified Gaia theory, now in its third incarnation, proposes that regulation at a state fit for life is a property of the whole system of life, air, rocks, and ocean. It contrasts with conventional wisdom, which sees life adapting to the physical conditions on Earth as life and the planet evolve their separate ways. This holistic vision is immediately appealing and contrasts with the perceived implications of evolution. Thus, it was greeted favourably inside and external to the scientific community because it allows other theories such as evolution to coexist with it, and the role of God can be incorporated without additional compromise.

However appealing though, Gaia theory has been found wanting when subjected to stringent scientific scrutiny. It has some strong supporters within the scientific community, such as the American biologist Lynn Margulis, whereas others, such as Richard Dawkins, consider it to be more a metaphor for life than a real scientific hypothesis. It does not make predictions that can be experimentally verified and, indeed, the timespans involved may make the construction of testable hypotheses impossible. However, it has encouraged thinking of the planet as an interconnected whole rather than as disparate parts (like Bohm's approach to the Universe), and some aspects of the Gaia hypothesis, such as long-term natural changes in ocean currents or weather patterns, may be evoked regularly by climate change sceptics in defence of their beliefs.

Science does not choose what it wants to believe (no one would choose the implications of quantum theory) — it demands rigour, proof, and verification. Hypotheses are built and then tested, allowing scientific fact to grow. Intrinsic to the scientific method is the pursuit of truth and the rejection of falsehood. It accepts what cannot be falsified but can be verified. The theory of evolution satisfies the scientific method and sits comfortably with all sciences that satisfy the same level of rigour and share the same compatible scientific foundations. It is a theory that some would like not to be true because it does offend on a spiritual and emotional level. But science, the most rigorous of critics, cannot refute it because acceptance is determined by scientific fact alone.

Today, science tends to proceed by gradual change, with additions and modifications to a current paradigm achieved through an interconnected scientific community — for instance, witness the time and effort taken to test and prove Peter Higgs' 1964 proposal of the so-called Higgs particle using the Large Hadron Collider at CERN. Yet when a new model for a concept is presented, it is often greeted with scepticism. Whether or not the details of the new model fit the existing data, other factors such as money, careers, pride, and belief can motivate heated defence of the old model or entrenched viewpoints. Even quantum theory was greeted originally with intense scepticism as it challenged the classical construction.

Darwinism and natural selection

Darwinism is the name given to the concept of the mechanism of evolutionary change. The central thesis is that in a varied population of organisms, only those individuals that are best adapted to the environment in which they live will survive and reproduce. Individuals less well-adapted will tend not to be able to reproduce through the competitive struggle with and indirect pressure from better-adapted individuals. The characteristics that make the better-adapted individual survive will thus become more common in future generations through their reproduction, whereas those of less well-adapted individuals will become extinct. Darwin called this 'struggle for survival' *natural selection*. It can be argued that the Giant Panda is an example of a species that is increasingly poorly adapted to its environment and heading for extinction; it restricts itself to mainly one food source (bamboo), its range is becoming more restricted due to human encroachment and agriculture, and from what is observed in captivity, its reproductive rate is poor.

A species' physical characteristics may change over time in response to external pressures. This means that new species that are incapable of interbreeding with the original species from which it evolved will result. Thus, natural selection acting on a varied population results in evolution. The finches of the Galapagos Islands are an example of this, as I will discuss later. Natural selection became known as the process whereby certain organisms are more successful from a reproductive point of view than others. As a result, they pass on their traits to the next generation in a disproportionate manner. The central point of Darwin's view was the separation found between the environmental problems presented, and the internal forces in the organism to provide solutions to these problems-with the most suitable solution being preserved.

Darwin based his theory on three observations and two deductions:

Observations:
1. An organism has a tendency to multiply in geometric progression.
2. The number of species remains constant over long periods of time.
3. All living things vary.

Deductions:
1. Based on the first two observations, he deduced that a constant struggle for life exists. There is constant competition between organisms to reproduce.
2. This process is natural selection. The organisms with favourable characteristics are more likely to survive and reproduce than those with less favourable characteristics.

The rule of life according to Darwin is to *adapt or die*. Darwin was aware that with a limited supply of food, populations of organisms cannot expand exponentially. He was also aware of the process of natural selection by predation. Here, predators act to maintain an equilibrium of prey in the population which, in turn, equilibrates the population of the predator.

From another perspective, the evolutionary purpose of natural selection is to increase the population of organisms that are closest to the optimal phenotype — the physical characteristics, as opposed to genotype, which is the genetic make-up — for the competitive environmental conditions wherein they reside. Since the terms genotype and phenotype will be used throughout this section, it is important to recall the difference between them and how they relate to each other. The genotype refers to an individual's entire collection of heritable genes — this is universally agreed upon. However, what is not agreed on is how this affects the phenotype.

The *Philip's World Encyclopaedia* defines phenotype as "physical characteristics of an organism resulting from heredity. Phenotype is distinctive from genotype, since not all aspects of genetic make-up manifest themselves". Hence, when modern reductionist evolutionary biologists who believe that the complexity of nature is understandable by reducing it to an interaction of its constituent parts state that "genotype defines phenotype", they imply that an organism's genes 'compute' the organism.

As Richard Lewontin states in his book *Human Diversity*, the phenotype of an organism is made of several aspects, namely its morphology, physiology, and behaviour, and these are temporally changing. Hence, an individual with a genetic tendency to be, say, overweight or a fast runner will only be one of these depending on how the environment *allows* this genetic trait to manifest; it is not set in stone. We will discuss in a later section Lewontin's views on the relationship between genes and the environment. However, phenotype hereon refers to this environmentally and temporally changing entity.

There are three main types of natural selection whose aim is to achieve the best result for the population for the set of conditions. These are:

1. **Stabilising** natural selection — this favours the mean (the arithmetic average or the sum divided by the number of individuals) at the expense of each extreme of the distribution. This process maintains the effect of directional natural selection.

2. **Directional** natural selection — this favours one of the phenotypic extremes, resulting in an eventual random distribution around the optimal phenotype.
3. **Disruptive** natural selection — this favours the two extremes at the expense of the mean.

These categories represent aspects of the entire process of natural selection.

No scientist doubts that the organisms of today have evolved over billions of years from organisms that were very different from them, and that most types of organisms have long been extinct. Extinction is the inevitable consequence of any species' existence, however successful it might be, and it is a natural process resulting from the differential survivorship of different forms. *Darwinian* theory is considered correct in its implication, but the reality of life's evolutionary processes is more complicated than merely survival of the fittest. In fact, it contains many matters of contention that we will discuss later in this section.

Adaptive radiation

Adaptive radiation is an idea that developed from the theory of natural selection. It describes the gradual formation of different species from a common ancestor through evolutionary processes where the adapted species becomes more specialised for a new niche. The most-well known example of this process is the case of Darwin's finches, first seen and documented by him in 1835 on his voyage around the Galapagos Islands (although it was the differences in populations of mockingbirds from island to island, a bird he had first seen on the South American mainland, that aroused his curiosity initially).

Here, the beaks of different finch species are adapted for the different diets accessible to the birds within their ecological niches across the different islands. Each finch possesses a beak specific to the task set by the particular food on the island they inhabit, such as broad beaks for cracking large seeds and narrow beaks for wheedling insects out of tree bark. It was supposed that these finches evolved from a more generalised ancestral island colonist that, over time, diverged into distinct species.

Darwin realised that the isolation of the specialised species, together with the observed inherent variation and competition for available niches, is responsible for the adaptive radiation. Specific to the islands, these finches are very similar in appearance apart from their beaks and their diets. Darwin had also observed something similar on the mainland with respect to the exclusive niches occupied by two distinct species of rhea. Thus, the way species appear is dependent on geography and environment.

Species generally arise through a process called *allopatric speciation*, which is a process whereby a once continuous population becomes split due to geographical change, usually over a long period of time, allowing for the formation of two new species. This phenomenon occurs because the isolated populations of the same species take on different evolutionary paths due to their existing among different pressures. They become so different over time that they would be unable to interbreed again, hence they evolve into separate species (over the shorter course of time, these would be referred to as *subspecies*). This is apparent with the distinct populations of giant tortoise found on the Galapagos Islands and the fate of 'Lonesome George', the last surviving tortoise from the island of Pinta. Moved to captivity, attempts were made to mate him with several young females from a closely related subspecies found on Isabella Island, but the three resulting clutches of eggs were all infertile.

What is interesting about the adaptive radiation seen in Darwin's finches though is that modern studies indicate that evolution is taking place in what may be termed 'real time' rather than over a very long period of time. The British evolutionary biologists Rosemary and Peter Grant started observing Galapagos finch populations on an annual basis in the early 1970s and found that the finches can evolve according to climatic conditions. Finches with intermediate-sized beaks struggle in times of drought when small seeds are scarcer, yet those members of the population with slightly larger beaks are more likely to survive and pass on their genes if they are able to turn instead to larger seeds as a food source.

Another example concerns the fish of Lake Victoria. Around 500 different species of cichlid have been noted here despite the lake being only about 15,000 years old, suggesting a very rapid (in evolutionary terms) degree of speciation from the original progenitors. Environment also plays a part in speciation here as there are distinct rocky and weedy areas to this vast African lake. Some species have evolved to have small jaws packed full of teeth suitable for foraging on plant material, whereas others have thicker jaws that are able to crush snail shells.

What really is notable about these diverse observations comes from molecular studies. It turns out that a gene encoding a secreted developmental protein called Bone Morphogenic Protein 4 (BMP4), which is involved in bone and cartilage formation, is highly expressed in both thick-jawed cichlids and thick-beaked Galapagos finches. Conversely, BMP4 is weakly expressed in fine-billed finches and softer-jawed fish. Thus, evolution is economical, using the same raw materials (i.e., genes) to fashion distinct anatomical features in different species.

An area of concern relating to Darwin's theory has been that of directional evolution, whereby some organisms appear to evolve in a particular direction for which some have claimed Darwin's theory cannot hold. Some organisms do evolve as if directed towards a predetermined goal. Lamarck suggested that organisms tend towards increasing complexity, an idea that Darwin rejected. An example of this supposed predeterminism is that of horse evolution (from *Eohippus*, the first horse), which tends towards greater height and fewer toes. The horse appears to tend towards a predetermined evolutionary goal and this temporal physiological change appears to be followed by other species, a process known as parallel development. *Orthogenesis* is the hypothesis that other related species tending towards the same goal do so not through evolution working according to natural laws but because species slowly transform due to some mysterious inner or external driving forces. Despite its appeal to creationists, it is not testable. This theory also conflicts with what is known as *neo-Darwinism* (see next section).

It is now known that the apparent linear or parallel development evolution is actually a process involving much branching and adaptive radiation into different niches rather than simple, multiple predetermined phenotypic goals. The process of evolutionary change in the physiology of the horse is the same as that of any species that changes with time.

Neo-Darwinism

Neo-Darwinism represents an incorporation of Darwin's theory of evolution through natural selection with the implications and development of the work of Mendel. This expanded version explains much of what was implied in the initial version but could not be explained without an appreciation of the importance of Mendel's work. It presents the idea that the adaptation of the organism to the environment occurs by natural selection acting upon small, inherited, variations which are initially non-adaptive.

Mutation is the ultimate cause of a new variation, and this mutation is preserved by inheritance. Although some genetic material has been shown to move during evolution from species to species by means of viruses, we will concentrate on evolution by selection/mutation. Some critics of neo-Darwinism claim that it does not account for rapid evolutionary activity interspersed with periods of inactivity. A reply could be that perhaps large genetic mutations result in larger phenotypic change, thus the inherent slowness of a neo-Darwinian change.

As well as the idea of sudden change, we must consider one of intermediary change. For example, the eye could not have evolved by mutation in an organism without an eye directly to a form that possesses an eye. However, any intermediary stage with an increased awareness of light direction or colour perception, or a move towards devoting more brain capacity to visual perception (e.g., around two thirds of the fruit fly brain is devoted to vision) would have been beneficial to the organism. An example here might be the evolutionary conservation of *eyeless*/PAX6 described in Chapter 4.

Mutations are heritable changes in the DNA sequence of genes. These can occur naturally or be caused artificially by radiation (X-rays and UV rays) and chemicals. The type of mutation depends on the nature of the chemical and the energy of radiation. High energy X-rays can cleave DNA, leading to rearrangement of the chromosomes. Lower energy UV rays can cause changes such as point mutations. Here, a DNA base of the wrong type is inserted at a particular location. Despite this, mutations are considered by some evolutionists to be the fundamental raw material of evolution and are the basis for variability in the population.

Natural selection preserves the organism with the most suitable phenotypic result of gene arrangement for the environment in which it lives. Good and bad mutations are passed to offspring in both asexual (prokaryotic) and sexual (eukaryotic) reproductive processes. However, sexual reproduction benefits populations of an organism because sexual populations are able to evolve more rapidly in response to a changing environment than asexual populations due to the ability to exchange chromosomes and therefore generate greater genetic diversity in resulting progeny. Furthermore, in sexual populations, deleterious mutations occurring in two individuals might not be passed on to their progeny.

Sexual reproduction also benefits the survival of the individual as well as the population. Asexual reproduction leads to genetically identical offspring whereas each result of sexual reproduction is genetically different. Hence, each might be better (or less well) adapted to the environment it encounters than the parent, but not be identically adapted. The English evolutionary biologist John Maynard Smith's analogy is that you have more chance in winning a raffle with ten different numbers than a hundred tickets with the same number.

As Mendel was essential to the formulation of neo-Darwinism, classical Mendelian genetics is named in his honour. Mendel's experiments on the common garden pea operated on the basis of characteristics being controlled by one gene (though at the time he did not know of the existence of genes), which show a simple dominant or recessive relationship between gene *alleles*. He noticed that recognisable traits such as flower colour or plant height were inherited independently rather than through blending in subsequent generations. He published his famous paper on the inheritance of traits in pea plants, titled *Experiments on Plant Hybridization*, in 1866.

This was only a few years after Darwin's book, *The Origin of Species*, yet because Mendel's paper was published in an obscure German periodical, it was not until 1900 that its full implications were realised. Thus, Darwin never knew of Mendel's work despite it already being in print for 16 years of Darwin's life — a sharp contrast with today's internet-based research that allows scientists to be aware of worldwide research as it is being done! It would be another 35 years before Mendel's work was rediscovered at the start of the 20th century.

Alleles are one of two or more alternative forms of the same gene, inherited from each parent. This combined inheritance occurs because the female gamete, the egg, and the male gamete, the spermatozoa, both of which contain a single or haploid copy of all genes of the organism, fuse during fertilisation and establish a new set of double or diploid copies. Dominant genes for a particular trait show themselves in the organism over a recessive gene for a different version of the same trait (e.g., eye colour, where having blue eyes is a recessive trait). Understanding alleles explains why traits are shown in offspring, and indeed explains the various inheritable traits that Mendel observed in the pea.

Take the rare hereditary condition of albinism as an example. An albino lacks pigment in the skin, hair, and eyes. Normal skin colour is caused by the amino acid phenylalanine being converted to tyrosine and finally to the pigment melanin. In an albino, the conversion of tyrosine to melanin is not possible. To explain dominant and recessive Mendelian genetics in action, let us denote 'A' as the normal, dominant gene for converting tyrosine to melanin and 'a' as the albino, recessive version of the gene that is unable to do this. So, why do we see albinism?

As most eukaryotes contain at least two copies of each gene, an individual will inherit one copy of the albinism gene (either 'A' or 'a') from each parent, so an individual that is 'Aa' (which we call heterozygous, meaning it has one of each allele, as opposed to homozygous, where both alleles are the same) for this trait will not show albinism as the 'A' allele is dominant over the 'a' allele. Let us now imagine that an 'Aa' male mates with an 'Aa' female. The probability for the offspring being albino (homozygous recessive) according to Mendelian genetics is one in four as shown in Figure 38. This is the only genotype that displays albinism in the phenotype. The genotypes AA (homozygous dominant), Aa, and aA (heterozygous dominant) that are possible from the mating would not show albinism in the phenotype as 'A' is dominant over 'a', even though heterozygotes carry the recessive allele.

As I mentioned, Mendel had no concept of genes (the *germinal units* that he said controlled characteristics are now called genes), but he did formulate two laws to explain the pattern of inheritance:

PARENTS	Father Aa	Father Aa	Father Aa	Father Aa
	Mother Aa	Mother Aa	Mother Aa	Mother Aa
Offspring	AA	Aa	aA	aa
Result	normal	Normal	normal	albino

Figure 38. Probability for albino offspring. Key: underlining indicates which genes are passed on to the offspring.

1. The first **Law of Segregation** states that a character exists as two factors, both of which are present in body cells but only one in sex cells, or gametes (ovaries and testes).
2. The second **Law of Independent Assortment** states that the distribution of factors to gametes is random.

His first law holds true but the second law only applies to allelic pairs found on different chromosomes.

Refining Darwinism as modern evolutionary theory — with the added knowledge of Mendelism (neo-Darwinism), population genetics, and molecular biology — provides us with a deeper insight into evolutionary processes than Darwin had. But before we look at different modern interpretations of Darwin's theory of evolution through the work of the American palaeontologist Stephen Jay Gould, Richard Dawkins, and Richard Lewontin, it is important to realise how profoundly Darwin's insights have affected our understanding of ourselves through sciences whose own evolution have been greatly affected by Darwinism. From the flourishing of our understanding of development, genetics, and comparative anatomy, we are able to answer fundamental questions about life, such as how species develop and why different species seem to evolve together.

Methods and insights of the theory of evolution

Evolution and development: Comparative anatomy

We know that species have evolved from common ancestors and scientists like to interpret this mechanism. Comparative anatomy, or homology, represents a method of comparing species' differences according to anatomy. Species that make up a larger group, such as a phylum, have many resemblances in relation to physical characteristics. For example, all chordates, the phylum to which all vertebrates including man belong, show a bilateral body plan with two eyes, two forelimbs, two hind limbs, and so on. During chordate development, each species passes through a *phylotypic* stage in which all chordates are almost indistinguishable. After this stage, the species diverge in structure.

As mentioned when we looked at development in Chapter 4, during the second half of the 19th century, there was much interest in the link between vertebrate development and the process of evolution. It was noted that the embryos of vertebrates are so similar that we cannot determine merely by looking at the early embryo whether it is, for example, a pig or a bird. Ernst Haeckel took such ideas and summarised them as *ontogeny recapitulates phylogeny*. Thus, the development of the individual repeats the evolution of the *phylum*, or the group to which it belongs. One way of viewing this is that when the organism is developing, it ascends its evolutionary developmental tree.

This *recapitulation evidence* is not considered today to be totally correct and recapitulation theory is regarded as pseudoscience. While some recapitulation is accepted, it is not widely believed that when, say, a human develops, he or she passes through fish and reptilian stages. Embryonic development is much more complicated than this, despite the fact that the evolutionary process uses genes, organs, or appendages common to earlier species to develop new body parts rather than design from scratch. For example, the wings of birds are thought to have evolved from the arms (or forelimbs) of feathered dinosaurs of which birds are the evolutionary descendants.

The preservation of a constant body plan between organisms despite different lifestyles has long been known. The hand of a human is structurally similar to the flipper of a dolphin, for example. Strong supportive evidence for the theory of evolution is the preservation of the phylotype between members of a phylum. However, from an evolutionary standpoint, it is thought that phylotypic conservation was forced on organisms so that gradual change could be adaptive.

Medical research and particularly advances in DNA manipulation techniques such as whole genome sequencing across multiple species has taught us a great deal about developmental stages in vertebrates. For example, the homeotic genes in *Drosophila* that organise body plan have their mammalian counterparts, as I outlined in the preceding chapter, and the evolutionary preservation of the defining region of these transcription factor genes and the homeobox domain coupled with expansion in numbers of Hox genes is crucial to the spatiotemporal structural development seen in vertebrates. The conservation of DNA sequence across species, and hence conservation of the encoded amino sequence of critical functional domains such as the homeodomain, proves the role of evolution in conserving useful genes and proteins for the continued construction of new and more complex organisms. Genetic profiling has established evolutionary links between species of different groups by comparing their DNA sequences.

Genetic comparisons are also useful the more related the species are since physical characteristics and anatomical similarities become too slight. Evolution is a conservative process. As mentioned above, nature does not tend to develop new anatomical structures; rather, it remodels existing ones during species development. If the organ is not remodelled, it becomes useless and vestigial, much like the human appendix which in herbivores is crucial for digesting the cellulose in grass and other plant material that makes up much of the herbivore's diet.

Species and populations

An area of interest in evolutionary theory is how populations and species develop. Populations may become reduced due to climatic changes, predation, disease, natural catastrophes, or even war. For example, there is concern that deforestation programmes reduce habitat size, thus reducing the 'gene pool' for the continued success of a species by creating smaller pockets of genetically isolated populations (a possible contributory factor in the decline of the Giant Panda). When such events occur, a reduced number of individuals of a species, which themselves may not be representative of the original gene pool, remain to pass on their genes to the next generation. This creates a bottleneck that can result in inbreeding and skewed genetic drift, or changes in allele frequencies between generations, due to an alteration in the gene frequency.

Thus, there is the danger that although the population can become large again after the bottlenecking, its genetic diversity may be reduced. Until random mutations can increase the population diversity again, the dangers of inbreeding are present, leading to organisms that are potentially less fertile or adaptable and further reducing the species' chance of survival.

Coevolution

Not only do species evolve in accordance with the environment, but they can evolve together for mutual benefit. Evolutionary interaction between plants and/or animals is a process known as *coevolution*. This term refers to pairs of species that have evolved in tandem for the benefit of both species. For example, birds feed on plants, and by this very act they disperse the seeds of the plant. There is a similar process seen between plants and insects through the pollen of the plant attaching to the body of an insect, which spreads it to another flower. Among animals, bats are also known as pollinators of certain plants. Many authorities tend to consider coevolution as referring to feeding relationships acting as selective pressures. For example, one particular species of cactus is toxic to all but one species of fruit fly, which has produced a cactus antitoxin and is thus able to uniquely exploit the feeding niche of that particular cactus.

In the sections that follow, the work of Stephen Jay Gould is used as the fulcrum around which to debate key aspects of life on Earth relating to how humans came to exist. In the discussion, the work of many scientists will be compressed into debates between Gould, Dawkins, and others so as to clarify the meaning rather than the historical progression of the ideas. This is because Gould represents what was considered a major challenge to Darwinian theory, though he did not mean it to be so. His ideas, popularised as a new version of Darwinism, were presented as an addition rather than a reappraisal of how evolution takes place.

Stephen Jay Gould and punctuated equilibrium

Stephen Jay Gould spent most of his academic career at Harvard and is one of the most well-known authors in popular science. In his book, *Wonderful Life: The Burgess Shale and The Nature of History* (1989), Gould presented his interpretation of the implications of the fossil findings from the Burgess Shale, a unique Cambrian oceanic cliff base formation found in present-day Yoho National Park, British Columbia. The Burgess Shale provided a huge number of fossils (about 80,000) representing animals whose body forms and parts were completely different from those found in animals existing today.

The American palaeontologist Charles Doolittle Walcott first found these fossils, which dated back to the Cambrian era (540–505 million years ago), in the early 1900s. Usually, fossils retain only the bony structures of organisms. What made the Burgess Shale remarkable was that the soft body parts of the organisms were fossilised as well. The unlikely combination of conditions that existed and followed where and when the creatures died as well as the subsequent rate of sedimentation made it ideal for the preservation of soft tissue.

Many of the fossils were sent to the United States National Museum in Washington, where they stayed for many years. After recent re-evaluation, it was found that much of Walcott's original categorisation of the fossils was wrong. He categorised many of the ancient animals by looking for relatedness and trying to fit them into modern taxonomic groups, yet some later, more detailed analyses showed them to be entirely different species. In short, the Burgess fossils appear to represent a burst of intense evolutionary creativity and experimentation with form.

There has been debate since 1940 about the mechanism by which evolutionary processes occur. Ernst Mayr suggested that some present-day birds evolve rapidly, a suggestion supported by the studies of the Grants on the bills of Galapagos island finches described earlier, but fossil evidence of the branching between forms would be rare or absent. If evolution were rapid between forms, the fossil record would show the former and latter stable states, but not the diversifying stages. Gould and the American palaeontologist Niles Eldredge supported this view and provided the contrasting terms *gradualism* and punctuated equilibrium to explain the opposing opinions. Gradualism is a term given to demonstrate slow evolutionary changes in a species. Eldredge and Gould proposed the idea of punctuated equilibrium in 1972 in a landmark paper entitled *Punctuated Equilibria: an Alternative to Phyletic Gradualism*.

However, it should be noted that Richard Goldschmidt of the University of California had argued the concept some 40 years earlier. This theory was based on the observation that many species appear suddenly in the fossil record while others remain unchanged over millions of years. However, what appears sudden in geological time is not sudden in genetic time. A few centimetres in rock can mean thousands of years, and that is not sudden in genetic time. Furthermore, genetic studies have shown that speciation can occur in timespans of only tens of generations.

If the fossil record is incomplete, then species can appear to change in fits and starts. But that may not mean that punctuated equilibrium is occurring; rather, it may be a false assumption from incomplete fossil records. Species studies have been performed showing that different species evolve at different rates, so debates on the two theories, gradualism and punctuated equilibrium, occur to this day. This debate is not about whether species evolve from other species (this is not in doubt) but rather about the mechanism involved.

In the opinion of many evolutionary scholars, punctuated equilibrium has received more interest than it deserves. The theory's persuasiveness is due more to Gould's energy, prose, and ability as a narrator to convince readers than a true reflection of what can be scientifically concluded from the data. Dawkins has called punctuated equilibrium a "minor wrinkle on the surface of neo-Darwinian theory". However, others of equal credibility consider it a valid explanation. Hence, although there are other theories that push the boundaries of pure Darwinism, punctuated equilibrium is discussed here as a credible modification. For one thing, it serves as an example of where a lack of data can result in the missing data being interpreted in different ways, as we saw for quantum theory earlier. Sometimes science progresses with a consensus of agreement while other times it reaches a fork in the road until more data shows the right path.

One problem is that fossil evidence normally provides no information about the soft body parts of an organism, which is the strongest indicator of differences. Without detailed records of the stages of species change, particularly of the softer body parts, it is impossible to determine the mechanism by which species change occurs. However, the Burgess Shale is a unique example of a soft-part fossil record of a specific era in our history, about 500 million years ago. Gould used this record information to promote his opinion of punctuated equilibrium, amongst other things. This is discussed at length in his book *Wonderful Life*, which we now turn to.

Wonderful Life: Decimation and diversification?

This book is both an historical account and an analysis of the Burgess Shale discoveries. Burgess was so important because without evidence of soft anatomy, it is not possible to understand the construction or diversity of ancient species.

The *Cambrian explosion* about 530 million years ago is the period of evolution of organisms on Earth for which the Burgess Shale fossils represent one geographically isolated small example. At the time of the findings, no other sites of soft tissue-preserved Cambrian life had been found, so deductions were made on Cambrian life from the findings in this small quarry. There have since been other finds elsewhere, but the fossils found at the Burgess Shale mark the advent of nearly all major groups of modern animals.

Even earlier (565 million years ago) at Mistaken Point, Newfoundland, creatures have been found. Yet, although they were the most successful species at the time and lasted for millions of years, the Mistaken Point creatures died out. Why? Because they had a simple fractal body plan with no way to evolve body parts that could adapt to the environment. They were evolutionary dead ends, but not so the organisms of the Burgess Shale. Despite Walcott's incorrect analysis of the fossils (he saw himself as a true follower of Darwin, hence proposing relatedness to known present-day groups), the real breakthrough came in the 1970s with the detailed reanalysis and interpretation of the fossils at the Smithsonian as well as from other visits to Burgess by Harry Whittington and his students, Simon Conway Morris and Derek Briggs.

The soft parts of the Burgess fauna were entombed in a variety of orientations, preserved as calcium and aluminium silicates due to the unique conditions in what became Burgess, rather than the usual carbon for traditional fossils. Due to the occurrence of multiple specimens in different orientations and of the same species, they were able to prepare accurate three-dimensional representations of the organisms for the first time. Gould drew many conclusions from this study and their implications are profound. For example, if we were to rerun evolution from the early days of the Burgess Shale, the chance of anything like human intelligence emerging would be minute.

Simon Conway Morris disagrees with this conclusion since he is not a supporter of punctuated equilibrium. In his 1998 book *The Crucible of Creation*, he argues against many of Gould's conclusions, not least the increasingly unpopular punctuated equilibrium. Primarily though, he rejects Gould's idea that if we could 'rewind the tape' of evolution and let it play again, then chance would favour a different selection and the world would contain different species. Hence, Gould saw that a lot of chance and randomness has led to what we see around us and that this run of events is just one of many possible outcomes (in the 'many worlds' interpretation of quantum theory discussed in Chapter 2, other evolutionary outcomes would exist elsewhere).

Conway Morris's belief is that the outcome of evolution is predetermined and has only happened once — that what happens is the only thing that could *ever* have happened. Predeterminism is discussed in Chapter 6, but being a believer in God, Conway Morris's interpretation of predeterminism would not necessarily imply that evolution is progressing along an inevitable course as determined by the interaction of force and matter since the Big Bang in a purely physical sense.

The first publication of a Burgess reinterpretation was in 1971 by Whittington, which served to not only reinterpret Walcott's conclusions but also provide a re-evaluation of the history of life. The Burgess Shale appeared to contain more types of creatures in terms of anatomical range than evidenced by all invertebrates alive today in the oceans. By extrapolating such conclusions from the Burgess Shale to evolutionary processes, the results pointed towards the need for a revision of the conventional progression of evolutionary processes, as depicted by the *cone of increasing diversity*.

In this picture of life's progression, species diversify from others with a net *increase* in the number of species over time. You can think of it like the trunk of a tree giving rise to large branches which then give rise to smaller ones, ad infinitum. The occurrence of diversifications is also considered to occur evenly with respect to time. This contrasts with Gould's 'stop-start' vision of the evolutionary process following his analysis of the Burgess reinterpretation.

Gould considered a new model based on *decimation and diversification* to be consistent with the Burgess reinterpretation. Here, there is rapid diversification of species where some evolve but others die out, and those that survive diversify further from a reduced number of starting species. Thus, the history of life is not a smooth continuum of development but rather one that is punctuated by brief episodes of extinction and subsequent diversification among the survivors of 'Life's Great Experiment'. This view of the evolution of life parallels Thomas Kuhn's vision of scientific progress — in science, there is every once in a while a paradigm shift in knowledge and then slow, accumulative progress on that theme;

punctuated equilibrium sees sudden disparity (possibly following a mass extinction) followed by gradualism.

The preservation of the soft body parts of the fauna of the Burgess Shale enabled deeper insight into the decimation-diversification process than had been possible previously. Gould considered the term 'decimation' carefully, considering the random sources of survival and death and the high overall probability of extinction. To fully understand the implications of his view of the Burgess reinterpretation, we must understand the difference and application of the terms *diversity* and *disparity*. Diversity can be applied to different systems; there is a *diversity of species*, meaning how many there are.

For example, horse diversity is low, meaning that there are few horse species (about ten, including donkeys and zebras). Diversity also applies to different body plans; that is, fundamental anatomical differences of design. The Burgess Shale presented a view of a large number of different and fundamentally new body designs, which indicates high disparity through a relatively small number of species (traditional view of diversity). How could such disparity in body plans have evolved in the absence of substantial diversity in the number of species?

When Gould spoke of decimation, he meant the reduction in the number and hence range of anatomical designs for life, not the number of species. Thus, the increase of species must have occurred from a reduced number of body plans. This is consistent with evolutionary processes as I described earlier in terms of nature using what is already at its disposal to evolve new parts rather than starting from scratch, and perhaps explains why early vertebrate embryos look so similar (a contestable point, admittedly). By calling the difference in body plans disparity, we therefore observe through the historical progression of life a *decrease* in disparity followed by a marked *increase* in diversity within the few surviving designs.

Gould's Burgess revision also suggests that with each hypothetical replay of life, there would be a different set of potential survivors and thus life as we know it would be different. We humans are therefore a chance event. It may seem discomforting, but we should accept that evolutionary pathways are unpredictable and we are the happy result of a random process! The result of evolutionary processes cannot be predicted from the outset. Conway Morris later concluded from analysing independent evolutionary paths leading to similar survival traits of species that the emergence of intelligence on Earth is not a fluke — that more than one path can lead to intelligence.

We know that eukaryotic cells appeared in the fossil record about 1.4 billion years ago and that the leap from prokaryotic cells to eukaryotic cells was perhaps the greatest leap in life's complexity. However, this leap was in fact mediated through a number of important transitions — the loss of the cell wall, the development of a new internal skeleton (a 'cytoskeleton', composed of microtubules and other supporting protein fibres), the development of new outer and inner membrane structures, the development of new functional organelles such as chloroplasts and mitochondria, and the removal of limitations on genome size. Each of these might be considered major transitions in themselves. Indeed, the British biochemist Nick Lane considers the evolution of the mitochondria as an unlikely event, but one that led to the development of complex life.

By losing the prokaryotic cell wall, the early eukaryotes were able to utilise a new way of feeding — engulfing and ingesting food, as we see in modern-day amoebae, for example — which aided their survival. Therefore, we can see that this transition was a monumental leap in complexity and potential. In John Maynard Smith and Eors Szathmary's book, *The Origins of Life*, they point out in some detail all the major transitions in the history of life on Earth that have led to the possibility of humanity. They also discuss the reasons for as well as how these might have taken place. In order of most ancient first, these are:

1. From replicating molecules *to* populations of molecules existing within compartments.
2. From independent replicating molecules *to* chromosomes.
3. From RNA (existing as a gene and enzyme) *to* DNA and protein as distinct functional forms.
4. From prokaryote *to* eukaryote.
5. From asexual clones *to* sexual populations (here, new individuals being produced by the division of a single cell into two cells as seen in prokaryotes is replaced by the fusion of gametes — most eukaryotes use this method).

6. From simple eukaryotic organisms lacking complex cell differentiation (protists) *to* animals, plants, and fungi.
7. From creatures living as individuals *to* the existence of colonies (e.g., sponges).
8. From primate societies *to* human societies with the associated advanced language capability and all that are entailed with it.

The duration between the appearance of the first eukaryotic cell and that of the first multicellular organism is longer than that from the Cambrian explosion to present. The Precambrian record reveals only one set of fauna of multicellular animals preceding the Cambrian explosion, the Ediacara fauna. The Ediacaran Period is the last period of the Neoproterozoic Era, preceding the Cambrian Period of the Palaeozoic Era. These fauna may represent a failed evolutionary experiment of multicellular life and, if so, are not ancestors for later creatures. They evolved, existed, and died out for whatever reasons that caused them to fail to adapt to the conditions they encountered.

Rather than Darwin's gradual rise to increasing complexity, the 100 million years from Ediacara to Burgess could have been witness to three different fauna types — Ediacara fauna, *Tommotia* (early cup and cap-like creatures found throughout the world), and the modern fauna, culminating in the maximal anatomical range of the Burgess. The Tommotian Age was a relatively short, 3 million-year period of the early Cambrian. To put this in context, there were 2.5 billion years of prokaryotic cells — the simplest level of complexity — and nothing else on Earth, then 700 million years of eukaryotic cells but no multicellular life. Then, in just 100 million years, the three major different fauna types appeared and led to what was seen at Burgess. In the half billion years since Burgess, we see massive diversity but no great increase in disparity — no new phylum from the Burgess complement.

To gain further insight into this, we need to clarify the classification of organisms. *Taxonomy* is the science of classification, and there are seven basic levels of increasing taxonomic inclusion:

SPECIES – GENERA – FAMILIES – ORDERS – CLASSES – PHYLA – KINGDOM

The Linnaean order of classification, named after the 18th century Swedish botanist Carl Linnaeus, contains further subdivisions:

Subspecies – SPECIES – subgenus – GENUS – tribe – subfamily – FAMILY – superfamily – suborder – ORDER – superorder – cohort – infraclass – subclass – CLASS – superclass – subphylum – PHYLUM – subkingdom – KINGDOM

Kingdom is the broadest grouping comprising Plantae, Animalia, and Fungi for multicellular organisms, Protista for single-celled eukaryotic organisms, and Monera for unicellular Prokaryota. In 1977, Carl Richard Woese divided the kingdom Monera into two separate kingdoms, Archea and Monera, based on phylogenetic studies of ribosomal RNA. About thirty-five phyla are thought to exist in the animal kingdom today, but this number may change in the near future after the data collected by the Sorcerer II Global Ocean Sampling Expedition, funded by the J. Craig Venter Institute, has been collated and released. These phyla include the modern-day arthropods, which includes over 1.1 million crustacean, spider, and insect species, and the chordates, which include all animals with a notochord (more than 100,000 species).

Thus, despite being a tiny quarry of a single location, the Burgess Shale appeared to contain the remains of up to twenty organism types that are *so* different from one another that they ought to rank as different phyla purely by virtue of their anatomical differences.

The Burgess fauna

The Burgess fauna therefore provided such evidence that necessitated a revision of biological evolutionary history on Earth. For example, the priapulids are burrowing worms and contribute little to modern diversity with only about fifteen species known. Yet the Burgess Shale consists of nearly as many *genera* of priapulids as the whole of modern Earth. Arthropods also present an example of how certain interpretations of the Burgess data conflict with evolutionary or phyletic gradualism being the sole causal factor or hypothesis that can explain species formation. Arthropods constitute about 80% of all modern animals. They contain a body of repeated segments through a phenomenon called *metamerism* and consist of a number of different species both extinct and extant, including trilobites, crustaceans, and insects.

Despite the variety of arthropod species, they can be grouped according to four basic anatomical designs — the still extant Uniramia, Chelicerata, and Crustacea, as well as the Trilobita which became extinct 225 million years ago. The classification of arthropods into subphyla is a contested issue. The typical modern classification is trilobites, chelicerates (e.g., spiders and scorpions), myriapods (e.g., centipedes), hexapods (insects), and crustaceans (e.g., crabs and woodlice). Hexapods and myriapods are sometimes grouped together as Uniramia.

Apparently, evolution settled on these few themes and stuck with them through the greatest diversification in the animal kingdom. However, in addition to these four designs, the Burgess Shale comprises at least twenty additional basic arthropod designs. Let us look at some examples of the Burgess fossils in more detail.

Marrella splendens, the most common Burgess arthropod, was the focus of four years of work for Whittington. In contrast to Walcott's interpretation, Whittington found that it bore no resemblance to trilobites, yet he tried initially to find existing phyla in which to place it. One could say that it was another Cambrian arthropod that existed beyond the range of modern groups, and that it illustrated that disparity had reached its peak at the outset and life continued with a process of decimation, not increasing variety of design — this was Gould's analysis. However, at the time of Whittington's analysis, this would have seemed too far-fetched an explanation and so, despite perhaps an inkling toward this radical view, an attempt was made to place it within existing groups, thus mirroring Walcott's approach.

Yohoia tenuis was the next arthropod studied by Whittington. It contained a body design unique among arthropods with a grasping front appendage dubbed the 'great appendage'. Despite placing it with the trilobites, he was not sure of this move. He then turned his attention to *Opabinia regalis* with little doubt that it was an arthropod. This organism was the turning point in Whittington's thinking.

Opabinia regalis was a rare organism in the Shale with about ten specimens and was considered the most primitive of all the arthropods found.

However, with further analysis, Whittington was unable to call *Opabinia* an arthropod or anything else yet described. It had some remarkable features; five eyes, a frontal nozzle reminiscent of the hose found on a vacuum cleaner, and the gut was a single tube with a u-bend in it. Whittington considered Yohoia and the other Burgess-segmented animals to be of uncertain affinities. Gould believes that information gained about this organism has taught us more about ourselves than has any other organism. Indeed, had it not been for his editor's input, *Wonderful Life* would have been titled *Homage to Opabinia*.

Another Burgess organism, *Nectocaris*, looked like an arthropod from the front but a chordate from behind. Like most of the Burgess organisms, it was only a few inches in length. Other Burgess organisms including *Odontogriphus* and *Dinomischus* were also difficult to classify. *Amiskwia*'s anatomy was well enough preserved by the Shale formation to preclude addition to any modern phylum. However, the one-inch *Hallucigenia* might be the organism of choice to display the Burgess disparity and uniqueness of design, such is its bizarre anatomy. It consists of tentacles on its back and walked on seven spikes. However, closely related specimens were later unearthed in the Yunnan province of China, which showed that this organism had been interpreted incorrectly.

In *The Crucible of Creation*, Conway Morris pointed out in his original interpretation that the organism was upside down. Later interpretation placed the spikes as lining the back. The closest present-day relatives of *Hallucigenia* incidentally are velvet worms, inhabitants of tropical rainforests. This change highlighted the difficulty of interpreting these fossils and clarified the uncertainty of claims about the Cambrian explosion.

Branchiocaris pretiosa also defied classification within recent arthropod groups, yet the common and similar-looking *Canadaspis perfecta* could be classified easily as a crustacean. This and other Burgess organisms of modern design showed that some of the Burgess experiments *were* successful and *can* provide us with clues about modern life's evolution on Earth. Gould wondered what could be inferred from the collection of *all* Burgess animals, including those that did and did not survive as a connection to later life.

By 1978, the organisms studied by Whittington, Conway Morris, and Briggs provided the possibility for a new account of how multicellular life might have evolved, and Gould saw how his model fitted the data.

For Gould, the seven years from the study of the organisms *Marrella splendens* (1971) to *Aysheia* (1978) represented a shift in perspective from a reappraisal of arthropod grouping to a new conception on the history of life. Four species, *Marrella splendens*, *Yohoia tenuis*, *Burgessia*, and *Branchiocaris pretiosa*, were arthropods, *Canadapsis* was part of a modern group, *Opabinia regalis* clearly was not an arthropod, and no one knew what to do with *Aysheaia*. Many other organisms were found and reinterpreted by Whittington, Briggs, and Conway Morris, each leading to the interpretation that the 'Burgess period' represented the greatest phase of experimentation and evolutionary flexibility that the Earth has seen.

Today, the distinct morphological differences between recognised groups occur because most of these initial experiments are no longer extant. Conway Morris made the discovery of *Sanctacaris* which appeared to be a chelicerate, the line that led to the horseshoe crabs, among others. Thus, with this organism, the Burgess Shale presented the forebears of all four modern arthropods groups discussed earlier. In addition, there were at least thirteen other lineages that did not survive. Why did some survive while others failed?

If we were given an example of each design, the four that did survive seem no more likely to have an anatomical advantage over any other. If we replayed life from these early seas, would the same groups survive and if not, would life be as we see it now? Could consciousness and even intelligence have evolved? Did we evolve due to the unlikely fortune that one of these groups did happen to be successful or that another failed? Despite their great work, Whittington and his students did make mistakes; such was the difficulty in interpreting the Burgess evidence. For example, what was considered to be an organism in itself turned out to be merely the mouthpart of another unique and unclassifiable organism, *Anomolocaris*. This perhaps is not surprising since this organism turned out to be by far the largest Burgess arthropod, up to three feet in length.

In summary, the Burgess Shale consisted of a range of disparity in anatomical design greater than that of all creatures in all the modern oceans — there were more than twenty unique designs of arthropod. The hypothetical evolutionary tree reflected by the interpretation of the Burgess fauna presents one of large morphological gaps among the survivors as most groups are removed by extinction. The radiation of the surviving lineages into a great diversity with restricted disparity of total form produces the extant groups we know now as classes and phyla.

Burgess: Cause and effect

The revision of the Burgess Shale interpretation poses two key problems about the history of life on Earth. First, how could such disparity arise so quickly or at all? The cause of the Cambrian explosion is unknown, but several possibilities have been suggested, including:

1. **'Snowball' Earth** — most of the Earth was covered in ice prior to the Cambrian in the late Neoproterozoic period. There was genetic isolation, but the earliest animal fossils appeared after this global freezing had passed.
2. **Oxygen limitations** — the early Earth atmosphere contained little or no oxygen, which is the product of billions of years of cyanobacteria photosynthesis. When low-level oxygen enabled animal life, it was of a small size and slow, which conformed to the gaseous possibilities.
3. **Nutrient stimulation** — the conditions on Earth induced or accelerated animal evolution through an influx of nutrients. Prior to the Cambrian, the oceans were low in oxygen and high in carbon dioxide. Multicellular organism development meant competition with bacteria for plankton. The bacteria numbers reduced and oxygen rose, enabling animal evolution. Here, radiochemical analysis and carbon dating provide some support. The $^{13}C/^{12}C$ carbon isotope ratio from early Cambrian deposits shows a drop in ^{13}C, which accumulates along the food chain and implies a drop in bacterial numbers, thus lending credence to this theory.
4. **Methane** — it is thought that massive methane emissions caused the *Permo-Triassic mass extinction* (see below) through global warming effects. A decrease in the $^{13}C/^{12}C$ ratio at the Ediacaran-Cambrian boundary followed by fluctuations throughout the early Cambrian has been noted. This decrease may be due to multicellular organism action or the release of methane due to dissociation of methane clathrates. If it is the latter, then global warming could cause extinction like that of the Permo-Triassic and provide the opportunity for diversification. However, it is not known how mass extinction would cause an increase

in disparity and diversity. Rather, extant animals would be expected to occupy new niches according to relevant fit. Thus, mass extinction does not fit the punctuated equilibrium model.
5. **Small developmental changes** — it is proposed that small innovations in the way an embryo develops may have resulted in rapid evolution of body forms. However, this also does not explain the increased diversity and disparity.
6. **Ecological innovation hypotheses** — these focus on different relationships between and induced by multicellular organisms. For example, the coevolution of plants and pollinators, or that of predator and prey, drives change in both parties. These theories explain perhaps rapid increases in diversity and disparity (e.g., Darwin's finches), but not the *timing* of the Cambrian explosion.
7. **Theoretical explanations** — new body forms must face little or no competition in the niche the organism occupies so that it has time to adapt. Thus, the greatest disparity is most likely to occur during the early stages of the diversification of animals. Furthermore, only the availability of niches prevents other potential phyla from developing. This theory explains why such an explosion occurred only once.

These represent possibilities for what caused the Cambrian explosion, but the focus here, and for Gould, is the second key problem about the history of life on Earth, namely what was the functional attribute or environment that set the pattern for what would survive and what would not? Would a different act of decimation at the same Burgess starting point have yielded the same groups and the same result as from Burgess's disparity?

Three kinds of evolutionary explanations have been suggested for the explosion leading to the Burgess Shale disparity:

1. There was an ecological barrel to fill, so there existed unparalleled opportunity and nearly every organism could find a place. Gould considered the Cambrian explosion too big and too diverse for such an explanation.
2. There is a directional history for genetic systems. It is conceived that Cambrian genes were simpler and more flexible than they are now, such

that they had fewer interactions with others than they do now. Therefore, due to the genetic complexity of modern organisms, they cannot spawn rapid new designs irrespective of the ecological opportunity.
3. There was early diversification and a later locking as a property of the system. The Burgess pattern of rapid disparity followed by decimation is considered a property of certain systems. Research has shown that such a large jump in design can yield success initially but falls to zero after time, which corresponds with the Burgess observation.

If life started with a few simple models and moved on, and any replay would yield the same results, then our evolution would be inevitable. However, with the Burgess interpretation, if life started with all its models present and constructed a later history from a few random models whose presence would be different on each theoretical replay of life, then we might never have existed and thus we are a random and unlikely occurrence in the history of life on Earth. The conventional argument for the Burgess data is that the losers — the designs that failed — were destined to fail by faulty anatomical construction. The winners were better adapted and survived as a result of their Darwinian edge.

With this view, it does not matter how many designs the Cambrian proposed since the better-designed formed the foundations for all later life. However, there is no evidence that the losers in the decimation were inferior in adaptive design to those that survived. However, this is a difficult analysis and conclusion to make since we are uncertain of Cambrian processes. What is true is that of the roughly twenty-five body plans Whittington and colleagues discovered, for which there were only one or two examples of each, four led to enormously successful extant groups, and the others died without trace.

Extinctions

Mass extinctions have been a key evolutionary driver in the course of life on Earth. While an unlikely cause of the Cambrian explosion according to Gould's way of thinking, others such as Dawkins and Conway Morris who do not regard punctuated equilibrium as correct see that mass extinction *does* present a feasible explanatory cause of the Burgess phenomena.

Although the cause of the Cambrian explosion is of course important, Gould was more interested in the flow of processes that led to *us* — if we are the result of a specific path, then why did this path occur rather than some other? I consider this a rhetorical question in the sense that there was no reason other than natural selection and chance. Indeed, by stressing the possibility of rerunning evolution and obtaining different results, he was mindful of the unpredictability, and chaotic nature, of life. Thus, the causes of mass extinctions fit these criteria, but not, sadly for Gould, his model. We should, though, discuss mass extinctions since their causes present conditions that affected how natural selection led to our existence.

Gould considered the Burgess reinterpretation to be as important a palaeontological discovery as the Luis Alvarez theory of mass extinction due to an asteroid impact at the end of the Cretaceous period, estimated in 2019 to be 65.76 million years ago, that wiped out the dinosaurs. However, the reason it has not received the same interest from the public and media is probably due partly to dinosaurs being more interesting in the public consciousness than miniature sea arthropods. Alvarez's generally accepted view on mass extinction by extraterrestrial impact has interesting correlations with Gould's view. Is there any pattern to who survives such an impact and who does not? One view is that the reasons for a species' survival in times of such an extinction event are very different from the causes for success in normal times.

About 175 million years ago during the mid-Jurassic period, there was a major change in the world that altered our history. Prior to then, the world consisted of one continuous ocean surrounding one huge continent. On this continent, the dinosaurs were very similar to one another — there was every opportunity for the creatures to pass throughout the single land mass. Furthermore, the climate was singular, consisting of long dry seasons and an intense monsoon season, a 'mega-monsoon'.

In the mid-Jurassic, the land mass broke, separating the Americas from Africa and Europe as we see it now, though their forms were different then. This separation by the Atlantic Ocean resulted in different climates developing between the new environments and dinosaur evolution started taking on different paths. Thus, reaching back to 175 million years ago, the fossil record shows different structural aspects of dinosaurs from these different regions which were, prior to the separation, the same. This is called *vicariance*.

The splitting of the landmass resulted in major climatic, volcanic, and seismic activity leading to mass extinctions. The creatures that were suited to the previously stable conditions were now subjected to altered environments, making them less well-adapted. Thus, geological change pushed biological change. Furthermore, it is thought that the ocean barriers prevented the movement of dinosaurs to more favourable climates. Being forced to exist within new boundaries also produced an evolutionary trend towards greater size in plant-eating dinosaurs as swell as a corresponding increase in the size of meat-eating dinosaurs that preyed upon them.

The dinosaur extinction at the end of the Cretaceous period resulted in about 60% of species going extinct, and it is thought that an impact in the Gulf of Mexico by an asteroid about ten kilometres wide and/or increased volcanic activity caused this extinction. Indeed, scientists have predicted that Earth has sustained over 50 million major collisions throughout its history, the majority during its first 100 million years. However, about 250 million years ago, approximately 96% of all organisms on Earth became extinct in what is believed to be Earth's greatest extinction event so far — the Permo-Triassic extinction.

The Permo-Triassic extinction has only recently been explained in a way that has led to broader acceptance, and for different reasons to that of the Cretaceous event. The extinction occurred in two phases. First, there was a significant increase in global temperature due to a huge release of lava in the region of modern-day Siberia. Billions of tons of molten lava were released over an area of thousands of square miles for a period of thousands of years. This caused a 5°C increase in global temperature, which was enough to cause some extinctions but not a mass extinction. However, the 5°C increase in global temperature was sufficient to cause a release of enormous quantities of methane gas, which was trapped within the Earth in a different form, leading to a global warming effect of a further 5°C.

The consequence was that over a period of about approximately eighty thousand years, the temperature of the Earth rose by 10°C, sufficient to turn temperate zones into deserts and bring about the mass extinction. It was also enough to melt ice caps. Thus, this was not a sudden extinction event like the one that ended the dinosaurs but a slow and gradual one. A global climate was created that favoured the continuation of only a few organisms over the vast majority, as those species that fitted the original environment were unable to survive the new conditions. In fact, it was the creatures that did survive these conditions that led to the evolution of dinosaurs. A similar situation is believed to have led to the success of mammals at the expense of dinosaurs 65 million years ago.

Therefore, Earth's extinctions have occurred through cosmic and local events that many species could not survive or adapt to. Today, humans may be able to predict and prepare for some events in order to prevent our extinction because technology is at a level that can provide advantages beyond our physiology. However, as some recent Hollywood films have depicted, some events are beyond even *our* technological capabilities. Some extinction causes, however, could occur as a *result* of our existence. Nuclear war is an example, global warming due to pollution another.

These are therefore amongst the most debated scientific and political topics today. I am not stating that the current climate change is going to cause our extinction or that it is entirely the fault of mankind's actions; rather, I am stressing that the Permo-Triassic extinction, and possibly others, shows us the effects that marked temperature changes on Earth can have on life. Extinctions were, and continue to be, an ever-present possibility. They are also an integral part of how we came to exist. Our ability to predict and react against extinction causes is due to our intelligence, and this appeared on Earth, apparently, due to extinctions and other pressures that redirected natural selection towards the course that resulted in us.

Although extinction is not a cause that fits Gould's vision of the Cambrian explosion, it is one of a number of feasible possibilities that *can* explain it. Since none have clearly been verified, then no harm is done to his vision. Gould's focus was on the processes *after* the explosion, and it is these that have caused much heated debate particularly between Gould and Richard Dawkins. Thus, before we look at that debate, let us state Gould's concluding interpretation of the Burgess fauna and the contrasting views of those who re-reinterpreted the fossils after that by Whittington and by Gould.

Burgess interpretation by Gould

Only 4% of organisms survived the Permo-Triassic extinction. For their genes, the extinction events were their sheer good fortune. Most survivors get through for specific reasons, yet traits that enhance survival during a mass extinction do so in ways that are incidental and unrelated to those that caused their evolution in the first place. It is feasible that an organism on the verge of extinction at the time of the cause of mass extinction might be, or become, better adapted to the new environment than organisms they were competing with unsuccessfully prior to the extinction event. For example, an extinction event might take out a major predator that sat at the top of a food chain due to lack of suitable prey to feed upon.

Thus, dinosaurs died out due to a rapid, unpredicted event that they could not adapt to. If not for this cataclysmic event, mammals would not have been presented with the environment that they adapted to so efficiently and we may not be here to discuss it.

Gould concluded that life evolved from the causal event or process of the Cambrian explosion by a pronounced decimation (after a rapid initial diversification of anatomical design) with an associated strong and perhaps controlling influence of randomness for selection. As a result of the Burgess work, Gould devoted much time to researching *bottom-heavy* evolutionary trees. That is, maximal diversity is reached relatively early compared to *symmetrical* or *top-heavy* systems. Bottom-heavy patterns like the Burgess represent early experimentation and later standardisation. Species may continue to increase, but diversification occurs within restricted anatomies. To clarify his point, there are nearly a million species of insects today with only three basic anatomical designs, yet Burgess provided twenty. Burgess seems to disprove the standard evolutionary view of the cone of ever-increasing diversity.

Burgess interpretation by Derek Briggs and Richard Fortey

Gould's theory of punctuated equilibrium seems to find its proof in Burgess Shale fossils and his enthusiasm in *Wonderful Life* is convincing. However, there are people who think that his enthusiasm and commitment to the idea produced an incomplete analysis of the *actual* data. Richard Dawkins, for one, thinks that punctuated equilibrium does not deserve the attention it has received.

What are the other more recent interpretations of the Burgess fossils? The British anthropologist Roger Lewin discussed in a 1992 issue of *Discover* magazine some of the conclusions by scientists who have suggested that Gould's vision was incomplete. In addition to the Burgess site, three other sites of Burgess-like fossils have been located — one in Greenland, one in Australia, and a third in China — suggesting a global distribution of such fauna. Conway Morris and the geologist John Peel studied the complete specimens of Cambrian slugs called halkieriids in northern Greenland in 1989. These were thought to be a series of creatures, but later proved to be different parts of the same organism. As such, what was considered as different phyla are in fact evidence of just one. By reducing the cases of Cambrian disparity, one wonders whether all Cambrian animals can be fitted into modern phyla and if so, is there no need for a massive extinction after the Cambrian explosion?

However, one must remember that we are comparing the disparity of what was *found* at the Burgess Shale — a small location — with that of *all* modern fauna, so we would expect far more in present times. Gould suggested that Burgess fauna showed greater disparity than would a comparable sample of modern animals.

Briggs became sceptical of Gould's theory in *Wonderful Life* when he and the British palaeontologist Richard Fortey re-examined the Cambrian arthropods. They argued that if there was a reduction in phyla after the Cambrian explosion, then diversity should also decrease within each surviving phylum, which means that the Cambrian arthropods should be much more diverse morphologically than their modern descendants. Briggs and Fortey used *cladistics* to measure morphological differences in the arthropods. Here, an evolutionary tree or cladogram is made (Figure 39) based on morphological characteristics to ascertain how different the Cambrian arthropods really were and to plot their relatedness to modern phyla. The cladogram constructed by Fortey and Briggs concluded that the Cambrian arthropods displayed no more morphological diversity than modern counterparts. Thus, they saw Gould's interpretation as wrong.

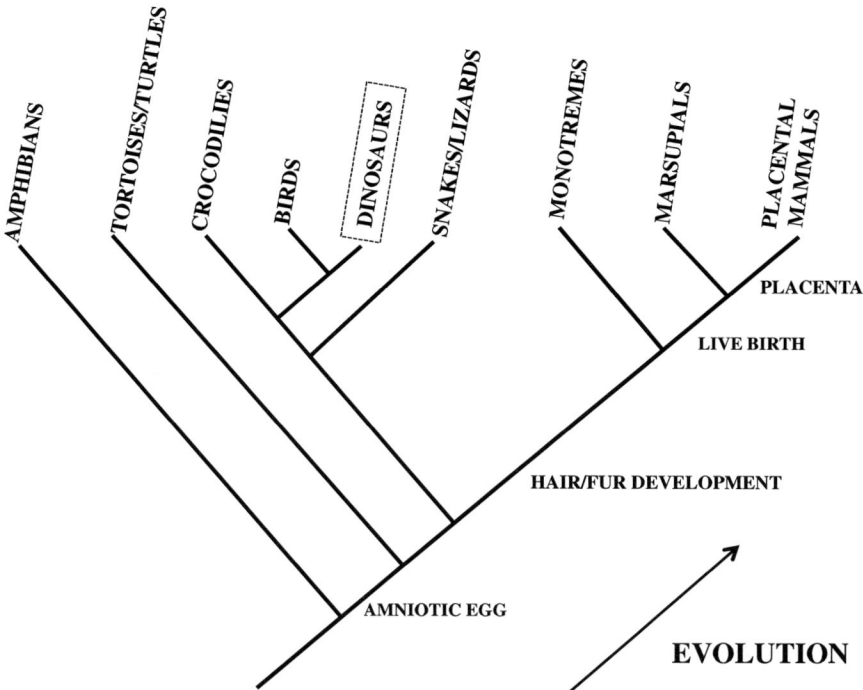

Figure 39. Example of a simple cladogram. Some key events that led to the evolution of distinct vertebrate classes (top of diagram, including the now extinct dinosaurs) are shown along the direction of evolutionary time (arrowed, bottom). These include the formation of an internal or amniotic egg, which characterises all modern birds and reptiles for example, and live birth — an event that separates the monotremes such as duck-billed platypus and echidna from all other mammals. A cladogram can be constructed to look at much finer degrees of relatedness, including DNA sequence homology between different members of a genetic family.

Of course, Fortey's and Briggs's conclusions were drawn from data that necessitated subjective interpretation of morphological differences to construct the cladogram. If they wanted a particular conclusion, the morphological similarities would seem more apparent to them than they would to Gould, who would not have wanted to see them. Furthermore, Gould stressed that cladistic analysis gives information on branching order, *not* on morphological disparity. So, the analysis would not clarify how different the organisms were, and Gould was stressing that they were *very* different. Further analysis by Briggs and Fortey claimed that the morphological data matched that of the branching data, but Gould argued that the methods to determine the significance of morphological differences in fossils are poor and thus cannot distinguish phyla, let alone species. Although Gould is no longer alive to defend his theory, it still exists as a feasible *addition* to Darwinian evolutionary theory since it is yet to be conclusively falsified.

Differences between Dawkins' and Gould's opinions

Dawkins and Gould have, in some aspects, differing views of the mechanism of evolutionary processes. We will leave aside their agreements, which actually apply to most of the theory and constitute the core of Darwinism, and focus on what they disagree about.

Dawkins, Gould, Richard Lewontin, the American philosopher Daniel Dennett, and the British evolutionary biologist John Maynard Smith have each written a number of books in addition to their academic publications covering every conceivable aspect of the theory of evolution. As the title indicates, this section will present the major differences in the opinions between Gould and Dawkins, for which the book *Dawkins Versus Gould — Survival of the Fittest* (2001) by Kim Sterelny was a source of insight.

Dawkins and Gould differed in their opinions on the nature of evolution as emphasised through heated print exchanges in the *New York Review of Books* and *Evolution*. Perhaps their academic backgrounds paved the way for their differences of opinion. Gould was trained by an ethologist and was sensitised to adaptive significances of behavioural patterns; he was a palaeontologist. In contrast, Dawkins is an evolutionary biologist. Gould believed that macroevolution is not microevolution scaled up, meaning what happens on the large-scale cannot be extrapolated directly from what happens on the small-scale. Sterelny considers Dawkins to be more correct in his view about evolution on local scales, whereas Gould is right about the relationship between events on small scales and those on the scale of palaeontological time.

Without God as a divine engineer, Dawkins agrees with Darwin that natural selection is the only answer to how complex adaptive structures came into existence. He believes that the history of evolution is the history of gene lineages, and the history of life is mostly an invisible war between gene lineages. Gould saw things differently; he was most interested in extinctions and their causes, which is why the Burgess Shale reinterpretation was of such interest to him. As you will recall, the basic anatomical designs of organisms all appeared at roughly the same time and no new ones have been invented since by evolution; rather, there is increase in diversity based on just a few set body designs.

From Dawkins's viewpoint

Dawkins believes that evolution is driven by selection according to the rule:

Competition + variation + replication = natural selection + evolution

He stresses the difference between *single-step* and *cumulative selection*. With single-step selection, where a new body design is preferable for an environment, a single giant leap in a single generation would not be possible. This constraint is overcome with the idea of cumulative selection. Here, if each generation is closer to the goal fit for the new condition in a non-Lamarckian sense, then it has an advantage.

As an example, the jump from a 'no eye' organism to a 'whole eye' organism cannot occur in one generation, but if each generation developed a form of photoreception or sensitivity to light that was an improvement upon the previous, it would be beneficial. Evolution towards this form continues until the optimum efficiency of the photoreceptor-enhanced, non-predetermined form is achieved. Once the eye has reached peak efficiency for that organism to exploit its environment, it need not evolve further. This is not a conscious predetermined evolution but rather the result of a potential niche existing for such a design.

The unit of selection for such a process is, of course, a lineage of gene copies. Gould rejected the idea that the characteristics of genes causally explain evolutionary changes in a population. He considered gene selection to presuppose a form of genetic determinism and argued that Dawkins oversimplifies the relationship between a particular gene and the characteristics of an organism that possesses it. The relationship between genes and organisms is complex and indirect. There is no simple link between genes and traits, such that no traits are directly linked simply to a particular gene. The two do not contest this, but Gould believed that Dawkins overstates their importance such that genes have phenotypic power. Dawkins stresses this in his book, *The Extended Phenotype* (1982).

Cumulative selection is accepted as fundamental to evolution, but what is questioned is whether the fundamental agents in evolution are gene lineages. Dawkins tries to convince us of this in *The Extended Phenotype*, wherein he talks of *outlaw genes* to explain his ideas. These genes promote their own replication at the expense of other genes within the organism. Being outlaws, they are 'selfish' — hence the title of an earlier book by Dawkins, *The Selfish Gene*. To him, they demonstrate that a gene's purpose is to replicate itself and it has evolved to ensure its survival.

However, we should note that relatively few vertebrate genes have been isolated and their DNA sequences determined in the mid-1970s when Dawkins wrote *The Selfish Gene* — he would not have known of functional redundancy and paralogous gene groups such as the myogenic transcription factors or mammalian homeobox genes that I described in Chapter 4. I also discussed how new insights into cell biology that stem from genomics, proteomics, and transcriptomics suggest an extremely complex system of regulatory control within the cell as shown by the recent discovery of 5,000 or so microRNA genes, each potentially regulating the expression of 400 protein-coding genes on average. When one factors in epigenetic effects such as methylation, whose effects we are only just beginning to unravel, it would seem that there are many potential checks and balances to regulate an outlaw's behaviour.

Mitochondrial genes are an example of outlaw genes. Mitochondria contain DNA and we inherit mitochondrial-encoded genes only from the mother, never the father. In 1987, using mitochondrial DNA and knowing its mutation rate, Alan Wilson of the University of California at Berkeley concluded that all our mitochondrial DNA was derived from a single version 200,000 years ago. This was the woman known as *Mitochondrial Eve*, who was the 'unknown' African female of our past from whom all of humanity's mitochondrial genes were inherited. Gould and Lewontin do not contest the existence of outlaws but share the opinion that Dawkins overemphasises them.

So what does Dawkins mean by having an 'extended phenotype'? This is where genes reach out into the world and promote their own replication, as is the case for the action of parasitic genes on host bodies. Extended phenotype genes are not outlaws, but these cannot be incorporated into a view of evolution that sees selection acting on individuals. In this case, Sterelny regards Dawkins's view of evolution as a more attractive proposition than that of Gould.

In *The Selfish Gene* (1976), Dawkins also discusses cooperation between individuals within a species. How could it have evolved and what causes altruistic behaviour where one individual acts in the best interest of another? Altruism differs from egoism ("is it good for me?") or hedonism ("does it feel good?"). It has been stated that acts of human altruism cannot be conclusively separated from either egoism and/or hedonism. For animals, it is possible in some cases that it is an inadvertent result of imperfect adaptation to the environment. A 'needs of the many outweigh the needs of the few' mentality may also apply, but from an evolutionarily programmed perspective.

For example, the way large shoals of small fish like anchovies swim 'as one' both creates the impression of a single large organism to predators and ensures that predators will only pick off individuals at the periphery. Of course, altruism in lower animals may also be an illusion. The evolutionary temptation to defect from altruistic behaviour and wear down the process from within the individual's group might be too great for such a process to evolve. If the group's lifespan is longer than the individual's, then the individual's selection clock runs faster than that of the group and has the more powerful effect. Thus, Dawkins sees cooperation as real but altruism as unreal.

Some animal species consist of non-reproductive individuals, such as worker bees. Why do the bees work for the unit when they cannot pass on their own genes? Darwin explains this behaviour by seeing the family (the worker bees derive from one Queen) rather than the individual as the true target of selection. Using Mendelian genetics, it can be said that one might sacrifice one's life to save two brothers or eight cousins, for example, since these combinations possess the same amount of the same genes as the individual. Thus, if such relatives are saved and they live on to reproduce through an individual's altruistic act, then the individual's genes will still be passed on indirectly to the next generation. If genes *govern* us, then these are fair trades from the gene's perspective. Behaviour may not actually occur in reality to produce such trades. Dawkins's denial of altruism may *appear* to show that genes do not govern us, but such a logical conclusion is flawed. Genes may not govern us, but not because of the denial of altruism.

As Lewontin stresses, the interplay of gene, organism, and environment together determine behaviour. Dawkins and Gould agree that gene selection is consistent with group selection. The latter describes the situation where alleles appear in populations because of the benefit to the group irrespective of its effect on the *individuals* of that group. By benefiting the group, they benefit the individual by enhancing its survivability from belonging to such groups. Similarly, deleterious mutations in alleles, such as the one that causes sickle-cell anaemia in Afro-Caribbean lineages, bring disadvantages for the health of the group. Thus, Dawkins agrees that individuals play a role in evolution and not only as a function of a group.

All evolutionary thinkers agree that many characteristics of organisms are not the direct result of selection. Some are by-products of selection for other characteristics. In Gould's influential 1979 paper, *The Spandrels of San Marco and the Panglossian Paradigm* (co-written with Lewontin), he introduced the term *spandrel* within an evolutionary context. Traditionally, spandrels are architectural features; they are the spaces that exist between arches and thus are not planned structural parts unlike the arch itself, but are forms that occur naturally as a result of the arch design. They are made ornate and thus become features themselves. Gould and Lewontin described features of organisms that arise as a necessary result of other selected features but are not built directly as a result of being favoured by natural selection as spandrels. Many features of human intelligence fit the spandrel concept. Dawkins disagrees, viewing them as non-adaptive by-products of evolution.

From Gould's viewpoint

Rather than considering adaptive complexity as the central problem of evolutionary biology as Dawkins does, Gould was more interested in large-scale patterns in the history of life, which are not explained by natural selection. His view of *extrapolationism* concerns the relationship between evolutionary processes within a species and their extrapolation to large-scale life history. Gould was strongly opposed to the traditional opinion that the processes of local populations generate evolutionary patterns; that is, the micro- to macro-extrapolation.

Dawkins is opposed to Gould's theory of punctuated equilibrium as was evident in his book, *The Blind Watchmaker* (1986). Punctuated equilibrium proposes that species do not gradually evolve into new species; rather, they arise by the splitting of parental species followed by speciation of the fragments. The implications of this process challenge those of extrapolationism. That is, it rejects the hypothesis that processes on the small-scale can be extrapolated to what happens on the large-scale. Gould emphasised the difference between diversity and disparity. We have studied this earlier, but to reiterate — diversity is the number of species in existence at the time whereas disparity is the number of basic anatomical body designs at that time. From these differences, he makes three bold claims about the history of life on Earth:

1. Disparity was at its peak around the time of the arrival of multicellular animals in the Cambrian period.
2. Little disparity has occurred since then.
3. Survival is *contingent*: if we replayed life from the early Cambrian with slight differences in the initial conditions, the survivors would be very different.

As we know, debate exists about point 1 and, thus, point 2. Point 3 is also a point of contention and it is untestable of course.

Gould's key concern was to put right the idea of evolutionary trends as scaled-up consequences of the struggle for life between organisms. The evolution of the horse is a good example to describe the different viewpoints. The extrapolationist view of the evolutionary development of the horse is that evolution saw a switch from browsing on trees to grazing on grass, resulting in morphological changes such as larger animals, larger teeth, and hooves evolving from toed feet. Gould's interpretation differed such that the horse lineage is species-diverse with many horse sizes and lifestyles. However, only a few species survived and those happened to be large, atypical horses, thus the average horse now is larger than its evolutionary ancestors as we can see from the fossil record.

To understand Gould's argument against extrapolationism more fully, we need to understand his ideas on mass extinction and punctuated equilibrium (as described in the previous section on Gould's interpretation of the Burgess Shale reinterpretation). Gould hoped to prove and appears to have succeeded in proving his case against extrapolationism for some aspects of evolutionary processes, as some patterns in the history of life conform to his proposal. That is, if there was a Cambrian explosion, we see the existence of evolutionary mechanisms operating other than those that occur at the scale of local populations.

Gould considered survival and extinction through periods of mass extinction to involve species selection. This selection is not visible in local populations and an inference is that major groups have disappeared, which would have otherwise survived. An example is how mammals came to prominence after the Late Cretaceous extinction, as that particular event wiped out the environment in which herbivorous and carnivorous dinosaurs flourished.

Dawkins talks of the power of selection to produce such diversity as dependent on slow and incremental operation. The Burgess Shale interpretation from Gould's viewpoint presents a problem to this idea, and Gould considered evolution to have worked differently during that period. Despite Gould's opinion that the Cambrian evolution was really explosive, there is the possibility that the last *common* ancestor of the animal phyla lived a long time before the Cambrian. One is not surprised to find in such heated debates that Dawkins considered Gould to overestimate the Cambrian disparity, just as Gould considered Dawkins to overstate the phenotypic power and reductive nature of genes which, if true, would have similarly major ramifications.

Gould thought that a misleading way to look at the history of life is one of a progressive increase in complexity. Types of life tend to become more complex as evolution builds lineages that increase in complexity over time, but most organisms have stayed the same over geological time scales (e.g., bacteria). The difference between the simplest and most complex organisms obviously increases with the progression of time. Yet, even on this matter, Dawkins and Gould disagreed. Gould considered complexity interesting as it is a measure of progress, whereas Dawkins sees evolution as progressive because life is becoming better adapted. Sterelny sees the difference in opinion to be due somewhat to Gould's seeing complexity as having a lower but no upper limit.

Perhaps what really happens in evolution is a blending of the best of both lines of thought, but with additions where both are wrong. How could Gould and Dawkins (and others) have such contrasting views on a subject, be so convincing about their own viewpoints, and be so convinced as to their correctness? Opinions on a subject are most vulnerable to influence when we have the least data on it. Additionally, we tend to adopt a line of reasoning that may be skewed as a result of it being presented to us in a certain way. This becomes the framework that our thought processes rely on and sets a path that is easier to continue on rather than to deviate from.

We are all victims of this human condition, and perhaps Gould and Dawkins were too with their initial steps into the evolutionary arena. Replay the history of their careers and swap their PhD projects, and perhaps then Dawkins would have been the advocate of punctuated equilibrium and Gould the reductionist! If the result of that rather Gouldian hypothetical scenario were so, it may say that our ability to extract truth from the interplay of theory, hypothesis, and experiment is weaker than our skill at manipulating the language of science to our own ends.

Before we move on to another 'big name' in this particular story of what evolution is and how it resulted in our existence, I should point out (using one particular example to stress the point) that although the early conditions determined the later effect, we should be mindful that throughout the unfolding of time on Earth to the present day, certain obstacles had to be addressed. Life could have taken a different course and we would not be here to deliberate the matter.

For example, consider the Carboniferous period 300 million years ago when enormous trees evolved in the struggle of plants for light. The wood, comprising lignin, was very tough in order to enable trees to grow to great heights and reach the sunlight before other plants. However, when the trees died, primitive fungi could not decompose the lignin, so CO_2 was locked in the wood. Over time, the oxygen content of the atmosphere increased from 20 to 30% (resulting, incidentally, in the growth of huge insects). It took fungi 50 million years to evolve into forms that were able to break down the lignin and allow the release of CO_2, restoring oxygen levels to those seen today. If fungi had not evolved this ability, the world today would be a very different place.

Richard Lewontin and the role of environment

Richard Lewontin has published many influential scientific papers and a number of books that consider the role of the gene, the organism, environment, and 'randomness' in the evolutionary process. In a particular environment, each genetic type (organism/s) in a population has a probability of survival and reproduction. This is the *fitness* of that type for that environment, and the *mean fitness* describes the average fitness for that population. Evolution is the change in frequency of different types from generation to generation. Thus, the mean fitness of the population changes as generations pass. If natural selection or survival of the fittest, where the best genotypic or phenotypic solution to an environment becomes more common and eventually characterises a new species is the only force operating on a population, then the mean fitness of the population can only increase.

Lewontin points out that evolution by natural selection is a process where different genotypes increase their fitness for a particular environment through survival and reproduction of those individuals that are best suited to it. However, some genotypes can reach greater fitness than others which, if in competition with fitter genotypes, will not survive. One genotype can only attain a fitness for an environment in accordance with the limitations defined by its genotype. There is no genetic foresight. Lewontin likens this to mountain climbing where fitness is like altitude and natural selection is like the compulsion to climb. Only the genotype that would be, say, Mt. Everest' would produce through evolution by natural selection the peak fitness for that environment. Genotypes of other mountains, however successful, would not reach that level of fitness since no mountain is higher than Everest.

Some of Lewontin's major ideas on evolution have been described in his books, *The Doctrine of DNA* (1991) and *The Triple Helix* (1998), from which I will clarify some key concepts.

The Doctrine of DNA

Darwin's explanation for evolution is that there was a universal struggle for existence as more organisms were born than could survive and reproduce. In the course of this struggle, more efficient organisms — better designed, cleverer, and better built for the purpose of life and survival — would leave offspring at the expense of inferior kinds. The consequence of this victory in the struggle for existence is evolutionary change. Darwin considered organisms to be acted on by the environment. They are passive objects while the environment is the active subject.

By alienating the organism from the outside world, the outside world then has its own laws independent of the organism and thus cannot be changed by the organism. With this view, the organism must adapt to the environment or else die. Lewontin sees this view as wrong because it does not reflect or show the correct relationship between organisms and the world they occupy. He sees that organisms, by and large, create their own living activities.

The ideology of modern science suggests that the correct way to study the world is to dissect it into its component parts and study the properties of these pieces that make up the world in isolation from one another. In different fields of science, this method is used with success, but many believe that it prevents access to a deeper level of truth by ignoring the whole (e.g., Bohm's implicate order and quantum physics; see Chapter 3) and its connections. Thus, there is no mutual dependency between the disparate parts; the causes are either internal or external.

From this perspective, living things are seen as determined by the internal factor — genes — and we will know what we *are* when we know precisely what genes we express and how the networking of different gene regulatory pathways functions. This view has implications for cloning, the use of the results of the human genome project, and 'personalised medicine' (e.g., revealing inherited cancer or heart failure susceptibility traits via whole genome genetic screening). Although the draft of most (92%) of the human genome sequence was published in 2003 after Lewontin's book was written, his concerns are still valid.

Currently, each new genome sequence reveals some 350,000 *single nucleotide polymorphisms* (SNPs), which are nucleotide differences with no direct effect on development or health from what is considered the 'norm' for that gene for that species, much unlike a mutation — they may be silent base changes in coding regions of genes that do not result in a different amino acid being incorporated into the peptide or within the scaffolding DNA between genes. This norm may have been derived from cell lines maintained *in vitro* or directly from human genome sequences, yet what can really be inferred as the norm when such a small percent of the total potential sequences are known? Even if the genome sequence was obtained for all people on the planet and complex statistical and phylogenetic analyses were performed to define common gene sequences (e.g., to humans in general, or to ethnic types or diseases), no sequence would be representative of *a* human and no sequence would define what it is to be human as a conscious, feeling entity.

Since the genome project sequence is not of 'your' or 'my' personal DNA sequence but rather a 'representation' sequence of humanity, Lewontin's holistic view is vividly pertinent. Of course, as more human individuals' genomes are sequenced, a 'truer' representative genome should be achieved. Sequencing the DNA of an individual now costs under $1,000 (the original sequencing effort cost in the region of $3 million) and it is predicted that up to 1.6 million human genomes may have been sequenced by 2017. However, that is still a tiny fraction of the total population and will inevitably include gene sequences that are common in the industrialised, so-called 'First World' while missing those that may be characteristic of other parts of the world.

Thus, as the industrialised West will be the principal market for genome sequencing and personalised medicine, the representative human genome will relate more to them than to our species as a whole. What genomic sequencing *can* do is to aid in defining predisposition to disease and response to drug types and to provide information of a physical nature that can aid in healthcare (hence the investment). It is also worth noting that certain diseases, such as heart failure and diabetes, or factors that impact on such health matters like obesity appear to be spreading outside of their 'traditional' base of North America and Western Europe as industrialisation becomes more widespread, especially in India and Asia, so the validity of a representative human genome is becoming less.

To think that the problems posed by the external world will be overcome if we possess the 'right' kinds of genes, and those with them can reproduce and pass them onto a new generation, is a view that regards us as the vehicles by which genes propagate themselves — in other words, we are just the vessels of their passage through time. Richard Dawkins is famously quoted as considering us as 'lumbering robots' whose genes create us, 'body and mind'. There is no doubt that these days we know a great deal about what genes are and how they work from a biological and functional perspective, such as DNA replication and gene expression, as we discussed earlier in the preceding chapter.

Yet, there is much to learn, especially concerning epigenetic events such as methylation of DNA, which is still poorly understood and seen as an environmental phenomenon. However, a common misconception is about the gene itself. It is not some internal object with a mind of its own and it is not self-replicating. Genes can neither make themselves nor express their proteins without help. Genes are, in the main, an encrypted instruction that must be decoded to produce a protein in accordance with a complex series of events involving multiple inputs of biological machinery.

As well as being an extrapolationist, Dawkins is famous for being a reductionist as I had mentioned earlier. Reductionism is a term that is used in many fields of human knowledge, such as philosophy, religion, science, mathematics, and linguistics. Scientifically, it generally refers to the idea that complex things can be understood by reducing them to an interaction of their constituent or causal parts — each with their own properties — or, philosophically, to mean that a complex system is just the sum of its parts.

Dawkins uses the term 'hierarchical reductionism' to show how complex systems can be described using a hierarchy of organisations, each describable in terms of objects one level down in the hierarchy. It proposes that internal forces beyond our control govern what we are as individuals. Thus, by this reasoning, the gene ultimately computes the mind and thus to know the gene is to know the mind. The external world also has its own laws, which we confront but do not influence. This perspective produces a picture that the genes are in us, the environment is outside us, and we are at the mercy of the pull between these internal and external worlds.

Adaptationism

Lewontin states there is no 'environment' in an independent and abstract sense — there is no organism without environment and there is no environment without organism. Organisms do not experience environments but create them. According to him, the neo-Darwinist view (e.g., that of Maynard Smith and Dawkins) of *adaptationism* must be replaced with a *constructionist* view of life.

In an evolutionary context, adaptationism attempts to distinguish products of adaptation from traits arising through other processes. Lewontin (and Gould) considers that neo-Darwinists exaggerate the influence of natural selection in shaping individual traits while ignoring other powerful factors that affect morphology and behaviour, such as developmental constraints. So, rather than organisms having to find environments and then either adapt or die, they *construct* the environment. Thus, Lewontin sees the environment as 'coded' in the organism's DNA in a reverse-Lamarckian way.

The environment of an organism is constantly in a process of being remade during the life of the organism. Organisms are able to determine the statistical nature of their environment in relation to its effects on them. That is, they are able to buffer for temporal and spatial changes and effect behavioural changes to best accommodate this. Organisms also change with the nature of signals from the environment; for example, an increase in temperature perceived by an organism causes internal physiological changes. Thus, an organism is complex and is more than the mere product of coded instructions. Another example is the cichlid species of Lake Victoria, which as a geological feature is only 15,000 years old, as mentioned earlier. In that time, different environments — rocky, barren regions versus sandy-bottomed, plant-rich niches — have shaped the jaw anatomy in these fish (sub)species, which presumably arose from just a few progenitor species.

Consciousness

Genes do not compute us (humans); they make us as big as we are, determine our physical limits, and enable a central nervous system to form with as many connections as it has. However, there are not enough genes to compute consciousness as an aspect of the structure of the central nervous system. Indeed, how consciousness works, what it really is, and what causes it remain unknown. As far as we know, it is a property of the brain that transcends its causal physical processes. In this respect, we should remember that we possess roughly the same number of genes as a mouse or a nematode worm.

Consciousness creates our environment and shapes its history and our future. For Lewontin, this is the correct understanding of the relation between our genes and the shape of our lives. Our DNA is a strong influence on our anatomy — it enables the formation of our complex brain. Making the brain possible, genes also make possible human nature, the limitations of which we do not know. Consider a man aged twenty and again aged fifty. At these different ages, he would still be recognisable both physically and mentally (psychologically) as being the same person. However, the matter that constitutes him at twenty is different from that aged fifty. How then can he be the same person?

The genes are the *instructions* for his physical make up. These instructions are retained for life so that as cells die and new ones are made, food can provide the energy and materials to construct the body in accordance with the genetic blueprint. In this way, the physical person is retained and if we leave it there, the reductionist viewpoint holds — the gene computes the organism. But genes also encode the neuronal network in the brain. Life's events strengthen, weaken, add, remove, and refine neurons and their connections, which is becoming evident from research using magnetic resonance scanning (MRI) of brains, and in a way that correlates with and constitutes the evolving mind throughout life. The life we choose moulds how the neuronal network develops and evolves.

We are not in conscious control of any of the processes that occur in our cells or of a large number of their cumulative effects (e.g., the coordinated effects of the different specialised cells that constitute the kidney). However, consciousness can control the actions of some coordinated systems of whose components we have no control over (e.g., flexing a muscle) or it can influence others (e.g., heart rate). Similarly, conscious thoughts are affected by various influences (e.g., external stimuli, the subconscious, unconscious, preconscious, and so on), so the totality of our being is a combination of the mental and physical, most of which we experience or are unaware of rather than control. This all leads to an important question — when stating 'I', to what is this 'I' referring?

When we think of another person, they present in our minds as their mental and physical characteristics. The person is like a 'thing' that we can consider. Yet, when we consider ourselves, we can consider our body in the same way, but not our minds. The mind, to which all things relate and are considered, seems spatially and temporally indistinct. But is the 'I' we refer to actually the mind? If we lost some part of our body in an accident, we would still be the same person. Even if we had neurosurgery and a part of the brain that enables the mind were removed, if we retained a mental sense of self (e.g., memories), we would be the same person. So, the fundamental aspect of what constitutes 'me' is not the physical matter or the appearance, but the mind. The mind directs the character that others recognise as one's self. The mind gives a sense of who you are, to which all things refer. Yet, although the mind is caused by the brain, it is a thing that defies temporal and spatial definition. We innately know what we mean when we refer to it, yet we cannot define it. I will turn to this difficult topic in the final chapters. Suffice to say, as the philosopher John Locke stressed, the continuity of mind and memory ensures that we are always the same person throughout life. Therefore, with respect to the human, the mind is a case that shows that factors additional to our genome determine who we are.

To summarise, although genes ensure our physical continuity (*what* we are) and provide the framework within which we can explore our potentialities, it is the experiences and choices through interacting with our environment that determine *who* we are. The human mind is a prime example of how reductionism fails to explain what a human being is. Consciousness cannot be explained by the mere physical interaction of the neurons that cause and contain it. The genetically encoded phenotype of all organisms interacts both with external and internal factors during life, producing an organism whose mental and physical attributes cannot be predicted according to the genome alone. Additionally, species evolve in accordance with random factors that cannot be controlled or accounted for. Lewontin discusses these issues that question reductionism in his later book, *The Triple Helix*.

The Triple Helix

After introducing the reader to the modern view of evolutionary biology, in which the Platonic ideals are rejected and actual variation between organisms is shown as what really needs to be explained, Lewontin turns his attention to development. We have discussed development as a process in Chapter 4, so we are better equipped to understand Lewontin's views on development from an evolutionary context.

The present direction of developmental biology is to understand how a fertilised egg differentiates into an embryo. With this direction, we see how with each round of cell division the embryo becomes more complex, with the establishment of anterior-posterior and dorsal-ventral axes within the body plan and specialisation or *differentiation* of cells into specific lineages. This process is driven to some degree by the activation of genes encoding transcription factors, whose protein products often function as activators but in some cases repress expression of a downstream gene or set of gene targets. The targets may encode other transcription factors and establish a regulatory hierarchy, and so the process continues.

What Lewontin is saying is that the role of development is seen as a regular sequence of stages through which the developing system passes and that the elucidation of these processes offers insights into what we are, just as a study of the processes that cause consciousness is *supposed* to provide insights into what consciousness 'is' (as will be discussed in Chapter 6). In this theory, the external environment has two roles: it acts as an external trigger to start the process and a minimal environmental condition must allow the unfolding of the internal programming.

At the genetic level, it has long been thought that animals possess similar programming for the positional development of body parts and that evolution adds and subtracts stages to this through gene signalling. We have seen this earlier with the case of homeobox genes in invertebrates (fruit fly) and vertebrates (mouse). Experimentally, the standard method for showing that a gene is important in a process is by finding a mutation in a gene that prevents the process under study from happening and then to manipulate it to prove the point.

Such was the case for understanding the development of the body plan in *Drosophila*, as mutants with recognisable phenotypes (e.g., white eyes versus red eyes, normal wings versus crinkled wings) could be easily generated by exposing adult flies to mutagens such as X-ray irradiation. However, this approach or conclusion is to some extent 'bad biology'. The gene may be expressed in many tissues, where its protein may interact with a variety of other tissue-specific or ubiquitously expressed proteins to bring about the particular phenotype of, say, a neuron in the brain or a cardiac muscle cell. Gene interactions are generally much more subtle in terms of organ-to-organ variability (or even cell-to-cell variability — witness the devastating effects of a single mutation that turns a healthy cell into a cancerous one), especially in higher organisms such as mammals, and the role of recently discovered hierarchical regulatory molecules such as miRNAs still leaves much to be discovered.

We cannot compute the animal even with the entire sequence of DNA at our disposal and unlimited computational power. We look different from other animals because of our genes, but as to why two people are different, genetic differences are insufficient and for some characteristics may be irrelevant as an explanation. There has long been much evidence that the ontogeny of an organism is the consequence of gene interaction, the temporal sequence of external environments throughout its life, and random molecular events with its cells. These must all be considered to give a proper account of the organism. The organism is not specified by its genes but exists as a unique outcome of an ontogenetic process that depends on the sequence of environments in which it exists.

Earlier, I mentioned Lewontin's view that genes do not determine the phenotype of the individual. Of course, some completely genetically determined characteristics such as blood group *are* determined by the genotype, but this is an exception rather than the rule. For example, identical twins living in different environments (e.g., at different altitudes, which would affect the metabolic rate) will develop differently — in this case, different body shapes and physiology, such as a bigger chest and larger lung capacity in the twin living at the higher, less oxygen-rich altitude. It is thought that genes determine the capacity of an organism — the maximum size, speed, and physical characteristics that it can achieve in a favourable environment. Thus, although an Olympic sprinter may have the genotype to be a fast runner, he would have to train and eat well to fulfil this genetic potential. Although genotype determines a physically achievable potential maximum for each, what is important is how each genotype responds to each environment rather than the potential maximum for each trait of that genotype.

Norms of reaction

Lewontin believes that the correct way to understand genes and organisms is through so-called *norms of reaction* graphs. For each genotype, there is a particular phenotype for each environment with a characteristic norm of reaction. A genotype does not specify a unique outcome of development but a 'norm of reaction'; that is, different developmental outcomes from different environments. In other words, genotypes produce different phenotypes for different environments.

Norms of reaction can reveal common misconceptions about the role of the environment in the relationship between genotype and organism. Geneticists use mutation experiments as a means to confirm that genotype specifies phenotype. The fruit fly *Drosophila* has long been used as a model organism for such experiments, yet its norms of reaction are often not characteristic of this relationship. For example, a useful mutation from a 'genotype determines phenotype' viewpoint would be one whose phenotypic difference from the normal, wild-type fly would occur in every individual carrying the mutation and over a wide range of environments. Geneticists would then state that the genetic effects are typical. However, the fact that *Drosophila* mutations do not act predictably is rarely clarified because the variable phenotypes observed for different environments would contradict a purely gene-determined phenotype.

The gene-centric view of development suggests that the morphology, physiology, and basic aspects of the organism are direct products of its genes. Other suggestions relating to aspects of the organism are viewed as superficial. However, if we analyse the fluctuating symmetry of bristles on the body of the fruit fly, for example, which are all encoded by the same genes, we see that the cause of this asymmetry is *developmental noise*. This non-trivial, non-genetically determined process is a consequence of the sort of random processes I mentioned earlier; random events within cells at the level of molecular interaction. Thus, the same gene cannot determine the outcome of its code as a result of this randomness. By including developmental noise in the process of development, the organism is seen to be determined neither by its genes nor environment but by an interaction between them with the inclusion of random processes. Thus, the organism does not compute itself from its genes nor from the information of its environments.

Adaptation revised

Darwin saw variation among organisms to be the result of an internal process, now known as mutation and recombination. This process does not respond to environmental demands. The environment presents problems and the organism achieves solutions through a random process. Here, adaptation is appropriate. Lewontin sees adaptive explanations as having a forward and backward form. In the forward form, which relates mainly to extant species, the problems posed to the organism are described on the basis of what is important to it. In the backward form, which relates mainly to extinct species, we observe a trait (usually through fossils) and determine what problem it solved. These explanations serve to show how the organism maps or mapped the demands of the environment through adaptation. Here, the organism is a passive object of external and internal forces, where problems are presented at random. Solutions to these problems are also generated at random.

A concept of the environment that is correct for our understanding of past evolution and future conditions needs to clarify the relationship between organism and environment. Organisms determine which elements of the external world are put together to make their environments and how these relate to each other and to themselves. Organisms determine what aspects of the outside world are relevant to them as a result of their shape and make up; they construct a world around them. They create physical relations with the outside world and constantly alter their environment. What is consumed by one living thing as energy and matter and then produced in another form is a resource for consumption for another.

If organisms are constantly adapting to the outer world, then as evolution progresses, species should be better adapted and live longer. However, the environment is constantly changing, so adaptation to yesterday's environment is of no advantage to that of today. Organisms modulate the statistical properties of external conditions as the conditions become part of their environment. This temporal and spatial modulation results in a smoothing out of variable environmental effects over their lifetime. Organisms differentiate with respect to space and time to enable detection of and reaction to the external environment. Of course, extreme examples of an organism failing to adapt to dramatic changes in its environment might be the devastating effect of *el Niño* upon coral reef life or the fragmentation of polar ice caps due to year-on-year global warming and its effects on polar bears.

Interestingly, signals from the physical world are integrated by organisms and transduced between different forms in accordance with their internal biology; for example, increased temperature causing a biochemical change inside the organism, such as temperature-dependent sex determination seen in reptile embryos. Of great importance is the difference in size of organisms, since it determines the effect of different environments on the organism as well as the organism's relation to it. Hence, Brownian motion (the random movement of particles suspended in a fluid) affects a microscopic organism but is of less importance to us; the reverse could be said of gravitation.

Cause and effect?

Lewontin is concerned about the view of the organism as distinguishable bits and pieces, each of which has a determined causal relation to each other component. By obstructing a practical understanding of natural phenomena, he considers this view to simplify the relation of parts to the whole and of *cause and effect*. This naïve reductionism is due to the nature of scientific work, which poses only those questions we are able to solve and solves only the questions for which our methods and concepts are adequate.

Nietzsche and Hume were strictly opposed to the inference that scientists make from the idea of cause and effect. To Hume, causality is useful only for picturing a process of events. Nietzsche realised that there is a continuum between cause and effect and that when scientists isolate and investigate events between cause and effect, they do not really see cause; rather, they infer what probably never occurs.

Lewontin sees this opposition between the molecule and organism, in this context, as wrong. Even by discovering all the genes as functional units in the production of proteins, we will not know the protein's function. Thus, we will not know how to assemble the gene/protein collective into a system with causal connections. The 'machine model' of life portrayed by the reductionist viewpoint leads us to ignore the most common characteristic of many physical systems, the dependence on initial conditions. Without taking into account the history of the organism, it is impossible to understand its situation. Evolution is a "historically contingent pathway through the space of possibilities", as Lewontin puts it. For example, the Indian rhinoceros and African black rhinoceros have one and two horns, respectively, because they are two alternative outcomes of the same selective process, but with different initial genetic conditions.

Genetic variation depends on mutation, but this is a rare occurrence (a new DNA mutation occurs maybe once in 100,000,000 gametes). The time span between the origin of a species and the time that a mutation occurs of just the right kind and of the right frequency to affect the selection process is of the same order as the lifetime of the species (about 10,000,000 years). Most mutations that would have been selected if they had occurred are never seen. A species must deal with the variation it already possesses.

Lewontin clearly feels that a reductionist approach to the study of organisms leads to not only incomplete answers about biological processes but also asking the wrong questions. An alternative approach is to go to the opposite extreme of reductionism and consider the world as a single, non-analysable structure of interactions that cannot be broken down without destroying their essence. However, a great deal has been achieved by the methodological strategy of reductionism despite its faults. Science needs to find boundaries for the near-independent subsystems that divide the biological world. For example, the extinction of a species will have a major effect on another species that depended on it for food, yet the effects will propagate through the biological world with degrees of influence ranging from major to none.

Three theories have been suggested that attempt to explain biological phenomena in terms of general properties of temporally changing systems:

1. **Catastrophe theory** suggests that systems change in time according to simple mathematical laws. Less than 0.01% of all species that have ever existed are alive today. Catastrophe theory hopes to show that extinction is a consequence of simple laws that allowed the species to spread initially. However, there is no evidence that such laws apply to biological systems.
2. **Chaos theory** developed to show that some simple dynamic systems reach equilibrium or oscillate in one range of parameters, yet pass from one state to another apparently randomly. This randomness can be predicted from the equations of the system. Chaos can be demonstrated using electrical circuits, but most of these are stable. The application and inference to biological systems is dubious.
3. **Complexity theory** provides the hope that complex biological systems possess laws that originate in the many interactions among the many parts of complexity itself. It remains to be seen if there is an application to the understanding of biological processes.

Lewontin thinks that we do not need new systems but rather a willingness to accept that biological systems occupy different regions in the area of physical relations than physico-chemical systems. Function cannot be understood without knowledge of shape and form. This logic applies to the study of life; whether we consider populations, cells, or even molecules, spatio-temporal relations must be accounted for when evaluating function. The interest in form from a biological perspective came with the solving of the structure of DNA in 1953, yet the role of DNA in biology has led to a scheme of explanation in biology that pays little attention to molecular structure and spatial relations.

For a correct path of understanding between gene and organism, we need to include phenomena that influence how the amino acid chain encoded by the gene becomes a three dimensionally, precisely folded protein of function. We have no idea what dictates the tertiary structure of a protein by reading the peptide sequence on its own — even today, computer programmes that predict secondary structure from the peptide sequence are fairly inaccurate. For the explanation of the development process, we must know the shape and internal environment of cells.

Lewontin thinks that progress in biology does not require revolutionary conceptualisations but rather new methodologies that enable the right questions to be asked and answered.

Gould, Lewontin, and Dawkins clearly present different ideas about some key aspects of evolutionary theory. Therefore, one or more of them must be wrong about certain issues of contention. That there is disagreement between such eminent scientists demonstrates both the complexity of the subject, and the fallibility of science to generate universally agreed views. Like any scientist in whatever discipline, their individual views on evolution will have been influenced by a multitude of scientific and personal factors, including the formative scientific years that focussed them on a particular collection ideas that resonated within them. Clearly, different pieces of information they each encountered served to contribute to, and mould, a paradigm of their 'truth' on the subject.

A scientist's quest for facts and truth, within any scientific discipline, is influenced by factors both inside and outside the actual data that pertains to the subject. The way an individual extracts objective scientific truth is unavoidably affected by issues (some of which even the scientist in unaware) such as peer pressure, ego, career concerns (e.g. obtaining research grant funding), religious views, that often lie outside the 'pure' goal of achieving objectivity.

These three scientists will have had access to the same vast repository of evolutionary data, yet many factors influence how it is interpreted. There is also an unavoidable, and high, correlation between what scientists generally tend to think is true about their subject of expertise, and the particular paradigm they were 'brought up on' (string theory is another case — see *Lost in Math*, by Sabine Hossenfelder) when their ideas were more malleable. One cannot escape the early influence of ideas on a blank slate, despite the journey of refinement of ideas that evolve from a certain foundation.

Furthermore, since scientific truth is relative (to human capacity), and not absolute, scientists (and philosophers) can attach a protective emotional defence of their views that is often rigidly impermeable to change, despite objective evidence contrary to their view (and evidence for a new 'truth' which was, ironically, their goal when they started). In the case of string theory, the search for the mathematical descriptions of reality that have to be 'beautiful' has resulted in little progress (the error of having a preconceived idea of how things *should* be rather than being open-minded to what results we observe).

Size matters

In *Why Size Matters* (2006), John Tyler Bonner makes some interesting observations about why organisms are the size they are and why this has profound consequences for us, as beings of higher-order consciousness, in terms of how we perceive the environment. Limitations on our size determine how we live and what we are capable of. If we were orders of magnitude larger or smaller, we would not have our abilities, but for reasons that are less than obvious.

Size determines the type of force that is dominant in an organism's existence. For an organism above 1mm in size, gravity dominates over cohesive forces. This domination increases with increasing size of the organism. Cohesion is the intermolecular attraction between similar molecules — cohesive forces explain phenomena such as surface tension. Being large creatures, humans are dominated by gravity while cohesive forces are not felt. Below about 1mm in size, cohesive forces dominate over gravity with increasing effect as organisms become smaller (e.g., we observe flies walking up walls, or across the surface of a pond).

Strength is also related to an organism's size. However, it does not increase linearly with size. Instead, it increases according to the formula:

$$\text{Strength} \propto \text{weight}^{2/3}$$

This means that small organisms are *proportionally* stronger than bigger ones. We see ants carrying objects bigger than themselves because as they are lighter than us, they are proportionally stronger.

Intelligence relates to size. The bigger the animal, the bigger the brain — in general — and the bigger the brain, the smarter the animal — also in general. I say 'in general' because there are cases that deviate from this trend. For example, blue whales are bigger than us and have bigger brains, but are less intelligent. Thus, intelligence depends not only on the size of the brain but also on the arrangement within. The endocranial volume of hominids has increased at a far higher rate than any other animal, including the great apes. In other words, we have been getting smarter quicker and our skulls have had to evolve to encapsulate our swelling heads.

Organisms on Earth have shown a general trend towards an increase in *length* during life's evolution. In the struggle for survival by natural selection, every niche is filled with organisms that can exploit it, and each is perfectly adapted to its niche. If not, another better-suited organism would come along or evolve and take over. However, in the case of size, there is always "room at the top" as Bonner puts it. A new niche is ever present and waiting for a bigger organism (but up to a point due to restrictions such as those imposed by parameters like gravity and food). Island gigantism is an evolutionary phenomenon that tends to occur on geographically isolated islands lacking a natural apex predator.

The lack of predation allows herbivores and other animals, particularly birds and reptiles, to grow larger and the fossil record shows many extinct examples such as the giant moa and elephant bird from New Zealand and Madagascar, respectively. The Galapagos Islands are, of course, famous for their several subspecies of giant tortoise. Interestingly, despite the steady increase in length of the whole organism, the cell size has remained the same. So, as organisms get bigger, the number of cells that comprise the organism increases.

The number of different cell *types* that comprise the organism has increased too. So, fans of metaphors can say that the organism has become more like a city where different specialists do different functions for the benefit of the whole. As discussed earlier, one of the great breakthroughs for life on Earth was the evolution of multicellular development. Prior to this, one cell had to carry out all functions. Thus, the result of multicellularity, increase in size of the whole organism due to available niches, and increase in number and types of cells, is the diversity of complex species we see today.

The bigger the animal, the slower the metabolic rate such that every organism with a heart (e.g., vertebrates) lives a life with approximately the same number of heartbeats. Thus, bigger animals with slower metabolic rates live longer because their quota of heartbeats are used up in a longer time frame. It is believed that all mammals appear to have a predetermined number of heartbeats in their life — about one to three billion as mentioned in Chapter 4. Hence, a mouse with a rapid heartbeat uses up its quota in just a few years.

The reasons for this metabolic difference are many, such as the fact that bigger animals like elephants have a smaller surface area to volume ratio. Thus, they can afford to have a slower metabolism as they lose heat less rapidly and need to expend less energy generating heat compared to small animals such as shrews or mice, which may burn off a third of their body weight in the cold just to keep warm. Bigger animals move slower because gravitational effects become an increasingly difficult force to overcome. The bigger the animal, the longer the time frame between generations, and this also applies to plants.

These and other trends demonstrate how the diversity of life on Earth coexists in an environment with common obstacles in the form of forces to overcome as well as flora and fauna to compete with and against. They show that despite the diversity of life, there are distinct rules on what can be done and within these rules, every opportunity is effected though natural selection.

iii) Mathematics and the Natural World

So far, we have made mentions of mathematical modelling in passing and acknowledged the power of computer programmes in determining relatedness of gene sequences and constructing cladograms that reveal evolutionary relatedness. But how does mathematics shape the natural world around us? In the final chapters, I will discuss mathematics, logic, mind, knowledge, and consciousness, linking all that we have discussed in this and the preceding chapters to produce a picture of what the world does, and can, mean to us. Scientifically, we use mathematics as a tool to assess the world and draw conclusions about it. From this analysis, we have found that mathematical rules and patterns are very much a part of nature itself.

The golden ratio

The *golden ratio* is as an example of how simple mathematical patterns are revealed in living systems. The number pi (π) represents the ratio of the circumference of a circle to its diameter. It has a value of 3.1415926…. There is no exact value — it is an irrational number. It cannot be represented as a fraction. The number of decimal places can continue indefinitely for the value of pi and we will not reach its true value. There is another irrational number called phi or tau (ϕ or τ) that has some very interesting properties in nature and shows that nature can evolve into mathematical rules. So, what is the number?

If I draw a straight line:

```
A                    C                    B
_____
    ⇐         x         ⇒⇐       1        ⇒
```

and make points on the line such that the ratio of the lengths AB/AC are equal to AC/CB, then what we have is the golden ratio. What is that? For the ratio AB/AC to equal AC/CB, there can be only one place on the line AB for the point C to take. Any other position for C will not produce this ratio. If we give a value to the distance from A to C as x and from C to B as 1, then we can calculate the value of the golden ratio by inserting x and 1 into the ratio formula. Thus:

$$x/1 = x + 1/x$$

By rearrangement:

$$x^2 - x - 1 = 0$$

This can be solved for x. For any *quadratic* equation of the form $ax^2 + bx + c = 0$, the value of x is given by:

$$x = \frac{-b \pm \sqrt{b^2 - 4ac}}{2a}$$

For the equation describing the golden ratio, this gives a value of x = 1.61803988749.... This number is the golden ratio.

What is the significance of this number from a biological perspective? Before we look at the biological meaning behind the golden ratio, let us look more at some mathematically interesting properties of this number. If we take the expression:

$$1 + (1 + (1 + (1 + \ldots \text{ ad infinitum, and solve for x, such that}\ldots$$

$$x = 1 + (1 + (1 + (1 + \ldots$$

Then this can be rearranged to give:

$$x^2 = 1 + 1 + (1 + (1 + (1 + \ldots \text{ (and we know } x = 1 + (1 + (1 + (1 + \ldots)$$

So we have:

$$x^2 = 1 + x$$

which rearranges to $x^2 - x - 1 = 0$, which we have shown gives us the value of the golden ratio.

Also, if we take the expression:

$$1 + 1/(1 + 1/(1 + 1/(1 + 1/\ldots \text{ ad infinitum}$$

and solve for x, such that:

$$x = 1 + 1/(1 + 1/(1 + 1/(1 + 1/\ldots$$

We know that $1 + 1/(1 + 1/(1 + 1/(1 + 1/\ldots = x$, so we have:

$$x = 1 + 1/x$$

This rearranges to give $x^2 = x + 1$, which is the same as $x^2 - x - 1 = 0$, once again giving us the golden ratio.

These simple and infinitely repeating algebraic expressions give us this special number, which comes from dividing a line at a specific point. The fact that they produce an irrational number is mathematically interesting, but what is especially fascinating is that this number correlates with physiological and behavioural properties of life on Earth. Consider this example — if a pair of rabbits is placed in an area, how many *pairs* of rabbits can be produced from that pair in a year if, every month, each pair begets a new pair that, from the second month on, becomes productive? The value for the number of pairs for each month continues like so:

1, 1, 2, 3, 5, 8, 13, 21, 34, 55, 89, 144, 233 .... et cetera

What is interesting about this sequence? How does it relate to the golden ratio? Taking the sequence of numbers, if we add 1 + 1, we get 2; if we add 2 + 1, we get 3; if we add 3 + 2, we get 5; if we add 5 + 3, we get 8. If we continue like this, we always arrive at the next value in the sequence. This sequence is called the *Fibonacci sequence*, named after the 12th century Italian mathematician Leonardo of Pisa, who was also known as Fibonacci and who introduced the sequence to western mathematics (it had been described in Indian mathematics).

This sequence, as we will see, relates to the golden ratio. Here are some other examples of its appearance in nature — the number of bees in each generation of a family tree increases according to the Fibonacci sequence. The number of stems protruding from the main stem of a plant for each rotation around its horizontal axis follows alternative numbers in the Fibonacci sequence — for example, eight stems for every three rotations, or five stems for every two rotations. The number of petals in a flower is often one of the numbers in the Fibonacci sequence.

Perhaps the most well-known example is the heads of sunflowers, which show two series of curves winding in opposite directions. The number of spirals is either 21 and 34, 34 and 55, 55 and 89, or 89 and 144. These are all numbers in the Fibonacci sequence. A similar thing is seen in pine cones and pineapples.

The shape of the shell of a nautilus also conforms to the Fibonacci sequence (Figure 40). This sea creature — a shelled cephalopod — has remained unchanged for millions of years and is considered a 'living fossil'.

Thus, the Fibonacci sequence presents itself as a solution by nature to many behavioural and physiological characteristics of both the flora and fauna of life on Earth. In fact, the spiralling of a galaxy conforms to a Fibonacci sequence, implying that this sequence reproduces the behaviour of much of what exists, whether living or not. Indeed, the number of permutations by which light can reflect from a mirror, if it reflects internally

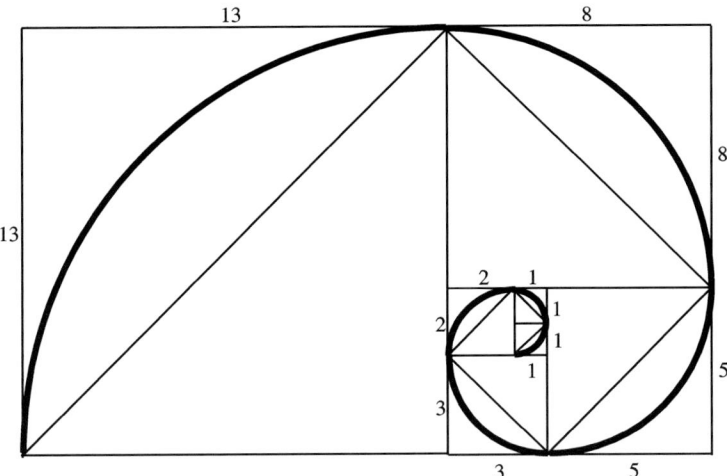

Figure 40. The shell of the nautilus. The golden ratio and the Fibonacci sequence can be mapped directly onto the shape of the shell of the nautilus. This special type of logarithmic spiral in the figure, created by joining opposite corners of squares created by the golden ratio, produces the shape of the shell of the nautilus.

once, twice, three, or more times between two panes of glass, equates to the numerical increase of the Fibonacci sequence.

However, although it also applies to non-biological phenomena on Earth, we should not get carried away and draw conclusions about the deeper significance of the Fibonacci sequence in nature but instead appreciate that it represents a naturally occurring, sometimes evolved solution to *many* biological and non-biological phenomena. Indeed, to draw significance beyond that would be to make the same mistake Stephen Wolfram made in his book, *A New Kind of Science* (see next section), where overemphasis is placed on the meaning behind the ability of simple programmes to produce both irregular and complex behaviour.

Each system is presented with its own reasons why the sequence makes biological or physical sense. Just as behaviour that is considered fractal in nature is seen in an increasing number of systems, so too will a tendency to the Fibonacci sequence continue to reveal itself as an appropriate solution to the pressures exerted on such systems. For example, in the case of the position of the branching stems around a main plant stem, this pattern enables maximal opportunity for light to reach the flowers emanating from the stems. It is the solution nature has found because plants with such a pattern prospered and the genes encoding such patterns survived.

We can now return to the question of what the Fibonacci sequence has to do with the golden ratio. Let us look at the Fibonacci sequence again:

1, 1, 2, 3, 5, 8, 13, 21, 34, 55, 89, 144, 233, 377, 610, 987 ...

If we divide the value of the next number in the sequence by the former number in the sequence, we get:

1/1 = 1
2/1 = 2
3/2 = 1.5
5/3 = 1.6666666
8/5 = 1.6
13/8 = 1.625
21/13 = 1.615385
34/21 = 1.619049
55/34 = 1.617647
89/55 = 1.618182
144/89 = 1.617978
233/144 = 1.618056
377/233 = 1.618026
610/377 = 1.618037
987/610 = 1.618033

As we progress to higher values in the Fibonacci sequence, we approximate closer and closer to the true value of the golden ratio. The value of the golden ratio cannot be calculated exactly and the number of Fibonacci numbers is infinite, so it is impossible to find both the final Fibonacci number and the value of the ratio. As Mario Livio points out in his book *The Golden Ratio* (2002), if we were to transmit the number phi, pi, or the *Feigenbaum point* (see below) into the Universe as an attempt to contact alien life, these numbers would tell the recipient that the transmitter (us) is intelligent as these numbers have a universal quality and their meaning to us will also be revealed to them, given that the rules apply everywhere in the Universe.

Prime numbers are numbers divisible only by themselves and 1, such as 1, 2, 3, 5, 7, 11, 13, 17, 19, and so on. There are many species of cicada in the world, most with relatively short lifespans, but the *periodical* cicadas, of which there are seven species, are extremely long-lived (13 or 17 years, although most of this is spent underground in the nymph stage). What is more, their local populations tend to be developmentally synchronised such that they all emerge and mature into adults within a very short span of time, which is a good tactic to avoid predation.

Gould reasoned in his 1977 essay *"Of Bamboo, Cicadas, and the Economy of Adam Smith"* that cicadas that mature at "prime number" year intervals have an evolutionary advantage when it comes to avoiding predation and being able to successfully pass on their genes to the next generation. For example, consider a bug that emerges only every 17 years — with a short period of adult life to boot — that is preyed upon by a predator with a five-year lifespan. This cicada population will only be troubled by a peak predator population every 85 (i.e., 5 × 17) years. In comparison, a cicada with a non-prime developmental cycle such as 12 years would be fair game for any predators with a two-, three-, four-, or six-year life cycle and could face regular 'boom or bust' scenarios of population crashes during those years that coincide with a peak number of predators.

It is an ongoing challenge to seek ever larger prime numbers (currently the largest number has over 17 million digits). However, as we count onwards from 1, we find that the distribution of primes becomes less common. In fact, the distribution relates very closely to a natural logarithm:

$$\text{Primes}/x \sim 1/\ln(x)$$

Meaning that the density (number) of primes below some number (x) is roughly the same as 1 divided by the natural log of that number. So, it is not only physical reality that follows logarithms as the solution or natural evolution of processes in response to problems but also the concepts we uncover that describe reality itself — we find logarithmic patterns as nature's solution to both what 'is' and the Platonically abstract ideas we discover that relate to them.

Is mathematics discovered or created? Is it 'out there' and it remains for us to find it out, or is it an abstract concept that only exists once created? My personal view is that mathematical concepts are out there in an abstract sense, like numbers, and have a universal meaning. They have an applicable meaning to the Universe they exist in. But mathematical objects have no objective reality. We can create the numbers one, two, and three or the meaning of addition and subtraction, but without consciousness of them, they do not exist. We have discovered their abstract meaning and application, and we continue to uncover deeper abstract connections. That which exists in the Universe — abstract, conceptual, or real — exists because the Universe permits what can or cannot be according to its physics. It is our job to find out these limits and what exists within them.

Fractals and chaos

Attempts have been made to understand the Universe by modelling complex systems, such as those that appear in life forms on Earth, using simple 'programmes' governed by non-mathematical rules. Stephen Wolfram, who devised the mathematical programme *Mathematica*, published a huge book titled *A New Kind of Science* (2002) that attempted to outline a fundamentally new way of modelling complex systems. With respect to life, it is known that complex equations fail to model biological systems, yet 'cellular automata' programmes can mimic results found in nature (e.g., tree branches, stream eddies, and leopard spots). However, his ideas were not universally well received by experts in the field as an attempt to explain life's processes, since many systems cannot be explained using such programmes. Criticism of this book included the that many of the conclusions had been made before and that new findings were speculative.

Chaos theory attempts to explain the complex behaviour of apparently chaotic systems that appear to show a fundamental level of order. These nonlinear systems display behaviour that cannot be predicted by supercomputers. Electrical circuits and weather patterns are examples of such chaotic phenomena. The flow of water changes from non-chaotic to chaotic behaviour when its path is hindered by a rock. Chaos theory shows that a tiny variation in the starting conditions of a chaotic system can result in an enormous difference in the result at some later time point within the system. When one ball strikes another and if this incident is somehow constrained to be the entire system, we can calculate the effect of the first ball on the motion of the second. This is determinism on a small scale. However, reality is not like that.

When you see a wave break, that is chaos. The billions of water molecules interact in such a way that even if we have all the data on their positions and velocity at one point and moment in space and time, we still cannot calculate them at the next. By exceeding experimental and theoretical limits, we can only model the outcome using chaos theory and statistical laws, which have been formulated to interpret this type of behaviour. They are very much a part of physics.

The French mathematician Benoit Mandelbrot (1924–2010) has investigated the interrelation between chaos and nature (chaos is intrinsic to nature). He is famous for the 'Mandelbrot set' fractal, which shows an infinitely deep structure following infinite iterations of its simple causative algorithm — a finite sequence of instructions used for a calculation. On greater magnification, it reveals novel intricacies superficially similar to the larger version and which repeat the common structure to infinite magnification. It is an example of complexity emerging from simplicity.

His work was an attempt to describe chaotic and dynamic systems as applied to the real world. Roger Penrose believes that the Mandelbrot set is not an invention but a discovery. It has been analysed along with other similar fractal algorithms in an attempt to understand how recurrent rules can produce complicated behaviour. Attempts have been made to use this science to distinguish biological 'agents' (e.g., molecules and cells) from their interactions (e.g., chemical reactions and evolution) and to ascertain how the computational properties of interactions account for what we see as 'beautiful' in nature.

Fractal geometry and chaos theory underwent a parallel development. Indeed, they are inextricably linked. For example, paralleling somewhat the deductions made by Darwin, the 19th century English economist Thomas Malthus observed that populations increase exponentially whereas food production increases linearly. The Belgian mathematician Pierre Francois Verhulst devised a model incorporating the concept of *negative feedback* that accounts for a realistic model of population growth. Here, the population in one year is a function of that of the previous year (hence, negative feedback). He devised a formula for calculating the predicted population in a year:

> If the population in one year is given by x,
> then the population in the following year is given by: $x_{next} = rx(1-x)$
> where 'r' represents a constant that can be adjusted according to the population.

By repeating this formula, it is possible to calculate long-term population behaviour. The repeated steps of an algorithm are known as *iterations*. For the formula given, if we are modelling some population, we can take a value of x that represents the population at one point in time, apply a value for r, and perform the algorithmic iterations. We will find that although the population rises and falls, it will eventually reach a steady-state level. However, for certain values of r, the population oscillates between two values known as *bifurcation points* and which repeat every two years — a process called *period-doubling*.

For a certain value of r, a period-doubling cascade appears on graphical representation where the bifurcations accumulate at a single point called the 'Feigenbaum point', named after Mitchell Feigenbaum. The interesting discovery is that this repeated doubling leads to chaos, but within this chaos exists elements of order. Thus, stable periodic behaviour and chaotic behaviour can both be integrated within the same algorithm.

In 1975, Tien Yien Li and James Yorke produced the first scientific publication linking this periodicity to chaotic behaviour, which ultimately led to the science of chaos theory. Feigenbaum showed that the ratio of distances between each bifurcation converged on the number 4.669201660910…. Experimental verification of this result proved it to be a principle of nature. The number is as real as π. Chaos, like the uncertainty principle and Gödel's theorem, represents another delimiting area of science on what we can know and what is unknowable.

Fractal geometry contrasts with the idealised forms of Euclidean geometry in that it can mirror some of the shapes seen in nature as mentioned earlier. The algorithms of fractal forms can present 2- and 3-D shapes that apparently mimic both biological and non-biological structures present in the Universe (e.g., clouds and galaxies). While it does not account for or explain all structures, its practical applications are already evident. From a biological perspective, fractal geometry is being used to detect early cancer cell formation because cancer cells differ from normal cells in that they are more 'crinkly' in appearance. Indeed, they display fractal properties that alter during cell growth. Detecting the fractal degree of the surface may provide some indication of the level of differentiation of the cell, thus indicating whether it is becoming cancerous or not.

Concluding Remarks

In this and the preceding chapter, we have examined the many wonders of the inner space of the cell, particularly with regard to how genes are expressed and can direct embryonic and fetal development, and looked at the role of evolution in shaping what we are now. Much discussion of evolution, of course, has occurred post-Darwin' — many of the scientists and philosophers of the Enlightenment, for example, believed in some element of divine influence at work in our development. Much focus, naturally, has been on evaluating the time-course of evolution from examples preserved in the fossil record, which has also raised questions about the relatedness of extant living species to long-extinct life forms.

A common misconception is that we (man) have evolved from 'lower' forms of life such as fish or frogs or reptiles with the passage of millions of years. This is not so — as evolution progresses and new species arise, it leaves in the fossil record examples of ancestral organisms that share some relatedness with extant species but are not the same as species living today. Indeed, a central tenet of *The Origin of Species* was Darwin's belief that all life on Earth has in its ancestry one common 'primordial' species.

In recent years, technological advances in bioscience fields as diverse as computer modelling, bioimaging, and genome sequencing have allowed even more precise assignment of organisms, both living and extinct, to particular taxonomic phyla or families. For instance, it is now widely accepted that modern birds share common ancestry with dinosaurs. The discovery in 2016 of the intact tail of a sparrow-sized, 99 million-year-old feathered dinosaur, preserved in a chunk of amber (fossilised secreted tree resin) and found in a Myanmar street market, was highly significant. When subjected to CT scanning and other techniques, it showed us for the first time how primitive feathers were attached to the skeleton of a dinosaur. What was striking was the similarity between the preserved feathers and those of modern birds. Primitive, certainly, but clearly related. The perfect preserving conditions of the resin that trapped this unfortunate and presumably tree-dwelling dinosaur even revealed the colouration of this tiny extinct creature.

This example brings to mind some of the early diary entries that Darwin made on his voyage on the HMS Beagle. Two years or so before he reached the Galapagos Islands, the Beagle had navigated the coast of Patagonia and, on several stops, Darwin had collected fossilised bones from a number of unknown extinct animals, including giant sloths and armadillo-like animals (now known to be glyptodonts, a family distinct from but also related to the modern armadillo family). As Darwin had seen (and been made to eat) armadillos on his trip, he was struck by the similarity between the bones of the fossilised animal and those of its living 'counterpart'. Gradually, as he made his way around the coast of South America, his observations on these and other birds and animals led him to speculate that perhaps the modern form had come to supplant and replace the now extinct relative within a common environment. It would be nearly 25 years before his ideas were published in the form of *The Origin of Species*, with its central theme of evolution by natural selection.

I described at length that extraordinary collection of much earlier fossils that is the Burgess Shale from 540 to 505 million years ago, and we saw how it provoked strong views on how evolution progresses, particularly with respect to how Darwin's vision of a process of gradual change (which we now explain at the gene level as being the steady accumulation of nucleic acid changes or mutations to give an individual a better chance of surviving and passing on its genes to its progeny) could be squared with a sudden burst of diversity and disparity as seen in the Burgess fossil evidence.

An article published in the scientific journal *Nature Communications* in 2015 discussed how increases in the oxygenation of Earth's surface environment led to the possibility of increased species diversity. About 800 million years ago, oxygen levels rose from about 0.1% to 2% of the present values and, with environmental events causing small spikes in oxygen levels, the possibility for larger Ediacaran animals to evolve resulted.

However, it is thought that around 540 million years ago, a significant rise in oxygen (about 10% of the current value) was enough to stimulate a sharp rise in the diversity and disparity of species. Although the development of animals into motile and macroscopic forms is known to be linked to the gradual increase in oxygenation of the Earth's surface environment, the *Nature Communications* article presented molybdenum isotope data to demonstrate that the extent of oxygenated bottom waters increased in step with early Cambrian bioradiation of animals and eukaryotic phytoplankton. Hence, as is the case with the interconnected web of knowledge that characterises the scientific method, evidence modifies our view of things.

Going back even further, fossilised cyanobacteria species have been found in pre-Cambrian *stromatolites* (fossilised mat-like structures built from microorganisms and solid matter) that date back possibly 2.7 billion years, maybe even as far as 3.5 billion years ago (though there is some dispute over this dating). Unfortunately, there is no supporting evidence for that immense stretch of time in which the first building blocks of life formed from the atoms swirling around in a hot and inhospitable younger Earth, but perhaps there is a clue in some living single-cell organisms that we now know have extremely ancient roots. We know that some organisms living today, particularly bacteria and invertebrates, are extraordinarily resilient, such as *Thermus aquaticus*, the hot pool-dwelling bacterium whose optimal temperature for metabolic function is a staggering 70°C or so.

As I described in the previous chapter, we have exploited these properties to create PCR technology, of course, but it makes one wonder how ancient a species *T. aquaticus* actually is and whether it is a reflection of what much of early, primitive unicellular life on our planet was like. *T. aquaticus*, which is regarded as a *hyperthermophile* as it lives at temperatures in excess of 60°C, is a *chemotrophic* organism. Chemotrophs are able to utilise simple carbon sources as the raw material for sustaining life through the use of methane or the oxidation of inorganic compounds such as hydrogen sulphide rather than photosynthesis to power their metabolism.

Similar organisms live in even more challenging conditions, such as chemotrophic bacteria found around deep sea hydrothermal vents that form where magma is especially close to the surface of the ocean floor.

The temperatures around such vents may reach 150°C; the lack of light renders photosynthesis impossible; there is effectively no oxygen; and the pressure is so high that water does not boil. Nonetheless, such vents are teeming with life from bacteria to worms, shrimps, and crabs. Many vent bacteria require temperatures of around 90°C to survive; as with *T. aquaticus*, their enzymes have evolved to be most active at such temperatures — either side of this temperature, enzyme activity drops off. Some forms exist symbiotically within giant gut-less worms that appear to have bypassed the evolutionary need to develop a gut, instead living off the products of chemotrophic metabolism produced by their passengers.

These findings are reminiscent of some hypotheses mentioned in Chapter 4, namely that eukaryotic cells, both plant and animal, may have evolved by ingesting different types of primitive single-cell organisms that gave rise to chloroplasts and mitochondria, respectively.

Carl Woese (1928–2012) was an American biophysicist and microbiologist who reshaped the history of evolution by comparing microbial organisms according to genetic relatedness rather than physical appearance and similarity. He achieved this by analysing 16S ribosomal RNA, a major component of the small subunit of the ribosome, from a variety of bacteria and so-called archaebacterial species, both thought at that time to be part of the prokaryotic kingdom. 16S rRNA accumulates nucleotide changes very gradually over time and therefore may be taken as a stable marker of evolutionary change. Work published by Woese in 1977 reclassified the archaebacteria as a distinct and ancient kingdom, 'Archaea', in its own right, distinct from bacteria and eukaryotes.

Thus, at a stroke, Woese redrew the tree of life by adding a third branch. The Archaea include bacteria that can endure environmental extremes, such as those that use sulphur as a source of energy, vent bacteria which are, of course, hyperthermophilic in nature, and extreme halophiles which can tolerate high levels of salinity. As a consequence, it is now accepted that the Archaea branched off from what Darwin referred to in *The Origin of Species* as the "one primordial form" early in the evolution of life on earth. Today, evolutionary science talks of the *Last Universal Common Ancestor* (LUCA) as the most recent life form to which all extant life on earth can trace ancestry, though 'recent' in this case means 3.5 to 3.8 billion years ago. LUCA is hypothesised to have been some sort of deep sea hydrothermal vent-dwelling organism, in accordance with what is known from the geological record for that period where it has been hypothesised that seas were hot, salty, and acidic due to prolonged periods of high levels of dissolved CO_2 during this turbulent and violently volcanic period of Earth's history.

A 2016 study based on an analysis of around 6 million protein coding gene sequences from a variety of prokaryotic genomes identified 355 protein clusters from over 280,000 that were likely to have been common to LUCA. These clusters suggest that LUCA would have been an anaerobic, CO_2-fixing thermophile that probably occupied a hydrothermal vent environment. Of course, it is to be expected that some scientists have presented alternative hypotheses that challenge the idea that all life on Earth can be traced back to a single organism.

We can go even further back in time and predict a world before the evolution of any organism thanks to what we know of nucleic acids and how evolution conserves gene sequence. RNA is a remarkably ancient molecule as Woese illustrated using 16S rRNA to construct accurate cladograms showing evolutionary relatedness. RNA may in fact represent the first complex molecule to have evolved; a single polynucleotide chain. Studies in the last few decades, including pioneering work from the labs of the American chemist Thomas Cech (b. 1947) and the Canadian-born molecular biologist Sidney Altman (b.1939), for which they shared the Nobel Prize in Chemistry in 1989, show that single-stranded RNA can have a catalytic function and self-cleave.

These findings lend credence to a hypothesis originally advanced by Woese, Crick, and the British chemist Leslie Orgel in the 1960s called the *RNA world hypothesis*. The hypothesis is that RNA was the original 'enzyme' and predates the evolution of protein enzymes with catalytic function. Such catalytic RNAs are called *ribozymes* and 16S rRNA, which occupies a major part of the small ribosomal subunit, is now recognised as a catalytic RNA. Indeed, this subunit provides key evidence for the functional role of a ribozyme as neighbouring amino acid residues are too far apart to form an active site for the catalysis of peptide bond formation. Other supporting evidence for this hypothesis comes from the observation that many key metabolic intermediates such as the co-factors AMP, ATP, and NADH are small ribonucleotides.

As mentioned in the previous chapter, RNA is much more labile (i.e., sensitive to degradation) than DNA and has poor and slow catalytic properties compared to enzymes, so it was likely to have been supplanted by DNA and proteins as the long path to cellular life evolved on our planet. In support of this possibility, scientists now are able to construct synthetic ribozymes in the laboratory in order to test their function. A synthetic RNA polymerase ribozyme, for example, was found to be capable of adding 20 nucleotides to an oligonucleotide primer over a 24-hour period. A slow start for the scientists, perhaps, but then evolution has the advantage of millions of years to perfect matters at the molecular level, and when nature has perfected something, there is little need to change it — indeed, change may be fatal and lead to extinction. At the gene level, we can clearly see this in the DNA sequence of ancient DNA-binding motifs such as the homeobox or in the example of the ability of the mouse PAX6 gene, which is involved in eye formation by being able to programme fly eye development in *Drosophila*.

I hope I have built a coherent picture of our physical selves and how we came to be here in this and the preceding chapter. By studying evolution and understanding the nature of life at the molecular level, we address the same 'big' questions as classical philosophers or physicists — what are we, what makes 'us' what we are, and where did we come from? Looking billions of years back in time and returning to our origins in the form of LUCA or even further back to how molecules such as RNA might have come to adopt a catalytic function, and then formulating testable hypotheses for such events, is no different from those physicists who created the conditions in the Large Hadron Collider that allowed the existence of the hypothetical Higgs boson (a marker of the very earliest moments after the Big Bang) to be determined.

Our unique minds have evolved to create scientific methods which, linked to human intellect and insight, have enabled us address questions relating to what our existence is and how it relates to us. How we have become — as far as we are aware — a uniquely self-aware organism and the nature of consciousness are questions that interest many from philosophers to physicists to neuroscientists. This is the subject for the final two chapters of this book.

6 Consciousness and the World

i) Introduction

Consciousness is something that happens in our heads most of our waking hours. The mind is free to think about anything, anytime. It can manipulate and contort the subject of thought so that it does not have to conform to the laws of physics, as is often experienced when dreaming. However, to interact with objective reality, the mind, in its freedom, has to distinguish what it does (and can do) with what is happening in the real world. Psychotropic drugs that alter conscious states, such as ketamine or LSD, have marked effects on this usually well-managed distinction.

We think of consciousness as our *experience* of reality, yet we do not understand how it works or what it really is. Why does something so personal and familiar present such difficulty when we attempt to understand it? In fact, there is no definition of consciousness that is generally agreed on. We know that it is 'inner' and that it is qualitative and subjective in the sense that it occurs in our minds, not outside. It has a 'what it is like?' aspect to it. As the psychologist Susan Blackmore states, there are some considerations we can be aware of that give us some idea of what it means:

1. *"What is it like to be a…"* from the American philosopher Thomas Nagel's famous article, *"what is it like to be a bat?"* If we ask such a type of question and acknowledge that there is something that we can be like, then that thing is by definition a conscious entity. We can ask about what it is like to be a bat, so a bat is conscious, but we cannot ask what it is like to be a stone, so a stone is not conscious.

2. *Subjectivity or phenomenality.* Consciousness means subjective or phenomenal experience. Thus, things are as they seem to be rather than as they are objectively.
3. The *mind-mind problem* is the subjective quality of experience, such as the blueness of blue or the smell of a thing; these qualities are termed *qualia*. Some philosophers claim that there is no such thing. The American Nobel laureate Gerald Edelman disagreed and thought that they evolve in a (higher) organism from the initial set of sensory discriminations that occur in the embryo.
4. The *mind-body problem*, which concerns how subjective experiences arise from objective brains.

Points 3 and 4 can be combined to be stated as the 'hard problem' of consciousness — a term coined by the Australian philosopher of mind, David Chalmers. If the connection between each issue here seems unclear, then perhaps we can summarise the whole problem of consciousness as two connected issues which, if solved, will explain what it is. These are:

A. The objective analysis of the minutiae of the processes that constitute a conscious experience, addressed using the scientific method. Francis Crick believed that it is caused by synchronised 40Hz signalling between the thalamus and cortex in the brain. Gerald Edelman thought that it involves reentrant mapping and his 'theory of neuronal group selection' (TNGS), which we will return to later. Roger Penrose suggests that consciousness manifests from the quantum and classical interplay across the microtubule quantum-entangled internal cytoskeletal states. This view requires a new type of physics that would be an all-encompassing revision of its current state. He believes that the mind is not like a computer, and that the non-computational aspect of the mind can be related to similar non-computational processes involved in the observer-induced collapse of the wavefunction to a macroscopic state. These theories will be discussed later. Other causal models exist, but the only feature that is uniformly agreed on is that consciousness occurs in the brain.

B. The subjective, qualitative, conscious experiences that are qualia. This is the "what's it like to be a..." problem. As Thomas Nagel pointed out, we cannot know what it is like to be a bat unless we *are* a bat; this is subjective knowledge. Even though you and I are human and I know what it is like to be a human, I only know what it is like to be the human Ben Webb, and not what it is like to be any other human. That knowledge is always subjectively private.

Although the American philosopher of language and mind John Searle claims it is a fallacy to state that we cannot have a scientific account of consciousness, he is clearly thinking of the mind-body problem rather than the mind-mind problem. Even then, knowing what *causes* it does not explain "what it is like", which is the essence of consciousness. Searle is neither a dualist nor a materialist, but believes in 'biological naturalism'. This view, reasonably, explains that consciousness is a part of nature and results from higher-level processes realised in the structure of the brain.

The integration of issues A and B denoted above leads to:

C. The mind-body problem (the 'hard' or difficult problem), which is a description of how the matter of the brain produces the conscious experiences of the mind. The problem is how a complete understanding of issue A (the causal mechanism) leads to issue B (the sensation). The question is how can objective, scientific knowledge of the processes that constitute the mechanism of a conscious experience (A above) tell us what that private, subjective experience is like (issue B)? At some point, irrespective of the complexity of our understanding of the causal process, some 'magic' occurs that converts mechanism (objectively knowable) to experience (subjectively knowable and private).

How can we make the object-subject transition possible? Indeed, the irony is that *that* magical leap from mechanistic cause to experience, which is the essence of consciousness, seems to be both the most important part and the one part we do not or cannot know. Those who believe that we are not wired to ever understand how this can occur are termed *mysterians* or *new mysterians* (e.g., the English philosopher Colin McGinn), a term coined by the philosopher Owen Flanagan, although McGinn used the name 'transcendental naturalism'.

Stating "when process 'x' occurs (which constitutes issue A), then qualia occur (constituting B)" is not enough because the transition between a causal process and a sensation with qualities that transcend its cause is not explained, but merely stated as a fact of occurrence. Indeed, the mysterians may be right in that no explanation for the transition between this cause and effect is satisfactory because moving from the object to the subject necessitates a 'jump'. Although human intellect recognises that explaining and understanding this is necessary, it cannot probe this jump due to either the structure of the mind, our methods of analysis, or reality itself.

One might ask, "Why does a particular conscious state, thought, or memory occur in the first place?" and "How does it link to a previous one?" Perhaps it is like this: when I am thinking of something, a unique integrated network of neural connections *causes* a conscious experience of it. Other unique connections, when drawn into conscious focus, can create other sensory experiences. The first conscious experience (of a sequence) may be the result of an integration of perception, mental and physical sensation, memory, and comprehension of this integration. Mood and analysis are some of the factors that may further affect and modify this experience.

As we can only be conscious of one thing at a time, the link between experiences, though always causal, may not necessarily be *consciously* causal. If one moves rapidly through a succession of fully conscious thoughts, the causal flow between them is obvious. However, if the link occurs within the subconscious (or *fringe-conscious*) such that no full conscious experience of them is achieved, then bringing the current content of the subconscious into full consciousness produces a conscious state that may *seem* to be unrelated to the previous one, when in fact a causal flow had occurred within a different part of the mind.

Although we are not consciously aware of its actions, the subconscious mind is able to perform multiple functions at the same time. Consider the facial recognition of someone we know. We do not consciously scan the features until a recognition pattern confirms the identity; instead, we perform this function subconsciously and rapidly and an affirmation occurs, then the conscious mind takes over with the interaction. Interestingly, data suggest that there are specific neurons whose purpose is for the recognition of a single thing. Considering that there are a hundred billion neurons with a hundred trillion interconnections in the human brain, it is certainly feasible.

As Richard Lewontin states, we are more than just the product of our genes. He was referring to the need to simultaneously consider the gene, organism, *and* environment to be able to define the organism fully. But it is the mind that defines our uniqueness. Genes encode, among other things, the structure of neurons; their connections in the brain are set during development. As organisms that experience, interpret, and understand the environment, we draw connections between things according to these experiences. Since neural connections create maps that link to the external world in a causal way, we strengthen and weaken these neural maps according to life's experiences. As such, our neural maps are continually modified and improved according to the objective world that defines them. The result is the flow between conscious, subconscious, fringe-conscious, and unconscious states and rational thought.

The American philosopher and pragmatist William James studied, among other specific topics relating to the mind, the correlation of thoughts and feelings with conditions of the brain. He considered 'mind' to be consciousness, and he introduced the term 'fringe-consciousness', related to consciousness and subconsciousness, to represent that which is accessible to introspection, such that ideas flowed to and from the conscious mind, aiding the conscious thought process.

The US-based Dutch neuroscientist Bernard Baars talks of a 'theatre of consciousness' to describe how we only have capacity for full conscious reflection of one thing at a time, much like a play on a stage — where the stage is consciousness and the play in progress is the thing being reflected on. The sensations, perceptions, thoughts, moods, and so on play on this stage that we are conscious of, where the 'audience' is the complicated and interconnected inner workings of the mind. Unlike a silent audience, however, these feed into the stage, shifting the focus of conscious attention.

It is clear that perceived inputs exceed the capacity for full conscious reflection of them. Yet, we have mechanisms for storage without immediate reflection. We can access these later either by choice or through subconscious linking. This inability to 'focus' on multiple inputs is not dangerous as reactions and responses are automatic.

Thought relates to the objective world such that what I *can* think is constrained by the reality in which I exist. I can push the boundaries and think of things that do not or cannot exist, but I cannot think of things outside my conceptual capacity. Reality, as presented to the type of organism I am, determines the limits for how I sense and perceive it as well as for thought itself. Ideas that are processed in the parts of our mind that are not within our conscious attention are brought to full conscious attention when they require further processing that is only possible using the abilities of full conscious analysis.

This interplay between different conscious states is not under our full control, but it has a positive role in creativity. There is a causal link between the neural maps that life has moulded and what can happen in objective reality. The mind grows as an inner theatre for creativity, relating ideas to feasibility within physical reality.

Creativity is a mental attribute of great importance to scientific work. The French mathematician Jacques Hadamard (1865–1963), famously associated with prime number theorem and the Riemann hypothesis, published a book in the 1940s called *The Psychology of Invention in the Mathematical Field*. In it, he recounted reminiscences of some significant mathematicians and physicists and their personal experiences of their creative processes, delving in some detail into the conscious-subconscious interrelationship and questioning where the spark of intuition originates. It concluded, surprisingly, that there is no common mechanism involved. Some individuals used symbolic imagery to manipulate ideas while others used words. This only adds further wonder both at the complexity of the mind and how much we still do not know.

Life is full of experiences constantly bombarding us. This information enters our mind and is processed. Even if we do not consciously consider this information, it can be assimilated. Part of the necessity of sleep, aside from resting our bodies, is to allow our minds to process the information we have received since last we slept. We become dysfunctional without sleep — our thinking processes slow down and clarity is lost. Information that enters the mind is often processed before it can be consciously contemplated because another snippet of information has distracted us before we can even begin to think about it. Sleep may enable the mind to process and make sense of different inputs that have been experienced and stored. It may enable information received to be oriented so that it can be acted on creatively.

Scientists and philosophers often speak of waking in the night with a 'eureka moment' for no *apparent* reason. From a biological viewpoint, a recent study (2015) demonstrated that certain brain cells shrink during sleep and this is associated with faster transit of cerebrospinal fluid (CSF) through the brain, possibly washing away toxins or misfolded proteins from neurons.

ii) The Unconscious: Accessing the Inaccessible

To understand the mind is one of the great goals of the human intellect — mind understanding mind. When considering the mind, people are often drawn with interest to its deep mysterious qualities, such as why only one thing can be considered at one time or where a thought originates. We are also fascinated by the consciously inaccessible states, such as the unconscious, partly because (in the case of the unconscious) it has such a profound affect on how we feel. Consciousness, as that most remarkable mental property, is taken for granted because it is with us every waking moment — it the immediate projection of ourselves.

Modern life, in western society, is complex. We have rapidly constructed a world that subjects the mind to myriad pressures that the human did not evolve to encounter. Psychological illnesses of one form or another are commonplace. Prescriptions for antidepressants are often the general practitioner's 'solution' to our inability to cope adequately with the stresses that our complex lives sometimes present us. Such drugs are big business for pharmaceutical companies, generating billions of pounds in revenue. Psychotherapy, counselling, and cognitive behavioural therapy, to name but a few, have also evolved to help the mind 'deal' with life more effectively in terms of health, happiness, and achievement. 'Mindfulness' is but the latest of these to be aggressively marketed as a way of coping with our busy, stressful lives.

Often, the unconscious mind is deeply associated with causing behaviour that makes one's existence more difficult. Not only the conscious mind but all states of consciousness are ultimately affected by inputs from physical reality. Each interrelates and contributes to the type of person we are and thus how we interact with the world. Of course, the fully conscious state is that which we have most control over and is the immediate means from which we address the physical world, but it is affected by both the unconscious and subconscious mind. As the unconscious is a deep and inaccessible part of the mind, it requires skilled and learned techniques to be probed. The fruit of this labour for the individual is supposed freedom following realisation from suppressed, repressed, or inhibitory patterns of behaviour. For our understanding of the mind, understanding what the unconscious 'is' demonstrates clearly that the mind, viewed as a whole, is one of the great challenges for 21st century science.

Carl Jung's unconscious

The study of the unconscious is a contentious issue. Much that has been presented on it has been refuted, rejected, revised, modified, and so on. This is much like scientific progression, but the study of the unconscious is not a science and thus not subject to the same type of scrutiny. Our knowledge of unconscious mental states is derived from conscious states. Unconscious mental states must be consciously thinkable; otherwise, it is a nonconscious brain process. There is some confusion over this, particularly concerning our innate ability to learn language. An unconscious state that cannot be made conscious and have intentionality is part of the nonconscious computational aspect of the brain's function.

The unconscious is a 'thing' of study in the psychoanalytic field, resulting from insights by Sigmund Freud (1856–1939). He studied medicine at the University of Vienna, where he also took courses in philosophy (in his early days he was a great admirer of Nietzsche) and biology. He went on to become a neurologist, and from this developed psychoanalysis. In his initial excursions into psychoanalysis, he dropped the physiological approach and used methods such as hypnosis. He also developed different methods such as associative free thought in an attempt to help patients recount traumatic memories that had negative influences on their behaviour, caused mental distress, yet of which they were unaware.

However, I do not wish to focus on Freud's work on the unconscious. It is that of his one-time collaborator, Carl Gustav Jung (1875–1961), that demonstrates how a model of the unconscious can be formulated with great creativity, be taken seriously, yet also prove to be highly controversial. His life and work was plagued with controversy, yet his influence on modern psychology and, of relevance here, the unconscious was significant. The existence of the unconscious mind, which could affect and act on the conscious mind, was known well before Jung became interested in it. He saw a difference between self and *psyche* — the psyche defines our conscious and unconscious, whereas the self represents the goal toward which the psyche is orientated. The psyche is divided into consciousness and the unconscious, which compensates the conscious. The unconscious balances the conscious attitude such that the individual is able to retain mental health.

In nine years spent working at the Burgholzli mental hospital in Zurich, Jung was confronted with numerous psychotic patients. There he concentrated his research into the reasons for the manifestation of the symptoms of schizophrenia. He developed word association tests, where patients were asked to provide immediate answers to carefully selected questions such that the response was not from the conscious process, which would cloud the subconscious origin, but from the unconscious. The unconscious, being the source of the effect of the trauma, would deliver answers to the test questions that would provide insight into the psyche of the individual.

Although the conscious is affected by the unconscious, conscious answers would serve no purpose to these questions since they stem from contemplative assessment of possible answers. Results from these tests confirmed Freud's views on the unconscious and, thus, started the collaboration between Freud and Jung. This collaboration was relatively short-lived due to differences in opinion, complicated by the unwillingness of each to compromise on their own increasingly contrasting opinions. Jung's key disagreement with Freud was their differing concepts of the unconscious. Freud conceived the unconscious solely as a repository of repressed emotions and desires, whereas Jung saw a deeper form of unconscious called the *collective unconscious*, where 'archetypes' resided.

Jung suggested that the archetype is the instinct's perception of itself just as consciousness is perception of life itself. In his construction of ideas about the unconscious, he integrated concepts of archaic images, symbols, and impulses. His 'Jungian analysis' was designed to probe the negative effect of the unconscious on an individual's behaviour and mental well-being, with the goal of achieving wholeness. Jung believed in 'individuation' — the psychological process of integrating the opposites — this being, in his mind, the central process of human development.

Jung divided psychic energy into two attitudes — extrovert and introvert. The extrovert is motivated from the outside and directed by external, objective factors. The introvert is the opposite, directed by inner subjection. He introduced four functional types of human temperament, grouped as two pairs of opposites; thinking and feeling, intuition and sensation. Thinking and feeling were termed rational as they evaluate experience and tell us what the thing is, and if it is good. Sensation and intuition were called irrational as they depend on perception. Within each pair, the 'superior' function will determine the individual's conscious orientation — this is called the 'differentiated' function, with the opposite being the 'undifferentiated' function. The other pairing of opposites then serve the pairing that affect the conscious.

Although not directly involved in contributing to our understanding the mechanisms of consciousness, Jung developed insights into the unconscious mind and how this is not only affected by our inherent make-up and life's experiences, but it also contributes significantly to how we react to the present.

The precise development and details of Jung's ideas are not pertinent here, but it is interesting to note that in some sense they have infiltrated the general psyche in many ways. For example, the popular Myers–Briggs Type Indicator (MBTI) is based on Jung's typology test. It is a well-known psychological type test, used widely as a tool in screening prospective employees. It produces a four-letter type formula (e.g., ESTP) based on four pairs of *dichotomies* (preferences): Extroverted or Introverted (1st letter), Sensing or iNtuitive (2nd letter), Thinking or Feeling (3rd letter), and Judging or Perceiving (4th letter), which are characteristics in an individual deduced from responses to specific scenarios and questions. The types define an individual's psychological preferences and indicates how he or she makes decisions, both personal and professional. The truth and validity of such tests are debated, principally due to the associated problems with this sort of self-reporting and one's truthfulness in providing answers to the questions.

Consciousness, the subconscious, and the unconscious are different aspects of the mind that, while accessible in some sense by objective analysis, require experience of them to really appreciate their existence. Consciousness is the 'feeling' that a mind has, whereas the subconscious and unconscious are aspects of the mind so-termed because of what they contain, how they affect us, and how we access them. Different conscious states are aspects of mental processes with clear differences. The conscious and subconscious are linked and enable the mind's interpretation of and interaction with reality. Consciousness *is* our awareness. The subconscious and unconscious affect our thoughts and behaviour but, unlike the subconscious, the unconscious is generally deeply (and negatively) affecting and something we are only aware of in a detached way.

iii) Consciousness: Accessing the Knowable?

The unconscious mind is clearly a powerful influence on the individual's psychological state. It affects mood and clarity of thought. However, despite its important role for the functioning of the mind, it is not a subject of scientific investigation. For the individual, it is accessed through skilled empathic knowledge by another human who understands human psychology. As a process, learning about the mechanisms of the mind can best be achieved by studying full consciousness. Although its mechanism may be similar to that of other conscious states, because it is the focal point of the mind and thus accessible, consciousness makes itself available for creative, scientific study. As the point of integration of conscious states, memory, and intellect, it is where the great ideas that have enabled civilisation to progress become apparent to the mind. It is the point of relation between the mind and the physical world.

Consciousness is a fascinating but elusive phenomenon; it is impossible to specify what it is, what it does, or why it evolved. The definition of consciousness according to the *International Dictionary of Psychology* is "the having of perceptions, thoughts and feelings of awareness". Perhaps it is only possible to define using terms that have meaning only if one knows how consciousness feels. Stuart Sutherland of the International Dictionary of Psychology thinks that "nothing worth reading has been written on it".

Consciousness is considered, somewhat contentiously, to be accessible by the scientific method. Recent research initiatives, such as Barack Obama's Presidential BRAIN Initiative or the Allen Mouse Brain Connectivity Atlas based at the Allen Institute for Brain Science in Seattle, aim to shed light on changes in gene expression in the brain; for example, during human foetal development or in mouse models of human diseases such as schizophrenia or autism. These may lead to prenatal diagnostic tests for susceptibility to certain conditions (which will undoubtedly raise its own philosophical issues), yet this is far from understanding what constitutes consciousness.

Many fall into the trap of equating consciousness with self-consciousness. To be conscious, it is only necessary to be aware of the external world. In self-consciousness, as Schelling pointed out, the self is both object *and* subject — the perceiver is the perceived. When one is conscious of some scene in front of us, we express it thus:

$$\text{Scene} \rightarrow \text{mind}$$

With self-consciousness, or thinking about being conscious of seeing the scene, we can express this thus:

$$\text{Scene} \rightarrow \text{mind} \rightarrow (\text{scene} \rightarrow \text{mind}) \rightarrow \text{mind}$$

A big problem for understanding consciousness is how this 'material', as consciousness, can refer to something that is in a conceptually different world (the mind relates to objective reality). This is the problem of *intentionality*, a concept whose importance is strongly defended by Searle, which means that the mind is aware of things and directed toward things (e.g., ideas or objects). For example, if I want a sandwich and think about the sandwich, then the sandwich is the intentional object of my mind. Intentionality is a property that humans possess which distinguishes them from computers (though some people disagree). Consciousness is directed towards intentional objects that are either physical or concern ideas that relate to things that are physical.

There are different kinds of intentionality too. For example, memories and beliefs have a mind-to-world direction of fit because they are intended to show how the world is, whereas desires have a world-to-mind direction since these represent how we want or plan the world to be.

I stress mind, not language, because Searle convincingly stresses that the intentionality of language is reducible to the intentionality of mind — in other words, the intentionality of mind is more fundamental than that of language. This is because, Searle claims, consciousness is observer-independent like the forces of nature. Language evolved in our species according to the possibilities of our physical brain and the needs that it would serve. Language constrains how we think and this determines what we say and how we construct our global and individual picture of the world. My intentional states, such as hunger, do not depend upon another person or mind to have meaning.

Language, however, is observer-dependent because it requires another person to have meaning (or rather, alone, I do not need language as I interact with intentional states internally). All intentionality is carried out against a background or in the context of a huge common or culture-specific set of beliefs. These are behaviours and expectations that exist as a result of being a function of our existing in a shared, social, and physical reality.

Consciousness, though experienced by everyone, is a difficult phenomenon to address both scientifically and philosophically. We probe its meaning in many contexts and for each there is much disagreement, indicating how much we still have to learn about it. What *is* agreed is that, essentially, it is not a thing but a process that occurs in our brains. It relates to the physical world in which it is embedded. It cannot touch or experience reality directly, yet its existence is a result of physical neuronal processes. It is the flow of sensations that gives life meaning, rather than just existence.

We started this section by attempting to define consciousness. We also defined the problems associated with understanding it, subjectively and objectively. Now we are in a position to look more closely at the possible mechanisms that describe how we have conscious states.

Neurons

Human cells are little different from those of other higher animals (we share 99.3% of our DNA sequence with chimps, after all), yet we possess unique abilities. These abilities are enabled by our brains, which can perform complex thought. This is "the active response of memory in every phase of life", and it includes the intellectual, emotional, muscular, and physical responses of memory. No other organism can integrate these functions so effectively.

The interaction between neurons constitutes the processes of the brain. The mind exists as a function of the brain. The mind is a hypothetical 'thing' that is supposed to account for the ability of the conscious being to feel, think, will, or behave. It is thought to consist of and control mental processes, which are biological in nature. Consciousness is a property of the mind. Hence, neurons provide the physical materials that underlie consciousness. It would therefore also be appropriate to describe neurons in a little more detail, since we will be discussing them often in this section in association with consciousness.

In Chapter 4, I discussed the functional components of a typical cell. We saw that all cells of the body, no matter how different in structure and function, have in common many essential or 'housekeeping' processes that are linked to key cellular functions such as metabolism and DNA replication. Patterns of tissue-specific gene expression during development create specific functional cells associated with different organs of the body. Likewise, the neurons of the brain and nervous system are unique in *their* functional requirement — *communication*.

Physically, neurons are diverse in appearance as necessitated by their function, but basically all neurons comprise three main elements — a cell body, from which sprout branching cytoplasmic projections called *dendrites*, and a singular cytoplasmic extension called the *axon*, which can reach significant lengths compared to the size of the cell body (some human axons extend for one metre, for example). Each neuron may display extensive branching, which is necessary for communication with other neurons. Since the insights of the Spanish neuroanatomist Santiago Ramon y Cajal (1852–1934), we know that neurons interact with other neurons via these projections, with information passing in one direction from the cell body to its extension (the axon) and on to the outer dendrites, where the signal is passed on to the input dendrites and cell body of an adjacent neuron.

Since thousands of dendrites can extend from each cell body, there are literally trillions of possible interactions between neurons. With so many interactions, there is an enormous potential for different mental processes and effects. The uniqueness of each human mind is determined somewhat by the neurons made during the development of that person, and the type of life lived by the individual affects how these pathways evolve and integrate.

How is this information transmitted and in what form? Coded information must pass along the axon as fast as possible in order to ensure an efficient system and it does this in the form of an electrical impulse, which passes along one neuron to another neuron via a junction called a *synapse*. Basically, the electrical impulse passes along the axon of the first neuron (termed a 'presynaptic' neuron) at up to 120 m/s to the end, where it reaches the synapse. The presynaptic end of an axon is specialised for manufacturing, storing, and releasing *neurotransmitters*, small molecules (e.g., acetylcholine, dopamine) that are released across the synaptic junction and picked up by receptors on the cell body of the adjacent 'postsynaptic' neuron.

The postsynaptic end of a neuron is specialised for converting chemical signals to electrical messages. This neuron is either excited or inhibited as a result of its receptor-binding neurotransmitters. Remembering that there may be many dendritic inputs to any cell body, if the overall postsynaptic potential sits above a threshold action potential stimulus, then the cell body will be triggered to fire an electrical impulse down its axon, resulting in a continuation of the signal received from the presynaptic neuron.

As there are no relative strengths of impulse, neurons either fire or do not fire. Thus, the input stimulus must be high enough to activate the action potential of the postsynaptic neuron for the signal to continue, and signals can pass within the brain and throughout the body via the nervous system at great speed. Different chemicals and receptors are utilised by the human brain for inhibitory and excitatory signalling; drugs that activate and inhibit such pathways are used to treat diseases such as Parkinson's and depression.

As well as utilising electrical impulses for transferring a message, some neurons use biochemical signals as their messaging system. Through second messenger molecules, the original signal is amplified and continued, much like the enzymatic protein kinase signal transduction pathways involving MAP kinases described earlier. There are also signalling mechanisms in the brain that act on a whole region rather than from one neuron to another. The diffusion of gases (e.g., nitrogen monoxide) to a particular region signals a desired effect on that region without the necessity of direct cell-to-cell signalling.

It is also worth mentioning at this point that neurons are not the only type of cell in the brain. Glial cells such as astrocytes or oligodendrocytes play a variety of roles — they provide structural support, lay down myelin which surrounds the axons and acts as an insulator for electrical conduction, and clear away neurotransmitters from synaptic junctions to prevent their build-up to toxic levels. Glial cells form the lymphatic system, a network of channels in close proximity to blood vessels of the brain which transport cerebrospinal fluid (CSF).

As mentioned earlier, recent studies on the molecular mechanism of sleep indicate that glial cells shrink during sleep, opening up these channels and improving the flow of CSF as shown by dye-tracing experiments in mice. This process potentially allows the washing out of toxins as well as T-amyloid, the key protein in the pathology of Alzheimer's disease. Studies in mice that had been injected with a tagged T-amyloid showed that it was cleared twice as fast from the brains of sleeping or anesthetised (unconscious) animals compared to those kept awake.

The neurons of the human brain are essentially no more complex in structure than those of an insect or nematode worm, so the complexity of mental function must result from the arrangement and number of neurons. Indeed, the human brain has a hundred billion neurons — by way of comparison, bees have about a million and nematodes a few hundred. It is clear that we possess the number and, importantly, the organisation of neurons to enable complex functions beyond the capacity of lower species. Later, we will discuss how arrangements of these neurons might produce higher functions such as consciousness. However, it has been suggested that such a search for how consciousness occurs and what it is through biological processes is a waste of effort because our minds and methods of analysis are not of the right type to be able to answer such a question. From the following description of our different attempts to understand consciousness, we will see how we might arrive at such a conclusion.

A complete physical analysis and description of the neural processes that *cause* a conscious experience say nothing of the experience itself. Since the experience is a component of the cause-effect whole (because it evolved to *have* an experiential element), then a description that fails to incorporate the experience is incomplete. So, as the experience says nothing about the causal elements either, then the objective and subjective elements of consciousness are much like complementary aspects of a quantum system in that they both comprise the whole, whereas neither alone achieve this.

Gerald Edelman

Gerald Edelman (1929–2014) was, like DNA pioneer Francis Crick, famous for work in two unrelated areas of science. He received his Nobel Prize for work on antibody structures, but his later interests turned to the mechanisms of consciousness.

His research in this area led him to the belief that we can understand ourselves from the activity of the brain. He thought that we must not think of the brain as a computer, but as an 'evolving' entity that arises through evolutionary time as well as during the course of our lives. He saw the abilities resultant from consciousness as enabled by a 'dynamic core' in the brain; a conclusion he made from physical experimentation. If this is correct, the debate about the mind-body problem is moving from being solely in the philosophical domain to one that involves scientific analysis.

How subjective experience relates to objectively describable events was what Schopenhauer termed the *world knot*. By describing the process of the dynamic core in the brain, Edelman hoped to untie this knot. He concluded from neurological and neurophysiological evidence that conscious processes are associated with distributed changes in neural activity in the thalamocortical system of the brain. Such changes in neural activity are integrated with fast and effective 'reentrant' interactions. These interactions are directly associated with the experience of consciousness only if they are highly differentiated and not uniform.

Edelman believed that three tenets of what he called 'Neural Darwinism', or neuronal group selection, are central for understanding the main neural interactions that are necessary for consciousness. The main tenets of this global brain theory are:

1. During the development of the brain, a collection of variant neuronal groups that are part of the neuroanatomy is formed. This is *developmental* selection.
2. During life experience, a secondary collection of neural circuits is formed because of changes in the strength of current connections. This is *experiential* selection.
3. Reentrant signalling between and among neuronal groups enable correlation of specific neural events both temporally and spatially.

Both 1 and 2 enable the variability and differentiation of different neural states that consciousness provides. The third tenet allows for the integration of these first two tenets. So, the theory of neuronal group selection (TNGS) can be summarised as follows:

1. Born with neural connections, and these…
2. Strengthen and weaken through life's experience, and…
3. Neural groups form and undergo reentry through parallel systems.

Multiple conceptually different stimuli are received, but how they are integrated into a unified conscious experience is called the *binding problem*. One possible answer is that stimuli link together to remembered pathways, which are groups associated with past similar experiences (and add to them). Reentry mapping creates a 'remembered present' as defined by Edelman, which binds these experiences together and enables consciousness of them.

How informative is consciousness? For Edelman, the issue is not so much how many independent pieces of information one conscious state can contain; rather, it is how many states are neglected when we are experiencing a single state at one moment (we can only concentrate on one thing at one thing). Informatively, consciousness is very effective since we can differentiate among billions of different conscious states within a fraction of a second.

Edelman was a scientist who believed in the existence of qualia. These have developed from the point at which the embryo is able to receive sensory information. For the quale of the pure sensation of, say, the colour red, Edelman explained this as a specific neural state defined by the integrated activity of all the neurons that make up the dynamic core. Thus, it is the discrimination of this one particular state from the billions of other states within the same core.

Edelman was well aware of the complexity of the reentrant system with the dynamic core, which he used to describe conscious experience. He believed that the evolutionary leap from simple nervous systems, where signals are exchanged within separate neural systems, to the complex one that enables these conscious processes was huge and transcendent. The simple systems would not have been (or are not) able to integrate signals (which the dynamic core does) to construct a scene from different signals. The dynamic core can do this from signals resulting from an individual's evolutionary and experiential history.

Edelman should neither be viewed as a Cartesian dualist (mind plus body) nor an idealist. However, he was not a reductionist in the sense of describing consciousness on the basis of quantum mechanical processes within neuronal microtubules as Penrose does, as we will come to later. In *his* search for the mechanism of consciousness, Penrose does not address the role of neurology and evolution, perhaps because he is an expert in quantum mechanics and not evolution or neurology. Thus, he ignores the role of that which he does not know about on an issue that requires it being paid some attention, at the expense of assigning unwarranted roles for a process he knows little about (see Penrose's book, *The Emperor's New Mind*, to draw your own conclusions). You cannot try and understand consciousness without acknowledging the functioning and evolution of the human brain.

Edelman was a reductionist in the sense that he recognised both mind and body as necessary for the development of consciousness. He did not see the human as a mind-body subject in the way that the existential phenomenologist Maurice Merleau-Ponty did. Indeed, he rejected phenomenology and introspectionism on the grounds that these put the observer outside of the key phenomena. It is true that one cannot, using only thought, analyse the underlying basis of conscious experience. However, Merleau-Ponty's ideas about being and perception through thought alone do provide insights into conscious experience.

With Edelman's impression of the human mind, we see how this differs from a computer's processing mechanism. He argued that we must not think of the brain as a machine in order to understand it. The American cognitive scientist Douglas Hofstadter sees more of a parallel between machines and minds, and he believes that the development of artificial intelligence (AI) follows the mechanisms of human thought. He implies that much of the function of the brain occurs as processes that are paralleled in 'intelligent' machines, though he does not explicitly call the mind a machine.

Summary of Edelman's process

According to Edelman's three tenets of Neural Darwinism, neuronal circuits develop in the brain, which produces large anatomical variation, and these undergo continual selection. Neurons that are activated together connect (fire together = wire together); behaviour and experience strengthen and weaken different circuits. The third tenet is reentry, which is the continual signalling from one brain region to another across parallel fibres. This is reentrant mapping and, together, these constitute Edelman's TNGS.

The thalamus is a structure in the forebrain that is associated with consciousness. Neurons radiate out from it to all parts of the cerebral cortex. Edelman believed that evolution of the reentrant thalamocortical system gave rise to the dynamic core, where the integration of multiple sensori-motor inputs can occur and be processed into a full conscious experience. Integrated activity creates a scene in the remembered present of primary consciousness, from which the animal can lay plans against. So, consciousness does not occur in a particular region of the brain, instead resulting from an interaction (reentrant mapping) between regions that are involved.

The dynamic core is the site where this interaction is integrated into a scene that mental processes can act on (i.e., relating the perceived external world to the analysed mental extrapolation of external reality). Neural activity in the dynamic core does not cause consciousness; it entails it. Thus, consciousness is not a thing but a process. A consequence of the TNGS is that brains are necessarily unique in terms of structure and dynamics (separate computers are identical in that they have the same hardware and software, but two brains are never alike).

Other advanced mammals may possess conscious abilities beyond primary consciousness (i.e., perception of the present without a sense of past, future, or the self or capacity to be conscious of being conscious) and have the rudiments of higher-order consciousness. Primates can manipulate objects and play while some birds can learn to use tools, for example. However, humans, with language and syntax, show the full flowering of higher-order consciousness. We have consciousness because the endocranial size of hominids rapidly increased with this language development-induced progress.

In 2014, the first complete map of the brain structure of a mammal was achieved, leading to speculation over how brain structures can correlate with the subjective experience of consciousness. A former collaborator of Edelman, Giulio Tononi, has developed a mathematical theory called *integrated information theory* that aims to determine what a structure needs in order to be conscious. More recently, a Japanese-American scientific team reported in the journal *Science* in 2017 that studies conducted in mice demonstrate that the brain makes two copies of memories of specific events; one for short-term use and the other for long-term storage, with each stored in different regions of the brain.

Short-term memories form in the hippocampus whereas long-term memories form in the cortex of the brain. The animal uses the hippocampal memories in the first few days, but the memories here appear to degrade with time, leaving the cortical memories intact. The scientists showed this by giving the mice a shock to induce memory and then using a light beam directed into the brain to turn groups of neurons on or off: for example, mice forgot the shock if the neurons in the hippocampus were switched off in this way within the 'early' period of remembering the shock event, but could recall the shock if the neurons in the cortex were switched on. Furthermore, blocking experiments indicated that the long-term memory in the cortex did not form if connection between the hippocampus and cortex was inhibited. These data add substance to Edelman's tenets of Neural Darwinism in terms of the brain and experiential selection.

Language: Consequence for consciousness — Edelman's thoughts

We do not inherit a language of thought; rather, the concepts are developed from the brain's linking of its own perceptual maps. Thought has a form of presyntax, meaning that it can occur in the absence of language. There is no brain-based inherited language acquisition device according to Edelman. Many believe that we genetically acquire an inherent ability to learn language, but Edelman's brain-based epistemology rejects this view. Language acquisition according to Edelman is *epigenetic*.

As mentioned briefly in Chapter 4, epigenetic modification of DNA by the addition of methyl groups, specifically at CpG pairs on a DNA strand, is a way of externally modulating gene expression independently of the set of genes that we have been born with. Consequently, this is a way for gene expression to be altered in response to changes in our environment. Epigenetics means that the organism is more than merely a product of its genes, just as consciousness is more than just the functional product of neural interactions. Indeed, consciousness transcends neural interactions.

So, language is not merely a genetic product. There isn't a set of genes that encode a language-acquisition device. Language acquisition is due to the structure of the brain, an ability that is a by-product of brain development, resulting from the increased size of the intracranial space and the cortex. Natural selection would, of course, act on those hominids that had acquired language skills due to the cooperative benefits resulting from the ability to communicate with one another. Language users would survive and thus the evolution of a syntax-using hominid would progress rapidly, and those without it would die out (all of this occurring pre-civilisation, of course).

The human brain was not designed to acquire knowledge. As Edelman put it, "evolution is powerful and opportunistic, but it's neither intelligent nor instructionistic". For animals, genotype = phenotype = selection. For humans, the side effect of the development of the brain following increases in endocranial volume and, thus, following the development and improvement of the use of syntax and language was the behaviour resulting from the improved brain power. This enabled civilisation to develop and everything else that results from this (e.g., the Richard Dawkins-coined *memes* — units of cultural intelligence), so each generation starts from a more advanced position than the last. Thus, technology and civilisation overrule the processes of evolution that apply to all other organisms.

Bernard Baars

Bernard J. Baars is a Dutch-born cognitive scientist whose specialty is conscious and unconscious brain functions. He is best known for his integrative theory called *global workspace theory* (GWT), which is a model for conscious and unconscious brain processes. There are similarities to Edelman's TNGS and, indeed, GWT continues to be developed by scientists working in the Neural Darwinism tradition of Edelman. 'Global workspace' refers to the role of conscious processes in the brain. Of course, as it is a theory, it is but one of many interpretations of the role of consciousness in the human brain.

Consciousness has been considered as principally within the domain of philosophy, but Baars has helped to show that traditional scientific methods can utilise empirical information and reveal much information relevant to it. The philosopher/psychologist William James and his *Principles of Psychology* were of considerable influence on him. By comparing matched conscious and unconscious brain processes, Baars uses this 'contrastive analysis' approach in experiments to study consciousness.

Although Francis Crick was more famous for co-discovering with James Watson the structure of DNA, Crick was also interested in the mechanism of consciousness, but he took a different viewpoint from that of Edelman and Baars.

Francis Crick

In Crick's book *The Astonishing Hypothesis* (1994), he stated that as long as a hundred years ago, there were three basic ideas relating to consciousness:

1. Not all operations of the brain relate to consciousness.
2. Consciousness relates to some form of memory (probably a very short term one).
3. Consciousness is closely associated with *attention* (William James dealt with the term 'attention' in the 19th century when he inferred that it requires the withdrawal from some things in order to deal with others).

Crick's ideas on consciousness were influenced by cognitive scientists such as Philip Johnson-Laird. He draws parallels between computer processes and higher brain function, such that many of the processes occur at the same moment and are not under our conscious control (in the case of the brain) or the computer's knowledge (so to speak). This view goes against Penrose's ideas of human thought and creativity and their correlation with AI, which are covered in his book *The Emperor's New Mind* (1989). Ray Jackendoff, another influence, is a cognitive scientist who sees the mind as a biological information-processing system. He is interested in what makes our conscious experience the way that it is. Considering the brain as an analogy of a complex mechanical computer, he argues that awareness is neither derived from perception nor higher-level thought, but from a level represented as an intermediate between sensation and thought.

It becomes clear that we are aware of little of our brain function and that much of the processes occur at a deeper level. We receive stimuli of which we are aware while processes occur of which we are not aware. Awareness is achieved again when conscious thought prepares us for speech or when we wish to know how we feel on a subject — speech is impossible without consciousness. Without speech, that *necessity* of consciousness is removed.

It is agreed by these scientists that consciousness is an active process and that information from it can feed into long-term memory. It is also agreed that short-term memory is additionally involved in its process. However, where Crick's work continued from theirs was that he was interested in the neurological structure of neurons in helping us to understand consciousness. He thought it impossible to understand fully the conscious process using philosophical argument alone.

To delineate the mechanism of conscious process, Crick looked at a certain aspect of consciousness. He made the assumption that people are not conscious of all the processes occurring in their brains, for which there is a consensus of agreement. For example, we are aware of memory but not the mechanism of memory. Another less well-accepted assumption of Crick's is that although he did not think that there is a single mechanism for *all* conscious processes, he believed that fully understanding one mechanism, such as pain perception, can lead to a greater understanding of other conscious mechanisms. As there are many forms of consciousness — for example, self-consciousness is an aspect of the conscious phenomena in itself — Crick chose to study a form that allowed hypothesis-driven experimentation of it. He chose visual consciousness and hoped that conclusions could be expanded to all other forms of consciousness.

Crick concluded that all aspects of the brain's behaviour are a result of neuronal activity — that is the 'astonishing hypothesis' he claimed in his 1994 book. Is that truly astonishing? Is it correct? Many think it to be an incorrect conclusion. If it were true, it might be astonishing because it is a form of biological reductionism. It removes the metaphysical, philosophical debate on our existence by focusing on the biological, physical nature of the brain as the vessel for consciousness.

The human mind is unique amongst minds. Is this due to neuronal arrangement or perhaps the nature of our neurons themselves? Human neuron proteins are transcribed and translated from essentially the same gene sequences as those of primates and other higher organisms, yet the final result of arrangement of these neurons creates a thing of unique ability. It seems likely that the arrangement, number, and group complexity, rather than the neurons themselves, are the causal factors for our mind's abilities. There is evidence that *Homo erectus* had discovered how to make fire and was using tools approximately 1.3 million years ago, and its brain size was double that of *Homo habilis*, which evolved 2.8 million years ago.

Our mental limitations are linked to our physical makeup. This limitation applies too to our comprehension of consciousness. A computer has limited capabilities based on its software and hardware. Even if we are not like a computer, the same applies to us. The more we learn, the more we see there is to know. Is there a limit to what there is to know? Furthermore, is there a limit to what we *can* know?

Roger Penrose

Mathematical theorems may evolve from the manipulation of axioms. These theorems relate internally to the system of axioms, which is a closed world of concepts. Science is different. Here, theorems are formed based on increasing knowledge of the real world. If the theorems can predict results that conform to experiment, then the theorem is good (until a better one comes along).

Penrose believes that the physical world emerges from the Platonic world of absolutes. More precisely, there is a timeless mathematical world 'out there' that describes the physical world and it is accessible to us. Thus, the world can be described by equations, but whether we humans have the insight to reveal them is another matter. He uses Einstein's theory of general relativity to demonstrate this.

Usually, scientists attain experimental knowledge of the physical world and then fit theories to the data, but Einstein was different with his general relativity. There was no experimental data against which to fit a model. His general theory, mathematical in nature, revealed what exists in reality and how it works. It is how the universe (space, time, and matter) works and the human mind (Einstein's) tapped into this understanding. Only later could experiments be designed that allowed his theoretical predictions to be validated and proven right.

Clearly, Penrose believes that because reality (as we know it) evolved from the singularity called the Big Bang, it is definable and understandable. He also believes that we are not yet capable of doing so because we are addressing the problems in the wrong way as we do not have the tools (yet) to address them correctly. In Chapter 2, I described how Penrose believes that a combination of quantum and classical physics is required to explain the Big Bang event, since no current model of understanding can describe the constituents and nature of the Universe that has resulted from the Big Bang. Let us use quantum physics to show why Penrose believes that there is a gap in our understanding of the Universe.

When you make a measurement of a deterministic quantum system, the rules are changed and probabilities are introduced. Thus, the collapse of the wavefunction renders a classical description of a quantum system *indeterministic* because the deterministic linear superpositions become probabilities of alternatives (and hence indeterministic) on measurement. Penrose believes that this process may be an approximation of a fundamental theory and that quantum theory, as it stands, is incomplete. Although some regard it as *the* fundamental theory, Penrose believes that a single theory should avoid the introduced indeterminism when the quantum-classical divide is bridged.

Penrose believes that quantum theory consists of both puzzles and paradoxes. The puzzles, such as wave-particle duality and entanglement, exist in the physical world and are real; they stand as examples of the strangeness of reality. He has no problem with the former, but he *does* with the paradoxes. These include the measurement problem, which he views as an indication that quantum theory is incomplete. The paradox of Schrödinger's cat is the most famous example of the measurement problem where the cat is in a superposition of being both dead *and* alive.

There are many ways of dealing with this problem, such as the many worlds interpretation where the Universe splits each time a measurement is made, the de Broglie/Bohm model with its pilot wave, or the Copenhagen interpretation where nothing is 'real' until measured and what is measured becomes real. However, Penrose believes that there is a contradiction when a classical, deterministic but probabilistic measurement is made out of a deterministic quantum system. The measurement-induced indeterminism changes the structure of the quantum mechanical system. Here, some new and unknown physics is required to smooth the transition.

If we also consider distantly entangled particles, such as those resulting from the decay of a spin-0 photon, special relativity limits the speed or time with which one can consciously attain information on what is measured. A density matrix can describe the probability of the combination (using bra/ket Dirac notation, $= \frac{1}{2} |+1\rangle \langle+1| + \frac{1}{2} |-1\rangle \langle-1|$), but one has to wait for the answer from the distant measurer of the reality of the correlation.

Density matrices like this also apply to the Schrödinger cat scenario where the distant entangled particles are replaced by live and dead cats. Again, although the cat is defined as live, dead, or both depending on your quantum philosophical viewpoint, only visualisation will show what is the case for *your* reality. Penrose calls this *(orchestrated) objective reduction*, where only one thing or the other happens objectively. Current quantum theory and classical physics cannot encompass this objective reduction in its formalism.

Penrose thinks that the problems of linking the classical to the quantum world are intertwined with the problems of consciousness. So, let us say something about different conceptions of how ordered matter can generate the experience of reality. I speak of ordered matter because the idea of panpsychism in its traditional sense — that basic physical constituents of the Universe have mental properties irrespective of whether or not they are part of living organisms — seems entirely untenable in the context of everything written here. Other than subtle differences, there appear to be four distinct views on the mind-body problem:

1. Proponents of 'strong AI' who believe that the processes of the mind produce consciousness and these can be simulated computationally.
2. Those (e.g., Searle) who believe that the processes of the mind produce consciousness, but while these processes can be simulated computationally, they will not produce consciousness.
3. Those (e.g., Penrose) who believe that the processes of the mind produce consciousness, but they cannot be simulated computationally. Indeed, Penrose states that mental processes cannot be simulated on any computer, whatever its capability. Since humans can evade the *Turing halting problem*, thought is therefore non-algorithmic. Essentially, the halting problem is that a computer, utilising an axiomatic system as its 'processor', will not know when to 'halt' a complex operation because its programming according to axiomatic rules prevents it from knowing if a problem is complex, solvable, or unprovable. That is, it will continue calculating forever even if the problem cannot be solved. Thus, by this view, thought is non-computable and non-computability is therefore the key to thought. Hence, the inference for AI has no meaning for Penrose, if intelligence is to be considered along the lines of human intelligence. From this perspective, since consciousness is not computable, the non-computability in the new physics must be exploited. This as yet undiscovered or perhaps non-existent physics will link the classical to the quantum world, unite general relativity with some variant of the Grand Unified Theory (GUT), and apply to the working of the brain.
4. Finally, there are those who believe that consciousness cannot be defined in computational or physical terms.

For those who believe that quantum physics is involved in consciousness, our inability to fully describe consciousness is either because, despite having the physics and mathematics to achieve it, we have yet to do so (not Penrose's viewpoint), or that a revision of physics is required and that this 'new' physics will enable it (Penrose's position). This revision may take many years if it is at all possible, and indeed whether or not this new physics is involved, David Chalmers believes that we are possibly 30 to 50 years away from understanding consciousness.

Let us compare Penrose's and Searle's viewpoints. For Searle, if the processes of the mind that cause consciousness are simulated computationally but do not produce consciousness, then they are not a true simulation of that which produces consciousness (i.e., the brain). Yet, if those components and processes in the brain that are responsible for consciousness were isolated from the brain, would they still produce consciousness? Both believe that brain processes cause consciousness, but that conscious states cannot be computationally generated when using artificial processes that simulate those of the brain. However, only Searle believes that the processes *causing* consciousness can be simulated.

Penrose considers the problem of understanding consciousness to be a scientific one. He sees the challenge as understanding the mental world in terms of the physical world. He does not give a definition of his interpretation of consciousness as he thinks that to attempt a definition would be to define the wrong thing, though he acknowledges elements of awareness that are passive (e.g., colour perception) and active (e.g., free will).

Although Penrose's main research contributions have been in cosmology, mathematics, relativity, and quantum theory, these concerns have suggested to him a connection between consciousness and unlocking the science required for a Grand Unified Theory/Theory of Everything (GUT/TOE). He thinks that the causal mechanisms of consciousness, when understood, will provide us with insight into the creation of a TOE. Or the opposite; that a TOE will provide insight into conscious processes. This suggestion that the brain calls upon a novel, unifying form of physics when consciousness is involved is a revolutionary idea to say the least and has received both strong support and criticism. Although not widely accepted (based on intuition), the idea is difficult to refute experimentally.

As Bertrand Russell tried to do for mathematics and Descartes did for the 'new philosophy', Penrose would like the terminology relating to the mind to be re-evaluated so that we can start from a set of truths. For example, he does not like the term 'intelligence' since it involves understanding, instead preferring the term 'insight'. From these types of thoughts, he reasons that AI is unlike the brain since physical actions of the brain evoke awareness, which can never be simulated by computational means. He has spent a great deal of effort trying to convince others of his belief that thought is different from computation. In this effort, Turing machines (any computer which performs its calculations in discrete steps, named after Alan Turing), Gödel's theorem, non-computability, improvable truths, and complex mathematics are discussed.

Penrose is also famous for 'Penrose tiling'. Here, simple geometric shapes termed *polyominoes,* which are planar shapes comprised of one or more square-shaped cells, are assigned rules by which they combine to form complex tiling patterns. Of importance here is the possibility of generating deterministic but non-computable patterns from these rules. That is, no programme can decide if a set will tile a plane. The link to the non-computable nature of consciousness, which relates to deterministic reality, is clear.

The physical cause of conscious experience is, almost universally, thought to involve neurons in the brain. Like most cells, neurons contain microtubules. These protein tubes are involved in many functions (described in Chapter 4), including cell division where they form the mitotic spindle. Microtubules are formed from the polymerisation of a basic unit, which is a dimer of two different forms of tubulin, named a-tubulin and b-tubulin. Polymerisation and depolymerisation of microtubules, a process regulated by phosphorylation carried out by specific protein kinases, is associated with the attachment and correct alignment of the chromosomes at the centre of the cell prior to division. However, mature neurons are non-dividing cells, so what is the function of microtubules in neurons?

Microtubules pack together laterally into two forms, termed A- and B-lattices, depending on how the dimers in adjacent microtubules interact with each other. The switching between the two forms may be acting in a signalling sense (on/off, equivalent to the 0's and 1's of binary computer code).

The crux of Penrose's argument is that quantum processes occur inside these subcellular neuronal microtubules because, being tubes, the inside is isolated from the external environment. Now, the consensus of opinion is that consciousness occurs globally across the brain, so Penrose's model would require a network of finely tuned and integrated microtubules. Within the isolated microtubules, quantum coherent activity is maintained and linked to tubulin conformations. As the EPR paradox and entanglement show that events separated in space can be considered as part of the same quantum system, then tubulin networks across the brain are feasible in the context of large-scale quantum coherence. Indeed, without a global ability, the idea has less credibility.

The microtubule walls and 'ordered' water outside the tubes are thought to maintain the isolation of the quantum oscillations inside. The separation of these oscillations from the outside are essential to prevent random leaps to the classical level. What is important for Penrose's idea is that quantum computations in the tubes occur long enough for the new physics to take place, and this involves non-computational processes that equate to the objective reduction of the quantum events — the result is conscious experience. These processes enable the type of thought that a computer cannot simulate and employ the type of physics that could unite deterministic quantum states with the classical level without probability involvement.

There is, of course, much debate over this about not only the physics but also simpler aspects such as the timing involved. For example, when considering free will, Penrose believes that he has shown that the time for it to act equates to the time taken for the new quantum behaviour, microtubule function, and non-computable processes to occur. However, this is not proof that his ideas are correct, but selected results of an inexact experimental science. Indeed, his ideas also suggest that at least one second is required for active thought to occur, but conversation is proof that this happens far quicker. Hence, experimental design needs to catch up with theory to provide a better testing ground.

However, it is an intriguing line of enquiry that will no doubt be explored in more detail. If it is proven correct, it would be a case of humans using their brains to understand both the fundamental mechanism of the brain and the rules of existence, and where the answer lies in the mechanism of the brain itself. Yet, even if the cause of consciousness is a quantum process, the physical apparatus (brain) we use to interact with the world is one that receives sensory information in the classical sense. So, our mental faculties have evolved to probe reality in a classical way. Moreover (if true), the objective reduction of the causal quantum processes of conscious experience still say nothing of the qualitative experience itself. *That* aspect remains a subjective, private experience and, as such, a mystery to the observer.

We have glimpsed at a few different views on consciousness, specifically those of Crick, Edelman, and Penrose. There are many other philosophers and scientists investigating it, each with their own interpretation. Some try to understand the actual mechanisms underlying consciousness whereas others focus on the qualia themselves (e.g., the English psychologist Nicholas Humphrey). The goal desired determines the type of strategy adopted to achieve it. Many contrasting views on consciousness exist because of the complexity of the subject as well as the relatively primitive methods with which we can investigate it (in relation to what is needed to get a complete picture). To obtain one that is universally accepted — and right — requires being able to ask the right questions and having the tools (mental, physical, and technological) to answer them. Unsurprisingly, there is much debate as to whether this is feasible.

John Searle (and more thoughts on Crick, Edelman, and artificial intelligence)

John Searle (b. 1932) has written an interesting account of his views on different philosophers' and scientists' accounts of conscious mechanisms. In his review, *The Mystery of Consciousness* (1997), he gives an analysis of the work of Crick, Edelman, Penrose, and Daniel Dennett III, among others.

By focusing on Crick, Edelman, and Penrose as well as their differences, we see that a common question — "what causes consciousness?" — leads to multiple solutions, despite each possessing the same tools (technology and the mind) at their disposal. Dennett believes that there is nothing about human consciousness that cannot be known by an advanced alien race studying it, but this must be wrong. He is ignoring the experience, although the word 'advanced' gives him room to defend his comment.

If one human cannot know for certain what another human feels when they experience something, then how could an alien? Furthermore, only *that* human can know *his or her* conscious sensation as it is a uniquely personal experience; I can attempt to guess what you feel when you 'see blue' because, as I am also human, I know how *I* feel when I 'see blue'. For the same reason, I cannot *know* the same for the alien because I am different. Even if the alien knew the causal mechanistic processes of human consciousness, understanding this is not the same as knowing consciousness.

It would thus know less about 'what it feels like' than the human who feels it. Clearly, when discussing consciousness, it should be clarified whether one is referring to its cause or the qualia.

One of the key points in Searle's analyses of different views on consciousness concerns AI. As already specified, there is the opinion among some researchers that the mind is just a computer programme. Thus, consciousness consists of computational processes. This is called the *strong AI* view (Dennett holds this opinion). The *weak AI* view is that brain processes cause consciousness, and these processes can be simulated on a computer. However, the computer simulation does not guarantee that consciousness will occur. Searle, Crick, and Edelman believe in variations of weak AI. As mentioned earlier, Penrose believes in neither strong nor weak AI.

When one looks at the different beliefs of these researchers regarding consciousness, one is drawn to their scientific training. Penrose is a mathematician and physicist. Thus, he draws on a version of quantum mechanics that requires an understanding of quantum gravity. Edelman and Crick, with their biological backgrounds (Edelman shared the 1972 Nobel Prize in Physiology or Medicine for his work on antibodies while Crick won his for elucidating the structure of DNA), used a more physiological approach.

Basically, the philosophers of mind divide into two camps — *dualists* and *monists*. Dualists believe that there are two kinds of phenomena in the world — minds and bodies. We are aware of what is in the world (objectively) and in our minds (subjectively). We are not aware of what is in the minds of others. Although psychological analysis affords insight, it does not provide knowing as traditionally conceived. Monists, on the other hand, believe that the world is made of one type of thing. Either way, the mind-body problem still exists where the mind, comprising thoughts and sensations, relates in some way to our interactions with the physical world. Let us deal with Penrose, Crick, and Edelman in succession and include some philosophical problems that Searle identifies with their prospective explanations of consciousness and the mind-body problem.

Penrose believes in three worlds: the physical world, the mental world, and the Platonic mathematical world. Each serves to ground the other (though it is not clear how). These worlds represent what is actually 'there', what exists in the mind, and what is to be discovered, respectively. Thus, the mind discovers (not creates) things about the physical world.

Penrose hopes to solve consciousness, ontology, and metaphysics with a form of quantum mechanics that does not exist yet (his 'new physics', as mentioned earlier). The reason he has decided that consciousness requires such physics is partly because he rejects the idea that consciousness can be supported by interactions between vast networks or maps of neurons (as Edelman suggested) and that the individual neuron is too large to be the functional element of conscious processes.

The noted philosopher of science Karl Popper dedicated considerable attention to issues relating to consciousness. Like Penrose, Popper talked of three different worlds describing reality — world one consists of objects, substances, and fields; world two of states of the human mind (conscious and subconscious), and world three of the products of the human mind. From this picture, he and the Australian neurophysiologist John Eccles (1903–1997) considered consciousness to be independent of the brain, which seems an implausible idea.

As we know, it was Gödel who proved that there are formal arithmetic systems that cannot be shown to be consistent or non-contradictory from within themselves, and Penrose uses this proof (and Turing's application of it within the context of a computer programme — see next section) to show that brains are not computers. There are certain mathematical questions that a formal system would try *ad infinitum* to solve, which a human would see as pointless to continue. We *see* it and give up, but the formal system is tied to trying forever. Penrose thinks that the implication from Gödel's work proves that weak AI is false. However, others believe that even though the mind cannot be simulated computationally, the units that create the mind can be.

However, in the case of the mind and consciousness, the whole is greater than the sum of the parts. The mind transcends the immediately apparent capacities that extend from the interactions of the causal neurons. A neuron is not a computer just because it is computable, nor is a brain a computer just because some of its parts and processes can be computed or simulated. Unlike a computer, the brain does not operate according to logical rules. No two brains are identical, even in genetically identical twins, unlike computers.

Developmental and environmental differences and life choices ensure that no two brains are alike — a 2015 study based on a small sample of genetically identical twins in which both were gay or one was gay suggests that epigenetic imprinting may account for the development of homosexual orientation. No computer programme or AI can account for the brain's output or behaviour. Although genes enable the brain, we are not born with enough genes (the estimated number of human genes currently stands at around 19,000) to specify the synaptic complexity of our brains, according to Edelman.

Some form of weak AI may be true. Penrose would be wrong to think that if weak AI were false, he is therefore right (if you think the Moon is made of cheese and I think that it is made of ice cream, and you prove that it is not made of ice cream, that does not mean it is made of cheese). More seriously, our non-computable mental abilities would not necessarily have to be relevant to non-computable elements. Neurons can still explain consciousness in causal terms. Penrose dismisses the neuronal explanation for consciousness despite the mathematical possibility that the very number of neurons in the brain, together with their interactive potential (i.e., networks and maps) with one another, presents a numerical interaction that could, from a certain perspective, account for consciousness.

Crick and Edelman believed that neuronal interactions produce consciousness, rather than an unknown quantum process within a neuronal constituent such as microtubules. Could Crick have been right in thinking that my free will is due to the behaviour of nerve cells and their molecules? If so, Searle points out some issues that Crick failed to address. For example, how does the brain go from electrochemical impulses firing between neurons to feelings? Searle makes it clear that qualia, and understanding qualia, is the problem of consciousness. Searle agrees with Crick that consciousness is an emergent property of the brain, such that complex sensations are emergent properties that arise in the brain from the interactions of its many parts. However, Crick thought that because our interpretations of reality can be wrong, we do not have knowledge of objects in the world.

Searle says that just because we are subject to illusions does not mean that we only have a symbolic interpretation of the world. What I see is what I see, not a symbolic form. However, Searle fails to stress or recognise that the sensation I experience following perception may not be perception itself, but an enriched sensation of it (as will be discussed further later). What is seen when looking at a cat, for example, is not the perceived visual input, but the sensation in the mind caused by it. The different aspects of our sensory experiences are combined into one that is single and unified. How this is achieved is the binding problem. Crick thought that this is the problem of how neurons act as a unit, and they do it by firing in synchronisation at a specific frequency (40 hertz).

Edelman thought that the billions of neuronal connections can produce consciousness when functioning as a network. He proposed this from the demonstration that the brain develops, in the individual, interconnected maps of neurons which become selected and strengthened, while other connections are eliminated through 'programmed cell death', also known as *apoptosis*. This is a normal developmental process that removes unwanted cells in order to form appropriate bodily structures. For example, as the appropriately named limb bud is refined *in utero* from a paddle-shaped appendage into a human arm and hand, cells apoptose within the 'spaces' between the digits of the hand in order to form the fingers and thumb. Thus, before a brain matures, it may lose neuronal connections which are in overabundance to necessity, while other groups are strengthened.

Using the idea of 'reentry' where signals pass between neuronal maps, Edelman showed that stimuli are received from different aspects of an object to produce patterns of neural groups, which are selected in maps. Different maps calculate different aspects of the observed object's reality (e.g., colour), and reentry mechanisms enable other maps to put repeatedly received sensory inputs (as maps) into order (e.g., to give an overall picture of an object; its colour, shape, movement, and so on). When the brain maps signals onto each other by reentry, Edelman proposed that this 'global mapping' coordinates perception and action.

Edelman said that higher-order consciousness (e.g., language) comes from primary consciousness (e.g., simple sensations). Higher-order consciousness is built from the processes that have primary consciousness, so Edelman must explain primary consciousness. For this, the brain must possess, among other things, a memory, a system for learning, and the ability to discriminate self from non-self. Searle points out that it is true that for an organism to possess higher-order conscious abilities, it must first be conscious.

Thus, Edelman thought that the development of syntax and semantics comes from the primary conscious abilities of the mind. We are not constrained by computable axioms. However, Searle points out that Edelman's functional descriptions can also be explained independently of consciousness. Edelman appeared to disregard qualia despite acknowledging their existence. For example, how warm is warm, and what does 'seeing red' feel like? *"Seeing Red"* is the title of Humphrey's 2006 book on conscious experience, where the feeling of seeing red is, obviously, the focus. Such subjective experiences should be explainable, but are considered unknowable by Edelman, as if my subjectivity is only for me in a knowable sense. The question remains — *how* do the physical structures of the brain cause consciousness?

These scientific descriptions attempt to delineate the remarkable ability we have of converting objective phenomena into inner, private, qualitative states of awareness. These qualitative states (or qualia) are, in essence, the 'being' of consciousness and they form the mind when associated with intellect composed of thought, perception, emotion, will, and memory. Indeed, research into consciousness uses the rational part of the mind to understand its most subjective property — the wondrous qualities of qualia. Whether an analytical approach will afford appreciation of what is essentially a personal, subjective state seems unlikely, even if we do work out the mechanism for their construction.

Machines that mimic intelligence (e.g., chess programmes) do not experience qualia and are not conscious. The only things we know that *are* conscious are living, organic minds which operate with input from the external world. Thus, is such input that resides outside the system of the intelligent 'thing' a prerequisite for consciousness? If so, one wonders how an artificial mind could be constructed with this capacity. The human brain possesses the property of consciousness as a function of its processes, which evolved in an organism that interacts with objective reality. When we think of an artificial brain, we imagine one that is a programme tied to its formalism, not one that interacts with inputs from the physical world. This form of an artificial brain is all that is presently possible. To produce consciousness and qualia, we know that an artificial brain would require greater than the minimal causal powers of our brains to produce them.

Formal programmes (as we understand them) render artificial minds susceptible to self-referential paradoxes that we, as minds with access to 'outside' the system, can overcome. To see through self-referential paradoxes, an artificial mind should possess something like human intuition, and this comes from existing inside and accessing outside the 'program' so that unfeasible solutions that may satisfy a rule will show as unfit for the physical world. This ability to access outside the programme and possess something akin to intuition may be a prerequisite for consciousness and perhaps, under the right circumstances, cause it. Thus, an artificial brain with access to reality outside its formal rules of programming will have overcome its intrinsic incompleteness and made a necessary leap towards the possibility for consciousness.

Consciousness is the *experience* of qualitative, subjective, mental states, so mimicking behaviour of what is known to be conscious is not consciousness. Behaviour is irrelevant where the ontology of consciousness is concerned because it is an inner state. So, what causes it? We have discussed possible explanations by Penrose, Crick, and Edelman, whose reasoning was based on cause and effect — something happens in the brain, causing consciousness. In other words, they believe that knowing the causal powers of consciousness allows it to be understood. Some say that information causes consciousness, but this seems unlikely because it is not a separate causal feature of the world. Information is relative to the observer whereas consciousness is internal and happens in the mind (which is why it is easy to take the dualist view of the existence of two worlds — the physical world and the world of the mind — rather than everything being explainable in terms of one world). The consciousness of each mind is embedded in and shares the same physical world, from which each receives inputs to access and constructs a personal mental world.

Consciousness is a process that cannot be reduced to something simpler. Observer-independent properties such as solidity can be reduced to its constituent molecular behaviour, but consciousness has a first-person subjective ontology and thus cannot be reduced to a form with a third-person objective ontology. While consciousness can be causally reduced to the behaviour of neurons, consciousness is eliminated if we consider just the neurons. Consciousness is an emergent property of neuronal behaviour, so consciousness only exists when it is experienced.

Unlike Crick, Edelman, and Penrose, who look at the cause and mechanism of consciousness, Humphrey tackles these experiences, its properties, and its evolution.

Nicholas Humphrey

Did consciousness evolve for a purpose, or was it just a 'fortunate' by-product of our evolution? It has been said that if we did not know that consciousness exists, it would be unnecessary to invent it because nothing points to its necessity. Nothing in the physical world has the features of consciousness, so it can be said that consciousness does not exist in the physical world. But, as we have conscious experiences to which the rules of physical reality do not apply, then all that consciousness 'is' is an experience of something in our minds. To return to Nagel's question, without consciousness, there would be no *thing* to be like. There would be no sense of self, which is the centre to which all that we do and think relates — it gives worth to meaning.

Edelman's TNGS may well prove to be that which enables an integrated conscious experience. How this binding problem is resolved is debated, but Edelman's solution involving reentrant mapping is consistent with Humphrey's ideas. However, while Edelman's ideas may well be the actual wiring processes of conscious experience, they say nothing of "what it is like" to feel something. That is, it says nothing of the sensation or experience. So, the study of consciousness consists of two distinct problems: the mind-body problem (i.e., how can a physical entity give rise to mental events? — the territory of Edelman, Crick, and Penrose) and the mind-mind problem (i.e., concerned with understanding the qualitative aspects of consciousness — for instance, the way that lemons smell or the colour red looks). The mind-mind problem is the part of the consciousness puzzle that Humphrey's ideas address, in addition to the 'hard' problem. So, what are Humphrey's ideas?

Einstein's equation $E = mc^2$ relates energy to mass and was discovered because the relationship between the clearly defined terms is empirically testable. But a conscious, subjective experience is dimensionally and conceptually different from the physical and objectively observed process causing it. This distinction means that even if a particular neural correlate is found to be responsible for a conscious sensation, it says nothing of the conscious sensation itself because it is not of the same form. Humphrey is well aware of this. Primitive animals receive a stimulus, which is perceived in some bodily way (e.g., light causing the animal to move towards it).

However, through natural selection, humans evolved a process where the stimulus perceived does not cause the physical reaction but a mental sensation. This sensation is not a direct physical reaction to the perceived, but a sensation that is contemplated and thus under the perceiver's control and reflected back on objective reality. So, the stimulus is perceived and a sensation is created, which is not a copy of that which is perceived but instead carries both information about the physical event in objective reality and how the perceiver feels about it.

The *inner eye*, as Humphrey termed it in the 1980s, is like a new sense organ in the brain that has a field of view that is of the brain itself rather than of the outside world. Phenomena are perceived and the inner eye selects information and presents it back to the brain in a form that reflects external reality, albeit in a processed, enriched form. It is possible to perceive the world without associated sensation, but sensation links the perceiver to the world and the subject to the object, such that the perceiver cares about the world and feels part of it.

Humphrey believes that we perceive something and have the mental sensation at the same time, so we think that it is the same thing when in fact it is not. The perception is one thing, which is a pure physical reception of the information from external reality according to our physical makeup, whereas the sensation is the mental construction from the phenomena (maybe according to Edelman's mechanisms). This sensation is purely the personal, subjective, conscious experience. Following perception, sensation is enabled, and reflection on this and back on the world makes one feel a part of it and, thus, care. Humphrey distinguishes perception from sensation in that perception is purely the direct input from objective reality that is achieved by our perceptive apparatus.

Without the sensation of perception — whether as a flowing integration of perception and sensation or a discrete process — the ability to perceive and survive still leaves the conscious individual feeling less a part of the world. There is obviously a Darwinian benefit for sensation over pure perception. However, strict Darwinians steer clear of consciousness in their evolutionary explanations of life because it appears to them to be their Achilles heel. Perhaps there is an evolutionary benefit for consciousness and, rather than being a thorn in the side, it is indeed further support for evolution by natural selection.

It is wrong to think that sensory categories such as colour exist independently of mind and language. A thing with colour has colour relative to the perceiver of colour. Without a perceiver, it merely has being. A recent internet 'meme', first posted on social media, concerned how different people saw an image of a particular patterned dress. Some saw it as blue with black stripes (its actual colour) whereas others saw it as white and gold. It has been likened to Wittgenstein's famous 'duck-rabbit' visual illusion, based on a 19th century German drawing of what looks like a rabbit's head when seen from one side but a duck's head from the other.

Colour itself is nothing but a property of a thing that is relative to and determined by that which perceives and senses it. The neuronal basis of consciousness tries to link neuronal activity with conscious sensation (e.g., 'seeing red'), but no correct definition of neuronal activity can *define* conscious experience. The former is objectively quantitative, the latter subjectively qualitative. Sensations have ownership (belong to subject), bodily location (invoke a part of the subject's body), presentness (sensations occur now), qualitative modality (one type of sensation), and phenomenal immediacy (all sensation is occurring now). So, the sensation is like a bodily expression.

The command signals following perception, which originally evolved to react physically to sensation, are encoded. Yet, with conscious sensation following perception, we do not react physically; rather, we monitor our own mental sensation that responds to it. Humphrey believes that we have both the primitive body-centred picture of what a stimulus is doing to the body as well as the advanced (possibly human-only), body-independent sensation of perception, which is not reactive in a physical sense to stimulus. We keep the primitive body-centred form of perception to stay abreast of world events (e.g., danger — the 'flight or fight' response), but most bodily responses to a stimulus reach the brain as virtual commands that are translated into sensation for analysis of action. So, the process is closed off from the outside world by the brain. An evolutionarily ancient reactionary response is felt, but action is *considered* following sensation. Whether these two processes exist or if the body-independent picture is functionally feasible and effective, and if indeed they are not extensions of the same process, are contentious issues.

The important fact is that rather than reacting directly to stimulus, the stimulus perceived and sensed in the brain enables us to not only control our response but, in terms of consciousness, have control of "what it is like". For instance, the perception of light does not only have a nonconscious reaction but also a conscious sensation over which we have some control as to "what it is like". Thus, drugs such as LSD affect our sensations more than our perception of the external world. When one bites an apple, different molecules stimulate receptors on the tongue and in the nose to generate the impression of the flavour and texture that we know from experience as 'apple'.

Similarly, when looking at a painting of 'Sunflowers' by Vincent Van Gogh for example, colour pigments applied in a particular pattern create the impression 'Sunflowers by Vincent Van Gogh'. Physical things translate causally into knowable sensations in the mind. The matter of the apple does not enter the mind, but eating one sets off a consistent flow of processes in the mind to generate the sensation 'apple', and with the benefit of long-term memory comes the ability to compare it to past apples eaten and evaluate the experience subjectively.

Philosophers term the essence of a conscious experience the 'X factor'. It is the private sensation (e.g., of feeling heat or pain, the taste of an apple, or seeing red) in the mind caused by physical processes in the brain. The flow and interaction of molecules and electrical signalling in the brain caused by an external stimulus or memory is sufficiently ordered and complex to produce this conscious property — one which transcends its cause. The mind translates the ordered flow of matter and electrical impulses which we can objectively understand in the brain into a solely subjective experience. This translation, defined specifically by the order, arrangement, and temporal flow of matter and electrical signals, ensures that the internal and external worlds are linked and consistent.

A moment in time might produce a stimulus that is perceived. The resulting sensation, of which we have control over "what it is like", has temporal depth. That is, the perceived stimulus is translated into a sensation in subjective time, thereby enabling conscious experience — the 'X factor', if you like. This might be one point extended in time or a coalescence of past, present, and future. The sensation in subjective time always relates at some level to a phenomenon in physical time. Time flows — the arrow of time is to the future as determined by the second law of thermodynamics. When a physicist talks of the present, it is part of the future becoming the present, then becoming the past. The subjective present as we experience it contains our conscious life. It is an awareness of the self and many things — indefinable by words but rich in meaning.

We cannot accurately verbalise our conscious content as language is an unfit tool for *that* job, but we can feel, control, hold on to, and experience it. Consciousness can act as an extended subjective present where the past, present, and future coalesce as a single unified experience while being instantaneous, with controlled repetition and duration. So, the X factor is how the mind converts the phenomenon perceived into a sensation that we have control over in terms of duration, repetition, past, present, and future. The primitive and biologically redundant responses to stimulus get privatised so that the incoming stimulus becomes closed off and internalised in the brain as a reentrant process. The sensation caused by the phenomena perceived feeds itself and is influenced by the primitive input of external stimulus, enriching the sensory, conscious experience.

Philosophical zombies

In philosophy, a *zombie* is a hypothetical 'person' who is objectively inseparable from a true person but who lacks qualia or conscious experiences.

Since philosophical zombies are logically possible, philosophers such as David Chalmers believe that qualia cannot be explained purely by physical properties. The idea of humans as zombies (and philosophers such as Dennett have ideas about consciousness suggesting that we are, indeed, zombies) is misguided, since zombies can perform complex tasks without conscious awareness only if they had learned how to do those tasks previously and consciously. Without subjective experience, the perceiver feels like a zombie, dissociated from the external reality perceived, whereas the individual who both perceives somatically and integrates this stimulus with reentrant central sensation (originally caused by stimuli and reinforced by memories and restimulation of those reentrant circuits) has an existence whose life is enriched and taken out of zombiedom. He feels important, not only with a sense of place but also feels part of the world.

Humphrey says that this moves humans from saying "I have experiences, therefore I am" to "I am because I have such experiences". He goes on to speculate that there is a genetic drive for such phenomena to evolve (where the sensation is distinct from the experience despite our being fooled that they are one and the same). By enriching our sensation of reality, we feel more a part of it, care more about it, want to be part of it, and thus increase our desire to survive and reproduce in it (preserving the genes along the route). Hence, for our survival as a species, the consequences of consciousness (as opposed to zombiedom) are advantageous because we can see the benefit of continuing our existence. With this idea, Humphrey found both a purpose for consciousness and why it evolved according to the rules of natural selection. However, earlier he expressed other (perhaps additional) reasons for the refinement of consciousness in man.

The Inner Eye

In his book *The Inner Eye* (1985), Humphrey describes how consciousness evolved to meet the human challenge of understanding and interpreting the behaviour of other human beings. Indeed, while we do not know what it is like to be a bat, we *do* know what it is like to be a human. Although behaviourism has shown, by its failure, that what goes on in the mind is not evident from behaviour and that the human mind is far more complex than that, our consciousness provides us with psychological insight into another's behaviour — its reasons and interpretation — through knowing our own thought-behaviour relationships and extrapolating them to others within the context of social situations.

So, human consciousness may be a by-product of the enlargement of the mind driven by the evolutionary advantage gained by improved cognitive abilities, but from this surprise ability comes the additional advantage of understanding and interpreting the behaviour of other humans. Such abilities arose from the time humanity took the first steps towards existing in social groups in Africa. Being able to understand behaviour from a consciously intuitive rather than behavioural stance would make an individual capable of reasoning about and predicting another's behaviour, thus enhancing survival.

Humphrey's idea at the time was that the genes that encode the neuronal networks constituting the conscious part of the mind may have evolved by natural selection to make the mind think it is distinct from the body. This, allied to the sensory enrichment of perception where the mind (to Humphrey) mistakenly believes that what it perceives *is* the sensation, seems to afford evolutionarily advantages. However, he was writing before the advent of genome sequencing and we now know, for example, that humans have less than 20,000 genes and that humans and chimpanzees share 99.3% of DNA identity. There are no unique human genes tailored to our unique brain function and consciousness. Whereas chimps exhibit a wide range of interactive gestures, consciousness gives us a far more sophisticated range of emotional gestures and responses which cannot be down to a very few changes in gene sequences.

Sensation separated from perception can enhance our analysis of the world. It need not be distorted since sensation is modelled from perception and, thus, from reality. The sensory enrichment and the mind's view of the world from its unique untouchable vantage point of access through bodily senses gives the mind the impression that the world is made for it. Our self-perceived importance of being embedded in reality is highlighted because, however rationally we reason that we are just an entity *in* reality, we *feel* that reality is for us because our own self is the one thing that is forever present for us.

So, two key errors the mind makes from a consciousness sense but which serve to enrich and enhance life are therefore:

1. The belief that sensation *is* perception when in fact they are different.
2. The belief that mind and body are separate things when in fact they interact with objective reality as an integrated unit.

John Searle dedicates much of his book, *Seeing Things as They Are* (2015), to refuting the 'bad argument' (as he calls it) that we cannot perceive the world directly and that we interact with our sensations of perceptions. Searle believes that we interact directly with our perceptions of the world because our reality would otherwise be our subjective reality of private experience. Here, illusions and hallucinations can mix — with the same status — with sensations derived directly from perceptions of the physical world which, to Searle, is unacceptable. Searle states that everything in the objective field is either perceived or can be perceived. Nothing in the subjective field is perceived, nor can it be perceived precisely, because the events in the subjective field consist of the perceptions of events in the objective field.

This view of Searle's is one position, yet it does not successfully refute the opposing interpretation. Let us look further into whether we perceive the world directly or as an enriched sensory experience of it.

Whichever view is correct must conform to the important issue of time. What we interact with in our mental experience of the objective world must be something effectively immediate in relation to the cause, otherwise there would be an obvious delay between what our senses enable us to perceive and our reflection on it. By 'effectively immediate', I mean that we are able to act on our mental experiences of the world as they happen and in a way that does not jeopardise our ability to act and react or survive.

Let us remind ourselves of the contrasting positions held by Searle and Humphrey and find a solution:

> **Searle:** We interact directly with our perceptions of the world because, if we do not, our reality would be our subjective reality of private experience.
>
> **Humphrey:** For body-independent sensation of perception (i.e., there is no disagreement on the body-dependent form), the stimulus perceived does not cause the physical reaction but a mental sensation. This sensation is reflected on and under the perceiver's control and reflected back on objective reality.

Both arguments are by eminent thinkers in their field and are the result of much research and analysis. Yet, contrasting views of the same phenomena cannot both be right. Indeed, Searle sees direct perception as applicable for all scenarios, and though Humphrey accepts in certain circumstances that the body-centred picture of sensory input exists, his body-independent view contrasts with Searle's thinking. So, can both views coexist? Is it possible that they actually represent extremes of the same view and, if so, how?

Our senses perceive, and it makes sense that these have evolved to present to the mind an ideal blend of richness and objective truth to enable the perceiver to interact most effectively with a world that he or she feels intimately connected to. Here, the enriched perception creates a sensation of the world, thought of by some thinkers as discrete from the perceived sense-data while by others as an evolved presentation of it through the combined sensory apparatus and brain.

Thus, as an extension to Searle's direct perception, the sensory enrichment that connects us to the world is still part of a singular process of perception of the objective world, but exists as an immediate, rich, and engaging experience. Humphrey's body-centred and body-independent mechanisms of experiencing the world may well be situation-specific extensions of this same process that our mental framework has evolved to accommodate. Sensation and raw perception are extremes of the same thing.

What Humphrey terms the 'body-independent process', where perception is the sensation we engage with, might be a sort of 'direct enrichment filter' from the perceptive apparatus. Here, information flows from the world to the mind and is enriched in the process. It is a one-way flow of information, enabling an immediate link between external events and mental experience of them. Clearly, we reflect on what we sense, yet what we sense is both what is perceived *and* the sensation of it, thus enabling a sense of immediacy. Of course, this is a simplistic view that emerges from trying to align wholly different descriptions under one paradigm, the purpose being to suggest that Searle's and Humphrey's views may not be so different.

In typical Searle style, he presents in his book the argument he aims to refute with a crude definition and then goes to great lengths to explain why it is false. Therefore, he appears convincing primarily because he is refuting a version of the argument that poorly represents the true picture of the opposing view. For perception of reality to be filtered through and into sensation in order to provide a rich subjective experience of the world presents a model that makes much sense. We are not simple data-processing machines where pure perception can be analysed, but are organisms that *feel* the world around us. That alone should be enough to convince us that mechanisms that enrich but not distort the perceived experience will bond us more to the world. Integrating our various physical perceiving apparatus with the mental processes that are stimulated by them results in subjective experience linking the subject to the object in an intimate and engaging way.

Of course, perceived stimuli are not going directly to our conscious centres, but are rather filtered through sensory receptive processes that have evolved to enhance, not distort, the sensations representing the objective world for the benefit (i.e., survival) of the organism.

The way we interact with physical reality and how we perceive and sense it have much to do with the age-old belief of the mind's separation from reality. Why do we think there is mind-body duality? Philosophers regard it as an unfortunate error (e.g., Descartes made this error), but even recognising these facts does not reduce their effect because it does not affect our *feeling* that it is the case — that is, telling me that perception is not sensation does not make me *feel* that perception is not sensation.

Humphrey believes that the mind evolving to think that it is separate from the body (even though, physically, conscious sensations map onto neural connections) would benefit human life by enhancing productivity through the generation of drives, goals, and creativity and engendering the feeling that we have something worth preserving. Any one of these may be seen as a positive evolutionary trait that confers a natural selective advantage and thus serve as a reason for its possibility. The mind thinking that it is distinct pushes our drives beyond eating, surviving, and reproducing to understand and transcend apparent limitations. Humphrey proposes that the enigmatic features of consciousness underlie its role in life.

Of course, the evolution of early hominid species is easier to understand in terms of the advantageous role of certain mental traits and psychological experiences than in modern man. The environment was more savage and less forgiving then than for us in modern circumstances. Think of a buffalo being attacked by a lion as an example to stress a point. Sometimes, it looks as if the buffalo gives up in such a fight despite there being an easy way (from our perspective) of overcoming the assault. Is it just lack of intelligence or something else that makes it resign so easily to its fate? Would the evolution of a sense of being or care for an innately rich connection to life provide it with a greater survival instinct? Although the buffalo does not possess the brain structure that allows for what is possible in a human, this example emphasises the survival value that deeper consciousness brings.

As well as the advantages of possessing a mind that thinks it is separate from the body, would the separation of sensation from perception also present a selective advantage in an evolutionary context? Yes, but so would rich and directly perceived experiences. Natural selection is the selection of traits that enhance reproduction and give advantages to the next generation. Minds that are rich in conscious experience are at an advantage over those that are not. Without the mind-body distinction felt, we would be drawn to the genetic drives of eating, surviving, and reproducing without the expression of conscious consideration.

Selection that enhances neural circuitry that makes the mind think that it is different from the body would require the production of mental sensations that feel different from body-conscious sensations. These distinct sensations also enrich the life of the person by encouraging the expression of this species-unique quality. It encompasses the drives for the enrichment, development, and progress of the species: science, art, music, and technological advancement. These result from the creativity enabled by the properties of mental imagery.

Humphrey believes that a mind that feels separate from the body serves two purposes:

1. It enhances the role of the expression of thought (creativity) in our present and future life and enhances intelligence through the desire to achieve.
2. The genetic changes that create the neural circuitry that fools the mind into thinking it is separate from body allows for a more advanced perceptual space. Such genetic changes would, of course, include the evolution of physical changes such as the development of an enlarged cranial space. In other words, sensations from perceptions are better constructed. They relate so well to the real world despite us thinking that they are purely perception. They are an excellent coalescence of what is out there in reality, how we feel about it, and what we want to do about it. Therefore, the advanced perceptual space provides an arena for enhanced intellectual creativity.

When Humphrey wrote *The Inner Eye*, he clearly thought that there was a strong genetic element to consciousness; perhaps even human-specific genes that enabled the levels of consciousness and intelligence we possess. As mentioned earlier and as discussed at length in Chapter 4, genetic analysis since the completion of the Human Genome Sequencing Project has modified our views. So, although point 2 above presents interesting views on the relation between sensation and perception, the genetic element for causing this is dubious. However, the evolution of enrichment of the process by which a perceived experience becomes a sensation, and the consequential experience of feeling connected to the world, would be advantageous for the individual and species (whether it is genetic, epigenetic, or through some other modification or arrangement).

Whether these events occur(red) or not is not known, so what do we know about what makes humans different?

1. Primate-hominid ancestors evolved.
2. Hominids split off from chimpanzees about 7 million years ago.
3. Hominid skull cavity size increased, and brain size increased with it.
4. Natural selection drives accumulation of advantageous traits, so perhaps a larger brain (which required a bigger skull) was necessary to support a bipedal existence.
5. More neural circuitry was laid down due to increased brain size, which gave more possibilities for neuronal interconnections, storage, and so on.
6. Consciousness was a by-product of this.
7. The genes did not alter much in sequence over the intervening 5 million years or so since the split (2), hence chimpanzees and man are 99.3% similar at the DNA level. There are no special genes for human consciousness.
8. Epigenetic modification that is human-specific may play a role.
9. The synergistic effect of having large cranial capacity, the pentadactyl limb, and existing in interdependent groups drove the need and capacity for communication, language, and intergenerational transference of knowledge, thus providing the space and means to evolve mentally.

An additional system that has evolved in the brain and mind that has natural selective advantage is the construction of a 3-D environment from a 2-D image. A 2-D image is perceived and projected onto the retina in the eye, after which what we experience as a sensation in the mind is a construction produced from the 2-D image together with other sensory inputs linked with memory and intellect. This 2-D image of the world, projected onto the retina, is converted into a neural representation as it passes to the primary visual cortex in the brain.

The complexity of the neural representation is due to repeated processing of visual input by specialised areas of the visual cortex for depth, angles, colour, and so on. Our brain has evolved to create a rich internal representation of what it perceives. The sensation produced in the mind from the external stimuli is far richer than the perceived stimulus alone and makes us feel part of the world and care about it, thus compelling us to live in it.

The three-dimensionality of sight is enhanced during the early stages of an organism's lifetime. We see things as 2-D objects, but as we exist surrounded by those objects, we learn what angles, colours, curves, and shapes look like and how they relate to what is actually there. The delay between perception and sensation, together with the brain learning during the lifetime how 2-D shapes and colours relate to 3-D objects, enables us to perceive and then sense the external world — through sight — as a 3-D environment. This, like the evolution of rich sensory experience, also provides an evolutionary advantage as it makes us want to engage with the world.

Direct perception is at the will of physical time, whereas we control the sensation in mental time by repeating, extending, and expanding it. This capability adds credence to Humphrey's body-independent view of sensation. Consciousness knows that it relates to the world but cannot interact with it. It is tied to the body and takes information from it to interpret the world. The mind cannot subjectively fully appreciate the world as it is dimensionally distinct (i.e., the mind cannot *feel* pain, cold, heat, and other sensations). Humphrey appreciates this and realises that the elusive X factor of consciousness cannot come from a full deconstruction of neuronal signalling. He is saying, for instance, that when

I see a red screen, although the light perceived comes in physical time, it is sensed in subjective time and can be expanded within different rules. So, the sensation of perceiving red is 'like' perceiving red through time and controlled by us.

We can make no complete definition of the X factor because it is a subjective quality. *Mirror neurons*, or 'monkey see, monkey do' neurons, have been identified which fire in the brain not only when an action occurs, but also when an action is observed in another animal. Despite this and the quality of empathy, the subjectivity of human consciousness ensures that what we feel is private. We can feel it and know what it feels like for 'me', but language fails to define it because that is designed for the shared, external, and objectively orientated physical world. There will always necessarily be a quality missing when we try to use objective tools to describe subjective experience, as Wittgenstein knew. So why try?

We all experience, yet it cannot be known whether your experience is like my experience. If I say "I feel hot", then you know what that means to you, but not to me. Consciousness is private on the *phenomenal* level where one person cannot know another's qualia of an experience or "what it is like", as well as on the *propositional* level where we do not even know that another person is having a conscious experience at all.

In summary, the mind is as it is due to evolution, whether or not our conscious richness was an accidental by-product of natural selection. Our neuronal circuits create rich subjective experiences, which constitute a mind that wants to understand how it relates to the world it interprets. The mind is embedded in the body, which is embedded in reality. The mind interprets its being in reality through the body in which it is embedded. It experiences its own subjective playing field, and those sensations are extrapolations from reality outside its own being.

Humphrey makes the insightful point that if we believe we exist due to a higher being who imbued us with rich conscious qualities, we should be mindful of the fact that one way consciousness won in evolution by natural selection was to encourage people to believe that they had *not* evolved by natural selection. To *believe* we evolved due to a higher being probably encourages us to live biologically fitter lives.

Soul Dust

In *Soul Dust* (2011), Humphrey's attempt to prove the resolution of the 'hard' problem, he starts by stating what he sees it as: "How can physical matter cause conscious experience?" To address this question, we need to know how we can utilise the tools we have to explain the conscious quality of experience produced by the brain.

I believe we can have a near-complete knowledge of conscious experience, but *not* of the same experience. We may one day be able to use the scientific method to obtain a physical, objective description of the physical processes that occur in the mind that correlate to a particular experience, or qualia. We can know or at least rationally hypothesise why qualia evolved — to make our body or, more fundamentally, our genes care about existing in a physical reality and strive to survive. The neural network that enables qualia and the selective evolutionary advantage it confers over one that *does not* produce the rich sensations of qualia may be, as Humphrey suggests, an evolutionary accident, but it is clearly a fortunate one from the vantage point of evolution by natural selection.

However, science does not allow me to know whether my subjective experience of, say, *thinking* of feeling rain on my face — let us call this 'event A' — is the same as your subjective experience of 'event A' even if you and I share the same physical reality, possess approximately the same physical being, and will have physical experience of 'event A' that lead to memories and qualia of it.

Thus, if we define me as person A (PA), you as person B (PB), knowledge of the processes causing the qualia of 'event A' as pEA, and knowledge of the actual *experience* of the qualia of 'event A' as qEA, I believe that we can only *ever* have knowledge of the following:

1. PA and PB can have pEA for both PA and PB.
2. PA can have qEA of PA but not of PB.
3. PB can have qEA of PB but not PA.

So, as I said, it is both yes and no. I can have complete knowledge of the cause for qualia to have evolved (a rational conclusion that it evolved for selective advantage). I also know how my experiences 'feel' and, through science, what processes occur in my brain when these felt experiences are happening. However, even if PA and PB were strapped to a machine and asked to think of event A and both produced the same readout indicating that the same physical processes occurred when they thought of event A, these results do not say that what PA and PB are *feeling* are the same. Moreover, neither PA nor PB has knowledge of qEA for their counterpart.

Knowledge of qualia and reality

The study of qualia consists of two distinct problems:

1. The mind-body problem, which is concerned with how a physical thing can give rise to mental events.
2. The mind-mind problem, which is concerned with understanding the qualitative aspects of consciousness, such as the way coffee smells.

The mind-mind problem is, of course, really part of the mind-body problem — it is the 'effect' part of the cause-effect relationship. Studying the mechanisms of the brain that cause qualia will probably tell us nothing about their qualitative aspects. Indeed, complete scientific knowledge of these causal processes relates little, in a conceptual sense, to the "what-it-is-like" aspect. Some believe that because the mind is caused by the brain and thus it is an unknown black box where qualia exist, then if we study the physical brain's mechanisms in hopes of revealing clarity about qualia, we will he left with interconnected smaller black boxes, but how these black boxes enable qualia will be no clearer.

If one browses the literature on the mind, one will find many viewpoints on the mind-body problem. Scientists and philosophers strongly defend their own opinions and oppose those of others. If the correct solution had been found or if it were easy to find, there would not be so many different and entrenched current positions. Why is the mind-body problem so 'hard'? Why are there so many different arguments about how to address it? Usually when many solutions to a problem exist and none are falsified, then the problem is either beyond the realms of science or so difficult that we are far from solving it. Is Colin McGinn therefore right in thinking that we do not possess the mental framework to understand — let alone solve — the mind-body problem, reality, and the infinite?

Let us take the concept of infinity. If we try to comprehend infinity, we simply cannot. We might think we can, but what we are understanding is the 'idea' of the infinite, not what it encapsulates. Just as we can state that there are infinite numbers, we cannot imagine what that really means. We can define space and time as infinite, but when we try to conceive of what that might mean, it overwhelms our capacity to do so. Because we are finite beings, the infinite extends beyond what we can know. We can understand the concept and manipulate it, but what this concept is transcends all possible categories of meaning and knowing we possess.

We cannot mentally encapsulate the infinite, yet we know what the concept means and how it relates to our conception of reality. We incorporate the infinite within a mathematical context to help us define our version of reality. Thus, we understand that we cannot encapsulate its essence, but know of its existence. Our models of reality are constructed in a way that buries this conundrum within the formalism. Our models essentially contain concepts we can manipulate, but not fully comprehend. Thus, understanding is a form of 'knowing about' without the need to 'know of'. By modeling reality that essentially uses knowledge of infinity within its formalism, we have a way of knowing how reality works without needing to know all of what it 'is' (which is impossible). Without the mental framework that makes possible the full integration of the infinite into our comprehension, we can only contemplate and understand the Universe within these confines.

The infinite is a part of the physical reality in which we are embedded and the conceptual reality we have constructed to describe it. We may one day construct a TOE that *describes* all phenomena and matter in terms that make sense to us, but the essence of that paradigm will essentially incorporate unknowable elements. If a TOE can describe all phenomena and matter, then why might that not be considered as *knowing* all phenomena and matter?

It would be like claiming we understand consciousness because we have delineated its physical causal processes. A mechanism for consciousness and a TOE that describes the processes and matter of reality would entail 'knowing' in a descriptive, causal sense. But consciousness possesses a 'quality' that transcends this description. Reality also presents itself as comprising intrinsically unknowable things and concepts. Thus, possessing knowledge of how things work and how they relate to other things does not provide knowledge of the innate nature of the thing, such as the way the person experiencing qualia knows "what it is like". A TOE would be within this constraint.

If reality is intrinsically unknowable, then *any* hope of completely 'knowing' it is obviously destroyed. If it is knowable, however, our minds may or may not be up to the task for any number of reasons, such as the complexity of nature or the form of thought that is used to analyse it (hence the alien thought experiment). Moreover, it may not be possible to encapsulate this knowledge under a single paradigm such as a TOE. Here, it may be only that which can be addressed objectively and by the scientific method that conforms to the paradigm. Subjective qualities like qualia may never fall under that banner.

If so, the irony would be that the qualities we know best, in a subjective sense, would be those that evade the very type of objective analysis some consider essential for us to claim that we really know reality. A TOE might describe the cause of subjective qualities, but not their nature. Since they *are* a part of reality, is the fact that science cannot address them an indicator that science produces a human-directed model of reality and not a true representation of how it works? Whether or not science can or will shift paradigmatically to incorporate experience is unknown, but it seems very unlikely.

The analysis of qualia presents many problems as stated earlier. Any shared language is as ineffective at describing 'feelings' as any scientifically-deduced causal mechanism is at revealing qualitative features. Indeed, since science is both objective and communicated, the difficulties posed in probing and clarifying the essence of qualia is doubled.

If I enjoy the smell of coffee and I observe you smelling coffee and you exhibit behavior to suggest that you are enjoying it, then I assume based on that behavior that you are having the same mental experience as I do when I smell it. However, I cannot be certain that what you feel is what I feel. No amount or type of communication between us can probe qualia to enable us to answer with certainty.

If qualitative experiences are knowable only to the one having them, then what of them do they know? The experience is not *known*: having the experience *is* the experience. There is a subtle difference between knowledge of the experience and knowledge of some 'thing' of physical reality external to the mind that causes a mental experience. For the former, the experience is the object and subject, whereas for the latter the object is the mental idea of its physical cause. Also, remembering an experience like smelling coffee is not the same as having the experience. One can remember what it is like, but *knowing* what it is like only happens during the experience.

Are subjective states a part of physical reality? In some sense they are like numbers because they are not considered physical and rely on a special type of matter (e.g., human consciousness) to have a form of existence. However, qualia differ in that they form a part of the human essence, whereas numbers are just abstract objects we use to make sense of the world. Yet, although qualia are experienced, we cannot say that we have isolated them by specifying the neuronal networks that cause them. They are a special property that is enabled by physical reality. They are unique in that we know them better than anything else in a subjective sense, and yet there is nothing we understand less objectively. They cannot be adequately defined, only experienced.

Problems with knowledge of qualia and reality

In 1994, David Chalmers wrote a paper stating that the hard problem of consciousness is far from being resolved. Subsequently, in the *Journal of Consciousness Studies*, 26 scientists, philosophers, neuroscientists, and other leaders in their related fields published their opinions on the matters raised by the Chalmers paper. Clearly, much remains to be decided.

When discussing qualia, we cannot be certain that the same phenomena are being considered because they are solely first-person mental experiences. Indeed, this is exemplified by the fact that there is debate over their very definition. Some philosophers and neuroscientists even deny their existence. Yet, if they are real, they present the strongest resistance to a physicalist and reductionist description of reality. The confusion about and debates over what they are are extensions of the question, "do they really exist?" Indeed, the credibility of many metaphysical positions pivots on the answers to these confusions.

Dennett, among others, does not believe that qualia exist. He arrives at this position by narrowing and refining their definition and generating criteria that they must fulfill in order to be considered real. In doing so, one finds it almost impossible to accept that what non-sceptics consider as qualia can conform to the (apparently) reasonable requirements.

Hypothetical scenarios are also constructed to refute the existence of qualia, and their ingenuity can certainly lead to quick and persuasive rejection of qualia. However, the unrealistic nature of the scenarios, unsubstantiated assumptions to support the arguments, and most importantly, failure to acknowledge that the experience *itself* is the key issue, often renders them as weak or as strong as the arguments supporting their existence. Thus, one is left with the fact that the "what it feels like" that goes on in our heads is certainly 'something', and every 'something' needs explaining. But are we capable of doing so? Is it even possible?

Physical description of subjective experience

Let us consider whether a purely physical description of the cause of these subjective experiences can be enough, such that nothing else is needed to encapsulate every aspect of their qualitative nature.

To describe the sensation of 'seeing red' to a blind person misses a quality. Language is not the tool for the job. Because I do not know what your experience is, only experiencing it can do it full justice. Indeed, two sighted people describing the sensation of 'seeing red' using the same language does not mean that they are having the same sensation, merely that the shared limitations of language apply to both experiences. Thus, as science must use a form of shared language, it is already hindered in its attempt to fully describe qualia.

Materialism and physicalism are similar philosophical positions, but in the philosophy of mind, physicalism is more appropriate since it has evolved in accordance with developments in physics. It is a form of monism that holds that everything that exists, including qualia, is explainable according to science. It is essentially a form of reductionism. Thus, physics, which describes energy, matter, space, time, force, and so on, can explain qualia too. Here, the mind is seen as a physical thing since nothing other than physical things exist. The mind is reducible to the brain and to its physical properties and processes.

Philosophical zombies, who are behaviorally or neurologically identical to you and I but do not experience qualia, are hypothetical beings that were constructed to facilitate the rejection of a purely physicalist description of reality. So, why are they a threat to physicalism?

Since everything about zombies is determined by physical facts and these are identical between zombies and normal humans, then the physicalist position rejects zombies. Most positions that accept the possibility of zombies also support some form of dualism where, although the *physical* world is describable in physicalist terms, the mental world is not. If zombies are a threat to physicalism, then they should be treated seriously. Yet if we adopt a common-sense approach to them, we might ask how it is that humans can be completely identical to zombies and yet possess a property that zombies do not. Why would both evolve?

Zombies fail in their destruction of physicalism if we believe that humans are all the same in an experiential sense, such that we all either exist as that which comes under the description of zombies, or none of us do. Intuition steers me to believe that the latter is true *and* that the mental experiences I have result from physical processes. But because these experiences have a quality that is unique in our understanding of reality, we are unable to provide an all-encompassing and wholly satisfactory description of them. Being solely qualitative, they exist outside the remit of the scientific method. But that fact does not destroy physicalism, merely we are incapable of addressing this intractable issue effectively in a scientific sense (hence it is more the domain of philosophers).

Qualitatively, qualia are untouchable by the scientific methods that are the basis of physicalism, yet they are described as a property of physical processes. So, it seems like a choice has to be made if this physicalist description (or 'admission', if we are being skeptical) is sufficient and final. Some believe it is while others say that qualia represent something more; some have argued that they are fundamentally unknowable while others believe that *we* are unable to know them.

David Papineau

Supervenience is a term that describes relationships between higher and lower levels of existence, where the higher level (e.g., atoms) is dependent on the lower level (e.g., elementary particles such as quarks). It is an important concept for physicalism because everything that exists in physical reality is caused by something else. Hence, the mental depends on the physical. Again, arguments against supervenience-based forms of physicalism exist.

In 1982, the Australian philosopher Frank Jackson formulated his 'knowledge argument' known as *Mary's Room*, which has caused considerable debate over its attack on physicalism. The argument goes like this: Mary, a neurophysiologist, is forced to study the world from a black and white room through a black and white monitor. Specialising in the neurophysiology of vision, she obtains through this black and white world all the physical information of what happens when we *see* a colour, but in terms of physical processes in the body and brain. The question is: when she goes outside and sees colour, will she have attained new knowledge in addition to what she has previously learned from the black and white world? Intuitively, one would assume that because she experiences colour, the associated qualia will be a new experience. This is new knowledge to that which she had of colour from just the physical information in the room. Thus, physicalism is incomplete or false, as not all information is physical.

Physicalist David Papineau refutes this rejection. First, the new experience that Mary has when she sees colour equates only to a new pathway of neuronal connections, which is a brain process. No new knowledge is gained. But what of the experience itself? This is why it is called the knowledge argument, because Mary knows something she did not know before as a result of the experience (you cannot know colour without experiencing it).

Dennett believes that Mary would know exactly what to expect of seeing red before actually seeing it. Thus, the whole experience would not provide or cause anything new and, by extrapolation, a scientific description of other causes of qualia would also be pre-known if appropriately explained. He seems to be expressing the pointlessness of having rich sensory experiences. If the sights and sounds of nature mean nothing, why do we care so much for things whose very value is in the experience it provides?

Papineau's second point is his belief that rather than having new knowledge of colour, Mary has a new concept of knowledge she already has, which leads her to new ways of thinking about it. This argument seems valid for a recollection of an experience, but not for having the experience itself. It seems to ignore that we are, after all, entities whose minds relate to the external physical world in a sensory way, and inputs from that world are powerful. Colour as experience is far more powerful than scientific knowledge of colour. Thus, the experience of colour cannot be considered only as a new concept of old knowledge. Yet, although it 'feels' so much more significant, it is possible that it is not so much new knowledge but rather that we place more value and attention on it. Hence, it may still be physical.

Let us return to Papineau's belief that Mary has no new knowledge when she sees colour for the first time, only that she has a new concept of it. This could happen because she had all other knowledge of colour except the experience of it, which is presented by seeing it outside the confines of her room. This new concept of colour is integrated with other knowledge of it. However, this seems valid only if she has had qualia of some thing before, which she would have had for sound, thoughts, memories, experiences, and so on.

Here, I am stating the conceptual similarity for colour-induced qualia with qualia from different phenomena. She would have had knowledge of the concept of qualia before, just not of colour. The knowledge she has of the concept of colour qualia is due to her knowledge of other qualia. Mary, at some point in the past, experienced qualia for the first time, and it was at this point that she acquired new knowledge (whether or not she was aware of this knowledge at such a young age when it happened). Physicalism must explain this knowledge.

The transfer from matter to imagination must be explained because it will have happened, and *that* is the key issue. If we are to believe that matter, force, space, and time generate *all* the functions and effects of the mind, then how this occurs and what the experience is must be explainable from a physical perspective.

A physicalist would state that the processes in the brain are sufficient to cause qualia. Few would doubt that qualia would not exist without them, but the debate emphasises how a physical description of the causal process does not map effectively onto the experience. A sequence of mental experiences is rich in texture and comprehension, and its depth intuitively feels greater than what can be described by physical interactions.

Until a clarification of what qualia are is agreed on, opinion as to their existence relates to definition. If the definition is that there is an experience going on in the brain, then there is debate over whether it is explainable in physicalist terms. If it is, then physicalism triumphs. If not, it fails. We will go on to see how McGinn, for example, believes that the physical or non-physical nature of qualia is a question our minds cannot answer. This transcendental naturalism view is such that although physicalism may, intrinsically, be true, we will never know if it is. Thus, by not knowing if it is true even if it is, we cannot say it is.

If Penrose is right about the non-algorithmic nature of thought, then knowing this would mean that we have a theory of physics that might equate to a TOE. However, if McGinn is right about transcendental naturalism, then the problem of qualia is unknowable. Are these views compatible? Yes, we will have the causal process, but the mapping of these thought processes as a means to understanding thought, and thought itself, presents its own unresolvable paradox. Indeed, the 'E' of the 'TOE' relates to causal mechanisms, and qualitative aspects are untouched.

Knowledge from the scientific method

The process of scientific study sees a scientist formulate a 'research hypothesis' stating an expectation to be tested. A statement is then derived that is opposite or counter to that research hypothesis called the *null hypothesis*. The null hypothesis is what is tested, and its rejection suggests that the research hypothesis is not rejected. Thus, we have a form of falsificationism. If our theory is not falsified, then we have not proven that it is wrong (though we have not proven it is right either). Indeed, we cannot prove that it is right for many reasons.

Some scientists think that hypothesis-driven science is poor science, but they fail to realise that what they are doing *is* hypothesis-driven science. What form the hypothesis takes and how strong it is is variable, yet without some concept of what one is doing, why one is doing it, what form of result one expects, and what the achieved results mean, any experimentation would be directionless. To prevent this from happening, experiments are carefully planned, and this planning is possible due to knowledge of the system being investigated. This knowledge is the foundation of hypotheses that enable the formulation of experiments whose results further understanding of the system.

Yet, as science increases our understanding of systems and things, this understanding is relative to many criteria. If we fail to recognise that we have constructed our experiments based on hypotheses whose formulation is entwined with conclusions from results obtained from past experiments, each of which could only ever be constructed according to the limitations of what type of being we are — physically and mentally — then we will assume falsely that the knowledge we acquire is some sort of absolute rather than relative truth.

We cannot avoid the many aspects of reality that we have so cleverly revealed indicating that we are receiving information constrained to:

1. Our experimental design.
2. Our physically enabled mental limitations to know a knowable or unknowable (to us or perhaps any conscious entity) Universe.
3. Our non-objective assessment point (we cannot achieve an objective point of assessment of reality — that is, we cannot achieve a 'view from nowhere' such that our view is not skewed).

Everything that we know is relative to the type of being we are, as a physical and mental entity. What we are physically determines what we can be mentally, and this determines our capacity to ask, answer, understand, formulate, and conceive. Inevitable limitations mean that our science is relative and thus the truth we seek is a relative truth. Our quest can only reveal knowledge relative to our capacity to understand the answers we obtain to the type of questions we are capable of asking.

I

When you listen to a thought, you are aware of not only the thought but also yourself listening to the thought, which implies that the 'I' is deeper than the thinking.

Our knowledge is acquired and added to that from the past, and so it goes on — this is progress. But this knowledge is skewed to the cultural and social context in which we live. Although science is supposed to reveal truth, how we incorporate such information into our knowledge of the world is affected heavily by factors far removed from the purity of scientific truth.

Language also defines how we relate to the world as individuals. There are between 5,000 and 10,000 different spoken languages in the world today. Within even the common languages, there are dialects and variations. The form each spoken language takes constrains the way the world seems to the perceiver because language affects how the mind thinks, which in turn affects what is and can be said. However, what is common is that they are a means for the inner self — the 'I' or 'me' — to communicate with others about the environment or shared physical reality.

If I ask "what is a man?", any answer will be relative. It is relative to the context of the question. What he is to himself is the very process of his mind in action over time, set against his memories and intellect. To others, he may be considered in the physical sense, the mental context, or maybe from an artistic point of view. But can a man be defined in his entirety by a definition? Is there such a thing as the true or innate nature of a thing, especially a conscious thing?

Does a reference to something always miss a quality that only the 'being' of the thing possesses? Does 'being' the thing under consideration define it totally? A rock does not have consciousness, so it lacks the 'being' that a conscious or self-conscious entity has. Is a rock possessed with a different type of being compared to a man? A rock merely 'is', and any description of it can only be in relation to the type of intelligent entity that chooses to describe it.

A conscious entity also 'is', but possesses both a type of being that can be described objectively by an intelligent entity (the type of which is relevant to the type of intelligence describing it) and another type that must be experienced. Man has no meaning to a rock or any other nonconscious entity, but has meaning both to himself and to other consciousness. While he and another consciousness can objectively evaluate him, only the man can experience his subjective self.

The 'I' that experiences the world is the part of the world you cannot experience. The same applies for each person and consciousness (as we know it). Their point of experience is not part of the world that another consciousness can experience, nor can one look into one's experiences and see them from the perspective of viewing the external world (when the subject is the object, the subject cannot be objective). I know what it *feels* like to me, but I cannot describe it. Language naturally evolved to be objective and designed for a shared, external reality (Wittgenstein's work was to try and untangle this web). If I try to describe 'me', then the linguistic tool I have at my disposal is a language that is ill-equipped for the job — I would be trying to describe the inner, subjective world with a tool that is suited for the outer, objective world.

What exists in the space and time of the physical world possesses qualities that language can address, and language can present an image to another mind that experiences the shared reality. Yet 'I', as a mind, is not physically located in space and time and thus, as a living 'process', defies the elemental construction of language. Any attempt to describe it can only create an assumption in another similar being of what is being described based on their assuming that they have the same sensation. Yet a description of a shared reality presents something that the recipient of the information can experience and probably has experience of, and hence knows what is meant.

So, the self is a process that gives consciousness to the physical body. When I experience myself, the subject is the object, and so the process under objective scrutiny is the subjective process itself — it is closed to analysis. 'I' may be a physical entity, but 'I' — as a self — am a process. This 'I' evaluates the physical world that my physical and mental self is embedded in to generate a mental map of meaning, against which my self acts to generate what I consider to be 'me'.

Although the expanse of the mind seems to defy location, and the idea of the mind and body as separate entities is appealing, one wonders if a being of our complexity and physiology could have a mind so different from how it is! The experience of 'me' that I have is because of the physiological limitations imposed on my being by the physical reality I evolved in. The matter that constitutes me, the forces imposed on me, my lifespan, my size, my environment, and countless other factors govern what produces my mind. Although it does not *have* to be as it is, these constraints determine what type of mind it can be. What is remarkable is that the matter that constitutes the human mind transforms the physical world of matter and force around it, as well as of it, into one of meaning, significance, and understanding.

iv) Free will

There are many views about the difficult subjects of free will and determinism (Figure 41). Experts hold many contrasting opinions, some of which I point out below. Free will has been discussed with the assumption that we all know what it means, but are we talking about the same thing (just as when people talk about God, do they mean the same thing)?

What is free will? Free will can be defined as the apparent ability to make choices free from certain constraints, principally determinism. It is the belief that we could have behaved differently than we did in the past, that we are the conscious source of our thoughts and actions in the present moment. Hard determinism claims that determinism is true and free will does not exist.

		FREE WILL	
		There is **NO** free will	There is free will
DETERMINISM	Reality determined	**HARD DETERMINISM**	**COMPATIBILISM**
	Reality **NOT** determined	**HARD INDETERMINISM**	**LIBERTARIANISM**

Figure 41. The compatibility of free will and determinism.

The term 'determinism' has a number of meanings, though causal determinism is the one of importance here. It states that future events are necessitated by past and present events combined with the laws of nature. Here, an entity that knows all the facts of the past and the present would be able to foresee the future.

Does free will exist? Philosophically, there are three approaches to this idea:

1. Determinism.
2. Libertarianism.
3. Compatibilism.

Since determinists and libertarians believe that behaviour is determined by past events, free will is an illusion to them. The deterministic view is simpler and clearer than that of the libertarian's, in that we simply have no free will — any action is a causally determined action resulting from a causally determined thought, which itself was predetermined through the unfolding of inevitable events from the Big Bang over time.

There are many libertarian views on free will — some invoke metaphysical entities such as the soul for execution of free will. However, the crux of the libertarian view on free will is that it requires indeterminism. Compatibilists believe that free will is compatible with determinism.

If the physical reality in which we exist was once an infinitely small point in spacetime (i.e., the Big Bang), then a logical conclusion would be that everything that exists (matter, force, and everything that resulted from its interaction) is determined from that event. If reality exists in a physical sense (which it does), then that 'event' possessed distinct and finite components that evolved over time. Thus, the unfolding of everything that 'is' and happens seems compatible with a deterministic view on free will. But that 'feels' incorrect — we feel as if our thoughts are freely determined. So, how can free will 'be' freely determined? How could this deterministic view be wrong?

If indeterminism is required for free will, why do libertarians believe that free will is an illusion? Quantum theory states that the Universe is indeterminate. But is it fundamentally indeterminate, or is only our knowledge of it at the fundamental level indeterminate (where it is, in fact, determinate in its existence but indeterminate for an entity such as a human to possess objective knowledge of it)? Libertarians believe that since the Universe is determinate, then free will is false as it must require indeterminism. This view is odd in that their certainty that the Universe is determinate is founded on as weak an evidence base as their belief that free will requires indeterminism.

How can free will be compatible with determinism as the compatibilists believe, and why must free will require indeterminism as the libertarians believe? I do not think that free will is compatible with true determinism, nor do I think that the libertarian view on indeterminism is correct. The libertarian view of indeterminate 'knowledge' of reality misses the point that the indeterminately known reality is finite and real (determined) in essence, yet merely 'hidden' from our objective approach. Thus, when this error is addressed, the question becomes merely: "can free will coexist with a determined finite reality?"

To answer this, we are of course assuming things from our finite, limited minds. We assume that if everything in the Universe came from the Big Bang, then there is a finite and potentially knowable reality of force and matter that emerges. If multiple universes coexist in a reality that extends dimensionally beyond our own Universe, then the determinism from the Big Bang, which determined our physicality, becomes an unknowable (in a TOE sense) determinism from sources external to our Big Bang. The effect on the unfolding of the interplay of matter and force by the other universe(s) on our own would be unknowable and yet, in the temporal flow of events, contribute to the predetermined events that happen and will happen (including the illusion of free will).

We cannot know whether such events happen, how or what their effect is, or if other universes exist (we are limited after all). Yet, if they do exist and interact with ours, then the effect of determinism on free will does not change essentially. This is because if other universes influence our Universe, free will would be compatible with determinism as the influence from outside our causal understanding (i.e., outside our Universe) remains an influence and thus affects or determines the temporal flow of events.

Free will is compatible with the libertarian view if this influence is seen as an indeterminate influence. Yet such indeterminism would neither lead to free will as a logical consequence nor automatically avoid the deterministic effect on free will imposed by the Big Bang.

External influences on our Universe *may* render our universe indeterminate. Yet, the problem here is that the determinism of our Universe and the influence of another (which is determinate within itself if it evolved from its own Big Bang), combined, are a determinate influence on what we see as free. The indeterminism we speak of is not innate but rather a consequence of our inability to define it (just like how chaos theory 'models' something that is innately knowable).

We cannot *know* if we are in control of our destiny or if we can be — due to both the nature of reality (as a physical constraint on true free will) and the context of the pressures and expectations imposed on us by ourselves and others (as a sociocultural constraint on the common-use meaning of free will, meaning to make choices).

Predeterminism and free will

To wholly accept that from the moment the Big Bang occurred, every event, every thought that happens and will happen is predetermined, represents a leap of faith that contradicts intuition. Someone recently said to me as we walked and looked into the sky, "An aircraft is far too complicated to be predetermined by the Big Bang." Yes, it seems complex, but even a single cell of a leaf, for example, is hugely more complex than an aircraft. We are likely to accept that a leaf cell is predetermined (through evolution acting over a vast period of time), but we elevate the aircraft's 'special' nature because it is of man's design — we are certainly quite biased towards our own achievements. Yet if a cell can be predetermined, it follows that so can a leaf, a flower, a tree, an ant, a mouse, a human, and all that a human inevitably thinks of and creates. Predeterminism seems so unlikely that we reject it, but in favour of what — supernatural beings, or the quantum indeterminate world which many consider too strange to understand? Is such a determined reality stranger than the fact that anything exists at all, or that the infinite is something conceptually and perhaps physically real? To be amazed by something is to be able to comprehend at least its meaning (Georg Cantor was driven from the realm of sanity by infinity).

Some things that we take for granted, when analysed, are more remarkable than we first imagined. The nature of our existence as a thinking being may be one such thing.

Is everything that occurs and has occurred predetermined by the Big Bang to the extent that my writing this particular sentence was predetermined, encoded in the constituents and processes that evolved in the moments of the Big Bang? Is everything that has happened, is happening, and will happen, an inevitable process of what must happen? Perhaps not. If there is influence on our Universe from another, then the answer could be 'no' since processes not encoded by the Big Bang are affecting what has, does, and will happen.

In *Quantum Leaps*, Jeremy Bernstein describes an alternative explanation as to how determinism can be avoided in a single Universe that evolved from a Big Bang: "It used to be said that the (Isaac) Newtonian universe evolved like clockwork. Once the initial conditions were given — the positions and momenta of all the particles — the future was completely determined. But if you could never precisely determine these initial conditions, as Heisenberg's uncertainty principle said, then you were liberated from this deterministic straightjacket." However, although the initial states cannot be determined through study by a conscious entity that also evolved from those initial circumstances, the conditions existed and, thus, had a definite (potentially definable) reality, rendering determinism (and predeterminism) feasible and real.

Perhaps we cannot know the answer. The human brain may be too simple to encapsulate all that is necessary to know a knowable universe (just as an ant cannot comprehend quantum mechanics). Furthermore, this Universe may be intrinsically unknowable, so knowing it lies outside our innate capacity and limitations to know. Yet, even if we *can* know a knowable universe and we are able to determine that the Universe is a predetermined flow of processes that must occur according to universal laws — and we are playing out those laws — does it actually matter? Does it change anything knowing this? It seems so, only in that we view it as the removal of free will from our actions. And that removal of choice and self-control eradicates the joy and purpose of our lives.

If free will is an illusion, it will be futile to consciously alter our actions in an attempt to demonstrate free will, since the conscious processes underlying this choice are caused by predetermined physical processes. Indeed, the feelings associated with trying to take control, which are the result of the conscious processes and ultimately our actions, would also be predetermined — we cannot change this if predeterminism is true.

If we accept that what we do is predetermined, then the thought of knowing our predetermination is already predetermined, *ad infinitum* — the Universe has encoded within itself the capacity for its physical constituents to generate a quality (conscious intelligence) that transcends its physical being. The matter knows not only of its existence, but also that what it does is according to predetermined, encoded rules.

If I am persuaded of the absolute determinacy of the world, then I could simply take the view that if I were to commit a crime, I was destined to do it by the initial conditions of the Universe. Any concept of my guilt in the matter would be meaningless. If everything is predetermined, then if I commit a crime and state that I should not be punished because I was destined to do it, then the answer could also be that the punishment, whatever it is, is also predetermined. The Universe would be a "que sera, sera" universe. But all this would be determined — actions, thoughts, consequences, and all. Absolute determinacy is potentially one of the most dangerous ideas imaginable, threatening to subvert all our ideas of personal responsibility.

If this is a predetermined universe, then living this predetermined life *feels* as if it were one where free will exists. How so? Since the 'feeling' of freedom does exist, then regardless of whether free will is real or not, the feeling of free will is at least real. So, the freedom that we feel would have evolved to be that way as part of a predetermined reality, including predetermined conscious processes. Since such a feeling has evolutionary advantages, one wonders if an intelligent living entity could evolve and exist without it.

The false feelings of free will result from mental processes whose causal events are predetermined. Additionally, the totality of cause and effect of an experience is not separated into predetermined (cause) and 'free' (effect) parts — all thoughts, decisions, and feelings would be predetermined. This predeterminism cannot be 'felt' as predetermined, because it is unclear how such a sensation that challenges the belief of being an intelligent, living entity would evolve. It would fail natural selection — a mental experience of predeterminism is unlikely to be consistent with the temporal experience of being a living entity. If predeterminism is real, it must exist in the conscious mind as a hidden illusion (perhaps through the process of natural selection), disguised by fake sensations of freedom. Ironically, these feelings of freedom are the illusion. The feeling of freedom renders every event of apparent choice an 'illusion of cause' by presenting it as an experience of some intelligent design.

In a predetermined world, the emotions of love, wonder, pain, excitement, and so on would be exactly the same as in a world where it were not true. So, if predetermination is possible but makes no difference, is it likely to be true?

Of course, we are talking about the illusion of free will in terms of a higher conscious entity — humans. For a simple organism such as an ant, predeterminism is easier to explain. There is no illusion; rather, the organism reacts to commands that are chemical in nature, which result from a predetermined temporal flow of cause and effect.

If one were to imagine that life on Earth were the only life in the Universe, and since we know that life that is capable of making choices evolved here, is it thus likely that when the first organism that made that first decision to, say, move this way and not the other, it had extinguished the possibility of describing the Universe in a wholly deterministic way?

John Bell: predeterminism, free will, and entanglement

John Bell was, perhaps with David Bohm, the quintessential physicist with a stronger interest in the philosophical ramifications of quantum theory than its direct application. When he was asked whether the Universe is deterministic, he replied that it was super-deterministic. He said this in the context of the quantum measurement issue where the 'experimenter' makes a 'free' choice. His conclusion was that not only is inanimate nature deterministic, but the experimenter who 'imagines' that he can choose what experiment to do is also predetermined.

When we consider the issue of entangled particles, the existence of free will produces a crisis. Here, if a measurement is made on one entangled particle, then this has immediate non-local consequences on the other remote, entangled particle. The result of measuring the other particle is causally influenced by this act. That is, a free conscious act of measurement of one entangled particle necessitates a violation of special relativity for the other remote particle.

Bell believed that if free will were an illusion and that we too are determined, then our causal involvement in the (result of) measurement is removed. He thought that if our 'choice' is not free and instead determined by the Universe, then no 'spooky-at-a-distance' communication (see Chapter 3) between the particles is needed because all aspects are predetermined (e.g., choices, qualities).

If free will were real, then it is one cause of the enigma of special cases where relativity is violated. Remove free will, consider it an illusion, and such cases may well be predetermined and no longer strange. They may seem like special cases of a predetermined whole where it is our limited access and assumptions of freedom that consider them as evidence of something different.

Physicalism, predeterminism, and free will

Hard determinism states that free will, as traditionally conceived, is an illusion. Indeterminism, however, does not mean the opposite is true. Rather, it renders free will possible. It also means that it could be a different type of illusion, yet one we find even harder to define.

Is a physicalist, materialist, or reductionist description of reality capable of describing every thing and process? Does such a description of mental process explain all that is? Is the totality of the subjective experience explained by the causal process, or is the 'feeling' additional? And, if so, would that additional thing be outside the remit of physicalism, physics, or materialism? Is the actual 'having the experience' *not* new knowledge of the experience, but rather the necessary result of processes that caused it? That is, the experience itself cannot be anything other than what it is.

If a physicalist description of consciousness is correct, then could we, by extrapolation, extend the conclusion to state that the future may be predetermined? This possibility may depend on a functional TOE (see below). Yet, to reiterate, the Big Bang is generally agreed on as the mechanism by which the Universe was formed. So, the properties of the particles and forces that immediately arose from the Big Bang as well as the new forces and particles that resulted during expansion are dictated by the conditions of the Big Bang.

At the large-scale level, galaxies formed under gravitational effects over time and complex systems like the human mind emerged. Yet they can all be traced back to the Big Bang by looking at the preceding variable, and the one before it, and before it, and so on. You can follow the movement of matter and energy back to the Big Bang. Thus, everything that exists is ultimately defined at some level by the initial conditions.

Currently, the Standard Model of physics links the fundamental forces (except gravity) and particles to describe the constituents of the Universe and how or why they interact. As we saw in Chapter 3, a physical TOE aims to link a GUT with gravitation. Such a TOE does not claim to predict the future, but to describe what happens in the present physical reality completely in terms of fundamental physical principles (the interaction of matter and force).

It is feasible that the Universe is intrinsically unknowable, indefinable, and random in its processes. Here, a TOE is impossible. However, even if the Universe were fundamentally definable under some paradigm, humans may not possess the mental capacity to formulate it.

So, let us assume that it is possible and we do possess the ability to formulate a TOE according to our conception of what one is. This theory is generally considered to be able to describe all biological and chemical phenomena in a reductionist context based on fundamental particle interactions. This, under physicalism, includes consciousness where 'feelings' (qualia) are nothing more than the result of the integrated complexity of neuronal interplay. So, a physicalist TOE describes all matter that exists, and every phenomena that emerge from physical things.

Even though my thoughts are composed of images and understanding rather than physical matter, they nevertheless emerge from physical matter (in the form of my brain) and are thus encapsulated under the paradigm of a physicalist TOE. Does that have any meaning when such a TOE can never encapsulate the essence of the feeling of thought? A TOE explaining all matter and interaction may define the process of emergent properties of matter such as thought, while those very properties possess a quality that is inaccessible to the very theory underlying its potential for existence.

Even if we possessed complete knowledge of the constituents of the Universe and had a TOE of a knowable universe, we would not be able to predict the future due to the complexity of the problem. Any calculation to predict future events would have to incorporate everything that is and has happened, rendering it both practically and theoretically impossible. But underlying this is the question of whether the future is predetermined. This question can be rephrased as: "Is reality determinate?" Is quantum indeterminism (to conscious observers) fundamentally determinate? Does our understanding of unknowable and chaotic events demonstrate not how these phenomena truly 'are', but how our models of them are limited? Physicalism would say so. Perhaps the quantum world is fundamentally determinate, but human access to it is indeterminate out of necessity imposed by the theory itself. The theory may also be a good but imprecise tool for modelling aspects of reality.

At present, we understand the world in classical and quantum terms, and they are incompatible. Accessing the quantum world requires making a measurement, which ends up preventing complete knowledge of it. Indeed, choosing what property to measure causes the complementary property to become unknown. Bohr said that the quantum world has no meaning until it is measured. Yet underlying this indeterminism (for conscious observation) is a determinate intrinsic nature; only measurement of it renders it indeterminate. Thus, *knowledge* of what 'is' is impossible, whereas the very existence of what is means that if nature has laws, then a predetermined future — of physical events at least — is feasible. I say 'at least' because the properties that emerge from and transcend physical processes may exist outside the remit of a TOE.

Looking at the problem from another perspective, for humans to know whether reality is predetermined or not requires subjective analysis of the objective world. Indeed, we cannot escape a position of reference and this skews our view. Indeed, our scientific method is innately referential to the type of being we are.

Thoughts seem to occupy a non-physical world. Yet, in a deterministic description of reality, these thoughts lead to actions that are predetermined. So, the thoughts themselves must be predetermined. Qualia would then be consistent with the physical processes that cause them at the time of their occurrence. If so, it is remarkable that qualia are encoded within the laws that govern reality and, despite being non-physical, induce causally predetermined acts. They exist within reality as a form of existence that transcends physicality.

Quantum measurement

Quantum indeterminism means a quantum object can be considered as not existing until measured, and when measured its existence conforms to the type of measurement. We cannot have complete knowledge of a quantum object. However, although our access to the reality of a quantum object may be incomplete, its innate existence is what it is.

In Chapter 3, we looked at some experimental studies that were set up to explore some of the peculiarities of quantum theory. Experiments in which light is passed through a polariser such a calcite crystal, which splits light into either horizontal (H) or vertical (V) polarised forms with regards to the plane of the crystal, show that a photon is not defined as either H or V until it is measured. The H-polarised photons, for example, are considered H-polarised only after measurement. The H or V polarisation after light passes through a calcite crystal is random, which seems to indicate its indeterminate nature.

Quantum mechanics may appear to be a spanner in the model of determinism. When one considers whether an electron is a particle or a wave, the 'measurement problem' occurs where the decision to observe either wave or particle activity ends up determining what the photon is. Thus, consciousness determines the future path. Yet, if the decision in the brain is predetermined, then the resultant photon behaviour is too. One could say that if this were true, the photon is *both* particle and wave — this alone negates determinism.

Is quantum physics incomplete? The apparent randomness of how a photon passes through the H or V polariser may be as much about our incomplete understanding as a suggestion of fundamental indeterminism. If one looks at this behaviour in a deterministic way, the photon exists and as such has properties that, when confronted with something like a polariser, it behaves according to. Our inability to understand or predict this behaviour does not mean that there is a lack of some fundamental explanation for it.

Is what happens in the quantum world predetermined by laws of physics that we do not understand? In the case of H/V polarisation of photons, is the randomness we observe (thinking they should be H or V and not random) due to our lack of understanding of the laws of physics? Perhaps humans are unable to completely know reality or, indeed, reality is unknowable — not necessarily meaning that it is chaotic, but that its mechanism defies our limited human means to delineate reality.

Consider the many worlds hypothesis, quantum non-locality, the theory of special relativity, hidden variable theories, chaos, and their relationship to fate. Each concept is innately intertwined with free will. Hence, as we develop our understanding of reality, its construction has different ramifications depending on whether we accept free will or determinism to be true.

Pierre-Simon Laplace was an 18th Century French physicist and mathematician who was famous not least for the idea of 'Laplace's demon', which posits that knowledge of everything *now* means that we can predict the future. Arguments against it may be fair (e.g., its incompatibility with indeterminism as well as computability issues), but they do not obviate the feasibility of a predetermined future. Why? Because although an intelligent entity may never be able to realistically know everything in the present (as a means to predict the future), the possibility of a defined and determined present and, thus, future remains intact. What is 'is', irrespective of whether it can be known (e.g., a star that exists but has never been seen).

Hidden variable theories are most easily demonstrated in situations where there are only a few possible outcomes to an experiment. An example is the polarisation of light, which is an instance of the 'superposition' principle (see Chapter 3). Measurement renders 'knowledge' about a potentially determinate system indeterminate, which means that the future cannot be predicted by human sentience, not that it cannot be predetermined.

Since predeterminism is a concept that requires sentience to conceive of and understand, then the question of predetermination only relates to sentience. Since sentient organisms (of the type that humans are) cannot know fundamental reality in a determinate way, then it appears that innate predeterminism and sentient indeterminism are compatible. Yet if the underlying fundamental reality is predetermined, then our actions and consequences of measuring it are predetermined.

It is easy to pass off predeterminism in many ways — by stating that our minds are too small to work it out, that the Universe may be unknowable (or perhaps knowable but not to us), that our point of reference prevents objectivity, or that we can only access deterministic reality in an indeterminate sense so that *our* world remains indeterminate and, thus, not perceived as predetermined. We are back to whether free will could be a component of a deterministic reality. If it is, how would free will choices be incorporated in a predetermined future? They would have to be predetermined. So, for free will to be consistent with predeterminism, it must somehow result in choices that caused predefined effects. This seems untenable. Indeed, the urge to reject attempts to justify predeterminism is due to it being such an unappealing idea.

Einstein trusted his theoretical instincts, and human feelings of free will are so strong because it is in our very essence — to remove it is untenable with the state of being human. Indeed, a human without free will does not seem human. But why should we accept causality and determinism for inanimate objects and yet think that a mind is free? Are we seeking an answer that is 'there' but requires an intellect greater than ours to comprehend? A cruel twist of fate is that we have the capacity and need to ask this question, but not the means to answer it.

If the Universe is part of a multiverse, then it is feasible that forces other than the Big Bang affect events in this Universe. Does the presence of those other forces change the idea of free will? If we exist in one Universe and hard determinism is real, then everything that does and will happen is predetermined, such as my future thoughts. With input from an external universe, does anything change? There are still 'determinations' of what happens, just that these are not from the singular, Big Bang-determined past.

What happens in our minds is an interplay of complex processes acting over finite space and time, and these are affected by the immediate past. So, the feeling of free will may be an illusion caused by the process of acting out inevitable thoughts, which implies that there is no escape from either the feeling of free will or there being no free will.

The mind is not separate from reality. While it is more free to roam than physical things, it is still constrained in some sense. Thoughts are a consequence of what is happening in the brain 'now', and what happens now is an inevitable consequence of what just was. Every thought that leads to an action is a causal process of past events evolving. Thus, the action that results is due not to free will as traditionally conceived, but rather to the natural unfolding of events. Is it possible that this unfolding can both be hard determinism while providing the sensation of 'free will'? Yes. As it feels free, the thought that it is determined feels wrong.

Can a universe allow an entity that has a mind to be free, whereas something without a mind must exist according to predetermined laws? Possibly, but where is the cut-off point? Is a rabbit free, or an ant or a virus? A virus lives, but rather than being a living thing *per se*, it is a conglomeration of complex molecules that require a living host cell in order to multiply. But aren't we too? How can we have one rule for the inanimate and another for the sentient or living in the same Universe? If reality *is* predetermined and complex organisms are part of reality, then surely they must all conform to the same rules.

It goes against everything we believe about ourselves if we are to accept that our will is not free and that we are merely playing out the course of matter and force acting over time, but at the same time create in our minds a sense of freedom. If this were true, why did I write this? Because I had to? Or because this is what was written for me since the Big Bang (regardless of possible interactions with other universes)? If we are to believe that something is true until proven false, then we cannot prove whether free will exists or not. We choose to believe it exists because it *feels* that way. Indeed, it *suits* us to believe that we are free despite being unable to prove it. But do we believe in it because we like or want it, and its very essence is sufficient to convince us that it is true and we are free?

While questions about the feasibility of free will take many forms, the principal question pertains to physicality — is it possible according to the laws of physics (i.e., is it compatible with quantum indeterminism)? And even if we agreed that it is possible under physical terms, there is the issue of considering the conscious entity. The refutation of free will is inconsistent on the grounds that the unknown subconscious cause of conscious action renders it not free, because denying any human process as free merely because we do not understand it yet is untenable. It is subject to being dismissed as we understand the brain better. Indeed, the subconscious is part of what or who we are and, thus, it is the part that affects our actions. The fact that it is not a fully conscious part does not refute free will.

Can we state that a quantum object is indeterminate because our physical means of accessing its reality is incomplete? Humans exist in a subject-object reality, in which only the idea of quantum determinism is possible. Yet reality exists, and to state that any quantum object is indeterminate is to define reality according to our mental and physical limitations in comprehending it. But the idea of an innately determinate quantum reality is feasible, only that our means of accessing it produces indeterminate limitations. Hence, if reality (i.e., matter and force in spacetime) exists and we are part of it, then it either exists indeterminately or is determinate.

In our limited way, we can comprehend the laws of physics and manipulate them for our own ends. The fact that we can predict and manipulate reality despite not understanding its underlying rules means that we have some insight into its processes. For example, electrons are quantum objects, yet their indeterminism does not prevent our understanding of molecular events — we use our macroscopic understanding of atoms in molecules to construct chemicals that prevent disease. The processes occurring in neuronal interactions also involve molecules, but their associated quantum indeterminism has no influence on our ability to extract useful information by classically addressing the processes — as has been the way of science in developing drugs and an understanding of the pharmacology of their action.

The mind consists of organised matter, and the resultant connections and intelligent consciousness are a consequence of how that mind works. How the mind works is the result of the processes that led to its existence. The choices we make are the complex interplay of both conscious and unconscious cause and effect.

So, is a criminal free to choose his crime, or was it predetermined? Is depression the result of nature, nurture, or predeterminism? Is life pointless if predetermined? Is it merely the experience of an inevitable unfolding event? Is there any difference between believing that life is about choices or one that is just about experiencing the inevitable unfolding of the one past-present-future existence?

Sam Harris

American philosopher and neuroscientist Sam Harris argues against free will because any intentional action is due to processes that cause them, of which we have no knowledge or control. His argument against free will is that although we understand the conscious mind as being determined by the subconscious, the subconscious is unknown to us, so we are not in control of the will for action.

We are also not in control of the genes that determine, to a certain extent, our nature. Yet that is no reason to doubt their influence on it. Indeed, although we do not understand subconscious processes, they are still a part of us and thus causally contribute to who we are in a significant way. Since the subconscious is in the mind, it is determined by the brain. Indeed, if the brain is predetermined, then everything it does is as well, including free will.

Just because we do not understand the subconscious-conscious interplay does not mean that there is reason to reject free will. Harris's argument seems separate from the real issue. To reject free will because of the unknown cause of conscious choice would mean that if science unravels the subconscious-conscious interplay, free will is restored. Yet, the reality of free will seems more fundamental than that which is revealed by the progress of human science. His is an argument not about free will being a predetermined illusion, but that conscious choice is not free due to unknown causal subconscious influences.

In *Free Will*, Harris asks, "How can we be 'free' as conscious agents if everything that we consciously intend is caused by events in our brains that we do not intend and of which we are entirely unaware? We can't." So, his view is that that any subconscious cause of a conscious thought prevents free will. Yet, is that subconscious cause not intrinsic to who we are? If we were to learn to access more of the processes of our mind, then as the awareness of deeper processes increases, does the argument *for* free will gain credibility since it deals directly with Harris's issues against it?

If we take Harris's argument to completion, free will cannot exist because the causative molecular events of subconscious processes are not known. Yet, it is not the fact that we cannot know what causes a thought that is the reason free will is an illusion (because science might one day find an exact causative molecular correlate for a thought), but that each molecular event is determined by past events and hence determines what the next event will be.

My actions and thoughts appear like decisions to me, but they may be merely experienced as time unfolds to reveal the inevitable. It is just that this 'decision' quality of conscious experience feels as if it were free. The marvel of the illusion of free will is that it so perfectly feels free. Perhaps it was evolutionarily necessary to be as such, but then again, it also has to be like this in a predetermined universe. But is it so unlikely for the Universe to unfold in such a way as to create an organism where free will feels 'free', yet is not? In a multiverse of universes, it is likely that one universe will exist that contains an organism that can contemplate free will.

Remarkable as that is, it is none more so than the fact that matter in the form of the human mind is sufficiently complex that its processes, acting over time, enable comprehension — matter has evolved a quality that transcends its mere physical nature. When we look at it deterministically, matter enters reality (at the Big Bang) and was on an inevitable path towards a form that enables its own comprehension. Who needs God(s) in a Universe so remarkable!

Free will as illusion?

In *The Little Philosophy Book*, Robert Solomon wrote: "According to quantum theory, the most basic events in the Universe, the behaviour of the most fundamental particles that make up all matter, are decided only by chance. Thus, the Universe is not deterministic." He goes on to ask whether an indeterminate Universe defines whether or not free will can exist.

Solomon believes that indeterminism acting in the brain's processes is much the same as a determinate Universe, where our actions are as if we were puppets to chaotic or predetermined events in the brain or the Universe, respectively. However, as a believer in free will, he suggests that indeterminism at the quantum level does not imply indeterminism at the macroscopic or street level of events. Although our decisions may be influenced in a cause-and-effect manner (e.g., if we are thirsty, we drink), we are free in a holistic sense to act out choices 'freely. Thus, although scientific determinism is false, practical determinism is intact. Put simply, the indeterminate causal processes of the macromolecular constituents of a human brain do not cause the 'mind' of that human brain to be indeterminate in its functioning.

I disagree with this. Solomon has decided that although the fundamental processes of a brain are innately indeterminate, they can lead to macroscopic determinate processes of consciousness that constitute free will. He is referring not to our knowledge of them but instead to fundamental indeterminism. Why would fundamentally indeterminate processes of something lead to determinate ones at a macroscopic level when the very nature of the causal processes are indeterminate? It seems like because he believes in free will and in indeterminism at the quantum level, the only way to resolve the two is to create some sort of magic that equates to making macroscopic determinism appear from indeterminate events. If quantum indeterminism is actually innately determinate (only our knowledge of them is indeterminate because of quantum duality), then the deterministic flow of events towards free will is not broken, and the illusion is real.

In Carlo Rovelli's short but illuminating *Seven Brief Lessons on Physics*, he asks how we can be free if our behaviour follows the predetermined laws of nature. He questions whether we escape this bind to determinism through the power of our freedom to think. Although he believes that if we could overcome the laws of nature in the context of free will, we would have found out how by now, he finds *his* solution to free will in our behaviour being determined by the laws of nature acting in our brains. Our behaviour is determined by what happens in our brains, not external factors. But isn't such reasoning either a call to some 'magic' happening or an illogical rejection of predeterminism?

Rovelli says that decisions are 'freely' determined as allowed by neuronal interactions. Referring back to Spinoza, he says that the 'I' and the 'neurons of the brain' are the same thing. He refers to the fact that we have as many brain neurons as there are stars in a galaxy and unimaginably more potential interactions between them. However, none of this satisfactorily excludes predeterminism from the *whole* process. That we are complex or that mental processes correspond to the 'I' are not arguments supporting free will. Indeed, to state that our behaviour is determined by natural laws and yet argue that our brains determine this behaviour freely (while constrained by those laws) seems like an illogical and improbable set of interdependent statements. Either we are free or not — those are the options. What magic allows this freedom to manipulate the laws of nature?

Some might say that if we consider predeterminism and the rejection of free will (whether or not an external universe interacts with ours) to mean that every effect at one moment in time is determined by the unfolding of events immediately prior to it, then this explanation also defines true free will. That is, free decisions are caused by events prior to that decision process. True, but there is a key difference. With free will, there are many possible outcomes in the future that are caused by the conscious act in the present. Without free will, there is only one inevitable outcome.

When we consider a brain of the complexity of a human's, does the existence of the 'illusion' of free will become harder to accept than in a simpler brain because we assume that intelligence would reveal the illusion? If so, then we only need to look at our own personal history of self-delusion to see that deception is clearly real and apparent. We can accept the idea of a simple organism in deterministic terms, responding to simple external stimuli according to internal reactive mental algorithms. But when the complexity of the human mind is the subject, where appreciation of music, art, feelings of love, and so forth are considered, how can we resolve all of this with an illusory free will? Is our rejection of predeterminism driven by ego, or a misunderstanding that predeterminism and lack of free will changes nothing really? If free will is an illusion, however, there are clear advantages for the mind to believe that we are in fact free.

Had this illusion evolved as being self-evident to the mind, or had science proved it, the lost sense of self might impact the drives and motives of an intelligent sentient being (ignoring the fact that in this case such actions would, themselves, be predetermined). Whether free will exists or not, it is to the advantage of the intelligent being to believe that it is real. It is possible that the mental part of our being that constitutes the areas involved in 'free will-related processes' has evolved in a way that projects the internal sensation of belief in free choice.

Colin McGinn states in *Mysterious Flame* that the cause of behaviour by mental states is nothing like the mechanical (physical) cause, the latter being the domain of which physics is concerned. Laws govern physical interactions. Beliefs do not make contact with action, so no comparable laws govern how behaviour evolves in the causal circumstances. That is, we do not know the nature of how mental states cause behaviour. Free will is mental causation in terms of the interface between mind and action. McGinn says that if we choose to believe in free will, we must accept that we have no understanding of the cause of 'free' choices. Belief in free will is not within the framework of traditional, physical, 'cause-and-effect' science.

McGinn says that the mystery of free will is that the way we are drawn towards trying to explain it cannot work. He says that if causes of actions are not free, it may be because the actions are predetermined by causal events, or that if the actions were not caused, then they are random and hence not free either. Thus, the rejection of free will may be because of either random or predetermined events, both of which negate freedom. However, his point stresses not whether free will is real or not, but that we do not have the mental and/or practical means to know one way or the other. Our cognitive abilities, which are very well fitted to delineating physical mechanisms such as protein synthesis, for example, are not at all suited to the task of figuring out how consciousness and free will work.

Gerard 't Hooft's view

Gerard 't Hooft of the University of Utrecht in the Netherlands won the Nobel Prize in Physics in 1999. He describes himself as "a determined determinist [who] would say that yes, you bet, an experimenter's choice what to measure was fixed from the dawn of time, and so were the properties of the thing he decided to call a photon". He adds, "If you believe in determinism, you have to believe it all the way" — each thought I have was not only determined by past thoughts, but by events billions of years ago.

't Hooft believes that there should be a deterministic theory underlying quantum mechanics. This theory must avoid the Bell inequality arguments that disallow a local hidden variable theory. He believes that hidden variables without local counterfactual realism can be constructed which explain why our world only *seems* to be quantum mechanical, without the need for pilot waves or a many worlds interpretation. Although hidden variables are often believed to cure the 'incompleteness' of quantum mechanics, 't Hooft clarifies that we require a revision of the dogma behind whether results truly violate either a deterministic theory or a strict adherence to an incomplete indeterminate model (an extension of Bohm's vision).

Currently, the belief is that a quantum theory of gravity that is consistent with the Standard Model will provide a complete model of quantum indeterminism — one that is alien to Einstein's intuitive ideal. However, 't Hooft believes that the way we address quantum indeterminism is the issue. He has disputed the validity of Bell's theorem on the basis of the superdeterminism loophole (a class of theories that evade Bell's theorem because they are deterministic), but his attempt to construct local deterministic models are met with scepticism because of the high accuracy of quantum theory in its current state as well as the fundamental implications of his ideas on the foundations of reality and free will.

't Hooft thinks that quantum indeterminism is an illusion hiding a deterministic set of rules that the Universe has obeyed since the Big Bang — rules that govern force, matter, everything. If we knew them, we could theoretically map the past to present to future of everything that happens in the Universe (no free will, as traditionally conceived).

Entanglement is a special case that demonstrates the connection of particles in a way that defies special relativity. Since quantum theory is incomplete without gravity, it is possible that everything is connected in a way that we have not yet realised. Uncovering how and why could allow quantum theory to be unified. Some believe that quantum theory is a description of reality, whereas 't Hooft sees it as a useful tool to describe an incomplete picture of reality that is fundamentally classical and deterministic in nature.

The entanglement of correlated particles is one example of what appears to be non-random, coordinated qualities. This correlation, John Bell argued, requires particles to actively communicate with one another (as in a non-local hidden variable model) or, as Bohr said, they are not real until measured, which 't Hooft's models do not allow for. So, to resolve this, 't Hooft has used the superdeterminism loophole. The idea is that physicists cannot fully control an experiment because the experimental setup is not independent of the processes that created the particles.

If we consider that free will is embedded in the complexity of the atoms in our brains, then the observer's choices with regards to 'measurement' decisions are just a consequence of the laws of nature. Hence, the role of the observer is nothing more than an aspect of the unfolding of a connected totality of events in the Universe. The experimentalists share a common past with the particles being tested (from the early Universe). This interdependence creates a selection bias that misleads physicists into thinking that no deeper level of physics explains particle coordination when in fact it can. Few accept this, for reasons given earlier.

Furthermore, the idea that the Universe is set up so that it stops you from doing an experiment that reveals its true nature is ever tougher to accept. The nature of the Universe is such that it fools you into making choices that imply things based on the illusion of free will, when in fact the particles (as well as you, the experimenter, and the particles in your brain) are also part of the Universe, so there might be harmonisation in some way between particles' properties and humans' measurement choices according to some underlying deterministic physics.

't Hooft believes that nature's laws are likely very simple and straight-forward, locality is preserved, and there is a strict separation between cause and effect. Essentially, everything is caused by deterministic laws. This view requires a move from the current position of knowing the statistical laws of, say, the decay of an atom towards a definite cause.

The link between connectedness and the Universe starting with a single Big Bang is clear in 't Hooft's ideas. Since everything and everybody in our Universe has a common past, they are correlated. We see special consequences of certain types of quantum correlations, but if the Universe at a deeper level is deterministic and describable in classical terms, then correlations of all things may become more evident — that is, describ-able at a deeper, connected level than merely saying we occupy the same Universe.

The predetermined self

The philosopher John Searle states that "the problem of free will is unusual among contemporary philosophical issues in that we are nowhere remotely near to having a solution". Why is this more important than other problems we do not have solutions to? Because to have our own freedom questioned is an affront to our conception of what the very nature of being human is. What would be remarkable is that if the Universe is deterministic and GUT equations are found that describe the interaction of matter and force to explain ALL phenomena, then human experiences of love, anger, *et cetera* as predetermined phenomena will essentially be embedded within these equations. Is that possible?

We accept that reality enables matter to arrange in a form that is conscious. Is consciousness any less remarkable than free will? From a purely emotional context, we can accept the possibility of consciousness as predetermined more than we can for free will, yet both are aspects of the same mind. It seems like that which relates to freedom is what we want to hold on to. Predeterminism challenges this freedom, and in doing so challenges our individuality. We find it hard to accept that the same 'freedom' as traditionally conceived free will also exists within a framework of determinism. The predetermined choices and decisions that we 'feel' are free are actually part of the illusory whole that comprises free will in a predetermined world.

The nature of the human mind is such that thoughts, emotions, and sensations are entwined with an automatic innate feeling that they are created by us because we are free, conscious entities. Hence, as we think that they can be different at any moment by choice, we have the freedom to control them. Thus, the idea of predeterminism feels wrong. Indeed, feelings and determinism seem to be mutually exclusive. The argument that such feelings could also be predetermined is yet another assault on our 'humanity' or existence as free beings.

How can the feelings that constitute freedom be predetermined? It certainly shatters existentialism ("we are condemned to feel deluded that we are free and yet know that we are not, and we cannot change anything"). We also do not have the evidence to prove or disprove free will. Like the idea of God's existence, we cannot prove it one way or the other. But we dismiss the idea of free will as predetermined because it feels wrong and we do not like it. Yet, if we see the possibility that the 'feeling' of free will is as much a process as is, say, the metabolism of glucose, then we are no longer hindered by the egocentric wish that this process is somehow different. However, unlike the latter example, the former lies outside the arena of science.

Does predeterminism mean that there is no point doing anything and resigning ourselves to fate? No, because whatever we do is predetermined, and whatever we feel still feels like there is a choice. It is all predetermined; our actions and thoughts — the thoughts of one individual resigning himself to doing nothing is predetermined. I should state that the meaning of 'fate' differs from that of 'predeterminism'. Whereas predeterminism is a single path from past to present to the future that is experienced, fate implies something different. Fate suggests a predetermined future for 'x' determined by some conscious entity 'y'. Fate seems to stray from the idea of pure physical predeterminism where what happens in the future is not some known goal to be reached, but is rather a natural consequence of the unfolding of events.

If it is only perceived loss of freedom that we object to when it comes to determinism, then is everything outside of conscious life acceptable as predetermined? But why would these processes be special merely due to their complexity or association with the human need to feel free?

Certainly, for matter to have evolved into a form such as humans that can understand and manipulate matter *seems* too fantastic to be inevitably determined. I stress 'seems' because the urge to reject it is driven first and foremost by emotion. But perhaps the Universe is after all too complex to comprehend for an entity embedded in it (whether predetermined or not), so a definitive answer will elude us.

It is feasible that the Universe cannot be understood since we are part of it and connected to it in an intimate way. Perhaps the entities that we are, what constitutes our minds, and the capabilities of our minds limit our comprehension within parameters determined by our nature. We can ask, but we may be unable to find truth. Truth is only relative to the limits defined by what we can ask and the tools we have at our disposal to formulate an answer. Truth will only ever be 'our' truth.

For example, consider the feeling of love for one person by another person. One school of thought would define it as a unique event for that person, evolving in an unknown way but freely determined by them. Another would say that it is defined exactly by the past, so the 'emotion' felt is just inevitable. Does that not destroy its beauty? Or is it our skewed impression of beauty, where it must be truly free to have value? The intensity of human feelings heightens the belief that the notion of ourselves as merely part of the unfolding of events in a determined Universe is wrong. Emotions are where the need to hold on to feelings of uniqueness are strongest, but just like intellectual thought and creativity, they may be part of the strangeness of a predetermined reality.

Whereas intuition may be grounded in subconscious processes where 'feelings' about right or wrong are influenced by years of learning that create deeper mental nonconscious mechanisms affecting our conscious decisions, emotion is different. Emotion is grounded more in what we want than what we would believe to be true should we be able to dissociate these feelings from the objective facts. We accept many strange phenomena in our intellectual quest to make sense of the world, but when we ourselves are challenged and presented as part of reality rather than as a free observer, we look to our instinct rather than logic to reject it. Whether free will exists or not really makes no difference since the experience is the same; we choose to believe in it because doing so allows us to convince ourselves we are special.

Predeterminism, TOE, and life on Earth

One might conclude that if everything is predetermined, then there must be a TOE to define it. We assume some law(s) could define this unfolding process in accordance with what exists in the Universe. A multiverse, human limitations, and the possibility that laws responsible for such a TOE may not exist (or remain unknown or unknowable to humans) are just three reasons why we may never find such a TOE. We have laws that give us the impression that we know how the Universe works to some extent, yet we think of these things with a finite and limited human mind.

A TOE that we seek would be defined by such human limitations. Even if it were complete, it would only address the questions we can ask. We cannot know if there are questions beyond our comprehension that we need to ask in order to complete it or, indeed, if such a goal is possible. A TOE, and not necessarily a human-formulated TOE, may be possible that can explain a determinate Universe. The Universe may unfold in a predetermined manner and yet do so in a way that cannot be defined by equations or a model that fits our methods of delineating universal laws.

If the Universe had no life and the quantum world is innately determinate, then we can accept that events unfold from past to present to future according to laws of interaction between matter and force. But If we do not accept this when intelligence is involved, then what level of intelligence is required before the predetermined process for events stops? Is there a minimum level of brain development in an organism that is necessary for it to be able to use free choice to direct its future?

Just as in the quantum world where it is impossible to define the exact distinction between the observer and observed, we can question a similar distinction for the brain. Does the simple brain follow predetermined rules, whereas the more complex brain enables a choice of different possible futures? If true, how can we define this distinction?

We accept that our minds are caused by processes in the brain that are chemical in nature. Can we not accept that the result of complex, evolved, and highly interactive chemical reactions in the mind produce a higher level of order whose effect (understanding, consciousness) transcends the causative physical process? Surely we can, and the choices ('free will') that these effects enable (i.e., we can manipulate the environment for our own good) are the ongoing effects of each process as they unfold over time. So, although the experience of consciousness seems personal and free, and free will itself is closely linked to the sense of self, both could be inevitable consequences of matter interacting in the brain.

Free will may represent ordered inevitabilities of the processes. In a human mind, the thoughts we will think tomorrow and the decisions we will make seem unknown and determined by the flow of choices we make. We think we have control over what they will be. Yet, this feeling of control is an innate illusion of the process of the physical events that constitute thought itself. The inevitable unfolding of the physical events that constitute the thoughts from today till tomorrow lead us to where we will be then. We think that this process is random, but it has unfolded as the matter that makes me, you, and everything in the Universe (and maybe others) go about their interactions.

The successful transition of mental choice to the physical execution of that choice enhances the belief of freedom and control over our path. We see it not as experiencing an inevitable unfolding, but as a self-directed path among many potential ones. It would have been impossible for matter to have evolved the complexity of the capabilities of the human mind without the associated sense of self and freedom. To feel rather than to merely comprehend, the illusion of free will is incompatible with a being that strives to understand the world around it.

Kurt Gödel and fatalism

It has been suggested that the application of Gödel's incompleteness theorem may provide one of the strongest refutations of predeterminism. As discussed in detail in Chapter 1, Gödel showed with this theorem that every unproved statement could be unprovable, and that for a large axiomatic system some proofs simply cannot be shown as true. Humans apply analytical systems as tools to try to understand reality. These systems may be simple, in which case they are complete and consistent (apart from truth-defining systems), or they may be complex, where they are incomplete and inconsistent.

Reality may be simple, consistent, complete, and knowable. In this case, we would need just a few fundamental particles (e.g., protons, neutrons, electrons) and forces (e.g., gravity, magnetism) to construct all that exists. The rules for these forces and particles were defined at the Big Bang. This scenario in consistent with predeterminism, fate, and fatalism. A way out of such a fatalist view could be intervention from another universe (with input external to our Big Bang, such as is possible in M-theory), if we were to see the intervention from a source outside our means of address as indeterminate rather than determinate.

If reality were complex, inconsistent, and unknowable, then no simple analytic system can know it. Complex systems cannot know it as no level of complexity can incorporate a complex system that encapsulates an unknowable reality. If we use the example that particles are equivalent to numbers of arithmetic and forces are equivalent to the functions of arithmetic, then if reality is sufficiently complex, it is neither consistent nor complete. If that is right and if our Universe is sufficiently complex (which it probably is), is it indeterministic?

An external universe influencing ours *could* make it complete and consistent, but also complex and indeterminate to a conscious mind. How could it make sense to human analysis? Any external influence is in some sort of harmony with our Universe. Our science has evolved to make sense of it, irrespective of whether reality is encoded solely by the Big Bang.

A simple system cannot encapsulate reality if reality is complex. A simple reality is knowable by a simple system, but this suggests fate and predeterminism. A complex system cannot know a complex reality either.

A complex reality is inconsistent (unknowable) — we can know parts of it, but not the whole. Thus, by treating reality as a system, our methods of analysis see it as knowable if it is simple. In a predetermined Universe, this would suggest few simple particles and forces (and a good chance for a beautiful GUT).

It has also been suggested that to correlate the Universe with a 'Gödel system' is wrong. To many, the idea that another universe (within a multiverse) could interact with ours and make it knowable is the wrong way to look at things. Other universes, if they do exist, probably do not interact with ours. Moreover, the idea that forces and matter of reality can be considered in the same way as the axioms and theorems of an axiomatic system might be pushing the bounds of credibility.

Role of the human mind in predeterminism

Consider the possibility of the Earth as being the only place in a finite universe where consciousness exists and thus the human mind is the most advanced form of consciousness. Would there be any reason why our mental processes extended reality from the realm of determinism to indeterminism? That is, if an inanimate, finite universe is predetermined and yet possesses the *possibility* for the evolution of sentient life, then if that life does evolve (as we know it has on our planet), does that evolved sentience transform a predetermined universe into one that is indeterminate? In essence, could reality — from the interaction of force and matter — enable the possibility of the formation of an entity whose existence renders determined processes indeterminate?

It seems highly unlikely that a universe can change. One would assume it to be either determinate or indeterminate, irrespective of what form force and matter produce in the unfolding of time. It seems hard to believe that the evolution of a species with a conscious mind is that which defines the deterministic state of a universe, as this would necessitate a type of entangled connection between the conscious mind and every other material part of the universe the instant that consciousness was realised.

Although input from an external universe would invalidate predeterminism from *our* Big Bang alone, it *does not* mean that predeterminism is possible from the combined influence of our Big Bang and any external universes. Indeed, if these combined influences determine action, then again free will is removed.

Whether we are *truly* free or not free but *feeling* free, the result is the same. Our minds are unable to grasp reality to know the truth of this dilemma. Although there must *be* a truth to it, we live *assuming* we have free will and control. We cannot alter whatever it is even if we were able to prove that it is not free (which would be interesting — the Universe inevitably creating a form of being that believes it is free and yet proves it is not, all as part of a predetermined, inevitable scenario).

Fortunately, although our minds are advanced enough to suffer the knowledge that there are things we want to know but cannot ever find the answer to, one thing we *are* spared is the possibility of finding out that we are a construction living out an evitable path without freedom (perhaps like a person finding out that they are a robot). Such a revelation would be a shock to the emotions, but it would not change anything as *feelings* are what they are, whether pre-encoded or not.

Types of free will

Incompatibilism

Here, free will and determinism are logically incompatible. In a deterministic universe, free will cannot coexist. That is, no world model that is deterministic in nature can allow free will to exist. The key consideration is whether people's actions are determined. Hard determinists are incompatibilists who accept determinism and reject free will. Metaphysical libertarians are incompatibilists who accept free will and deny determinism.

Metaphysical libertarianism

Metaphysical libertarianism claims that determinism is false and free will either exists or is possible. This is an incompatibilist viewpoint which subdivides into non-physical, physical, or naturalistic theories. Non-physical theories hold that a non-physical mind overrides physical causality, so physical events in the brain that lead to actions do not have purely physical explanations. Will, beyond physical reality, is deemed to play a role in the decision-making process.

Libertarianism that does not involve removing physicalism requires physical indeterminism, such as subatomic particle behaviour based on probabilities. Physical determinism based on physicalism implies that there is only one possible future.

Free will by chance and determination

William James's model of free will was two-stage. For the first, the mind develops different possibilities for action. In the second, the will selects one option. This model attempts to reconcile libertarian free will with the existence of irreducible chance, like quantum indeterminism in modern times. If an event is caused by chance, then indeterminism would logically be valid. Although some philosophers conclude that this would undermine the possibility of certain knowledge, some go further in believing that chance would make the whole state of the world independent of any earlier states.

Compatibilism

Compatibilists believe that determinism is compatible with free will. They see determinism as irrelevant or of little importance. What matters is that an individual's will is the result of his or her own thoughts and not caused by some external force.

Free will as unpredictability

Dennett supports a compatibilist theory of free will. Here, if one rejects supernatural influence, then since chaos puts limits on the precision of our knowledge of the current state of the world, the future is poorly defined for all finite beings. He states that the only well-defined things are 'expectations'. The ability to do 'otherwise' only makes sense when dealing with these expectations and not with some unknown and unknowable future. According to Dennett, since individuals have the ability to act differently from what anyone expects, free will can exist.

The philosopher Ted Honderich believes that determinism is true, but both compatibilism and incompatibilism are false. He rejects indeterminism because quantum phenomena are not events located in space and time but are rather abstract. Thus, his rejection of indeterminism is not the fundamental nature of quantum reality, but our indeterminate access of it — we have indeterminate access to a determinate fundamental reality, while we treat the world classically in a determinate sense. Since we treat the world in a deterministic way and the quantum world is fundamentally determinate, the indeterminate access to it does not matter. Even if they are micro-level events, they do not seem to have relevance to how the world is at the macroscopic level.

In *Breaking the free will illusion* (2014), 'Trick Slattery argues against free will using simple logic. He states that anything that happens (and we are considering events of human action) is either caused deterministically, or is not. If deterministic, then it could not have occurred any other way. Such events clearly do not involve free will. If events are *not* caused deterministically, then they have occurred for no reason, in that they can neither be *controlled* by anyone's conscious will (since we cannot reason by indeterminate, uncontrollable, processes), nor determined through a causal chain. This view is one of hard incompatibilism. Free will is excluded because whether events are determinate or indeterminate by cause, they aren't controlled by conscious will.

Since the Universe must be determinate and/or indeterminate, if solely determinate then we have our answer for thought (the exclusion of free will). If fundamental indeterminism is real, then how can any mental process occur if this indeterminism is involved in thought? It seems logical that rationality, reason, and any mental computation cannot function unless under the control of that which thinks. If indeterminate, as Ted Honderich says, quantum processes in the mind could be too small to affect the large scale classical events that comprise thought. So even if reality *is* indeterminate in nature, free will doesn't exist whether we consider indeterministic effects part of thought processes or not.

If most (perhaps 95%) of our mental processes are not occurring in full consciousness, and what occurs in our conscious mind derives from these deeper mental events (and their conscious interplay with the temporal experience of the senses), then this has ramifications on free will. The deeper mental events are no doubt a unique function of that particular being's mental framework and, thus, what a person consciously thinks (chooses) is affected (determined) by them- the freedom of the will could be considered lost to these unknown deeper events. It could also be argued, however, that the deeper, non-conscious, mental processes must derive from somewhere, and we are left with hard determinism.

One may wonder how the issue of free will and determinism affects the concept of morality and, further still, punishment, within a civilised society. Indeed, if someone's behaviour is predetermined, is he to blame? It is a complex issue, and a detailed analysis of this can be found in James Miles's book, *The Free Will Delusion: How We Settled for the Illusion of Morality*. Here, it is suffice to stress the point that one must understand that morality is still intact if you believe in hard determinism (hard incompatibilism). Even though a person's bad behaviour would be predetermined, and they had no choice but to act that way, they must still be punished for it (e.g. be removed from society to prevent harming those who uphold the law). But they mustn't be *blamed*, because they had no choice. Thus, we cannot humiliate or kill an offender, but remove them from the opportunity to continue the offense (or such like, depending on the severity). Society is as safe under philosophical determinism, but blame is removed from the equation. If it were possible to assimilate that into one's consciousness (as difficult as assimilating the illusion of free will), perhaps people and society in general would be less segregated.

Influences

Science started off by portraying the Universe as deterministic. Here, it was thought that the information was there and, if gathered, total knowledge of the future was possible, as was the prediction of the future. Modern science mixes deterministic and stochastic theories. Quantum mechanics has cast doubt over the fundamental deterministic nature of the Universe, and the quest for a (possibly impossible) TOE is ongoing.

Dennett has stated that because of chaos and epistemic limits on the precision of our knowledge of the current state of the world, the future is poorly defined for finite beings. Only 'expectations' are well defined. This argument seems weak because it defines free will of action based on the limited comprehension one can have on what the possibility of action is. We are concerned about whether the action is inevitably predefined (including the thought) or truly free.

It is easy to think that predeterminism makes sense for non-mental processes, such as the motion of planets. Can predeterminism and free will as an illusion lie side by side in the same Universe? We would need to accept that the 'quality' of consciousness *is* the physical process — that the feeling of free will as 'free' is equivalent to the associated mental processes. For one thought to be inevitable, every preceding thought must also be, so the truth of the inevitability of one thought is the truth of the inevitability of all. The meaning of thought can be conceived of as a higher-level order that is defined by a lower-level order and whose properties cannot be extrapolated as a function of the lower-level order.

The external universe or universes can impact ours such that events progress not according to a determination from the Big Bang, but also from 'plus external influences'. Therefore, at a defined time, t, events progress from there such that a complete knowledge of the Universe at time t will not enable a prediction of events at t+x because in the intermittent time (x), the influence of the external universe is real but unknown. A thought at time t is affected by the totality of internal and external universal influence at time t. At time t+x, the processes in the Universe between t and t+x have been influenced by internal and external universal components, so the structure of the mind at t+x that constitutes a choice has been determined by influences that are internally predetermined by the Big Bang and external from other universe(s).

So, thoughts exist in a universal space that is constantly redetermined by the totality of influential inputs from all reality. As each thought is generated, the influences for that thought may be many and both internal and external.

Brain states are determined by internal and external factors. My brain state at some moment in time, denoted by t, is followed at time t+x (where x is a minute step forward in time) by a new brain state. The flow from time t to t+x and so on defines the temporal flow of thoughts. The distant future (time t+x+x...) is reached by multiples of infinitely small moments, and each moment follows the former in a way that presents minute changes in brain state. Added together, the distant future brain state (and thought) seems more likely to be predetermined than if seen only at the start and the end.

My choice to do this or that, and feelings associated with decisions, are influenced by the past and present interplay of force and matter within me as well as by my environment. The feelings, choices, and actions *are* part of these processes. The sensation of free will is not something that acts in response to and independently of the force and matter that constitute my physical being and environment. For that to be true, the sensation would have to exist outside of the influence of spacetime, which is illogical since it evolves as a quality from the physical neural interplay in my mind.

Although the 'feelings' of choice and free will exist in the mental domain, apparently distant from the rules of physics, they *are* a quality of the brain's interactions, whose states that cause the sensations are entirely determined by these total physical influences. Thus, my sensation of and belief in free will are both encoded by the determining of past and present influences, despite existing as a mental entity within me in a manner that *appears* free from the rules of physical reality. By being embedded in reality, they are not only a part of but also determined by it. Although mental, they are not independent of the causal physical process and are indeed wholly determined by it. And since they are determined by it, the brain state they cause is the physical manifestation of the mental experience of 'free will'.

Questioning free will

That which lies outside the observable Universe could be affecting the observable Universe in a way that precludes predeterminism (e.g., imagine that the Universe is proceeding along its predetermined path, and then a parallel universe extracts matter from it such that any event in future from that event cannot be predetermined from the Big Bang because components and forces from the Big Bang have taken on a path not determined by it). However, whether a parallel universe extracts or adds matter to ours, this always means that at any moment in time, the next moment is determined by the matter and force interaction preceding it.

Of course, predeterminism is easier to accept in a Universe without external input. But if external universes affect ours, predeterminism is still explicable with the addition of matter. Yet, if external universes extract matter, it is harder to explain. Here, a Big Bang-determined path is redefined by external events. If external universes add and/or extract matter from our Universe, then we have little chance of a TOE. Indeed, if such events occur, it would be unlikely that we can make sense of the reality we exist in.

Can we reject predeterminism and as a result re-establish free will as a valid function of interactions with an external universe? If we think such interactions render the universe indeterminate, it would be ironic to reject predeterminism in the context of free will because it would again rely on the intuition that we truly are free, not that anything physical has changed besides the source of matter and force evolving over time.

To accept free will purely on the grounds that external universes render predeterminism impossible (from a Big Bang) is to ground an intuitive belief in something that is not only unverified but also likely unverifiable or unfalsifiable. We *know* that we exist in a Universe and the Big Bang is its most likely cause. Under this paradigm, free will as an illusion is a reasonable assumption. To reject this assumption (where an external universe extracts from ours) presents a scenario so far out of our intellectual comfort zone that arguments for and against free will are likely to be driven more by emotion than by reason or scientific data.

If other universes affect ours in a significant way, would it not impact on our ability to make sense (in terms of laws) of our Universe? Whether external universes input, extract, do both, or neither, at any one moment the mind will be affected by a continuity of stimuli. In terms of the effect on free will, if external universes extract or add, then that does not induce free will but more likely redefines the determined conditions.

It makes intuitive sense that if all matter and forces were defined at the Big Bang, then an enclosed universe is determined — that all that happens and will happen, including qualia, is according to rules. Thus, what *will* happen is the only thing that *can* happen. Thus, if I commit murder, for example, I was always going to murder, and it is just my misfortune than I am the collection of matter that is both conscious and performs this act.

The fact that we make sense of the Universe in a predictive sense leads logically to questions about the limits of understanding, and of *our* understanding. Answers are constrained to the limits of our questions and our capacity to both ask and comprehend. Although it might seem like a cop out to say that we do not have the mental construction to comprehend how reality is, it seems to me to be closest to the truth. Only arrogance on our part overrides the frustration of wanting to know and being able to ask but not understand, and this may blind us to the strong possibility that the

Universe is either innately unknowable or knowable only to an intellect of a type vastly superior and different from our own.

We know that science progresses and ideas, laws, theories, and concepts change as we know more. So, when is the truth reached? How do we know if it is ever reached? And can it ever be reached? Wittgenstein said that to know the limit, we need to know the other side. That, we cannot do. Perhaps we truly *know* nothing (remember the legend that Socrates considered himself wise because he alone knew that he knew nothing) — we can only have useable 'information' that is subject to revision.

To 'know' something differs between that of objective physical things, subjective experience, and of concepts and ideas. We cannot know a physical entity in a subjective way. The type of knowing we have of physical things is that which relates to how well we can determine its matter constituents, predict its behaviour, and so on. That *type* of knowing is constrained by the limitations of our framework of science. Knowledge of concepts *is* subjective.

For example, let me return to the concept of redness. Red is the emission of electromagnetic radiation of a defined wavelength that we have called 'red'. We might assume that each human perceives the same feeling for red. But this 'redness' is relative to what we 'are', just as the same thing would be conceived of as different to an alien whose physical and mental makeup were different from ours. This 'redness' is knowledge that is not only unique to the species, but also to the individual. Yet, as a group, we can point to a red thing and say 'that is red'. We agree what red is, but what that means to the individual is unique.

A concept such as 'addition' was potentially already 'there' from the beginning of the Universe and could only be what it is — one 'thing' plus another 'thing'. Without intelligence or some form of consciousness, this addition of those two things does not exist — the things just 'are', in a physical sense. The 'twoness' is the result of intelligent appreciation of that fact. If we go back to our alien observer, would this twoness be the same as for us? It would have to be. It does not relate to the nature of the perceiver, but to the 'twoness' itself. So, does that mean we can really 'know' such concepts, in that what they are is universal to any sentient form? Again, we need to be mindful that they are constructions of the human mind.

The concept of addition was created by a sentient being — it does not exist by itself. It does not have to exist just because we have realised or comprehended the concept. There are many concepts about reality that are potentially 'out there' that we have yet to uncover. Perhaps some other intelligence has realised some fundamental concept that we have not. For them it is real, but for us it is not. So, what is real in this sense is constrained by our limitations.

The platonic existence of abstract objects exists in a third realm, distinct from physical things, in that they do not exist at a particular time and place and possess matter as is the case for concrete objects, or *concreta*. So, some ideas may be true (like 'addition') but beyond our comprehension, but it does not make them less real than those that we do understand. Furthermore, some ideas we believe to be true may turn out to be wrong. But if we take one that we are certain is correct, such as addition, can we state this certainty as absolute? Only insofar as the truth of it is as true as our belief in our own existence. The truth of each is in accord with our concept of a belief system, itself constrained by our mental and physical being.

All knowledge is relative to what we are. To 'know' implies completion where nothing more can be added, but elements of absolute truth about any thing (or the implications of an idea or concept) must, essentially, evade us. For any conception of truth, whether it be about something physical or ethereal, presents unique reasons why the truth we have, or seek about it, cannot be anything other than 'relative' truth — relative to what we (as humans) are.

To assume we have absolute knowledge of a concept or thing is to assume that we know the boundary of knowledge. But we cannot know the boundary. We 'know' relative knowledge. As Wittgenstein stated (*Tractatus Logico-Philosophicus*; 5.61), "We cannot say in logic 'the world has this in it, and this, but not that', for that would appear to presuppose that we were excluding certain possibilities, and this cannot be the case, since it would require that logic should go beyond the limits of the world; for only in that way could it view those limits from the other side as well. We cannot think what we cannot think; so, what we cannot think we cannot say either."

We are limited and finite, and all we that know must relate to what these limitations entail. We cannot know what that is because we cannot see beyond what our physiology or mental framework allows. We cannot comprehend a form of knowing greater than our own, nor what knowing would be to that form of intelligence.

A GUT would define physics, chemistry, and biology as physical processes, but would not define everything. It would explain objective knowledge of these things within the constraints of what we decide objective knowing is (with limitations defined by our minds and technology), but it can neither know what truth is (we cannot know what physically induced boundaries of knowledge are, just what *our* boundaries are) nor, even within our limits, access the nature of physical being (we cannot know a thing as it is in-itself, to itself). We infer about an underlying non-local reality from measurement, but cannot truly know it since we exist in the realm from which we infer (not from where it is inferred).

A GUT is a model that makes sense to us for explaining phenomena and how things interact. Whether it is part of truth or only that which makes sense to the limitations of verifiability and falsifiability we are capable of, we cannot know. If we can only imagine within limits (which is true) and then create a theoretical model (constrained by these limits) that is testable and proven right (which we may do), then this model is right only in proving that there is alignment between our imagination, theory, testability, verification, and falsification. Although this is rare, it is not to be confused with truth, because even though we cannot imagine beyond this model (in the sense of what may be real and true), we know that it is limited by our conceptual possibilities and that these relate more to our limitations than to the possibility, feasibility, or truth of a deeper structure and conception of reality than we *can* imagine.

There are questions we have asked but are as yet unable to answer or know if they are answerable. There are questions we are yet to ask, and there are questions we can never ask — perhaps because they involve concepts outside of human language or thought, or are beyond the capacity of man, yet which, if we could ask and answer them, might provide deeper answers about our being.

Ilya Prigogine

The Nobel-Prize winning chemist Ilya Prigogine (1917–2003) wrote in his 1996 book *The End of Certainty* that determinism is no longer a viable scientific belief. He suggested that the more we know, the less we can accept determinism. It is interesting that his lack of belief in the validity of determinism was as strong as 't Hooft's favouring of determinism. The fact that two scientists and Nobel laureates have the same information and yet chose opposing views of such fundamental importance implies not only that our knowledge is incomplete, but also that emotion, intuition, and feeling play a key part in the decision-making process, and selective information is used to support it.

Prigogine cited the examples of weather systems and organisms as unstable systems and argued that they are explainable not in deterministic terms but in chaotic or probabilistic terms. Yet, this example points to more of a lack of sufficient information to describe such systems than a refutation of determinism. A deterministic description would be possible with more information, rather than reality preventing a fundamental limitation to attaining such information.

Prigogine tried to convince about the lack of validity of determinism using the concepts of irreversibility and instability. Since all processes in deterministic physics are time-reversible, he said that determinism denies the arrow of time. But it is known that we do not have a theory that is foolproof and explains all phenomena fundamentally. Deterministic physics evolved before quantum physics. The equations may imply that time-reversibility is feasible, but the world does not work like that. One could reject all multidimensional string theories merely for the apparent absence of these dimensions.

Colin McGinn

Like the study of the Universe's constituents and processes, fully understanding consciousness may be a subject of investigation that is doomed to failure. We assume that because we are intelligent, we can, in due time, understand everything around us, including ourselves. Is that an assumption formulated from reason or arrogance?

There are some, like the British philosopher Colin McGinn, who believe that we can never fully understand how the physical processes of the brain produce conscious experience. McGinn thinks that this task is not intrinsically impossible but, rather, it requires a type of understanding that lies beyond human intellectual reason — our minds are not set up to understand this aspect of what they do. The type, not degree, of complexity that constitutes the mind defies comprehension by the type of complexity that it is. He takes this conclusion further by stating that the difficulty we have in resolving many philosophical problems, such as free will, the self, and knowledge, is due to the innate makeup of the human mind. Intractability exists because there is no objective correlation between how the human mind works and what it is trying to solve in the physical world.

McGinn questions whether the Universe (or reality) is fundamentally unknowable, or that to know it would require reasoning that we do not intrinsically possess. If reality *is* unknowable, it explains why we can neither know it nor solve the mind-body problem. If reality is fundamentally knowable, there is no reason why our minds would possess the intellect and insight at the right level to understand it or solve the mind-body problem (see Figure 42). In a knowable universe, are the two linked? Penrose thinks

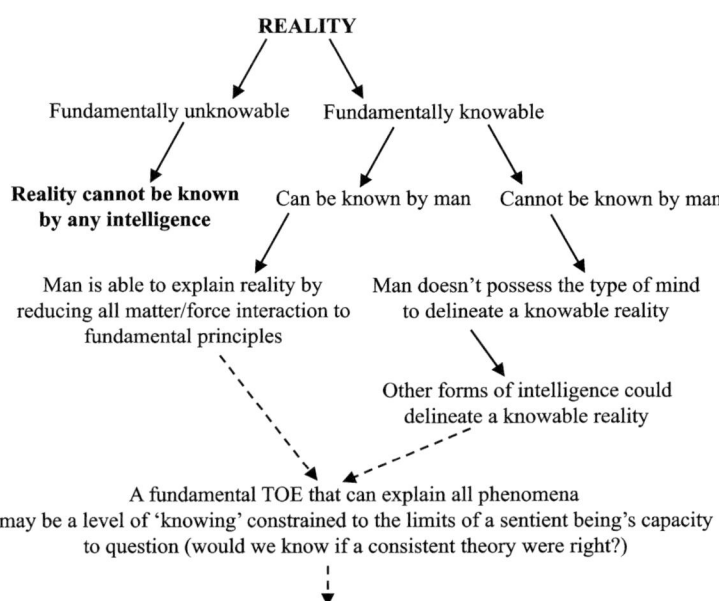

- If the form of 'knowing' is skewed toward the type of questions a being can ask, can we know the fundamental laws discovered are truly fundamental?
- Since 'knowing' is a conscious phenomena, can a theory be complete without encompassing the subjective experience (or is the 'experience' of knowing something equivalent to the mental processes causing it)?
- There are different types of 'knowing'- things definable by scientific method and those not (e.g. conscious experience). Yet, the concept of infinity lies within scientific method but cannot be consciously grasped.
- Thus, 'knowing' reality is a species-relative thing, and the truth of it is coloured by the subjective value we put on different forms of knowing (e.g. is the infinite completely known or not at all)

Figure 42. Knowability of reality. Some considerations for whether we can know reality and what this knowledge of reality might mean.

that solving the mind-body problem in a knowable universe will help us to understand the Universe.

We cannot solve the mind-body problem because we cannot know reality. Whether reality itself is actually unknowable is not the issue — *we cannot know whether it is knowable or not*, so therefore it follows that the mind-body problem is inherently unsolvable. If we were conscious organisms of a form that could tap into the secrets of reality, then we would possess the capacity to know the self. As things stand, it seems like the question of whether quantum indeterminism is a property of reality (a fundamentally real limit to knowability) or caused only by the incompatibility of our mental and physical makeup with accessing knowable truth is irresolvable. So, the mind is our only means to assess reality and the mind itself, and its solutions are those that are possible by the nature and application of its intellect and insight. McGinn's conclusions about human limitations are not defeatist, but are founded from logic, language, reason, and evidence.

As discussed in Chapter 5, Gould and Lewontin argued for the existence of *spandrels*, or phenotypic characteristics that developed during evolution as side effects of true adaptive changes by natural selection, in *The Spandrels of San Marco and the Panglossian Paradigm*. If the increase in brain size was correlated with increased intelligence and thus increased survivability, then could consciousness be a spandrel of sorts, only mental and not physical? Noam Chomsky has suggested that our language faculty evolved as a spandrel. As the brain enlarged, structural changes produced the possibility of language despite there being no evolutionary reasons for it.

Chomsky views human intelligence as a collection of cognitive modules, each one responsible for tackling some unique aspect of physical and social reality. However, one that would be required to solve the mind-body problem is absent. The task is there, but the tool does not exist. Hence, this problem transcends our innate makeup. Whether or not consciousness was a 'fortunate' by-product of the evolution of the human brain — and Humphrey sees that consciousness *does* present an evolutionary advantage, as I have mentioned — there appears to be no reason why there would be a selective advantage for having brains that are capable of addressing this problem (Figure 43, below). Of course, this all presupposes that a brain such as ours is of a form that could, with different arrangements, solve such a problem, and that such a problem is even fundamentally solvable.

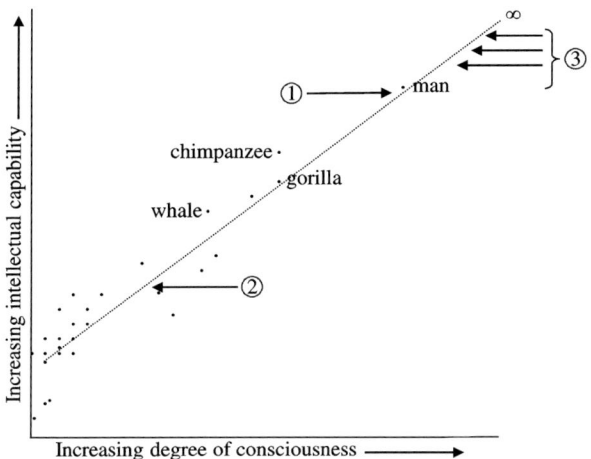

Figure 43. Hypothetical plot of the relationship between level of intelligence and degree of consciousness. There is probably an approximate linear relationship — the higher the intelligence, the greater the level of consciousness. Point ② represents the minimum threshold where it is psychologically advantageous to be conscious and, thus, organisms that possess the most limited form of consciousness appear here. Whether or not the mind-body problem is knowable, point ① represents the threshold limit where *some* assume that it is possible to achieve this knowledge. If reality is knowable but not to humans, then where on the line is the level necessary to solve these problems (represented by point ③). There is no reason why we should be more or less advanced than organisms at this point (i.e., assuming that there is a point on the line relating to knowability). ∞ (infinity) represents the possible unknowability of the Universe and, hence, the mind-body problem.

Chomsky explained that we learn languages through the application of the innate language acquisition cognitive module, and that learning additional languages is easier if they employ rules of grammar that are similar to our main language. Thus, if the task is to learn a new language with the same rules as the first, then we have the cognitive module as a tool to achieve this.

Chomsky's insights have considerable bearing on McGinn's 'mysterian' view on the mind-body problem. Physical reality is constructed of matter, which exists primarily as atoms, ions, and molecules. Whether living or inanimate, this matter interacts with other matter in both simple and complex systems according to causal relationships. Modern science is a delineation of these processes. Language also consists of elements that interact according to grammatical rules. Thus, although language is not material, it is conceptually similar to physical processes in that rules (replacing material laws) determine how it functions. McGinn realised that there is a cognitive structure shaping our knowledge of the world and that this structure is not appropriate for the mind-body problem.

McGinn presents a model called DIME — an acronym he uses to describe how philosophical theories tend to address difficult problems such as free will and consciousness. For such problems, he states that philosophers domesticate (D) them, reduce them to something irreducible (I) or magical (M), or eliminate (E) them — perhaps by denying the phenomena as real. McGinn sees attempts to solve these types of problems as futile because they elude our method of reasoning. We are cognitively shut off from such problems.

Reason is the human capacity to rationalise, think, and argue intelligently. The grammar of reason is biologically innate, and we can use this for the abstract manipulation of concepts. This particular grammar is to reason what universal grammar is to language. It is what McGinn calls 'Combinatorial Atomism with Law-like Mappings' (CALM), which states that we can understand things that conform to CALM principles, but not those that do not.

CALM

The CALM conjecture describes how simple 'atomic' elements (be it atoms, words, or whatever the basic unit of the system is) combine and map together. This works for language, mathematics, and aspects of physical reality. For systems like these, we can map combinations or arrangements of the fundamental constituents of that system in ways that accord to defined laws (constructed or delineated by our minds through subjective and objective analysis) to produce understandable, interpretable effects. Of course, the understanding of each is incomplete, but there is a relationship between the fundamental part and the whole that they constitute which we can interpret. This does not work for the mind-body problem because there is no mapping.

Where words combine by rules into meaningful phrases, CALM allows abstract manipulations of simple concepts, be they real or conceptual in nature. In the manipulation, if a theoretical object changes over time, CALM guides us to find laws, concepts, and theories that describe the change. This enables us to do science effectively because the objective physical world, or the world of mathematical and physical concepts, can be broken down, conceptualised, and manipulated using this tool. CALM can help us theorise how components change over time and this can lead to understanding. This is science. However, philosophy (or science) of the kind that deals with concepts such as consciousness and free will must comprise ideas whose concepts do not conform to the CALM conjecture, so our tools to delineate these ideas or phenomena are futile.

For instance, consciousness is a part of reality, but we are not wired in a way that allows us to understand it. Perhaps we are actually unable to understand it how we *want* to understand it, or think we *could* or *should* understand it. That is, we understand it in ways that do not convince us that we have a firm grip on it, like we do for other things discussed herein (this 'convincing' is perhaps what conforming to CALM would enable). Indeed, although we know things about consciousness, the tools we use to understand it — and which we use to understand other things in an experimentally testable and theoretically provable way — produce unsatisfactory answers. The solutions exist as theories and hypotheses that can only appeal (or not) to our emotional rather than rational selves. According to McGinn, those philosophers and scientists who *try* to tackle these subjects find that their conclusions are merely intellectual tangles devoid of true insight. In essence, we do not have the tools to understand certain things that are fundamental for a complete understanding of reality.

Dennett, for example, would consider this view too gloomy and pessimistic. Yet, he would also concede that during the link between what the mind physically does and what it produces, there is a step where we have to say 'and then the magic occurs'. Is that acceptable when it does not fit the CALM conjecture? Consciousness, as 'what it is like', transcends causative processes. Yet, the process observed and the subjective experience felt do not map, so no advancement in our understanding of the physical process of consciousness will get us any closer to bridging that gap. In the CALM conjecture, the neuronal processes do not map onto the conscious experiences that extend from them.

Paradoxes of language do not pose a problem to the mind because as we exist and experience both outside and inside the mind, we can see when linguistic paradoxes ("what's written on the other side of this piece of paper is false") occur. A formal axiomatic version of such a paradox would pose a problem to a computer programme that is constrained to its formalism. The hypothetical zombie does not have conscious experience. However, humans are not zombies and *do* have conscious experience, so the question of the zombie is irrelevant.

Humphrey thinks that we need to define what must be achieved to be considered universally acceptable as a solution to the mind-body problem, otherwise we cannot ever know whether we will achieve it or whether we have achieved it. In an article by McGinn titled *"Can We Solve the Mind-Body Problem?"* (1989) in the philosophical journal *Mind*, he concludes that the mystery of the mind-body problem persists and evades our best efforts. He says that the time has come to admit that "we cannot solve the mystery of how the water of the physical brain is turned into the wine of consciousness". Nearly thirty years on, little has changed.

View from nowhere

Relativity treats the observer and observed as separate in that the observer must be assigned coordinates in spacetime. Quantum physics must also view the observer as integrated in the quantum system. Bohr knew that both classical and quantum physics failed to achieve a perspective outside the system, or a 'view from nowhere, as Thomas Nagel called it.

In general, the subjective and objective view do not serve the same purpose. When attempting to achieve an objective point of view, we place ourselves and our subjectivity in a broader conception of the world that strives to see the world as if it is a 'view from nowhere'. However, Nagel believes that it is very difficult to integrate subjective and objective perspectives, yet a world that incorporates the reality of each is needed.

There is no god-like perspective of reality where it can be known 'absolutely as it is in itself'. Mathematical descriptions are relative to us and relate to relationships of reality's components, confirmed or refuted by experimental verification. The fact that we can neither incorporate ourselves, the measurer, in the analysis nor integrate our physical and mental limitations means that any description is incomplete as an absolute.

We cannot know a quantum system completely. For example, both wave and particle properties are required for a complete view, but measurement precludes the simultaneous revealing of both. David Bohm saw quantum theory as a calculus that enabled predictions of results while nevertheless being devoid of fundamental explanations of events, thus rendering it incomplete. As discussed in Chapter 3, Bohm tried to develop a theory that challenged the functional paradigm. Indeed, for him, the wave or particle nature that is revealed is just how the implicate (or enfolded) true order of reality unfolds and reveals itself to us in an experiment.

The fact that we are conscious entities experiencing the physical world means that there is a subjective and objective element to our reality that cannot be avoided. The component that assesses is the subjective self (the mind), and all that is external to this is the objective world. Yet the matter that constitutes the machinery of the mind constitutes both subject and object. So 'the view from nowhere' is the ideal, but perhaps represents another impossibility.

7 Mind-Knowledge-Meaning

i) Are We Asking the Right Questions?

Colin McGinn believes that we can never fully understand how the physical processes of the brain produce conscious experience. His views have often been oversimplified and inaccurately represented by some to try and demonstrate the failure of this defeatist attitude. I find this unfair. To state a being's limitations is not defeatist if they are in fact real. Meaning can be found in life whether or not there are limitations imposed on our understanding of reality, by reality.

Let me take the opposed stance to a defeatist attitude and see where we lie with the hard problem. Perhaps Edelman was right with his TNGS and that certain neuronal connections activate in the brain when qualia occur in our minds. Although this account provides a physical cause of the conscious process, all it says is that when this *happens,* mental experience occurs. It does not say what the feeling is.

Perhaps there is some sort of 'theatre'-type process occurring in the mind when qualia occur. This theory is somewhat like Humphrey's idea of sensation. Humphrey has enlightened us on two issues of consciousness: firstly, the reason for it in an evolutionary sense — to make us care for and feel part of the external physical environment — and, secondly, the perception-sensation distinction.

He provides a neat description of what sensation is in his book *Seeing Red*. When I look at a tomato, red light from it travels to my eye and I create an internal expressive response. Humphrey says that I engage in 'redding'. I monitor what I am doing to discover what is happening to me — perception becomes sensation. The representation I form of my response is the sensation of red. So, to have the sensation of red means to observe my own redding.

I see red as a signal, but the sensation is my conscious observation of my own way of seeing red. Another person will have their own appreciation of how red that 'red' is — their own redding. Here, Humphrey has described a plausible distinction between pure perception of the external world and how sensation (qualia) results from the internal monitoring of what is happening when the perceived signal enters the brain. The pure signal information processing is the perception, whereas the involvement of the mind with the processed perceived information is the production of the sensation of red. I perceive red, but I feel red when I process the information that equates to the perceiving.

This process of creating qualia from internal analysis of the perceived input, although not defined, can easily be considered variants of Edelman's TNGS and Baars's theatre (and no doubt countless other models). It is not so hard to form multiple and broadly similar theories of what causes qualia. However, even with such descriptions, it still says nothing of the experience. I know what I feel when I see red, but I can never know what you feel.

In *Soul Dust* (2011), Humphrey introduces the term 'ipsundrum', which is an illusion-generating mental creation in response to stimuli. A sensation is generated when I reflect on something that I perceive in physical reality, and this sensation is mentally associated with the physical cause. This ipsundrum is not a physical thing, but a mathematical object. It is a dynamic pattern of neural activity whose properties become visible at the level of a computation that integrates what happens over time. Although it depends on reentrant feedbacks, it differs from Edelman's TNGS, not least in that it depends on something like Hofstadter's 'strange loops'.

In *I am a Strange Loop*, Hofstadter suggests that one can derive a coherent and robust account of consciousness from logical manipulation only. He proposes that a sufficiently complex string of symbols can act as a substrate for consciousness. He suggests that consciousness is an emergent consequence of low-level brain activity, which is an idea that Humphrey has assimilated into his own model of the ipsundrum. In particular, the abstract patterning which he terms a strange loop (related to the self-referential structure of Gödel's incompleteness theorem) forms the basis of both theories — it is at the core of Hofstadter's and an essential element of Humphrey's. But we see that the mechanism and not the feeling is described — the 'hard' problem is addressed by avoiding the essence.

One is mindful of the fact that Humphreys' key expertise is psychology, whereas Hofstadter's is logic and computer science, and both use their expertise as the foundation of their solution to consciousness. Penrose's key expertise is quantum theory, which he believes is at the core of a solution to consciousness. The fact that many experts of diverse specialties can find support for the validity of their solution to this ineffable problem suggests two things — either that they are all so convincing as individuals and yet cannot all be true, so we are far from a real solution, or that a solution cannot be found. Or perhaps we are trying to answer a question for which we have no idea what a solution would even equate to.

It is odd too that although consciousness emerges from a biological brain, some of these diverse solutions apply physics, mathematics, and logic without any reference to the living, evolving, and embedded nature of the human mind and brain.

Two problems remain unresolved and are perhaps unresolvable. McGinn believes that the human mind is unable to resolve these problems and that they could be unknowable:

1. Third person knowledge of subjective experience will forever escape scientific analysis. For all the knowledge about the physical processes happening in our brains when conscious, the sensation is private and we can never *know*, in a scientific and objective sense, if the qualia we feel are like those that another person feels for the same type of input (e.g., seeing red).
2. To state that we understand how the processes of the brain produce conscious experience is not the same as knowing what processes are occurring when one has a conscious experience. How the physical processes of a certain type translate to feeling requires a type of objective analysis that encapsulates what happens when physical process transcends into feeling — this is out of the remit of science as it is, or probably can be.

If we possess minds that evolved according to something like Edelman's TNGS, then neuronal groups wiring and firing together seems feasible. Over time, the wiring and firing modifies — in accordance with additional external input — memory, conscious thought, and factors associated with living. This produces an ever-changing wiring and firing 'structure' that represents the wiring and firing of billions of neurons at any one moment. In so doing, a mental 'shape' is created (a changing combination of connections of neurons over time), which correlates to a conscious feeling.

This is a feasible simplistic representation of the correlation between the physical structures in the brain and how they interrelate and cause consciousness. Yet, the 'magic' event of the feeling seems inexplicable. Perhaps we are seeking an answer to the hard problem in a way that cannot be solved, as McGinn suggests. It is possible that as the interactions between neurons over time must have an effect, the effect is the feelings we have as consciousness. Thus, the hard problem would be answered by the statement that "the physical processes of certain interacting parts of the brain ARE qualia because the same physical processes cause qualia".

ii) Mind

Philosophers are sceptical about what neuroscience can tell us about these issues, whereas many neuroscientists think that philosophers have had long enough to attempt a solution and have not succeeded. Philosophers consider that whatever scientists do, the first-person and third-person perspective on consciousness cannot be reconciled — that is, the gap will not be bridged — so how sensation and experience are generated from neuronal function will remain unsolved.

Humans are intelligent conscious beings that experience mental sensations. These are considered representations of the physical world external to the mind, constrained by their causal physiological limitations but intellectually acted upon as if they represent how the real world 'is'. Thus, the sensations provide the background against which we use intelligence and insight to make sense of the physical and mental world. Computer programmes differ in that they are constrained solely to the programme's formalism.

In Edelman and Tononi's book *Consciousness* (2001), the introduction to Chapter 16, which is entitled 'Thinking', makes it clear that they think human mental processes exceed those of computers. In their retort to the question, "what goes on in your head when you have a thought?", they admit that "the neural basis of consciousness supports the conclusion that an awful lot goes on in the brain every time we have a thought, most of it in parallel and of an awe-inspiring complexity and richness of association. A good deal of its information having a complexity that's far beyond the capabilities of present-day computers". That, of course, still applies.

Consciousness is something that happens in the brain and is, thus, intimately linked to biological processes. It is matter being aware of matter, but where is the mind? Although I know that it is associated with my brain, it does not feel like it is in my head and instead seems to follow my senses, which experience the world outside the mind. An answer that encapsulates a human's sense of being alive and embedded in a world seems far removed from the possibilities of analysis by scientific methods. In this respect, we might wonder whether trying to address the location of conscious experience has any meaning. Does 'location' only have sense when applied objectively?

Conscious states are caused by the brain and so must reside in the brain, but their effect as experience has no defined location in space or time. Indeed, the experience transcends physical space and time. Objects and phenomena of the real world, distinct in place and time, are reflected on as unique and personal experiences in the form of qualia. What your mental sensation of a real object or experience is, qualitatively, is unique to you.

We assimilate and interpret information about reality from the senses and feel that *that* provides us insight into the truth of the world. Yet intellectually, we know that is not the case. It is our version of reality. Our senses of sight, smell, audition, touch, and taste are all constrained by biological limitations. Indeed, in addition to these five traditional senses, other senses such as pain, heat, cold, and acceleration also constitute mental sensations which feed our intellect, insight, and analysis. Our thoughts, constrained by logic and language, affect our interaction with and interpretation of reality. However, *by* being a living, intelligent, and conscious being that interacts with the world (unlike a formal programme), we possess the capacity to be creative and imagine things beyond physical feasibility.

Although our access to knowledge is finite and limited, the mental world enables us to investigate ideas beyond the constraints of physical laws and test our inventiveness. This occurs mainly consciously, but there is interplay with different conscious states, including that of sleep.

Once something in physical reality is consciously or subconsciously noticed, a memory or map (i.e., neural correlate) of it is made such that it can be manipulated in hypothetical scenarios within different conscious states. How this is done depends on many factors such as the context of the interaction with it, individual psychology, neural connections, life choices, intellect, knowledge, and so on. The object in physical reality that causes a mental sensation is an object of shared experience, yet the mental representation and meaning it causes in minds is private. Real objects must conform to physical laws, but their mental representations can be placed in different scenarios and distort physical laws. The ability to construct private mental representations of components of physical reality and manipulate how they may relate to other objects, ideas, forces, concepts, and so forth in hypothetical scenarios is the essence of creativity. Without this ability, our creativity as well as technological, cultural, and social development would have been severely restricted.

Memory

Memory is essential for language, thought, and consciousness. For a memory to be made, something must obviously 'happen' in the brain. Yet we know we have different types of memory — reading requires short-term memory of the last few words to enable continuity, whereas some things are remembered for all of one's life. An elderly person affected with dementia may lack short-term memory but recall things from their childhood. So, what are the different processes that constitute the different types of memory?

'Working' memory is like a tank, filling and emptying continually with sensations that are experienced. It is always full and it is required to make sense of the continuity of the experience, such as watching a film. Although it is essential for understanding language, little of the content of this type of memory is retained for long-term storage. Short-term memories are quite unstable in the brain and easily forgotten, and physical and chemical changes in the brain are required before they can be transferred to long-term memory. Emotional response, prolonged mental effort, and stress are just some factors that result in electrical, synaptic, chemical, and even genetic responses that contribute to the retention of memories. The difference between short- and long-term memories may be that only the latter result in changes in the production of neurons or synapses.

Memories are, of course, required for everyday living. The information needed for interaction with the external world has been learned, memorised, and stored in logically associated modules in the brain such that behaviour or remembering occurs unconsciously, or recall is easy through accessing a particular organised module. These associated modules are the reason why thinking of something reminds one of something else, and only on analysis does one realise why the association has been made.

Specific parts of the brain function for particular types of *necessary* memory. How to walk or ride a bike are learned and never forgotten, but they also require a different type of storage from that for, say, remembering a telephone number. It is clear, however, that particular memories have a physical basis and a particular location (of events) in the brain. Indeed, it has been shown that 'exercising' a type of memory affects the size of that part of the brain involved in its storage (e.g., the hippocampus for spatial memory).

The detailed process of how memories are stored is beyond the capability of current scientific methods. However, studying memory in the simplest organisms provides insight into how they *may* occur in humans. Indeed, since we likely evolved from the same organisms as all life on Earth did and hence share common genes, this reductionist approach is useful in many aspects of science. The nematode worm *Caenorhabditis elegans* (*C. elegans*) is an ideal model organism for study as we know exactly how many cells it has — 959 in the case of an adult hermaphrodite, of which 302 are neurons.

In the 1960s, Eric Kandel used the giant sea slug, which has about 20,000 neurons, as a model organism to understand memory storage and extrapolating these insights to how human memory works, if not in the details then at least from a functional process standpoint. In 2000, he was awarded the Nobel Prize for his efforts. What did he show? The chemical mechanism of short- and long-term memory storage in the slug is conserved *throughout* the animal kingdom. Experiments showed that the neurotransmitter serotonin causes increased second messenger (cAMP) production in certain neurons, which activates a protein kinase that phosphorylates an ion channel and results in a prolonged action potential in a nerve. More serotonin causes a stronger impulse.

Enzymes are a huge family of biological catalysts, and specific enzymes called phosphatases function by removing phosphate groups from proteins (i.e., acting in opposition to protein kinases). For a dephosphorylated ion channel, this removal results in cessation of the impulse. Thus, this short-term memory requires no gene effect (i.e., no activation or repression of gene expression) but instead involves modulation of proteins (kinases and phosphatases) already present. For long-term memory, cAMP-activated kinases enter the neuron cell body and, through transcription and translation, result in the expression of certain genes (e.g., cAMP-response element-binding protein (CREB), a transcription factor). A 2015 study on *C. elegans* revealed that training worms to associate a particular smell with food led to activation of over 750 genes in neuronal cells in a cAMP-dependent manner. These activated genes and their proteins reinforce synaptic strength and contribute to new synapses being formed. Thus, short-term memory enhancement can result in long-term memory through genome effects. Just as exercise can activate the expression of genes relating to muscle production, merely thinking about things can cause the expression of genes relating to memory.

Mind, matter, and knowledge

Of the processes we think we *do* understand about both the mind and the physical world, can we be sure that our scientific analysis produces meaningful data? On the one hand yes, because what we know works in that the information can be used predictably. This is verification and falsification in action. But on the other hand, the answer is also no because our understanding is built on foundations that include chaos, indeterminism, probability, and so on, all of which prevent complete knowledge. Furthermore, this framework is constructed by the finite human mind, which means that knowledge of the world is relative to what *we* are and in no way *necessarily* relates to what is happening in reality.

Let us use some examples to summarise our position. Knowledge of different aspects of the world presents problems determined by the type of question asked. If I am asked if there is an apple in my hand when I am holding an apple, I can ignore issues suggested in the previous paragraph and give an answer based on understanding what the intent of the question is. If I am asked "what is an apple?", then different criteria must be considered. Additional to the formal rules of language is 'understanding', which results from it being a living, shared process. Thus, "what is an apple?" can produce different answers, each correct in its own way. An apple can be many things — an object, a fruit, food, a particular species, a complex arrangement of molecules, and so on.

What a thing 'is' is what it is in itself. Any other meaning of what something is can only be contextual. Take myself as an example. I am a brother, a son, and a scientist — these definitions concern how I relate to others within a social context. I am also a human being composed of proteins, fats, DNA, and other molecules — these are my physical constituents. I have conscious sensations, feelings, thoughts, and emotions — these are subjective experiences 'known' only to me. Each is a conceptually different aspect of what I am. All are true, so what am I? I am each of these things and they are not mutually exclusive.

There is an element of truth to the knowledge we acquire, but we have physical constraints that determine our intellectual limits, which are unlikely to be the same as those of an alien intellect with a different kind of mind and scientific method. Thus, *facts* about nature are properties of nature that make sense to us because they are obtained in a way that accords with our physical being and, thus, method of analysis.

Can we ask whether knowledge that we define as truth is absolute, or is 'truth' just *our* most accurate picture of how things are? Mental and physical limits necessarily bind us to the types of questions we can ask and what we can answer. We cannot ask what we cannot conceive of, and things do exist in some sense that we will never conceive of. Thus, we are cognisant of the fact that some truths, especially those about physical reality, might be valid only for cases that we can apply them to.

But what about the truth of ideas? Are they a purer truth? We can state that $3 + 3 = 6$, which we believe to be an absolute truth. Is it an absolute truth only upon establishment of axioms by which we can define 3, +, =, and 6? Those axioms are not absolute as we cannot prove them to be true, and this holds in the general case. Mathematics is, at its essence, logical extrapolations from a set of axioms. The axioms must be assumed, hence they are not absolutely true. It seems like we cannot be sure of anything — for physical forms, the descriptions of truth are constrained to the type of being we are and thus cannot be universal. For truth of ideas, as fundamental axioms must be taken as given and assumed, they cannot be absolute.

Humans have unique insight into their own nature, which is deeper than that possible through objective scientific analysis. We can scientifically analyse human and inanimate objects and obtain scientific knowledge of both. The knowledge of the inanimate object, while limited, can address all its properties, but this is not true for a living, conscious thing. Qualia are subjective, knowable only to that which produces them, and inaccessible to scientific method. Thus, by definition, living entities exclude aspects of their self to objective analysis.

So, our possible scientific and philosophical analyses of reality relate, unavoidably, to *our* mental processes. The nature of questions we ask, methods of address, and consequences of analysis are constrained by what we can possibly achieve as limited by nature. For anything we analyse, whether physical or conceptual, there are contextual limits to what the information means, not least because we as analysers are limited by our physical and thus mental construction.

In a sense, there are three types of objective knowledge of physical things:

1. We can know an inanimate object through the scientific method.
2. We can know another sentient being through the scientific method, but we cannot know its mind.
3. We can know ourselves through the scientific method and have access to our own minds.

Water, for example, is known as constituting oxygen and hydrogen. We can analyse it and define it according to what it is constructed from. When experiencing one's thoughts and qualia, we cannot gain similar objective insight into what these experiences are despite owning and controlling them. We cannot break them down into something simpler, even if they are constructed as such. We have access only to the full experience. Thinking involves this full experience and any possible constitutive, deeper property cannot be isolated because doing so would require experiencing it, and we only experience the *full* experience.

Allow yourself to engage in a flow of thoughts and then attempt to gain insight into them. Nothing can be learned about the property of the experience. The mind is not designed to probe its own thinking experience and gain insight into it. It evolved to interpret inputs from outside itself. The mind is good at looking 'out' to the world and then analysing it internally, but not so good at understanding its innate nature. Objectively, the mind understands the simplest description of things in terms of 'being' and 'non-being'. As 'being' can be defined as 'that which nothing lacks', it therefore encapsulates everything that exists. Conscious and nonconscious entities have different types of being.

'Being' (something that *is* — like, say, a stone) and 'conscious being' (something that has awareness) are clearly very different things. The mind is not physical but the result of interactions between physical things (neurons) in the brain. The mind-body problem is the relation between these different types of being. The solution, if it is possible, entails a process which the human mind did not evolve to do.

Clearly, the human mind is highly intuitive and intelligent in its interaction with the physical world. It is clearly more advanced than any other living entity on Earth. But what of computers, a technological product of the human mind? Earlier, we asked "is the mind a computer?" or "can a programme be conscious?" Could a computer be creative like a human? Some deny the possibility that a computer can 'think'. In the next section, we investigate differences between humans and computers and expand on what defines our unique attributes for acquiring knowledge of the world, before finally defining how real that knowledge is.

iii) Limits of Knowledge

Jacob Bronowski discussed the cultural evolution of humankind in *The Ascent of Man* (1973). Beautifully, simply, and enthusiastically presented by a man who oozed compassion, he emphasised all parts of humankind's evolution through science, religion, and aspects relating to our creativity, such as art and architecture. It is a celebration of man and ultimately positive in its outlook. In it, Bronowski stated that there is no absolute knowledge and that all information is imperfect. With this, he indicated the limitations to how much credence we should pay to our unravelling of the laws of nature.

Thus, our quest for truth will always be limited by the possibility that it could all be wrong. What we see as testable truths may just be our 'best-fit' interpretations of observations. Yet, as we use our knowledge to progress technologically, there is at least an element of 'worthwhile' truth to it. We can only work with the mental and physical tools we have and evolve along the course that our progress has cut.

Numbers and the infinite

Humankind has developed technologically by understanding and manipulating the concept of number. By identifying and applying rules to number manipulation and relating these to the world around us, an increasingly complex understanding of mathematics and physics has evolved. This process started with simple whole numbers (integers) and simple shapes (e.g., the circle) and their relations. Yet a number is not a thing but an abstract concept. They exist in the sense of Platonic idealism, but not as atoms exist. They require consciousness for their discovery, rather than possessing an innate physical existence.

Platonic realism states that mathematics does not create 'objects', but discovers them (like discovering a new planet). Thus, mathematical 'objects' exist prior to discovery rather than being created. The equation $E = mc^2$ was discovered by Einstein as a relationship that is a truth of physical reality, and the equation represents how an aspect of reality behaves. He did not create the behaviour; rather, he discovered the equation that describes the behavioural truth.

Platonism states that such 'objects' (e.g., concepts and classes) do not belong to the physicality of spacetime, but to a domain accessible only to the intellect. This domain presents the perfection of forms, which are represented in reality as imperfect forms. The perfect circle I have in mind cannot be matched in the phenomenal world. For instance, we take the 'number' 6.55 for granted, but this had to be 'created' by man. It exists only in the mind of intelligence since there isn't a '6.55', yet there can be 6.55 of this or that. Once a number is conceived, its existence is applicable to reality.

After the Big Bang, the meaning of number was there' in terms of what it *could* mean. Number potentially existed, but needed a mind to 'discover' it. Without a conscious entity to conceive of or manipulate such concepts, a property such as 'three' atoms has no meaning. Without intelligence, the three atoms just exist, behaving according to physical laws and their innate being. Intelligence enables the understanding of these laws. To probe the essence of physical reality, the mind must construct concepts so that ideas can be modelled and tested. Among the most fundamental of concepts is the idea of number.

As our knowledge of mathematics increased, we continued to identify patterns and interesting relations between numbers. Since numbers are inextricably linked with reality, further understanding of their relations served to improve our knowledge of what reality is. Indeed, numbers and their relationships are the foundations of mathematics. This is the language of physics, which is the fundamental describer of physical reality.

We associate the concept of infinity with numbers and, indeed, it is a concept used in the mathematical field. However, until Georg Cantor made it his life's work to understand this enigma, grasping infinity as anything other than a mathematical abstraction or tool had eluded all the great mathematicians before him. The number 3 can be imagined when applied to physical 'things'. We can imagine three oranges, for example. However, we cannot imagine infinity, applied or not. Yet infinity, despite being knowable only as a concept, is inextricably linked with every part of reality. Its unknowability but valid applicability is as much a part of reality as is quantum indeterminism.

Galileo had tried, unsuccessfully, to understand the infinite. He took a circle and from its centre drew, and assumed, infinite diameters to the circle's circumference. Here, he thought that all possible radii were drawn. However, if a larger circle that shared the same centre were drawn outside this circle (thus encapsulating it), then as the radii reach the larger circle's circumference, gaps appear between the radii. This enabled 'new' radii to exist, but if infinite radii had already been drawn, how was this possible?

Galileo concluded that humans could only apply infinity but not comprehend it (perhaps he was a mysterian), and he gave up any further attempts to understand it.

Why is infinity so important? It is an essential element of mathematics and, thus, the construction of our science that describes reality. It is part of reality, even if in an abstract sense. To merely apply but not understand infinity is to ignore possible insights that this fundamental component can provide about how reality is. Although we may never be able to imagine infinity as we do a material object, to gain insight into what it means provides a deeper understanding of not only mathematics but also reality itself.

Gödel and Tarski: Logic, truth, and intuition

The modern computer's performance is linked to Gödel's theorem. The computer is the embodiment of Hilbert's original dream of a formal system — one that is complete, consistent, decidable, and thus contradiction-free. However, it is susceptible to the issues of an axiomatic rule-follower. Furthermore, the theorem implies that there can never be an antivirus programme in a computer that will not alter the programme being protected, but that will detect programmes attempting to alter the programme being protected.

Gödel wanted to prove that humans can follow concepts outside the formalism and identify paradoxes intuitively, whereas formal systems cannot. His theorem *did* prove the incompleteness of formalised systems, but there is still debate about whether the human brain is like a computer or whether a mechanical brain can match the capacities, in all their conceptual glory, of the human brain. Intuition was important to Gödel in that this ability is what distinguishes the living mind from that of a computer. He considered mathematical intuition to be as true and reliable as sensory perception.

This belief in the importance of human intuition was key to Gödel's friendship with Einstein. Although Gödel's role in the development of general relativity is not well documented in the scientific literature, Gödel did make important contributions to understanding the theory. This interest must have been spurred when he and Einstein worked together at Princeton University. Their walks to and from work are the stuff of legend. Einstein said that the favourite part of his day was the honour of walking home with and talking to Gödel. Einstein's friendship as well as his shared belief in the capacity for human insight to extract truth from the *knowable* Universe were especially important to Gödel.

By a logical application of Einstein's field equations, Gödel showed that time stands still. While correct as a feasible interpretation of the equations, Einstein felt intuitively that it was wrong in the context of how things happen in the physical rather than mathematical world.

Einstein's and Gödel's faith in human intuition was decisive for whether a theory 'felt' right. Einstein's genius was linked to his insight and intuition. He felt that he knew whether some scientific idea about the nature of reality was right or wrong, as if possessed with a deep connection with reality. Gödel was insightful and brilliantly logical, which enabled him to make great strides in the field of mathematical logic. Yet, reality is not an abstract concept to be proven or disproved according to logical rules. Einstein had a feel for reality that Gödel lacked. Gödel's work on relativity produced intriguing results, but history has noted that strange things *can* happen when a logician plays with the equations of nature and pays no attention to intuition or what 'really' happens.

Nevertheless, Gödel's greatest legacy was his incompleteness theorem. At the time he presented it to the world, Hilbert had believed that mathematics could be completely axiomatised in a logical way. Being a positivist, Hilbert tried to formalise all mathematics, but Gödel's theorem proved this to be an impossible task. Thus, Gödel was essentially saying to the greatest mathematician of the time that "your dream is doomed to failure, such an axiomatisation can never happen". Hilbert sought consistency, not truth, in a complete formalised system of logic and mathematics. Gödel destroyed the hope of both consistency *and* truth. So, the theorem's conclusions were not 'satisfying' as it did not give an answer that added something that was missing from Hilbert's formalism. Rather, it explained why the systems were prone to falsehoods. It said that Hilbert could only ever achieve an essentially incomplete formalised system.

Gödel's theorem explained many things — Russell's paradox, Cantor's proof of why the universe of set theory is not a set, and even why humans and computers are conceptually different in the sense that human minds are not computers. His work shared similarities with that of Cantor and Boltzmann before him in that his revolutionary ideas conflicted with those of the time and, thus, he did not receive the immediate credit he deserved. This is typical of work that presents a paradigm shift to the accepted views of the time.

Gödel also shared similarities with Cantor and Boltzmann in another sense. After his incompleteness theorem, he decided to address the subject of infinity using logic and continue working on the problems that had driven Cantor to deep depression and possibly madness. This endeavour was risky considering Gödel's own fragile psychological makeup and his lack of popularity among fellow logicians (he had, after all, shown logic is internally inconsistent). Indeed, after Einstein died, he felt increasingly fragile, paranoid, and isolated. As Gödel probed the infinite, he, like Cantor, drove himself to despair. He died weighing barely 90lbs, apparently having starved himself to death due to fear that people were trying to poison him.

When one considers the famous paradoxical statement "all Cretans are liars" by the Cretan philosopher Epimenides, the brain cannot make sense of it *if* it sticks to the logical rules of the statement. However, obviously we can 'see' the flaw, which a computer cannot, because we also exist outside the rule-following system of analysis. The inescapable incompleteness of a complex formal system was seen by Gödel but not by Bertrand Russell or his contemporaries, because they were caught by the apparent clarity and infallibility of the notion of 'class'.

Human thought, insight, and understanding cannot be reduced to a set of rules, so we are not impeded by the same constraints. For a paradox such as Russell's Paradox (basically a problem of set theory where a set can be defined as both a member and not a member of itself, leading to a disturbing paradox: see Chapter 1), human minds are capable of resolving the paradox as access to external physical reality adds to the analytical system, providing information that 'shows' what cannot be.

Gödel's 1931 proof depended on writing a self-referential mathematical statement in the same way that the Epimenides paradox is a self-referential statement of language. Thus, the genius of Gödel linked self-referential statements with number theory. Gödel also realised that the symbolism of Newton's *Principia* could be replaced with numbers. From this, he made the *Principia* its own subject. Thus, a formula of the *Principia* could say, "This formula cannot be proven using the rules of the *Principia*."

One must not assume after Gödel's findings about systems such as the *Principia* that mathematicians did not try to find a mathematical way out. Hilbert thought that he had found a way to prove the consistency of a system that was comprehensive enough to contain all arithmetic (e.g., *Principia*) by using what is known as *metamathematics*. Mathematics represents the formal systems that mathematicians use, whereas metamathematics is the discussion and theorising about mathematical formal systems. "2 + 2 = 4" is a mathematical statement; "2 + 2 = 4 is true" is a metamathematical statement. Gödel concluded, however, that it is impossible to give a metamathematical proof of the consistency of a system such as *Principia* unless the proof uses inferences alien to the derivation theorems within the system. Furthermore, metamathematical considerations were already intrinsic to Gödel's incompleteness theorem.

So, whereas the *Principia* aimed to formalise mathematics, it actually displayed the incompleteness of 'complete' formal arithmetic systems. Not only is the system of the *Principia* incomplete, it is *essentially* incomplete. Goldbach's theorem demonstrates this. Presented in 1742 in a letter to the leading mathematician of the time, the Swiss Leonhard Euler, this theorem states that every even number is the sum of two primes. No example has ever been found to refute this, yet no proof has been found to show that this conjecture applies to all even numbers.

So, the arithmetical statement may be true, but is non-derivable from axioms of a formal version of number theory. Remember, proof and truth relate to our capacity for interpretation of reality and may not relate to ultimate truth (as in the case of Kant's noumenal world). Ultimate truth, if possible and in any sense real, is of no use to us as we deal with the phenomenal world. Only that which we interact with at the same level has phenomenal truth.

All formulas constructed by man that are not (yet) falsified by experiment can be seen as representing Platonic truths, and yet we must ultimately accept that they present truths according to the limits of insight and testability by our physical and mental making. What lies as ultimate truth, if indeed there is such a thing, may forever be unknowable to us.

From Gödel's work, we can say that number-theoretical truths can only be produced in an inconsistent axiomatic system (the axiomatic method involves accepting without proof certain propositions as axioms, such as the two angles of a right-angled triangle equalling the right angle when added together). Thus, whatever axiomatic system is used, provability is weaker than truth. However, despite the incompleteness of number-theoretical truths, the world still functions. Numbers as abstractions are different from numbers which we use to create physical reality. It seems like there is some transition between the reality of numbers and those on paper.

The Hungarian-born physicist and priest Stanley Jaki (1924–2009) was among the first to link Gödel's theorem with a TOE. He, and later Stephen Hawking, believed that Gödel's theorem implies that any theory of physics that claims to be a GUT or TOE will be incomplete. Indeed, since a TOE must be complete, it must also be inconsistent. Jaki and others believed that a theory formulated as a finite number of principles and known for certain as 'final' is impossible.

The Polish philosopher Alfred Tarski (1902–1983) clarified during the same year as Gödel's proof that the inference from this incompletion of classes, as demonstrated by these self-referential paradoxes, is that there is no complete language of science. If any scientific statement contains the term 'is true', it becomes bound by the same paradox demonstrated by Epimenides's statement.

The American logical philosopher Saul Kripke showed that there are different levels of truth. There are 'necessary truths', which apply in *all possible worlds*, and 'contingent truths', which are applicable to *certain circumstances*. That I am typing these words is a contingent truth because I might have done something else, according to Kripke. That prime numbers are not divisible by any whole number other than themselves is a necessary truth, because it applies in all possible cases. What I will say, and have done, about truth here relates to truth from a formal approach. However, if I say that there are nine planets orbiting our Sun (if we accept Pluto as a planet), then this is a truth, but one that is conceptually different from formal truth. It can only be proven untrue by experimentation.

Thus, in the real world of physical things rather than abstract concepts, axiomatic systems, and the like, falsification is the best way to determine if something is true. Furthermore, it is only true until proven false. So, physical truth is not ultimate, unquestionable, and irrefutable truth; rather, it is that which has not yet been shown to be wrong. Does this mean that logical truths are purer and deeper in their meaning? Maybe so.

Tarski showed that truth is a property of sentences, not of the world. Important for any definition of truth is the distinction between an *object language* and a *meta-language*. A sentence in English (or some other natural language), such as 'grass is green', asserts something of another sentence. This is characteristic of a meta-language. English is its own meta-language, which is what Tarski called a 'semantically closed' language. The formal language of mathematics, logic, and computer programming are 'semantically open', and Tarski believed that only semantically open languages can have a definition of truth. For natural languages such as English, the object language and meta-language are identical, leading to paradoxes such as that of Epimenides. Conscious users of such language can identify some such paradoxes due to intuitive insight outside the paradoxical system.

Given Tarski's statement that truth is a property of sentences and not the world, then the statement "all even numbers aren't odd" is true for language, but not the world. Language can also include statements such as "what I'm saying is false", making it prone to self-referential paradoxes. Language is used to relate to the external world, yet to know when a proposition is paradoxical requires the ability to conceive the proposition and interpret its sense. Since thought processes, as interplay of imagery, symbolism, and words, are not understood as a process, we do not know the rules that apply when the mind thinks. But we are looking at how language and thought relates to reality and truth. Knowledge of these things is knowledge for some conscious thing (us).

Truth is only possible for an open language because it can be ascribed from 'outside' the language via meta-language. Thus, Tarski was pessimistic about the possibility of truth for a natural, closed language, such as those that human beings speak. Furthermore, by using an open language, computers cannot be intelligent since they are unaware of the Epimenides-type paradoxes that occur when object and meta-languages are identical.

How does this affect scientific truth? It does not make science a waste of time, but we have to accept that for any experimental result where a conclusion is found or a truth is stated, that truth is bound by self-reference and is only correct within these confines. Put simply, we cannot do meaningful science without stating that this or that is true. Yet, when we do, this language creates self-references that lead to paradoxes.

Thus, we appreciate that the methods we use to delineate and understand the world around us are limited. Fortunately, mathematics, science, and logic work in a useable sense, despite utilising paradox-prone systems.

If I say that something is true about physical reality, such as "protein X activates protein Y in human cells", and this statement is the result of scientific experiment, then it is considered true because the experiments provide results that verify it. It continues to be accepted as true until another experiment falsifies the result. As we have seen, that is the scientific method. However, truths from the scientific method are not necessary truths but working models of truth from a particular context.

Stating that something analysed through phenomena is true cannot serve as actual or necessary truth because we have no way of knowing that it cannot be falsified. Truth about physical things is knowledge of those things in terms of how they relate to and are perceived and interpreted by an entity with limits. Thus, our physical and mental limitations that prevent us from attaining absolute truth, together with the fact that physical truth relates to these limitations, means that ultimate or noumenal truth of physical things is meaningless — it is always a point of knowledge on a path to an unattainable truth.

Truth has a different type of meaning for knowledge of concepts, relationships, ideas, and the like than it does for knowledge of the innate properties of physical things. However, the former relates to the latter. Knowledge of an idea may be complete because it can be encapsulated in its entirety in the mind, but the idea relates to physical reality. This linkage requires a change or a contortion of form, rendering knowledge of the innate nature of physical reality incomplete. Let us be mindful of the fact that our knowledge of physical things is formulated using ideas and concepts, which manipulate information extracted from physical reality. Although the mind assesses reality, it is also part of reality, so it cannot be entirely objective about what it is part of. It has to be affected by reality at some level.

We try to be objective when we think about a part of physical reality, but the subject-object division can never be fully attained. Knowledge and truth must be understood as relative for a finite, limited, and conscious entity who is embedded within reality. David Bohm paid more attention to this than did most of his contemporaries and attempted to construct an understanding of reality as a whole and implicate order, where everything is connected and interdependent. His description of quantum theory on these grounds is ingenious in that his non-local, hidden variable description of reality preserves realism while removing the philosophical dilemmas intrinsic to the Copenhagen interpretation of quantum theory (i.e., a quantum 'object' is not real until measured).

The nature of physical reality, external to our minds, is addressed by the scientific method. Ideas can be manipulated in the mind to be free from the physical constraints of the laws of material physics. Although ideas are part of reality and thus conform to the laws of reality (if there are any), they are not constrained to the laws of physics that apply to their physical counterparts outside the mind. Thus, the mind can investigate possibilities for reality that do not actually happen and, in doing so, help to reason about what does happen. However, the 'freedom' of thought is still only free in the context of being constrained by what the mind is — a part of the reality that *is*.

When I think about how things are, those thoughts cannot be anything other than what is possible for a being that exists in reality. The mind cannot construct its mental imagery around a world it has not experienced; it relates to the one in which it is embedded. The laws of physics apply to matter and its interactions and processes in external reality, whereas how reality *is* determines what the mind is and, thus, what it can do. We cannot think of what reality is not.

So, the mind can think of things that can and cannot happen, and together with the intellect, it interprets what does happen. That is, the capacity to think of both what can and cannot happen — even without knowing if it cannot happen — married with intellectually analysing and interpreting the results of things that do happen, gives us the capacity to reason why they happen. If the mind were constrained by the same rules of physical reality as that of the body, then we would not have such a huge capacity for creativity.

The thought of a physical thing produces a mental representation of it. Here, while it can then be in the mind, 'that' being is of a form that is alien to its reality. That representation is what is analysed and extrapolated back onto the objectively real counterpart, for which we claim to have attained some truth of. The interplay of mental, sensory, and physical manipulation of physical things as well as the ideas of them generates knowledge of both the thing itself and the idea of it.

Knowledge attained this way conforms to our 'version' of reality. It comprises whatever we experience as the phenomenal world and it is what our minds, physiology, language, systems of analysis, logic, temporal-binding, and so on limit us to. Beyond that (which Leibniz conceived of as omnipotence and is thus accessible only to God), what constitutes the 'true' reality that *is* is something we acknowledge as perhaps Kant's noumenal truth, but it is of a form that we do not or cannot know.

Although J. B. S. Haldane said that "the world may be stranger than we are capable of imagining" and d'Espagnat believed that the true nature of reality is veiled from our access, they were both referring to a knowable reality but which is not knowable to us (as mysterians believe). Only omnipotence can 'know' all reality in the way that we can 'know' our own conscious states.

Implications of Gödel's theorem

Gödel's theorem is a much-abused result in mathematic logic because the implications that have been extrapolated from the theorem extend beyond what it really says. There are two common misunderstandings:

1. The first is that Gödel's theorem imposes a fundamental limitation on knowledge and, thus, physics and mathematics, which is simply not the case. The theorem applies to deductions from axioms, which is only one of many sources of knowledge we use as a tool to understand reality.
2. Some say that that Gödel's theorem proves the impossibility of AI. That is, machines cannot think. Since machines are evolving very rapidly, it is a brave assumption, but the conclusion is based on a simple argument — since axiomatic systems are equivalent to Turing machines (see next section) and computers are close approximations of this, and as there are truths that cannot be deduced by such axiomatic systems, then there are truths that cannot be obtained by computers. As humans can achieve these truths (results) since we are not bound by such rules, therefore our mind cannot be represented by a computer and thus we are not computational machines. However, saying AI is impossible by

such an argument follows a thread of logic where there is no unequivocal proof.

Douglas Hofstadter and artificial intelligence

Gödel uncovered problems relating human intelligence to AI. Thus, it seems appropriate to mention here some of the points made in Hofstadter's 1979 book, *Gödel, Escher, Bach: An Eternal Golden Braid*. This book addresses how a self can come from inanimate matter. Hofstadter uses the conclusions of Gödel to question whether words and thoughts follow formal rules.

Ultimately, Hofstadter thinks that the answer is yes, provided one goes to the lowest level — that of the hardware (i.e., the neurons, of which the human brain possesses about a hundred billion) — to find the rules. This is because when we think — and thoughts represent the software — we continually change the rules, but the hardware that is composed of neurons remains the same, so their rules do not change. They can only act in a neuronal way, such as the release of neurotransmitters, firing of synapses, *et cetera*. Furthermore, accessing our thoughts enables us to change the rules, but we cannot change our neurons except through the action of a third party, such as surgery or an accident.

His book assesses the impact of Gödel's finding on computers and intelligent systems, particularly that of humans and the future of AI. It compares AI with human intelligence, speculates on the limits for AI, and assesses how Gödel's findings about self-reference impact on human thought about our own brains, minds, free will, and consciousness. The book does not analyse whether a machine could collapse a wavefunction and, thus, whether intelligence and consciousness are linked to quantum reality. If a machine could collapse the wavepacket, then (human) consciousness would lose its unique role in the solution to the measurement problem. Hofstadter questions how thought can be supported by the hardware of the brain. From this, he discusses the relation between concepts and neural activity. He questions what all human brains have in common.

There is a lengthy analysis of the argument put forward by the Oxford philosopher John Randolph Lucas that Gödel's theorem demonstrates that human thought cannot be seen as mechanical, which Hofstadter finds flawed. Hofstadter is, however, in the minority by thinking that machines can be conscious. Lucas claims that Gödel's theorem proves that mechanism is false and that minds cannot be explained by machines. Lucas emphasises that there are some statements of number theory that humans can make which are true, and yet a computer is blind to their truth and cannot be programmed to see, thus making humans more intelligent.

Hofstadter sees this as wrong due to the issue of being able to 'Gödelise' (as Hofstadter terms the operation) or make the dimensional jump. Thus, humans are able to come out of the self-referential loop, but computers will have to be programmed to deal with such loops (although we cannot predict all of them) or AI must be advanced enough to enable the computer to do so itself.

The future of AI seems to be that as the intelligence of machines evolves, the mechanisms converge with those of human intelligence. Hofstadter sees all intelligence as variations on a single theme and that for machines to achieve human intelligence, their mechanisms must parallel those of human thought. But if they parallel human thought, that is saying that to have human mental attributes is to have human-like mental processes, which is not really claiming much. The achievement will be to artificially create what we do in our minds. Whether machines will ever be able to do this is another question. If such a solution is achieved, then it confirms that human-like mental processes produce intelligence, but not whether a wholly distinct mechanism can.

It seems unlikely that AI can generate qualia, irrespective of the form of AI model, because as Humphrey convincingly speculates, the richness of sensory experience, which is clearly linked to qualia, evolved by natural selection. Thus, *all* human mental attributes that constitute consciousness evolved in a mind within a body that interacts with a physical world. Without this interaction, the rich experience of sensation and qualia would seem less important. A machine, without *needing* these qualities to evolve and also not having to evolve at all under selective pressure, exist as hardware and software through a different course. Machines are human constructions whereas humans are the crowning achievement of the toughest test — billions of years of evolution. Without the sensations from experiencing objective reality, mechanistic parallels of human thought will lack the essence that characterises it.

It is interesting that Lucas thinks that minds cannot be explained as machines, because it brings to mind some ideas on this subject by Heidegger. He stated that by existing, a human has a mode of access to the world that cannot be rendered explicit in theory. Thus, a computer can never be constructed to possess the ability to understand contexts and situations that living beings such as humans take for granted. Heidegger generated this view from the idea that by contemplating the world, even when we attempt to be objective about it from a neutral stance, this objectivity is already an interpretation.

The parts of the world we contemplate are posited as more real than others. When this idea is used to compare machines and mind, it seems that our holistic understanding of the world creates an interpretation through intelligence that, if mimicked by machines, will be deficient in the crucial areas of sensual appreciation and interaction and render them less able. Heidegger was clearly mindful that a mind interacting with objective reality possesses qualities that one which is purely internal to its own processes does not.

In *Gödel, Escher, Bach: An Eternal Golden Braid*, Hofstadter compares biological and non-biological self-reproducing entities (e.g., computer programmes and DNA molecules) and their relation to external mechanisms that enable this self-reproduction (e.g., computers and proteins, respectively). While DNA is not self-reproducing, it can be replicated within a complex multi-protein/DNA mechanism involving the actions of various enzymes upon DNA, as we have seen in Chapter 4. However, it can be considered self-ordering, given the specificity of Watson-Crick base-pairing such that the base adenine (A) always pairs with thymine (T) while cytosine (C) pairs with guanine (G). Thus, during DNA replication and cell division, each strand acts as a template to construct the correct counterpart strand of the double helix. Hofstadter analyses the similarities between biological and non-biological mechanisms by which information travels between levels of a system.

He goes on to discuss methods of discerning the presence of 'thought' in a machine, paying particular attention to the pioneering work of Alan Turing and his famous 'Turing test' (or 'imitation game'), which sets out to determine whether machines can think. He investigates the model and goal for AI, leading to speculations on the concept of creativity and how self-reference impacts society (e.g., science probing science, governments investigating governmental wrongdoing). He questions how Gödel's theorem affects such processes, especially that of how the human brain can think about itself.

Before we look in more detail at some of the points raised, it will be appropriate to say a little about the enigmatic character that is Turing and his work relating to these issues.

Alan Turing

Alan Turing (1912–1954) lived a relatively short and tragic life, but in it he achieved much. He is most famous for his association with both the development of computer science and cracking the German Enigma code during World War II. His influence was wide-reaching.

In his pioneering work on the application of mathematical logic to computer science, he came up with the idea of what has come to be immortalised as a *Turing machine*. This is a simple theoretical computer with an infinite length of tape on which to store data, and it works by moving back and forward along the tape according to a programme. The programme itself can be stored on the tape, and these machines are called *universal Turing machines*.

Of importance here is that he proved, in an influential paper in 1936 using the idea of the Turing machine, that no algorithm can determine whether any arbitrary programme halts. This is called the halting problem and it is Turing's version of Gödel's incompleteness theorem. Indeed, the ideas and proofs of Turing's solution to the halting problem are similar to those of Gödel's incompleteness theorem. Turing's work on the halting problem placed Gödel's theorem in a different and more digestible context. It clarified and refocused Gödel's incompleteness theorem by stating the specific problems with computability and unknowability.

The halting problem is a problem of decision-making in the context of computability theory. It asks, "If there is a programme with a finite input, and there is both unlimited time and memory for the programme to execute its function before halting, then will it ever halt on some particular input?" Thus, the halting problem asks whether the programme will run forever or finish running given the input.

Turing programmes either halt when a result is achieved or continue *ad infinitum*. Turing's 1936 paper proved that there is no mechanical procedure that tells us whether a Turing machine performing some calculation on an input will halt given that input. That is, a general algorithm that can solve the halting problem for any programme/input (data) pair *cannot* exist. Thus, for Turing machines, the halting problem is undecidable (remember that Gödel proved that any formal axiomatic system will essentially include internal undecidable propositions).

The halting problem was, in fact, one of the first problems that was proven to be undecidable. While the halting problem relates to Gödel's incompleteness theorem in structure and applies to computability, it also has ramifications for the difference between humans and computers as well as whether humans are machines. Indeed, this was a key concern and point of interest to Turing, and his views on the subject differed from Gödel's. Gödel believed that a human could halt an unprovable problem because we possess what a computer does not — intuition. We can see 'outside' of the problem, just like we can *see* the paradox of Russell's paradox, and determine if it would be a lost cause to persist.

It is believed that Turing considered (or hoped for) the human mind to be a machine, whereas Gödel thought that the mind was different. Gödel, like Einstein, believed that human intuition was the essential element behind creativity and the resolution of paradoxes that purely formal systems of analysis were susceptible to. However, Gödel's need to *prove* intuition was logically impossible, and his failure to do so was part of the reason why he lost his grip on sanity and starved himself to death. Like Cantor and his search for the continuum hypothesis, Gödel's mind could not find a solution because the problem's boundaries exceeded the mechanism of human thought.

Turing was interested in whether machines can think. He set out his ideas to test whether machines can demonstrate intelligence in his 1950 paper, *Computing Machinery and Intelligence*. Here, he proposed a *gedanken* experiment with a hypothetical test that he later termed the *Turing test*. In it, one person acting as the experimental judge converses with another person and a machine, both of which are behind a panel so the judge cannot determine which is which by sight. A keyboard and screen are used so that no voice gives the game away. The machine and person attempt to appear human, and the judge must determine who is the human (knowing that only one is). If the human judge fails to detect the human, then the machine passes the test.

John Searle has proposed an argument against the Turing test in many of his publications on mind and consciousness (since his 1980 paper, *Minds, Brains and Programmes*). His *'Chinese room' gedanken* experiment stresses a misinterpretation of or by the Turing test. Searle believes that software could pass the Turing test merely through the manipulation of symbols of which it has no comprehension. Therefore, although the software is mimicking human behaviour, it is not thinking like a human and thus its ability to pass merely indicates the test's flaws. Why is it called the Chinese room experiment? If a programme receives Chinese character input and produces new Chinese character output such that a Chinese-speaking human believes that the programme speaks Chinese, then the programme has passed the Turing test.

Moreover, it might seem convincing that the programme *understands* Chinese. But Searle points out that if he had a book that translated the programme into English, then he could manipulate the Chinese characters just as the programme did without understanding the meaning of any of the characters. Thus, it becomes a case of the manipulation of meaningless symbols according to instructions rather than true understanding. In doing so, he would produce the same results as the programme and thus pass the Turing test. Although he knows no Chinese, according to the test he is fluent. Searle takes things further and stresses that although rule-following computers can rapidly present correct answers, they cannot 'understand' in the same way a conscious human mind can.

The study of incompleteness, undecidability, unknowability, and infinity has caused misery and desperation for many who have been seduced by their paradoxes. Whether this is due to the innate psychological makeup of those able and driven to probe the depths of these subjects or the fact that the subject matter itself is innately unsettling and controversial remains a matter of debate. Like Gödel, Boltzmann, and Cantor, Turing suffered, albeit for different reasons. Living as a homosexual early into the Cold War during the repressive 1950s in Britain and working on matters of national importance, Turing was subjected to treatment that would be considered a violation of basic human rights today. He was injected with female hormones to quash his homosexuality, causing his body and mind to change and driving him to suicide. For an excellent intellectual biography of this great man, see *Alan Turing: The Enigma of Intelligence* by Andrew Hodges.

Strange loops and artificial intelligence

Hofstadter talks of the strange loop. which is a phenomenon that occurs whenever one moves up or down through the levels of a hierarchical system and finds oneself back at where one starts. This characteristic of an incomplete axiomatic system permeates art and music.

In M. C. Escher's drawing *Waterfall*, the centre defines the strange loop. The drawing must, essentially, be incomplete. It is a pictorial version of Gödel's theorem. Another of Escher's work, *Circle Limit I*, is a Euclidean representation of Lobachevskian space. Thus, Escher's work, in its many forms, constitutes graphical illustrations of aspects of human knowledge where understanding is essentially or otherwise incomplete. Johann Sebastian Bach's canons and fugues also display the strange loop effect. Therefore, Escher and J. S. Bach's works are musical and artistic representations of the Epimenides Paradox, which Gödel's theorem explains (hence the title of Hofstadter's book, *Gödel, Escher, Bach: An Eternal Golden Braid*). As stated earlier, Hofstadter sees this effect in many places, even in the biological world (e.g., in the flow of information between DNA and protein).

The border between intelligence and non-intelligence is a hazy one. Hofstadter believes that strange loops, which possess rules that change themselves, are at the core of intelligence. Since the human mind is so complex, it is difficult to see how we can fully understand human intelligence. We may develop deep insight into complex mental processes, but the understanding will be limited by the mechanism of our mental framework. Because of an inherent property of intelligence that allows humans to jump out of the tasks they are performing and survey what has been done, humans are not stumped by the Epimenides paradox.

To understand intelligence itself, we are caught in the trap of trying to use something (the mind) to understand the quintessence of that thing (intelligence), which is a case of the self analysing the self. Can we really step back from or out of ourselves to evaluate ourselves, notwithstanding the fact that we are using the same mechanism to interpret itself? We are limited by the rules governed by what we are made of and how these can function. Objectivity about the subject — our own mind — is difficult.

Is understanding human intelligence a catch-22 situation? To be free from the constraints described above, one must be non-human to analyse it. But being non-human prevents us from knowing what it is to *be* human. Must one experience something to know it? But with this argument, are we even able to analyse the intellect of any species on Earth (e.g., chimpanzees)? As we continue to realise, the level of understanding and 'truth' that we attain is that which is useably beneficial but not a statement of fact about absolute truth. All truth is *our* human truth, and even that is 'true' until falsified or when a new version takes its place.

Since Turing's ground-breaking work on computer intelligence in the 1950s, scepticism was already present that machines would never be kind, resourceful, beautiful, friendly, amusing, capable of falling in love (the 2013 film *Her* uses this idea as its central theme), the subject of their own thought, and such like. Many of these doubts are still current. They are qualities that exist in a sentient entity that interacts physically with its environment.

The computer gaming and AI specialist Arthur Samuel (1901–1990) thought that no computer 'wants' to do anything because computers are programmed by someone else. There is the argument that only in the hypothetical scenario of a computer programming itself from zero would it have its own sense of desire. But by that same argument, only if a human designed himself and chose his own wants could he be said to have a will of his own. Thus, this argument does not differentiate the human from the machine. As AI progresses, the comparison with human intelligence demonstrates divergence in some aspects but convergence in others. The likelihood of complete convergence is remote.

As AI programmes become more 'intelligent', their 'worldview' will increasingly diverge from ours. As intelligence is tied to speed of thought, perception, and thus physical capabilities to assimilate information, the concepts of each would accordingly differ to describe the world. As the programme would undoubtedly have a different hardware and software from a human, its perspectives on what counts as important would be different too.

Two points exemplify differences when comparing the potential for AI with the human brain. First, human intelligence extends from an interacting entity. Human processes have been subject to external environmental pressures that have guided and determined all that a human is (although the mind of the human has overcome these pressures somewhat and possesses properties that transcend the physical). The mind of the human exists in, interacts with, and is part of a body that responds to the senses — we hear, see, smell, taste, and touch — and each of these influences our mental process. AI cannot possess this same interaction. A machine is mind, whereas a human is mind-body.

The mechanism of brain function can be mimicked, but the mind, which is affected by physical reality, is unique to an entity that 'experiences' life. The mind is more than the sum of its parts. It is more than its mechanism because its mechanism is driven and affected by not only what it physically is but also all that it interacts with — the world around us.

While AI software is prone to Gödelian paradoxes, the human mind can see through them and sense their futility because it interacts with physical reality. If, like AI software, we existed purely as a mental state, then these paradoxes would affect us too. By being a mind-body that interacts with the physical world which is external to the programme, we are freed from these paradoxes because the sensory input from the physical world acts as the additional information necessary to make an incomplete analytical system complete, thus closing the loop. Furthermore, our minds care to know about the world because it is inextricably linked to physical reality through the body.

Present in different levels of our mind are the interpretations of all that our senses have experienced, which affect and are affected by our conscious thought. Perhaps AI can mimic a brain's function, but it seems highly unlikely that it will ever be like the mind of a living thing. Hofstadter says that the brain is rational but the mind may not be, and this is to our evolutionary benefit (somewhat like Humphrey's view on the richness of conscious experience). The process of human thought incorporates the ability to reconsider what is considered; a machine may be faster, but its solution to a problem is its one and only solution.

The second point is that despite human existence being facilitated through natural selection, there was no predetermined goal for intelligence or consciousness. The idea that humans with a richer sensory experience have a greater chance of survival and the idea that natural selection is 'looking' for this capacity from the start are not the same thing. The point here is the goal for AI. Evolution does not have conscious foresight for the development of an unknown process that will benefit the genes that contribute to this ability, but those *with* this ability are more likely to survive and reproduce. AI *has* a goal — intelligence. In addition, it has man as a template of what intelligence is, and it is man too who models AI on this very template.

Given that human intelligence and all its sensory richness evolved under the constraints of its hardware's machinery (DNA, fundamentally) in a non-goal-orientated direction, why does AI research follow brain function so closely when it has the luxury of designing from scratch and with a specific purpose? Is it because the brain is the only model we know that works, that the brain is seen as 'as good as it gets', or are we on the wrong path for creating the best possible AI? Do the limitations that result from Gödel's theorem restrict our path to the one that we follow? Only time will tell.

The British philosopher of mind, Peter Hacker, states in his book *Wittgenstein* that we need not fear that machines will out-think us, but we should fear that they might lead us to cease to think for ourselves. Hacker says that while machines do not lack computational power, they do lack animality. There is a fundamental difference here between humans and machines. The root of thought as we 'know' it is desire, suffering, hope, and frustration, not mechanical computation. Machines cannot think as we do because they cannot feel. They do not experience qualia. They are a thinking machine, not a mind functioning from a brain that is part of a sensory and interacting organism.

In *The Psychology of Invention in The Mathematical Field*, Hadamard discusses about how scientists know they have produced the correct result to some problem without consciously thinking about it. That is, they know they have the correct result by virtue of a mere 'sensation', which they know will be proven correct through conscious thought. This is part of being 'alive', and while machines might be able to achieve more than we can computationally, there is an additional element that extends from being alive which a programme will not experience because they do not interact with sensations caused by living both inside and outside the programme.

A machine cannot feel emotion or sensations resultant from perception. Creativity, a part of intellect, is dependent on these. Trying to programme and compute sensation in an AI context will not simulate it appropriately. Sensation is an effect that comes from outside the programme, which cannot be simulated internally. To achieve sensation would require sensation to be programmed as part of the necessity for the survival of the programme, which is currently impossible.

Reality

What we see of the world around us is not the reality itself, but our interpretation of it that has been enabled by the integration of perception, sensation, intelligence, and accumulated knowledge. About 300 years ago, it was wrongly thought that we could know the nature of the world without empirical considerations. Our strongest sense is sight. We use vision to generate our impression of the world, yet what we see is not exactly what is there but merely our impression of it according to our particular physiology.

Different animals possess differently composed visual systems. For instance, some insects perceive wavelengths we cannot, and snakes see in the infra-red region consistent with heat emitted from warm-blooded prey. Thus, the images received by their brains (irrespective of interpretation) are different from ours. With so many species existing on Earth with their differing complexities of visual systems, the perceived realities will be different. It is all relative.

To know reality requires sentience. Asking what reality means to a rock is meaningless. A rock exists to you or I, but not to itself. If life had never existed in the Universe, then there would be no sentience to perceive reality. So, reality is only relevant and meaningful when it relates to matter in a form that considers it meaningful. It makes sense according to the way it is perceived, analysed, and interpreted. Thus, the brain, body and senses must be essentially linked to the reality in which it exists. Without the interpretable correlation between stimulus, perception, and sensation, we would not be able to make sense and manipulate it for our benefit.

iv) Mental Prowess

The human mind is more advanced than that of any other organism such that we have become able to adapt and use our environment and make ourselves the masters of the Earth. We are less efficient than many species in terms of our senses and physical abilities, but it is our mental superiority that has given us the all-important edge. It enables us to have more control than any other organism for ensuring our survival.

Animals almost exclusively learn only what is necessary for survival, whereas humans are different. Practically everything distinguishing humanity from all other life is a consequence of the mind. Because of our dominance, survival is easy and thus energy is focused on advancing knowledge, culture, leisure, and so on. As such, the gap widens in many ways between humanity and all other life. Genetically, we are similar to many species, but the human mind has made us into a unique species.

Early man

In *The Inner Eye*, Humphrey suggests that what defined the evolution of early man from his ape ancestors in Africa was not the use of the thumb or walking upright, but the ability and necessity to work with others as a social group. Gorillas have relatively large and complex brains, but at the same time have a relatively uncomplicated life in practical terms. However, their group social interactions are so complex that they push their cognitive abilities to the maximum in the context of being good gorilla psychologists. Modern humans utilise their cognitive abilities in a similar way to survive and succeed in complex societies. However, we would not fare well in the primitive environment from which we and our cognitive abilities originated and evolved.

Does this mean that the move toward social behaviour was the driving force for the enlargement of the human brain and its associated abilities? It seems at least partly so. The idea is that the brain's size and ability expanded through necessity, in naturally selective survival terms, ever since early man made the step towards a socially interactive existence in Africa several million years ago.

Humphrey suggests that as the lush African forests became steadily drier through climactic change, precursors of early man split into groups that either moved to the plains (becoming early man) or stayed in the forests (remaining as apes). In the plains, the need became apparent for socially complex interdependent groups to form in order to enhance survival. Natural selective pressure favoured those groups that worked better together as a unit, and so the smarter ones who solved practical and social problems would pass their genes on to the next generation.

Neanderthal man had bigger brains than Homo sapiens, and yet they still died out. They are thought to have died out because they had smaller social networks than *Homo sapiens*. Also, when they died out some 40,000 years ago, it was coincident with a cold spell and changes to flora and fauna, so perhaps they proved less adaptable to climatic change than *Homo sapiens*.

As mentioned previously, mirror neurons in the brain fire not only when an action is done, but also when it is observed. The US-based neurologist Vilayanur Ramachandran believes that about 50,000 years ago, these became so sophisticated in humans as to cause a rapid evolution of this ability, leading to the possibility for a complex culture. This view ties in with Humphrey's ideas, and mirror neurons link to the innate psychological ability. However, it was only until 10,000 years ago that humanity invented agriculture. Here, hunting was replaced by farming and gathering by sowing. From this point on, humankind was able to focus on issues other than (or in addition to) survival. Word of mouth was replaced by the written word, which allowed each generation to start a little ahead of the one before. The application of our mind through culture, society, and technology led to the level of advancement we see today.

Ironically, however, although human consciousness probably evolved to enable people to relate to one another through innate psychological abilities, it has also enabled the construction of a type of modern society that now threatens the need for this ability. Modern human cultures, technically less advanced than the first world of western civilisation, consist of individuals who are more in tune with the components of their everyday existence. They tend to have an intimate knowledge of the environment, other people, and things with which they interact. Although we are more culturally, sociologically, and technologically advanced, we accept people and things according to the rules of society. We 'accept' people and products without need for this innate evolved ability. Humphrey sees us as increasingly subservient to the machinery of the society we have constructed and as increasingly divorced from our natural surroundings.

We accept things according to the way our society works, and the way it works is that in most cases, who and what we interact with is the end result of a process. Who is the doctor we visit at hospital, and where did the food we eat come from? We do not know, or care, so long as it is packaged in a way that we feel comfortable with, in the way that society tells us is OK. Now, much is assumed and taken care of for us as long as we comply with the system into which we are integrated. The intimate knowledge our more socially and culturally primitive human ancestors had of their world is far removed from our own structured existence.

Cultures aside, do these considerations provide a feasible explanation for why there has been such an advance in effective mental prowess of hominids over the past 500,000 years? There has been a significant increase in brain size from early man to modern man. The brain of *Australopithecus* was about a third the size of that of *Homo sapiens*. Humans originally diverged from the line that led to other living primates about 14 million years ago (although some data suggest that hybridisation may have occurred until as recent as 4 million years ago). Up to 2 million years ago, brain size increased slowly. However, in the past 2 million years, brain size has nearly tripled, mainly in the region of the frontal cortical lobes. This region is responsible for processing and integrating multiple, diverse information. It relates the self to the world and enables planning.

More importantly for this argument, the visual centre in the brain has increased considerably. This increase in size equates to development that results in an enhanced ability to adapt the environment for our benefit and is an evolutionary improvement through necessity. The density of brain cells in the human brain has also been found to be double that of chimpanzees. Of equal significance is the improved use of the manipulation of the pentadactyl limb on the hand. We are far more developed in this area than are the apes.

In this half million or so years of development, the physical foundations were being cemented that have enabled us, in the last few hundred years, to become technologically advanced. Comparing this with other evolutionary leaps in the history of biological life on Earth, we can perhaps say that giant strides in development occurred in the transition of the prokaryotic cell to the eukaryotic cell, from single-cell life to multicellularity and, in a far shorter duration of time, the enlargement and increased complexity of the human mind.

So, what made us become so different from all other creatures? The ability to adapt the environment to the benefit of the individual rather than the other way round would provide a distinct advantage over prey and enemies. Resultantly, a whole new avenue of potential history was open to early man. As Bronowski said, "human evolution is being dominated by human culture". He meant that with our early mental development, a new path for evolution had opened that was not possible for other organisms.

Modern man

The geneticist Steve Jones believes that humans are no longer evolving, and one reason for this is due to a lack of older fathers. In modern times (in western society), in a 29 year-old father for example, there have been approximately 300 cell divisions between the sperm that made him and the ones he passes on. For a 50 year-old father, there are over 1,000. The latter increases the likelihood that beneficial DNA changes such as polymorphisms are included in the progeny, hence causing greater genetic diversity.

Perhaps, however, since the timespan of human evolution is measured in thousands of generations, it is difficult for any scientist to assess adequately the effect of polymorphisms within their own lifetime. Evolution 'in real time' may hold for Darwin's finches on the Galapagos Islands, as noted by the studies of evolutionary biologists Peter and Rosemary Grant over the past 30 years or so, but perhaps not for *Homo sapiens*. Indeed, the complexity of human social reality means that evolution by natural selection has very little meaning.

It seems that our ability to learn and build with each generation increasingly removes the human component necessary for it to function.

We are becoming dependent on and intertwined with technology. This is, on the whole, beneficial for humankind in terms of progress.

Perhaps it is a good thing that testing hypotheses and interpreting data cannot keep pace with creativity and slows progression, as it affords us some time to reflect and gives our non-unified global morality time to accommodate. History has taught us that that our aggressive, greedy, exploitative, selfish, and wasteful nature often predominates over insights we have accumulated from past errors. We see but too often choose to ignore. These negative traits will continue to prosper so long as societies reward them in the short-term. Perhaps our awareness as mortal beings and the fundamental driving force of evolution expressed in a highly intelligent, conscious being necessitates a huge paradigm shift in society for us to preserve the world we have before it is too late.

Learning

To the uninitiated, science can appear bafflingly complex. Anything new presents obstacles for mastery, whether it is physical or mental in nature. Every scientific idea in existence had to be conceived, theorised, and conceptualised. Of course, individuals vary in aptitude and the human race demonstrates huge extremes in ability for physical and mental excellence. For each, ability increases with nurture.

For intellectual pursuits, such as learning about science, the knowledge and confidence that an individual acquires while stimulating the mind about the subject enhances the potential for deeper insight into it. The more we learn and understand, the more formed, accurate, and constructively malleable the mental playing field is on which to exert one's creativity on the subject. For science, the reward from learning about the physical construction of reality is that it enriches life. It provides an honest, logical framework from which a measured perspective on existence is possible. It gives sense and meaning to the way the world works.

Thought

Thoughts do not just appear; there must be a stimulus. Not just an external stimulus that we react to, but also one of an internal origin that leads to conscious assessment. We talk of incubation followed by illumination of a thought. We incubate the idea, where no conscious thought is perceived, and then it is made apparent by illumination in full consciousness.

Thought and its processes has long caused debate. The philologist Max Muller claimed that thought is impossible without words, whereas George Berkeley said that words are the impediment to thought. Perhaps the mechanism of thought differs for different people (Hadamard was convinced of this). Many great creative minds utilised different symbolic and linguistic methods to achieve their insights. If there are different mechanisms that *can* be used in thought processes, then it seems that different people favour do one over another, although what physiological and/or psychological reasons define this difference is unknown.

It is clear that thought is more rapid than our ability to verbalise it. Verbalising thought is a translation where the symbolic images of the interaction between our conscious and subconscious mind is converted to a language that we have created for mutual understanding. Schopenhauer stated that thoughts die the moment they are embodied with words. Indeed, their form changes to one with constrained limits. It has also been suggested that when we allow our minds to wander, we think in images and these weaken when full, voluntary consciousness is attached. John Locke and John Stuart Mill believed that complex conscious ideas can only be considered in the presence of words. However, many scientists, especially those involved in the study of abstract concepts, will strongly disagree (see later).

One can sometimes be aware that, following a specific external stimulus, one has fully formed ideas about a subject even though one feels certain that they had not previously consciously formulated them. Therefore, such 'preformed ideas' *appear* to be rationalisations that occurred in a nonconscious way. If this were the case, then the *apparent* job of the conscious mind would be to articulate them, internally and externally. Then, although I *consider* my conscious self as the sole arena of reason, my deeper, subconscious values, intellect, and psychological states present to my conscious mind for articulation the 'type' of feelings I have about a subject in accordance with a coalescence of these contributory factors (determined by the life that moulded my psychological and intellectual profile). The idea is that, worryingly, the type of person we are is the deeper, unconscious self and that what we are conscious of is just an expressed version of this (whereas we *believe* we are always showing our true self).

Although the inner states appear to be the dominant force of the overall character, the intellect rationalises our (psychologically characteristic) intuitive thoughts and feelings in the conscious mind, so the inner impulse reaction is consciously reinterpreted before expression.

Perhaps fringe-consciousness, the closest thing to full-attention consciousness, enables us to rationalise our opinions on the multiple inputs of information we receive each day. In this way, we can nonconsciously evaluate phenomena according to our conscious mental makeup *and* keep up with the amount of information perceived and sensed, leaving the focus of our conscious mind for issues of primary concern.

v) Can We Know Reality?

As was discussed in Chapter 3, consciousness has implications for the 'measurement problem'. Where does the collapse of the wavepacket occur? Is it when the needle on the measuring device registers it, or perhaps when consciousness becomes aware of the needle registering it? If consciousness collapses the wavepacket, where and when does this actually occur?

As consciousness is a process, the collapse can only be defined as occurring over a span of time (and space). When consciousness of the needle registering the collapse occurs, this *process* of recognition cannot state the collapse as having occurred at a *point* in spacetime. Intuitively, one feels that it must occur immediately rather than over some hazy transition. So, rather than having a problem with a machine causing the collapse, we create a new one by transferring the cause to the mind. Namely, either there is no causal *point* of collapse caused by consciousness, or we need to probe the conscious process more deeply to identify how such a causal moment can exist.

We have discussed how it might not be possible to know physical reality given that we might not possess the type of mind that can know it, regardless of whether reality *is* innately unknowable. That aspect of knowing relates to making sense of the world. Absolute knowledge of physical reality as it is may be impossible. We cannot imagine the innate nature of a quantum object; we can merely intellectually rationalise it.

Niels Bohr's insight

For the measurement problem, regardless whether consciousness causes the collapse of the wavepacket, there can be no collapse without consciousness. Consciousness either causes it or is required for the design of systems that *do*. Without consciousness, there can never be an experiment to determine the 'real' state of a quantum system. In the Copenhagen interpretation, without mind to measure and isolate a real property (relative to consciousness), the distinction between a measured and quantum state is meaningless.

Bohr realised that when we apply classical mechanics to objects on the macroscopic level, we are experiencing a macroscopic illusion. Our descriptive apparatus is dominated by visual experience, which is out of the range of quantum phenomena. Thus, although it appears that we live in a quantum mechanical Universe, the classical physics that represents a higher-level approximation of quantum dynamics is of a form that is more in tune with our macroscopic interaction with reality as physical selves interacting through an embedded conscious mind. Hence, Bohr was not a determinist.

Physics does not find out how nature is, conceded Bohr, it tells us what we can say about nature. Clearly, he understood the relative aspect of our knowledge — there was no arrogance in assuming that we are revealing absolutes. Rather, information achieved reflects as much about us as it does about the reality we inhabit. Scientific knowledge discloses the subjective character of existence, according to Nadeau and Kafatos. Our physical characteristics constrain the type of knowledge we achieve, irrespective of how efficiently our minds expand the horizons of physical limitations.

Einstein, like Bohr, was aware of our relative standpoint in assessing reality. He knew that the words and language we use to describe reality have evolved in a way that naturally describes reality according to old, classical concepts. He and Bohr knew that we inevitably use classical descriptions and mental conceptions of reality since we are macroscopic perceivers.

vi) The Quantum Versus Real Division

Absolute knowledge about physical reality may be beyond us, but what about the knowledge we *do* acquire and how it relates to us? If I, the subject, observe an object through spectacles, then the spectacles are part of the subject. But as I move the spectacles away from my face, when do they cease to be the subject and start to be the object? Of course, it is to do with focus, but there is a murky boundary for the transition. Here lies the issue of how a part of physical reality can be both part of that which interprets physical reality and part of the reality that is interpreted.

This reminds one of the unclear boundary when a measurement is made of a quantum superposition. In *that* case, where is the collapse of the wavefunction occurring — the *process* of consciousness causing the *point* of collapse? Von Neumann stated this, rather murkily, as the point of interaction with a large object. Wigner deduced that it was the eye, then the brain, and then consciousness. Both demonstrate difficulties present in making definite statements about the relationship between the observer and the observed.

Reality is veiled from us, but we know *of* it. As comprehension of the distinction between 'real' and veiled reality is itself an intellectual idea, which in itself exists because of the capacity for matter to interact and produce a property that transcends matter, it enables experimental design to reveal properties of reality in a form that is recognisable to the type of being looking for it. Thus, we inevitably recognise and understand what is revealed because we conceived the theories and designed the machines to produce data that are compatible with our paradigm.

The collapse is presented to the machine which registers it, and then to the mind which understands it. As the model to identify the collapse is designed by consciousness, can we assign its cause to consciousness? According to the Copenhagen interpretation, the quantum world becomes real when measured. But measurement is more than indication, it is understanding too. As a machine is not conscious, it cannot understand, so the machine registering the collapse without conscious awareness of it is irrelevant. But a cat is conscious, so can it register and cause the collapse? No, because it does not understand what it is seeing. What then of a human who registers the collapse, but who does not understand what he or she is seeing despite having the capacity to — does he or she cause it?

Is awareness of the meaning of the machine's registration of the collapse important, and how can understanding its meaning cause it? Nothing has physically happened in the minds of the cat or different persons that *physically* cause the collapse. We assume that if one understands the measurement problem and the collapse is registered by part of a machine that is designed to cause it, then consciousness of this by the comprehending brain is what caused it. The experiment enabled it, the machine registered it, the eye observed it, and the mind comprehended it. This comprehension part seems illogical, yet so is the idea that something that does not understand the details can cause it. How can conscious understanding cause it, and yet how also could conscious non-comprehension cause it?

However, does it not also make sense that if the needle registers the collapse, whether it is understood or not, it has happened? No. Humans who recognise the collapse do so because they are involved in some way that permits them to understand the implication of the machine registering it. The collapse has occurred because of and relative to the human model of what that collapse means. Only by understanding that the collapse relates to a division between the superposition of a quantum system and a real' quality of it does the registration of the collapse mean just that.

To a machine or some consciousness that does not understand this, such as a cat, the needle on the machine pointing to 'collapse' could mean anything. A cat's eye may pass information of the collapse to its brain or a machine may register it. But a mind that understands what the collapse means is still necessary for knowing that this collapse presents information of a superposition state.

vii) Concepts that Limit Our Knowledge of the World

We can now summarise some of the concepts, many of which are interconnected, that limit and determine what we can 'know' of the world around us.

Relating to our physiology

Everything we know is relative to the type of being we are — a physical and mental entity with finite capacities. Our physically enabled mental abilities limit our ability to know a universe that is knowable or unknowable (to humans or perhaps any conscious entity). What we *can* know is limited by our physiological and mental makeup.

Consciousness as qualia exists in the brain due to processes of the brain. The brain is constituted of molecules, which comprise of atoms. Thus, atoms in certain arrangements can generate phenomena that are a transcendent quality of aggregated matter — matter comprehending itself. So, whereas matter is physical, in our minds this physicality underlies a far more profound property — the order of the interactions of matter in the brain space constitutes the wonders of the mind.

Since the building blocks of all physical components of our Universe are fundamentally the same, it is the arrangement of these constituents in the mind that enable it to be what it is. The wonder of the mind is self-evident, but as such we can easily forget or fail to recognise this staggering quality that can emerge from matter. Given that the act of comprehension is constrained to the qualities enabled by the components of physical reality, one wonders whether our comprehension of what reality 'is' is just a constrained and limited form of understanding. We cannot be objective and have a 'view from nowhere'. We are embedded as a finite, limited entity. We cannot achieve a fully objective assessment of reality.

The qualitative properties of consciousness are only knowable in the first-person sense and are inaccessible through objective scientific analysis. This cannot probe nor can language describe the essence of conscious sensation. If through scientific investigation one hopes to encapsulate the 'X factor' of consciousness through the description of its causal biological mechanism, then one is doomed to failure.

Relating to our access to reality

The behaviour of chaotic systems such as the weather can only be approximated due to the practical impossibility of acquiring complete knowledge of them. Statistical mechanics is used to approximate the behaviour of systems involving large numbers of particles according to formulated laws.

Quantum theory suggests that there is a fundamental limit to our ability to know reality and that properties at the quantum level that are knowable to us are dependent on the type of measurement made. This indeterminate viewpoint of reality is not appealing, but alternatives to this Copenhagen interpretation that attempt to create a more realist view require assumptions that are even stranger:

The measurement problem and the quantum-macroscopic interface: A superposition defines a quantum object. To access the quantum world, one must measure it, and by doing so one changes it. How we measure it determines what property of it we can know. Knowledge of the whole remains indeterminate according to limits defined by Heisenberg — this is the orthodox explanation. Superpositions have been observed in fundamental particles, atoms, and even small molecules, but they are not common in large-scale objects, such as humans.

The murky boundary between subject and object: When does something cease to be part of the subject and become part of the object (e.g., moving spectacles gradually away from the face when observing something)? Are devices we use to measure quantum properties an extension of the subject or part of the object?

Non-locality: Experimental proof of the violation of Bell's inequality reveals the Universe to be non-local. Entanglement involving four photons has been shown experimentally. The Bell inequality is not suited to test four-particle entanglement, and yet the result has been used to demonstrate the extreme contradiction between quantum mechanics and local realism: reality at the quantum level is not local. However, information we can 'use' must conform to special relativity and is local in a communicatory sense.

We could define two kinds of realism: There is epistemological realism, where science must adhere to rules and procedures to function, gain knowledge, and progress. There is also metaphysical realism, where physical reality has an existence independent of observation. The latter underlies the former, but we do not 'live' in it as such; rather, we infer it when we make a measurement of it. Thus, we understand that it is there, but by existing as organisms in an interactive, divided world from where measurements of the underlying, causal world are made, we are as detached from it (in a social sense) as we are to the implications of special relativity.

Relating to our knowledge about reality

There are infinite orders of infinity. We can conceive of them mathematically, but they cannot be grasped in a traditional sense. For example, we know that there are infinite natural numbers, but we cannot know them because the list is, quite simply, infinite. The infinite is everywhere in our physical and conceptual existence. Yet, knowing *of* the infinite is not the same as knowing the infinite. The former is knowable, the latter is intrinsically impossible.

The scientific method underlies how we extract information about the world. It presents knowledge that is relative to us, including our experimental design limits and our capacity to interpret, rather than to some fundamental truth.

What is truth? The idea that truth is "a property of sentences, not of the world" has more recently been challenged. In practical scientific terms, the physicist Richard Feynman said, "We never are definitely right, we can only be sure we are wrong." Truth is only possible for a semantically open language like a computer programme and not the semantically closed English language, because it can be ascribed from 'outside' the language in a meta-language. Thus, the human mind can assess whether something is true about a computer programme by being outside it. Nothing is outside a closed language as it is its own meta-language, so no truth can be assigned to it. Thus, truth that the human mind ascribes to the world is only relative truth.

As language, thought, and reality are not connected in a seamless flow, unavoidable alterations of meaning occur when they interrelate. The French philosopher Jacques Derrida realised that we use language to think and communicate, but there is no way of knowing how it relates to reality outside language. Since our processes of reason are constrained by linguistic rules and yet reality is not, thus reality lies beyond our capacity to understand it. To communicate thoughts, we use a shared language. Being conceptually different from thought and also limited by rules, language cannot fail to further distort ideas.

Physical reality may be *intrinsically* unknowable. If so, it explains why we cannot know it. Moreover, we may never *know* if it is unknowable, so we keep trying to know it. Conversely, even if we could determine physical reality to be knowable, we may not possess the physical and mental capacity to know it. Here, the brain organisation required to generate concepts capable of knowing it may be of a level of complexity that lies beyond an organism of our construction.

It is impossible for the finite human mind to know if there is nothing more to know of reality (i.e., that knowledge is complete) because we cannot conceive of knowledge beyond our mind's finite boundaries of capability. A theory of reality that appears complete may be so, but it may also only relate to an incomplete model. Our search for absolute truth might be like counting upwards in the search for the highest number without being aware of the concept of infinity.

Ever since Hume's attack on causality, scientific inductive reasoning tells us that experimental results inform us about the likelihood of something happening, and not if it does or will happen with certainty. Our entire scientific edifice is constructed on the inductive reasoning of causality, although we have no fundamental proof of why things occur — rather, given that they occur, our explanations are within the context of them occurring. Thus, if all of reality as we see it were a hoax, our descriptions would be nothing more than a valid description of this hoax. Scientific realism is the belief that there is a real world existing independently of the mind and, for science and philosophy to advance our understanding of reality, believing this to be the case seems to be the wisest option, especially since we cannot prove otherwise.

Many postmodernist thinkers see science as a succession of paradigms that are allied to current cultural trends. Cosmology, for example, has moved through paradigms that are Aristotelian, Ptolemaic, Copernican, Newtonian, and now, Einsteinian. Are we getting closer to the truth, or are the modifications of models more allied to the complexities of society? If the postmodernist view is true, science will be more of an indication of how society is and thinks than of how reality actually is. I do think that we are getting closer to an unreachable 'true' model of reality — a closer approximation of how things work. Yet this can only be a fine-tuning of how reality relates to us — its innate nature is hidden. If we are not 'wired' in the right way to know reality and given that we are constrained temporally, physically, and mentally, then we can only ever expect to know a fraction of what *is*.

Historically, it was believed that knowledge about reality cannot be attained by pure thought. Yet if the tools of objective science are not up to the task either, then where do we stand in finding truth? We realise that 'truth' about reality is truth relative to the type of being that *Homo sapiens* is, both physically and mentally. So, in order to progress, we link all knowledge attained from the same scientific conceptual framework, mindful of its limitations but also building an integrated and consistent whole to achieve a more accurate description of reality.

viii) My Position

Penrose's position on consciousness appears feasible because of the non-computability. It draws on and clarifies the difference between programmes and human mental processes without being inconsistent with physicalism. On the other hand, Edelman's position is also appealing because it states that the integration of neuronal groups can generate the necessary complexity and diversity for our mental world without having to accommodate any new physics. These are two well-reasoned explanations for the cause of qualia. But do they also encapsulate the essence of the experience and, if not, how do we do that? If they do, then physicalism appears to be a strong philosophical position.

Physicalism is appealing to a scientist. The idea that everything, including consciousness, is reducible to matter and force makes logical sense in the context of the Big Bang. Some think it removes the mystery and 'magic' that encapsulates the essence of conscious experience, but I disagree. Given that we will never know *why* anything exists at all, just that it does, and that all that exists does so from a point in spacetime called the Big Bang, then from a scientific point of view in a reductionist sense, everything *should* be explainable.

However, the second point that counters physicalism is that although clearly there are processes occurring in the brain that cause consciousness, knowing that they do and what they are still leaves an unanswered explanatory gap between this cause and the experience. To others, a scientific description of the processes of consciousness *is* the description of these experiences.

For science, where real world verifiability and falsifiability are paramount, the untestability of the zombie problem (alongside other hypothetical, unprovable philosophical constructions proposed as a means to destroy a complete physicalist view of reality) renders it outside of the scientific method. Yet it can be assessed from an intuitive stance within a scientific context and since we are either all zombies or none of us are, then a rejection of their existence must result from anyone asking whether or not they do exist. If we conclude that zombies do not really exist, and I do not believe that they do, then why worry about the problems they cause for physicalism if they did? The 'hard' problem is hard enough as it is.

If physicalism withstands zombiedom, then why is it difficult to believe that when one feels emotions while remembering some key event in one's life, for example, the feelings aroused are reducible to chemical and electrical activity in our brains? No amount of complex scientific theorising and experimentation elucidating these processes nor analysis of how such a process has evolved can diminish the intuitive doubt that something more is happening *during* the experience.

Where does this leave us? It could be said that when we think progress is being made on the 'hard' problem (the functional causal element of consciousness), we are actually going around in circles. We always stumble at the 'gap' — the link between cause and effect. We never seem to get closer to this link between the objective delineation of the cause and the subjective experience itself, irrespective of advancement in physics and neuroscience, because no method *can* encompass both aspects.

Is our search for that which encapsulates the subjective experience in an objective way a search for something non-existent? Is the search driven by the erroneous intuition that because the experience is so rich and different from anything physical, it cannot be defined in physical terms? At present, the debate circles around a stalemate because one side cannot *prove* the experience to be physical while the other cannot prove that it is more than that.

I am drawn to the distinction between being and knowing when considering the meaning of our understanding of the mind-body problem. Nature consists of physical things and forces. Yet knowing them is a relative concept in the sense that describing and explaining their nature reveals what they are according to our criteria of what knowing them is. Although our models make sense to us, the nature of this knowledge might take a different form for a different type of intelligence.

Is the scientific method's inability to objectively address the mind due to the incompatibility between the 'being' of the mind and 'knowing' this being? Being is innate, known only subjectively, whereas knowing is relative and thus cannot be known objectively. As such, scientific analysis of the causal processes of the being of consciousness does not encapsulate its innate being. The being of consciousness *is* the subjective experience, which is the emergent property of its causal physical processes, just like how glowing is a property of heating a metal rod.

However, although specific physical processes in the mind are equivalent to certain conscious states, a physical description of mental processes *does not* describe our mental world, including qualia. The former implies that subjective states emerge from physical processes, whereas the latter implies that these subjective states are not explicable in objective terms. If we believe that qualia are unknowable, then that is because either we believe that reality is fundamentally unknowable or our minds do not possess the type and/or level of complexity required to define qualia in objective terms. This is transcendental naturalism, a philosophical view that is consistent with predeterminism.

There are four main positions of knowability that relate to the mind-body problem and our comprehension of reality:

1. Reality is unknowable. If unknowable, no intelligence can understand it because it cannot be known. If everything exists in an unknowable Universe, then knowledge of it cannot be absolute, but be relative to the type of intelligence addressing it.
2. Reality may be unknowable to intelligence, but humans aren't able to know whether it is knowable or unknowable.
3. Reality is knowable to some form of intelligence, but humans do not possess the type of mind that is able to know reality objectively.
4. Reality is knowable to us. We can explain all phenomena according to physical laws.

I hold a variant of positions 1 and 2 in that I believe:

Everything is predetermined, so consequentially free will is an illusion. For predeterminism and free will as an illusion to be feasible, one would need to accept that the 'quality' of consciousness (the X factor, the qualia) could be equivalent to the physical brain processes causing that conscious state.

When we make a decision on some matter considered (e.g. whether to make a cup of tea), the *feeling* we experience associated with the decision seems to be consistent with it being a 'free' choice. However, could that feeling not also be equivalent and identical to the mental processes occurring during that feeling, from a physical process perspective? That is, the feeling is not just caused by the physical processes, but *is* the physical process in the context of how it is experienced. So, if the processes could be predetermined, so too the feelings.

The *feeling* of freedom during choices is actually the way we experience such causal mental processes. The 'feeling free to choose' is a fortunate by-product quality of certain mental states. It isn't actual freedom, but evolved to feel that way. Fortunate, because it gives value to human existence. We *feel* alive and in control.

If reality is intrinsically unknowable, no form of intelligence can ever know if this unknowable reality is unknowable or just difficult to know. However, determinism and the illusion of free will can still be consistent if this version of reality were the case. Conscious beings that do or could exist would have finite temporal and spatial limitations imposed on them by reality itself. These limitations, while enabling of consciousness and reason, may prevent a mind that is complex enough to comprehend the whole of reality from existing. That is, a mind that is more complex than is feasibly possible to evolve in this finite Universe would be needed to know it, or it may just be unknowable by design. To question the feasibility of reality being knowable outside the bounds of what is possible for a sentient being would be meaningless.

If reality *is* knowable, the knowledge consistent with knowing it could be of a form that requires intelligence so different from our own that we may not be able to understand it. Such knowledge could encapsulate the properties and interactions of all of reality within a deterministic context where free will is also consequentially an illusion.

For position 3, even a GUT that does explain all phenomena would not mean that we have made reality knowable, but rather that the questions *we* address have been answered. We have no means of knowing if we have formulated the questions whose answers demonstrate complete knowledge of reality.

For any metaphysical truth, knowledge of qualitative experiences of conscious entities transcends knowledge of the physical components that cause it and is inexplicable by a paradigm relating to force and matter. Subjective experience cannot be known other than to that which causes and experiences it. Objective knowledge of that same experience will be incomplete according to any model of reality. Although the causal elements and material process of the experience could be known, the qualitative experience will be essentially private.

ix) What Am I?

An apple is seen as something complete. Eat half of it and we are left with half an apple — this seems simple. But what of yourself? If we look at a person and say that he or she is so-and-so, does this encapsulate the person? Of course not; there is all that is going on in that person's mind that adds so much more. But what is it that constitutes 'me'?

If I lose a leg, I am still me. In ten years' time, I will still be me despite changing in appearance and size. The matter that comprises me is constantly changing, so is it the mind that is me? Even then, the memories, knowledge, thought, neural connections, and matter have changed. Indeed, one thing that is certain about me is that I am changing all the time, yet with a continuity that links my past self to my present and future selves.

One could answer that question by referring to our physiological construction that has been ascertained by accumulated scientific knowledge, but by doing, so the point I want to stress would be missed. Only humans ask, "What am I?" Therefore, by referring solely to physiology, we group humanity with all other things, which can *more* effectively be defined physiologically than can humans. Thus, when asking "what am I?", the question is more profound.

If we want an answer that can encapsulate the question's true meaning, then scientific analysis seems to provide little insight. Indeed, we do not know if science can provide an answer that can do justice to such a question and afford meaning to a being that *feels*. A scientific answer can only leave one wanting because it is orientated to defining our being in physical terms. But if physicalism is real and our feelings are just a natural transcendent product of physical processes, then we are left in a quandary.

We reject current science as being able to address the question of qualia satisfactorily, yet if everything *is* physical, then science *is* the tool. Does this lead us to transcendental naturalism where an answer that is compatible with a complete scientific paradigm is possible? This could be true. Such a form of science that defines us, our feelings, and all of reality under a single model could exist. Here, there would have to be no *magic* that turns matter into mental experience, but rather a model where the experience naturally evolves from matter without making us lose our sense of being more than just a complex collection of atoms. We cannot imagine the details of such a model since such science, if it is even possible, evades us.

Heidegger's philosophy of being addresses human existence in a way that is far removed from science. Yet it is a complete philosophical attempt to analyse what human existence is. Heidegger's Dasein defines human 'being'. His philosophy accepts that the description of Dasein is limited by thought, language, minds, technology, society, and such like, and that this is part of the meaning of the description. Dasein is modelled by society, which in turn is defined by Dasein, which subsequently models what Dasein is.

Rather than searching for an ever deeper level of scientific description of ourselves, which can never encapsulate our essence, Heidegger's phenomenology of being does not try to describe an absolute truth. Instead, it tells us what human 'being' is in the world we have made. Dasein is not scientific, but describes what humans *are* as determined by how our social constructions mould Dasein. In such a description, science has little input in defining humans in the world.

Although Dasein has little concern with scientific analysis of the Universe, Heidegger believed that what science tries to tell us about the Universe is the only useful way of accessing it. However, as science knows full well, it is not absolute truth. Dasein tells us that science is a social construct that reveals what it can within limitations. Under these terms, "what I am" is a thing in progress, indefinable to you or myself because I am ever changing — I change in my lifetime, and we change in accordance with the time in which we live as moulded by society and technology.

Dasein fails where science fails in our need to know the relation of the mind-body to the reality in which we are embedded. However, the difference is that Dasein diverts from this issue to define itself within the world it exists, whereas science faces it head-on. In doing so, although science comes up wanting in terms of definite answers, it provides the only thing we can ever really expect from it — useable information that is relative to what we are.

x) Man and Reality

This book has described the thoughts behind the generation and application of key concepts that have shaped our understanding of our place in the physical world. These include the philosophical, the physical, the chemical, and the biological.

The link between different areas of scientific and philosophical thought demonstrates that although science is the master of technological progress, both science *and* philosophy are essential for our future understanding of the world around us as well as who we are. Indeed, science is firmly rooted in ancient philosophical schools of thought.

The conclusions we draw from our analysis of physical reality is that our knowledge of it, though huge, is determined and constrained by how we are constructed. For all our inventiveness and technological know-how, which have blossomed over the past hundred years, our insights relate to our physiological and mental makeup. While technology affords us a window into the nature of reality that far exceeds what our physiology alone is capable of, every aspect of our analysis is constrained to a form that is determined by what we are.

If the Universe evolved from the Big Bang, then everything that exists is reducible to that cause in some way. A true TOE should fully encompass consciousness and the indeterminate, since these exist in reality. Any model of reality we *can* generate essentially conforms to our capacity to imagine and test. Truth that extends beyond our capabilities, whether it is that which we recognise or concepts we cannot even conceive of, evades any possible TOE. Yet this unknowable aspect may be essential for a true TOE.

Although the individual exists as part of a society of people, we are all aware of our uniqueness and mortality. We are born into the world and as we progress through our life, this awareness raises age-old questions such as "what am I?", "why am I here?", and "what is existence?" that philosophers first and scientists later came to ask. What the world means to each mind and what solutions are considered a resolution to such questions are also unique. As a species, we address common issues collectively in the hope of resolving problems to enhance our survival, reduce suffering, and increase pleasure. Yet, for the individual, more fundamental than these concerns is the need to know what we are and our place in the Universe.

We may live a life driven by the necessities and expectations of the society in which we exist, and these may vary from culture to culture as well as within a culture, but common to all cultures across all times is the sense of wonder as to what we are and our place in the grander scheme of things. Some people may never question things and are content to merely accept things as they are and exist within this acceptance. But just as we strive to improve the practicalities of our existence, it is in our human nature to wonder and to hope that we can answer within our lifetime the fundamental issues that relate to what we all are. We seek meaning in our existence, and one's search for meaning is fulfilled according to the individual and the likelihood for resolution is, to some extent, both cultural and sociological.

How can science help the individual find meaning? An accurate scientific description of reality would provide a framework against which to construct one's own sense of meaning. But if the Universe is fundamentally unknowable, then the framework is an unstable one. If we do not have the physiological makeup required to know a knowable reality, then it is a conditional and relative one. Indeed, we are mindful that there is no apparent reason why our species possesses exactly the necessary mental capacity that enables us to know reality. Whatever scenario is the case, satisfactory answers to the meaning of life are set against a background of knowledge about reality that is determined by the ability of the human mind.

If I ask "what am I and why am I here?", science can address the physical side in terms of scientific concepts. But if one wants meaning that defines the nature and quality of mind, then philosophy and spirituality have as much to say as science does. The scientific method works for what it is designed for because it produces answers that fit the type of questions we ask, namely practical solutions to objective problems.

All questions relate to the mind. But if what I am is the ever-changing pool of emotions, intellect, and thought which constitutes consciousness who sees, hears, smells, tastes, and interacts with a physical world through the body, then how can a scientific description of this physical world satisfy something that is not physical itself? Any description cannot overcome the divide between the non-physical mind and the physical world. The mind wonders and cares about the world. Perhaps our inability to reach the meaning that the mind desires is a blessing in disguise. Why? Because the world remains an enigma, the mind will never stop wondering about it.

It is the relentless curiosity, ingenuity, and creativity of the mind acting collectively through the various scientific means that permit us to apply it that has enabled human civilisation to progress this far. In addressing the physical world, science is mankind's crowning achievement. But if philosophy becomes science only when knowledge of that subject is achieved, then the age-old questions that arise from the mind's search for its own sense of meaning seem destined to be beyond the domain of science.

The relationship between man and reality is the relationship between all that *is* and a carbon-based, spatially, and temporally constrained organism that lives for about 75 years on average, weighs about 70 kg, and has a brain that possesses matter ordered in such a way as to possess the ability to comprehend. Irrespective of our knowledge of reality or our solutions to the meaning of our existence, we are surely a marvel of reality itself and, as such, must continue to move forward by asking probing questions for the sake of our past, present, and future.

References

The following list presents reference sources for the writing of this book. Those recommended to readers who want more detailed explanations of the individual topics discussed and which excel in exposition and content are indicated with an *.

Acheson D (2002). *1089 and All That*. Oxford University Press.
Agar J (2001) *Turing and the Universal Machine*. Icon Books UK.
Albert DZ (1994) *Quantum Mechanics and Experience*. Harvard University Press.
Annas J (2002) *Plato: A Very Short Introduction*. Oxford University Press.
Arand D (2015) *Truth Evolves*. Createspace.
*Arieh B-N (2008) *Entropy Demystified*. World Scientific Publishing.

    (Bold attempt to explain the 'unexplainable' — entropy.)

Aristotle (1986 edition) *De Anima (On the Soul)*. Penguin Classics.
Atkins P (2007) *Four Laws that Drive the Universe*. Oxford University Press.
Aurelius M (1964 edition) *Meditations*. Penguin Classics.
Austin JL (1962) *Sense and Sensibilia* (ed. GJ Warnock). Oxford University Press.
Avise JC (2007) *On Evolution*. The John Hopkins University Press.
Ayer AJ (1972) *Bertrand Russell*. Chicago University Press.
Ayer AJ (1984) *Ludwig Wittgenstein*. Penguin.
Ayer AJ (2000) *Hume: A Very Short Introduction*. Oxford University Press.
Ayer AJ (2001) *Language, Truth and Logic*. Penguin Modern Classics.
Ayers M (1997) *Locke*. Phoenix.
*Baars B (2001) *In the Theatre of Consciousness*. Oxford University Press.

    (A psychologist's view of consciousness as a stage, the mind as the theatre, and the audience as the mental and physical stimuli and processes feeding into it. Highly credible.)

Baggott J (1992) *The Meaning of Quantum Theory*. Oxford University Press.

*Baggott J (2004) *Beyond Measure*. Oxford University Press.

(A survey of the development of quantum physics from 1900 to present, paying particular attention to its interpretation. Excellent.)

Baggott J (2005) *A Beginner's Guide to Reality*. Penguin.

*Baldwin T. ed. (2004) *Maurice Merleau-Ponty: Basic Writings*. Routledge.

(Merleau-Ponty was one of the great albeit less well-known philosophers of the 20th century. His analysis of perception was, I think, far more profound and well thought out than even Sartre and Heidegger.)

Bais S (2005) *The Equations*. Harvard University Press.

Bais S (2005) *Very Special Relativity*. Harvard University Press.

Ball P (2001) *Stories of the Invisible*. Oxford University Press.

Barnes J (2000) *Aristotle: A Very Short Introduction*. Oxford University Press.

Barnett L (1948) *The Universe and Dr. Einstein*. William Morrow.

Barrow JD (1999) *Impossibility*. Vintage.

Bars I, Terning J (2009) *Extra Dimensions in Space and Time*. Springer.

Begelman M, Rees M (1998) *Gravity's Fatal Attraction*. Scientific American Library.

Bergmann PG (1992) *The Riddle of Gravitation*. Dover Publications.

Berman D (1997) *Great Philosophers: Berkeley (The Great Philosophers)*. Phoenix.

Bernasconi R (2006) *How to Read Sartre*. Granta.

*Bernstein J (2011) *Quantum Leaps*. Harvard University Press.

(Entertaining and informative perspective on Bell's theorem.)

Berry R (2000) *Freud: A Beginner's Guide*. Hodder and Stoughton.

*Blackburn S (1999) *Think*. Oxford University Press.

(Good introduction that illuminates how great historical thinkers have tackled central themes of philosophy.)

Blackburn S (1996 edition). *Oxford Dictionary of Philosophy*. Oxford University Press.

*Blackburn S (2006) *Truth*. Penguin.

(Good survey of historical address of this most important concept.)

Blackmore S (2005) *Consciousness: A Very Short Introduction*. Oxford University Press.

Blumberg ML (2010) *Freaks of Nature*. Oxford University Press.

*Bohm D (1980) *Wholeness and the Implicate Order*. Routledge.

(Bohm develops a theory of quantum physics that attempts to bring matter, existence, and consciousness together into a complete system. Fascinating and far-reaching in its ambition.)

Bohm D (1985 edition). *Unfolding Meaning*. Ark.
Bohm D, Peat FD (1989) *Science, Order and Creativity*. Routledge.
Bondi H (1980) *Relativity and Common Sense*. Dover Publications.
Bonner JT (1962) *The Ideas of Biology*. Dover.
Bonner JT (1993) *Life Cycles*. Princeton University Press.
Bonner JT (2000) *First Signals*. Princeton University Press.
Bonner JT (2006) *Why Size Matters*. Princeton University Press.
Braver L (2014) *Groundless Grounds: A Study of Wittgenstein and Heidegger*. MIT Press.
Brenner WH (1999) *Wittgenstein's Philosophical Investigations*. State University of New York Press.
*Bronowski J (1973) *The Ascent of Man*. Back Bay Books.

(Accompanied the popular TV series, correlating scientific development with the marvel of humankind.)

Bronowski J (1978) *The Origins of Knowledge and Imagination*. Yale University Press.
Browne J (2006) *Darwin's Origin of Species: A Biography*. Atlantic Books.
*Bullock A, Trombley S. eds. (2000). *The New Fontana Dictionary of Modern Thought (paperback edition)*. Harper Collins.

(Essential book of explanations of terms that have shaped the modern world.)

Calder G (2003) *Rorty*. Weidenfeld & Nicholson.
Calder N (1979) *Einstein's Universe: The Layman's Guide*. Penguin.
Campbell CA (1945) *Philosophical Lecture Notes*. Glasgow University Press.
Cartledge P (1998) *Great Philosophers: Democritus (The Great Philosophers)*. Phoenix.
Chaitin G (2006) *Metamaths*. Atlantic Books.
Changeaux J-P, Connes A (1998) *Conversations on Mind, Matter and Mathematics*. Princeton University Press.
Charlesworth B, Charlesworth D (2003) *Evolution: A Very Short Introduction*. Oxford University Press.
Clark T (2001) *Routledge Critical Thinkers: Martin Heidegger*. Routledge.
Clegg B, Pugh O (2012) *Infinity: A Graphic Guide*. Icon.
Close F (2004) *Particle Physics: A Very Short Introduction*. Oxford University Press.
Close F (2009) *Nothing: A Very Short Introduction*. Oxford University Press.
Coleman JA (1990 edition) *Relativity for the Layman*. Penguin.
Coles P (1999) *Einstein and the Total Eclipse*. Icon.
Coles P (2001) *Cosmology: A Very Short Introduction*. Oxford University Press.
Comte-Sponville A (2005) *The Little Book of Philosophy*. Vintage.
Comte-Sponville A (2008) *The Book of Atheist Spirituality*. Bantam Press.

Conway Morris S (1998) *The Crucible of Creation: The Burgess Shale and the Rise of Animals.* Oxford University Press.

Conway Morris S (2003) *Life's Solution: Inevitable Humans in a Lonely Universe.* Cambridge University Press.

Cornell J. ed. (1992) *Bubbles, Voids and Bumps in Time.* Cambridge University Press.

Cottingham J (1997) *Descartes.* Phoenix.

Coyne JA (2009) *Why Evolution is True.* Oxford University Press.

Crawford D (2000) *The Invisible Enemy.* Oxford University Press.

Crawshey-Williams R (1970) *Russell Remembered.* Oxford University Press.

Crease RP (2009) *The Great Equations.* Robinson.

Crick F (1958) On protein synthesis. *Symp Soc Exp Biol* **12**: 139–163.

Crick F (1970) Central dogma of molecular biology. *Nature* **227**: 561–563.

Crick F (1994) *The Astonishing Hypothesis.* Simon & Schuster.

Crossley JN (1990) *What is Mathematical Logic?* Dover.

Damasio A (2006) *Descartes' Error.* Vintage.

*Darwin C (1998 edition) *The Origin of Species.* Wordsworth Editions Ltd — Jeff Wallace introduction.

(Written in 1859 — startling for its courage, insight, and scope.)

Davies P (1981) *The Edge of Infinity.* Penguin.

Davies P (1984) *Superforce: The Search for a Grand Unified Theory of Nature.* Counterpoint.

Davies P, Brown J eds. (1986) *The Ghost in the Atom.* Cambridge University Press.

Davies P, Brown J eds. (1988). *Superstrings: A Theory of Everything?* Cambridge University Press.

Davies P (1995) *Are We Alone?* Penguin.

Dawkins R (1976) *The Selfish Gene.* Oxford University Press.

*Dawkins R (1982) *The Extended Phenotype.* Oxford University Press.

(More detailed analysis of Dawkins's views on evolutionary biology than *The Selfish Gene.*)

Dawkins R (1986) *The Blind Watchmaker.* Penguin.

Dawkins R (1995) *River Out of Eden.* Phoenix.

Dawkins R (1996) *The View from Mount Improbable.* Penguin.

Dennett DC (1995) *Darwin's Dangerous Idea.* Penguin.

Derbyshire J (2004) *Prime Obsession: Bernhard Riemann and the Greatest Unsolved Problem in Mathematics.* Plume Books.

Descartes R (1968) *Discourse on Method and the Meditations.* Penguin Classics.

D'Inverno R (1992) *Introducing Einstein's Relativity*. Oxford University Press.

Dixon O (2019) *Who the Hell is Friedrich Nietzsche?: And What is His Philosophy All About?* Bowden & Brazil.

Du Sautoy M (2017) *How to Count to Infinity*. Quercus.

Dyson FJ (1999) *The Sun, the Genome, and the Internet*. Oxford University Press.

Dyson FJ (2000) *Origins of Life*. Cambridge University Press.

*Edelman G, Tononi G (2001) *Consciousness*. Penguin.

> (The best description of the probable physical cause of consciousness I have ever read.)

Edelman G (2004) *Wider than the Sky*. Penguin Allen Lane.

Edelman G (2006) *Second Nature: Brain Science and Human Knowledge*. Yale University Press.

Edmonds D, Eidinow J (2001) *Wittgenstein's Poker*. Faber & Faber.

Einstein A, Lorentz HA, Weyl H, Minkowski H (1924) *The Principle of Relativity*. Dover Publications.

*Einstein A (1952) *Relativity: The Special and General Theory (15th edition)*. Bonanza.

> (By the man himself; very readable with few equations, but Wheeler's book is easier.)

Einstein A (1923; 1983 edition). *Sidelights on Relativity*. Dover Publications.

*Eldredge N, Gould SJ (1972) Punctuated equilibria: An alternative to phyletic gradualism. In TJM Schopf (eds), *Models in Paleobiology*. Freeman, Cooper, pp. 82–115.

> (The key paper introducing punctuated equilibrium.)

Eldredge N (1996) *Reinventing Darwin*. Phoenix.

Emsley J (2001) *Nature's Building Blocks*. Oxford University Press.

Epstein LC (1985) *Relativity Visualized*. Insight Press.

Ewing AC (1951) *The Fundamental Questions of Philosophy*. Routledge and Kegan Paul.

Farmelo G (2009) *The Strangest Man: The Hidden Life of Paul Dirac*. Faber.

Feyerabend P (1995) *Killing Time*. University of Chicago Press.

Feyerabend PA (2010) *Against Method*. Verso.

*Feynman RP (1990) *QED*. Penguin.

> (A great populariser of difficult ideas, and this, being his own, is clearly close to his heart.)

*Feynman RP (1998) *Six Easy Pieces: The Fundamentals of Physics Explained*. Penguin.

(Small volume but covers many topics; from the basics of atoms and physics to one of the best explanations of wave-particle duality that I have ever read — not as easy as Feynman suggests.)

Feynman RP (1999) *Six Not-So-Easy Pieces: Einstein's Relativity, Symmetry and Space Time*. Penguin.

Feynman RP (1999) *The Meaning of it All*. Penguin.

Fleisch D (2008) *A Student's Guide to Maxwell's Equations*. Cambridge University Press.

Ford K, Hewitt P (2012) *101 Quantum Questions: What You Need to Know About the World You Can't See*. Harvard University Press.

Freeman WJ (2000) *How Brains Make Up Their Minds*. Phoenix.

Freud S (2005) *Forgetting Things*. Penguin.

*Gamow G (1985) *Thirty Years that Shook Physics*. Dover Publications Inc.

(Interesting and amusing account of the generation of quantum physics.)

Gamow G (2002) *Gravity*. Dover.

Gardiner P (2002) *Kierkegaard: A Very Short Introduction*. Oxford University Press.

Gardner M (1997) *Relativity Simply Explained*. Dover.

*Gensler HR (1984) *Gödel's' Theorem Simplified*. University Press of America.

(Excellent simplification and explanation of Gödel's theorems.)

Gödel K (1992) *On Formally Undecidable Propositions of 'Principia Mathematica' and Related Systems*. Dover Publications.

*Goldstein R (2006) *Incompleteness*. Atlas Books.

(Good non-mathematical description of Gödel's theorem, though Yourgrau gives better insight into the man while Nagel and Newman explain the theorem better).

*Gould SJ, Lewontin RC (1979) The spandrels of San Marco and the Panglossian paradigm: A critique of the adaptationist programme. *Proc R Soc Lond B Biol Sci* **205**(1161): 581–598.

(The key paper introducing spandrels.)

*Gould SJ (1989) *Wonderful Life: The Burgess Shale and the Nature of History*. Hutchinson Radius.

(Enthusiasm flows throughout this account of the work and implications of the reinterpretation of the Burgess fauna.)

Gould SJ (2002) *The Structure of Evolutionary Theory*. Harvard University Press.

Gowers T (2002) *Mathematics: A Very Short Introduction*. Oxford University Press.

Gray J (1998) *Great Philosophers: Voltaire (The Great Philosophers)*. Phoenix.

Gray J (2002) *Straw Dogs*. Granta.

*Grayling AC (2001) *Wittgenstein: A Very Short Introduction*. Oxford University Press.

(Perhaps this or Ray Monk's *How to Read Wittgenstein* is the best place to start on Wittgenstein.)

Greene J (1975) *Thinking and Language*. Methuen.

*Greenstein GS (2019) *Quantum Strangeness*. MIT Press.

(Deep and readable analysis of Bell's Theorem.)

Gribbin J (1984) *In Search of Schrödinger's Cat*. Black Swan.

Gribbin J (1998) *The Search for Superstrings, Symmetry, and the Theory of Everything*. Back Bay Books.

Gribbin J (2010) *In Search of the Multiverse*. Penguin.

Griffith M (2012) *Free Will: The Basics*. Routledge.

Hacker PMS (1997) *Wittgenstein*. Phoenix.

*Hadamard J (1945) *The Psychology of Invention in the Mathematical Field*. Princeton University Press.

(Account and analysis of how historically great scientists have explained the nature of their creative thought. Fascinating.)

Hager T (1995) *Force of Nature: The Life of Linus Pauling*. Simon & Schuster.

Hagger N (2009) *The New Philosophy of Universalism: The Infinite and the Law of Order*. O Books.

Hall R (1991) *Unravelling the Universe*. Channel 4 Television.

Halpern P (2010) *Collider: The Search for the World's Smallest Particles*. John Wiley & Sons.

Hanfling O (1997) *Great Philosophers: Ayer (The Great Philosophers)*. Phoenix.

Harris S (2012) *Free Will*. Free Press.

Hawking S (1988) *A Brief History of Time: From the Big Bang to Black Holes*. Bantam Press.

Hawking S, Penrose R (2000) *The Nature of Space and Time*. Princeton University Press.

Hayman R (1997) *Nietzsche*. Phoenix.

Heaton J (1999) *Understanding Wittgenstein*. Icon Books UK.

Heaton J (2000) *Wittgenstein and Psychoanalysis*. Icon Books UK.

Hebra A (2003) *Measure for Measure*. The John Hopkins University Press.

*Heidegger M (1927) *Being and Time*. Blackwell.

(Difficult to read, but one senses that importance is hidden within poor exposition.)

Heidegger M (1993) *Basic Concepts*. Indiana University Press.

*Heisenberg W (1962) *Physics and Philosophy*. Penguin.

(Interesting insight into one of the originators' defence of the Copenhagen interpretation.)

Henry J (1997) *The Scientific Revolution and the Origins of Modern Science*. Palgrave.

Herbert N (1988) *Quantum Reality*. Bantam Doubleday.

Hey T, Walters P (1987) *The Quantum Universe*. Cambridge University Press.

Hey T, Papay G (2014) *The Computing Universe: A Journey through a Revolution*. Cambridge University Press.

Hintikka J (2000) *On Gödel*. Wadsworth (Thomson Learning).

Hirstein W (2001) *On Searle*. Wadsworth.

Hodges A (1997) *Great Philosophers: Turing (The Great Philosophers)*. Phoenix.

Hodges W (1977) *Logic*. Penguin.

Hoffmann B (1983; 1999 edition) *Relativity and its Roots*. Dover Publications.

*Hofstadter DR (2000: 20th anniversary edition). *Gödel, Escher, Bach: An Eternal Golden Braid*. Penguin.

(Using Gödel, Bach, and Escher, Hofstadter explains how he sees that a self can come from inanimate matter. The book correlates artificial with human intelligence and argues the differences between them.)

*Hollingdale RJ (2001) *Nietzsche: The Man and his Philosophy*. Cambridge University Press.

(Fascinating account of Nietzsche the man, and how events in his life affected and directed his philosophy- by one of the most respected translators of Nietzsche's works.)

Holmes J (2002) *Depression: Ideas in Psychoanalysis*. Icon Books.

*Honderich T ed. (1995). *The Philosophers: Introducing Great Western Thinkers*. Oxford University Press.

(From Socrates to Sartre, a number of experts introduce the work and lives of the western world's greatest philosophers. A great place to start in philosophy to find out how ideas interrelate and have evolved.)

*Honderich T (2002) *How Free are You?* Oxford University Press.

(Excellent defence of hard determinism.)

*Hossenfelder S. (2018). Lost in Math.

(Highly readable critique of the physics community's search for beautiful mathematical descriptions of reality- revealing this effort often to be bad science.)

Hoyle F (1964; 2005 edition) *Of Men and Galaxies*. Prometheus.

Hume D (1748; 2004 edition) *An Enquiry Concerning Human Understanding*. Dover.

Humphrey N (1986) *The Inner Eye*. Oxford University Press.

Humphrey N (1993) *A History of the Mind*. Vintage.

*Humphrey N (2006) *Seeing Red: A Study in Consciousness*. Harvard University Press.

> (A different and illuminating perspective on qualia — excellent).

Humphrey N (2006) Consciousness: the Achilles heel of Darwinism? Thanks God, not quite. In: J Brockman (ed), *Intelligent Thought: Science versus the Intelligent Design Movement*. Vintage, pp. 50–64.

Humphrey N (2007) The society of selves. *Phil Trans R Soc B* **362**: 745–754.

*Humphrey N (2011) *Soul Dust: The Magic of Consciousness*. Quercus.

> (Follow up to *Seeing Red* — 'explaining' the hard problem.)

Inwood M (2000) *Heidegger: A Very Short Introduction*. Oxford University Press.

Iredale M (2012) *The Problem of Free Will: A Contemporary Introduction*. Routledge.

Janaway C (1994) *Schopenhauer*. Oxford University Press.

Janicaud D (2005) *Philosophy in 30 Days*. Granta.

Janicaud D (2005) *On the Human Condition*. Taylor & Francis.

Jaspers K (1966) *Kant*. Harcourt.

*Jeans J (1981 edition) *Physics and Philosophy*. Dover.

> (Although written in the 1940s, it is a lucid and beautifully written account of quantum and classical physics and their relations to various philosophical views.)

Jenkins M (2000) *Evolution*. Hodder & Stoughton.

Jensen ON (2004) Modification-specific proteomics: Characterization of post-translational modifications by mass spectrometry. *Curr Opin Chem Biol* **8**: 33–41.

Joad CEM (1944) *Philosophy*. English Universities Press Ltd.

Johnson C (1997) *Great Philosophers: Derrida (The Great Philosophers)*. Phoenix.

Johnson G (2000) *Murray Gell-Mann and the Revolution in Twentieth-Century Physics*. Jonathan Cape.

Jourdain PEB (1956; 2007 edition) *The Nature of Mathematics*. Dover.

Jung CG (1957; 2002 edition). *The Undiscovered Self*. Routledge Classics.

*Kant I (1783) *Prolegomena to Any Future Metaphysics (1977 translation; by J Ellington)*. Hackett.

> (Kant's summary of the great *Critique of Pure Reason*.)

Kanterian E (2007) *Ludwig Wittgenstein (Critical Lives)*. Reaktion Books.
Keller EF (2010) *The Mirage of a Space Between Nature and Nurture*. Duke.
Kierkegaard S (2001 edition). *Johannes Climacus: Or a Life of Doubt*. Serpent's Tail.
*Knoll AH (2003). *Life on a Young Planet*. Princeton University Press.

(A Harvard professor's view on the first 3 billion years of life on Earth, including the Cambrian explosion.)

Kolata G (1997) *Clone*. Penguin.
Körner S (1990 edition) *Kant*. Penguin.
Kripke SA (1982) *Wittgenstein: On Rules and Private Language*. Blackwell.
*Kuhn TS (1996 edition) *The Structure of Scientific Revolutions*. The University of Chicago Press.

(A controversial analysis of how science evolves through paradigm shifts.)

*Landau LD, Rumer GB (1960; 2003 edition) *What is Relativity?* Dover Publications.

(Simple and elegant.)

*La Rochefoucauld FDDL (1959 edition) *Maxims*. Penguin Classics.

(Written in France in 1665, this book of insight into human nature in a social context still leaves one nodding in agreement while smiling — it seems we haven't changed!)

Leavitt D (2006) *The Man Who Knew Too Much*. Phoenix.
Lechte J (1993). *Fifty Key Contemporary Thinkers: From Structuralism to Postmodernity*. Routledge.
*Leslie J (1989) *Universes*. Routledge.

(Interesting philosophical volume on the anthropic principle — was the universe designed for life?)

Lesmoir-Gordon N, Rood B, Edney R (2000) *Introducing Fractal Geometry*. Icon Books.
Lewin B (1995) *Genes V (2nd edition)*. Oxford University Press.
*Lewis PJ (2016) *Quantum Ontology: A Guide to the Metaphysics of Quantum Mechanics*. Oxford University Press.

(Superb metaphysical analysis of the possible meaning of different interpretations of quantum theories.)

Lewis PB (2012) Arthur Schopenhauer. Reaktion.
*Lewontin RC (1993). *The Doctrine of DNA*. Penguin.

(Questions the validity and necessity of the Human Genome Project. Written before completion of the sequencing of the genome, but its issues are equally valid and thought provoking today.)

Lewontin RC (1995) *Human Diversity*. Scientific American Library.

*Lewontin RC (1998) *The Triple Helix*. Harvard University Press.

>(A brilliant book. Its central focus is that for us to understand living things, we must think of genes, organisms, and the environment not as separate entities but as a whole.)

Lewontin RC (2000) *It Ain't Necessarily So*. Granta.

Livio M (2002) *The Golden Ratio*. Review.

Lovelock J (1979) *Gaia: A New Look at Life on Earth*. Oxford University Press.

*Magee B (1973) *Popper*. Fontana Press.

>(A lucid introduction to Popper's contribution to modern philosophical thought.)

Magee B (2016) *Ultimate Questions*. Princeton University Press.

Mahon B (2004) *The Man Who Changed Everything: The Life of James Clerk Maxwell*. John Wiley & Sons.

Malcolm N (2001) *Ludwig Wittgenstein: A Memoir*. Cambridge University Press.

Maldacena J, Susskind L (2013). Cool horizons for Entangled black holes. *Fortschr Physik*, **61**(9): 781–811.

Mandelbrot BB (1977) *The Fractal Geometry of Nature*. W. H. Freeman.

Maor E (1994) *e: The Story of a Number*. Princeton University Press.

Maor E (2017) *To Infinity and Beyond: A Cultural History of the Infinite*. Princeton University Press.

Martin R (2000) *On Ayer*. Wadsworth Notes Series.

Martin S. ed. (1993) *The Sayings of Friedrich Nietzsche*. Duckworth.

Maslin M (2004) *Global Warming: A Very Short Introduction*. Oxford University Press.

Matthews PH (2004) *Linguistics: A Very Short Introduction*. Oxford University Press.

*Maudlin T (2002) *Quantum Non-Locality and Relativity: Metaphysical Intimations of Modern Physics*. Blackwell.

>(Excellent description of Bell's theorem, non-locality, relativity, and the measurement problem.)

Mayblin B (2008) *Introducing Logic*. Icon.

Maynard Smith J (1998) *Shaping Life: Genes, Embryos and Evolution*. Weidenfeld and Nicholson.

Maynard Smith J, Szathmary E (1999) *The Origins of Life*. Oxford University Press.

McEvoy JP (1995) *Hawking for Beginners*. Icon.

*McEvoy JP (1999) *Introducing Quantum Theory*. Icon.

>(Looking at the cartoon layout hides the fact that this is a technically accomplished introduction to the history and science of some of the key issues of quantum theory.)

*McFarland E (1998) *Einstein's Special Relativity*. Trifolium Books Inc.

(Simple introduction to special relativity in action.)

McGilchrist I (2012) *The Master and His Emissary*. Yale University Press.

*McGinn C (1993) *Problems in Philosophy: The Limits of Enquiry*. Blackwell.

(Detailed analysis of the human possibility to comprehend and solved the deeper fundamental philosophical problems such as free will.)

*McGinn C (2000) *The Mysterious Flame: Conscious Minds in a Material World*. Basic Books.

(Lucid explanation of why we may not ever be able to understand the mind-body problem or reality itself.)

McGinn C (2002) *The Making of a Philosopher*. Scribner.

McGinn C (2016) *Inborn Knowledge: The Mystery Within*. MIT Press.

*McGuinness B, Von Wright H. eds. (1997 edition). *Ludwig Wittgenstein: Cambridge Letters: Correspondence with Russell, Keynes, Moore, Ramsey, and Sraffa*. Blackwell.

(Provides a deeper insight into the workings of the man — academically and personally.)

McLeish K (1998) *Aristotle*. Phoenix.

Merleau-Ponty M (1945; 2002 edition). *The Phenomenology of Perception*. Routledge.

*Merleau-Ponty M (1968) *The Visible and the Invisible*. Northwestern University Press.

(Incomplete by the time he died, this work marks true progress from Heidegger's *Being and Time*.)

Merleau-Ponty M (2004) *The World of Perception*. Routledge.

*Mermin ND (2006) *It's About Time: Understanding Einstein's Relativity*. Princeton University Press.

(To get a *real* feel for relativity, this is the easiest entry before delving into other works that involve rigorous mathematics.)

*Miles JB (2015) *The Free Will Delusion: How We Settled for the Illusion of Morality*. Troubador Publishing.

(Clear and fascinating analysis of determinism and free will.)

*Milner B (2001) *Nuclear and Particle Physics*. Cambridge University Press.

(Ever wondered what radioactivity is or how a nuclear reactor works? This small and concise book has it all.)

Mollon P (2000) *The Unconscious*. Icon Books UK.
Monk R (1991) *Ludwig Wittgenstein: Duty of Genius*. Vintage.
Monk R (1996) *Bertrand Russell: The Spirit of Solitude*. Jonathan Cape.
Monk R (1997) *Bertrand Russell*. Phoenix.
Monk R (2005) *How to Read Wittgenstein*. Granta.
Morgan NG (1989) *Cell Signalling*. Open University Press.
Morris R (2001) *The Evolutionists: The Struggle for Darwin's Soul*. Freeman.
Myerson G (2002) *Sartre's Existentialism and Humanism: A Beginner's Guide*. Hodder & Stoughton.
Nabel G (2009) The coordinates of truth. *Science* **326**: 53–54.
Nadeau R, Kafatos M (2001) *The Non-Local Universe: The New Physics and Matters of the Mind*. Oxford University Press.
*Nagel E, Newman JR (2002 edition) *Gödel's Proof*. New York University Press.

(Written in 1958, this work is still probably the best simple introduction to the meaning of the theorem.)

*Nagel T (1987) *What Does It All Mean?* Oxford University Press.

(Great simple summary of the key philosophical problems — compact, concise, and correct.)

Nagel T (1989) *The View from Nowhere*. Oxford University Press.
*Nelson Q (2007) *The Slightest Philosophy*. Dog Ear Publishing.

(Excellent defence of naïve realism.)

Nidditch PH (1962) *The Development of Mathematical Logic*. Routledge.
Nietzsche F (1961) *Thus Spoke Zarathustra*. Penguin.
Nietzsche F (1974; Kaufmann edition) *The Gay Science*. Random House.
Nietzsche F (1977) *A Nietzsche Reader*. Penguin Classics (selected and translated by RJ Hollingdale).
Nietzsche F (1993) *The Birth of Tragedy*. Penguin.
Nietzsche F (1994) *Human, All Too Human*. Penguin.
Nietzsche F (2001) *Beyond Good and Evil*. Cambridge University Press.
Nietzsche F (2001) *The Gay Science*. Cambridge University Press.
Noble D (2008) *The Music of Life*. Oxford University Press.
Norsen T (2002) *An Introduction to Bell's Inequalities and Non-Locality*. Objective Science.
Norsen T (2002) *Quantum Mechanics and Non-Locality*. Objective Science.
Norsen T (2002) *Hidden Variable Theories*. Objective Science.
Norsen T (2002) *Bells' Inequality and the Case for Super-Fast 'Entanglement' Interactions*. Objective Science.

Norsen T (2002) *'Non-Locality' and Realism: A Brief Discussion*. Objective Science.

Norsen T (2006) *Against Realism*. Elsevier.

Nurse P (2020) *What is Life: Understanding Biology in Five Steps*. David Fickling Books.

O'Hara S (2004) *Nietzsche: Within Your Grasp*. Wiley.

Ohno S (1972) So much 'junk' DNA in our genome. *Brookhaven Symp Biol* **23**: 366–370.

Okasha S (2002) *The Philosophy of Science: A Very Short Introduction*. Oxford University Press.

Olbers W (1826) *Uber Die Durchsichtigkeit Des Weltraumus*. Bodes Astronomisches Jahrbuch.

Omnes R (1999) *Understanding Quantum Mechanics*. Princeton University Press.

*Pais A (1982) *Subtle is the Lord: The Science and the Life of Albert Einstein*. Oxford University Press.

(Pais provides us with a definitive text on the work and life of Einstein.)

*Pais A (1991) *Niels Bohr's Times, In Physics, Philosophy and Polity*. Oxford University Press.

(A great physicist in his own right, Pais does justice to the work of perhaps the most pivotal figure in the formulation of modern quantum theory.)

Palmer D (2006) *Seven Million Years*. Phoenix.

Palmer DD (1996) *Kierkegaard for Beginners*. Writers and Readers.

*Papineau D (2002) *Thinking About Consciousness*. Oxford University Press.

(A powerful defence of physicalism.)

Papineau D (2012) *Philosophical Devices: Proofs, Probabilities, and Sets*. Oxford University Press.

Parr HC (1997) *Time, Science and Philosophy*. Lutterworth Press.

Pears D (1997) *Wittgenstein*. Fontana.

Peat FD (1997) *Infinite Potential: The Life and Times of David Bohm*. Helix Books.

*Penrose R (1989) *The Emperor's New Mind*. Oxford University Press.

(This volume contains a detailed explanation of Penrose's idea that classical relativity and quantum theory can only be united with a completely new form of physics, the development of which requires human rather than artificial creativity.)

Penrose R (2000) *The Large, the Small and the Human Mind*. Canto, Cambridge University Press.

Penrose R (2005) *The Road to Reality*. Vintage.

Pesic P (2001) *Labyrinth*. MIT Press.
Pesic P (2003) *Seeing Double*. MIT Press.
Petzold C (2008) *The Annotated Turing*. Wiley.
Pierantozzi DC (2019) *Cantor and Infinity*. Independently published.
Pinker S (2005) *Hotheads*. Penguin.
Planck M (1915; 1998 edition) *Eight Lectures on Theoretical Physics*. Dover Publications.
Plant R (1997) *Hegel*. Phoenix.
Plato (1960 edition) *Gorgias*. Penguin Classics.
Plato (2003 edition) *The Republic*. Penguin Classics.
*Polkinghorne JC (1984) *The Quantum World*. Penguin.

(An expertly written introduction to quantum theory with few formulae; perhaps the best understanding one can achieve without the use of quantum theory's mathematical language.)

Polkinghorne JC (2002) *Quantum Theory: A Very Short Introduction*. Oxford University Press.
Polster B (2004) *Q.E.D.: Beauty in Mathematical Proof*. Wooden Books.
*Popper K (2002 edition) *The Logic of Scientific Discovery*. Routledge.

(Written by the father of the scientific method, in which falsifiability is introduced.)

Popper K (1994) *Knowledge and the Mind-Body Problem*. Routledge.
Prager J (2001) *On Turing*. Wadsworth Notes Series.
*Price H (1996) *Time's Arrow*. Oxford University Press.

(Philosophical insight into why the past affects the future, and not the reverse.)

Priest G (2000) *Logic: A Very Short Introduction*. Oxford University Press.
*Priest S (1998) *Merleau-Ponty*. Routledge.

(Brilliant summary of this great underrated philosopher's work.)

Prigogine I (1997) *The End of Certainty: Time, Chaos and the New Laws of Nature*. The Free Press.
Putnam H (1999) *The Threefold Chord: Mind, Body, and World*. Columbia University Press.
Quine WV (2003) *Pursuit of Truth*. Harvard University Press.
Quinton A (1998) *Hume*. Phoenix.
*Rae A (1986) *Quantum Physics: Illusion or Reality?* Canto, Cambridge University Press.

(Another excellent introduction to quantum theory that is similar in level to Polkinghorne's book but with a more philosophical slant, which is a good thing!)

Rae A (2005) *Quantum Physics: A Beginner's Guide*. Oneworld publication.
*Rae A (2013) *Reductionism: A Beginner's Guide*. Oneworld publication.

(Clear, rigorous, and insightful treatment of reductionism.)

Rae A (2016) *Quantum Mechanics* (6th edition). Routledge.
Ramachandran VS (2005) *A Brief Tour of Human Consciousness: From Impostor Poodles to Purple Numbers*. P I Press.
Randall L (2012) *Higgs Discovery: The Power of Empty Space*. Bodley Head.
Raphael F (1998) *Popper*. Phoenix.
Redfern M (2004) *Earth: A Very Short Introduction*. Oxford University Press.
*Rees M (1999) *Just Six Numbers*. Weidenfeld & Nicolson.

(Explains, through six physically imposed numbers, how the universe's existence and ours is finely balanced.)

*Rees M (2002) *Our Cosmic Habitat*. Weidenfeld & Nicholson.

(Few can match Rees's enthusiasm in making fascinating topics relevant and memorable.)

Rees M (2002) *Before the Beginning: Our Universe and Others*. Free Press.
Rees M (2004) *Our Final Century?: Will the Human Race Survive the Twenty-first Century?* Arrow.
Rees M (2004) *Our Final Hour: A Scientist's Warning*. Basic Books.
Rees M (2011) *From Here to Infinity*. Profile Books.
Regis E (2008) *What is Life?* Oxford University Press.
Reichenbach H (1980 edition) *From Copernicus to Einstein*. Dover.
Ridley A (1998) *Great Philosophers: Collingwood (The Great Philosophers)*. Phoenix.
Robinson D (1999) *Nietzsche and Postmodernism*. Icon Books. UK.
Rogers B (1999) *Pascal*. Routledge.
Rose S (1966) *The Chemistry of Life*. Penguin.
Rucker RVB (1977) *Geometry, Relativity and the Fourth Dimension*. Dover Publications.
Russell B (1950) *Unpopular Essays*. Allen & Unwin.
Russell B (1961) *Has Man a Future?* George Allen & Unwin Ltd.
*Russell B (1967 edition) *The Problems of Philosophy*. Oxford University Press.

(Written over ninety years ago, but arguably still the best introduction to philosophy.)

Russell B (1968) *The Art of Philosophising*. Littlefield Adams Quality Paperbacks.
Russell B (1997) *ABC Of Relativity* (5th edition). Routledge.

Russell B (2007 edition) *Introduction to Mathematical Philosophy*. Spokesman Books.
Sagal PT (1994) *Mind, Man and Machine: A Dialogue (2nd edition)*. Hackett.
Sardar Z (2000) *Thomas Kuhn and the Science Wars*. Icon Books.
*Sartre J-P (1948) *Existentialism and Humanism*. Methuen & Co. Ltd.

(*Being and Nothingness* simplified and made readable; a classic.)

*Sartre J-P (1963) *Nausea*. Penguin.

(Sartre's first '*existential novel*' presenting the ideas of existentialism with his flair for writing.)

Sartre J-P (1972 edition) *What is Literature?* Routledge.
Sartre J-P (1984) *Existentialism and Human Emotions*. Citadel.
Sartre J-P (1989) *Being and Nothingness*. Routledge.
Sartre J-P (1990) *Iron in the Soul*. Penguin.
Sartre J-P (1994) *Sketch for a Theory of the Emotions*. Routledge.
Sartre J-P (2001) *The Age of Reason*. Penguin.
Sartre J-P (2001) *The Reprieve*. Penguin.
*Scarani V (2003) *Quantum Physics*. Oxford University Press.

(Presents quantum concepts such as entanglement and interference simply using a novel approach of experimental rather than theoretical physics, thus shedding light on Bell's inequality.)

Schlick M (1920; 2005 edition) *Space and Time in Contemporary Physics*. Dover.
*Schopenhauer A (1995) *The World as Will and Representation (Volume 1)*. Dover.

(Underrated.)

Schott B (2002) *Schott's Original Miscellany*. Bloomsbury.
Schrödinger E (1944) *What is Life?: With Mind and Matter and Autobiographical Sketches*. Canto.
Schumacher EF (1993) *Small is Beautiful: A Study of Economics as if People Mattered*. Vintage.
Scruton R (2001) *Kant: A Very Short Introduction*. Oxford University Press.
Scruton R (2002) *Spinoza: A Very Short Introduction*. Oxford University Press.
Scruton R (2017) *On Human Nature*. Princeton University Press.
Searle JR (1980) Minds, brains, and programs. *Behav Brain Sci* **3**: 417–424.
Searle JR (1992) *The Rediscovery of the Mind*. MIT Press.
Searle JR (1998) *The Mystery of Consciousness*. Granta.
*Searle JR (1999) *Mind, Language and Society*. Basic Books.

(Well-written account of Searle's key works — intentionality, consciousness, and social reality — unified.)

Searle JR (2004) *Mind*. Oxford University Press.
Searle JR (2014) *Seeing Things as They Are*. Oxford University Press.
Seneca (2018 edition) *On the Shortness of Life*. Benediction Classics.
Sexton E. (2001) *Dawkins and the Selfish Gene*. Icon Books.
Sharp DWA. ed. (1983) *The Penguin Dictionary of Chemistry*. Penguin.
Sim S (2001) *Lyotard and the Inhuman*. Icon Books.
Singer P (1983) *Hegel*. Oxford University Press.
Singh S (1997) *Fermat's Last Theorem*. Fourth Estate.
Siracusa J (2008) *Nuclear Weapons: A Very Short Introduction*. Oxford University Press.
Slattery T (2014) *Breaking the Free Will Illusion for the Betterment of Humankind*. Working Matter Publishing.
Smith B. ed. (2003) *John Searle*. Cambridge University Press.
Smith L (2007) *Chaos: A Very Short Introduction*. Oxford University Press.
*Smolin L (2006) *The Trouble with Physics*. Penguin.

(Criticism of the unifying claims of string theory.)

Solomon RC (2008) *The Little Philosophy Book*. Oxford University Press.
Sompayrac LM (2019 edition) *How the Immune System Works*. Wiley-Blackwell.
Sorell T (2000) *Descartes: A Very Short Introduction*. Oxford University Press.
Squires E (1985) *To Acknowledge the Wonder: Story of Fundamental Physics*. Institute of Physics Publishing.
*Squires E (1990) *Conscious Mind in the Physical World*. Institute of Physics Publishing.

(Excellent discussion of the relationship between the conscious mind and reality.)

*Squires E (2000) *Mystery of the Quantum World*. Institute of Physics Publishing.

(Like Rae's book, but perhaps a little easier to grasp.)

*Sterelny K (2001: 1st edition; 2007: 2nd edition) *Dawkins Versus Gould*. Icon.

(Compares and contrasts the views of the two.)

Stevens A (2001) *Jung: A Very Short Introduction*. Oxford University Press.
Stewart I (1995) *Nature's Numbers*. HarperCollins.
Stokes P (2003) *100 Essential Thinkers*. Arcturus.
Storr A (2001) *Freud: A Very Short Introduction*. Oxford University Press.
Strathern P (1997) *Newton and Gravity*. Arrow Books.
Strathern P (1999) *Turing and the Computer*. Bantam.
Strawson G (2019) *Things that Bother Me*. New York Review of Books.
Stroll A (2006) *Wittgenstein*. Oneworld Publications.

Stryer L (1995) *Biochemistry (4th edition)*. W. H. Freeman & Co.
Styer DF (2000) *The Strange World of Quantum Mechanics*. Cambridge University Press.
Sutherland S (2007) *Irrationality*. Pinter & Martin.
*Svensmark H, Calder N (2007) *The Chilling Stars*. Icon.

(Provides evidence for the role of the stars in 'global warming' effects.)

Tanner M (1998) *Schopenhauer*. Phoenix.
Tanner M (2000) *Nietzsche: A Very Short Introduction*. Oxford University Press.
Thomas L (1978 edition) *Lives of a Cell: Notes of a Biology Watcher*. Penguin.
Thompson M (2009) *Me*. Acumen.
*Thorne KS (1994) *Black Holes and Time Warps: Einstein's Outrageous Legacy*. Papermac.

(Interesting account of the development of cosmological research from someone intrinsically involved.)

*Tomonaga S-I (1997) *The Story of Spin*. Chicago University Press.

(Technically difficult, but a great analysis of an aspect of quantum theory.)

Trefil J (2003) *Cassell's Laws of Nature*. Cassell.
Treiman S (1999) *The Odd Quantum*. Princeton University Press.
Turing AM (1936) On computable numbers, with an application to the entscheidungsproblem. *Proc London Math Soc 2*, **42**: 230–265.
Turing AM (1937) On computable numbers, with an application to the entscheidungsproblem; A correction. *Proc London Math Soc 2*, **43**: 544–546.
Turing AM (1950) Computing machinery and intelligence. *Mind* **236**: 433–460.
Turing AM (1952) The chemical basis of morphogenesis. *Phil Trans Roy Soc London B* **237**: 37–72.
Tweed M (2003) *Essential Elements: Atoms, Quarks, and the Periodic Table*. Wooden Books.
Veltman M (2003) *Facts and Mysteries in Elementary Particle Physics*. World Scientific.
Vilenkin NY (1995) *In Search of Relativity*. Birkhauser Boston.
Walker R (1998) *Kant*. Phoenix Paperbacks.
Warnock M (1970) *Existentialism*. Oxford University Press.
Watkins M (2002) *Useful Mathematical and Physical Formulae*. Wooden Books Ltd.
Watling KJ ed. (2001) *The RBI Handbook of Receptor Classification and Signal Transduction (4th edition)*. Sigma-RBI.
Watson JD (1968) *The Double Helix*. Penguin.

Webster R (2003) *Freud*. Phoenix.
*Weinberg S (1977) *The First Three Minutes*. Fontana.

(Surprisingly readable account of the first three minutes of the universe.)

Weinberg S (1993) *Dreams of a Final Theory*. Vintage.
Wells D (1986) *Curious and Interesting Numbers*. Penguin.
*Westfall R (1993) *The Life of Isaac Newton*. Canto.

(Well-researched account of the scientific work and character of Newton.)

*Wheeler JA (1990) *A Journey into Gravity and Spacetime*. Scientific American Library Paperbacks.

(Special and general relativity made interesting and enjoyable.)

*Whitaker A (2006) *Einstein, Bohr and the Quantum Dilemma: From Quantum Theory to Quantum Information*. Cambridge University Press.

(The best of the bunch alongside Baggott in terms of a philosophical analysis of non-locality and Bell's theorem.)

White M, Gribbin J (1993) *Einstein: A Life in Science*. Simon & Schuster.
White M, Gribbin J (1996) *Darwin: A Life in Science*. Simon & Schuster.
Wilczek F (2008) *The Lightness of Being: Mass, Ether, and the Unification of Forces*. Basic Books.
Williams B (1998) *Great Philosophers: Plato (The Great Philosophers)*. Phoenix.
*Williams C (1980) *Free Will and Determinism: A Dialogue*. Hackett.

(Hypothetical philosophical discussion on hard determinism.)

Wittgenstein L (1922) *Tractatus Logico-Philosophicus*. Routledge.
Wittgenstein L (1969) *On Certainty*. Blackwell.
*Wittgenstein L (1973) *Philosophical Investigations*. Blackwell.

(Reveals the workings of his unique insight.)

Woit P (2006) *Not Even Wrong*. Jonathan Cape.
Wolfram S (2002) *A New Kind of Science*. Wolfram Media Incorporated.
Wrathall M (2005) *How to Read Heidegger*. Granta.
Yourgrau P (2005) *A World Without Time*. Allen Lane.

Index

A
Abellán, Carlos, 303
adaptationism, 450
adaptive radiation, 408–410
aether (ether), 103, 122–124, 126, 139
ageing (and relativistic effects), 121, 130, 136, 153, 157–158, 175
Age of Enlightenment (Age of Reason), 3, 7, 9
albinism, 413
alleles, 412–413, 442
alternative mRNA splicing, 355–356, 368
Altman, Sidney, 477
altruism, 441–442
Alzheimer's disease, 381, 494
amino acids, 317–319, 325, 343, 355–358, 363, 369, 385
    post-translational modification of, 365, 367–369
    structure (primary, secondary, tertiary & quaternary), 319, 459
    types of side chain, 317–318
analytical philosophy (symbolic logic), 22, 73
Antennapedia (*Drosophila* mutation), 377, 383, 386
anthropic principle, 163, 178, 228, 397–398
antimatter, 165, 183, 233, 279–280, 282, 285
Aristotle, 1–2, 11, 20–23, 28, 52, 60, 64, 66, 77, 84–85, 97
    and causality, 73
    and the Lyceum, 20
    '*Organon*,' 52
artificial intelligence (AI), 498, 510, 613, 619
    strong versus weak viewpoints, 443, 461
Aspect, Alain, 247, 249, 256–257, 260, 263, 273, 278, 302
Astronomical units (AU), 114
atherosclerosis, 339, 373
atomic number, 193–194, 212, 279, 289, 306
ATP (adenosine triphosphate), 331
    role in metabolism, 367
Avogadro's number, 193
axiomatic set theory, 35, 37–38, 571, 607–608, 612, 617, 619
Ayer, A.J., 19
    '*Language, Truth and Logic*', 19

B
Baars, Bernard, 483, 500–501, 592
    and global workspace theory, 501
    'theatre of consciousness,' 483

Bacon, Francis, 52, 97
Baggott, Jim, 249, 277–278
   'Beyond Measure', 277
Balmer, Johann, 206, 209
Balmer series, 209–215
Barbour, Julian, 276–277
   'The End of Time,' 276
Barish, Barry, 108
Beeckman, Isaac, 61
Bell, John, 245, 302, 550, 564
   and determinism, 544, 566, 572
   and entanglement, 504, 508, 550
   and work of Alain Aspect, 247
   inequality theorem, 76, 245–247, 251, 256–257, 263, 273, 278, 302, 563
Bentham, Jeremy, 73
Berkeley, George, 8, 17, 61, 72, 440, 629
Bernstein, Jeremy, 548
   'Quantum Leaps,' 548
big bang, 105–118, 149, 160–179, 203, 266, 291–292, 303, 421, 478, 504, 545–552, 556–557, 560, 564–565, 570–571, 576–578, 603, 638, 644
   and free will, 149–150, 164, 303, 545–548, 556, 564, 578
big crunch, 118–119, 160–161
bioinformatics, 366, 372–373
Birch and Swinnerton-Dyer conjecture, 138
black-body radiation, 185, 197–199, 202, 204, 217, 221, 226
black holes, 107, 113, 156, 161, 163, 168, 179, 241
   and Hawking radiation, 107
   and Schwarzschild metric, 157
   and Schwarzschild radius, 156
block universe, 149–150
Bohm, David, 218, 220, 245, 251, 257, 259, 262, 264, 267–271, 278, 301, 447, 550, 589, 610
   thoughts on reality, 398
   'Wholeness and the Implicate Order,' 267–268
Bohr, Niels, 25, 110, 189, 207–215, 219–221, 225–229, 235–236, 240–241, 249, 258, 263–264, 278, 302, 307, 553, 564, 588, 611, 631–634
   and bright line spectra, 205
   and entanglement, 504, 508, 550
   Copenhagen interpretation, 182–185, 190, 218–220, 228, 236–241, 248–251, 257–266, 274, 277–278, 298, 611, 631–634
Boltzmann, Ludwig, 123, 126, 194–197, 200, 204, 605–606, 618
   and kinetic theory of gases, 192, 195, 198, 227
Bonner, John Tyler, 340, 392, 461
   'Why Size Matters,' 461
boomeranging, 152
Born, Max, 188, 221–222, 227, 229, 236
Bose, Satyandra, 280–281
Brahe, Tycho, 101–102
Briggs, Derek, 420, 427–428, 435–438
bright line spectra, 205–208
   and Fraunhofer lines, 205
Bronowski, Jacob, 7, 241, 601
   'The Ascent of Man,' 601
Brout, Robert, 293

bubble universes, 177
Burgess Shale, 417–430, 435–436, 439, 444, 474
    description of Burgess fauna, 420, 425, 428, 434, 436
    interpretations by Briggs and Fortey, 437
    interpretations by Gould, 417, 420–422, 430, 435–436, 444

C

Cambrian explosion, 419, 424, 427, 429–432, 434–436
Cantor, Georg, 25, 30, 547, 603
    and set theory, 25, 37–38, 605
cardiac myocyte, 329, 338–340, 356, 372
Carnap, Rudolf, 18
Cartan, Elie, 155
catastrophe theory, 459
causality, 21, 44, 73, 76, 88, 182–183, 457, 556, 572, 637
Cech, Thomas, 477
cell-based therapy ('tissue engineering'), 309, 374
cell theory, 314
central dogma of molecular biology, 343, 354
Chalmers, David, 480, 506, 521, 535
chaos theory, 459, 470–472, 547
Chase, Martha, 342
chemotrophic bacteria, 475
chloroplast, 314, 316–317, 332, 423, 476
Chomsky, Noam, 50, 584–585
chromatin, 346, 349, 357, 361, 368–369, 372, 376
    modification of, 368

    role in gene expression, 325, 490
    structure, 369
cladistics, 436–437
Clauser, John, 302–303
Clausius, Rudolf, 191, 194
cloning (DNA), 348–349, 354, 361, 387
collapse of wave function, 186, 189, 218, 220, 228, 237, 244, 265–267, 480, 504, 632
    and consciousness, 86, 95, 269, 273, 512, 543, 586, 596, 613, 618
Combinatorial Atomism with Lawlike Mappings (CALM), 586
comoving time, 107
comparative anatomy, 414–416
comparative genomics, 365, 376–377
compatibilism and free will, 573
compatibilist, 545–546, 573
complexity theory, 459
Compton, Arthur, 141, 188
Compton effect, 141
conjugation (in bacteria), 348
consciousness, 48, 60, 65, 70, 76, 79–88, 95–96, 148–152, 165, 188, 228, 236, 244–245, 257, 269–278, 308, 342, 479–535, 542–543, 551–554, 558–602, 613–614, 618, 622, 625, 629–634, 638–645
    and artificial intelligence (AI), 498, 510–516
    and brain structure, 96, 276, 451, 480, 483, 490, 492, 499, 501–503, 507, 511, 513, 527
    and evolution, 463, 497–498, 518, 526, 530, 571, 583–584
    and free will, 544, 563, 587

and predeterminism, 547, 549–550, 556, 566, 571
and qualia, 480–482, 496, 510–511, 513, 515, 521, 530–532, 534–540, 552, 554, 578, 591–595, 600, 614, 622, 634, 638, 640, 643
and quantum theory, 96–99, 105, 109, 115, 123, 127, 140–142, 164, 181–190, 195–199, 207, 210, 216–218, 220–221, 227–229, 233, 236–238, 240–241, 244–280, 290, 294–295, 300–303, 307–308, 405, 419–421, 504–507, 545, 550, 554, 560, 564, 589, 593, 611, 634
and self, 76, 87, 395, 490, 502, 542–543
and the collapse of the wavefunction, 264, 504, 632
and the mind-body problem, 481, 495, 505, 511, 517, 532, 585, 601, 639–640
and veiled reality, 632
the 'hard' problem, 480–481, 517, 531, 535, 591, 593–594, 639
role of neuronal microtubules in quantum mechanisms, 480, 497, 508–509, 513
'X factor' of consciousness, 521, 529–530, 634
Conway Morris, Simon, 420–422, 427–428, 431, 436
'The Crucible of Creation,' 420, 427
Copenhagen interpretation (of quantum theory), 182–190, 218–220, 228, 236–241, 248–251, 257–258, 263–266, 274, 277–278, 298, 505, 611, 631–634
Copernicus, Nicholas, 97, 101–102
'Doctrine of the Rotation of Celestial Bodies,' 101
correspondence principle, 221
cosmic antigravity, 116, 167, 173–174
cosmological constant, 160, 167
Couch Adams, J, 56
counterfactuals, 186, 258
Crick, Francis, 46, 342, 354, 480, 495, 501
and central dogma of molecular biology, 343, 354
and DNA structure, 46, 323, 342, 345, 354, 357, 384, 495, 501, 615
'The Astonishing Hypothesis,' 501
cyclotron, 283

D

dark energy, 167, 174, 294, 301
dark matter, 160, 167–168, 173–174, 176, 293, 301
Darwin, Charles, 7, 395–396, 401
and adaptive radiation, 408–410
concept of one common ancestor, 396
Darwinism, 405, 414, 499, 501
Darwin's finches, 409, 627
neo-Darwinism, 410–412, 414
'The Descent of Man,' 403
'The Origin of Species,' 396, 399, 401, 412, 473–474, 476
theory of natural selection, 396, 401, 408

voyage of 'HMS Beagle,' 401–403, 406, 409–410, 414, 420, 424, 438, 447, 471–474, 627
dasein, 85, 643–644
Dawkins, Richard, 367, 404, 414, 434, 436, 449
    and reductionism, 367, 449, 452, 457–458, 503, 536
    on 'outlaw' genes, 440
    'The Blind Watchmaker,' 443
    'The Extended Phenotype,' 440
    'The Selfish Gene,' 440–441
    views on evolution, 373, 460
    on work of Gould, 373, 414, 419, 431, 434, 438–441, 444, 460
de Broglie, Louis, 188, 190, 217–219, 223–225, 245, 264, 505
    and pilot waves, 190, 218, 245, 264, 505, 563
    and quantum theory, 98, 181, 187–188, 270, 300, 507
    and veiled reality, 632
decoherence, 236–237
deconstructionism, 18, 64, 90
Democritus, 11
Dennett, Daniel, 438, 510–511, 521, 536, 538, 573, 575, 587
Derrida, Jacques, 18, 90, 636
    'of Grammatology,' 91
Descartes, Rene, 7–8, 10, 17, 23, 60–68, 71, 74, 85, 91, 97, 507, 526
    Cartesian system, 62, 65, 68
    'cogito ergo sum,' 62, 64–65, 85, 97
    criticism by Derrida, 91
    'Discourse on the Method,' 62
    'Le Monde,' 61
    'Meditations,' 62
    on substance (*res cogitans* versus *res extensa*), 63
    'Principles of Philosophy,' 61–62, 64
d'Espagnat, Bernard, 95, 268, 274–276, 278, 612
    and free will, 52, 563–564, 569, 576, 640
determinism, 87–88, 149, 164, 182, 188, 196, 235, 245–247, 251, 439, 471, 544–573, 580–582, 641
development (biological), 347, 356, 361–362, 365–366, 369–393, 410, 414–416, 421–423, 429, 443, 448, 453–456, 459–462, 471, 473, 475, 478, 483, 488
    and environment, 483, 512, 577
    and evolution, 169, 365, 381–382, 392, 410, 414–416, 423, 443, 453, 462, 473, 622, 627
    and fruit fly (*Drosophila*), 377, 386–387, 389, 411, 417, 453, 455
    and gene expression, 355–357, 361, 365, 369, 376–377, 449, 492
    and methylation, 380
    cardiac development, 372, 383
    dynamic random processes, 376–377
    homeodomain (homeobox) factors and body plan, 415
    skeletal muscle development, 337, 339, 354, 360
developmental noise, 60, 455–456
DeWitt, Bryce, 164

diabetes, 311–312, 336, 448
dialectical materialism, 75–78
    thesis and antithesis, 75, 77
Dirac, Paul, 182, 185, 189, 221, 226, 229–230, 233, 236, 279–280
    and quantum algebra, 182, 221
    Dirac equation, 233
    Dirac units, 185
DNA (deoxyribonucleic acid), 46, 297, 308–310, 315, 319, 341–365, 370, 373, 377, 380, 387, 403
    as agent of heredity, 342
    and gene number, 310, 313, 351, 356, 365, 368, 373, 384, 451
    and RNA transcription, 355, 359–360, 366, 369
    central dogma of molecular biology, 46, 343, 354, 357
    complementary DNA (cDNA), 353–354
    DNA cloning, 387
    DNA mutation, 309, 351, 366, 368, 382, 386, 388, 411, 458
    DNA polymerase, 344, 349–350, 352, 354
    DNA sequencing, 349, 352, 354, 365–366, 370, 377
    hydrogen bonding (Watson-Crick base pairing), 319, 332, 344–345, 350, 352, 365
    methylation, 369, 380, 440, 449
    polymorphisms, 382, 447, 627
    recombinant DNA, 348
    replication, 327, 344–345, 349–351
    structure of, 323, 342, 377
Doctor of Philosophy (PhD or DPhil), 3, 95
Doppler effect, 136
double-slit experiment, 216–218, 235, 245–246
Drake equation, 171
Drosophila melanogaster, 377
    eye development, 389–390, 478
    Hox genes and development of body plan, 384
Dyanokov, Mikhail, 108
Dynamic random processes (in development), 376–381

E

Eccles John, 512
Edelman, Gerald, 480, 495–498, 500–501, 510–512, 514–517, 592, 594–595, 638
    '*Consciousness*' (with Giulio Tononi), 499
    on 'Neural Darwinism,' 498–499, 501
    theory of neuronal group selection (TNGS), 480, 496, 498, 501, 517, 591–592, 594
Ediacaran Period, 424, 475
Ehrenfest, Paul, 188, 199, 210, 221
eightfold way, 285, 287
Einstein, Albert, 7, 25, 29, 59, 93, 99, 103–107, 120–129, 137–142, 152, 155, 158–159, 185–192, 197, 204–207, 217–219, 229, 237–241, 252, 302, 307, 310, 504, 604–606, 637
    and EPR paradox, 127, 237, 239, 241, 245–246, 258, 508
    and intuition, 61, 605
    and photoelectric effect, 120, 197, 204, 217

and wave/particle duality, 215–218, 229, 235, 260–261, 263, 295
Einstein train, 132
$E=mc^2$, 120, 218, 238, 517, 602
influence of Lorentz, 129
influence of Mach, 124
theory of general relativity, 59, 98, 105, 136–141, 160–161, 189, 290, 295–301, 504, 604
theory of special relativity, 98, 105, 117–134, 139–144, 185, 204, 233, 240–241, 249, 258, 264, 279, 283, 292, 505, 555, 635
Einstein-Cartan geometric field equation, 155
electroweak theory, 290–291
elementary particles, 177, 183, 186, 218, 282, 288, 295–297, 303, 538
empiricism, 10, 12, 17, 19, 24, 52, 59–60, 67, 70–75, 79–80, 93
  and Bishop Berkeley, 8
  and Hume, 17, 457
  and Locke, 17, 67, 70–72, 74
  scientific empiricism, 52
  view of Kant, 268
endoplasmic reticulum (ER), 314, 316, 329
energy hill, 159
Englert, François, 293
entanglement, 146, 186, 237, 240–241, 246–247, 249, 251–252, 257, 261, 263–264, 268, 504, 508, 550, 564, 635
entropy, 159–161, 191–192, 195–196, 200, 277, 321
enzymes, 317, 319–322, 324–328, 332, 335, 348–351, 354–356, 359, 361, 363, 367, 369, 379–380, 476–478, 598, 615
  allosteric interactions, 322, 326
  and glycolysis, 332
  catalysis, 320–321, 477
  in chromatin remodelling, 361
  in DNA replication, 351
  inhibitors of enzyme function, 322
  MAP kinase signalling, 326–327, 331, 377
  restriction endonucleases, 348
  turnover number, 321–322
epigenetic modification of DNA, 370, 500, 528
Epimenides's (liar) paradox, 27, 606, 608–609, 619
epistemology, 7, 22–24, 30, 71, 500
Euclid, 16, 25, 34, 161–162
  'Elements of Geometry,' 16
eukaryotes, 316, 329, 350, 413, 423, 476
eukaryotic cells, 171, 315, 317, 340, 346, 349, 357, 362, 371, 423–424, 476
  appearance in evolutionary history, 316
  components of, 289, 299, 306, 338
event horizon (Schwarzschild singularity), 156
Everett, Hugh, 164, 177
evolution, 308–317, 340, 347, 351, 365–370, 376, 381–382, 389–411, 414–423, 426–447, 453, 456, 460, 462, 469–471, 473–478, 497–500, 516–518, 526–531, 547, 571, 584, 601–602, 614, 624–625, 627–628

adaptationism, 450
adaptive radiation, 408–410
and brain development in hominids, 99, 379, 411, 500, 526
and Burgess Shale fossils, 419, 435
and consciousness, 463, 497–498, 518, 526, 530, 571, 583–584
and development, 89, 410, 414
and organism size, 455, 458–459
cambrian explosion, 419, 424, 427, 429–432, 434–436
coevolution, 416–417, 430
comparative anatomy, 414
comparative genomics, 365, 376–377
cone of increasing diversity, 421
Darwinism, 405, 410–412, 414, 417, 419, 438, 495, 498–499, 501
decimation and diversification, 419, 421
directional evolution, 410
exon shuffling, 370
gradualism, 418–419, 422, 425
natural selection, 309–312, 381–382, 392–411, 432–434, 438–439, 442, 446, 450, 462–463, 474, 518, 522–523, 530–531, 549–550, 584, 614, 622, 627
neo-Darwinism, 410–412, 414
origins of life on earth, 399, 423
punctuated equilibrium, 54, 417–420, 422, 430–431, 435–436, 443–445
ribosomal (r)RNA genes and evolution, 357

speciation, 402, 409, 418, 443
existentialism, 10, 76, 80–87
and Heidegger, 78, 84, 90–91
and Kierkegaard, 82–83
and Sartre, 82
exotic particles, 112, 165, 284, 297
extinction events, 432–433, 435
and Burgess Shale fauna, 419, 435
extinction of the dinosaurs, 432, 434
permo-triassic mass extinction, 429, 433–434

F

falsification (principle) and scientific enquiry, 56, 58, 60, 74, 93, 298, 309, 598, 608
fatalism, 570–571
fate (of the universe), 106, 160
Feigenbaum point, 468, 472
Fermi, Enrico, 280
Feyerabend, Paul, 54, 93
'Against Method,' 55
Feynman, Richard, 98, 110, 218, 230, 302, 636
Feynman diagram, 232
'Feynman Lectures in Physics,' 218
'QED,' 183–184, 230–232, 265, 291, 296
Fibonacci sequence, 466–468
FitzGerald, George Francis, 129
Flanagan, Owen, 482
forces, 102–108, 113, 119, 149, 152–154, 163, 167, 175–179, 184–185, 207, 267, 279–301, 306, 319, 406, 410, 449, 456–463, 491, 544, 551–571, 577–578

Fortey, Richard, 435–436
Foucault, Michel, 24, 90, 92
Fourier analysis, 225
Fournier, Jacques, 112
fractals, 112–113, 467, 470–473
   and Mandelbrot set, 471
Franklin, Rosalind, 342
Fraunhofer, Joseph von, 205
Fraunhofer lines, 205
free energy, 320–321, 334
free-float, 143, 152–153, 155, 157, 159
free will, 52, 57, 79, 149–150, 164, 277, 303, 507, 509, 513, 544–551, 555–566, 568–569, 572–578, 582, 586–587
   and hard determinism, 544, 551, 556–557
   and predeterminism, 149, 548, 570
   as illusion, 149, 303, 545, 550–551, 559–563, 574–575, 578, 640–641
Frege, Friedrich Ludwig Gottlob, 22–23, 27, 37–39, 42, 86
   and quantification theory, 16, 23
   and symbolic logic (analytical philosophy), 22, 73
   'Begriffsschrift,' 22–23, 27, 37, 39, 86
   'Grundgesetze,' 27
Freud, Sigmund, 486–487
Friedman models and expansion of the universe, 161
fringe-consciousness, 483, 630
fruit fly (*D. melanogaster*), 377, 386–387, 389, 411, 417, 453, 455
fundamental (elementary) particles, 183, 186, 218, 282, 288, 295–296, 303
fuzzy logic, 18

G

Gaia hypothesis, 404–405
Galapagos Islands, 401, 406, 408–409, 462, 474, 627
Galilei, Galileo, 7, 404, 603
Gell-Mann, Murray, 230, 284
   and the eightfold way, 285, 287
gendanken (thought experiment), 127–128, 132, 147, 227, 238–239, 261, 263, 617–618
   delayed-choice experiment, 261, 263–264
gene editing, 372–373
gene expression, 310, 315, 325–327, 341, 343, 346, 353–358, 361–362, 365, 368–371, 376–377, 381–382, 386, 490, 492, 500
   central dogma of gene expression, 46, 343, 354, 357
   in development, 356, 361–362, 368–369, 371, 376–381, 500
   epigenetic modulation by methylation, 370, 500, 528
   housekeeping genes, 360, 369
   mechanisms of gene regulation, 368
   transcription, 326–327, 343, 346, 353–355, 357–362, 369–370, 372, 374–380, 382–385, 389
   transcription factors, 326–327, 359–362, 369, 372, 375–380, 382, 384–385, 389
   translation, 320, 346, 353, 358–359, 362–365, 371, 378
gene pool, 416
general relativity, 59, 98, 105, 120, 136–141, 146, 153, 160–161, 189, 251, 290, 295–296, 300–301, 504–506, 604

contribution of Minkowski, 140
extension by Kaluza, 295
free-float, 143, 152–153, 155, 157, 159
interval, 126, 144, 148, 153, 157
gene structure, 313, 316, 323, 366, 384, 387
    exons and introns, 355–356
    promoters and enhancers, 359
genome, 95, 309, 315–316, 331, 343, 351–354, 357, 365–368, 371–372, 376, 380–384, 388–389, 415, 423, 447–448, 452, 473, 523, 598
    comparative genomics, 365, 376–377
    gene number and sizes, 443
    human genome, 95, 309, 315–316, 331, 351, 367–376, 384, 447–448, 528
    human genome sequencing project, 95, 447–448, 528
genomics, 310, 365–366, 376–377, 395, 440
    comparative genomics, 365, 376–377
geodesics, 153
Ghirardi–Rimini–Weber theory (GRW), 220
Gilbert, Walter, 370
global workspace theory (GWT), 501
glycolysis, 332–336
Gödel, Kurt, 15, 23–31, 34–38, 92, 194, 508, 512, 570–571, 593, 604–619
    and Cantor, 25, 31, 34, 38, 194, 605–606, 618
    contribution to Einstein's work on general relativity, 189

criticism of Russell & his work, 23
incompleteness theorem, 15, 24, 37, 92, 570, 593, 605–607, 616–617
golden ratio, 463–468
    and Fibonacci sequence, 466–468
Goldschmidt, Richard, 418
Gould, Stephen Jay, 373, 414–422, 427, 430–446, 450, 460, 469, 584
    and decimation and diversification, 419, 421
    and punctuated equilibrium, 417, 419–420, 422, 431, 435, 443–445
    and spandrels, 442, 584
    'Wonderful Life-The Burgess Shale and The Nature of History,' 417, 419–425, 435–436
gradualism, 418–419, 422, 425
grand unified theory (GUT), 108, 265, 269, 279–280, 290–295, 299–300, 317, 506–507, 552, 565, 571, 581, 608, 641
Grant, Rosemary and Peter, 409, 418, 627
graviton, 107, 289, 296, 298
green fluorescent protein (GFP) reporter gene, 361
Griffith, Frederick, 341
GRW, 220
GUT, 108, 265, 269, 279–280, 290–291, 294–295, 299–300, 317, 506–507, 552, 565, 571, 581, 608, 641
GWT (see Global Workspace Theory)

H

Hacker, Peter, 622
Hadamard, Jacques, 484, 622, 629
   'The Psychology of Invention in The Mathematical Field,' 484, 622
Haeckel, Ernst, 390, 415
haemoglobin, 317, 322–325, 351, 365, 374
Haldane, J.B.S., 109, 612
Harris, Sam, 558–560
   'Free Will,' 557, 569, 577
Hawking, Stephen, 98, 107, 159, 299, 608
   Hawking radiation, 107
Heaviside, Oliver, 122
Hegel, Georg, 9, 25, 66–67, 75–78, 87, 90
   'Encyclopaedia of the Philosophical Sciences,' 77
   influence of Kant, 67, 76–78, 607
   influence of Spinoza, 9, 43, 76, 561
   'The Phenomenology of Mind,' 76–77
Heidegger, Martin, 9, 24, 48, 78, 81, 83–86, 90–91, 615, 643
   and dasein, 85, 643
   'Being and Time,' 48, 83, 86
Heisenberg, Werner, 25, 182, 189–190, 221–224, 226, 229, 233–236, 248, 635
   and correspondence principle, 221
   and matrix mechanics, 223
   and uncertainty principle, 30, 174, 190, 219, 234–236, 238–239, 266, 548
Helmholtz, Hermann, 122, 190–191, 194
Hershey, Alfred, 342
Hertz, Heinrich, 127
hidden variables, 240–241, 246, 250–251, 255–264, 271, 278
   and John Bell, 245–246, 302, 564
   contribution of von Neumann, 632
Higgs boson, 95, 288, 291–293
Higgs, Peter, 288, 292, 405
Hilbert, David, 16, 27, 34–35, 37, 138, 211, 604–605, 607
   Hilbert space, 211
Hippocrates, 2
histone acetyltransferase (HAT), 369
histone deacetylase (HDAC), 327, 369
histones, 327, 346, 357, 369
Hobbes, Thomas, 61, 73
Hodge Conjecture, 138
Hofstadter, Douglas, 172, 498, 613
   and AI, 172, 498, 592–593, 613–616, 619–623
   and strange loops, 592–593, 619–623
   'Gödel, Escher, Bach: An Eternal Golden Braid,' 613, 615, 619
   'I am a Strange Loop,' 592
homeobox/homeodomain (Hox) genes, 378, 380, 384–389, 415, 440, 453, 478
   in Drosophila development, 385–390, 415, 478
   in mammalian development, 384, 388–389, 415
homeotic mutations, 377, 386, 388
Honderich, T, 573–574
Hooke, Robert, 103, 314

Hox genes, 378, 380, 384–389, 415, 440, 453, 478
Hoyle Fred, 106
Hubble, Edwin, 106, 119, 167
    Hubble constant, 106
    Hubble flow, 106–107
    Hubble radius, 175
    Hubble's law, 106, 119
Hume, David, 8–9, 12, 17, 19, 58, 61, 67, 73–75, 91, 457, 637
    'An Enquiry Concerning the Principles of Morals,' 73
    causality and inductive reasoning, 56, 73
Humphrey, Nicholas, 510, 515–531, 584, 588–593, 614, 624–626
    and Philosophical zombies, 521, 537
    on evolution, 411, 446, 460
    'seeing red', 515, 519, 536
    'Soul Dust,' 531, 592
    'The Inner Eye,' 518, 522, 528, 624
Hund, Friedrich, 213
Hund's rule, 213
Husserl, Edmund, 77, 80–81, 84, 87, 90–91
    'Logical Investigations,' 80
hydrogen bond, 319, 332, 344–345, 349
    in DNA (Watson-Crick base pairing), 319, 332, 344–345, 350, 352, 365
    in protein structure, 324, 381

I

idealism, 10–11, 13–14, 20, 25, 72, 75, 86–87, 602
immune system, 328–329
immunoglobulins (Ig), 328–329, 365
incommensurability, 93
incompleteness, 4, 15, 24, 27–30, 35, 37, 92, 593, 604–608, 616–618
indeterminism, 5, 30, 86, 504–505, 545–564, 571–574, 584, 598, 603
    and free will, 52, 544–551, 563–564, 569–577, 587
    quantum indeterminism, 30, 86, 188, 258, 553–564, 573, 584, 603
infinity, 4, 31–34, 198, 265, 533, 547, 585, 603–604, 606, 618, 635, 637
insulin, 318, 325–326, 335–336, 356
intentionality, 486, 490–491
interferometry, 108, 122, 246, 258–259, 318
interval, 126, 144, 148, 153, 157, 469
isotopes, 193, 279, 305–306, 475
isotropy, 107

J

Jackendoff, Ray, 502
Jackson, Frank, 538
    and 'Mary's Room' *gendanken* (thought experiment), 538
Jaki, Stanley, 608
James, William, 79, 483, 501, 573
    'Pragmatism', 10, 78–79
    'Principles of Psychology', 79, 501
Jeans, James, 9, 198–199, 202
Johnson-Laird, Philip, 501
Jung, Carl, 486–489
    and archetypes, 487

K

Kafatos, Menos, 273, 631
Kaluza, Theodor, 295

Kant, Immanuel, 7, 9, 12–14, 17, 22, 61, 67, 73, 76–78, 84, 86–89, 93, 95, 268, 274, 607, 612
    criticism by Frege, 22, 86
    criticism by Heidegger, 9, 78, 84, 86
    'Critique of Pure Reason', 12–13, 17, 76, 86
    'General History of Nature and the Theory of the Heavens', 12
    influence of Hume, 9, 67, 73, 76
    influence on Hegel, 9, 67, 76–78
Kepler, Johannes, 101–103, 159
    laws of planetary motion, 101–102, 159
Kierkegaard, Søren Aabye, 82–83
    objective *versus* subjective truths, 82–83
Kirchhoff, Gustav, 198, 205
Krebs (TCA) cycle, 333
Krebs, Hans, 333
Kripke, Saul, 608
Kuhn, Thomas, 53–54, 92–93, 307, 421
    'The Structure of Scientific Revolutions', 54

L

Lamarck, Jean Baptiste, 396, 402, 410
    'transmutation of species,' 396
language, 5–6, 11, 15–27, 30, 38–53, 59–60, 64–65, 85–94, 99, 159, 166, 182, 222, 268, 270–274, 300, 424, 445, 481, 486, 491, 499–500, 514, 519–521, 528–536, 542–543, 581–587, 595–599, 603–612, 629–643
    and Chomsky, 50, 584–585
    and evolution, 445, 500, 584
    and logic, 15–30, 38–47, 91, 584, 595
    and memory, 514, 596
    and Nietzsche, 86, 89
    and Searle, 481, 491, 514
    and Wittgenstein, 17, 24–25, 30, 39–52, 59–60, 64, 85, 89, 91–93, 270, 543
    criticism by Derrida, 91–92, 636
    language games, 49, 93–94
    meta-language vs object language, 609
Laplace, Pierre-Simon, 235, 555
    'Laplace's demon,' 555
Large Hadron Collider (LHC), 57, 94–95, 283–294, 297–299, 405, 478
Larmor, Joseph, 137
Leibniz, Gottfried, 12, 17, 61–62, 66, 68–70, 137, 612
    'Monadology', 70
    monads, 69–70
    'Theodicy', 68
Lenard, Philipp, 203
Le Verrier, U., 56
Lewontin, Richard, 373, 391, 407, 414, 438, 440, 442, 446–448, 450–460, 483, 584
    and adaptationism, 450
    and consciousness, 451–453, 483–484
    and constructionist viewpoint, 450
    and norms of reaction, 455
    and spandrels, 442, 584
    on genes and environment, 373, 391, 407, 442, 446, 450, 452, 454–455, 458, 483
    'Human Diversity', 407
    'The Doctrine of DNA', 446–449

'The Triple Helix', 391, 446, 452–453
liar (Epimenides) paradox, 27
libertarianism and free will, 572–573
Linnaeus, Carl, 425
   taxonomic definitions, 424
Livio, Mario, 468
   'the golden ratio', 463–470
Lobachevskian space, 162, 619
locality, 152, 237, 239–241, 243, 245–251, 257–258, 271–273, 555, 565
   and John Bell, 245–247, 249–251
Locke, John, 8, 17, 61, 67, 70–74, 452, 629
   'An Essay Concerning Human Understanding', 70–71
logic, 7–8, 11, 14–52, 55, 58, 63, 68, 77–81, 85–6, 89–91, 97, 109, 272, 300, 312, 459, 463, 568, 574, 580, 584, 593–5, 604–616
   and Aristotle, 2, 20–23, 77, 97
   and Frege, 22–23, 35, 37–38, 42, 86
   and Gödel, 15, 23–24, 27, 29, 35, 37–38, 604–613, 617
   and Hegel, 77–78
   and Husserl, 80–81
   and language, 15–17, 19–22, 25, 27, 30, 38, 40–47, 91, 584, 595
   and limits of knowledge, 7, 23, 30
   and mathematics, 15, 20, 22–26, 29, 35, 38, 463, 600, 604–610, 612, 616
   and Wittgenstein, 7, 9, 17, 25, 30, 38, 40–47, 49–52, 86, 580
   deductive logic, 14, 80

first-order logic, 15
fuzzy logic, 18
inductive logic, 8, 20, 58
   in scientific method, 404, 638
   scientific method, 18, 46, 52–53, 55, 57, 78, 97, 404, 605, 610
sorites paradox, 17
symbolic logic (analytical philosophy), 15, 22–23
truth-values, 18, 46
logical positivism, 14, 18–20, 28, 38, 40, 93, 123
   and Aristotle, 20–22, 28
   and Cantor, 30–34, 37–38, 606, 617
   and Frege, 22–23, 38, 86
   and Gödel, 23, 27, 34–37
   and Popper, 30, 55, 93
   and Russell, 23–30, 42
   and Vienna Circle, 18–19, 45, 56
   and Wittgenstein, 38–52, 92
loopholes (quantum), 257, 302–303
Lorentz, Hendrik Antoon, 129, 137, 139, 142, 188
   Lorentz-FitzGerald contraction, 129, 137
   Lorentz transformation, 129–130
LUCA (Last Universal Common Ancestor), 476–478
   and Darwin's 'one primordial form,' 476
Lyotard, Jean-Francois, 93–94

M

Mach, Ernst, 123–124, 126, 129, 142
Magee, Bryan, 55, 58, 60
Maldacena, J., 241
Malus's law, 254

Mandelbrot, Benoit, 471
many worlds hypothesis, 164, 266, 555
Margulis, L., 404
Marxism, 55, 75–76
Marx, Karl, 69, 76
Mary's Room thought argument, 538
matrix mechanics, 182, 190, 221–224, 226, 233, 236
Maxwell, James Clerk, 103–104, 122, 127–129, 142, 179, 192, 194, 196, 198
   and electromagnetic wave theory, 104, 122, 127, 142, 182, 216, 226, 229
   and kinetic theory of gases, 192, 198, 227
   Maxwell distribution, 194
Maynard Smith, John, 382, 388, 412, 423, 438, 450
   'Shaping Life', 382, 388
   'The Origins of Life' (with Eors Szathmary), 423
McGinn, Colin, 481–482, 532, 540, 562–563, 582–588, 591, 593–594
   and mysterians ('transcendental naturalism'), 481–482, 585
   and reality, 532, 540
   Combinatorial Atomism and Lawlike Mappings (CALM), 586
   'Mysterious Flame', 562
Meinong, Alexius, 28
memory, 16, 75, 80, 95, 452, 482, 489–492, 499–502, 514–515, 520, 529, 594, 596–598, 616
   molecular basis in model organisms, 324
   short-vs long-term memory, 499, 597

Mendel, Gregor, 341, 347, 386, 402, 411–413
   Mendelian inheritance/genetics, 347, 386, 402, 412–413
Merleau-Ponty, Maurice, 82, 86, 497
metabolism, 308–312, 317, 334–338, 365, 385, 463, 475–476, 492, 566
   chemotrophic metabolism, 476
   electron transport chain, 334
   glycolysis, 332–336
   Krebs (TCA) cycle, 333
   Metabolic rate and size, 454
   oxidative phosphorylation, 332–334
metabolomics, 366
metamathematics, 607
metaphysics, 9, 12–13, 17, 20, 24, 41, 44, 61–62, 65, 76, 79, 94, 97, 512
   and Aristotle, 20–21, 97
   and Descartes, 12, 17, 61–62
   and free will, 79, 545, 572
   and Kant, 61, 95
   and Leibniz, 61
   and Mach, 123
   and Nietzsche, 89
   and Wittgenstein, 9, 17, 41, 44, 91
   Metaphysical libertarianism, 572–573
   metaphysical realism, 272–273, 635
   natural philosophy and science, 9
Michelson-Morley experiment, 122, 129, 139
microarray, 366
microtubules, 340, 423, 480, 497, 508–509, 513
   in cytoskeleton, 340, 423
   as molecular motors, 336

role in quantum mechanism of consciousness, 480, 497, 508–509, 513
Miles, James, 575
Milky Way, 113, 115, 171
Millikan, Robert, 204
Mill, John Stuart, 73, 629
Mills, Robert, 138
mind-body problem, 65–66, 72, 95, 187, 267, 276, 480–481, 495, 505, 511, 517, 532–533, 583–588, 601, 639–640
Minkowski, Hermann, 140
Mitchell, Morgan, 303
Mitchell, Peter, 334
mitochondria, 314, 316, 333–334, 338, 423, 440, 476
    Mitochondrial genes, 440
'Mitochondrial Eve,' 440
molecular mass, 192–194
molecular motors, 336–341
momenergy, 154–157
momentum, 102, 141, 154, 158–159, 207–210, 218–224, 233–235, 238, 246–248, 258
    and uncertainty, 219, 233–235
monads, 69–70
Moore, George Edward (G.E.), 25, 43, 51
morphogenesis, 376, 393
Mullis, Kary, 352
multiverse, 118, 149–150, 169–170, 173–179, 400, 556, 560, 568, 571
    and Tegmark classification system, 177
mutations, 309, 324, 351, 362, 366–368, 371–372, 374, 377, 382–389, 392, 396, 411–412, 416, 440, 442, 448, 453–458, 474

gain-of-function *versus* loss-of-function mutations, 386
homeotic mutations in development, 377, 386, 388
Myers-Briggs test, 488
myocardial infarction, 339
myoglobin, 322–325
mysterians (new mysterians), 481–482, 585, 604, 612

N

Nadeau, Robert, 273, 631
Nagel, Thomas, 479, 481, 588
    view from nowhere, 541, 588–589, 634
natural selection (see evolution), 309–312, 381–382, 392–411, 432–434, 438–439, 442, 446, 450, 462–463, 474, 518, 522–523, 530–531, 549–550, 584, 614, 622, 627
Navier-Stokes equation, 138
Ne'eman, Yuval, 285
    and the eightfold way, 285, 287
Neural Darwinism, 495, 498–499, 501
Neurath, Otto, 18
neurons, 310, 368, 451–454, 482–485, 491–503, 508, 512–516, 530, 561, 594, 597–601, 613, 625
    and Alzheimer's disease, 381, 494
    and consciousness, 86, 95–96, 451–452, 480–485, 491–502, 512–516, 519, 523, 529, 543, 586, 594, 613
    and memory, 452, 491–492, 499, 514, 594, 597–598
    in animal models, 373, 376
    mirror neurons, 530, 625
    neuronal group selection (Neural Darwinism), 495

neuronal reentry, 495–496, 514
structure and synapses, 493, 597, 613
Newtonian mechanics, 97, 119, 140, 185, 208
Newton, Isaac, 7, 9, 12, 14, 56, 59, 68, 94, 97, 99, 102–104, 123, 129, 137
   and light, 127, 230
   and natural philosophy (physics), 9
   laws of motion, 102, 104
   laws of universal gravitation, 103
   'Principia', 15, 26–30, 35, 37–38, 71, 103, 606–607
Nietzsche, Friedrich, 7, 64–69, 75, 84–90, 457, 486
   'Beyond Good and Evil', 89
   'Thus Spoke Zarathustra', 86
nominalism, 11
noumena, 9, 13–14, 17, 67, 77, 88–89, 93, 268, 274, 607, 610, 612
   rejection by Hegel, 9, 67, 77
nuclear energy/power, 104, 202, 279–306

O

(orchestrated) objective reduction, 505, 509
Occam's razor, 164
Ohno, Susumo, 367–368
Olbers's paradox, 111–112
ontogeny, 390–392, 415, 454
origin of life on Earth hypotheses, 399–401
orthogenesis, 410
'outlaw' genes, 440
oxidative phosphorylation, 332–334

P

Papineau, David, 538
   and 'Mary's Room' thought argument, 538
   and supervenience, 538
parsec, 114–115
Pauling, Linus, 342
Pauli, Wolfgang, 189–190, 210–215, 221–222, 280, 287, 294–295
   and Pauli exclusion principle, 190, 211, 280, 294
Peano, Giuseppe (Peano arithmetic), 26
peer review, 4, 94
Peirce, Charles Sanders, 78
Penrose, Roger, 118, 150–151, 160–163, 187–188, 236, 291, 471, 480, 497–517, 540, 593, 638
   and big bang/Big Crunch, 160
   and mind-body problem, 480–481, 495, 505, 511, 517, 532–533, 583–586, 588
   and objective reduction, 505, 509
   and Penrose tiling, 508
   and quantum mechanism of consciousness, 163, 236, 497, 502, 505–512, 516–517, 593, 638
   and quantum theory, 163, 187–188, 480, 497, 504, 506–507, 509, 512
   and 'three worlds,' 150–152, 511
   'The Emperor's New Mind,' 497, 502
   views on artificial intelligence (AI), 498, 502, 506, 511–513
Perelman, Grigory, 139
periodic table, 193, 211–213, 215, 220, 279, 289

perturbation theory, 184
Perutz, Max, 323
phenomenology, 10, 76–77, 80–82, 86
   and Husserl, 77, 80–82, 84, 87, 90–91
   and Merleau-Ponty, 82, 86, 497
   and Sartre, 82
phenotype, 381, 386, 407–408, 413, 440–441, 452, 454–455, 500
   'extended' phenotype, 440–441
   relationship to genotype, 407
philosophical zombies, 521–522, 537, 638–639
phosphorylation, 320, 325, 327, 332–334, 355, 358, 365, 368, 370, 508
   MAP kinases, 326–327, 331, 377, 493
   protein phosphatases, 325, 367, 598
   receptor tyrosine kinases (RTK), 326
photoelectric effect, 190, 197, 203–204, 216–217, 226
photoionisation, 201
photosynthesis, 429, 475–476
physicalism, 536–538, 540, 551–554, 573, 638–639, 642
   and free will, 52, 640
   and philosophical zombies, 521, 537
pilot waves, 190, 218, 220, 245, 262, 264, 505, 563
Planck, Max, 96, 129, 167, 174, 181, 187–189, 197–208, 220–224, 229
   and black-body radiation, 185, 197–203, 217, 221
   Planck length, 174, 181, 296

Planck's constant, 181, 200, 204, 207, 234
Planck time, 96, 167, 174, 181
Planck units, 208
planetary motion, 101–102, 159, 209
Plato, 1, 10–11, 13, 20, 22, 24, 64, 85–87, 150, 163
   and idealism, 10, 13–14, 20, 25, 72, 75, 86–87
   'Republic,' 86
   'Theory of Ideas,' 11
Platonic realism, 25, 103, 150–151, 453, 602
Platonic world, 150, 152, 453, 503, 511
Poincaré conjecture, 138
Poincaré, Henri, 27, 137
polarisation of light, 242–243, 246, 254, 554–555
polymerase chain reaction (PCR), 351–354, 356, 387, 475
polymorphisms (in DNA), 382, 390, 447, 627
   single nucleotide polymorphism (SNP), 447
Popper, Karl, 30, 52, 55–60, 74, 93, 150, 298, 311, 512
   and falsification, 58, 298, 581, 598
   on language, 30, 44
population genetics, 396, 414
post-structuralism, 92
pragmatism, 10, 78–79
   and James, 29
   and Peirce, 79
predeterminism, 149, 410, 421, 547–556, 561–562, 566–571, 576–578, 640

and free will, 544–551, 563–564, 569, 572, 576–577, 587
and GUT/TOE, 269, 507, 548–578, 640
and mind, 481, 615, 619
and physicalism, 536, 551–554
and the quantum world, 258, 568, 574

Prigogine, Ilya, 581–582
'*The End of Certainty*', 581

prions, 377, 380–381

prokaryotes, 171, 315–316, 350, 355, 360, 411, 423–425, 477, 627
difference from eukaryotes, 423

promoter, 359–362, 369–370, 376, 380

protein kinase signalling, 325, 327, 331, 367, 493, 508, 598
in gene expression, 325, 490

proteins, 46, 310–330, 336–374, 378–390, 416, 449, 454, 458, 478, 598–599, 615
amino acid and protein structure, 317–318, 324–325, 357, 363–365, 369–371, 381–385, 448, 459, 477
and chromatin, 361
and prion diseases, 380
enzymes, 317–328, 332, 335, 348–356, 359–363, 367–369, 379–380, 476–478
protein modifications and activity, 310, 325–327, 355, 370
protein synthesis (translation), 320, 346, 353–365, 370, 378, 563, 598

proteolysis, 325

proteome/proteomics, 310, 366, 370, 372, 440

Ptolemy, 100–101, 637

punctuated equilibrium, 54, 417–420, 422, 430, 435–436, 443–445

P vs. NP, 138

Pythagoras, 2, 11, 74, 133

Q

qualia, 480–482, 511, 513, 515, 521, 530–540, 553–554, 578, 591–595, 600, 614, 622, 634, 638, 640, 643
and artificial intelligence (AI), 498, 511, 614
and consciousness, 95, 269, 273, 512, 523, 543, 586
and philosophical zombies, 521, 537
and reality, 265, 268–269, 532, 535

quanta, 181–182, 189, 200–201, 204, 273

quantification theory, 16, 23

quantum algebra, 182, 221

quantum chromodynamics (QCD), 184, 265, 291, 296

quantum electrodynamics (QED), 183–184, 230–233, 265, 291, 296
and Feynman, 218, 230–232, 235, 266, 297, 302

quantum entanglement (see entanglement)

quantum field theory (QFT), 184–185, 229–230, 233

quantum indeterminism, 30, 86, 188, 258, 553–564, 573, 603

quantum measurement problem, 236, 266, 550

quantum measurements and the 'measurement problem,' 220, 236, 244, 257, 265–267, 504–505, 550, 554–558, 613, 630–631, 633, 635

quantum mechanics (or quantum physics/ theory), 98, 110, 127, 131, 177, 183–188, 217, 221–229, 233, 238, 244–256, 261–262, 267–272, 276, 292, 295, 299–301, 497, 505, 511–512, 548, 554, 563, 575, 631, 635
   and consciousness, 86, 273
   and Copenhagen interpretation, 182–185, 190, 218–220, 228, 236–241, 248–251, 257–266, 274–278, 298, 505
   and delayed-choice *gendanken* (thought experiment), 261
   and determinism/indeterminism, 5, 30, 86, 548, 554
   and hidden variable theory, 243–245, 247, 251, 255–257, 261, 264, 269, 302, 563
   and Standard Model, 184, 282, 288, 290–294, 296, 298, 300–301
   and string theory, 177–178, 188, 294–296, 298–300, 460
   and uncertainty, 30, 84, 182, 185, 190, 219, 234–236, 238–239, 266, 398, 427, 472
   philosophical implications according to Bohm, 245, 257, 267, 301, 563
   quantum mechanical probability, 227
   relationship to QFT & QED, 184
   Schrödinger's cat, 189, 227–228, 505
   Solvay conference, 188–189, 238
quantum numbers, 70, 190, 209, 211, 215, 220–221, 225
   and orbital filling, 213
Quine, W.V.O., 93

R

Ramsay, Frank, 43
rationalism, 12–13, 17, 60–71, 93
   and Descartes, 12, 17, 60–66, 71
   and Kant, 12–13, 17, 60–61, 93
   and Leibniz, 12, 17, 61, 68–70
   and Spinoza, 61, 66–68
Rayleigh (Lord), 198–199, 202
Rayleigh-Jeans law, 198, 201
realism, 8, 11, 86, 245, 249–252, 257, 260, 271–273, 301, 602, 611, 635, 637
   epistemological realism, 635
   metaphysical realism, 272, 635
   Platonic realism, 602
reality, 1, 4, 6–14, 17, 21, 25, 28–31, 40–47, 51–59, 63–67, 70–72, 75–85, 88–110, 117, 120, 131, 141–151, 164–176, 181–188, 194–196, 220, 228, 231, 234–250, 257–258, 261–279, 291–293, 298–309, 395–398, 408, 442, 460, 469–471, 479–491, 498, 504–518, 521–560, 564, 566–615, 621–623, 627–646
   and 4-D spacetime, 144, 149, 153
   and determinism, 164, 235, 245, 471, 544–558, 566, 571–572, 582, 641
   and free will, 52, 544, 547, 551, 563–564, 569, 572, 576–577, 587
   and scientific method, 53–59, 97, 166, 269, 534–537, 553, 599, 611, 645
   and the quantum world, 105, 187, 195, 237, 258, 265–267, 275, 278–279, 505, 553, 555, 568, 574

objective reality, 1, 77–78, 96, 470, 479, 484, 490, 515, 518, 523–524, 614–615
'veiled' reality, 268, 274–276, 278–279, 612, 632
recombinant DNA, 348
redshift, 112, 115–116, 119
reductionism, 367, 449, 452, 457–458, 503, 536
   in biology, 315, 459–460
   in philosophy, 1, 3, 39–40, 61, 486, 521
Rees, Martin, 9, 110, 166, 400
   'Our Cosmic Habitat,' 170, 399
Reichenbach, Hans, 18, 103
relativity, 29, 59, 93–146, 153–162, 175, 181, 185–189, 204, 233, 238–241, 249–251, 258, 263–283, 290–301, 307, 398, 504–507, 551, 555, 564, 604–605, 635
   general relativity, 8, 105, 120, 136–141, 146, 153, 160–161, 189, 251, 290, 295–296, 300–301, 504–506, 604
   special relativity, 98, 105, 112, 117–129, 134–142, 162, 185, 204, 233, 239–241, 249–251, 258, 263–265, 279–283, 292, 505, 551, 555, 564, 635
relativity of simultaneity, 128
renormalisation, 184
restriction endonucleases, 348
reverse transcriptase, 353–354
reverse transcription, 343, 353–354
Riemann, Bernhard, 35, 137, 139
RNA (ribonucleic acid), 46, 308, 317, 327, 343, 346, 353–355, 357–359, 364, 371, 423, 477–478

messenger RNA (mRNA), 327, 343, 357–358
microRNAs (miRNA), 357, 368, 371–372, 454
nuclear RNA (snRNA), 357
ribosomal RNA (rRNA), 357, 364, 425, 476–477
ribozymes (RNA enzymes), 327
RNA interference (RNAi), 371
RNA world hypothesis, 477
small cytoplasmic RNAs (scRNA), 357
splicing & alternative RNA splicing, 355–359, 368, 370
transfer RNA (tRNA), 364
Rovelli, Carlo, 561
   'Seven Brief Lessons on Physics,' 561
Russell, Bertrand, 23–30, 34–35, 37–40, 43, 55, 68, 73, 107, 120, 402, 507, 605–606, 617
   'A History of Western Philosophy,' 24
   and Frege, 23, 27, 38–39, 42, 86
   and Gödel, 23, 27, 29–30, 34, 37–38, 606, 617
   and Wittgenstein, 24–25, 30, 39–40, 42–43
   classes/sets, 26, 28
   'Principia Mathematica' (with A.N. Whitehead), 26, 30, 35, 37–38
   Russell's paradox, 26–27, 38, 605, 617
   theory of descriptions, 28
   theory of types, 27–28
   'The Principles of Mathematics,' 26

S

Sanchez, Francisco, 64
Sanger, Frederick, 315, 349, 370
Sartre, Jean Paul, 81–82, 86–87, 90
   '*Being and Nothingness*', 87
Schmidhuber, Jürgen, 397
Schopenhauer, Arthur, 17, 87–89
   '*The World as Will and Representation*', 88
Schrödinger, Erwin, 182, 189–190, 223–226, 233, 236, 240, 263, 266
   Schrödinger's cat, 189, 227–230
   Schrödinger wave equation, 224–225, 236, 250, 266
Schwarzschild, Karl, 153, 156
   and black holes, 156–157
   Schwarzschild geometry, 156–157
   Schwarzschild singularity, 156
science & scientific method, 6, 52–59, 74, 82, 97, 166, 269, 308–309, 341, 366, 405, 475, 480, 490, 501, 531–544, 553, 595–600, 610–611, 636–639, 645
   and dialectical materialism, 75–78
   and Popper, 52, 55–60, 74, 298, 311, 512
   and pragmatism, 78
   and Wittgenstein, 47, 92
   Baconian method, 52
   falsification, 56, 58–60, 74, 93, 298, 309, 540, 581, 598, 608
   multi-disciplinary approach (in biology), 309, 373
   objectivity *versus* subjectivity, 82
   thesis, antithesis and synthesis, 75–77
   work of Feyerabend, 52–53, 55, 93
   work of Kuhn, 52–53
search for extra-terrestrial intelligence (SETI), 166
Searle, John, 481, 510–516, 523, 565, 618
   and The predetermined self, 565
   'Chinese room' *gendanken* (thought experiment), 618
   '*Seeing Things as They Are*', 523
   '*The Mystery of Consciousness*', 510–511
self, 5, 9, 15–16, 27, 47, 63, 76, 82–89, 308, 311–317, 326–328, 340, 348–349, 375, 393–395, 449–452, 477–478, 487–490, 498–502, 514–523, 542–543, 548, 562, 565–569, 582–584, 589–593, 600, 606–616, 620, 626, 629–634, 642
sentience in the universe, 165, 571
   and Drake equation, 171
   and predeterminism, 571
   views of Martin Rees, 166
seven-transmembrane domain (7TM) receptors, 331
sickle cell anaemia, 324, 442
signalling cascades, 326, 376
single nucleotide polymorphisms (SNPs), 447
skeletal myocyte, 337, 360, 375, 381
   and skeletal muscle development, 337, 360, 375, 383
Slattery, 'Trick, 574
sliding filament theory of muscle contraction, 337

Smith, John Maynard, 382, 388, 412, 423, 438
   'Shaping Life', 382, 388
   'The Origins of Life' (with Szathmary, Eors), 423
Smolin, Lee, 298, 300–301
   'The Trouble with Physics', 300–301
social constructs, 643
Socrates, 11, 21, 40, 82, 85, 95, 579
Solomon, Robert, 560
   'The Little Philosophy Book', 560
Solvay conference, 188–189, 238
Sommerfeld, Arnold, 140, 209
spacetime, 34, 96, 108, 113, 129, 137, 140–149, 152–159, 176, 272, 296, 298–300, 545, 558, 577, 588, 602, 630, 638
   and black holes, 156–157, 241
   and string theory, 295–300
   boomeranging, 152
   contributions of Poincaré and Riemann, 137
   curvature, 143, 152–157, 160
   momenergy, 154–157
   Schwarzschild singularity, 156–157
special relativity, 98, 105, 112, 117–144, 162, 185, 204, 233, 239–241, 249–251, 258, 263–265, 268, 279–283, 292, 505, 551, 555, 564, 635
   and entanglement, 240–241, 249–251, 263–264, 268, 550–551, 564, 635
   and EPR paradox, 127, 237–242, 258, 508
   and time dilation, 129, 134, 136, 141
   contribution of Lorentz, 129, 137, 139, 142, 162
   Einstein train, 132–134
   influence of Mach, 123–124, 129
   twin paradox, 131, 134–140
speciation, 402, 409, 418, 443
Speusippos, 20
Spinoza, Baruch, 39, 66–68
   'ethics', 1, 7, 20, 22, 45, 66
   'Principles of Descartes Philosophy', 61, 66–68
   relation to Descartes's work, 65–66
   'Short Treatise on God, Man, and His Well-Being', 66
   'Tractatus Theologico-Politicus', 66
Sraffa, Piero, 49
Standard Model of physics, 168, 177, 184, 288–301, 552, 564
stem cells, 311, 372–376, 383, 393
   cell-based therapies, 309
   induced pluripotent stem cells (iPSC), 375
Sterelny, Kim, 438, 441, 445
   'Dawkins vs Gould: Survival of the Fittest', 438
strange loops, 592, 619–623
string theory, 177–178, 188, 294–300, 315, 460
Strutt, John William (Lord Rayleigh), 198
subatomic (fundamental/elementary) particles, 56–57, 64, 98, 104, 109, 113, 119, 141, 183–188, 230–235, 279–306, 310, 573
   and string theory, 177, 188, 295–300, 315, 460
   and uncertainty, 233–235

Higgs boson, 288, 291–293, 478
Standard Model of elementary
 particles, 282, 288
subjective experience, 80, 481,
 495, 499, 517, 520–521,
 525–526, 530–531, 536–537,
 551, 579, 587, 593, 639–642
 types, 19–21, 27–29, 47, 63, 69,
  74, 94, 138, 148, 176, 272,
  280–285, 289, 295, 316, 319,
  328, 333, 337–339, 356–358,
  370, 374–376, 407–408,
  421–425, 444–448, 462, 476,
  488, 507, 565, 572–575, 586,
  596–597, 599–601
subconscious, 451, 482–489, 512,
 557–559, 568, 629
 and Harris, 558–560
 and Jung, 487
 fringe-consciousness, 483, 630
subjective experience, 80, 480–481,
 495, 499, 515–520, 525–526,
 530–531, 536–537, 551, 579, 587,
 593, 599, 639–642
 and philosophical zombies,
  521–522, 537
superdeterminism loophole, 564
supersymmetry (SUSY), 296–298, 300
supervenience, 538
Susskind, Leonard, 241
syllogisms, 21, 28, 52, 77
synapses, 493, 597–598, 613
synchrotron, 283–284
systems biology, 372–373, 375
Szathmary, Eors (with John Maynard
 Smith), 423
 'The origins of life', 399–401, 423

T

tabula rasa, 71
Tarski, Alfred, 608
taxonomy, 424
TCA (Krebs) cycle, 333
Tegmark, Max, 177
theory of everything (TOE), 98,
 106–109, 169, 177, 184, 269,
 275–280, 287–294, 299, 507,
 533–534, 540, 546, 551–553, 568,
 575–578, 608, 644
 and predeterminism, 557–554,
  568–569, 640
 and quantum basis of
  consciousness, 109, 275, 507
theory of neuronal group selection
 (TNGS), 480, 496–501, 517,
 591–594
thermodynamics, 159–160, 190–200,
 204, 320, 332, 521
thesis and antithesis, 75, 77
't Hooft, Gerard, 563–565, 581
 and superdeterminism, 564
Thorne, Kip, 108, 159
time dilation, 95, 120, 129, 134–136,
 141
time travel, 159–160
Tononi, Giulio, 499, 595
 '*Consciousness*' (with Gerald
  Edelman), 595
transcription (of messenger RNA),
 327, 343, 346, 355, 357–359
transcription factors, 326–327,
 358–362, 369–385, 389, 415, 440,
 453, 598
 co-factors, 361
 gene families, 375, 383

homeobox genes in fly development, 380, 440, 453
homeobox genes in vertebrate development, 387–390, 440
in skeletal muscle development, 360, 383, 385
transcriptomics, 366, 440
transgenic animal, 360–362, 373, 380, 388
knock-out mice, 372–373, 380, 388
translation (protein synthesis), 48, 320, 346, 353, 358–365, 371, 378, 520, 598, 629
post-translational modification, 358, 365, 367–369
truth, 5–18, 21–26, 37, 42–47, 53–72, 77–83, 89–105, 119, 123, 139, 149, 151, 158, 163, 188–189, 241–242, 265, 270–272, 291–293, 299–300, 309, 405, 445–447, 460, 488, 525, 541–542, 567–572, 576–584, 595, 599–614, 620, 636–637, 642–644
and language, 19, 609
scientific truth, 91, 460, 542, 609
truth tables, 45
Turing, Alan, 19, 27, 393, 508, 615–619
and the halting problem, 506, 616–617
Turing machine, 508, 612, 616–617
Turing test ('imitation game'), 19, 615, 617–618
twin paradox, 131, 134–140

U

ultraviolet catastrophe, 197, 199
uncertainty principle, 30, 174, 190, 219, 234–236, 238–239, 266, 472, 548

unconscious, 19, 451, 482, 485–489, 494, 500–501, 558, 597, 630
and Jung, 486–489
universe, 4–6, 12, 22, 34, 53–55, 61–69, 76, 79, 95–100, 105–121, 137–139, 148–152, 160–182, 191–197, 203, 211, 224, 228, 240–241, 246, 249–251, 257–258, 265–267, 271–283, 290–295, 299–303, 315, 395–400, 405, 468–473, 504–505, 533, 541, 545–585, 605, 623, 631–635, 640–645
and determinism, 88, 245, 544, 546, 556, 566, 572–548, 556
and locality, 240, 251
block universe, 149–150
expansion of our Universe, 106, 116, 118, 160–161, 168, 173–175, 294
fate of (Big Crunch), 108, 118–120, 160, 168, 173–176
knowability of, 5, 108, 149, 548, 553, 583–585, 605, 640
multiverse, 118, 149–150, 169–170, 173–179, 550, 556, 571
origins of (big bang), 106, 161, 163, 179, 299, 478
universal conditions, 112, 159–166
UV rays, 411

V

vacuum fluctuations, 159
veiled reality, 268, 274–276, 278, 632
velocity of light, 98, 112, 116, 121–139, 147–148, 153, 164, 170, 174–175, 181, 219, 261, 293
Verhulst, Pierre Francois, 471

verification (principle), 19, 472
vicariance, 433
vienna circle, 18–19, 45, 56
view from nowhere, 541, 588–589, 634
von Neumann, John, 229, 244–245, 632

W

Walcott, Charles Doolittle, 417
Wallace, Alfred Russell, 402
Watson-Crick base-pairing rules, 344–345, 364–365, 615
Watson, James, 342, 501
wave mechanics, 182, 221, 223, 225, 229, 233
    and Schrödinger, 221, 223, 229
    contribution of Lorentz, 129
    Schrödinger wave equation, 224–225, 236, 250, 266
wave/particle duality, 215–220, 229, 235, 260–261, 263, 295
Weiss, Rainer, 108
Wheeler, John Archibald, 99, 107, 142–144, 153–155, 164, 250, 261
    'A Journey into Gravity and Spacetime', 142
    and Delayed-choice *gendanken* (thought experiment), 261–264
Whitehead, Alfred North, 26
Whittington, Harry, 420–421, 426–428, 431, 434
    and Burgess re-interpretation, 421
Wien, Wilhelm, 199
Wigner, Eugene, 228, 236
Wilkins, Maurice, 342
Wilson, Kenneth, 184
Wittgenstein, Ludwig, 7–9, 17–19, 23, 30, 38–52, 59–60, 64, 84–86, 89–97, 270, 530, 579–580, 622
    and language, 17, 24, 41, 43–45, 47–49, 51, 59
    and logic, 25, 40–41, 44, 51
    and Russell, 23–30, 42
    '*Blue*' and '*Brown*' books, 41
    on certainty', 24, 41
    influence of Sraffa, 49
    'Philosophical Investigations', 40–41, 43, 47, 49
    '*Tractatus Logico-Philosophicus*', 19, 39–45, 47, 49, 580
    truth tables, 45
Woese, Carl, 476
    and RNA world hypothesis, 477
Wolfram, Stephen, 148, 467, 470
    'A New Kind of Science', 467, 470

X

Xenocrates, 20
Xenophanes, 11
'X factor' (in consciousness), 520–521, 529–530, 634, 640
X-rays, 188, 323, 342, 344, 411, 454

Y

Yang, Chen-Ning Franklin, 138
Yang-Mills Theory, 138
Young, Thomas, 216

Z

Zeillinger, Anton, 303
zinc finger transcription factors, 383–384
    retinoid receptors in development, 385
zombies (see philosophical zombies), 521–522, 537, 638–639
Zweig, George, 284